THE LINGUISTIC CYCLE

The Linguistic Cycle

LANGUAGE CHANGE AND THE LANGUAGE FACULTY

Elly van Gelderen

OXFORD
UNIVERSITY PRESS

Oxford University Press, Inc., publishes works that further
Oxford University's objective of excellence
in research, scholarship, and education.

Oxford   New York
Auckland   Cape Town   Dar es Salaam   Hong Kong   Karachi
Kuala Lumpur   Madrid   Melbourne   Mexico City   Nairobi
New Delhi   Shanghai   Taipei   Toronto

With offices in
Argentina   Austria   Brazil   Chile   Czech Republic   France   Greece
Guatemala   Hungary   Italy   Japan   Poland   Portugal   Singapore
South Korea   Switzerland   Thailand   Turkey   Ukraine   Vietnam

Copyright © 2011 by Oxford University Press, Inc.

Published by Oxford University Press, Inc.
198 Madison Avenue, New York, New York 10016

www.oup.com

Oxford is a registered trademark of Oxford University Press

Library of Congress Cataloging-in-Publication Data
Gelderen, Elly van.
The linguistic cycle : language change and the language faculty / Elly van Gelderen.
    p.   cm.
Includes bibliographical references and index.
ISBN 978-0-19-975605-6; 978-0-19-975604-9 (pbk.)
1. Linguistic change. I. Title.
P142.G45   2010
417'.7—dc22   2010010907

1 3 5 7 9 8 6 4 2

Printed in the United States of America
on acid-free paper

Contents

List of Figures

List of Tables

Preface and Acknowledgments

IN THIS BOOK, I examine instances of what Hodge (1970), Tauli (1958), and others have called the linguistic cycle. Some well-known cycles involve negatives, a cross-linguistic change of full negative phrases to words to affixes and of full verbs to negative auxiliaries; verbal agreement, where full pronouns are reanalyzed as agreement markers; aspect, when adverbs become aspectual markers; and articles, when demonstrative pronouns are reanalyzed as articles and then as affixes. Grammaticalization clines show the same but without the focus on renewal.

One aim of the book is to provide descriptions of several cycles in a variety of languages and language families and types, for example, Afro-Asiatic, Athabaskan, Austronesian, Creoles, Indo-European, Niger-Congo, Pama-Nyungan, Salish, Uralic, and Uto-Aztecan. These descriptions should be interesting to linguists working in a variety of frameworks. Another aim of this book is to offer a structural way to account for grammaticalization and cyclical change. I will propose that Economy Principles (formulated within the Minimalist Program) account for these cycles, in particular the Feature Economy Principle. Using Minimalist Principles provides a unique way to look at the cycles.

The book also offers some thoughts on language typology and on language evolution. It is organized to first show cycles of head marking in part I and then to go into dependent marking in part II. Head and dependent marking are essential in describing the typology of a language and therefore could be seen as macrocycles. The other cycles (negative, aspect, and future marker) discussed in part III are less crucial to the overall typology of a language but do contribute to it. They could be seen as microcycles.

I started thinking about this book while at the Center for Advanced Study in Oslo in the fall of 2004, at the invitation of Jan Terje Faarlund. Out of the research group assembled in Oslo came a conference in Rosendal (Norway) in May 2005 and a follow-up in Oslo in December 2005. All of this was Jan Terje's initiative. The Rosendal papers were published as *Grammatical Change and Linguistic Theory: The Rosendal Papers*, edited by Thórhallur Eythórsson, and my chapter in that volume forms the basis for this book. This work has also benefited from comments by anonymous referees and the editors of the *Journal of Germanic Linguistics, Linguistic Typology, Studia Linguistica*, and *Transactions of the Philological Society* (my articles in van Gelderen 2007, 2008d, 2008e, and 2009a) and by those of the chapters in *Variation, Selection, Development: Probing the Evolutionary Model of Language Change*, edited by Regine Eckardt, Gerhard Jäger, and Tonjes Veenstra, in *Historical Syntax and Linguistic Theory*, edited by Paola Crisma and Pino Longobardi, and in *The Prehistory of Language*, edited by Rudie Botha and Chris Knight. Many ideas in these articles and chapters can be found in this book, though they are substantially changed. At a fairly late stage, I benefited enormously by spending a month at the Max Planck Institute for Evolutionary Anthropology in Leipzig. Certain aspects became much clearer in my mind. Thanks to Bernard Comrie for making this stay possible.

I would also like to thank audiences in the United States and Canada, in Tempe, Tucson, Tsaile (Arizona), Cold Lake (Alberta), Ann Arbor (Michigan), New Haven (Connecticut), New Orleans (Louisiana), Corvallis (Oregon), Madison (Wisconsin), Tulsa (Oklahoma), and Montréal (Quebec), and elsewhere, in Aarhus, Berlin, Munich, Padua, Venice, Naples, Trieste, Bergamo, Stellenbosch, Paris, Osaka, Tokyo, and Seoul.

Special thanks are due to Werner Abraham, Harry Bracken, Terje Lohndal, Gary Miller, Lynn Sims, Olena Tsurska, Johanna Wood, and Hui-Ling Yang for encouragement and extensive discussion and comments. Viktorija Todorovska provided editorial comments on the first half of the book. For comments (and native speaker judgments), I would like to thank (in alphabetical order) Mohammed Al-Rashed, Mariana Bahtchevanova, James Berry, Binyam, Michela Cennamo, Yi-Ting Chen, Guglielmo Cinque, Jan-Terje Faarlund, Aryeh Faltz, Ahmed Gul, Richard Ingham, Daniela Kostadinovska, Lorene Legah, Yoko Matsuzaki, Marianne Mithun, Frans Plank, Christer Platzack, Cecilia Poletto, Keren Rice, Willem de Reuse, Siri Tuttle, Marc Richards, Marit Westergaard, and Mary Willie. Many thanks to Peter Ohlin, Brian Hurley, Jennifer Kowing, Robert Milks, Jenny Wolkowicki, Ashwin Bohra, and three anonymous reviewers and to Bruce Matsunaga for help with the cover.

Note on Glosses and Abbreviations

As mentioned in the first chapter, I simplify glosses where appropriate. For instance, when discussing negation and the agreement on the verb or demonstrative is not relevant, I leave that information out.

A, AP	adjective/adverb, adjective phrase/adverb phrase
AAVE	African American Vernacular English
ABL	ablative Case
ABS	absolutive Case
ACC	accusative Case
ACT	active voice
ADE	adessive
AF	actor focus
AGR, AGRP	agreement, agreement phrase
ANT	anterior
APPL	applicative
ART	article
ASP, ASPP	aspect (both position and gloss), aspect phrase
ATTR	attributive
AUX	auxiliary
AxPrt	axial part (nominal part of the PP)
BNC	British National Corpus (for abbreviations following BNC in citations in examples, see list of works at http://www.natcorp.ox.ac.uk/XMLedition/URG/bibliog.html)
CdES	Un Corpus d'entretiens spontanés
C	complementizer
CAUS	causative marker (in gloss)
CI	conceptual-intentional system
CL	classifier in gloss (both nominal and verbal)
CLDT	clitic left-dislocated topic
CM	Case marker in gloss

CONNEG	negative main verb marker
CONT	continuous
COP	copula in gloss
CP	complementizer phrase
CSE	Corpus of Professional Spoken American English (for abbreviations, see references)
CVC	Cape Verdean Creole
CVE	Cajun Vernacular English
D	determiner
DAT	dative Case
DEC	declarative
DEF	definite marker
DEM	demonstrative
DET	determiner
DIM	diminutive
DIST	distal in gloss; distributive
DOE	Dictionary of Old English Corpus (see references)
DOM	differential object marking
DP	determiner phrase
DSD	desiderative (Yaqui)
DSM	differential subject marking
DUR	durative
EMPH	emphatic
EPP	Extended Projection Principle: forces movement
ERG	ergative Case
EXCL	exclusive
F	feature; or future (in gloss); or feminine (in gloss)
FACT	factive
FE	Feature Economy
FIN	finite, position in tree and used in gloss
FOBJ	finite on object nouns, used in gloss
FOC	focus marker
FP	functional phrase (F stands for any functional category)
FUT	future
FV	final vowel (Bantu)
GEN	genitive in gloss
H	human (Micronesian)
HC	Helsinki Corpus (see references)
HPP	Head Preference Principle
HT	hanging topic
ICE	International Corpus of English
i-F	interpretable feature
IMPF	imperfective
INCL	inclusive
IND	indicative

INDEF	indefinite marker
INE	inessive Case
INF	infinitive
INT	intransitive
INST	instrumental Case
IRR	irrealis
IV	instrument voice
KP	kase phrase
LAT	lative Case
LIG	ligature
LF	logical form
LMP	Late Merge Principle
LOC	locative marker
M	mood
N, n	noun, light noun
Neg, NegP	negation, negative phrase
NEG	negative (in gloss)
NF	nonfeminine or nonfuture (in glosses)
NP/nP	noun phrase/(light) noun phrase
NM	nominalizer or noun marker
NOM	nominative case
NONPST	not past
OBJ	object in gloss
OBL	oblique in gloss
OCC	occurrence, forces movement; alternative to EPP
OED	*Oxford English Dictionary*
OM	object marker
OPT	optative (in gloss)
OT	Optimality Theory
OV	object verb
P	preposition/postposition or plural (in gloss)
PAL	pronominal argument language
PART	participle; partitive case
PASS	passive
PC	*Peterborough Chronicle*
PF	phonological form; or perfect(ive); or patient focus
phi-	person and number features
PHON	interface to SM system
POSS	possessive in gloss
PP	Prepositional/Postpositional Phrase
PRED	predicate marker
PRES	present in gloss
PRO	null subject
PROGR	progressive
Pron	pronoun

PROX	proximal in gloss
PRT	particle in gloss
PRTV	partitive case
PST	past in gloss and features
Q	question; qualifier in gloss; quantifier position
QP	quantifier phrase
QUA	qualifier in gloss
RC	relative clause
REAL	realis
REFL	reflexive
REL	relative marker (in gloss)
S	singular or strong ending on adjectives (in gloss)
SBJ	subjunctive
SEM	interface to CI system
SM	sensorimotor system; or subject marker (in gloss)
Spec	specifier
SS	same subject
SU	subject
T	tense
TH	theme (also in gloss)
TMA	tense, mood, aspect
TOP, TopP	topic (position and gloss), topic phrase
TP	tense phrase
TR	transitive marker
TV	transitive verb marker
u-F	uninterpretable feature
UG	Universal Grammar
V/v	verb/light verb
V-2	verb-second
VO	verb object
VOC	vocative Case
VP/vP	verb phrase/(light) verb phrase
W	weak ending on adjectives
WALS	*World Atlas of Language Structures*
X	any head
XP	any phrase
%	unattested
#	number feature, or pause in transcription
=	clitic boundary
/	repetition in transcription
1P	first plural etc.
3MS	third person masculine singular and similar forms
1S	first singular
2P	second plural and similar forms
I, II, and similar	noun classes

THE LINGUISTIC CYCLE

1

THE LINGUISTIC CYCLE

An Introduction

THIS BOOK EXAMINES cyclical change and shows how that change provides a unique perspective on the language faculty. According to one definition in the *Oxford English Dictionary*, a cycle is a "period in which a certain round of events or phenomena is completed." Toward the end of the cycle, similar events start again, but they are (slightly) different and happen at a different pace. The changes are therefore unidirectional.

With the exception of studying the negative cycle, generative linguists have not seriously examined the idea that language change is cyclical.[1] However, the emphasis within the Minimalist Program on principles not specific to language, in conjunction with universal grammar, has prompted generative linguists to look for Economy Principles. I argue that cyclical change provides insight into the principles governing the language faculty: Economy Principles are the reason for linguistic cycles.

Early descriptions of cycles or cyclical change can be found in Condillac (1746), Tooke (1786–1805), Bopp (1816), and Humboldt ([1822] 1972) but, apart from work by Tauli (1958), Hodge (1970), Greenberg (1978), Givón (1978), and Katz (1996), not much recent research has been done on linguistic cycles. Thus, the current state of research is not much better than in 1972, when Robin Lakoff wrote that "there is no mechanism within the present theory of transformational grammar that would allow an explanation" (1972: 173–174). There is even outright rejection of the idea of linguistic cycles. For instance, Newmeyer (1998: 263–275, 2001) dismisses unidirectional change as does Lightfoot (e.g., 2006a: 38). Others, such as Traugott and Dasher (2002: 87), claim that the number of counterexamples to unidirectionality is small and not systematic. I take this approach and have not dealt with the occasional counterexample.

---

1. More work on the negative cycle has started to appear. For instance, in 2008 and 2009, one-day events on the negative cycle took place in Birmingham (http://www.lhds.bcu.ac.uk/english/cycles-of-grammaticalization).

In this book, I argue that cycles are the result of reanalysis by the language learner and I attempt to provide an explanation of this phenomenon within generative grammar, that is, within the Minimalist framework. I argue that the real sources of change are internal principles that bias the learner toward certain structures. This is very different from models such as Lightfoot's (2006a, 2006b) and Westergaard's (2009) that examine how much input a child needs to reset a parameter. According to Lightfoot, "children scan their linguistic environment for structural cues" (2006b: 32); therefore, change comes from the outside, that is, it is triggered by variable data. The challenge for this type of an account is to determine the external triggers. I, on the other hand, argue that change mainly comes from the inside (allowing of course changes in the input due to external factors as well).

I have four goals in this book. One major objective is to provide examples of linguistic cycles: the head-marking cycle (from subject and object pronoun to subject and object agreement) in chapters 2 and 3 and the dependent-marking cycle in chapters 5 and 6. Changes in the copula are related to the agreement cycle and will be discussed in chapter 4. These are major cycles, or macrocycles, in that they change the overall typology of a language. Other cycles are the future and aspect cycles (chapter 7) and the negative cycle (chapter 8). These are minor cycles, or microcycles, in that they do not change the typological characterization of a language. For all cycles, I explore what the typical steps in the cycles are, where they start, and how they renew themselves.

Another objective is to show that Economy Principles (present in the initial cognitive system or Universal Grammar of the child) can account for parts of linguistic cycles. In van Gelderen (2004),[2] I apply this approach to some instances of grammaticalization. In this book, I examine full cycles. I argue that Economy Principles, in particular Feature Economy, are responsible for the various stages of linguistic change. Loss of semantic features occurs when full verbs such as Old English *will* with features such as [volition, expectation, future] are reanalyzed as having only the feature [future] in Middle English. The features can then be considered grammatical rather than semantic. The grammatical features come in two kinds, features that are interpretable at the conceptual-intentional interface and those that are uninterpretable at that interface but functioning to link two positions. I use Feature Economy to explain this change: semantic features are not economical in the computation since they make the elements to be combined inert. Interpretable features are slightly more economical in their interactions since they can value uninterpretable features. Uninterpretable features act as probes and are the most economical in keeping the derivation going. Hicks (2009: 204) characterizes Feature Economy (not his term) as "establish[ing] dependencies where possible." I see Feature Economy as the main force behind the linguistic cycle; semantic features become grammatical features, which in turn need semantic ones again.

A third objective of this book, pursued throughout but summarized in chapter 9, is to argue that some of the cycles (e.g., the agreement cycle) are relevant in the typological classification of languages and others (e.g., the negative cycles) are not. Heine et al. (1991: 246) argue that there is "more justification to apply the notion of a linguistic cycle to individual linguistic developments" than to changes from analytic to synthetic and back to analytic. Synthetic morphology includes both head marking and dependent marking. Nichols (1992: 46–96) uses a

---

2. I use the Dutch convention of prefixed Dutch names. Thus, *van Gelderen* will appear as *van Gelderen* in the text but will be listed as *Gelderen, Elly van* in the references.

complex typology in which languages are assigned points for head or dependent marking. She considers head and dependent marking in the clause, the NP, and the PP and finds a consistency (if dependents are marked in the NP, they are also marked in the clause and the PP). One of her other conclusions is that head marking and dependent marking "are about equally frequent overall" (1992: 95) even though certain geographic areas prefer one or the other. These conclusions are important for cyclical change but are outside the scope of this book. Thus, I have not looked at the marking of grammatical relations inside the NP or PP, and will not be looking at cycles involving change from head marking to dependent marking and back.

Baker (2001) has suggested macroparameters. Following Sapir, he argues that a language has a basic character. Thus, the choice of polysynthesis, for example, implies that the language will have many other characteristics. Some of the changes discussed in this book show that Baker's macroparameters are not valid since a change in the polysynthesis "'parameter'" does not necessarily trigger a change in other parameters, as would be expected in Baker's approach. I try to find a compromise between Baker's (2001 and 2008a) approach and a parametric approach involving only features, as in much recent work by Chomsky.

The final objective of the book is to argue that research into language change can provide insight into the shape of the earliest human language and how it evolved. Typical answers to the question of how language evolved are put as either adaptive/gradual evolution (Pinker & Bloom 1990; Givón 2009) or as gapped evolution (Chomsky 2005). Chomsky asks two questions: Why is there language at all? and Why are there so many languages? The answer to the first question is that a major evolutionary shift occurred, enabling the operation Merge. Currently, that is the main component of language: "the core principle of language, unbounded Merge, must have arisen from some rewiring of the brain" (Chomsky 2008: 9). To answer the second question, externalization may have developed later and may not have involved a genomic change: "the reason might be that the problem of externalization can be solved in many different and independent ways, either before or after the dispersal of the original population" (Chomsky 2008: 10). I will argue that cycles may show us how languages develop. Chapter 10 is devoted to language evolution.

In section 1 of this chapter, I provide some background on grammaticalization and cycles as well as a list of cyclical changes. Section 2 introduces the Minimalist Program and Economy Principles. Section 3 examines language acquisition data that may provide evidence for Economy Principles. Sociolinguistic factors interfere with economy, as I show in section 4 (though I will not focus on this in the remainder of the book). In section 5, I discuss the relevance of economy to language typology and in section 6 methodological issues. Section 7 provides an outline of the rest of the book.

1. Grammaticalization and Cyclical Change

1.1 GRAMMATICALIZATION

As is well known, grammaticalization is a process whereby lexical items lose phonological weight and semantic specificity and gain grammatical functions. The best-known examples of lexical elements changing to grammatical ones are verbs being reanalyzed as auxiliaries and prepositions as complementizers. There are also grammatical elements that are reanalyzed into more grammatical ones.[3] These changes necessitate renewal and the entire process is sometimes referred to as a *linguistic cycle*. As Mithun (2000a: 232) says, "morpheme order often does reflect the sequence of grammaticalization of affixes: those affixes closest to the root are indeed the oldest, and those on the periphery of words can be seen to be more recent additions."

Grammaticalization was identified early on but was established as a term only in 1912 by Meillet. Works such as Lehmann ([1982] 1995) and Traugott and Heine (1991) have inspired many linguists to pay closer attention to this phenomenon, especially in a functionalist framework. Recently, there have been structural accounts of the cyclicity of the changes involved. Van Gelderen (2004, 2008a, 2008b, 2008e, 2009b), for instance, discusses Economy Principles that help the learner acquire a grammar that is more economical and, therefore, more grammaticalized. Wu (2004), Simpson and Wu (2002a, 2002b), Roberts and Roussou (2003), Eckardt (2006), and Roberts (2007) provide formal accounts of grammaticalization, especially change "up the tree." Roberts and Roussou use "upwards reanalysis" (2003: 205). Fuß (2005) argues for a morphological reanalysis when existing inflection is defective. The phonology of grammaticalization has been scrutinized by Schiering (2006), who shows that the phonology is not always reduced.

Grammaticalization is a descriptive term and I use *reanalysis* to emphasize the role of the child acquiring the language. Technically, it is not *re*analysis since a child hears language and analyzes the linguistic input in the most economical way. This may result in a grammar different from that of an earlier generation, which leads linguists to refer to the phenomenon as reanalysis. Grammaticalization is thus seen as following from the innate properties of the language faculty and the task of the linguist is to unearth the principles. Examining unidirectional language change provides a unique window on the principles of the language faculty.

The changes involved in grammaticalization can be schematized as in (1), where (1a) represents the morphosyntactic changes and (1b) the changes in argument status.[4]

(1) a. phrase > word/head > clitic   > affix   > o
     b. adjunct > argument > (argument) > agreement > o

Once the change reaches the right side of (1), renewal and borrowing bring new words and phrases into the language, starting the grammaticalization chain all over again. Table 1.1 lists some well-known English examples of lexical elements reanalyzed as grammatical ones.In (2) to (7), I provide examples of the six changes listed in table 1.1: (a) exemplifies the earlier lexical use and (b) the later grammatical use. Most of these are cases where the lexical and grammatical items occur during the same stage of the language: Modern English has *go*, *have*, and *to* as both lexical and grammatical categories, as shown in (2), (3), and (4), but the lexical category is the earlier one. The grammaticalization of *on* in (5) resulted in its loss, so the grammaticalized form (5b) disappeared. In the case of *for* (6) and *after* (7), the lexical use in (6a) and (7a) has disappeared (renewed by *in front of* and *behind/following*), but the grammatical use remains.

---

3. Andersen (2008) distinguishes lexical elements becoming grammatical, which he terms *grammation*, from grammatical elements becoming other grammatical elements, which he calls *regrammation*.

4. See Siewierska (2004: 261–262) for slightly different clines.

TABLE 1.1

Instances of Grammaticalization

	V>AUX		P>AUX		P>C
go	motion > future	to	direction>mood	for	location>time>cause
have	possession>perfect	on	location>aspect	after	location>time

(2) a. I told Cowslip we were **going** before I left the burrow. (BNC-EWC 3181)
    b. Anne can HAVE her Mini. . .. Cause I's **gonna** get me a BMW.(http://www.
       inkycircus.com/jargon/2006/09/anne_can_have_h.html)

(3) a. I **have** a garden.
    b. I **have** seen the garden.

(4) a. The highway **to** Phoenix
    b. I didn't expect **to** find you here. (BNC-FPM 899)

(5) a. Above them **on** the balcony terrace, Alina Petrovna stood . . .(BNC-FYY 1799)
    b. *and iuunden þene king. þær he wes **an** slæting*
       and found the king there he was on hunting

       'and they found the king where he was hunting' (Layamon, *Brut*, Caligula, 6139, in
       Brook & Leslie 1963)

(6) a. *hlynode*   ***for***   *hlawe*
       made-noise   before   mound

       'It made noise before/around the gravehill' (*Beowulf*, 1120, in Klaeber [1922] 1941).
    b. I would prefer **for** John to stay in the 250 class. (BNC-ED2 626)

(7) a. *Ercenberht rixode **after** his fæder*

       'E. ruled after/following his father' (Chronicle A [entry for the year 640], in
       Thorpe 1861)
    b. **After** she'd hung up, she went through into the kitchen. (BNC-GWO1402)

Once an element reaches the right side of (1), renewal takes place and we have cyclical change.

1.2 THE LINGUISTIC CYCLE

Hodge (1970: 3) calls the cyclical phenomenon where "one man's morphology was an earlier man's syntax" the 'Linguistic Cycle.' *Spiral* is another term for cycle[5] (see Gabelentz [1901] 1972: 256; Hagège 1993: 147); it emphasizes the unidirectionality of the changes: languages

---

5. *Cycle* is also a technical term in a generative derivation. Currently, *phase* is more commonly used in that context.

TABLE 1.2

Cycles

Subject Agreement

demonstrative/emphatic/noun > pronoun > agreement > zero

Object Agreement

demonstrative/pronoun > agreement > zero

Copula Cycle

demonstrative > copula > zero

Case or Definiteness or DP

demonstrative > definite article > "Case" > zero

Negative

a negative argument > negative adverb > negative particle > zero

b verb > aspect > negative > C

Future and Aspect Auxiliary

A/P > M > T > C

do not reverse earlier change but may end up in a stage typologically similar to an earlier one. Jespersen (1922:428–429) uses spirals when he criticizes the concept of cyclical change. His criticism is based on his views that languages move toward flexionless stages in a unidirectional manner. Jespersen's views are not correct: languages and families such as Finnish, Altaic, and Athabascan increase in morphological complexity.

The changes in (2) to (7) represent small steps in certain cycles, the auxiliary cycle in (2) to (5) and the clausal one in (6) and (7). This is true for other cycles as well. The negative cycle is well established for Indo-European, in Jespersen ([1917] 1966), for example, though some of these changes had been identified early on by Gardiner (1904) for Egyptian (see van der Auwera & de Vogelaer 2008). The article or definite cycle has been discussed by Tauli (1958) and more recently by Lyons (1999). Scholars have also argued that cycles affect morphological type. Hodge (1970) examines the rise and fall of overt morphology in Egyptian. He argues that a cycle occurred in Egyptian: Old Egyptian morphological complexity (synthetic stage) turned into Middle Egyptian syntactic structures (analytic stage) and then back into morphological complexity in Coptic. This cycle is discussed here as the agreement cycle (see particularly chapter 2). Tauli also considered the changes involving agreement cyclical. Table 1.2 lists full cycles up to the point where they are renewed by an element similar to the leftmost in the cline.

In the next section, I will provide some background on the syntactical framework used. This will enable us to examine grammaticalization and the cycle in a structured, explanatory way.

2. Minimalism, Economy, and Cycles

In this section, I will review the Minimalist Program, the basic clausal structure, Economy Principles, and cycles.

2.1 THE FRAMEWORK

In the 1950s, Chomsky's generative model offered an alternative to behaviorist and structuralist frameworks. Chomsky focuses not on the structures present in the language/outside world but on the mind of the language learner/user. The input to language learning is seen as poor (the "'poverty of the stimulus'" argument): speakers know so much more than what they have evidence for in the input. How is this possible? The answer to this problem, Plato's problem in Chomsky (1986a), is Universal Grammar (hence UG), the initial state of the language faculty, a biologically innate organ. UG helps the learner make sense of the data and build an internal grammar. In the 1980s, UG was seen as consisting of "principles" (true in all languages) and "parameters" (choices to be made depending on the language).

Currently, the role of parameters and of UG in general is considered much less important than it was in the 1980s. Parameters now (Chomsky 2004, 2007) consist of choices of feature specifications as the child acquires a lexicon. All parameters are lexical and determine linearization; therefore, they account for the variety of languages. Baker, while disagreeing with this view of parameters, calls this the Borer-Chomsky Conjecture (2008a: 156, 2008b: 353): "All parameters of variation are attributable to differences in the features of particular items (e.g., the functional heads) in the lexicon." I briefly discuss parameters in section 5.

Initially, many principles were also attributed to UG. At the moment, however, the emphasis is on principles not specific to the language faculty (UG), but to "general properties of organic systems" (Chomsky 2004: 105), "'third factor principles'" in Chomsky (2005, 2007). Chomsky (2007: 3) identifies three factors crucial in the development of language.

(1) genetic endowment, which sets limits on the attainable languages, thereby making language acquisition possible; (2) external data, converted to the experience that selects one or another language within a narrow range; (3) principles not specific to FL [faculty of language]. Some of the third factor principles have the flavor of the constraints that enter into all facets of growth and evolution. . .. Among these are principles of efficient computation.

The third factor is divided into several types, including principles of efficient computation, which are "of particular significance in determining the nature of attainable languages" (Chomsky 2005: 6). The Economy Principles discussed later, and reformulated in terms of Feature Economy, are probably also part of more general cognitive principles, thus reducing the role UG plays. If children use Economy Principles in building their internalized grammars, there should be some evidence for this in the way language changes.

2.2 BASIC CLAUSAL STRUCTURES

In a pre-Minimalist system (e.g., Chomsky 1986b), a clause consists of an outer layer (the complementizer phrase, or CP), an inner layer (the tense phrase, or TP), and a thematic layer that contains the verb and its arguments (the traditional verb phrase, or VP). The outer layer is responsible for encoding discourse information and linking one clause to another, the inner layer is involved in the marking of tense and agreement through morphology or auxiliaries, and the lowest layer determines the thematic roles. Each layer can be expanded: when the sentence is negative, a NegP is added.

In this framework, syntactic structures are built by using general rules, such as that each phrase consists of a head (X) and a complement (ZP) and specifier (YP).

(8)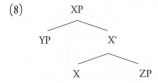

This holds for both lexical (N, V, A) and grammatical categories (C, D, T).

In the Minimalist Program (Chomsky 1995, 2001, 2004, 2007), phrase structures are abandoned in favor of a general rule Merge. Merge combines two bundles of features; from Merge, the relations in (8) follow automatically. As Boeckx (2008: 75) explains, following Chomsky (1995), the three levels in (8) can be seen as follows: "a minimal projection [X in (8)] is a lexical item selected from the lexicon, . . . a maximal projection [XP in (8)] is a lexical item that doesn't project any further, . . . an intermediate projection [X' in (8)] is . . . neither minimal not maximal." For convenience, I continue to use the levels in (8) as well as specifier, head, and complement in what follows.

In a Minimalist approach, a Modern English derivation proceeds in four steps. First, items are selected from the lexicon. Chomsky (2007: 6) suggests the lexicon has "atomic elements, lexical items LI, each a structured array of properties." Abstracting away from features, a lexical array could be {saw, it, T, Martians}. Second, the elements are merged, as with *saw* and *it* in (9), and one of the heads (in this case V) projects to a higher VP.

(9)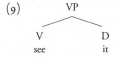

There is some debate as to whether there is an additional labeling operation and which elements are selected for Merge. The labels in (9) are added for convenience only (Chomsky 2004, but see Lohndal 2006). Most likely, it is the theta requirements that make sure *saw* and *it* merge and not *saw* and T.[6]

Third, after adding a (small) v and subject *Martians* to (9), as in (10), functional categories such as T (and C) are merged to vP. Agree ensures that features on v and T find a noun with matching (active) features to check agreement. When agreement is checked so is what is often referred to as Case (at least in many languages, but see Baker 2009 for languages without this connection). Following Pesetsky and Torrego (2001),[7] I will call this tense rather than nominative and aspect rather than accusative. So, v and T have interpretable tense and aspect features but uninterpretable phi features. They probe (search) for a

---

6. Chomsky (2005: 13, 2007: 11) suggests that certain heads have edge features that drive Merge, both external Merge, as in (9), and internal Merge. These edge features overlap with uninterpretable features and EPP features, and I ignore them in this book.

7. Williams (1994: 11–12) is perhaps the first to argue that an NP has tense: "Nominative NPs are simply tensed NPs."

nominal that they c-command to agree with. The v finds this nominal in *it* and T finds this nominal, or goal, in *Martians* and each element values its uninterpretable features, which then delete.

The final structure looks like (10) where the features that are not "'struck through'" are interpretable and not subject to elimination. The subject moves to Spec TP: it is merged from an internal position for language-specific reasons (EPP or OCC).[8]

(10)

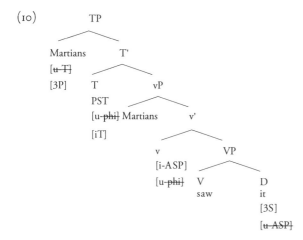

A difference in this line of thought from arguments such as Chomsky (1995: 277–278) is that I see the case features on T and v as interpretable. This means that at LF they are interpreted, as finite and transitive respectively. The derivation in (10) uses early lexical insertion, that is, a lexicalist approach, as in Chomsky (1995, 2004). In this book, nothing hinges on this. The CP layer is not indicated in (10).

At some point, the derivation has to be handed over to the sensorimotor (SM) and conceptual-intentional (CI) systems external to the syntax. This is done through the interfaces PHON and SEM, corresponding to PF and LF in older frameworks. This emphasis on language-external systems is formulated as (11).

(11)   Strong Minimalist Thesis
        Language is a perfect solution to interface conditions (Chomsky 2007: 3)

Thus, the syntax has to satisfy the requirements of the external systems, which is achieved via the interfaces PHON and SEM. The former is responsible for linearization and externalization, for example, what is spelled out in (10) (see Nunes 2004 for an account on how to decide which copies to spell out). For the CI system, two aspects are relevant: the theta structure (determined in English through position but in other languages through inherent

---

8. Many have indicated that EPP or OCC features are non-Minimalist since they are not interpretable at the interfaces; see, e.g., Stroik (2009: 7). I assume they will at some point turn out to be relevant to the CI interface.

Case) and the discourse information. The topic and focus can be determined through aspect together with Case (Abraham 1997; Philippi 1997), through definiteness markers, or through position, as in Chinese, where indefinite objects and subjects appear toward the end of the sentence, as (12) and (13) show.

(12) a. *chi* *le* ***fan***   Chinese
          eat   PF   rice

          'I ate some rice.'

      b. ***fan*** *chi* *le*
          rice   eat   PF

          'I ate the rice.'

(13) *Lai* *le* *yi* *ge* *ren*   Chinese
      come   PF   one   CL   man

      'A man came.' (Li & Thompson 1981: 20; Yi Ting Chen, p.c.)

As Chomsky (2002: 113, 2008) points out, the semantic component expresses thematic as well as discourse information:

> In "what John is eating what," the phrase "what" appears in two positions, and in fact those two positions are required for semantic interpretation: the original position provides the information that "what" is understood to be the direct object of "eat," and the new position, at the edge, is interpreted as a quantifier ranging over a variable, so that the expression means something like "for which thing x, John is eating the thing x." (Chomsky 2008: 8)

Two mechanisms are responsible for this: external and internal Merge, respectively. Merge is essential, and it is the core of the derivational system. Through Merge, binary and hierarchical relationships between the merged elements form. We refer to the merged constituents as heads, complements, and specifiers. Merge, thus, brings with it the principles in (14).

(14) **Principles connected with Merge**
      a. Merge involves projection, hence headedness, and heads and phrases
      b. The binary character of Merge results in either:

(i)   (ii)

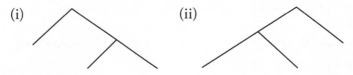

      c. There is c-command of the specifier over (the head and) the complement, resulting in the special nature of the specifier.
      d. There is recursion.

A lot can be said about each of these principles. For instance, Kayne has argued (1994) that all languages are right-branching as in (bi). This means that there are no headedness parameters.

Within Minimalism, Principles of Economy have played an important role. For instance, Rizzi (2004: 224) argues that Relativized Minimality is an Economy Principle "that appears to be a natural principle of mental computation." "'Fewest steps," "'last resort," "'least effort'" are all relevant in syntactic derivations (see Chomsky 1995; Zwart 1996; Collins 1997; Fox 2000). This means that, in building derivations, there are ways to resolve ambiguous structures. Economy is part of the syntax, the I-language, and not the processing system, the E-language, as in Hawkins (2004: 31). In the remainder of this section, I outline a few Economy Principles.

2.3 THE HEAD PREFERENCE, LATE MERGE, AND FEATURE ECONOMY PRINCIPLES

Lightfoot (1979: 121) introduces an Economy Principle, the Transparency Principle, that "requires derivations to be minimally complex." His focus is on the child's postulating of underlying structures that are close to their surface structures. In current Minimalism, the emphasis is not on simplifying the distance between numeration and the sensorimotor interface, but the spirit of Lightfoot's proposal is simplicity of representation and this will be relevant in the principles discussed here. Van Gelderen (2004) justifies principle (15),[9] which is at work in the internalized grammar due either to UG or to general cognitive principles. This principle holds for external Merge (projection) as well as internal Merge (movement).

(15) **Head Preference Principle (HPP):**
      Be a head, rather than a phrase.

In accordance with the HPP, a speaker will build (16b) rather than (16a), if given evidence compatible with either. The FP stands for any functional category; a pronoun (as well as an adverb or a preposition) is merged in the head position in (16b), but occupies the specifier position in (16a).

(16)   a.   FP   b.   FP

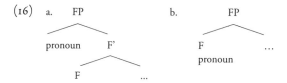

Hawkins's (2004) efficiency principle has a Minimize Forms Principle, a less specific one than the HPP and a performance principle. Optimality Theory has Economy Principles as well: STAY ("do not move") and TELEGRAPH ("do not spell out FCs"). These OT constraints are ordered differently cross-linguistically, unlike the Head Preference and Late Merge ones.

The Head Preference Principle is relevant to a number of historical changes (table 1.3): whenever possible, a word is seen as a head rather than a phrase. In this way, pronouns change

---

9. Within a Distributed Morphology framework, Embick and Marantz (2006: 25) discuss the hypothetical principle Lexical Preference, which says "use a word rather than a phrase if they express the same features."

TABLE 1.3

Examples of the HPP

Specifier > Head	Specifier > Head
Demonstrative pronoun *that* to complementizer	Demonstrative pronoun to article
Negative adverb to negation marker	Adverb to aspect marker
Adverb to complementizers (e.g., *till*)	Full pronoun to agreement

from emphatic full phrases to clitics to agreement markers, and negatives change from full DPs to negative adverb phrases to heads. This change is slow since a child learning the language will continue to encounter a pronoun as both a phrase and a head. For instance, coordinated pronouns are phrases as are emphatic pronouns. If they remain in the input, phrases will continue to be triggered in the child's grammar. In the case of pronouns changing to agreement markers, the child will initially assume the unmarked head option, unless there is substantial evidence that the pronoun is a full phrase.

A practical issue here is how to distinguish between specifiers and heads. Sometimes, this is difficult and that is why they are reanalyzable by the language learner. Specifiers are full phrases and can be modified and coordinated, and they occur in certain positions; a coordinated or modified element is never a head, and head movement is usually recognizable. Table 1.4 summarizes this.

There is a second Economy Principle in early Minimalism (e.g., Chomsky 1995: 348). To construct a sentence, we need to select lexical items from the lexicon, put them together, or merge them, and move them. In Early Minimalism, Merge "comes 'free' in that it is required in some form for any recursive system" (Chomsky 2001: 3) and is "inescapable" (Chomsky 1995: 316, 378). Move, on the other hand, requires additional assumptions. This means that it is less economical to merge early and then move than to wait as long as possible before merging. This is expressed in (17).

(17)   **Late Merge Principle (LMP):**
       Merge as late as possible.

Principle (17) operates most clearly in heads. Thus, under Late Merge, (18a), with the auxiliary base generated in T, is preferable to (18b), with the auxiliary in a lower position and moving to T. See also Kayne (1999). The LMP accounts for the change from lexical to functional head or from functional to higher functional head frequently described in the grammaticalization literature (e.g., Heine & Kuteva 2002).

(18)

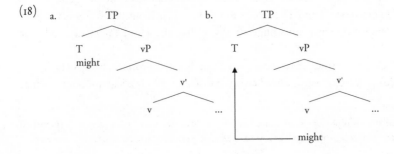

TABLE 1.4

Specifiers and Heads

	Specifier/XP	Head/X
Coordination	Yes	No
Modification	Yes	No
Movement	Quite free	To head positions such as T and C

Late Merge also accounts for lexical phrases becoming base generated in the functional domain, as with certain prepositional phrases in Middle English as well as certain adverb phrases. Van Gelderen (2009a) develops this idea in detail:[10] from an original VP-adverbial PP, as in (19), to a frequent preposing, as in (20), to a reanalysis in the specifier of the higher CP in (21).[11]

(19)   *hu*   *hit*   *Hringdene*   **after**   **beorþege**   *gebun*   *hæfdon*
      how   it   Ring-Danes   after   drinking   lived   had

      'how the Ring-Danes were doing after their drinking.' (*Beowulf*, 116–117, in Klaeber [1922] 1941)

(20)   *Æfter þysan com Thomas to Cantwarebyri*

      'After this, Thomas came to Canterbury.' (Chronicle A [entry for 1070], in Thorpe 1861)

(21)   *for* [**efterþan þet** *þe mon bið dead*] *me leið þene licome in þere þruh*
      Because after-that that the man is dead they lay the body in the tomb

      'After the man is dead, they put the body in the tomb.' (*Hic Dicendum Est*, in Morris 1872, 51: 4–5)

Structure (22a) shows the more recent representation and (22b) the earlier one. Under LMP, (22a) is preferable.

(22)

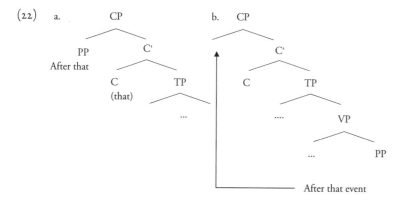

---

10. For instance, there is a temporal change involved as well that is not immediately relevant here and therefore left out.

11. On the distinction between *adverbial* and *adverb*, see the beginning of chapter 7.

In Roberts and Roussou (2003), if a functional category chooses Merge over Move (F^*_{merge} over F^*_{move}), the element that used to satisfy F^*_{move} does not have to satisfy F^*_{merge}. It could be another lexical item. In my proposal, it is important that a lexical item has actually moved to the functional category. This is different from Simpson and Wu's (2002a, 2002b) Lateral Grammaticalization, where a reanalyzed item does not have to have been internally merged (i.e., moved).

Certain lexical items are "prone" to a reanalysis under the LMP. For instance, non-theta-marked elements can wait to merge outside the VP (Chomsky 1995: 314–315). I will therefore argue that if, for instance, a preposition can be analyzed as having fewer semantic features and being less relevant to the argument structure, it will tend to merge higher (in TP or CP) rather than merging early (in VP) and then moving. How does the LMP work in practice? Assuming a lexicalist hypothesis in which a lexical entry "contains three collections of features: phonological . . . semantic . . . , and formal" (Chomsky 1995: 230), an LI such as the light verb *go* might have the semantic features [motion, future, location]. If *go* occurs with another verb, such as *bring*, one of the semantic features of *go*, in this case [future], need only be activated. Thus, a biclausal structure can be avoided. The examples of grammaticalization given in table 1.1 are all instances of Late Merge. I have added a few others in table 1.5.

Chomsky (2001) uses the terms external Merge for the initial Merge (the traditional Merge) and internal Merge when an element merges for a second time (the traditional Move). Since Move is seen as a special case of Merge, that is, Remerge, it is not less economical than Merge (see Chomsky 2001, 2005: 12). One could argue that (17) is still valid since the special Merge, that is, internal Merge, requires additional steps. Traces are no longer allowed; they would introduce new material into the derivation after the initial selection and therefore copies are included in the derivation, as in (10). Move/internal Merge is not "Move" but "'Copy, Merge, and Delete.'" Since the derivation contains more copies of the lexical item to be internally merged, and since those copies have to be deleted, (13) could still hold as an Economy Principle. In addition, Chomsky (2005: 14) suggests an important difference: external Merge is relevant to the argument structure, whereas internal Merge is relevant for scope and discourse phenomena. This establishes a crucial difference between the two operations.

It is also possible to think of syntax as inert and reformulate Late Merge in terms of feature change and loss. This is currently the thinking about linguistic variation: parametric variation is due to different features connected to lexical items. Starting with Chomsky (1995), the features relevant for and accessible during the derivation are formal. Formal features can be interpretable (relevant to the semantic interface) or uninterpretable (only relevant to move elements to

TABLE 1.5

Examples of the LMP

On, from P to ASP	VP Adverbials > TP/CP Adverbials
Like, from P > C (*like I said*)	Negative objects to negative markers
Modals: v > ASP > T	Negative verbs to auxiliaries
To: P > ASP > M > C	PP > C (*for him to do that . . .*)

certain positions). Interpretable features are acquired before uninterpretable ones, as Radford argues (2000), but are later reinterpreted as uninterpretable, triggering the functional/grammatical system. The same happens in language change. Changes in negatives can be explained by arguing that their (initially) semantic features are reanalyzed as interpretable and then as uninterpretable, as in (23). Phrases like *never* have interpretable negative and phi features that are searched for by a probe in a functional category. Once the phrase is reanalyzed as a head (e.g., Old English *ne* 'not'), another element is required. One could therefore argue there is a principle at work, as formulated in van Gelderen (2007, 2008a, 2008b, 2009c), namely (23).

(23)   **Feature Economy**
      Minimize the semantic and interpretable features in the derivation, for example:

Adjunct		Specifier		Head		affix
semantic	>	[iF]	>	[uF]	>	[uF]

The change represented in (23) occurs in the case of the negative cycle as well as the subject cycle: the interpretable person (and gender) features of a full pronoun are reanalyzed as uninterpretable when they become agreement.

(24)   **Subject Agreement Cycle**

emphatic	>	full pronoun	>	head pronoun	>	agreement
[i-phi]		[i-phi]		[u-1/2][i-3]		[u-phi]

This is compatible with Chomsky's (1995: 230, 381) views on features: "formal features have semantic correlates and reflect semantic properties (accusative Case and transitivity, for example)." This makes sense if a language learner uses the semantic features in the derivation, these features turning into interpretable ones so to speak. Chomsky assumes that uninterpretable features need to be valued and I follow that, but see Pesetsky and Torrego (2007) for the alternative that +/- valued is independent from +/- interpretable.

In (23) and (24), I connect heads with having uninterpretable features. I think that is correct and could be made to work. Due to the number of features a head can have, this is sometimes hard to be consistent about, however. A major problem in the approach I develop regarding Feature Economy is that the status, number, and use of features is still very fluid in Minimalism. Proliferation of features needs to be avoided. In the concluding chapter, I will briefly discuss this.

Schütze (1997, 2009) uses an Accord Maximization Principle which is very similar to (23) and Hicks's Principle in (25) comes close to Feature Economy. He justifies Feature Economy as a component of Merge (Hicks 2009: 204).

(25)   **Maximize Featural Economy**
      Establish dependencies via syntactic operations where possible.

Unvalued features are more economical since they allow the relevant dependencies to be established '"for free" by syntactic means. This principle provides the rationale for the change from semantic to uninterpretable features. It also explains why there may be a difference in Feature Economy where uninterpretable features of the probe and those of the goal are concerned. Those of the probe keep the derivation going.

Based on van Gelderen (2008e, 2009a), I briefly review how the grammaticalization of prepositions discussed earlier as (19) to (22) can be seen in terms of Feature Economy and Late Merge. In chapter 7, a slightly more elaborate version appears. A preposition such as *after* has semantic features (e.g., [time, order, past]) and phonological ones (two syllables, etc.). These are not accessible during the derivation, though [time] may be interpretable, as in Pesetsky and Torrego (2004). In addition, there are formal features, which are accessible during the computation and include categorial,[12] Case, and phi features, at least in Chomsky (1995: 230–232). Assuming that prepositions have unvalued phi features, they value the Case of the DP in their domain.[13] So, the Case of the DP is valued after agreement with an appropriate probe (I use ACC to show the Case features but nothing hinges on this choice).

(26)

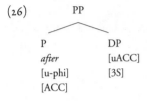

Thus, there is a formal uninterpretable and unvalued feature [u-phi] that makes prepositions into probes (see also Baker 2008a: 112–114). This is the feature relevant for the derivation; other features are a burden on the computational system since they do not keep the derivation going. Language learners thus use (23) to eliminate [ACC] from the lexical item, i.e. they select it with fewer features. With the interpretable [ACC] feature removed, the features of *after* are as listed in (27a), making it a C looking for interpretable phi features from a goal that doesn't need to value its case, that is, as in (27b).

(27)   a.   *after*
            [u-phi]

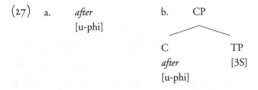

Thus, we have gone from (19) to (21). The same changes occur with *like* and *for* and a number of other prepositions. For instance, Higashiizumi (2006: 69–74) provides a good overview of how temporal prepositions are reanalyzed as causal. The uninterpretable, unvalued features of C will probe into the clause it c-commands and find a goal in the lower TP to value its phi features. It is well known that CPs (as subjects) trigger third person singular agreement on the verb. This is expected if the complementizer has phi features (that are overt in many languages).

---

12. In later work, following Marantz (1997), lexical items are seen not as specified for category but as roots that are nominalized or verbalized through Merge with an n or v.

13. This accounts for the difference between a preposition and an adverb: the former needs an NP in its complement, the latter does not.

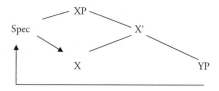

FIGURE 1.1. The linguistic cycle

Chomsky (2004, 2007: 3–4) argues that we need to attribute as little as possible to UG and rely instead on principles not specific to the language faculty. Many Economy Principles, including (15), (17), and (23), fall into the latter category in that they reduce the computational burden.

Like the Head Preference Principle, Late Merge is a motivating force for linguistic change, accounting for the change from specifier to higher specifier and head to higher head. These principles help language learners reanalyze their linguistic input. I have reformulated the LMP as a Feature Economy Principle; the same can be done for the Head Preference Principle. When phrases are reanalyzed as heads, they lose semantic and formal features, as we will see.

2.4 CYCLICAL CHANGE

The two principles just mentioned, and their reformulations in terms of Feature Economy, account for grammaticalization, and Feature Economy is responsible for cyclical change. Let's see in more detail what happens when we combine the effects of the HPP and the LMP. Figure 1.1 shows how a specifier can be reanalyzed as a head (through the HPP) and how the specifier position can be filled by a phrase from a lower layer (LMP).

This scenario works perfectly for changes where a negative object such as Old English *na wiht* 'no creature' becomes a specifier (LMP) and subsequently a head *not* of a NegP (HPP).

A stage not yet accounted for is the shift of the head to zero, as in the case of negative heads: Old English and Modern French *ne* and *n't* are null in many varieties of Modern English. The main reason for head deletion is head movement of other heads: the auxiliary moving via the Neg(ative) head to C may lead to feature syncretism (where one word has two functions). Words such as *won't* and Old English *nis* 'not-is' tend to be reanalyzed as expressing only one feature. See Faarlund (2008: 231), who argues for the principle in (28).

(28) **Null hypothesis of language acquisition**
   A string is a word with lexical content.

He explains that "[i]n terms of acquisition and reanalysis, this means that the child misses some of the boundary cues, and interprets the input string as having a weaker boundary (fewer slashes, stronger coherence) at a certain point" (2008: 236), as in (29).[14]

(29) ///>//>/
   halli///hino   >   hall//inn   >   hall/en   Stages of Norwegian
   stone this   stone the   stone the

---

14. For independent reasons, the form *hallen* is not used and is ungrammatical, but Faarlund uses (29) for the morphology.

Roberts and Roussou (2003: 16, 200, 210) similarly rely on "simplicity" and "simpler representations" to help the acquisition process. These are fleshed out further (2003: 200, 210) and rely on feature syncretisms like Faarlund: if one lexical item "spell[s] out the features of two (or perhaps more) heads" (2003: 200), a reanalysis can take place since syncretism is not economical.

However, it is not clear that avoiding syncretism is most economical. One could argue that there are two possibilities, as stated in (30) and (31).

(30)   Movement links two positions and is thereby economical; that is, assume
        uninterpretable features and movement.

(31)   Avoid syncretism; iconicity is economical; that is, assume interpretable features.

Feature Economy favors (30) since it keeps the derivation going. If you select two words from the lexicon with only interpretable features, they will not interact or merge.

As a result of (23), one needs "new" features. Once the functional element has lost its semantic and interpretable features, it becomes a probe looking for an element to value its uninterpretable features. I assume it can value these with elements that are themselves inactive; otherwise renewal would not take place. Some elements are straightforward renewers: demonstratives have phi features and adverbs temporal or spatial ones. A few are given in table 1.6 and will be discussed in later chapters.

Representative cycles can therefore be seen as (32), rather than as (1) or (23). This indicates that there are two types of cycles for certain elements. In chapters 2, 3, 4, and 6, the change represented in (32a) is exemplified; in chapter 7, (32b) is relevant, and in chapters 5 and 8, both are.

(32)   a. Adjunct   >   Specifier   >   Head   >   o
            semantic   [iF]   [uF]   --
        b. Head   >   (higher)   Head   >   o
            [uF]   [uF]
            [iF]

Cyclicity is mentioned only three times in Hopper and Traugott (2003). They talk about grammaticalization as a "continuously occurring phenomenon" (2003; 124) and point out

TABLE 1.6

Examples of Renewal

Agreement	Emphatic pronouns/nouns
Case	Demonstratives
Future	Verbs of motion
Negative	Minimizers/Negative DPs/Negative APs

that the cyclical model is "extremely problematic because it suggests that a stage of a language can exist when it is difficult or even impossible to express some concept" (2003; 124). Having a probe with uninterpretable features automatically look for another element avoids such a stage, I think.

Before ending this section on economy, I'll add a brief note on analogy, which has been a major explanatory principle for hundreds of years and shows similarities to economy. Meillet ([1912] 1958: 13) is famous for emphasizing both phonetic regularities and analogy in morphological paradigms in linguistic change. "La recherche des lois générales, tant morphologiques que phonétiques, doit être désormais l'un des principaux objets de la linguistique."[15] Within the morphological laws, he recognizes two principles, analogy and grammaticalization ([1912] 1958: 130–131) where analogy is mainly restricted to paradigmatic regularity. After him many others have used this concept, such as Kuryłowicz (1964) and Anttila (1989). Kiparsky has claimed that the "*direction* of analogical change is optimization of the evaluation measure" (1982: 203–204) provided by UG. Thus, the child choosing between grammars that fit the data it encounters will choose the morphological representation that is more regular. Most examples in Kiparsky (1982, 2000) involve lexical/paradigmatic relationships and are therefore different in range from the Economy Principles mentioned above. Lightfoot (1979: 347–348) notes that "analogy plays an extensive role in syntactic change" because UG puts constraints on the levels of opacity. Fischer (2007: 135–145) also invokes analogy as playing a very important role in language change. Her examples involve cases of grammaticalization such as *going to* reanalyzing as a future on analogy of the Auxiliary + bare infinitive pattern; "it in fact joins another token-set" (2007: 145). Analogical reasons have been criticized for their looseness and their arbitrariness, but in Fischer's Construction Grammar framework they are less loose.

Thus Feature Economy is responsible for the linguistic cycle. In the next section, we will see how these principles are at work in language acquisition.

3. Economy and Language Acquisition

Acquisition data are difficult to interpret. If the child uses the pronoun *me*, is that a full phrase (as in adult English), an N head, or a D head? In this section, with data taken from the CHILDES database, I first show that children use what look like heads rather than phrases, in accordance with the HPP, though this may be for more general reasons. I then argue that children also create grammatical/functional elements from lexical ones (the LMP), and use what looks like Feature Economy when they develop beyond the lexical word stage.

3.1 HEAD PREFERENCE

Children are well known for using single lexical words in the early stages, as in (33), from the two-word and telegraphic stages (age is given as year followed by month, followed by day if relevant).

---

15. "Research of general laws, both phonetic and morphological, must from now on be one of the main goals of linguistics" (my translation).

(33) a. all gone (Allison, 1;4.21, Bloom 1973)
     b. walk school (Allison, 1;8.21, Bloom 1973)
     c. baby eat cookie (Allison, 1;10, Bloom 1973)
     d. sit down right here next truck (Allison, 1;10, Bloom 1973)

There is no evidence of overt coordination in Allison's speech at age 1;10, as (34) shows. This is expected if only heads are used.

(34) horse cow
     'horse and cow' (Allison, 1;10, Bloom 1973)

The earliest pronoun produced is given in (35), a dislocated structure, the only one in the file for age 1;8.

(35) Mommy **you** wiping (Allison, 1;8.21, Bloom 1973)

No files for Allison were collected between 1;10 and 2;4. At age 1;10, there are no pronouns; at age 2;4, pronouns are used correctly, as (36) shows.

(36) a. **she** (i)s not eating snack right there (Allison, 2;4, Bloom 1973)
     b. **I**'m gonna sit on here (Allison, 2;4, Bloom 1973)
     c. oh **I** don't want drink it (Allison, 2;4, Bloom 1973)

The first use of demonstratives with nouns,[16] clearly making a head into a phrase, is eight months later than (35), namely (37).

(37) a. want eat **my snack** (Allison, 2;4, Bloom 1973)
     b. where **the chair** mommy (Allison, 2;4, Bloom 1973)
     c. it **a puddle** from juice I spilled (Allison, 2;4, Bloom 1973)

This suggests that there is an initial preference for heads. The same is true for other children. Peter (Bloom 1970) uses both *I* and *me*.

(38) a. I writing
     b. I'm writing

(39) a. me found it # I find it
     b. me take it off # no me take it off
     c. me too # go home
        (all from Peter, 2;1.18, Bloom 1970)

---

16. There are earlier instance of modification, as in (i) and (ii), but these are compounds:

(i) there baby cup (Allison 1;10, Bloom 1973)
(ii) more apple juice (Allison 1;10, Bloom 1973)

Even though *I* and *me* could be phrases in (38) and (39), there are no instances of coordination of (pro)nouns.

If we consider a more complex phenomenon, that is, the choice between a *wh*-relative (in the specifier position in adult language) and no relative or *that* (a head), the same preference for heads holds. Using data from four children, Diessel (2004: 137) shows that when the children start to produce relative pronouns, out of 297 relative clauses, 165 have *that*, 6 have *who* (all by one child), and 126 have no marker. This shows that children avoid phrases completely. The 6 instances of *who* can be argued to be heads since *whom/to who* do not occur. The percentages are 56 percent *that*, 42 percent zero, and 2 percent *who*. In the CHILDES-Kuczaj corpus (Kuczaj 1976), Abe produces 82 percent *that* relatives, as in (40) and 18 percent *wh*-relatives. There is no evidence that the *wh*, as in (41), is not a head, however, since they are never full phrases.

(40)   **a dragon that** was this little (Abe, 4;0.16)

(41)   You know **the round part where** they dig (Abe, 4;1.5)

Abe's use of *who* is sometimes in direct imitation of a caregiver, as in (42).

(42)   FATHER: no the person **who** eats em.
        CHILD: the person **who** eats em? (Abe, 3;1.8)

So one could argue that adults may already be avoiding phrases. Researchers estimate that in adult speech *that* (or zero) relatives appear 80–90 percent of the time, as opposed to 10–20 percent in written genres.

3.2 LATE MERGE AND FEATURE ECONOMY

Lexical categories are acquired before grammatical ones. For instance, Clark (1971) and Friederici (1983) have shown that lexical prepositions are acquired before grammatical ones, and more recently Littlefield (2006: 148–149) has done the same. Among the lexical ones, spatial prepositions are acquired before temporal ones (Tomasello 1987). I demonstrate in this section that children seem to turn lexical categories, such as prepositions, into grammatical ones, such as complementizers, seemingly without explicit input. This means they are employing Feature Economy, reanalyzing semantic features as grammatical ones.

In order to argue decisively that language change is determined by principles at work in acquisition, it would be great if children completely abandoned using the lexical item with semantic features in favor of using the grammatical item. However, most languages have words that are ambiguous between lexical and grammatical status, such as prepositions and complementizers. Pronouns may be an instance of a clear change from lexical use to grammatical use. In what follows, I provide instances of words ending up doing double duty, so to speak: first as lexical words and then as both lexical and grammatical words.

Josefsson and Håkansson (2000: 398) argue that Swedish "children first acquire the PP and then, directly after that the subordinate clause": (43) first and then (44).

(43)   *precis **som** en kan/ **som** en kanin*
        just like a rab/ like a rabbit

(44) *grisen, den **som** heter Ola*
    pig that who is-called Ola (Embla, 2;3.4, both from Josefsson & Håkansson 2000: 410)

According to Josefsson and Håkansson, the children do not start using complementizers at all until they have reached a 90 percent use of prepositions in obligatory contexts.

In the CHILDES-Kuczaj corpus, English *like* and *for* are used similarly to their use in Swedish. Initially, the child uses *like* as a lexical category only, as in (45) to (48), and later adds the complementizer, as in (49) and (50).

(45) **like** a cookie (Abe, 3.7.5)

(46) no the monster crashed the planes down **like** this **like** that (Abe, 3;7.5)

(47) I wan(t) (t)a show you something # I mean **like** this thin? (Abe, 3;7.5)

(48) I feel **like** having a pet do you? (Abe, 4;8.20)

(49) watch it walks **like** a person walks. (Abe, 4;9.19)

(50) Daddy # do you teach **like** you do [//] **like** how they do in your school? (Abe, 4;10.1)

This is all the more interesting in that the caregivers in the transcript use *like* as a C only after *sound* or *look*, as in (51). Although the child may have heard the use of *like* as a C in another context, it could also be a spontaneous invention by the child guided by Late Merge.

(51) ABE'S FATHER: it looks **like** some birds have eaten some of the bread. (Kuczaj file 206)

The situation with *for* is similar to that of *like* although *for* is used by the caregivers both as complementizer and preposition. Initially, the preposition is used to express benefactor thematic role, as in (52) and (53). Later, this meaning is extended to time, as in (54), and more abstract use in (55) and (56).

(52) Mom # this white one **for** me? (Abe, 2;7.18)

(53) this picture is mine **for** myself (Abe, 2;7.18)

(54) how long you grow up **for** a minute (Abe, 2;9.27)

(55) Mom # I'm glad you are making a rug **for** out in the hall. (Abe, 2;8.14)

(56) this uh be a cave **for** [/] **for** # what you say? a Thanksgiving one this uh be a cave. (Abe, 2;11.6)

The first target-like C is in (57). Another month and a half later, Abe produces his second one (at least on the transcripts we have), namely (58), and three months later the third one (59).

(57)   yeah and I said I was waiting and waiting **for** you to come and I [/] (Abe, 3;2.1)

(58)   this crocodile was standing around waiting **for** someone to drop around and what did he see when he saw it? (Abe, 3;3.18)

(59)   yeah maybe it's time **for** it to rain we'll have a storm. (Abe, 3;6.26)

Abe continues to use *for* as a preposition, as in (60), as well as a complementizer in (61).

(60)   a.   two Dad # how come some people have cookies **for** lunch sometimes? (Abe, 3;7.5)
       b.   ok then we could go way # way # way down from the stairs and dig **for** that rock I saw (Abe, 3;7.5)
       c.   because people don't use hatchets **for** hunting butterflies (Abe, 3;7.5)

(61)   it's not too high up # but I'm waiting **for** Silver to get ready. (Abe, 5;0)

The total number of *for* complementizers before infinitives, as in (62), by adults in this corpus is thirty-five. This makes the situation different from that of *like* where no such input exists.

(62)   ABE'S FATHER: ok # go ahead and call me when you're ready **for** me to play are you still playing by yourself?

The total number of sentences with a complementizer *for*, such as (61), that are uttered by Abe is twenty-one. There are a few nontarget like sentences like the one in (63).

(63)   CHILD: ropes.
       MOTHER: what for?
       CHILD: **for cows to catch with**.
       FATHER: for what?
       CHILD: **for cows to catch with**. (Abe, 3;0.7)

The HPP predicts that if there is evidence for a pronoun to be both a phrase and a head, the child and adult will analyze it initially as a head unless there is also evidence in the grammar (e.g., from coordination) that pronouns function as full DPs. Feature Economy helps the child reanalyze a lexical element as a grammatical one. For instance, when *for* and *like* are used as complementizers, they "exchange" some interpretable for uninterpretable features. All cross-linguistic variation is therefore in the lexicon. I will now turn to some other evidence for Feature Economy from acquisition data.

Radford (2000) argues that interpretable features are acquired before uninterpretable ones, but are later reinterpreted as uninterpretable, triggering the functional/grammatical system. His data show that pronouns appear late; nouns carrying interpretable Case and phi features are used instead. See (33), repeated here as (64).

(64)   baby eat cookie (Allison, 1;10, Bloom 1973)

The Case features are then reanalyzed as uninterpretable, according to Radford.

Radford also argues that verbs with *-ing*, as in (38a), initially carry interpretable aspect features, later reanalyzed as uninterpretable. One can debate the correct analysis (e.g. one can argue that the features of *-ing* remain interpretable in the adult grammar and that the auxiliary carries the uninterpretable features); all evidence seems to suggest that children start out with interpretable features. It would be good to investigate all instances where currently uninterpretable features are postulated and see how the child represents these.

If the acquisition picture sketched is accurate, acquisition (and maturation) of features mirrors the grammaticalization process and provides evidence that Feature Economy, as in (23), is a cognitive process driving language change.

4. External Factors to Language Change

Many historical linguists see language change as determined by two kinds of factors. There are internal reasons for change, such as those instigated by the Economy Principles or by "Ease," as in Jespersen (1922:261–264), which deal mainly with the articulatory ease of pronunciation. Children acquiring a language use these principles to analyze their input. This probably also happens in the case of creoles. As Mufwene (2001) claims, there is a feature pool of constructions that learners choose from for various reasons (internal as well as external ones). There are also external factors for language change such as a need on the part of speakers to be innovative, polite, creative, or conservative. I will discuss the latter briefly in this section since the remainder of the book emphasizes internal factors.

External factors include pragmatic ones. The urge of speakers to be innovative may introduce new, loosely adjoined elements into the structure. Hagège (1993: 153) uses the term *Expressive Renewal*. Speakers may want to be explicit and therefore chose full phrases rather than heads. One source of new specifiers and words is borrowing. Heine and Kuteva (2005: 3) give examples of *wh*-interrogatives being expanded to relatives in Tariana under the influence of Portuguese, where interrogatives and relatives share the same form. The same pattern occurred in the history of English: *wh*-pronouns were used in questions but were later extended to relative contexts under the influence of French (see van Gelderen 2004: 88). Heine and Kuteva (2005: 73) give many other examples, such as Tariana speakers renewing their evidentials by using Portuguese expressions such as *eu vi* 'I saw'. Lehmann (2002: 20) provides other examples of renewal: Latin *ante* 'before' gets an *ab* prefix to become French *avant*; Latin *ille*, which had become reduced, was reinforced by **eccu illu* to Italian *quello*, as we will see in chapter 6.

Another external factor is the need of society to be conservative and prescriptive. This may stop change altogether. In the chapters that follow, we will examine some examples. For now, I will mention stranding and negatives, where prescriptive rules in English are very strong. Considering economy, a principle such as (65) is expected.

(65)   **Stranding Principle**
       Move as little as possible.

This principle has been used to explain why speakers in English typically front the DP, as in (66) to (69), rather than the full PP in (70) and (71) or the full quantifier phrase in (72) and (73). I have given examples from Modern and Middle English.

(66)   **Who** did you talk to ~~who~~?

(67)   *Quilc men mai get wundren on* 'which men may yet wonder about' (Genesis and Exodus 3715, in Morris 1865, from Denison 1993: 132)

(68)   **The children** might have been all ~~the children~~ reading happily.

(69)   **The roote of riȝtwis men** shal not ben al ~~the roote of riȝtwis men~~ moued. (Wyclif, *Proverbs* 12.3 [1382], from *OED*)

(70)   **To whom** did you talk ~~to whom~~?

(71)   **fro hwat** he scal his sunne uor-saken (HC MEI)

(72)   **All the children** might have been ~~all the children~~ reading happily.

(73)   The sterres also and **all the fyrmamente** she maketh to retorne abacke. (Caxton, *Eneydos*, 23.87 [1490], from *OED*)

Preposition stranding in English, as in (66) and (67), started in the thirteenth century (Denison 1993: 125–127). It is preferred under (65) and it is estimated that in speech 86 percent of prepositions are stranded while in writing only 7 percent are. This difference between spoken and written data points toward strong prescriptive pressure. According to Diessel (2004) and Snyder (2007), young English speakers produce only stranded constructions, as in (74) and (75), but as adults they are taught to take the preposition along, as in (76).

(74)   **where**'s the bolt go **in** (Peter, 2;1.18 Bloom 1970)

(75)   those little things **that** you play **with** (Adam, 4;10, Diessel 2004: 137).

(76)   things **with which** you play

The data on quantifier-stranding, or quantifier-float, are not as straightforward. Unexpectedly, pied-piped instances of the quantifier *all*, as in (72), are quite popular in English (see Wenger 2005), so something else must be going on. Floating quantifiers are very infrequent in child data.

Bullokar's grammar from 1586 contains stranded prepositions, but one century later, most grammarians prescribe against its use: Poole (1646: 38), Dryden ([1691] 1965: letter 17), Lowth ([1762] 1967), and Coar (1796). Yáñez-Bouza (2004, 2007) finds that these prescriptivists indeed had an influence on the language. On the basis of an analysis of 285 different works on grammar written between 1700 and 1800, she argues that the proscription against stranding goes back to the seventeenth century and has a real influence on usage, especially in the eighteenth century. Other languages may have prescriptive pressure as well (see Oppenrieder 1991). As chronicled in great depth in Fleischer (2002), in many varieties of German, preposition stranding is frequent though some describe it as "älter oder umgangssprachlich" (137). It is also common in North American varieties of French; see for example Roberge and Rosen (1999).

Some languages do not strand prepositions even though they have no obvious prescriptive tradition. There is something in their grammars that disallows preposition stranding. Van Riemsdijk (1978) and Hornstein and Weinberg (1981) discuss this phenomenon early on. For preposition stranding to be allowed, the stranded preposition and the verb need to be adjacent: *talk* and *to* in (66). This is also the case in (77), from Jacaltec, a Mayan language, and in many languages of the Kru family, as in (78), from Gbadi.

(77)   *mac*   *chach*   *to*   **munil**   *yin*   Jacaltec
          Who   you   go   work   for
          'Who are you going to work for?' (Craig 1977: 15)

(78)   *tablE*   *yI*   *wa*   *kE-lO*   *lilE*   **klU**   *jIlE*   Gbadi
          table   WH   they   FUT-FOC   food   on   put
          'It is the table they will put the food on.' (Koopman 1984: 54, but tones left off).

Law (1998) offers another explanation: if a language has D-to-P incorporation, preposition stranding is not allowed. This holds in many of the Romance languages as well as in Dutch and German (see chapter 3, section 7). Formulating the exact grammatical constraint against preposition stranding is not important here. I just wanted to show that English speakers allow it even though prescriptive grammar does not.

As for negatives, at least since the eighteenth century, there has been such a prohibition against multiple negatives to express sentential negation that, even though an overt negative object in (78) with a negative *n't* would be expected, this will not happen in most standard varieties of English. Thus, the negative cycle is not continuing in the way one expects it.

(79)   I can't do **nothing** for you either, Billy.(Ken Kesey, *One Flew over the Cuckoo's Nest*, 118)

To renew the weakened negative *–n't*, *never* is used instead, as in (80). Even in (80), prescriptive rules say to use *never* only when you mean "at no time, not ever."

(80)   a.   I **never** saw the outline of a plane, just this incredible ball of flame. (BNC-CH2 12700)
        b.   No, I **never** see him these days (BNC-A9H 350)

The adverb *never* seems to occur in the same position as *not/n't* because it typically follows the auxiliary and precedes the main verb. It must, however, be in a specifier position since the auxiliary moves across it and since it can be modified as in "almost never."

Jespersen (1922) formulates this tension between internal and external reasons for change as a "tug-of-war" and says: "the correct inference can only be that the tendency towards ease may be at work in some cases, though not in all, because there are other forces which may at times neutralize it or prove stronger than it" (1922: 262). It may be that the new utterance is hard to understand, for instance, and is not economical for the hearer. Lightfoot (1979) distinguishes between "changes necessitated by various principles of grammar" and those "provoked by extra-grammatical factors." Gabelentz uses "Deutlichkeit" ('clarity') and "Bequemlichkeit" ('comfort') as important (competing) factors, as in the well-known passage in (81).

(81)   Nun bewegt sich die Geschichte der Sprachen in der Diagonale zweier Kräfte: des Bequemlichkeitstriebes, der zur Abnutzung der Laute führt, und des Deutlichkeit-striebes, der jene Abnutzung nicht zur Zerstörung der Sprache ausarten lässt. Die Affixe verschleifen sich, verschwinden am Ende spurlos; ihre Funktionen aber oder ähnliche drängen wieder nach Ausdruck. Diesen Ausdruck erhalten sie, nach der Methode der isolierenden Sprachen, durch Wortstellung oder verdeutlichende Wörter. Letztere unterliegen wiederum mit der Zeit dem Agglutinationsprozesse, dem Verschliffe und Schwunde, und derweile bereitet sich für das Verderbende neuer Ersatz vor ... ; immer gilt das Gleiche: die Entwicklungslinie krümmt sich zurück nach der Seite der Isolation, nicht in die alte Bahn, sondern in eine annähernd parallele. Darum vergleiche ich sie der Spirale. (Gabelentz [1901] 1972: 256)[17]

For many of the early twentieth-century (structuralist) approaches, the emphasis on ease implies an emphasis on performance factors, or E-language, as for example in Hawkins (2004). In the approach used in this book, I explain some of the "Ease" principles as part of the I-language.

Merge, I assume, is universally available since it is a UG principle. Morphology differs from language to language. If we believe that, at the conceptual-intentional interface, both thematic and discourse/scope information have to be marked, we need morphology or posi-tion to indicate this. If Merge was the crucial evolutionary jump, morphology and other options come later. These various options arise through grammaticalization, and I assume formal principles account for these changes. Differences between languages arise because they are in different stages of a particular cycle.

---

17. "The history of language moves in the diagonal of two forces: the impulse toward comfort, which leads to the wearing down of sounds, and that toward clarity, which disallows the wearing down to destroy the language. The affixes grind themselves down, disappear without a trace; their functions or similar ones, however, require new expression. They acquire this expression, by the method of isolating languages, through word order or clarifying words. The latter, in the course of time, undergo agglutination, erosion, and in the meantime renewal is prepared: periphrastic expressions are preferred ... always the same: the development curves back toward isolation, not in the old way, but in a parallel fashion. That's why I compare them to spirals" (my translation).

TABLE 1.7

Morphological and Syntactic Markers

	Semantic	Grammatical	Discourse
Adpositions	Yes	(Some)	(Some)
Case-inherent	Yes	No	No
Case-structural	No	Yes	No
Agreement	No	Yes	No
Aspect	No	(Some)	Yes
D	No	(Some)	Yes
"Word order"	No	Yes	Yes

5. Typology and Parameters

Three types of languages are often recognized: isolating (Chinese, creoles), dependent marking (Korean, Malayalam), and head marking (Navajo). They represent the different ways that semantic, grammatical, and pragmatic (definiteness/specificity) information may be coded in one language. In some languages, semantic roles are marked through dependent marking (Case or adpositions), grammatical relations through agreement, and pragmatic information through word order or articles, but in most cases these overlap. The result is a varied morphology, as can be seen in table 1.7, and which I work out in more detail in chapter 5.

In this book, I will ascribe the difference between head-marking and non-head-marking languages to different stages of the agreement cycle. As I show, the setting changes fast in some languages without too many other characteristics changing. For instance, the Northern Athabascan languages lack object polysynthesis whereas the Southern ones have it; otherwise, the two are quite similar. This is a problem for approaches such as Baker's (2001: 183) hierarchy of macroparameters. Figure 1.2 provides a simplified version of Baker's hierarchy.

The choice is between polysynthesis and no polysynthesis. Polysynthetic languages treat adjectives as nouns or verbs, and that is the second parameter to set. Nonpolysynthetic languages have many parameters to set. One familiar parameter is headedness. It is clear that there are many problems with this, as pointed out in Baltin (2004: 551). The main objection is that the approach has a flavor of arbitrariness and is difficult to envision as part of UG. How would this have come about as an evolutionary shift?

It is possible to rephrase Baker's macroparameter hierarchy in terms of features and see differences between languages as different feature choices, as is common in Minimalism. I attempt to show this possibility in figure 1.3, which I will add to in chapter 9. This means that languages could be head marking, dependent marking, both, or neither. It goes against the current thinking that both phi and Case features are relevant for all languages. Other attempts involving features are found in Biberauer and Richards (2006), Richards (2008a), and Roberts and Holmberg (2010).

In approaches such as these, the choices are not deep and are feature based. This means that the child gets hints to pay attention to features, which would have to be part of UG. The

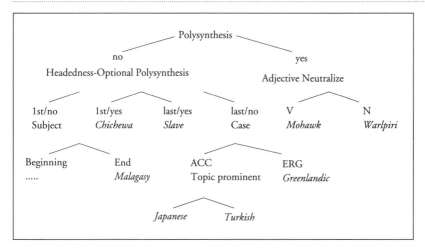

FIGURE 1.2. Baker's simplified macroparameter hierarchy

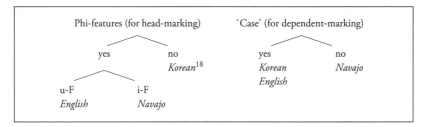

FIGURE 1.3. Feature macroparameters

differences expressed in figure 1.3 are also in accordance with the view that parameters are only relevant to lexical items.

6. Methodological and Practical Issues

To find evidence of cycles and cyclical change, I have read many grammars (and am grateful to the careful work of the authors), but haven't done that in a typologically and geographically systematic way. Where relevant, I have consulted the online *World Atlas of Language Structures* (www.wals.info) to get an idea of where certain phenomena might be found. Since I use a variety of languages and stages of languages, the examples I found constitute only the tip of the proverbial iceberg and rely heavily on Indo-European languages and languages of North America. For contemporary languages, I use data mainly from grammars, the Internet, and corpora. This brings up the issue of competence versus performance, I- versus E-language. Finding a pattern in a spoken corpus shows that there is something systematic going on: repeatedly finding *shouldof* and *shoulda* in contemporary texts (as well as those from the fifteenth century)

---

18. Baker (2008a: 39, 153) argues that T is not a probe in Japanese, which is similar to not having probing phi features; the same would hold for Korean.

indicates that something interesting is happening with modals and perfect auxiliaries. Similarly, if first (and second) person pronouns are "repeated" more than third person ones, this indicates an important difference between those persons in the language. This difference cannot be attributed to performance but must be determined by the I-language.

The corpora used include the 100-million-word British National Corpus or BNC (thetis. bl.uk), the fairly small French Corpus d'entretiens spontanés or CdES (www.uwe.ac.uk/hlss/ llas/iclru/corpus.pdf), the Helsinki Corpus of older English texts or HC (see Kytö 1993 for a description of this corpus), the *Time* magazine corpus (http://corpus.byu.edu/time),and the 2-million-word Corpus of Professional Spoken American English (www.athel.com). The last one is abbreviated here as CSE and contains transcriptions of committee meetings (COMM), faculty meetings (FACMT), and White House briefings (WH). The BNC has been made very user-friendly by Mark Davies's interface (http://corpus.byu.edu/bnc/). With many of these texts, I have used the concordance program MonoConc. I have also made use of individual electronic texts, made available by the Oxford Text Archive and the Dictionary of Old English project (DOE) at the University of Toronto. The latter is wonderful in that it allows one to search all of Old English. For languages such as Norwegian, Swedish, Dutch, Urdu/Hindi, and French, I have used Google searches. The choice of which to use depends on the size of the query. For instance, if looking at all instances of *me*, it is more convenient to select a smaller corpus.

Mostly, I provide bibliographical references for the primary sources (e.g., King Alfred's works and the *Poetic Edda*), but in some cases I use only electronic resources (e.g., Jane Austen's and Ken Kesey's novels). Therefore, if the reference can be found easily, as on the Internet, it will not be listed in the bibliography. I did not want to clutter up the bibliography with works I use only once or twice as example sentences.

I simplify glosses where appropriate but have kept the glosses as much as possible as they were in the original source. When discussing negation and the agreement on the verb or demonstrative is not relevant, I leave that information out. Once in a while, I have left special characters out, such as tones in Chinese sentences, since native speakers say they can get the meaning without them in a full sentence. Data from corpora and Google searches often incorporate unusual spellings or punctuation. I have left these as they were in the original.

It is often very hard to decide which name of a language to use. I have been pragmatic rather than always politically correct simply because it is impossible to be the latter. This results in inconsistency. For instance, Chipewyan is an older name that is well known to linguists but the speakers prefer Dëne Sųłiné (even though they are not in agreement about the spelling of it). I have therefore used Chipewyan/Dëne Sųłiné. I have tried to use language names that were explicitly chosen by their speakers, as with Tohono O'odham instead of Papago, and Athabascan (with *b* and *c*) rather than Athabaskan. Other problems arise using umbrella terms like Persian, French, Mandarin, Urdu/Hindi, and of course English.

7. Outline

This book consists of four parts. The first two examine how arguments are marked and how changes in this marking proceed in a cyclical fashion. Part I, which contains three chapters, deals with a cycle of head marking, that is, increase and loss of subject and object agreement. Part II discusses dependent marking, sometimes called Case. It has two chapters, one on the origin of Case, the other on definiteness. Part III looks at how temporal, modal, aspectual, and negative information is expressed and how this is cyclical as well. Part IV contains two chapters on how cycles are important for work in typology and language evolution.

Part I

2

THE SUBJECT AGREEMENT CYCLE

GIVÓN (1976), ARGUING that agreement markers arise from pronouns, says "agreement and pronominalization . . . are fundamentally one and the same phenomenon" (1976: 151). In this chapter, I show that emphatic and demonstrative pronouns can be reanalyzed as subject pronouns, which in turn can be reanalyzed as agreement and later be lost. I refer to this series of changes as the subject agreement cycle or subject cycle. Subject agreement is frequent, as Bybee's (1985) estimate of 56 percent verbal agreement with the subject shows and Siewierska's (2008) of 70 percent. Subjects aren't the only arguments involved in this kind of cycle; object pronouns can also become agreement markers, as I will show in the next chapter.

Cross-linguistically, there are many examples of the subject agreement cycle, both synchronically and diachronically. Lambrecht (1981), among others, shows that the Modern French pronoun is an agreement marker accompanied by an optional topic. Jelinek (1984, 2001) has argued that in Athabascan, Arabic, and Australian languages, the agreement morphemes are arguments. Katz (1996) has considered the status of the subject pronoun in diachronic stages of Hebrew and Finnish. In this chapter, I classify these stages in terms of phrase structure and provide examples. I also suggest reasons for why one stage is reanalyzed as the next and explain why first and second person start the cycle and behave differently from third person. As the pronoun is reanalyzed, the gender features are lost.

In section 1, I provide background information on the subject cycle as well as on Minimalism as it relates to the subject cycle. I also list the criteria for distinguishing between arguments and agreement. This section discusses Economy Principles such as Feature Economy and Specifier to Head as relevant to the subject cycle and closes with a formulation of the subject cycle's structural stages. In section 2, I examine one stage of the cycle in Hindi/Urdu and Japanese and another one in English and French. In Hindi/Urdu and Japanese, subject pronouns are real arguments, but in English and French they are becoming agreement markers. If the Economy Principles are as important as I argue they are, one would expect fast change. In section 3, I present data from creole languages that are in flux. Sections 4 and 5 examine possible cycles in polysynthetic languages. Section 6 investigates where and why the subject agreement cycle starts and how renewal takes place. Section 7 examines pronouns in relation to complementizer heads.

1. The Subject Agreement Cycle

Arguments can be expressed synthetically (through agreement) or analytically (through pronouns). This has been recognized for a long time (see, e.g., Hodge 1970 for Egyptian) and is not a coincidence because subject agreement arises through incorporation of subject pronouns into the verb. The two ways of expressing an argument are related diachronically.

1.1 THE CYCLE

The typical stages of the subject agreement cycle are provided in (1). Note that third person pronouns typically derive from demonstratives as in (1a). In (1b), I have added the cline for first and second person pronouns, which derive from emphatic pronouns, often oblique ones, or nouns.[1]

(1) a. demonstrative > third person pronoun > clitic > agreement > zero
     b. noun/oblique/emphatic > first/second person pronoun > clitic > agreement > zero

For instance, the Latin demonstrative *ille* 'that' is reanalyzed as the French article *le* 'the', the third person subject pronoun *il* 'he', and the third person object pronoun *le* 'him'. As we will see later, the French pronominal *il* is on its way to becoming an agreement marker. The originally oblique emphatic pronouns *moi* 'me' and *toi* 'you' are becoming first and second person pronoun subjects, respectively. The differences between (1a) and (1b) reflect the well-known views of Benveniste ([1966] 1971) that first and second person pronouns and third person ones function differently: the former have their own reference while the latter need to refer. I will argue that this means the third person has either deictic or gender features whereas first and second person are pure person features.

The changes in (1) have been studied extensively. According to Tauli (1958: 99, based on Gavel & Henri-Lacombe 1929–1937), the Basque verbal prefixes *n-*, *g-*, and *z-* are identical to the pronouns *ni* 'I', *gu* 'we', and *zu* 'you'. Givón (1976: 157) assumes that Bantu agreement markers derive from pronouns. As early as the nineteenth century, Proto-Indo-European verbal endings *-mi*, *si*, and *-ti* are considered to arise from pronouns (e.g., Bopp 1816). Hale (1973: 340) argues that in Pama-Nyungan, inflectional markers are derived from independent pronouns: "the source of pronominal clitics in Walbiri is in fact independent pronouns." Likewise, Mithun (1991) claims that Iroquoian agreement markers derive from Proto-Iroquoian pronouns and Haugen (2004: 319) argues that Nahuatl agreement markers derive from earlier forms. Fuß (2005) cites many additional examples.

1.2 AGREEMENT VERSUS ARGUMENTS

Distinguishing an argument from an agreement marker is notoriously difficult. An argument is assigned a theta role by the verb or by entering a construction via Merge (e.g., Hale &

---

1. Third person pronouns infrequently derive from nouns as well. I leave out the possible verbal origin of pronouns, i.e., through reanalysis of an inflected auxiliary.

Keyser 2002). They are often nominals or pronominals. Nominals need not be arguments; they can be topics, that is, adjuncts, in which case they cannot be quantified or focused. In the case of topic nominals, it is not immediately clear which element in the sentence bears the theta role. Agreement markers bear no theta roles.

As to the syntactic status, agreement markers are always heads and nominal arguments are typically phrases. Pronouns can be either heads or phrases. Agreement markers cannot be coordinated, but full pronouns can be. Thus, coordination forces the appearance of full pronouns, as in (2) and (3) from Malagasy (from Pearson 2001): (2) contains a "weak" pronoun *–ny* and (3) a full pronoun *–izy* in the coordinated nominal.[2]

(2) *Hita-**ny*** *tany*   *an-tokotany*   *i-Koto*   Malagasy
     see-*3*   there   DET-garden   Koto
     'She/he/they saw Koto in the garden.'

(3) *Hitan'* ***izy*** *sy*   *ny zaza*   *tany*   *an-tokotany*   *i-Koto*   Malagasy
     see   *3S* and the child there DET-garden Koto
     'She/he and the child saw Koto in the garden.' (Pearson 2001: 43)

In a Minimalist framework, agreement is represented through uninterpretable person and number features on a probe, such as T. These features need to find an element with interpretable features to agree with. The feature status will be important when we discuss change.

As mentioned earlier, pronouns can be either heads or phrases. Everett (1996: 2, 20) sees pronouns, clitics, and agreement as epiphenomena of where the phi features are inserted. I will argue that much depends on whether the phi features are interpretable or not and on what other features are present. According to Cardinaletti and Starke (1996: 36), pronouns can be "deficient heads," "deficient XPs," or "non-deficient XPs" (XPs being full phrases). Phrases can be coordinated and modified; they bear theta roles and occur in specifier positions. Pronominal heads bear theta roles, but cannot be modified or coordinated since that would render them nonheads. Finally, what look like agreement morphemes may or may not bear theta roles, but they are definitely heads.

Zwicky and Pullum's (1983) criteria for distinguishing agreement from nonagreement (a pronominal head in my discussion here) include the fact that agreement is obligatory and has a fixed position (see also Mithun 2003). The criteria I use to distinguish agreement from full pronouns are summarized in table 2.1.

These criteria will be relevant in the agreement cycle since full pronouns develop into agreement markers. Note that "clitic" is not used here since it is hard to define even though, in the chapters that follow, I occasionally use the term *clitic* to indicate a head that has lost some independence but not its theta role. In polysynthetic languages, markers on the verb are connected to theta roles, hence the agreement with and without a theta role.

1.3 MINIMALISM, ECONOMY, AND THE SUBJECT CYCLE

As mentioned in chapter 1, Chomsky (2007: 3) identifies three factors crucial in the development of language: (1) genetic endowment (or UG), (2) external data, and (3) principles not

---

2. In examples throughout, any instances of "s/he" have been spelled out for clarity.

TABLE 2.1

Pronouns versus Agreement					
	Theta role	XP or X	Fixed Position	i-Phi	Language
Full pronoun	Yes	XP	No	Yes	Hindi/Urdu, Japanese
Head pro-Noun	Yes	X	No	Yes	French, (English)
Agreement	Yes	X	Yes	Yes	Navajo, Old English
(in polysynthetic languages)					
Agreement	No	X	Yes	No	Hindi/Urdu, etc.

specific to FL, such as principles of efficient computation. In the spirit of the last one, also known as third factor, van Gelderen (2004) identifies two principles that account for language change and may be good candidates for principles of efficient computation: the Head Preference and Late Merge Principles.

(4) **Head Preference Principle (HPP):**
Be a head, rather than a phrase, that is, "analyze something as small as possible."

(5) **Late Merge Principle (LMP):**
Merge as late as possible.

For the subject cycle, this means that a speaker will build structures like (6a) rather than (6b), if given evidence that could point to either. A pronoun (or an adverb or preposition) is merged in the head position in (6a), but occupies the specifier position in (6b).

(6) a.

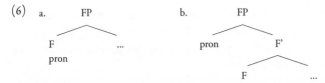

In this way, pronouns are reanalyzed and go from emphatic full phrases to clitic pronouns to agreement markers. This change is slow since a child learning the language will continue to encounter the pronoun as both a phrase and a head. For instance, coordinated pronouns are phrases as are emphatic pronouns. If they remain in the input, phrases will continue to be triggered in the child's grammar. Lightfoot (e.g., 2006b) examines how much input a child needs before it resets a parameter, as for example from OV to VO. In the case of pronouns becoming agreement markers, the child will initially assume the unmarked head option and keep it, unless there is substantial evidence that the pronoun is a full phrase.

How is Late Merge relevant for the subject cycle? Under Late Merge, the preferred structure would be (7a), with the pronoun base generated in T, rather than (7b) with the pronoun base generated in a lower position and moving to T.

(7) a.

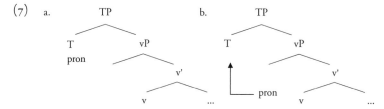

When subjects are full pronouns, they are relevant to theta marking in the lower domain as well as to checking the person and number features of the higher T. After they are reanalyzed as higher heads, a new element for theta marking is assumed (possibly null) and the higher head no longer moves.

It is also possible to reformulate the two principles in terms of feature change and loss. This is preferable since it allows us to see cross-linguistic variation as located in lexical items, not in the computation. Changes connected to the subject agreement cycle occur when the interpretable person (and gender) features of a full pronoun are reanalyzed, i.e. selected from the lexicon, as uninterpretable when they become agreement. Topic/emphatic pronouns have semantic phi features that can be reanalyzed as interpretable and subsequently as uninterpretable. The reanalysis means that the phi features are reanalyzed from interpretable on the (pro)noun to uninterpretable on T as part of the agreement, as in (8).

(8) **Feature Economy**

Adjunct	Specifier	Head	affix
emphatic >	full pronoun >	head pronoun >	agreement
[semantic]	[i-phi]	[u-1/2] [i-3]	[u-phi]
		[u-#]	

The features [u-1/2] [i-3] indicate that the cycle starts with first and second person features, an assumption underlying many accounts. In section 6, I will account for this difference by arguing that first and second person pronouns are structurally simpler and can therefore be incorporated more easily.

As far as theta roles are concerned, emphatic pronouns have none, pronouns have them, and agreement does not. Theta-checking/probing differences are not indicated in trees.

1.4 THE MECHANISMS BEHIND THE CYCLE

The stages of table 2.1 are represented in figure 2.1. In stage (a), the nominal and pronominal (abbreviated as *pron* to avoid confusion with *pro* in pro-drop) are both in the specifier position of TP having moved there from a lower position where their theta role was determined. In (b),[3] the pronoun moves to the head position as a head. In (c), the pronoun is reanalyzed as agreement in T, which triggers the need for another nominal element, usually the topic. The cycle then goes back to stage (a). We could take the renewing topicalized DP in English and French to originate inside the vP and to move up, as in Boeckx & Grohmann (2005). This means that in stage (c) the topicalized DP moves to a Top position whereas in (a) the DP would just move to the Spec of TP.

---

3. See the appendix for more detail on stage (b).

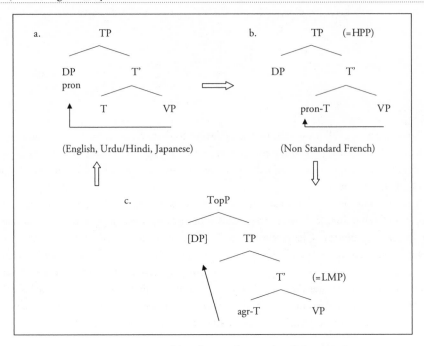

FIGURE 2.1. Stages of the subject cycle using the HPP and LMP

The transition from (a) to (b) is expected under the Head Preference Principle and that from (b) to (c) under the Late Merge Principle.

After stage (c), there will also be loss of agreement inflection, also known as deflection. Double marking is rare, that is, marking the subject both through pronouns and inflection (see Cysouw 2003). Aalberse (2009) develops an interesting approach in terms of the relationship between sociolinguistic forces and internal economy in the loss of inflection. Studies in syncretism are important to examine how inflection is lost. For instance, Baerman and Brown (2008) say that second and third person singular agreement forms are often identical. This is an important aspect of the cycle but one that would require a long discussion.

Figure 2.2 shows the stages of the subject cycle using Feature Economy. I have added both [phi] features and [T] features. As in Pesetsky and Torrego (2007), the latter involve what is traditionally seen as Case. In (a), the phi features in T act as a probe and value their person and number with the DP (or pronoun) lower in the clause; the [u-T] of the DP is valued at the same time (as "nominative"). In (b), the pronominal head is reanalyzed as having fewer features. For instance, the [u-T] features on this goal are absent (but, as we'll see, gender will disappear too).[4] In (c), the pronoun in T has just [u-phi] and needs to probe for another DP (empty or not).

Roberts (2010: 66) sees a clitic/head in stage (b) as a situation where valuation of the features, as in (9), is the same as movement since the features from the goal are "copied" on the probe. When the features of the goal are all included in those of the probe, the goal becomes

---

4. As mentioned in chapter 1, I differ from, e.g., Chomsky in allowing a goal with just interpretable features. However, in (b), we could say that the pronoun is reanalyzed as having some of its phi features as [u-F].

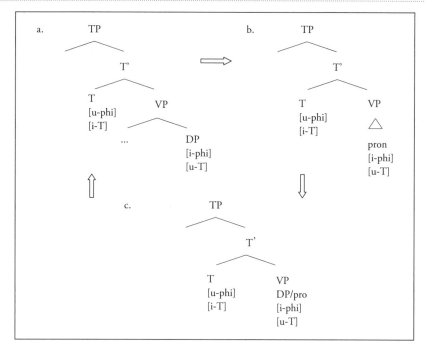

FIGURE 2.2. Stages of the subject cycle using Feature Economy (... indicates an optional phrase)

invisible, so to speak. The reanalysis is that, instead of moving as in figure 2.1, the head stays where it is, but the result is as if it had moved.

(9) Before valuation: T [Pers:__, Num:__] clitic [Pers: 3, Num: S]
       After valuation: T [Pers: 3, Num: S] clitic [Pers: 3, Num: S]

I adopt Roberts's position except that I think this scenario is relevant only with first and seond person pronouns/agreement. Third person pronouns typically have (interpretable) gender and deixis, so are not as readily identical to T. Therefore, they lag behind and are either included after reduction of gender and deixis, as in Italian *I*, or as zero. This will be explored further in section 6.

In (9), after valuation, the result can be a reanalysis of the pronoun as T [u-phi], as in colloquial French and some varieties of Italian, or as [i-phi] in polysynthetic languages. The latter choice would not be economical under Feature Economy and is extremely rare, perhaps only attested in the rise of object polysynthesis in Southern Athabascan. In polysynthetic languages, the subject and object markers in sentences such as (10) look like affixes and that would mean the arguments are empty *pro* and the language is radically pro-drop.

(10)   pro   pro   ***yi-ni-ł-tsą́***   Navajo
                    it-you-CL-saw

          'You have seen it.'

The "affixes" can also be seen as pronominal arguments, having [i-phi] features, and bearing a theta role. In that case, they do not need empty *pro* and can be characterized by the absence of specifiers in the TP layer. In section 4, I discuss these analyses and their relevance for the agreement cycle.

An important consideration in the agreement cycle is the occurrence of pro-drop or null subjects (and objects). When the (pro)noun is optional, it is not clear if the theta role is tied to the agreement marker (and an argument is superfluous) or if an empty argument pronoun is present that bears the theta role. The occurrence of pro-drop is therefore not decisive for determining the stage in the cycle even though the question is relevant. Rizzi (1982: 154) ties the occurrence of pro-drop to rich agreement in languages such as Italian: *pro* is licensed by agreement. This is still accepted as one way of licensing pro-drop. To account for pro-drop in languages such as Chinese that lack agreement, Huang (1984) suggests that pro-drop can be licensed in a language that lacks agreement completely (Chinese), but not in one that has partial agreement (standard English). Roberts and Holmberg (2010: 49) propose a hierarchy, shown in figure 2.3.

If their analysis is accurate, pro-drop is connected to the stages of the cycle since the cycle is based on the choices of [phi] features. Languages with radical pro-drop, that is, without [phi features] would not be subject to the subject agreement cycle. This is certainly true for Chinese.

Like the reformulation of Baker's parameter hierarchy discussed in chapter 1, the hierarchy in figure 2.3 ties features to typological stages. The advantage of figure 1.3 is that dependent marking is added as independent of agreement and that there is less depth in the choices.

Neeleman and Szendroi (2008) have suggested that the morphological shape of the pronoun determines if the pronoun can be left out or not (though they still allow context-sensitive spell-out rules where full agreement licenses a zero spell-out). If the pronoun has agglutinative morphology and different parts of the pronoun are spelled out by different spell-out rules, there is pro-drop. Thus, the Japanese pronoun *watasi-ga* 'I-NOM' has a very identifiable Case morpheme *–ga*. This allows the top layer of the pronoun to be spelled out as *-ga* whereas the NP part can be spelled out as *watasi*. If it is the morphological shape of the pronoun and not the type of [phi] features that determines if pro-drop occurs or not, pro-drop is expected to occur at any stage in the agreement cycle, but that is not the case.

I now turn to descriptions of the stages of the cycle represented in figure 2.2.

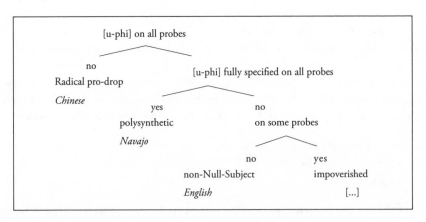

FIGURE 2.3. A hierarchy of pro-drop, from Roberts and Holmberg 2010: 84

2. Full Pronouns to Heads

In this section, I look at examples from stage (a) in figures 2.1 and 2.2 and the transition to stage (b). Section 2.1 shows that in Hindi/Urdu and Japanese pronouns and nouns have the same status, that is, stage (a). Sections 2.2 and 2.3 discuss English and colloquial French, respectively. In English, first (and second) person pronouns are moving toward loss of independence, that is, stage (b). In colloquial French, most speakers have already reached stage (b). In Egyptian and Celtic, discussed in section 2.4, pronouns and agreement are complementary. This makes sense if pronouns and agreement are the same phenomenon, but spelled out in different positions, that is, stage (b).

2.1 STAGE (A): HINDI/URDU AND JAPANESE

A clear example of stage (a) is Urdu/Hindi, where the pronoun is phonologically not reduced, as in (11), and can easily be modified, as in (12).

(11) *mē* 'I', *tum* 'thou', *woo* 'she/he', *ham* 'we', *aap* 'you', and *woo* 'they'

(12) a. *ham log* 'we people'
      b. *aap log* 'you people'
      c. *mē hii* [1S-FOC] 'I'

Pronouns get similar Case endings to full nominals, as (13) and (14) show, and are in similar positions relative to the verb, that is, they need not be adjacent to it, as in (15) and (16).

(13) *mē*   **nee**   *us*   **ko**   *dekhaa*   Urdu/Hindi
      I   ERG   him   OM   saw
      'I saw him.'

(14) *aadmii*   **nee**   *kitaab*   **ko**   *peRhaa*   Urdu/Hindi
      man   ERG   book   OM   read
      'The man read the book.'

(15) **mē**   *kahaanii*   *likhtii*   *hū*   Urdu/Hindi
      I-NOM   story   writing   am
      'I am writing a story.'

(16) **woo aadmii**   *kahaanii*   *likhtaa*   *hē*   Urdu/Hindi
      that man-NOM   story   writing   is
      'That man is writing a story.'

Pronouns can also be coordinated, as in (17). When coordinated, they have the same form as when they are not coordinated, unlike in the Malagasy examples in (2) and (3).

(17) **mē**   *or*   **merii**   **behn**   *doonō*   *dilii*   *mēy*   *rehtee*   *hē*   Urdu/Hindi
      I   and   my   sister   both   Delhi   in   living   are
      'My sister and I are both living in Delhi.'

The agreement on the verbs is full and pro-drop occurs. Urdu/Hindi also has relatively free word order and rarely uses expletives. Both of these features are compatible with its pro-drop character.

Could Urdu/Hindi be a language where agreement (or pro) bears the theta role and the subject (pro)noun is the topic? Butt and King (1997) have argued that nominative subjects are focused. This means they are not in topic positions. An example of a focus marker is *too* in (18).

(18) **Mē** **too** *us see* *kahũuga*   Urdu/Hindi
     I   FOC   he to   tell-FUT-3MS

     'I'll certainly tell him.' (Barker 1975: 1: 213)

Japanese has pronouns that are very nominal (Noguchi 1997). Kuno (1973: 17) notes that Japanese "lacks authentic third person pronouns." Instead, it uses pro-drop or full nouns. These nominal pronouns can be modified, as in (19), and vary according to politeness level.

(19) *tiisai*   *kare*   Japanese
     small   he

The Case marking and topic suffixes on pronouns are identical to those of full nouns, as shown in (20), and they can be separated from the verb, as shown in (21).

(20) *watakusi* *wa*   /   *Yoko*   *wa*   Japanese
     1S   TOP   Yoko TOP

     'As for me/Yoko, . . .'

(21) *watakusi* *ga*   /   *Yoko*   *ga*   Japanese
     1S   NOM   Yoko NOM

     'I/Yoko . . .'

(22) *watashi-wa* *kuruma-o* *unten-suru*   *kara*.   Japanese
     I-TOP   car-ACC   drive-NONPST PRT

     'I will drive the car.' (Yoko Matsuzaki, p.c.)

Typically, pronoun heads cannot be code switched. Japanese pronouns, however, can be code switched in many cases, as in (23), so they must be phrases.

(23) *watashi-wa*   drove the car   Japanese-English
     I-TOP

     'I drove the car.' (Yoko Matsuzaki, p.c.).

Thus, in Urdu/Hindi and Japanese the subject pronoun is a specifier. This is stage (a) of figure 2.1.

Could the Japanese pronominal subjects be topics? Like full nominals, they can sometimes occur in topic position and be marked for it, as in (22), but they need not be, as (24) and (25) show.

(24) *kondo-wa*   **watashi-ga** *kuruma-o*   *unten-suru*   *kara*.   Japanese
     this time-TOP I-NOM   car-ACC   drive-NONPST PRT

     'This time, I will drive the car.' (Yoko Matsuzaki, p.c.)

(25)	*kondo-wa*	*kuruma-wa*	**watashi-ga**	*unten-suru*	*kara.*	Japanese
this time-TOP	car-TOP	I-NOM	drive-NONPST	PRT

'This time, as for the car, I will drive.' (Yoko Matsuzaki, p.c.)

In terms of features, the pronouns and DPs are full phrases at this stage and carry the traditional Case and phi features. The T probe values its own phi features as well as the Case features on the DP (the [u-T] ones). Languages such as Korean and Japanese may have no T with [phi] features (see figure 1.3 in chapter 1 and figure 2.3). That possibility is not crucial for the formulation of the subject agreement cycle since these languages would just not be subject to the cycle.

2.2 STAGE (A) GOING ON (B): ENGLISH

In English, Case is not very relevant, except on pronouns. Even there, the difference between nominative and accusative/dative is not straightforward (e.g., Quinn 2005). I argue that the nominative (*I, she/he,* etc.) is really the head and the accusative (*me, her/him,* etc.) the phrasal variant. I show how the modification and coordination of the head and fully nominal variants differ and also how first and second person pronouns are often repeated if separated from the verb.

English nominal subjects, like subjects in general in Urdu/Hindi, are phrasal and in the specifier position since they can be modified, as in (26), and coordinated, as in (27).

(26) **that book's rejection by ten publishers (he had still not heard from The Applecote Press, Chewton Mendip)** had made him a little nervous of putting pen to paper. (BNC-ASS 2596)

(27) To pay for these new weapons, **the Pentagon and the Office of Management and Budget** have proposed a number of cuts in other accounts. (http://www.d-n-i.net)

English pronouns are less clearly phrasal since they are not often modified and coordinated. In the British National Corpus, I checked the use of the definite article followed by an adjective followed by *he* and found no instances where the adjective modified the pronoun.[5] The coordinated *she and he* occurs 8 times in the BNC and *he and she* 19 times. The pronouns by themselves, on the other hand, are very frequent: there are 640,714 instances of *he* and 352,865 of *she*.

(28) while **he and she** went across the hall, Jasper appeared, running... (BNC-EV1 2028)

The reason that sentences such as (28) are rare may have to do with Case. When pronouns are coordinated, they show an accusative/oblique case in colloquial speech, as in (29).

(29) **Kitty and me** were to spend the day there... (by the bye, **Mrs. Forster and me** are *such* friends!) (Austen, *Pride and Prejudice*)

---

5. There are 178 instances of the sequence *the*-adjective-*he*, but these are of the kind in (i).

(i) ... and told me that my funghi marinati was the best he'd ever had ... (BNC-ACK)

Pronouns on their own are marked as nominative: *I, she, he, they, we*; coordinated and modified phrasal pronouns show accusative/oblique Case: *me, her, him, them, us*. The latter are in topic position. Quinn (2005) surveys the distribution of morphological Case on pronouns and notes that "case considerations still influence the distribution of pronoun forms. . . . However, . . . this case influence is weakened by a trend towards invariant strong forms" (2005: 2). One could therefore argue that there are no nominative and accusative forms, just heads and phrases.

English has examples where the nominative pronoun is repeated because this nominative subject is adjoined to the head in T when possible, as in (30) to (32). This means the language is between stages (a) and (b) in figure 2.1. Sentence (30) is from a piece of creative writing, (31) is spoken, and (32) is from a sports TV broadcast.

(30) She's very good, though **I perhaps I** shouldn't say so. (BNC-HDC)

(31) if I had seen her, er prints **I maybe I** would of approached this erm differently. (BNC-F71)

(32) **I actually I**'d like to see that again. (BNC-HMN 901)

The same repetition occurs with second person, as in (33) to (35), and infrequently with third (in the BNC), as in (36).

(33) then it does give **you maybe you** know a few problems. (BNC-J3Y 72)

(34) **You maybe you**'ve done it but have forgotten. (BNC-FUH 1047)

(35) Erm **you actually you** know you don't have to say I'm. (BNC-JYM 79)

(36) Erm **he perhaps he** remembered who he was talking to and what it was all about. (BNC-JYM 1176)

Subject pronouns are not repeated after VP adverbs such as *quickly,* at least in the BNC, as we would expect if pronouns are in the T position.

(37) a. %I quickly I . . .
  b. %I completely I . . .

As I discuss in section 6, contraction of the subject and the auxiliary is much more frequent if the former is a pronoun. This has been noted by Hiller (1988) and Rickford and Blake (1990) and is to be expected assuming a head preference.

Answers to questions such as (a) are typically (b), as mentioned in Siewierska (2004: 17), expected if *I* is an agreement head and cannot occur on its own.

(38) a. Who did this?
  b. *I/I did

Another sign that nominative pronouns are becoming agreement is that there is a frequent emphatic in English. It is in the accusative/oblique form of the pronoun, *me* in (39a) and (39b), occupying a topicalized position.

(39) a. **Me,** I've been a night person longer than I can remember. (BNC-GVL 335)
      b. **Me,** I was flying economy, but the plane, . . . was guzzling gas. (BNC-HoM 36)

The topics in (39) are hanging topics (HT), as opposed to clitic left-dislocated topics (CLDT), because one can have (40) with a topic marker *as for* and because the Case of the topic and the pronoun inside the clause does not match. This distinction is based on Cinque (1990):

(40) **As for me, I** am rooting for my beloved Red Sox to win the World Series.(https:// www.was.org/Usas/USChapter_files/Newsletter/October04.pdf)

As opposed to Italian (see Belletti 2008), English allows pronominal HTs, as in (40). Using Boeckx and Grohman's (2005) framework that both HTs and CLDTs involve movement, I will later suggest a way to reanalyze a topic into a subject, that is, from stage (c) of figure 2.1 into stage (a).

In English, the emphatic is most acceptable with first person, as in (39) and (40), and second person, as in (41). With third person or an indefinite, it is unattested, as (42) to (44) indicate. This shows that first and second person start the change.

(41) **You,** you didn't know she was er here. (BNC-KC3 3064)

(42) %**Him,** he . . . (not attested in the BNC)

(43) %**Her,** she shouldn't do that. (not attested in the BNC)

(44) %**As for a . . . ,** it . . . (not attested in the BNC)

If the subject is being reanalyzed as agreement, what happens when the auxiliary inverts in questions, that is, when it moves to C? There are a number of varieties of English where this movement does not take place, as in (45) from African American Vernacular English (AAVE), as in Green (1998: 98–99), and (46) from Cajun Vernacular English (CVE), as in Winters (2008).

(45) a. ***What I'm*** *go'n do?*   AAVE
         'What am I going to do?'
      b. ***How she's*** *doing?*   AAVE
         'How is she doing?'

(46) a. ***When you can*** *visit me?*   CVE
         'When do you want to visit me?'
      b. ***Which books you can*** *loan me?*   CVE
         'Which books can you loan me?'
      c. ***Who they shouldn't*** *talk to?*   CVE
         'Who shouldn't they talk to?'

This pattern, where pronouns do not invert, may also occur in relatively Standard English with first and second person. So, though third person pronouns and full nouns occur on their own when the modal moves to C, as in (47) to (49), first and second person do not appear this way in corpora searches, as indicated by (50).

(47) What else **could possibly he** be?(http://driftglass.blogspot.com/2006/10/ file-under-police-dog-whistle-politics.html)

(48) **Might possibly the human race** now achieve its broader destiny?(http://my. athenet.net/~dickorr/Sovran's_Eye1.html).

(49) **Could possibly the third set numbers** stand for letters, characters, rather than words? (http://forums.steinitzpuzzlers.com)

(50) % **might/could/will possibly I** (not attested on a Google search or on the BNC)

This shows that the third person pronoun is more syntactically independent than first and second person pronouns, that is, it occupies a specifier position; first and second person nominative pronouns are heads.

In section 6 below, I suggest that first and second person pronouns are always the first to appear adjacent to the verb, as in (30) to (35), and to be accompanied by additional topics, as in (39) to (41). I now turn to colloquial French.

2.3 STAGE (B): FROM STANDARD TO COLLOQUIAL FRENCH

French is one of the Romance languages that has lost pro-drop and some verbal agreement and has developed clitic subjects. The development I discussed for English pronouns has gone further in French, as linguists have known at least since Lambrecht (1981). I show that the (non-standard) French pronoun is often analyzed as an agreement marker. As before, I will examine modification, coordination, and position relative to the verb. The pronoun is also frequently accompanied by a full nominal or emphatic pronominal in topicalized position. Modern written French is different from the spoken language. I will therefore discuss different varieties and the terms *colloquial French* and *standard French*. I use *French* when referring to all varieties.

In Old French, subject pronouns are optional and forms such as *je* in (51), from the twelfth century, are used for emphasis.

(51) *Se **je** meïsme ne li di*   Old French
      If I myself not him tell

      'If I don't tell him myself.' (Cligès 993, from Franzén 1939:20)

This sentence is of course ungrammatical in Modern French, since the pronoun needs to be adjacent to the verb. Modification and coordination are also rare with pronouns in Modern French but not in Old French, as Kaiser (1992: 151) shows in detail. I examined a thousand occurrences of *je* in the spoken Corpus d'entretiens spontanés and did not find a single instance of a pronoun modified by a PP or another word. There were no coordinated pronouns, as in (52), either.

(52) **Je et tu . . .*   French
      I and you

This lack of modification is not true for third person, as (53) shows.

(53) *et c'est **elle qui** a eu la place.*   French
      and it-is her who has had the place
      'and she had the place.' (CdES)

The regular pronoun is never independent from the verb, as shown in (54). In (54), *écris* must be preceded by a subject pronoun; the same is true of the verb in (55) and (56). As Tesnière (1932) points out, French is a synthetic language with an analytic orthography.

(54) a. *Je lis et j'écris*   Colloquial French
          I read and I-write
      b. **Je lis et écris*
          I read and write

(55) *J'ai   vu   ça.*   French
      I-have   seen   that

(56) **Je probablement ai vu ça*   French
      I probably have seen that

Lambrecht (1981: 6) and Schwegler (1990: 95) mention the elimination of clitic-verb inversion, as in (57). Instead, one hears (58a) and (58b).

(57) *Où   **vas-tu***   Standard French
      where go-2S

(58) a. ***tu   vas   où***   Colloquial French
          2S   go   where
          'Where are you going?'
      b. *que   **tu   vas***
          that   you   go
          'Are you going?'

Auger (1994: 67) argues the same for Quebec colloquial French, saying that only second person clitics appear postverbally. De Cat (2005: 1199, 2007: 14) argues that there is still frequent inversion; her data from Belgian, Canadian, and French French show that inversion, as in (57), occurs only 2 percent of the time in yes/no questions in Belgian French and only 21 percent in the same context in Canadian French. In her spoken French French data, there is no inversion in yes/no questions. In Belgium 40 percent of *wh*-questions are inverted, but in Canada and France only 1 percent and 2 percent are inverted, respectively.

Zribi-Hertz (1994: 137) provides instances of quantifiers as subjects with pronouns preceding the verb as well, as in (59). Since quantifiers cannot be topics, the subject pronoun is indeed an agreement marker and there is no empty null subject.

(59) a. ***Tout le monde il*** *est beau,* **tout le monde il** *est gentil*   Colloquial French
      all the world he is beautiful, all the world he is gentle

      'Everyone is beautiful, everyone is nice.'
      (Zribi-Hertz 1994: 137, from a film title)
   b. ***Personne il*** *a rien dit*
      person he has nothing said

      'Nobody said anything.' (Zribi-Hertz 1994: 137)

The occurrence of (59) makes French and some varieties of Italian different from polysynthetic languages though it has been argued that Romance is becoming polysynthetic.[6]

If the subject pronouns are being reanalyzed as agreement markers on the verb, how can this happen where other clitics precede the verb also in Standard French, such as the negative and object in (60)?

(60) *mais* **je** **ne**   *l'ai*   *pas*   *encore* *démontré*   Standard French
      but   I   NEG   it-have   NEG   yet   proven

      '. . . but I haven't yet proven that.'
      (*Annales de l'institut Henri Poincaré* 1932: 284 [found using Google])

It turns out that sequences such as in (60) are very rare in colloquial French. As is well known, the negative *ne* is fast disappearing and object clitics are being replaced by *ça*, as in (61).

(61) *j'ai*   *pas*   *encore* *démontré*   **ça**   Colloquial French
      I-have NEG   yet   proven   that

      'I haven't yet proven that.'

In Fonseca-Greber's (2000: 127) study of spoken Swiss French, forms such as *je* 'I' always precede the finite verb. If they were anything but agreement, this wouldn't be the case. Fonseca-Greber also shows that all emphatic pronouns (except for *eux* 'them') are accompanied by the subject marker. With proper nouns, the percentage is lower, around 75 percent for person names and 35 percent for place names (321). Definite NPs have additional pronouns around 60 percent of the time, with human singulars the highest (329). Doubled "pronouns" occur frequently with indefinite subjects, on average 77 percent.

(62) ***une omelette elle*** *est comme ça*   Spoken Swiss French
      an omelet she is like this

      'An omelet is like this.' (Fonseca-Greber 2000: 335).

(63) *si un:* ***un Russe i*** *va en france*   Spoken Swiss French
      if a Russian he goes to France

      'If a Russian goes to France.'   (Fonseca-Greber 2000: 335)

Quantifiers are the least likely to be doubled, about 20 percent of the time.

---

6. Kayne (2005: 7) uses the Romance data to cast doubt on polysynthesis as a macroparameter.

(64)   *c'est que **chacun il** a sa manière de . . .*   Spoken Swiss French

     it is that everyone he has his way of

     'Everyone has his own way of . . .' (Fonseca-Greber 2000: 338).

This is the last stage before the pronoun is reanalyzed as an agreement marker. Once that happens, quantifiers generally occur with the clitic/agreement marker. Sentence (64) is rare because the pronominal *il* would be bound. For the same reason, colloquial French does not allow (65) (yet).

(65)   ***Qui il** est allé?*   Colloquial and standard French

     who he is come

     'Who has come?'

However, Lambrecht (1981: 30) reports a switch from standard (66a) to colloquial (66b).

(66)   a.   *C'est moi **qui** conduis*   Standard French
        b.   *C'est moi **qu'je** conduis*   Colloquial French

          It is me that I-drive

          'It is me that drives.'

     The features involved in the change to agreement in (52), (54), (55), and (58) are person features (and possibly number). Third person pronouns are more complex in French (and English) in that gender is also involved. The features of T in stage (b) of figure 2.2 would never be identical unless gender is also lost, and *i* or *e* is the agreement for third person singular. We see this has happened in varieties of Italian in (110) to (113).

     If *je* and *tu* are agreement markers, is French pro-drop or is a new subject already present? Sentences such as (67) are very frequent but not yet obligatory. This makes colloquial French pro-drop. In the CdES, there are 2,097 instances of *je* and 152 of these are preceded by *moi*.

(67)   ***Moi** je suis un blogueur*   Colloquial French

     Me I am a blogger

     'I am a blogger.' (http://www.radical-chic.com/?2009/03/03/910-moi-je-parle-vrai-comme-sarkozy)

Evidence from code switching points to the fact that *moi* 'me' (as well as *toi* 'you', etc.) is an emphatic, or possibly a subject, resulting in a grammatical switch. In Arabic, the agreement morpheme on the verb has a theta role (or there is an empty subject with a theta role) and a subject is therefore optional. If present, it has to be emphatic. This is true in code switching in (68) as well. In (69), the emphatic Arabic does not suffice and a French *tu* is needed, evidence that *tu* is part of the French agreement morphology.

(68)   ***moi** dxlt*   Arabic-French

     I went-in-1S

     'I went in.'

(69)   ***nta tu** vas travailler*   Arabic-French

     you you go work

     'You go to work.' (Bentahila & Davies 1983: 313)

This may show that the emphatic is in the argument position, as in stage (a) of figure 2.1, at least for first and second person pronouns.

French is thus in transition between having subject arguments expressed analytically and having them expressed synthetically. As one would expect, different varieties of French are in different stages. French pronouns show more evidence of agreement status than English ones. As I discuss in section 4, these languages are unlike polysynthetic languages in that they have quantifiers, as in (59). In the next subsection, I examine a stage where pronouns can be considered to incorporate into the verb without the emergence of a new emphatic element.

2.4 PRONOUNS AND NOMINALS IN COMPLEMENTARY DISTRIBUTION: EGYPTIAN AND CELTIC

In some Australian languages (Dixon 1980), Old Egyptian and Coptic, and some modern Celtic languages, the pronoun is in complementary distribution with the agreement marker. Siewierska and Bakker (1996) note that these languages are rare. To their knowledge, a strict complementarity occurs only in Celtic and the Amazonian language Makushi. This complementarity has been explained as the result of incorporation of the pronoun into V or C (Willis 1998: 217). The phenomenon fits with the general direction of the subject cycle in that the pronoun is reanalyzed as head. In Welsh, we'll see (expected) renewal.

Reintges (1997: 62–66) shows that full nominal subjects and pronominal subjects in Old Egyptian have a different distribution (with eventive verbs). In (70), there is only a perfective marker on the verb, whereas in (71) the pronominal subject is combined with the initial verb.

(70) *ʿḥ̣ʿ-n*   *Pjpj* *ḥr* *mḥt(y)* *pt*   *ḥnʿ-f*   Old Egyptian
stand.up-PF Pepi at   north   heaven with-3MS

'(King) Pepi has stood up with him at the northern side of heaven.'
(Pyramid Texts, 814b/P, from Reintges 1997: 62)

(71) *ʿḥ̣ʿ-k*   *χnty-sn*   Old Egyptian
stand.up-2SM in.front-3P

'You stand in front of them.' (Pyramid Texts, 255b/W, from Reintges 1997: 62)

Reintges argues that the endings are incorporated pronouns that occupy the same (original) positions as full nominals.[7] The same remains true in a later stage, Coptic. When a full nominal subject is present in Coptic, the markers on the auxiliary or verb are absent, as (72) and (73) show.

(72) *hən* *te-unu*   *de*   *a*   *pe.f-las*   **meh** *ro-f*   Coptic
in   the-hour PRT   PF   the-his-tongue fill   mouth-his

'Immediately, his tongue filled his mouth.'

(73) *a-f-ent-əs*   *ehun* *e-t-pɔlis* *rakɔte*   Coptic
PF-he-bring-her PRT   to-the-city Alexandria

'It (the ship) brought her into the city of Alexandria.' (Reintges 2001: 178)

---

7. Old Egyptian also has a stative paradigm and here Reintges (1997) argues that the verbal endings are agreement markers since they are obligatory.

The Celtic languages vary in the use of agreement with overt subjects. Middle Welsh has three sets of (preverbal) pronouns, but even the least emphatic ones are full phrases (Willis 1998), as in (74).

(74) ac   **ef**   ehun   yn y   priawt person a   'e gwylwys Middle Welsh
      and   he   himself in his own   person PRT   3S-ACC watched

      'and he himself watched it in person'
      (*Cyfranc Lludd a Llefelys*, 141–142, from Willis 1998: 136)

In (74), *ef* 'he' is separated from the verb and also modified. Willis argues that by early Modern Welsh this situation has changed radically and modified and coordinated pronouns are very rare. This shows that a reanalysis to head has taken place.

There is a stage where the pronouns are doubled, as in the eighteenth century (75). This doubling occurs typically with first person pronouns, expected if *fi* is a head.

(75) **Mi**   af   **fi**   'n   feichiau trosti   Early Mod Welsh
      I   go   I   PRT   surety   for-her

      'I'll act as surety for her.' (*Enterlute Histori*, 50.6, from Willis 1998: 213)

None of the modern Celtic languages shows agreement between the verb and the subject if there is a full DP subject, as (76a) and (76b) from Modern Welsh show.

(76) a. *Gwel**odd**   y   dynion   ddraig   Welsh
         Saw-3S   the   men   dragon
      b. *Gwel**san**   y   dynion   ddraig   Welsh
         Saw-3P   the   men   dragon

      'The men saw a dragon.' (Borsley & Roberts 1996: 40)

An analysis of pronominal subjects in these languages is given in (77); the pronoun is a head moving to T together with the verb. Other analyses are possible but the main point is that when the subject is a pronoun this happens, expected if the pronoun is a head.

(77)

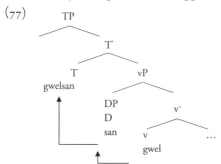

Modern Welsh optionally has an emphatic pronominal subject with an inflected verb, as in (78), but this is impossible in Irish, as shown in (79).

(78) Gwelsan   **(nhw)**   ddraig   Welsh
      Saw-3P   they   dragon

      'They saw the dragon.' (Borsley & Roberts 1996: 40)

(79) *chuirfinn* (***mé**) *isteach* *ar* *an* *phost* *sin*   Irish
      put.1S.   I   in   on   ART   job   DEM
      COND

'I would apply for that job.' (McCloskey & Hale 1984)

These sentences would be analyzed as in (80): the emphatic is being reanalyzed as specifier of the TP and *san* in (78) is agreement in T.

(80)

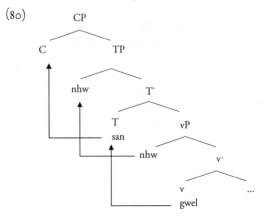

This structure is as in stage (a). So Celtic first shows a full phrasal subject in (74), then a head in (75), and then a phrasal pronoun in (78) for Welsh. This is a full cycle: stage (a) of figure 2.1 is reanalyzed as (b) and then as (c).

I'll now discuss a language where complementary distribution between the pronoun and the full nominal cannot be explained by the difference between head and full phrasal status. In Macuiltianguis Zapotec, in the unmarked word order VSO, the DP subject in postverbal position and the subject marker on the verb are in complementary distribution, as (81) and (82) show.

(81) *Ruuni* **naanquí'yà'** *yíínató'*   Macuiltianguis Zapotec
      ruuni   naan quí'=ya'   yíína=tó'
      do   mother of-my chili=DIM

'My mother is making yellow mole.' (Foreman 2006: 227)

(82) *Ttuttu* *saa* *ribiia-**yà'***   *ttu* *bia*
      each   day   get.on-1SNOM   a   horse

'Everyday, I ride a horse.' (Foreman 2006: 109)

When the word order is SVO, as in (83), the subject is marked twice, so to speak, by the nominal and the nominative clitic on the verb. In (84), the doubling is shown for a fronted pronoun. Foreman (2006: 242) argues convincingly that the subjects in (83) and (84) are in topic positions, and that the clitics are the arguments, base generated in the same position as full DPs.

(83) **Naanquí'yà'** *ruunyé* *yíínató'*   Macuiltianguis Zapotec
      naan quí'=ya'   ruuni=yé yíína -tó'
      mother of=my   do =3FNOM chili=DIM

'My mother is making yellow mole.' (Foreman 2006: 236)

(84) **Ìntè'**   *bettiyà'*   *ttu*   coneeju   Macuiltianguis Zapotec
      ìntè'   betti =ya'   ttu   coneeju
      1sNOM   kill =1sNOM   a   rabbit

      'I killed a rabbit.' (Foreman 2006: 194)

If the DP and the clitic are indeed in the same position in (81) and (82), Macuiltianguis Zapotec is in stage (a) of the subject cycle, and pro-drop is not permitted (Foreman 2006: 282). Foreman's (2006: 249) tree is as in (85) for (86), where the verb on its way to T moves and adjoins to the adverb but where crucially the pronominal subject cliticizes last.

(85)

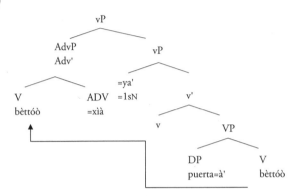

(86) *Bèttóòxìàyà' puertà'*   Macuiltianguis Zapotec
      bèttóò =xìà =ya'   puerta =à'
      close =quickly=1S   door

      'I quickly closed the door.'

Thus, if this analysis is right, Macuiltianguis Zapotec provides an instance where a pronoun is not tempted to behave like a head. It might be necessary to look at the other Zapotecan languages to find which direction the change is going. VSO seems to be basic to many of them (Grimes 2000).

    In some languages, therefore, the full noun and pronoun have the same categorical status (Egyptian and Macuiltianguis Zapotec) and in some (e.g. Welsh), that status is changing. I'll now turn to creoles.

3. From (a) to (b) Faster: Creoles

In this section, I examine whether creoles move faster in losing pronouns and renewing them. The two creoles I look at are Palenquero and Cape Verdean Creole.

    Palenquero, a Spanish/Portuguese creole based on Kikongo, is described in detail in Schwegler (2002). It shows a set of pronouns reflecting a change in stage in progress. It also provides evidence for a start with first and second person singular.

    For the singular, there are preverbal emphatic forms, as in (87) (also used for objects), as well as bound pronouns, as in (88). These represent two stages.

(87)   **ele**   *bae*   *ku*   *yo*   Palenquero
     she/he   go   with   I

     'She/he goes with me.'

(88)   **i-ta**   *minando*   *pegro*   Palenquero
     I-AUX   look   Pedro

     'I am looking at Pedro.' (Schwegler 2002: 278)

The singulars do double, as in (89), in particular in the first person.

(89)   **Yo**   **i-sabé**   *eso*   *nu*   Palenquero
     I   I-know   that

     'I don't know that.' (Schwegler 2002: 280)

Schwegler (p.c) says that there is a person hierarchy with first person (singular) being more doubled. The emphatic pronouns *yo, bo, ele* 'I, you, she/he' derive from the Spanish or Portuguese subject pronouns, but the more clitic-like person markers *i*, as in (88) and (89), and *o* and *e* in table 2.2 derive from Kikongo. Palenquero also has noninversion of the subject and the verb in questions, which is expected if the pronoun is an agreement marker. Schwegler (2002: 282) says that the system has remained remarkably stable, but that this may be due to external reasons.

    According to Baptista (2002), Cape Verdean Creole (CVC) subject pronouns are similar to English and French, except that many more stages are represented and there doesn't seem to be a person hierarchy. The regular pronoun *n* needs to be adjacent to the verb or TMA marker, as in (90), but it is not yet obligatory, that is, an agreement marker, as (91) shows.

(90)   **N**   *ta*   *favora-l*   *dretu*   CVC
     I   TMA   favor-him   well

     'I favor him a lot.' (Baptista 2002: 47)

(91)   **Ami**   *pega*   *na*   *kel*   *livru*   CVC
     I   catch   in   this   book

     'I studied this book here.' (Baptista 2002: 50)

TABLE 2.2

Pronouns in Palenquero

	Pre-V	Independent
1S	*i*	*yo*
2S	*o*	*bo*
3S	*e*	*ele*
1P	—	*suto*
2P	—	*utere*
3P	—	*ané*

TABLE 2.3

Pronouns in CVC

	Regular	Emphatic
1S	*n/m*	*mi/ami*
2S	*bu*	*bo/abo*
3S	*e*	*el/ael*
1P	*nu*	*nos/anos*
2P	*nhos*	*nhos/anhos*
3P	*es*	*es/aes*

The topicalizable nonclitic *ami* does not need to be adjacent to the verb, as (92) shows.

(92) Mas **ami,** N ta trabadja azagua   CVC
       but   I,   I   TMA work   rainy season
      'As for me, I work during the rainy season.' (Baptista 2002: 50)

The long forms can also appear together (Baptista 2002: 51): one is in TOP (or focus), the other in the Spec of TP.

(93) **Ami, ami** pega na kel livru li   CVC
       I,   I   catch in this book here

Example (94) is also possible, and it prompts Baptista to provide a structure with the long pronoun *mi* in the specifier position (of AGRsP) and the short *n* as the head.

(94) **Mi** **N** odja bonberu   CVC
       I   I   see   exterminator
      'I saw the exterminator.' (Baptista 2002: 257)

Mi and *n* can be combined to *mi'n,*[8] which I take to mean that *mi* too is becoming a head.

According to Baptista, the situation is similar for the other pronouns, though not many examples are given. The forms are listed in table 2.3.

Creoles provide evidence of lots of forms, doubling, and renewal of the pronoun by a topic. In the case of Palenquero, renewal starts with first person.

4. Polysynthesis? Navajo, Spanish, and Varieties of Italian

In this section, I provide some background on polysynthetic languages and offer two different analyses for these languages,[9] focusing on Navajo. In this chapter and the next, I am concerned only with agreement, and therefore the term pronominal argument

---

8. The CD audio version that accompanies the book makes this clear, as does Baptista (p.c.).

9. In this chapter, I discuss only subject polysynthesis. In the next chapter, I discuss object polysynthesis.

language (PAL) is better, but polysynthetic is more common. Polysynthetic languages consistently mark agreement as well as other grammatical information, such as aspect and mood. I argue that colloquial French, Spanish, and some varieties of Italian, even though they share many characteristics of polysynthetic languages/PALs, do not fit this classification (contra, e.g., Ordóñez & Treviño 1999). When there is change in polysynthetic languages, there is either a loss of (poly)synthesis, as in Malinche Nahuatl (Hill & Hill 1986)[10] or an increase (e.g., in object polysynthesis in Navajo). I account for this too.

In section 1, there was an example from Navajo and I presented two possible analyses. One, represented by Jelinek (1984), has the agreement marker bearing the theta role. In that model, polysynthetic languages are called pronominal argument languages. For instance, in Navajo (95), the subject and two objects are marked on the verb and the full nominals are optional.

(95) *bínabinishtin*   Navajo
      b-í-na-**bi**-ni-**sh**-tin
      3-against-around-3-Q-1S-handle-IMPF

      'I teach it to him.' (Young & Morgan 1987: 223)

Jelinek (1984), in examining Warlpiri, argues that languages have either lexical or pronominal arguments. In nonconfigurational languages "clitic Pronouns [are] Verbal Arguments" (1984: 43) and all nominals are adjuncts. Jelinek's version of this difference/parameter is (96).[11]

(96) **Configurationality Parameter**
      a. In a configurational language, object nominals are properly governed by the verb.
      b. In a . . . non-configurational language, nominals are not verbal arguments, but are optional adjuncts to the clitic pronouns that serve as verbal arguments. (Jelinek 1984: 73)

Baker disagrees with the assertion that the agreement affixes are arguments, though he characterizes the properties of the languages in similar ways to Jelinek and also argues that the nominals are adjuncts. His approach is that "the morphemes on the verb do not *replace* conventional argument phrases . . . but . . . *reinforce* them" (Baker 1995: 15). Baker (2001) proposes the macroparameter in (97).

(97) **The Polysynthesis Parameter**
      Verbs must include some expression of each of the main participants in the event described by the verb (the subject, object, and indirect object). (Baker 2001: 111)

---

10. Hill and Hill (1986) observe mostly the loss of noun incorporation in Mexicano, not the other characteristics. What struck me in their transcripts was the topicalization, as in (i):

(i) *In   the   tlen   mo-tōca?*   Mexicano
     TOP   you   what   2S-name

     'As for you, what is your name?' (82)

11. Initially, nonconfigurational languages are defined as having free word order (e.g., Hale 1983, 1989), but later the emphasis shifts away from word order because Navajo has relatively strict word order and languages with free word order such as German can be accounted for through scrambling. There is structure to nonconfigurational languages.

As outlined in chapter 1 (see figure 1.2), Baker considers this the main macroparameter, though I will discuss it independently from the other parameters. He distinguishes between subject and object polysynthesis (2001: 148, 149), which I believe is accurate. That, however, weakens his macroparametric approach.

The approaches of Baker and Jelinek are similar in that they assume an adjunct status for the nominal; see also Mithun (1987). They differ, however, in how they approach agreement. I will rephrase the two approaches in terms of [phi] features and indicate how each would account for change.

In Baker's approach, a tree for a transitive verb with a simplified VP might look like (98). I have added the features, but Baker assumes the pro elements in specifier positions. These empty arguments make polysynthetic languages very close to nonpolysynthetic ones, such as English.

(98)

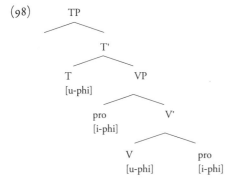

In the case of the loss of polysynthesis, the pro in argument position in (98) would be replaced by a nominal. There are a number of ways to account for this, such as adjunct incorporation (van Gelderen 2008a). A change toward polysynthethic status, as we'll see happening, that is, toward a structure such as (98), would involve the arguments becoming the adjuncts and empty pro elements serving as goals for the probes in T and V. It is harder to think of a third factor (as in Chomsky 2005) reason for this change.

Jelinek's basic tree would look like (99), where I have added the features. Notice the lack of uninterpretable features.

(99)

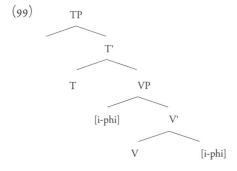

A change from a polysynthetic to a nonpolysynthetic language in this model occurs when the interpretable [i-phi] in (99) is reanalyzed as uninterpretable [u-phi], triggering the need for DPs or pro to provide the interpretable [i-phi] features. This is expected under Feature Economy. The change toward a polysynthetic language, that is, toward (99), involves loss of the probe and its uninterpretable features and the use of goals as both goals and probes. That is similar to stage (b) and fits with figure 2.3: the presence or absence of a probe (nonpolysynthetic vs. polysynthetic) may be a basic parametric choice, if Roberts and Holmberg (2010) are right. For this reason, I will adopt Jelinek's analysis.

Thus, what makes languages polysynthetic is the absence of a probe and the status of the nominal. I will now provide some of the arguments given by Jelinek, Baker, and others to show that all pronouns and nominals are adjuncts. In polysynthetic/pronominal argument languages: (a) nominals (DPs as well as independent pronouns) are optional, as in (100) from Navajo; (b) sentences with more than one nominal are rare, as indicated in (101); (c) there are no anaphors and nonreferential quantified DPs; and (d) there is minimal embedding.

(100) *Nanishté*   Navajo
       na-ni-sh-té
       around-you-I-carry.IMPF
       'I am carrying you around.'

(101) *(Shi)*   *(diné bizaad)*   *yínishta'*   Navajo
       I   Navajo language   1-study
       'I am studying Navajo.'

The optionality of nominals is expected if they are adjuncts, as is the fact that they are specially Case marked in some languages. Regarding (c), Baker (1995: 49) makes the point that anaphors such as "himself" would be adjuncts and hence outside the c-command domain of the real subject. Some scholars have argued that quantifiers are adverbial (Faltz 1995; Jelinek 1995). Thus, in (102), *altso* 'all' is not a quantifier with scope over the entire sentence; it has scope only over the adjacent DP.

(102) *má'ii*   *altso*   *dibé*   *baayijah*   Navajo
       coyote   all   sheep   3–3-ran-away
       'The sheep ran away from all the coyotes' or

       'All the sheep ran away from the coyotes.' (Jelinek 2001: 18)

Regarding (d), Hale (1989) notes that (non)configurationality is confined to constructions, not languages, and that sentential complements such as (103) and (104) in Navajo have to be configurational, even though Navajo as a whole is nonconfigurational.

(103) *Shi-zhé'é kinta'nígóó deesháál nízin*   Navajo
       my-father Flagstaff-to FUT-1-go 3-want
       'My father wants to go to Flagstaff.' (Hale 1989: 300)

(104) *doogááł ní*   Navajo
       3-arrive 3-said (disjoint reference)
       'He said that he arrived.' (Willie 1991: 143)

Baker (1995: 452–495) says that polysynthetic languages avoid embedded arguments. Constructions such as (103) are rare in Navajo; the preferred embedding strategy is nominalization, as in (105).

(105) *honeesná-nígíí yoodlá*   Navajo
       3.win-NOM 3.believe (free reference)
       'He believes he won/he believes the winner.' (Willie 1991: 178)

In sections 2.2 and 2.3, I show that the subject agreement cycle starts with first and second person. There is evidence for this from Navajo, and the other Athabascan languages, for the same development because the first and second person pronouns are much closer to the verb stems than third person ones. Young and Morgan (1980) put first and second person in position VIII and what they call the deictic third person ones in position V, that is, much more to the left and away from the stem. The deictic third persons indicate subjects that are not present, unspecified, or areal. The definite third person is zero. Rice (2000: 181) confirms this for other languages. Section 6 provides more data on this asymmetry.

The characteristics of Navajo just discussed indicate that the nominals are adjuncts. The role of agreement is prominent and resembles the stage of a number of Romance languages. I first provide a few examples where this seems to be the case and then show that neither Spanish nor Italian dialects are being reanalyzed as polysynthetic languages. Instead, they are back in stage (a) of figures 2.1 and 2.2 and follow the cycle. The same holds for colloquial French. "Real" polysynthetic languages are special in the choice of [i-phi] on heads since they lack specifiers.

In Spanish and standard Italian, subjects are optional and one could argue that the agreement, shown in bold in (106) and (107) for Spanish, is the argument.

(106)   *(Muchas tribus)* **buscaban**   *la opotunidad*   *de rebelarse*   Spanish
        many tribes   sought-3P   the opportunity   to rebel
        'Many tribes sought to rebel.'

(107)   a. (nosotros) buscáb**amos**
           'we sought'
        b. (vostros) buscab**ais**
           'you sought'
        c. (ellos, ellas) buscab**an**
           'they sought'

Ordóñez and Treviño (1999) show that preverbal overt subjects pattern with left-dislocated objects in ellipsis, extraction of quantifiers, and interpretation of preverbal quantifiers. Postverbal subjects do function as arguments in Spanish (though Ordóñez & Treviño 1999 do not take this into account); quantified subjects are grammatical as are embedded objects. So Spanish has agreement, pro-drop, and frequent topicalized subjects, but its nominals still function as arguments.

The situation is similar in standard Italian, but there is an incredible diversity in the dialects. In Venetian Italian, full nouns and pronouns can be doubled, as in (108); indefinites, however, cannot be doubled, as shown in (109).

(108)   ***Ti te*** *magni sempre*   Venice
        you you eat always
        'You always eat.'

(109)   ***Nissun (*el)*** *magna*   Venice
        nobody he eats
        'Nobody eats.' (Poletto 2007: 5)

In section 6, I discuss this definiteness hierarchy in Italian. In other varieties, especially Northern ones such as Trentino and Fiorentino, all of these are grammatical, even the quantified one, as in (110) to (113). That means that these varieties are "back" to stage (a) in figures 2.1 and 2.2.

(110) **Nisun** **l'ha** **dit** **niente**   Trentino
     nobody he-has said nothing
     'Nobody said anything.' (Brandi & Cordin 1989: 118)

(111) **Tut** **l'è** **capita** **de** **not**   Trentino
     everything it-has happened at night
     'Everything happened at night.' (Brandi & Cordin 1989: 118)

(112) **Tuc i panseva**   Albosaggia (Northern Lombard)
     Everybody they thought.
     'Everybody thought.'

(113) **Vargù al ruarà tardi**   Albosaggia (Northern Lombard)
     Somebody he will-arrive late
     'Somebody will arrive late.' (Poletto 2007: 6)

Colloquial French, as discussed in section 2, patterns with Spanish and Italian dialects. All seem to resemble Navajo in the importance of agreement. The agreement marker, however, doesn't have a theta role since the nominal doesn't have to be an adjunct (as it does in Navajo). There are in fact some overt subject arguments. This shows that the languages are in stage (a). Polysynthetic languages, on the other hand, are in stage (b) without uninterpretable features. In the next section, I examine some changes in those languages.

5. Loss of Polysynthesis/PAL

In this section, I examine the loss of polysynthesis. Again, it is probably better to speak of a pronominal arguments language than a polysynthetic one since we are only considering the marking of the subject here. For convenience, however, I use *polysynthetic*.

First, I briefly discuss this loss in Pama-Nyungan, following Jelinek (1987), and then I turn to a similar loss in the history of English. A similar loss is said to have occurred in the Eskimo-Aleut family. Fortescue (2002) argues that Proto-Eskimo-Aleut was as polysynthetic as present-day Greenlandic Eskimo, but that Aleut is undergoing a shift away from polysynthesis. For instance, it has auxiliaries for tense, mood, and aspect and only marks third person objects on the verb. I will not examine this claim because of the lack of detailed data.

Jelinek (1987) argues that Proto-Pama-Nyungan was a pronominal argument language where nominals were adjuncts. Dyirbal, a Pama-Nyungan language, evolved from an accusative PAL into a split ergative non-PAL. The older stage, still represented by Warlpiri, has (pro)nominals adjoined and the real arguments marked through inflection on the auxiliary (in second position), as in (114) and (115).

(114)   *Wawirri*   **kapi-rna**   *panti-rni*   *yalumpu*   Warlpiri
        kangaroo   FUT-1S   spear-NONPST   that

        'I will spear that kangaroo.' (Hale 1983)

(115)   *Ngarrka-ngku*   **ka-Ø**   *panti-rni*   Warlpiri
        man-ERG   PRES-3S.NOM-3S.ACC   spear-NONPST

        'The man is spearing it.' (Hale 1983)

In Warlpiri, there are separate pronouns, and they are Case-marked like full nominals. This prompts Jelinek (1983: 80) to consider them as adjuncts and the markers on the auxiliary as nominative and accusative marked arguments in (116).

(116)   *ngajulu-rlu*   *ka-rna-ngku*   *nyuntu-Ø*   *nya-nyi*   Warlpiri
        I-ERG   PRES-1NOM-2ACC   you-ABS   see-NONPST

        'I see you.' (Hale 1973: 328; Jelinek 1983: 80)

Dyribal becomes a split ergative language marking ergative/absolutive on nominals and nominative/accusative on pronouns. Because of the absence of an auxiliary with third person agreement, the nominal was reanalyzed as an argument; the ergative and absolutive in (117) "became grammatical cases" (Jelinek 1987: 103).

(117)   *yabu*   *numa-ŋgu*   *bura-n*   Dyirbal
        mother-ABS   father-ERG   saw

        'Father saw mother.' (Jelinek 1987: 102)

The ergative Case derives from an instrumental. Since Dyribal has no auxiliary verb, the nouns and pronouns are the arguments. This series of changes can be explained with the reanalysis of T with [i-phi] as T with [u-phi].

As mentioned earlier, Modern English is in stage (a), perhaps heading toward stage (b). Old English and Early Middle English, I will argue, are in transition from polysynthetic to nonpolysynthetic. Bonneau and Pica (1995: 135) similarly argue that Old English developed from a system in which complement clauses, relative clauses, and DPs "were interpreted as adverbials to a system in which they are interpreted as arguments of the verb." I will argue that DPs and CPs are not arguments and that Old English verbal subject agreement is argumental, that is, [i-phi]. Evidence for this can be found in the overt verbal agreement, the *-est* ending in (118), that eliminates the need for a full subject with all kinds of subjects, as in (119) (cf. van Gelderen 2000: 121–149).

(118)   *ær ðon ðe hona creawa ðriga mec onsæcest*
        before that that rooster crows thrice me-ACC deny-2S

        '**You** will deny me three times before the rooster crows.' (*Lindisfarne Gospel*, Matthew 26.75, in Skeat [1881–1887] 1970)

(119)   *þæt healreced hatan wolde medoærn micel men gewyrcean*
        that palace command would meadhall large men to-build

        'that **he** would order his men to build a big hall, a big meadhall.' (*Beowulf*, 68–69, in Klaeber [1922] 1941)

Null subjects are especially numerous with third person singular and plural pronouns. This kind of pro-drop continues up to the mid-thirteenth century. Berndt (1956) estimates that in some Old English texts only 20 percent of subjects are overt. Pro-drop is particularly frequent with third person pronouns, which I come back to in section 6 when I discuss the person split.

Old English verbal agreement distinguishes person and number separately. In addition, subjects in the traditional sense are often optional. Starting in the fifteenth century, a topic appears, as in (120) and (121), without being clearly integrated.

(120)   *As for þe toþer.tway enemyes. wich ben . . . seruauntes to hem. . . .. mowe sone be ouer come. whan here lordis and maystris ben ouercome*

'As for the other two enemies, which are servants to them . . . [they] must soon be defeated, when their lords and masters are defeated.' (*The Tree of xii frutes*, 149.11–14, in Vaissier 1960)

(121)   *As for the secunde þinge wiche longith to a religious tree þat is plantid in religioun: is watering*

'As for the second thing which pertains to a religious tree that is planted in religion is watering.' (*The Tree of xii frutes*, 5.8, in Vaissier 1960)

Pronominal argument languages also do not have object reflexives (Baker 1995: 53). The absence of reflexive pronouns in Old English is well known (Faltz 1985); simple pronouns, as in (122), function reflexively.

(122)   *Ic on earde bad . . . ne **me** swor fela*
        I on earth was-around . . . not me-DAT swore wrong

'I was around on earth . . . I never perjured myself.' (*Beowulf*, 2736–2738, in Klaeber [1922] 1941)

Quantifiers, or as Lightfoot (1979) calls them, prequantifiers, are quite complex in Old and Middle English. They are inflected as adjectives, many have an adjectival meaning (*eall* means 'complete'), and some have pronominal functions. This shows they are more referential, like quantifiers in polysynthetic languages. Carlson (1978) explains why quantifiers are not a separate category in Old English. The two reasons I find interesting are that prequantifiers can occur together, as in (123), and can modify a pronoun, as in (124).

(123)   *Mid childe hii weren **boþe two***
        With child they were both two
        (Layamon, *Brut*, Otho, 1200, in Brook & Leslie 1963, from Carlson 1978: 308)

(124)   ***Ealle we** sind gebroðra . . . and **we ealle** cweðað*
        All we are brothers . . . and we all say (*Aelfric Homilies*, 1: 54.8, from Carlson 1978: 320)

In pronominal argument languages, clausal arguments are unexpected since it would be difficult to represent them on the verb. Sentence (125) shows lack of embedding. Note, however, that this does not occur consistently: there are instances of embedded sentences even in Old English.

(125)   *An preost was on leoden. laȝamon wes ihoten. he wes leouenaðes sone. liðe him beo drihten. he wonede at ernleȝe. at æðelen are chirechen* A priest was among people. Layamon was called. He was Liefnoth's son. kind him be God. He lived at Areley. at lovely a church 'There was a priest living here, called Layamon. He was the son of Liefnoth, may God be him kind. He lived at Areley, at a lovely church.' (Layamon, *Brut*, Caligula, 1–3, in Brook & Leslie 1963)

If subject pronouns are adjuncts in Old English and agreement is the real argument, how are subjects Case-marked? It can be argued that there is a split Case system for subjects and objects, objects being assigned inherent Case (by the V, Adj, or P) and subjects nominative Case (which is really a definiteness marker). In (126), the subject is nominative and the object *him* is dative because the verb *forscrifan* 'proscribe' assigns a goal theta role.

(126)   *siþðan*   *him*   *scyppend*   *forscrifen* *hæfde*
        since   3S-DAT   creator-NOM banned   had

'Since the creator had banned him.' (*Beowulf* 106, in Klaeber [1922] 1941)

Inherent Case depends on the theta role, is assigned by V, and can be genitive, dative, or accusative. It is more frequent on third person pronouns than on first and second person ones (van Gelderen 2000). There is theory-internal evidence that pronouns can serve as reflexives in Old English. This can be accounted for through inherent Case in a system such as Reinhart and Reuland (1993).

In Old English, subjects are adjuncts with nominative Case that marks definiteness or specificity while objects have inherent Case. Thus, Old English Case is interpretable (in terms of Chomsky 1995) as is agreement. The loss of inherent Case around 1200 triggers the checking of uninterpretable Case features in functional categories, starting with the most definite nominals.

As we saw, a number of the key characteristics of pronominal argument languages also hold for Old English. Like in Navajo, the grammatical specifier position (Spec TP) is not present. This means that Old English stage (b) has been reanalyzed as Modern English stage (c), that is, (a).

6. Stages in the Cycle: The Importance of Phi Features

In this section, I address several questions:

1. What is the typical "start" of the reanalysis of a subject pronoun as an agreement marker and of the topic as subject pronoun?
2. What constitutes an explanation for this?
3. What is the source of renewals? How can this systematic source be explained?

Siewierska (2004: 263–268) and Fuß (2005: 1–21) review several possibilities to account for (1), as does Ariel (2000). I look at the start of the cycle in 6.1 and explore various accounts in 6.2. I opt for the one already mentioned in section 1.4, the element with the fewest features can be reanalyzed most easily, although I think there is room for more work on (2). In 6.3, I address (3), that is, the source of renewals. I argue the source depends on whether an element has phi features or not.

6.1 THE START: PERSON AND DEFINITENESS

I already discussed how first and second person pronouns are the first to be reanalyzed in colloquial French, English, Palenquero, and Navajo, and we'll see how this process occurs in Cree, Old English, Italian, Palu'e, Jacaltec, Dutch, and Old Norse. As is known from

the work of Forchheimer (1953), Ingram (1978), and Cysouw (2003), pronominal paradigms vary quite a lot across languages, though first and second occur most frequently,
and more persons are distinguished in the singular than the plural (or dual). Bybee (1985:
54), examining twenty-eight languages that mark subject agreement, finds that third person is less often marked than first and second person; see table 2.4 for subject and object
agreement.

Mithun (1991) shows that in North American languages first and second person have different grammaticalization patterns from third person pronouns. For example, in Algonquian
languages, such as Cree, first and second person agreement is a prefix and third person agreement is a suffix, as in (127).

(127)   a. ***ni**-nēhiyawān*   Cree
          1S-speak.Cree

          'I speak Cree.'

       b. ***ki**-nēhiyawān*   Cree
          2S-speak.Cree

          'You speak Cree.'

       c. *nēhiyaw-**ēw***   Cree
          speak.Cree-3S

          'She/he speaks Cree.'
          (data from Monica Brown, from Mithun 1991: 87)

In Athabascan, the third person marker is in a different position in the verbal complex (see,
e.g., Cook 1996 and Mithun 2003). It is more to the left of the stem than first and second
person are, indicating a later date of the change.

In Indo-European languages, it is fairly clear where the cycle starts. In Old English, the third
person pronoun is dropped more often than first or second person pronouns. This means that
first and second person pronouns are the first to be reanalyzed as obligatory arguments. That
number is not as relevant as person is shown in table 2.5. This is as expected if number is also
part of the set of phi features to be checked in T as argued in section 6.2. Axel (2007: 315) shows
a similar split in three Old High German prose texts. In Modern English, first and second
person pronouns again lead the changes, as we've seen in section 2.2, leading the cyclical
changes. These are more like agreement markers, that is, marked with uninterpretable features.

Poletto (1993, 2004) shows that there is a person hierarchy in Italian dialects. In the Italian
of Venice, first and second person pronouns must be doubled, as in (128a), definite nouns
may be, as in (128b), but quantified nouns cannot be, as in (128c). (Examples [128a] and
[128c] are repeated from [108] and [109]).

TABLE 2.4

Person Differences as Marked on the Verb

Agreement	Of First	Of Second	Of Third
Subject	24 (86%)	26 (93%)	13 (46%)
Object	13 (93%)	13 (93%)	6 (43%)

From Bybee 1985: 54, but rearranged

TABLE 2.5

	Null versus Overt Subject in Old English Parts of Lindisfarne Manuscript		Parts of Rushworth Manuscript	
1S	9/212 (96%)	9/656 (99%)	6/191 (97%)	21/528 (96%)
1P	0/53 (100%)	1/120 (99%)	1/44 (98%)	2/100 (98%)
2S	16/103 (87%)	22/308 (93%)	12/90 (88%)	22/226 (91%)
2P	10/206 (95%)	21/428 (95%)	20/168 (89%)	62/302 (83%)
3S	445/116 (21%)	1292/225 (15%)	223/246 (54%)	995/186 (16%)
3P	263/108 (29%)	618/154 (20%)	130/141 (52%)	528/124 (19%)

From van Gelderen 2000, based on Berndt 1956

Percentage of full subject is in parentheses. See van Gelderen (2000: 132–133) for more background on these manuscripts.

(128)   a. ***Ti te** magni sempre*   Venice
          you you eat always

          'You always eat.'

       b. ***Nane (el)** magna*
          John he eats

          'John eats.'

       c. ***Nissun (*el)** magna*
          Nobody he eats

          'Nobody eats.' (Poletto 2007: 5)

As mentioned in section 3, in some other varieties, all of these are grammatical, even the quantified one in (129).[12] These varieties are in stage (a). They are not in stage (b) because in that stage quantifiers do not occur.

(129)   ***Gnun a** m capiss*   Torino
        Nobody he me understands
        'Nobody understands me.' (Poletto 2000: 142)

---

12. There is, as many have pointed out, a difference between universal quantifiers and negative or existential ones. Poletto (2007: 6) provides the following difference.

   (i)   *Bisogna   che   **tuti**   i   faga   citu*   Bellinzona
         necessary   that   everyone   they   make   silence
         'It is necessary that everyone is silent.'

   (ii) ***Quaidun**   telefunarà   al   prufessur*   Bellinzona
         Somebody   will-phone   to-the   teacher

   Universal quantifiers are typically doubled by a plural and more easily left dislocated. Poletto argues that this is because they are interpreted as [+specific]. Her explanation for the doubling hierarchy has to do with the number of features: the more features, the easier the doubling. Doubling is more economical because the feature will be checked through the clitic and the entire element (e.g., DP) does not have to move.

TABLE 2.6

Overt Subjects in Spanish

	S (%)	P (%)
1	18.9	6.3
2	15.9	8.6
3	9.2 (M) 11.2 (F)	3.7 (M) 11.2 (F)

From Rosengren 1974: 237

TABLE 2.7

Mexican Spanish, Overt Subject

Person/Number	%
1S	24.4
2S	12.5
3S	8.2

From Lopez 2007

In Spanish, overt subjects are more frequent in first person and second person than in third. Rosengren (1974) examines theater texts from Spain written between 1945 and 1968 (totaling 330,000 words) and his results for overt subjects with present indicative verbs are shown in table 2.6. Similar differences have been reported for other varieties of Spanish. For instance, in Mexican Spanish, overt subjects appear in accordance with the person hierarchy too, as Lopez (2007) shows (see table 2.7).

I'll now turn to a different stage in the cycle, that is, the one where cliticization starts. Here too, we'll see a split. In the history of English, contraction of pronouns to the left of verbal elements starts with first person around 1600, as in (130a) from 1608 and (130b) from 1630 (both taken from the early Modern English part of the Helsinki Corpus).

(130) a. **Ill** haue another foole, thou shalt dwell no longer with me. (Robert Armin)
       b. **I'le** be at hand to take it. (Thomas Middleton)

In early Modern English, contraction with first person is more frequent. In Shakespeare's *The Merry Wives of Windsor*, there are 213 third person masculine singular pronouns and 10 of those are contracted (5 percent). Of the 745 first person singular pronouns, on the other hand, 74 (10 percent) are contracted (X^2 4.898, $p < .05$). In Modern English, this is harder to calculate since second person is used as an impersonal pronoun as well, especially in spoken English.

In a study of contraction in twentieth-century newspapers, Axelsson (1998: 94ff.) finds only a few contractions with full nouns. Many of them involve personal, company, or geographical names and simple nouns of one syllable, as in (131). Names can be seen as D heads and therefore able to incorporate. There are only a few instances where such an analysis is problematic.

(131)   **Hat's** the way to do it.

(Axelsson 1998: 97)

An additional example of first person starting the agreement cycle comes from Palu'e, a Malayo-Polynesian language of Indonesia. Donohue (2005) reports that Palu'e is a language without agreement but that the first person *aku* 'I' can be free or cliticized to the verb, as in (132a) and (132b). Only one of these can appear, as (132c) shows. Sentences such as (132b) are ambiguous and might lead to reanalysis of the pronoun as agreement marker. It is the ungrammaticality of (132c) that stops this reanalysis.

(132)   a. ***Aku***   *pana*   Palu'e

1S   went

b. ***Ak-****pana*

1S-went

c. *****Aku***   *ak-pana*

1S   1S-went

'I went.' (Donohue 2005)

As we saw in sections 2.2 and 2.3, definite nominals are ahead of indefinite nominals in being doubled by a subject pronoun or clitic, as (133a) and (133b) from standard spoken French show; as we saw earlier, (133b) is grammatical in Swiss French.[13]

(133)   a. ***cette chanson*** *elle est pour toi*   Standard spoken French

this song she is for you

'This song is for you.' (song title)

b. ****une omelette*** *elle est comme ça*

an omelet she is like this

'An omelet is like this.'

The reason for this is that indefinite phrases, containing quantifiers, are difficult to have as topics. Therefore, unless the doubled pronoun has been reanalyzed as agreement, sentences such as (133b) are not possible. The same happens in dialects of Italian as well as in ancient languages. Garrett (1990: 228, 234), for instance, shows that doubling in Lycian only occurs with definite NPs.

Once the pronoun is reanalyzed as agreement (i.e., as u-phi), it will find a new DP and that DP is often a topic. The renewal occurs if the topic changes its movement from Spec vP to Spec CP to movement from Spec vP to Spec TP. This would be a grammaticalization "down the tree" but one obeying Feature Economy.

Combining person and definiteness, we get a hierarchy as in Silverstein (1976), presented in (134a). I have added what I think the features are in (134b). Apparently, Silverstein meant this hierarchy to be used in a binary way, that is, put one line in and the nominals on the left pattern the same way while the ones on the right do so in another way.

---

13. It is peculiar that indefinite third person pronouns are grammaticalized as agreement before definite ones, as discussed by Mithun (1991) for many North American languages. I have nothing further to say on this.

(134)   **Definiteness Hierarchy**
    a.   1/2   >   3   >   definite   >   indefinite/quantifier
    b.   [ego]/[tu]   [-ego]/[-tu]
            [i-gender]   [i-loc]   [u-T]

Third person has always been considered different (see Benveniste [1966] 1971) and I express that in (134) by means of [i-gender] for Indo-Eurpean languages. However, as we'll see in the next section, third person pronouns differ cross-linguistically in other features as well. Third person pronouns will therefore become agreement last since they have to "lose" those additional features.

6.2 ACCOUNTS FOR THE STAGES

In section 1, I provided an account of the agreement cycle using Economy Principles. In this section, I discuss other accounts and then return in more detail to my own account and fine-tune it with respect to where the cycle starts.

6.2.1 Givón's Topic, Ariel's Accessibility, or Frequency?

In Givón's (1976) account, topicalized nominals turn into subjects. This is sometimes called the NP-detachment hypothesis: agreement markers develop from resumptive pronouns in topicalized constructions, such as (135a). The topic is then reanalyzed as subject, as in (135b).

(135)   a. That man, **he** shouldn't be . . .
          ↓
   b. That man he-shouldn't be

Ariel (2000: 211) and Fuß (2005: 9–10), among others, argue against Givón's account. Fuß suggests that Givón would predict the changes starting in the third person, which is not the case. Ariel examines the stages in Hebrew and argues that they do not show a lot of topicalized nominals. She also cites evidence from Celtic (see section 2), Swahili, and Australian languages where pronouns and agreement are in complementary distribution, which one wouldn't expect in Givón's account. I have argued that this complementarity comes about by movement of the (pronominal) head. Ariel (1990, 2000), on the other hand, argues for an accessibility theory.

    A (simplified) accessibility hierarchy is provided in (136): agreement and pronouns represent different points on a continuum of accessibility marking. A speaker chooses between these on the basis of the mental accessibility of what is referred to.

(136)   zero < poor agreement < rich agreement < clitics < unstressed pronouns < stressed
       pronouns < demonstratives < full name
       (part of the accessibility scale, Ariel 2000: 205)

A personal pronoun is more accessible in the speaker's mind than a noun is. Ariel suggests that first and second person are more accessible than third person and can therefore be marked by agreement rather than a full pronoun. Third persons are less accessible and therefore marked by either pronouns or nouns. This need for third persons to be additionally marked also explains the use of demonstratives for third persons, a more marked form for a less accessible person, and the use of topic drop for (highly accessible) first person in English (*Hope to see you soon*). She concludes that "first and second person referents are consistently highly accessible, but third person referents are only extremely accessible when they happen to be the continuing discourse topic(s)" (Ariel 2000: 221).

There are, of course, counterexamples from languages that have third person agreement but not first or second. Ariel mentions English third person singular present marking. However, that doesn't mean third person starts the cycle since we know that first and second person English pronouns were historically used as subjects before third person ones, as shown in section 6.1. The same is true of German (van Gelderen 2000: 136; Axel 2007: 315), as also mentioned earlier.

Another account of the person differences is the frequency-driven one, espoused by several scholars. Siewierska (2004: 266–268) provides a brief review and points out that the frequency of certain pronouns is so dependent on text type that it is hard to use this to explain person differences. Spoken narratives contain a lot of third person subjects (and objects) but regular dialogue has a lot of first and second person.

I will now turn to other explanations and look at the problem through a Minimalist lens.

6.2.2 Person, Definiteness, and Feature Economy

Poletto's explanation of the person hierarchy involves feature checking. First and second person marking involves more features than third person. Therefore, in the case of first and second person, the verb has too many features to check and a clitic pronoun appears as an auxiliary element, that is, it "is a sort of substitute for a verb" (2000: 147). Poletto argues that rather than the verb checking all the features in separate functional categories, the clitics or agreement markers do this more economically. She asserts that pronoun doubling is more frequent with those elements that have more functional information and that the number of features to be checked causes the doubling. She explains the definiteness hierarchy in (134) by a universal order of checking domains: first and second below third, below plural, and so on. I will also use features, but argue something different.

I have claimed that there is a cognitive principle, Feature Economy, assisting the acquisition process and that DPs and other elements already acquired by the child are then also used with fewer semantic and interpretable features. Uninterpretable features enable a smooth derivation. The consistency with which certain interpretable features disappear first, in other words, are reanalyzed as uninterpretable, needs to be explained, however. In section 4, I mentioned briefly that in Old English, third person pro-drop is more likely than first or second person. I argued that this is an indication that the third person [phi] features on the verb may be [i-F] and that no checking takes place. But what gives the different pronouns a different feature? I will use the insight by Roberts (2010b), who argues that if checking of all features looks like movement, reanalysis as a higher position is possible. This is of course more likely with first and second person since they have fewer features.

Many have suggested that first and second person pronouns have more deictic features. Déchaine and Wiltschko (2002) argue that pronouns differ cross-linguistically in their phrase structure. In English, first and second person pronouns project to a DP, as in (137a), but third person ones project to a Phi-P, as in (137b).

(137)

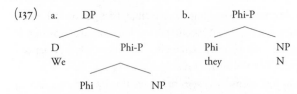

These trees predict the opposite from what we saw evidence for earlier: (137) would predict a full (first and second person) DP to be "harder" to cliticize than a smaller (third person) Phi-P.

I will suggest the opposite from Déchaine and Wiltschko, namely that first and second person are pure phi features (person and number) whereas third person has more features. I also argue that third person pronouns vary cross-linguistically in their features. They can include gender, as in (134), or +/- referential, as in (138).

(138)

Empirical evidence for the difference between can be found in languages that use first and second person pronouns as reflexives, as shown in (139) from Dutch and (140) from late Middle English, but not third person ones.

(139) a. *Ik waste **me***   Dutch
          1S washed 1S
          'I washed myself.'

     b. *Jij waste **je***
          2S washed 2S
          'You washed yourself.'

     c. *Hij waste ***hem*** (ungrammatical with *hem* as reflexive)
          3S washed 3S
          'he washed himself.'

(140) a. *I put **me** in youre wise governance*
          'I am putting ***myself*** under your wise control.'
          (Chaucer, "Wife of Bath's Tale," 1231)

     b. *And softe unto **hymself** he seyde*
          'And softly, he said to himself' (Chaucer, "Knight's Tale," 1773)

One explanation for this is that first and second person pronouns have only person features, and not other features (deictic ones), and this makes them coreferential with another entity. The reason that (140a) disappears from (standard) English has to do with a restructuring of the pronoun system in which the object pronoun is the phrasal variant.

In Old English, third person pronouns can also function as reflexives, as in (141), indicating a lack of refential or deictic properties. Pintzuk (1996) argues that they are clitics and this would fit with reduced referentiality.

(141)   **him** *bebeorgan ne con*
      him hide not can
      'He could not hide himself.' (*Beowulf*, 1746, in Klaeber [1922] 1941)

Kiparsky (2002) argues that Old English personal pronouns are not used deictically, do not head restrictive relative clauses, and are not used as predicates. Pronouns, according to him and Traugott (1992: 171), express the discourse topic whereas demonstratives indicate a change of topic. They both quote (142) as evidence for the different roles of the demonstrative and personal pronouns. The first two pronouns *hi* and *him* continue previous topics but the demonstrative *se* changes the topic to the angel.

(142)   **Hi** *habbað mid* **him** *awyriedne engel, mancynnes feond, and* **se** *hæfð and weald. . .*
      'They have with them corrupt angel, mankind's enemy, and he [the angel] has power over. . .' (Ælfric, *Homilies* 2:488.14, from Traugott 1992: 171)

The use of topic change in Old English may be indicated by demonstrative pronouns, as *se* does in (142), but it also indicates emphasis, as in (143).

(143)   *þæt fram ham gefrægn Higelaces þegn, god mid Geatum, Grendles dæda;*
      that from home heard Higelac's thane, strong with the Geats, Grendel's deeds
      se *wæs moncynnes mægenes strengest on þæm dæge*
      he was mankind's kin's strongest in that day
      'When Higelac's thane heard about Grendel's deeds, (he) was at home in Geatland. **He** was the strongest man alive at that time.' (*Beowulf*, 194–197, in Klaeber [1922] 1941)

Third person pronouns are thus variable in their feature content. Mithun (2003) investigates the affixes in polysynthetic languages. She argues they can indeed be referential and definite in Yup'ik and Navajo. These are affixes that I have argued have interpretable features.

We see thus that the person split is due to differences in the feature content of the personal pronouns. First and second are pure person, but third person pronouns may have other features. I have suggested gender and deixis here, but the precise formulation remains for further research.

6.3 SOURCES OF RENEWAL

If reanalysis as agreement involves the phi features and renders those uninterpretable, it is to be expected that renewal comes from other sources of phi features. As mentioned in section 1, these are emphatic or oblique pronouns, demonstratives, and nouns.

Third person pronouns (e.g., Latin *ille* to Modern Romance *le*, etc.) are created from demonstratives, and the deictic features on the D of this pronoun, I argue, are the reason they grammaticalize as agreement late. Third person pronouns are the last to show pro-drop, as in the history of English, and often result in zero agreement, possibly a sign that the deictic features cannot incorporate as agreement.

In many languages, the agreement and the pronoun look alike, as in (144) from Navajo. This makes sense if agreement has a pronominal source (even though *shí* in (144) may ultimately be a verb with subject marking).

(144)	**shí**	*éiyá*	*Lena*	*yinishyé*		Navajo
	I	TOP	Lena	1S-called		

'I am called Lena.'

If –sh– were ever lost, it is to be expected that *shí* would be "recruited," as well as the second person pronoun. The paradigm for both pronouns and agreement is given in table 2.8 and gives some insight into earlier sources of the renewal of the agreement morphology. What subject agreement and free pronouns have in common is the first and second person singular forms. As can be seen the dual and plural numbers must be a recent addition, with *da* marked in a different position on the verb, and third person is not marked. We have very little evidence of dual pronouns grammaticalizing as agreement.Third person is more complicated and occurs in a different position, and different prefixes occur depending on the type of subject. For the Northern Athabascan languages, Cook (1996: 107) suggests as the origin of one of the third person prefixes a plural marker.

Another example of a renewal that comes from the original pronoun is shown in Khalkha. Comrie (1980, 1981: 210–211) discusses Mongolian languages developing subject agreement from the subject pronoun. His example for the older pattern is as in (145a) and (145b). The newer pattern is seen in Buryat (146).

(145)	a.	**bi** *med-ne*	Khalkha
		I know-PRES	

       'I know.' (Comrie 1980: 91)

       b. *med-ne* **bi**

(146)	**(bi)** *jaba-na-b*	Buryat
	(I) go-PRES-1S	

       'I am going.' (Comrie 1980: 91)

This means the pronoun grammaticalized but presumably was still in use.

TABLE 2.8

Navajo Subject Agreement and Independent Pronouns

	S	Dual	P	S	Dual	P
1	-sh-	-iid-	da + iid	shi	nihi	danihi
2	-ni-	-oh-	da + oh	ni	nihi	danihi
3	-ø-	-ø-	da	bi	bi	daabi

Fourth person, indefinite, and areal left out

Many Asian pronouns derive from nouns (see Cysouw 2003 and Babaev 2008): Indonesian *saya* 'I' originates from 'servant, slave', but is now the regular first person, as in (147). Thai is reported to have over twenty first and second person markers, all derived from nouns. In (148), also from Indonesian, the second person still has the lexical meaning of 'father'.

(147) **Saya** *tinggal* *di* *Bali*   Indonesian
       I   live   at   Bali

       'I live in Bali.'

(148) **Bapak** *tinggal* *di* *sini*   Indonesian
       Father   live   at   here

       'Do you-honorific live here?' (Sneddon 1996: 162)

Demonstratives and nouns provide sources of [phi] features, as expressed in (149). Note that demonstratives would have deictic features, and complicate the picture. These features explain the different grammaticalization steps.

(149) The cycle of phi features
       noun   > emphatic subject > pronoun   > agreement > zero
       [i-phi]   [i-phi]   [i-phi]/[u-phi] [u-phi]
       [sem]

Steele (1976) mentions that in some Uto-Aztecan languages the clitics in second position (i.e., following the first element) are derived from independent pronouns. This can still be seen in one of the daughter languages. In Tohono O'odham (150), *'añ* is reduced from the first person pronoun *'a:ñi*.

(150) *'a:ñi* *'añ*   *s-ba:bigĭ* *ñeok*   Tohono O'odham
       I   1S-IMPF   slowly   speak-IMPF

       'I was speaking slowly.' (Zepeda 1983: 18–19)

Tohono O'odham is polysynthetic with the optional subject pronouns in topic position. Sentence (151) suggests that the auxiliary is in the CP domain since the person marker is cliticized to the Q head.

(151) *N-o*   *hegam* *hihim*   Tohono O'odham
       Q-3.IMPF   they   walk-IMPF.P

       'Are/were they walking?' (Zepeda 1983: 14, 21)

In Yaqui, another Uto-Aztecan language, *ne* 'I' is related to the independent first person pronoun *'inepo*. The morphological form of pronouns is varied in Yaqui. Clitics have longer and shorter forms, depending on the stems they attach to. There are examples of first person *né* (Dedrick & Casad 1999: 42) occurring in second position and of *-ne*, of the independent form *'inepo*, and of a reduced form *'inep-* combined with an object clitic. There is also a doubling: *'inepo-ne* for first person singular and *'empo-'e*, as in (152), and emphatic subjects, where *-la* attaches to the full pronoun *'inepo-la* or the reduced one *'inep-ela* that mark focus, as in (153) for first person plural.

(152) *'émpo-'e   káa   'áman   wée-éan*   Yaqui
      you-you   not   there   go-ought

'You ought not go there.' (Dedrick & Casad 1999: 243)

(153) *'ítepo-la   'áma   tawa-babae-k*   Yaqui
      we-only   there   remain-DSD-PF

'We stayed there by ourselves.' (Dedrick & Casad 1999: 244)

If -*la* is a focus marker, this might suggest that the independent form is in the specifier of the FocP and it could be that the longer pronoun is originally a copula verb and agreement marker. Steele provides (154), which has the subject both in second position as well as attached to the verb.

(154) *Kwarénta péso dyáryota-**ne ne**-kóba íani ínine*   Yaqui
      Forty peso daily-I I-earn now here

'I make 40 pesos a day here.' (from Steele 1976: 553)

Tohono O'odham, like Luiseño, marks its auxiliary with subject and aspect and is therefore a subject pronominal argument language. Many other Uto-Aztecan languages (such as Hopi) do not mark the subject on an auxiliary. In these, the pronominal argument was lost and replaced by the adjunct, but the cycle of (149) might start over again.

Harris (1978) discusses the evolution of 'disjunctive' and 'conjunctive', that is, emphatic and clitic, pronouns in Romance languages. Old French, which is pro-drop, has first and second person *je* and *tu* for nominative and *moi* and *toi* for accusative emphatic. After the loss of pro-drop, *je* and *tu* become the regular clitic pronouns and *moi* and *toi* become the emphatics for both nominative and accusative. The two stages are represented in table 2.9, in accordance with the changes suggested in (149). In (155), these changes are represented with features, pointing toward a loss of features in the history of language.

(155) Old French   Standard French   Colloquial French
       iCase   uCase   uphi
       iphi   iphi

TABLE 2.9

Changes in French First and Second Person Singular Pronouns

	Old French		>	Modern French	
	Emphatic	Regular		Emphatic	Regular
Subject	*je/tu*	zero		*moi/toi*	*je/tu*
Oblique	*moi/toi*	*me/te*		*moi/toi*	*me/te*

From Harris 1978: 117 and Schwan 1925: 179–180

Third person pronouns in French derive from demonstratives, as expected, and include definiteness in some forms. According to Foulet (1919: 108–109), the forms for masculine singular are *il, lui, li,* or *le,* for feminine singular *ele, li,* and *la.* The various plural forms are *il, eles, les eus,* and *les eles.*

So far, I have looked only at agreement patterns classified as nominative-accusative, not at ones referred to as ergative-absolutive. Hofling (2006), Law et al. (2006), and others have examined the history of ergativity in earlier Mayan. The evidence points to similar renewals, but possibly with third person. The same is true with Balochi, as I show.

Robertson (1980) discusses the changes in the Mayan language family. The ergative agreement marker is always a prefix, but the absolutive is variant and can therefore be argued to have changed recently. The agreement markers and independent pronouns are given in tables 2.10 and 2.11 for Jacaltec, an agglutinative VSO language, spoken in Guatemala and Chiapas, Mexico.The absolutive marker is the closest to the independent form and is therefore the most recently renewed, in accordance with Robertson.

As to the start of the cycle, it is most likely to be the first and second person again, since third person pronouns, as in (156a), are obligatory and leaving out the third person subject, as in (156b), results in ungrammaticality.

(156) a. *x-Ø-s-watx'e*   *naj te' iiah*   Jacaltec
ASP-ABS3-ERG3-make he the house

'He made the house.' (Ordóñez 1995: 331)

TABLE 2.10

Agreement Markers in Jacaltec

ERGATIVE	S	P	ABSOLU-TIVE	S	P
1	*hin/w*	*ko/x*		*in*	*oŋ*
2	*ha/haw*	*he/hey*		*ač*	*eš*
3	*s/y*	*s/y . . . eb'*		*Ø*	*Ø . . . eb'*

From Robertson 1980: 13; 15
The variants are preconsonantal/prevocalic respectively. Craig (1977) has *cu/x* for *ko/x* and *ach* for *ač*.

TABLE 2.11

Independent Pronouns in Jacaltec

	S	P
1	*ha(yi)n*	*ha(yo)n*
2	*hach*	*hex*
3	*naj/ix*	*heb/hej*

From Craig 1977: 101–107

b. *x-Ø-s-watx'e   e'   iiah
    ASP-ABS3-ERG3-make the house

    'He made the house.' (Ordóñez 1995: 331)

First and second person agreement is incompatible with having an overt first or second person pronoun as the subject or object, as in (157). This makes it look as if the agreement is more clitic-like, as in Celtic.

(157) a. *ch-in-axni*   (*hayin)   Jacaltec
          ASP-ABS1S-bathe IS

          'I bathe.'

      b. *x-Ø-w-il*   (*hayin) *ha-man*
          ASP-ABS3-ERGl-see IS   your-father

          'I saw your father.' (Ordóñez 1995: 331)

With aspect markers, the agreement is "split" between the auxiliary and the verb, a remnant of an earlier biclausal structure.

(158) a. *ch-ach*   *toyi*   Jacaltec
          ASP-ABS2 go

          'You go.'

      b. *ch-ach*   *w-ila*
          ASP-ABS2 ERGl-see

          'I see you.' (Craig 1977: 90)

Balochi is a split ergative language and both subjects and objects of all types of cases can appear on the verb. In (159), it is the ergative agent. The forms are not ergative, though, but are object clitics (Gibertson 1923: 71).[14]

(159) *mai*   *goš*   *buriϑaɣant-iš*   Balochi
      me   ear   cut.off-they

      'They cut off my ears.' (Gilbertson 1923: 73, 117, from Korn forthcoming: 11)

More work is needed here to determine the start of this cycle.

Returning to the three questions posed at the beginning of section 6, we have seen that the typical start of the subject cycle is with first and second person pronouns (question 1). I have sought to provide an explanation in the features of pronouns (question 2). Pronoun renewal (question 3), after pronouns have become agreement markers, is found in other pronouns, demonstratives, and nouns. The reason for this particular source is that phi features need to be renewed and these elements are good sources of those. Universally, third person seems to include more deictic features and hence its source is typically a demonstrative. I'll now turn to some variations on the subject cycle.

---

14. In the related Harzand dialect of Tati, agents of ergative verbs have markedly different pronominal clitics (Korn 2008: 7), but it is unclear what their derivation is.

7. Agreement in C

In this section, I examine languages where the subject pronoun is more connected to the complementizer than to the tense or inflection. Fuß (2005) makes the distinction between I-oriented and C-oriented clitics. Earlier, I examined the development of the former and now I focus on the latter.

I will argue that in some languages the finite verb moves to C (or Fin), as in (160). These have [u-phi] in C, and are therefore C-oriented.

(160) **Ga** *jij*   *daar*   *vaak*   *heen?*   Dutch
      go   you   there   often   to
      'Do you go there often?'

The (pronominal) subject needs to be adjacent to the verb in C for many speakers, as the ungrammaticality of (161) shows.

(161) *__Ga__* *vaak* __*jij*__ *daar* *heen*   Dutch
      go   often   you   there   to
      'Do you go there often?'

The inflection on preposed verbs, as in (160), is different from that on postsubject verbs, as in (162).

(162) *Jij* **gaat** *daar* *vaak* *heen*   Dutch
      you   go   there   often   to
      'You (seem to) go there often.'

In subordinate clauses, the complementizer is in C, as in (163a), and C without the verb also has a special relationship with the subject. In (163a), for example, for many speakers, adverbs cannot come in between, as (163b) shows.

(163) a. ... **dat ie** *gisteren zou aankomen*   Dutch
              that he yesterday would arrive
      b. *... **dat gisteren hij/ie** zou aankomen
              that yesterday he would arrive

              'that he'd arrive yesterday'

This means that we can argue that (certain) subject pronouns can be agreement markers on C. Sentences such as (164) and (165) provide further evidence.

(164) ... **da-k** *daar*   *niet*   *heen*   *wil*   Dutch
          that-I   there   not   to   want
      'that I don't want to go there'

(165) *Da* *ken-**ik***   **ik**   Flemish
      That know-II
      'I know that.'

De Vogelaer and Neuckermans (2002: 236) provide the paradigm for Dutch inverted and non-inverted verbs with the doubled subject pronouns, as in (165), and maps of the Dutch-speaking areas where they occur, mainly in Flanders and Brabant. The doubling shows that the clitic has become an agreement marker and C is a probe looking for interpretable phi features. De Vogelaer and Neuckermans (2002: 242) conclude that sentences without inversion are more pragmatically marked. The least acceptable are the third person ones. The noninverted doublings are not acceptable.

Example (166) gives an analysis for Dutch where C is a probe and checks its features with the pronoun. Either the verb moves to C or a complementizer appears. It is possible to reanalyze that situation as one where the pronoun is the agreement on C, hence (165).

(166)

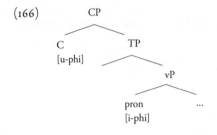

The reanalysis/change to a stage where the pronoun is agreement can be explained as Feature Economy: C is reanalyzed as a probe with [u-phi].

In Old Norse (Boer 1920: 210; Eythórsson 2004; Faarlund 2004: 35), first and second person pronouns may cliticize on the verb, as in (167) from 500 CE. In Icelandic, *hygg ek* can be *hykk* 'think-I'. The Old English and Old High German second person singular -*st* derives from the Germanic/Indo-European second singular pronoun (Lühr 1984), as in (168).

(167) *hariuha   haitika   farawisa*   Old Norse
       Hariuha   named-I   danger-knowing

       'I am called Hariuha, the one who knows danger.' (*Sjælland bracteate*, 2:1, from Krause 1971).

(168) . . . *mec onsæc-**est***   Old English
       . . . me betray-2S

       '. . . you betray me.'

Middle Dutch (Royen 1929: 487) and colloquial Dutch have a clitic, as in (169). Middle English has *hastow*, *wiltow*, and other forms, as in (170), Old High German has (171), Farsi *umad-esh* 'came-he', and Alemannic (172).

(169) *da kank nie doen*   Brabant Dutch
       that can-I not do

       'I can't do that.'

(170) *Se**tow** this people?*   Middle English

'See you these people?'
(*Piers Plowman* 468, in Skeat 1886)

(171) *ni wane the**ih** thir gelbo*   Old High German
NEG think that-I you deceive

'Don't think that I deceive you.' (Otfrid,
Evangelienbuch, 1: 23, 64, from Somers
Wicka 2007)

(172) *hätt-**er** gseit*   Alemannic
has-he said (Giacalone Ramat 1998: 117)

Many of these stages then double the pronouns, as in Old Norse (Boer 1920) in (173), where the full pronoun is base generated in an argument position.

(173) **Fanca**   *ec*   *mildan mann*   *eþa*   *sva*   *matar*   *goðan,*   Old Norse
found-I-NEG   I   mild   man   noble   and   food   good

'I found none so noble and free with his food.'
(*Hávamál* 39, from http://etext.old.no/Bugge/havamal.html)

Thus, for subject pronouns being reanalyzed not as T (as in French) but as C, the person and definiteness hierarchy is relevant and renewal does occur.

8. Conclusion

As we can see, then, subject pronouns change to agreement markers, agreement markers disappear, and pronominal subjects renew, and we can classify the stages of the cycle using phrases, heads, and [phi] features. Pronominal argument languages, though relevant to the subject cycle, represent a special stage.

The cyclical changes discussed here can be seen as brought about by certain cognitive or third factor principles as in Chomsky (2005, 2006), in particular by Economy Principles. Language change is triggered by reanalyses of linguistic data. Words with just semantic features are inert, but reanalyzed with grammatical features, they are computationally active.

What do these cyclical changes say about feature architecture? In section 6, I have suggested that a third person pronoun is more complex and grammaticalizes into agreement later. The complexity is due to additional features of deixis and often gender. First and second person are pure person features whereas third person has a D.

Appendix: From DP to D

Figure 2.1 gives a very broad description of the change from DP to D. I will be more specific here. Theta-marked subjects are merged in the specifier of vP. When the pronoun is a phrase, it moves from specifier of vP to specifier of TP or another functional category above vP in languages such as English.

The next stage is the result of the fact that the language learner reanalyzes the pronoun as a head. Chomsky (1995: 249) says "a clitic raises from its [theta]-position, and attaches to an inflectional head. In its [theta]-position, the clitic is an XP; attachment to a head requires that it be an Xo." Thus, in its vP-internal position, the subject is a phrase, but it later moves as a head. This movement is complex since it interacts with the movement of auxiliaries. Let's assume a simplified VP shell like (174) where the main verb *see* moves to v.

(174)

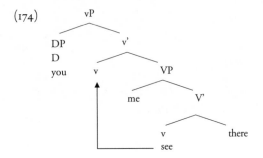

The subject then moves as a head (internal merge) to T. On its way to T, it can move through other heads, as in (175).

(175)

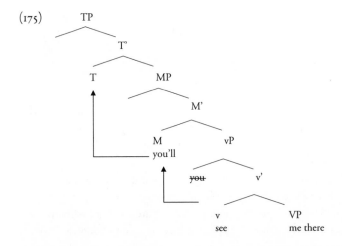

(176)   You'll see me there.

Initial Merge of the pronoun is in the specifier because of theta checking. The T position has uninterpretable phi features and probes for interpretable phi features to agree with. It finds these in the subject pronoun. The next stage is when the pronoun is seen as late merged in T, and reinterpreted as being T with uninterpretable features and as a prefix, as may be happening in French.

Before the change is complete, topicalization occurs. These cases of topicalization look like hanging topics and are standardly (Cinque 1990; Belletti 2008) seen as base generated outside the clause. If we analyzes these topics as originating in the vP, as suggested in for example Boeckx and Grohmann (2005), we get (177).

(177)

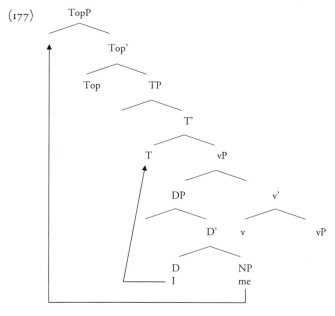

After the nontopic pronoun is reanalyzed as agreement, the DP will be used as goal for phi features, and move to Spec TP instead.

3

THE OBJECT AGREEMENT CYCLE

LIKE SUBJECT PRONOUNS, independent object pronouns can attach to verbs to become dependent heads. They can subsequently be reanalyzed as agreement markers and disappear. This increase and decrease in head marking can be named the object cycle. The phenomenon is widely attested in the Afro-Asiatic, Bantu, Dravidian, and Indo-European language families. In this chapter, I will discuss examples from those languages as well as from Austonesian, Athabascan, and Uto-Aztecan.

Marking subject and object arguments on the verb may constitute polysynthesis. Even among closely related languages, the degree of polysynthesis of the arguments differs. For instance, among the Uto-Aztecan languages, Tohono O'odham and Cahuilla mark subjects and objects on verbs, Yaqui has some object agreement but no subject agreement, and Luiseño doesn't mark objects (Jacobs 1975: 105) and marks subjects only for number (Kroeber & Grace 1960: 137). Different varieties of Spanish display similar variation, as does Athabascan.

To explain the marking of objects on the verb, Harrison (1978: 1093) postulates a verb-object attraction process and Tomlin (1986) formulates a verb-object bonding principle. However, compared to subjects, objects are less tightly connected to verbs. Siewierska's (2008) data show that 70 percent of languages mark the subject on the verb, while only 60 percent mark the object. In addition, in many languages, such as Athabascan, the subject affixes are closer to the verb root, which shows that they were attached to the verb before the object affixes. As in chapter 2, for convenience, I use "clitic" to indicate a head that has lost some independence but not its theta role.

The need for object marking on the verb is hard to characterize: is it the definiteness or animacy of the object that is relevant? Richards (2008a: 139) accounts for differential object marking (DOM) and a number of other effects by arguing that "[p]erson in the syntax just is animacy/definiteness at the (semantic) interface." As we'll see in this chapter, there is a lot of variation as to what starts the object cycle across languages, and I will therefore suggest a relatively uncreative solution of what sets the cycle in motion: animates and definites just happen to be in the right configuration. This makes them different from DOM.

This chapter is organized in terms of the stages of the object cycle. In section 1, I discuss what an object is and provide an abstract example of a complete cycle. As in the previous chapter, I also provide criteria for distinguishing between pronouns and agreement markers. In section 2, I provide examples of stage (a) from Urdu/Hindi, Japanese, Malayalam, and Mokilese, in which the object pronoun is a full phrase. In section 3, I discuss English, Persian, Cape Verdean Creole, and a few Semitic languages as instances of languages that are moving toward or are already in stage (b), where the pronoun is an agreement head. Section 4 examines varieties of Spanish, Southern Slavic, Bantu, and Austronesian languages as examples of stage (c), and section 5 examines Athabascan, since some languages of this family may have undergone a reanalysis from (b) to (c). Uto-Aztecan is a family on its way from (c) to (a)/(b) and is discussed in section 6. Sections 7 and 8 examine other objects and changes with verbs relevant to valency issues.

1. Objects, Agreement, and the Cycle

This section is divided into three parts. In the first part, I discuss what counts as a (direct) object; in the second, I give an example of the object cycle and a representation of the structural changes involved; and in the third, I provide the criteria for distinguishing between pronouns and agreement.

1.1 WHAT IS A (GRAMMATICAL) OBJECT?

It is not always clear why languages need to mark grammatical objects in addition to semantic objects, such as theme or goal, and pragmatic roles, such as quantifier or topic. Grammatical subjects bind reflexives and are responsible for control; direct objects have fewer structural properties.

It is often difficult to distinguish between an object and an adverbial. An object may trigger agreement on the verb and be marked by structural Case on the object DP. It can also be passivized and is typically not optional. An adverbial, on the other hand, is not marked on the verb and may get semantic, but not structural Case. It cannot be passivized and it is optional. Native speakers differ, however, with regard to whether *the pool, the field*, and *to her* are objects or adverbials in (1) to (3).

(1) They swam in **the pool**.

(2) They crossed **the field**.

(3) I gave a book **to her.**

As mentioned, passivization of objects is grammatical but that of adverbials is not; objects are obligatory but adverbials are optional. These differences can be used as tests to show that *the pool* in (4) is an adverbial and *the field* in (5) an object. As the question marks indicate, the judgments are not uniform across speakers. The indirect object *to her* in (6) is even harder to classify.[1]

---

1. The judgments are by American native speakers in an undergraduate grammar class.

(4) a. ?The pool was swum in.
   b. They swam.

(5) a. The field was crossed.
   b. */?They crossed.

(6) a. ?She was given a book to.
   b. ?I gave a book.

Languages typically have no more than one subject and two objects; all three are either separate constituents or can be marked on the verb in highly polysynthetic languages. Some languages employ a combination of these two strategies. In most of this chapter, I will consider constructions with one object. In section 7, I discuss indirect, prepositional, applicative, and other objects.

1.2 THE OBJECT CYCLE

For ease of exposition, I will now provide a fictitious example of a full object cycle, using English words. Let's say that a language has a fully independent object pronoun, as in (7). Since this pronoun can be coordinated and modified and need not be close to a verb, we will say that it is a full phrase.

(7) I saw yesterday **her** (and him).   Fictitious example

A possible next stage is for speakers to optionally analyze this object pronoun as a head, as in (8). This head cannot be coordinated or modified and is phonologically dependent on the verb. The phi features of the pronoun $\prime r$ would be interpretable, probed by the verb with uninterpretable phi features.

(8) I saw **'r** (*and him).   Fictitious example

As I will argue in section 3, this could be the stage present-day English is in.
   The next stage might be for the object to weaken and to be reanalyzed as an agreement marker with [u-phi]. Once it had these features, it would be renewed through an emphatic or some other form, as in (9).

(9) I saw(**'r**) **HER.**   Fictitious example

The emphatic in (9) is phrasal and the cycle can start over again. A possible cline would be (10).

(10) phrase   >   head   >   agreement   >   zero
    [i-phi]   [i-phi]   [u-phi]
    [u-Case]

   Figure 3.1 shows one way of representing the object cycle. For simplicity, there are only two layers in the vP shell. In stage (a), the main verb moves to the light verb v and, depending on the language, to T. This is the stage for (7): the object pronoun is phrasal and in a specifier

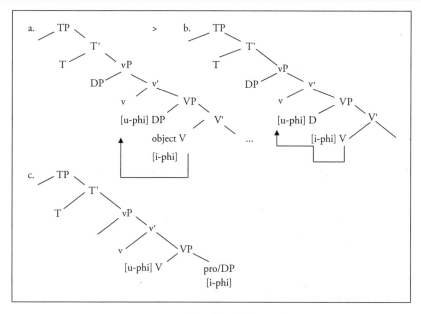

FIGURE 3.1. The (direct) object cycle

position. As mentioned earlier, pronouns can be either heads or phrases. If they are heads, they are "picked up" by the verb on its way to the light v, as in (b), a representation of (8). Under the Head Preference Principle, this is the preferred situation. In this stage, there can be no additional coreferential full nominal, that is, the pronoun and nominal are in complementary distribution. In stage (c), the pronominal head is reanalyzed as a higher functional head, that is, as a set of uninterpretable features on v. This stage could have a *pro* or another phrasal (pro)nominal as an object inside the VP. It is similar to (a) *after* a loss of object pro-drop.[2] Object polysynthesis can be represented as (b), but as explained in the previous chapter in the discussion of subject polysynthesis, the v would lack [u-phi].

A more elaborate vP shell is possible. Much recent work has expanded the VP with a vP and an inner aspect phrase. Ramchand (2008), for instance, posits an initiator phrase, a process phrase, and a result phrase. For my purposes, the exact names do not matter. Therefore, I adopt a structure such as in (11) with three layers and a vP where all arguments are in specifier positions.

(11)

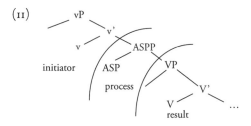

<hr />

2. I will avoid the term *clitic doubling* since it is unclear whether the doubled element is in an argument or an adjunct position.

In the previous chapter, I argued that it is unusual for the third person pronominal subject to be reanalyzed as subject agreement due to its additional deictic features (at least in many languages). With respect to object agreement, there is enormous diversity as to what starts the cycle. Animate and definite object pronouns of all persons are reanalyzed as object agreement but there is no obvious pattern. Indefinite objects, like indefinite subjects, are the last to be incorporated because, when they are doubled, they have to be arguments and the doubled pronoun is then agreement. Figure 3.2 shows that in stage (a), there is checking with a full DP. I assume there is no EPP feature on v to cause movement of the DP. When a pronoun is the object, as in (b), it can be taken out of the lexicon with fewer features. After valuation of [u-phi], the evidence for a separate pronoun is not evident. Stage (c) renews the pronoun that has been reanalyzed as agreement.

As we know, the subject cycle starts with first and second person pronouns. The object cycle, on the other hand, starts with first and second person pronouns (in Uto-Aztecan and Swahili) or with third person (in Persian most likely) or with definite objects (in Macedonian). With the emphasis on animacy, it is interesting to note that object agreement often retains gender, unlike subject agreement. Differential object marking, discussed in chapter 5, will show the same starting point of animate and definite objects. Richards (2008b) argues that syntactic [person] is semantic animacy/definiteness, and I assume that that's what is grammaticalized in the case of objects. The reason definiteness, in addition to animacy, is also important is the presence of the [ASP] features: only definite and animate DPs appear in the relevant configuration. It would be necessary to look at the pronominal features of each language to come up with a precise reason. I have not done that.

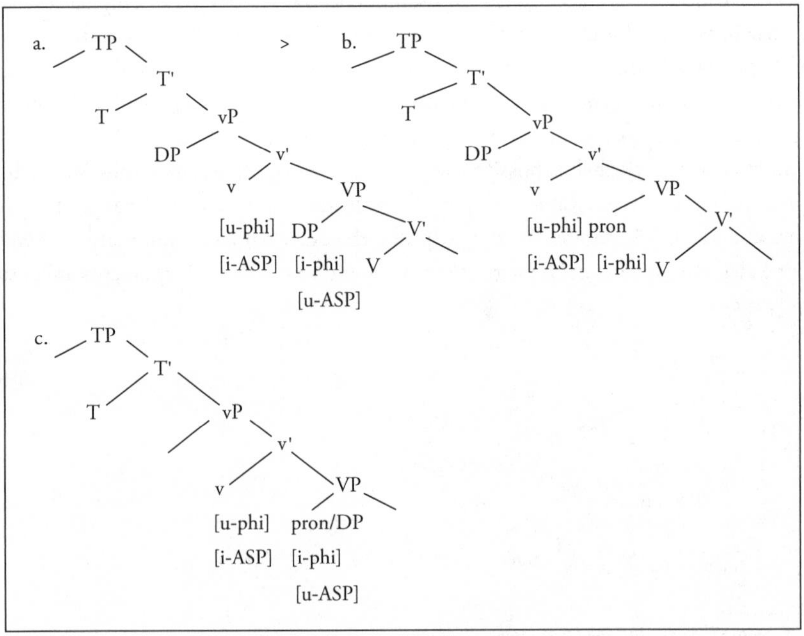

FIGURE 3.2. The (direct) object cycle in terms of features

1.3 AGREEMENT, HEADS, PHRASAL PRONOUNS, SUBJECTS AND TOPICS

The status of full DPs and pronouns is not completely clear in many languages. In the previous chapter, I provided the criteria for distinguishing the different stages of subject pronouns. I do the same for object pronouns in table 3.1. As in chapter 2, I assume that agreement can have interpretable features in polysynthetic languages.

The term *clitic doubling* is used when a pronominal head is optional, as in (12); *agreement* is used when the marking is obligatory.

(12) *zri-x-t*   **umcic**   Taqbaylit Berber
      saw-I-it   cat
      'I saw the cat.' (Tsakali & Anagnostopoulou 2008: 340)

It is not always clear whether that head, or clitic, has a theta role. Some other examples of object agreement and clitic doubling may be helpful. As Tsakali and Anagnostopoulou (2008) show, clitic doubling occurs in Taqbaylit Berber (12), Greek, Albanian, and Bulgarian (13); French, on the other hand, has participle agreement and clitics, but no clitic doubling, as shown in (14).

(13) *Vidjah* **(go)** *Ivan*   Bulgarian
      I-saw   3S   Ivan
      'I saw Ivan.'

(14) *Paul* *les*   *a*   *repeintes*   (*les tables*)   French
      Paul   them-ACC   has-3S   repainted-3P   the tables
      'Paul has repainted them [the tables].'

How does one distinguish between the doubled clitic *–t* in (12), the clitic *les* in (14), and the agreement marker *–es* in (14)? In (14), the clitic *les* counts as an argument; hence, an additional DP *les tables* is not possible. In the varieties of French where clitic doubling occurs, past participle agreement is ungrammatical, as (15a) and (15b) show. This indicates that the doubled pronominal head has taken over the function of agreement.

TABLE 3.1

Object Pronouns versus Agreement

	Theta role	XP or X	Fixed Position	i-phi	Language
Full pronoun	Yes	XP	No	Yes	Hindi/Urdu, Japanese
Head	Yes	X	No	Yes	Persian, English
Agreement	Yes	X	Yes	Yes	TohoNo O'odham, Navajo
Agreement	No	X	Yes	No	Yaqui

(15) a. *Il*   **m'a**   *mis*   *sur*   *la*   *liste*   Variety of French
          he   1S-be-3S   put   on   the   list
      b. **Il* **m'a**   *mis-e* **moi** *sur*   *la*   *liste*
          he   1S-has-3S   put-F   me   on   the   list

      'He has put me on the list.' (Tsakali & Anagnostopoulou 2008: 346)

Tsakali and Anagnostopoulou's account depends on how the full DP is associated with the sensorimotor interface: "in a split-checking derivation the associate receives contradictory information with respect to where it should be pronounced, by both the Clitic Phrase and the Agr-OP" (2008: 344). In (15b), *moi* 'me' cannot be unambiguously associated with either the clitic *m* or the agreement *e*. I assume that the clitic doubling and agreement options are different stages in the cycle that are in complementary distribution since they are both heads.

Very relevant here is the status of DPs: are they adjuncts (topics) or arguments (subjects) and, when topics, what kind? De Cat (2007: 64) provides some criteria: individual level predicates force the "subject" into a topic position and "cause" clitic doubling, as in (16a), while stage level predicates do not, as in (16b).

(16) a. *Le*   *malais*   *c'est*   *difficile*   French
          DEF   Malay   it-is   difficult

      'Malay is difficult.' (De Cat 2007: 77)

      b. *Le*   *directeur*   *est*   *là*

      'The   director   is   there.' (De Cat 2007: 77)

Even clear topics can either be moved to a topic position (left dislocated) or to a higher position (hanging). The criteria for determining the type of topic involve sensitivity to islands (although this has been disputed), doubling, and prosodic characteristics. Table 3.2 lists the criteria for distinguishing between subjects and topics. As mentioned in chapter 2, one can argue that even hanging topics can be moving.

We'll now examine some of the stages of the object cycle.

TABLE 3.2

Arguments versus Topics

	Hanging Topic	Dislocated Topic	Argument
Position	Above ForceP[a]	Spec TopP	In vP
Pause	Long	Less long	Least long
Island sensitive	(No)	(Yes)	N/a

E.g., DiscP, Benincà 2001

2. Fully Phrasal Pronominal Objects: Stage (a)

Urdu/Hindi is in stage (a): pronouns appear either as unmarked or oblique forms, as shown in table 3.3.

Examples of object pronouns are given in (17) and (18); the preferred construction is (18) with the object marked by *-ee* (Barker 1975: 141). The object does not cliticize onto the verb since an adverbial can intervene in (17).

(17) *mēy* *nee* ***us*** ***ko*** *gher* *me* *dekhaa*   Urdu/Hindi
      I ERG him/her OBL house in saw-3MS
      'I saw him/her in the house.'

(18) *mēy* *nee* ***usee*** *dekhaa*   Urdu/Hindi
      I ERG 3-OBL saw-3MS
      'I saw her/him.'

In the previous chapter, Japanese subject pronouns were shown to be phrasal. Object pronouns can be modified in the appropriate context and are also phrasal. They can be Case marked, as in (19), and need not be adjacent to the verb.

(19) a. *watashi-wa* ***kare-o*** *mimashita*   Japanese
        1S-TOP 3S-ACC saw
        'I saw him.'

     b. kare-wa ***watashi-o*** mimashita
        3S-TOP 1S-ACC saw
        'He saw me.' (Yoko Matsuzaki, p.c.)

Malayalam, a Dravidian language, has both subject and object pro-drop and no verbal agreement. The pronouns are phrasal, as shown in (20).

(20) *Raaman* ***awan-e*** *sneehikunnu*   Malayalam
      Raman he-ACC love
      'Raman loves him.' (Jayaseelan 2000: 18)

TABLE 3.3

Pronouns in Urdu/Hindi

	Unmarked	Oblique
1S	*mēy*	*mujh(ee)*
2S	*tum*	*tujh(ee)*
3S	*woo*	*us(ee)/us ko*
1P	*ham*	*ham(ee)*
2P	*aap*	*aap ko*
3P	*woo*	*un(hee)*

In addition, the system has three kinds of honorific marking, three persons and genders as well as number and deixis. As expected, it is easy to code switch between an English verb and a Malayalam object pronoun, as in (21).

(21) They saw **enne**   English/Malayalam
                me

'They saw me.' (Anju Kuriakose, p.c.)

Urdu, Japanese, and Malayalam are dependent marking languages, to use Nichols's (1992) term. These typically have independent pronouns. Therefore, certain stages of the subject and object cycles may coincide with stages of the Case cycle.

Some non-dependent-marking languages also show evidence of cyclical changes in pronouns. Song (1994) surveys object pronouns in a number of Nuclear Micronesian languages. Some approach agreement markers, as in (22); some are clitics, as in (23); and others are quite independent, as in (24), where no distinction is made in form between a subject and object pronoun.

(22) *Nga   kihte-l   **Sah***   Kosraean
     I   feed-3S   Sah

'I am feeding him.' (Lee 1975: 61)

(23) *Kidi-o   nglalis-**ie***   Ponapean
     dog-DET   bit-me

'That dog bit me.' (Rehg 1981: 229)

(24) *Ih   ka-mwinge-hla   **arai***   Mokilese
     She   CAUS-eat-PF   them

'She fed them.' (Harrison 1976: 87)

The object pronouns in Mokilese can be moved and are therefore considered independent forms by Song (1994: 539). In addition, the pronominal paradigm is quite elaborate and the forms are phonologically strong. The first person singular is *ngoah(i)* and the second singular is *koah/koawoa*, and there is no distinction for subject or object. Harrison (1978: 1095–1098) argues that the Mokilese pronouns are the result of replacement by focus pronouns, so that the Nuclear Micronesian languages all show different stages of the object cycle. In section 4, I discuss Micronesian more fully, in particular Marshallese.

3. Persian, Cape Verdean Creole, English, and Semitic: From Stage (a) to (b)

In this section, I discuss the transition from (a) to (b). Persian has independent as well as dependent pronouns and could therefore be in transition. Object pronouns in Cape Verdean Creole are close to the verb and doubling is possible only with human DPs. Modern English, Arabic, Hebrew, and Coptic show that pronominal and nominal objects are in complementary distribution and are therefore in stage (b).

3.1 PERSIAN

Subject marking in Persian is accomplished through an optional independent pronoun, such as *man* 'I', and an ending on the verb, such as *-am* in (25a). Object pronouns come in two varieties, *-ash* 'him' in (25a), which resembles an agreement marker, or an independent pronoun, *u* in (25b), which is often preceded by a preposition.

(25) a. *(man)* *pursed-am-ash*   Persian
         (I)   asked-I-him
         'I asked him.'

      b. *az*   *u*   *pursidi?*
         from   3S   asked-2S
         'Did you ask him?' (Lazard 1957: 100)

Thus, Persian has two kinds of object pronouns: dependent and independent, as shown in table 3.4. Lazard suggests that the difference in use is determined by formality in that the dependent pronouns ('suffixes personnels') are part of the colloquial language. This is of course expected if it is in a later stage of the cycle.

The independent pronouns are phrasal. In distribution, they resemble nominals: *shoma* in (26) is modified by a relative clause and *to* in (27) has a direct object marker, *ra*. The independent pronouns function as subject pronouns, as in (25), but do not "double" objects, although this is changing in contemporary Persian, according to Lazard (1957: 104).

(26) *shoma-i-ke*   *dust*   *na-dashte-id,* ...   Persian
         2P-REL-that   love   NEG-have-2P ...
         'You who have not loved ...' (Lazard 1957: 101)

(27) *to-ra*   *dust*   *dar-am*   Persian
         2S-OM   love   have-1S
         'I love you.' (Lazard 1957: 104)

In addition to subjects, the independent pronouns in table 3.4 are used for oblique objects; the dependent ones are used for possessives as well as for oblique objects.

TABLE 3.4

Persian Object Pronouns

	Dependent	Independent
1S	*-am*	*man*
2S	*-et*	*to*
3S	*-ash/-esh*	*u/an*
1P	*-(em)an*	*ma*
2P	*-etan*	*shoma*
3P	*-ashan*	*ishan/anha*

Unlike the independent pronouns in (26) and (27), the dependent forms cannot be modified or have the definite object marker *ra*. Compare the independent object *to* 'you-2S' in (28) to the dependent *-et* in (29).

(28) ***to-ra***   *didam*   Persian
     2S-OM   saw-1S
     'I saw you.' (Lazard 1957: 103).

(29) *did-am-**et***   Persian
     saw-1S-2S
     'I saw you.'

As (30) shows, the dependent object pronouns are in complementary distribution with full pronouns. This means that the former are not agreement markers yet.

(30) ****to-ra***   *didam-**et***   Persian
     2S-OM   saw-1S-2S
     'I saw you.'

Ghomeshi (1996: 149) argues that subject and object marking on the verb are "the spell out of F features that identify noun phrases in argument positions," but that object markers absorb case and are therefore incompatible with full objects. I think it makes more sense to argue that the object markers are still arguments.

Lazard (1957: 182–183) presents evidence for a further development: when the object is a clear topic, the pronominal ending is also present, as in (31). Lazard claims that this use is colloquial and that the doubling occurs with objects marked by the DOM *-ra*; this fits the reanalysis of the verbal object clitic as third person agreement.

(31) a. *sib-o*   *xord-am-**esh***   Colloquial Persian
         apple-OM   ate-1S-3S
         'As for the apple, I ate it.' (Ghomeshi 1996: 241)

     b. *to*   ***u-ro***   *xub*   *ne-mishenasi-**sh***
         you   him-OM   well   NEG-know-3S
         'You, you don't know him well.' (Lazard 1957: 182)

At first glance, there doesn't seem to be a person preference for the innovation in (31), since the doubling apparently also takes place with second and first person. If we look at the paradigm of table 3.4, however, the shape of the third person independent pronoun is very different from that of the dependent one: *-esh* doesn't look like *u/an*. In Classical Persian, *-ash* (Lazard 1957) was used only for animate objects. Since *u* is used for 'she/he' and *an* for 'it, that', it could be that these are later renewals, related to the demonstrative (Phillott 1919: 69). One could speculate that this means that the third person *–esh* became dependent before the first and second person forms, which still resemble the independent forms.

Several South Asian languages are also said to show a development toward the use of dependent pronouns: Kashmiri, and supposedly also Punjabi, Sindhi, Pashto, and Balochi (Grierson 1895; Tauli 1958: 99). Butt (2004), based on data from Akhtar (1999), shows that Punjabi has second and third person nonnominative markers on the verb that replace arguments, as in (32).

(32) *xat*   *likhia=i?*   Punjabi
       letter.MS.NOM   write.PST=2S

'Have you written the letter?' (Akhtar 1999:282)

These are used for all arguments (except nominative-marked ones). I think the start of this change with third and second person is interesting.

Having shown that object pronouns in Persian are developing into heads and possibly agreement markers, I turn to Cape Verdean Creole and to the history of English.

3.2 CAPE VERDEAN CREOLE AND ENGLISH

Creoles have fluid pronouns and, in this section, I first provide an example from Cape Verdean Creole to show what the source of the object agreement is and where it may start. I then turn to English.

In table 2.2, I listed the emphatic and subject pronouns. The pronouns used for object are very similar to the subject ones. The object pronoun is always to the immediate right of the verb, as in (33a), and can be doubled by a pronoun or DP only if it is human, as in (33b).

(33) a. *N*   *ta*   *favora-l*   *dretu*   CVC
           I   TMA   favor-3   a lot

'I favor him a lot.' (Baptista 2002: 48)

       b. *(A)el/João*   *N*   *gosta*   *d'el*
            Him/João   I   like   of-him

'Him/João, I like him.' (Baptista 2002: 240–241)

The third person singular *el* and plural *es* lose their vowels next to the verb but there is no other evidence that one or the other is further ahead in grammaticalization. Unlike the subject, where a full emphatic pronoun may appear, objects have to appear in their short forms.

In the previous chapter, I argued that Old English was pro-drop and that possibly the agreement on the verb was argumental. In this section, I first ask if there is any evidence that the object is pronominally marked on the verb as well. Then, I discuss early Modern English where the change from stage (a) to (b) is occurring.

In Old English, there is minimal object agreement on past participles; it occurs mostly in number, never in person. This is typically not enough to identify the object argument; therefore, the object is not dropped even though the number is marked on the participle in (34).

(34) *þæt he us hafað þæs leohtes bescyrede.*
       that he us has of-the light deprived-P

'that he has deprived us of the light.' (Genesis 393, Junius, in Krapp 1931: 15)

Object drop, as in (35) and (36), is much less frequent than subject drop (cf. Visser 1963–1973: 1: 97–188; van Gelderen 2000: 147–9). Many later cases of apparent object drop, as in (37), have to do with valency changes, which I discuss in section 8.

(35) *hie . . . leton holm beran | geafon on garsecg*
      they let sea bear gave on ocean
      'They let **him** bear the sea, and gave **him** the ocean.' (*Beowulf*, in Klaeber [1922] 1941: 47–49)

(36) *þonne his ellen deah*
      then his courage lasts
      'when his courage lasts **him**.' (*Beowulf*, in Klaeber [1922] 1941: 573)

(37) *ðæt he sona forðæm hreowsige*
      that he soon therefore repents
      'that he therefore soon repents.'
      (Alfred, *Pastoral Care,* Hatton, in Sweet [1871] 1934: 165.21)

Thus, in Old English, there is no evidence of head marking of the object on the verb. In later stages of English, however, we witness the beginning of such a cycle.

In Old and Middle English, object pronouns are phonologically robust and not contracted though they are usually placed in special (preverbal) position. By Early Modern English, contraction becomes more common. Partridge (1964: 150) shows that after 1600 the contraction of pronouns becomes widespread. Although Shakespeare uses it sparingly, Fletcher uses the contracted form abundantly, as table 3.5 shows for Fletcher's *Bonduca* as compared to three of Shakespeare's plays.

(38) Hear how I salute *'em*.
      (Fletcher, *Bonduca*, 3.1)

Examples from the Helsinki Corpus (EMODE periods 2 and 3) are given in (39) to (43). Most are third person objects, both singular and plural, but none of them is doubled as they are in the colloquial Persian (31).

(39) And when Mistresse Briget lost the handle of her Fan, I took't vpon mine honour thou hadst it not. (Shakespeare, *Merry Wives of Windsor*, 2.2)

TABLE 3.5

Object Reduction in One Play by Fletcher and Three by Shakespeare

	Bonduca	*Cymbeline*	*Winter's Tale*	*Tempest*
them	6 (7%)	64 (96%)	37 (82%)	38 (75%)
'em	83	3	8	13
Total	89	67	45	51

Based on Partridge 1964: 151

(40) I'le giue't you instantly.
      (Middleton, *A Chaste Maid in Cheapside* [1630]).

(41) that they eat with me, and that I oblig'd 'em in all things I was capable of. (Aphra
      Behn, *Oroonoko*)

(42) Yes sure I thinke I haue her measure about me, good faith 'tis downe, I cannot
      show't you, I must pull too many things out to be certaine.'
      (Middleton, *A Chaste Maid in Cheapside*)

(43) But she, as if she had resolved never to raise her eyes to the face of a man again, bent
      'em the more to the earth, when he spoke. (Aphra Behn, *Oroonoko*)

In spoken Modern English, third person contraction, as in (44), is still more common
than first or second person, as in (45). Doubling of the pronoun by a full DP is possible only
if the latter is a topic, as in (46).

(44) If you see'm, tell'm to save me a seat.   Colloquial English
      'If you see him/them, tell him/them to save me a seat.'

(45) ?If he sees'yu, . . .
      'If he sees you . . .'

(46) a. You saw'm, that producer.
      b. That guy, you hate'm.

This person split could come about for a variety of reasons: for example, third persons may
be used more frequently as objects. In the British National Corpus, this is true, as the
numbers in table 3.6 show.

Third person (masculine) singular objects occur more often in this 100-million-word corpus than first person singular ones, especially when compared with subjects.

When given a chance, object pronouns in English are immediately next to the verb. Using
the American *Time* Magazine Corpus, I searched phrasal verbs followed by pronominal
objects and both the particle *up* alone and *up* followed by a (personal) pronoun. Table 3.7
lists the frequency of objects intervening between a verb and the particle *up* as well as objects
following the verb and particle.

The contrast is striking. The typical pattern for pronouns is as in (47) and for nouns as in
(48), though (49) also occurs.

TABLE 3.6

Numbers of Subject and Object Pronouns for First and Third Person

	Subject	Object	Total
First	869,460	131,452 (13%)	1,000,912
Third	640,736	153,653 (17%)	794,389

$p < .001$

TABLE 3.7

Objects with a Verb and *up* in the *Time* Corpus 1923–2006

	V + Pronoun + *up*	V + *up* + Pronoun
me	275	0
us	102	0
you	180	0
him	1050	3*
her	350	0
it	**2157**	6
them	865	0
art+N	244	1830

(47) just then Miller Huggins stepped in and pled with her to **make it up** with Tiny for the sake of the Yankees (*Time* 1923)

(48) Determined to invest no more capital to **clean up the mess** (*Time* 1952)

(49) I'm here to **button this thing up**, barked National Recovery Administrator Johnson one day last week (*Time* 1933)

The three instances of *him* following *up* are all as in (50), that is, there is no option to analyze the pronoun as a head since it is coordinated. The six instances of *it* following *up* involve the verbs *go up it* and *climb up it* and are not phrasal; therefore, they are not included in table 3.7.

(50) Chen needled the Japanese so spectacularly that they made a special expedition to **mop up him and his men** (*Time* 1941)

The frequencies indicate that English objects are being incorporated. Later, I will show that another change is interfering with the object cycle, the particle being incorporated into the verb. English pronominal objects are a good example of stage (b) since they are in complementary distribution with full argument DPs, as (51) shows. As in Persian, doubling is possible with an adjunct DP indicated by a pause, as in (51b).

(51) a. *They wanted to clean it up the mess yesterday.
      b. They wanted to clean it up yesterday, the mess.

Thus, the history of English shows a few indications that an object cycle started, possibly first with third person.

3.3 AFRO-ASIATIC: SEMITIC AND BERBER

In Egyptian Arabic, the object pronoun and an argument nominal are in complementary distribution (Jelinek 1989: 121), as in (52). There are no freestanding object pronouns.

(52) a. *šuft-uh*   Egyptian Arabic
saw.1S-him
'I saw him.'
b. *šuft il-walad*
saw.1S the-boy
'I saw the boy.'

Nominals and object agreement are also in complementary distribution in Coptic (53) and in biblical Hebrew (54).

(53) a. *hetaß pe-rome*   Coptic
'kill   a-man'
b. *hɔtßə-f*
'kill-him' (Reintges 2001: 178).

(54) a. *uberaktiy 'otah*   Biblical Hebrew
bless   her
'I will bless her.'
b. *uberaktiyha*
bless-her (Genesis 17.16, from
http://lists.ibiblio.org/pipermail/b-hebrew/1999-September/004360.html)

In Arabic, if the object is a topic or right-dislocated, that is, an adjunct, the pronoun appears, as in (55) and (56).

(55) *il-walad, šuft-uh*   Egyptian Arabic
the-boy, saw.1S-him

(56) *šuft-uh, il-walad*   Egyptian Arabic
saw.1S-him, the-boy
'I saw the boy.' (Jelinek 1989: 121)

This shows that Arabic is in stage (b). More evidence for this is that Arabic cannot have an object pronoun without object marking on the verb, as (57) shows.

(57) a. *šuft-ik*   Standard Arabic
saw.1S-2FS
b. *šuft-ik   ʔinti*
saw.1S-2FS   you.2FS
c. **šuft   ʔinti*
saw.1S   you
'I saw you.' (Shlonsky 1997: 197)

Berber, another member of the Afro-Asiatic branch, has object clitics as well, as argued in Ouali (2008), and shown in (12) and (58). Indirect objects can optionally be doubled, as in (59), but not direct objects.

(58) *wshix-**as-t**   Tamazight Berber
      gave.1S-3S-it
      'I gave it to him.' (Ouali 2008: 81)

(59) *wshix-(**as**)   lektab   i-Fatima*   Tamazight Berber
      gave-3S   book   to-Fatima
      'I gave the book to Fatima.' (Ouali 2008: 112–113)

Berber shows something that a number of languages do: it starts the cycle with the more animate object, namely the indirect one.

As I have shown in this section, Persian, Cape Verdean Creole, and early Modern and Modern English objects are definitely well on their way toward stage (b), as are the ones in Arabic, Coptic, Hebrew, and Berber. Most of these show a third person start and a doubling in the case of animate and definite objects.

4. Spanish, Southern Slavic, Bantu, and Austronesian: Stage (c)

In this section, I examine some languages that provide evidence of stage (c) or moving toward it.

4.1 VARIETIES OF SPANISH

As shown by Jaeggli (1982), in standard Spanish the object clitics *la, lo, las,* and *los* are in complementary distribution with full nominals.

(60) *Vimos **la casa de Maria***   Standard Spanish
      1P-saw the house of Maria
      'We saw Maria's house.'

(61) *****La vimos **la casa de Maria***   Standard Spanish
      it 1P-saw the house of Maria

As in Arabic, doubling is obligatory with pronominal objects, as in (62), which indicates that change is starting.

(62) **lo**   vimos   **a**   **él**   Standard Spanish
      him   1P-saw   OM   him
      'We saw him.'

In many varieties, the change has gone further: in Porteño or River Plate Spanish spoken in Argentina, Uruguay, and Paraguay (Suñer 1988), Andean Spanish, and Amazon Spanish, doubling occurs with a (specific) nominal, as in (63), that may or may not be preceded by the case marker *a*.

(63) *Pedro   **lo**   vió*   *a*   ***Juan***   River Plate Spanish
      Pedro   him   3S-saw   OM   Juan
      'Pedro saw Juan.'

Mayer (2003) describes Limeño, the Spanish spoken in Lima, which shows the first stage of clitic doubling. In this variety, proper names may optionally be doubled by a pronominal form, as in (64).

(64) *De repente **la** vió a **Grimanesa** bajando las escaleras*   Limeño Spanish
Suddenly her saw CM Grimanesa descending the stairs

'Suddenly, she/he saw Grimanesa coming down the stairs.' (Mayer 2003: 21)

This is similar to the initial stages of subject doubling.

In other varieties, the Case marker is not present and there is no definiteness or animacy restriction on the direct object. Hill (1987) shows that speakers of Malinche Spanish (spoken in the area of Puebla and Tlaxcala in Mexico) have clitics and nominals without a Case marker, as in (65).

(65) **lo**   trae   **un**   **chiquihuite**   Malinche Spanish
it   he-brings   a   basket

'He brings a basket.' (Hill 1987: 74)

Franco (1993) in his survey of object agreement across languages concludes that there is much variation. The southernmost areas of Latin America, where Southern Cone Spanish is spoken, tend to have object agreement, like Basque Spanish. Franco's criteria include strict adjacency to the auxiliary or verb, fixed order, and obligatory co-occurrence with accusative objects.

If the pronoun has indeed become agreement, it should be able to double with a quantifier. In standard Spanish, this is not the case, as (66) shows; in Southern Latin American and Basque Spanish, on the other hand, doubling is possible with a genderless marker *le*, as in (67).

(66) *****A**   **quién**   **lo**   *viste*   Standard Spanish
to   who   3M   saw-2S

'Who did you see?'

(67) *A*   **quién**   **le**   *viste*   Argentinian Spanish
to   who   3M   saw-2S

'Who did you see?' (Franco 1993: 141)

4.2 SOUTH SLAVIC: MACEDONIAN AND BULGARIAN

As Kalluli and Tasmowski's (2008) edited volume on clitic doubling shows, there is a great deal of variation in Southern Slavic. Doubling is one of the Balkan Sprachbund's characteristic features and all languages in table 3.8 are part of that Sprachbund. As is obvious, the differences are many. According to Tomić (2006),

[i]n the Easternmost Bulgarian dialects clitic-doubling of both direct and indirect objects is strictly dependent on discourse factors—only topicalized (direct or indirect) objects in the Left Periphery are clitic-doubled. As one moves south-westwards, the role of definiteness and specificity in clitic-doubling increases. In the West-central and South-western Bulgarian dialects *in situ* objects can also be clitic-doubled, though often they are interpreted as

TABLE 3.8

Balkan Clitic Doubling

Macedonian	All definite direct objects (DOs) and all indirect objects (IOs)
Albanian	All IOs, DOs instantiated by first and second person pronouns, and all nonfocal/nonrhematic DOs
Romanian	All full personal and definite pronouns, preverbal indirect objects and not [-specific] DPs, postverbal direct object DPs introduced
By adposition	*pe*, and postverbal indirect object DPs that are not [-specific] or [-human] goal
Greek	No obligatory context, except with *olos* 'all'
Bulgarian	All objects that are interpreted as experiencers and nonexistentials

topics. Further westwards, the role of discourse factors in clitic-doubling gradually disappears. In the majority of the Macedonian dialects all definite direct objects and all specific indirect objects are clitic-doubled. In the South-westernmost Macedonian dialects, however, the specificity effect disappears and the doubling clitic can be left out, even when the indirect object is obviously specific. Bare indefinite indirect objects, which can never be specific, can here also be clitic-doubled. Thus, at least in the case of indirect objects, the doubling clitics get very close to becoming mere case markers.

Tomić's description illustrates several stages of the bject cycle. In Macedonian, the pronominal heads/clitics "are closest to complete grammaticalization, that is, to becoming mere case markers which formally distinguish direct and indirect objects from subjects, in another Balkan Slavic language, Bulgarian, clitic-doubling is predominantly dependent on discourse factors" (Tomić 2008: 1).

In Bulgarian, the doubling appears only in pragmatically marked circumstances, preferably with topicalized objects, as in (68), repeated from (13).

(68)   *Vidjah*   **(go)**   *Ivan*   Bulgarian
        I-saw   3S   Ivan
        'I saw Ivan.'

As Tomić emphasizes, there is a lot of regional variation in Bulgarian (and Macedonian).

In Macedonian, the direct object has to be "doubled" by a clitic, such as *ja* in (69) and *go* in (70), although some speakers only use *nego* when emphasized.

(69)   *Daniela*   **ja**   *kupi*   *kniga-ta*   Macedonian
        Daniela   3FS   bought   book-the
        'Daniela bought the book.'

(70)   *Daniela*   **go**   *poznava*   **nego**   Macedonian
        Daniela   3MS   knows   him
        'Daniela knows him.' (Daniela Kostadinovska and Victorija Todorovska, p.c.)

If the nominal is an indefinite, as in (71), the preverbal pronoun does not appear.

(71)　*Daniela　kupi　　edna kniga/knigi*　　　　　　　　　　　　Macedonian
　　　Daniela　bought　one book/books.
　　　'Daniela bought a book/books.'
　　　(Daniela Kostadinovska and Victorija Todorovska, p.c.)

In Southwestern Macedonian, indirect object doubling takes place even in the case of indefinite objects, as (72) shows.

(72)　***(Mu)***　*go　dade　　pismo-to*　**na　dete**　　　Southwestern Macedonian
　　　3S-DAT　3S　gave.3S　letter-DEF　to　child
　　　'She/he gave the letter to a (mere) child.' (Tomić 2006)

South Slavic languages mark definite objects by adding to the nominal a pronominal/clitic head. The next step would be to start this doubling in all cases, with focused DPs as well, for example.

The source of the doubling is pronominal: Bulgarian and Macedonian third person masculine *go* is a shortened form of the full pronoun *nego,* second person *te* shortened from *tebe,* first person *me* from *mene,* and so on. From table 3.8, no uniform start of the cycle becomes obvious. In Albanian, first and second person are doubled first but there is no such evidence in Macedonian and Bulgarian. Native speakers of the latter languages show no preference for doubling of certain persons.

4.3 BANTU

Bantu languages are moving from complementary distribution between object markers (OM) on the verb and overt DPs to obligatory agreement. The origin of the OMs probably is preverbal pronoun (see Givón 1976, 1979: 243–244; Wald 1979: 506), as expected in an agreement cycle. Wald (1993: 331) says that "the OM has never become an obligatory verb inflection in most Bantu languages, though there is relatively recent motion in this direction among the Central East Coast languages, including Swahili." Bresnan and Mchombo (1987) also show that object markers in Chichewa are in complementary distribution with full objects in certain positions but are changing to (obligatory) agreement markers. Riedel (2009) shows that there is an enormous variety of object marking in the Bantu family but she argues that all such marking is agreement and not pronominal. Indeed, in these languages, there is a great deal of variability in how objects (and subjects) are represented. Marten, Kula, and Thwala (2007: 259) identify seven microparameters for object markers in Bantu languages; this indicates that the languages are in flux. I will give some examples from Kinande, Zulu, and Swahili that show cyclical change.

Baker (2003: 109) examines Kinande, a Bantu language that like Chichewa has optional OMs. In (73a), there is no verbal marker referencing *eritunda*; in (73b), an OM, *-ri*, appears on the verb and the nominal *eritunda* is an adjunct. This means Kinande is in stage (b). (As is usual with Bantu languages, the agreement is indicated through numbers in the gloss.)

(73)   a. *N-a-gul-a   eritunda*   Kinande
           1S-T-buy-FV fruit.5
           'I bought a fruit.'
       b. *Eritunda,   n-a-ri-gul-a*
           fruit.5   1S-T-OM5-buy-FV
           'The fruit, I bought it.' Baker (2003: 109)

The situation is similar in Zulu: if objects are marked on the verb, as in (74a), the nominal objects have to be in dislocated/adjunct positions, according to Buell (2002) (see also van der Spuy 1993), and shown in (74b). This means that the OM in (74a) is still the argument.

(74)   a. *A-bafana   ba-ya-sihlupha   i-salukazi*   Zulu
           2-boy   2FOC-7-annoy   7-old.woman
           'The boys annoy the old woman.' (Buell 2002)
       b. *W-a-pheka   i-zambane   u-Sipho*
           1-PST-cook   5-potato   1-Sipho
           'Sipho cooked a potato.' (Buell 2002)

Incidentally, the situation is similar with Zulu subjects since agreement is optional. If agreement is present, as in (74b), the subject has moved out of the VP. If it is absent, as in (75), an expletive agreement marker of noun class 17 occurs.

(75)   **Kw-a-pheka**   *u-Sipho   i-zambane*   Zulu
       17-PST-cook   1-Sipho   5-potato
       'Sipho cooked a potato.' (Buell 2002)

In Swahili, the verb must have a subject marker (SM) and may have an object marker when the object is definite, as in (76) and (77); indefinite inanimate objects, as in (78), need not be marked. First and second person objects are always marked since they are definite.

(76)   *mwanamke   a-li-wa-angalia   watoto*   Swahili
       woman   SM-PST-OM-watch   children
       'The woman watched the children.' (Wald 1993: 326)

(77)   *ni-li-ki- soma   kitabu*   Swahili
       1S-PST-it-read   the-book
       'I read the book.' (Givón 1976: 159)

(78)   *ni-li-soma   kitabu*   Swahili
       1-PST-read   a-book
       'I read a book.' (Givón 1976: 159)

Thus, Swahili is moving toward stage (c). Wald (1979: 516), in an analysis of spoken Swahili, shows that there is a lot of variability in which objects trigger OM, but that first and second person objects always trigger an OM since they are "human and definite." Definiteness, however, is much less of a factor than is animacy. The inanimate indefinites are marked by means of an OM only 11 percent of the time, whereas definite humans are marked 90 percent. Riedel (2009: 44–45) shows that object marking in Sambaa, a language neighboring Swahili, is sensitive to human objects, rather than to animate or definite. In keeping with this, it is also first and second person objects that are obligatorily marked on the verb, as (79a) shows for second person, and not third person, as (79b) shows. (Note that all free pronouns are emphatic, however.)

(79) a. *N-za-**ku**-ona*   *iwe*   Sambaa
        1S-PF-OM2S-see   YOU

        'I saw YOU.'

    b. *N-za-(**mw**)-ona uja*
        1S-PF-OM-see DEM

        'I saw HIM/HER.' (Riedel 2009: 45–46)

4.4 AUSTRONESIAN: INDONESIAN, BUGIS, AND MARSHALLESE

Van den Berg (1996) discusses some historical changes in the Austronesian language family. He argues that the original focus system (well-known from Tagalog) is lost and the verb becomes "conjugated," that is, goes from stage (a) to stage (c). Himmelmann (1996) argues the same, but Cysouw (2003) show that the link isn't perfect. Harrison's (1978) data show that the history of Micronesian also provides evidence for an object cycle.

In this section, I provide examples of various stages. I first show that Indonesian is in stage (a), with minimal evidence of stage (b). Kambera has object agreement for definite objects and Tukang Besi has agreement with definite, affected objects, which means these are in stage (b). Bugis shows remnants of a voice system being replaced by agreement, that is, stage (c). Obligatory agreement is first evident with definite objects and the source of the agreement is pronominal. I also consider Micronesian.

Indonesian, a western Malayo-Polynesian language, has many types of pronouns, most of which look like they are in stage (a), especially since there are many (honorific) nouns that substitute for pronouns. In a few cases an object is affixed on the verb, as in (80a); this usually happens with verbs marked by the active voice marker *men-*, but not with other verbs, as (80b) shows.

(80) a. *Dia*   *mengambil*   *kue*   *itu*   *lalu*   *memakan-**nya***   Indonesian
       he   ACT-took   cake   that   and   ate-it

    b. *Dia*   *mengambil*   *kue*   *itu*   *lalu*   *makan-(***nya**)*
       he   ACT-took   cake   that   and   ate

       'He took the cake and ate it.' (Sneddon 1996: 165)

I assume that *men-* is in v and that this is somehow relevant to the start of the cycle. In (80b), the object is dropped probably because an object needs to be licensed by a voice marker, *men-*, in v. First and second person can also be attached to the verb but, since there is no doubling by a nominal and the process is optional, all these forms (including [80a]) are still arguments and not agreement.

Kambera, a Central-Malayo-Polynesian language, has obligatory object marking on verbs when the object is definite, as in (81), but not when it is indefinite, as in (82a). It could be that it had an earlier stage with only animate definites but that is no longer the case. A definite object without the object marker *nyà* is ungrammatical, as (82b) shows.

(81)   *Mbàda*   *manahu-da-**nyà**-ka*   ***na***   ***uhu***   Kambera
        already   cook-3P-3S-PF   the   rice
        'They have already cooked the rice.'

(82)   a.   *Mbàda*   *manahu-da-ka*   ***uhu***   Kambera
           already   cook-3P-PF   rice
        b.   **Mbàda*   *manahu-da-ka*   ***na***   ***uhu***
           already   cook-3P-PF   the   rice
           'They have already cooked some rice.' (Klamer 1998: 68)

Klamer (1997: 918) writes that "[t]he cliticization of transitive objects is determined by definiteness, unlike subjects. In other words, definite objects of simple transitive verbs MUST be cliticized on the predicate and their coreferent NPs are always optional, while indefinite objects cannot be marked with clitics but must be expressed by full (indefinite) NPs."

In Tukang Besi, a Nuclear-Malayo-Polynesian language, object agreement occurs when the object is affected and the aspect is perfective, as in (83a). In this case, the object is preceded by the nominative article, that is, "is assigned pragmatic prominence" (Donohue 1999: 153). In case of a nonaffected, there is no object marker on the verb and the article preceding the object is nonnominative; the sentence is nonperfective, as in (83b).

(83)   a.   *No-'ita-**aku***   *na*   *iaku*   Tukang Besi
           3realis-see-1S.OBJ   NOM   1S
           'He saw me.'
        b.   *No-'ita*   *te*   *iaku*
           3realis-see   CM   1S
           'He is looking at me.' (Donohue 1999: 135)

The use of the object markers is determined by givenness rather than by definiteness, according to Donohue, and is perhaps a type of voice marking as in the Philippine languages. The source of the object marker is pronominal; for example, *aku* and *iaku* in (83a) are clearly related, but so are the others, except perhaps the third person, as table 3.9 shows. This may show that the cycle started with third person since that form is the least recognizable.

Bugis, a Western Malayo-Polynesian language, is like other languages and families on (Southern) Sulawesi in that it marks subjects and objects on the verb. The marking on the verb shows an ergative-absolutive pattern. The set of markers is quite similar across the languages and there is a definiteness effect: only definite objects are marked, as is clear from (84a) as opposed to (84b).

(84)   a.   *Na-baca-i*   ***boq-ev***   Bugis
           3ERG-read-3ABS   book-ART
           'He is reading the book.' (Hanson 2001)

TABLE 3.9

Pronouns and OMs in Tukang besi

	Free	OM
1S	*iaku*	*-aku*
2S	*iko'o*	*-ko*
3S	*ia*	*-'e*
1(non-S)	*ikami/ikita*	*-kami/-kita*
2P	*ikomiu*	*-komiu*
3P	*amai*	*-'e*

From Donohue 1999: 113

    b. *Mab-baca-i*   **boq**
      AF-read-3ABS   book
      'He is reading a book.' (Hanson 2001)

If the object is not marked on the verb, a voice marker (AF in [84b]) appears. The classification of this language as a focus or an ergative system is quite complex (see, e.g., Hanson 2001). If, as van den Berg (1996) and Himmelmann (1996) assume, the inflected verbs are an innovation, the innovation occurs with definite nominals.

In Micronesian, another branch of the Austronesian language, there are number of changes that are represented by different stages in various languages. Languages such as Marshallese have innovated (1) new forms of first and second person emphatic and object pronouns and (2) object pronouns that can optionally be doubled by clitic-like elements. I will describe the pronoun situation in some detail in this language and then compare it with what Harrison says about the Micronesian family.

In Marshallese, two sets of pronouns occur, an emphatic and an object pronoun, as well as subject agreement clitics (Harrison 1978; Willson 2008: 18, 22). The absolute/emphatic pronouns are used in topic position but, as (85) shows, they are optional.

(85) (***Na***) *i-j*   *yokwe* *ajiri* *ro* *nej-ū*   Marshallese
     1S   1S-PRES love child the CL-1S
     '(Me,) I love my children.' (Willson 2008: 21)

The emphatic pronoun is also used in coordination, as in (86), to emphasize objects, and for subjects in verbless clauses.

(86) ***Kwe*** **na** *im* *Mona,* *kōj-jil*   *e-naaj*   *umum* *nan* *bade* *eo*   Marshallese
     2S   1S and Mona 1P-three 3S-FUT bake   for party the
     'You, me, and Mona, the three of us will bake for the party.' (Willson 2008: 21)

A free object pronoun is used in (87), although this form can be used only for humans; for nonhumans, a marker that looks more like agreement is used, as in (88).

(87) *E-ar*   *denōt*   *er*   Marshallese
      3S-PST   slap   3P.H

      'He slapped them (the boys).' (Willson 2008: 19).

(88) *E-ar*   *denōt-i*   Marshallese
      3S-PST   slap-3P.non-H

      'He slapped them (the fish).' (Willson 2008: 19).

I discuss the latter in the following paragraphs. Willson (2008: 31) doesn't consider these markers transitive, but Harrison (1978) does.

As (85) to (88) show, there is also a subject marker; these elements are all provided in table 3.10. Notice that only first and second person singular object forms are distinct (as well as third person plural subject). This suggests that the first and second person singular pronouns are innovative. Table 3.10 confirms that suggestion.

Harrison (1978: 1081) reconstructs the pronouns for Proto-Micronesian as in table 3.11 and argues that in the precursor of Proto-Micronesian, the emphatic and object pronouns were the same in function and syntax, as they still are in Mokilese: "all pronominal object marking was by means of absolute pronouns" (1978: 1082). As table 3.11 shows, in Proto-Micronesian, the emphatic pronoun is also used as the object in the plural, but in the singular the two types of pronouns are distinct. First and second person are VP-internal enclitics, according to Harrison (1978: 1082), and the third person is a verbal suffix. The current situation in Micronesian is a continuum, as shown in table 3.12. Harrison explores the differences among languages and argues that, in some languages, the verb-object attraction "was impeded . . . by the process of final vowel deletion, which created canonical shapes unamenable to the eventual suffixation of object pronouns" (1978: 1100).

As mentioned, some transitive verbs have optional object markers. There are two kinds: one for pronouns and DPs, as in (89), and another one for plural nonhuman objects, as in (90).

TABLE 3.10

Pronouns in Marshallese			
	Emphatic	Object	Subject
1S	*na*	*eō*	*i*
2S	*kwe*	*eok*	*kwō*
3S	*e*	*e (human only)*	*e*
1P.INCL	*kōj*	*kōj*	*kōj*
1P.EXCL	*kōm*	*kōm*	*kōm*
2P	*kom(i)*	*kom(i)*	*kom*
3P	*er*	*er (human only)*	*re*

Adapted from Willson 2008

TABLE 3.11

Pronouns in Proto-Micronesian

	Emphatic	Object
1S	**ngai*	**ai*
2S	**koe*	**ko*
3S	**ai*	**a*
1P.INCL	**ki(t,t')a*	**ki(t,t')a*
1P.EXCL	**ka(ma)mi*	**ka(ma)mi*
2P	**kamiu*	**kamiu*
3P	**ira*	**ira*

Adapted from Harrison 1978: 1081

TABLE 3.12

Object Continuum in Micronesian

ABSOLUTE Only	ABSOLUTE+CLITICS	CLITICS Only
Mokilese, Pingelapese[a]	Ponapean, Marshallese, Kosraean[b]	Gilbertese, Trukic[c]

From Harrison 1978
[a]E.g., (24) in text [b]E.g., (22), (23), and (87) in text [c]E.g., (92) in text

(89)   *E-ar*   *pukot-e*   *(kōj)*   Marshallese
       3S-PST   look.for-OM   1P
       'He looked for us.' (Willson 2008: 32)

(90)   *E-ar*   *denōt-i*   *(kweet*   *ko)*   Marshallese
       3S-PST   pound-OM   octopus   the
       'He pounded the octopuses.' (Harrison 1978: 1075)

When the OM is present, the pronominal and DP objects (if the latter are nonhuman) are optional. However, sentences with topicalized objects must have an overt OM on the verb, as in (91); this indicates that the OM is an argument, not an agreement marker, at least in Marshallese.

(91)   a. *Juuj*   *eo*   *a-ō,*   *e-ar*   *lo-e*   Marshallese
          shoe   the   POSS-1S   3S-PST   see-OM
          'My shoe, he saw.'
       b. **Juuj*   *eo*   *a-ō*   *e-ar*   *lo*
          shoe   the   POSS-1S   3S-PST   see
          'My shoe, he saw.' (Willson 2008: 34)

Harrison (1978: 1068) reconstructs transitive verb markers for Proto-Micronesian that resemble the Marshallese OMs: *-a* for singular nominal objects and *-i* for pronominals, plural objects, and plural nonhuman objects. According to him, these are nicely reflected in Gilbertese (92) to (94).

(92) I   noor-a   te   ika   Gilbertese
      1S   see-TV   the   fish
      'I saw the fish.' (Harrison 1978: 1068)

(93) I   noor-i   waa   akanne   Gilbertese
      I   see-TV   canoe   those
      'I saw those canoes.' (Harrison 1978: 1068)

(94) I   noor-i-a   Gilbertese
      1S   see-TV-3S
      'I saw her.' (Harrison 1978: 1073)

Harrison (1978: 1069) further says the transitive markers have been lost in Marshallese, Kosraean, and Ponapeic and that "Marshallese evidence for an earlier *-i/*-a* contrast is far from straightforward" (1072) since the reconstructed *ia* does not correspond to the third person *e* [ɛ]. He excludes other possible sources. Thus, the object pronouns in the Micronesian languages illustrate various stages of the object cycle. In some (Mokilese), there are only free pronouns, in others (Marshallese), there are pronouns as well as clitics, and in yet another group (Gilbertese), there are only agreement markers.

As far as I can tell, the sources for object markers in Austronesian are pronominal but the start is unpredictable: possibly first with voice markers in Indonesian and Tukang Besi, with definite DPs in Kambera, and with first and second person pronouns in Marshallese.

5. Polysynthesis in Athabascan

I will now provide evidence for an increase of object polysynthesis in Athabascan. Scholars know that in Southern Athabascan languages such as Navajo, both subject and object markers are obligatory on verbs, as are pronominal and oblique objects. Rice (2003: 72) assumes that the Southern pattern is an innovation. As I have already argued for polysynthetic subjects, polysynthetic objects can be represented as having [i-phi], without a probe with [u-phi] in v. I will first discuss the Northern languages and suggest that even some of these are changing, and with interesting complex starting points, as Gunlogson (2001) points out.

Northern Athabascan languages such as Ahtna, Slave, and Dogrib display complementary distribution between nominal objects, such as *tuwele* 'soup' in (95a), and verbal affixation, *be-* in (95b).

(95) a. sú   **tuwele**   k'ágoweneli   Slave
         Q   soup   2S-taste
         'Have you tasted the soup?'

b. *sú*   ***bek'ágoweneli***
   Q   3S-2S-taste
   'Have you tasted it?' (from Jelinek 2001)

This is also the case with oblique and pronominal objects, as in (96), where the nominal oblique *ndéh* 'land' appears without a marker on the postposition or on the verb.

(96) ***ndéh***   *ts'ę*   *gohndíh*   Slave
     land   from   1S-IMPF-love
     'I live from the land.' (Rice 2003: 53)

A similar complementarity between object and agreement marker occurs in Kaska, Salcha, and Chipewyan/Dëne Sųłiné. In (97a), (98a), and (99a), the object marker is present but not the nominal, and in (97b), (98b), and (99b), the nominal is but the object marker is not.

(97) a. ***meganehtan***   Kaska
        me-ga-ne-o-h-tan
        3S-at-ASP-3S-CL-look
        'He looks at her.'
    b. ***ayudeni***   *ganehtan*
        girl   at-ASP-3S-CL-look
        'He looks at the girl(s).'

(98) a. ***i-ðəɬΦœ***   Salcha
        3S-Q-3S-CL-kill
        'He kills it.'
    b. *šos*   *ðəɬΦœ*
        šos   ð-O-ł-Φœ
        bear   Q-3S-CL-kill
        'He kills a black bear.' (Tuttle 1998: 106)

(99) a. *dɛnɛyu*   *nɛɬʔį*   Chipewyan/Dëne Sųłiné
        man   looking
    b. *yɛ-nɛɬʔį*
        3-looking
        'He is looking at him.' (Richardson 1968: 4)

Doubling of the object is possible in topicalization (Gunlogson 2001: 376). If the object is clearly topicalized, the object marker/pronoun appears on the verb. Compare the topicalized (100a) to the nontopicalized (100b).

(100) a. ***gah***   *tlį*   *nidhą́ą́*   ***te-ye-déhnde***   Slave
        rabbit   dog   far   3–3-chased
        'The rabbit, the dog chased it a long way.' (Rice 1989)

b. *tłį*   *nidhą́ą́*   *gah*   ***tedéhnde***
dog   far   rabbit   3-chased

'The dog chased the rabbit a long way.' (Rice 1989)

The same phenomenon occurs in Gwich'in, Slave, and Kaska, where the pronoun is normally the subject, as in (101), and the object need not be marked. If, unexpectedly, the pronoun is the object, as in (102), the nominal subject is seen as a topic and hence needs to be doubled.

(101)   *eskie*   *nénetał*   Kaska
eskie   né-Ø-ne-Ø-tał
boy   TH-3S-ASP-CL-kick

'She kicked the boy.'

(102)   *eskie*   *néyenetał*   Kaska
eskie   né-ye-Ø-ne-Ø-tał
boy   TH-**3O**-3S-ASP-kick

'The boy kicked her.' (Jelinek 2001: 25)

The phenomena in (101) and (102) can be explained as in other languages we considered: the pronominal object marker in (101) counts as an argument. Since it is in complementary distribution with a nominal object, we can say that it moves to the verbal complex, unlike the full nominal. This is why Kaska is not truly object polysynthetic. In true polysynthetic languages, there is no complementarity between the nominal and pronominal.

Rice (1989: 1016–1018) shows that with human plural objects in Slave, "the plural object pronouns are present," as in (103). This is probably an innovation and fits with the tendency for Athabascan to undergo increase in object polysynthesis.

(103)   *deneke*   *goghάyeda*   Slave
people-P   3-see-4P

'She/he sees the people.' (Rice 1989: 1017)

Babine-Witsuwit'en, a northern Athabascan language, has only indefinite DPs, as in (104a), in complementary distribution with verbal agreement (Gunlogson 2001; Jelinek 2001); the definite ones can be doubled, as in (104b). This fact points to a change toward a more polysynthetic stage.

(104)   a. *dinï*   *hida*   *nilh'ën*   Babine-Witsuwit'en
man   moose   at-3-look

'The man is looking at **a moose**.'

b. *hida*   ***dinï***   *yi-nilh'ën*
moose   man   3-at-3-look

'The moose is looking at **the man**.'

(Gunlogson 2001: 374)

With proper name objects, and definite and possessed objects, the *yi*-object marking is obligatory.

Navajo, a representative of Southern Athabascan, has optional nominals, as the counterparts of Slave (95) in Navajo (105a) show; the marker on the verb can never be left off, as (105b) shows.

(105)   a.   *('atoo')   yí-ní-dlą́ą́'-ísh*   Navajo
             soup   3S-2S-eat-Q
             'Did you eat the soup?'
        b.   **ní-dlą́ą́'-ísh*
             2S-eat-Q
             'Did you eat it?' (Jelinek 2001: 23)

From Slave and Babine-Witsuwit'en, we see that the start of the cycle is possibly with human/definite objects. The object markers are similar to the subject ones, as in Navajo, but there are specialized forms for animate, unspecific, and areal objects. They all occur in the same position (Young & Morgan 1987, position IV) so, unlike in the case of subjects, we cannot draw any conclusions as to these representing different stages in the grammaticalization process.

The trend in the Athabascan languages seems to be toward more object polysynthesis. The presence of noun incorporation, as in (106) from Slave, is relevant here. Rice (2008) shows that the most archaic Athabascan languages, Ahtna and Koyukon, have retained noun incorporation, but Navajo, Apache, and the Pacific Coast languages have not. The other languages are in between, mostly with some object noun incorporation. She argues that "incorporation came to be in competition with agreement" (2008: 375)

(106)   *léh-**xu**-de-k'a*   Slave
        together-tooth-CL-grind
        'She/he grinds her/his teeth.' (Rice 1989: 650, 658)

In the more archaic languages, subjects as well as objects can be incorporated. Navajo and the other Southern languages, however, lack productive incorporation but show remnants of it, as in (107) and (108).

(107)   ***t'a'i**-di-l-ta'*   Navajo
        wings-Q-CL-move quickly
        'to flutter its wings' (Young & Morgan 1987: 711)

(108)   ***tsi**-naa-'eeł*   Navajo
        wood-ASP-float
        It floats around (= 'boat')

It could be that when pronouns are reanalyzed as the bearers of [i-phi] and nominal arguments as adjuncts, the nominals can no longer incorporate.

There are differences in polysynthesis in the Athabascan family. Slave has subject but not object polysynthesis, for example; Navajo has both. Though Rice (2000, 2008) and Rice and Saxon (2005) do not assume a pronominal argument analysis for Athabascan languages, the differences between the Northern and Southern languages fit with such an analysis. The Southern languages are in stage (b) with [i-phi] features in both T and v.

As to the start of the cycle, definiteness seems a factor in Babine-Witsuwit'en and animacy in Slave. Can we find out where the Navajo markings started? As shown in the previous chapter, the subject markers show a person split in that first and second person are closer to the verb than third person, indicating an earlier grammaticalization. The first and second person object pronouns are very similar in shape to the subject forms (see table 2.7), but the third person object can have many shapes depending on animacy, definiteness, and other factors (see Young & Morgan 1987: 64–65). A third person object appears if the subject is third person but, since its position is the same as that of first and second person objects, we cannot conclude anything on where the cycle started.

6. Uto-Aztecan: the rise and fall of polysynthesis

Langacker (1977) has reconstructed Proto-Uto-Aztecan morphosyntax and argued that both subject polysynthesis and object polysynthesis arose at some point and were then lost in most cases. The loss represents a change from stage (a) to (b) and back to (a), as I will show. Steele (1976) also argues that Proto-Uto-Aztecan pronouns develop into agreement markers, as does Haugen (2004, 2008). This much seems to be uncontroversial. Different Uto-Aztecan languages have developed in different ways; in some (Tohono O'odham), object polysynthesis has remained, in others (Yaqui) it has not. I will show that these developments fit the object cycle. I start with a language that has clear object polysynthesis, Tohono O'odham.

In Tohono O'odham, subject agreement is marked on the auxiliary verb in second position and object agreement on the participle (regardless of whether the object precedes or follows the verb). Since the independent object occurs with agreement, this is object polysynthesis. In (109) and (110), the third person subjects are marked as 'o and the plural object by means of ha in (109) and by means of ñ in (110).

(109) *Gogs 'o **ha-huhu'id** hegam* Tohono O'odham
      dog is/was P-chasing them/those
      'The dog is chasing them.'

(110) *Ceoj 'o 'añi: **ñ-ceggia*** Tohono O'odham
      boy is/was me 1S-fighting
      'The boy is/was fighting me.' (Zepeda 1983: 34)

Obligatory object marking, as in Tohono O'odham, also occurs in Nahuatl and Cahuilla. As Munro (1989: 114) mentions for Pima, the use of independent pronominal (subjects and) objects is rare, as expected in a polysynthetic language.

The Tohono O'odham paradigm for dependent and independent pronouns appears in table 3.13. As mentioned in the previous chapter, many of the dependent pronouns look like short forms of the independent ones.

In Yaqui, subject pronouns occur as either free or dependent pronouns in second position. Object pronouns are typically independent, as in *enchi* in (111), where the subject pronoun *inepo* is also a free form.

TABLE 3.13

Tohono O'odham Object Pronouns

	Dependent	Independent
1S	*ñ-*	*'a:ñi*
2S	*m-*	*'a:pi*
3S	-	*hegai*
1P	*t-*	*'a:cim*
2P	*'em-*	*'a:pim*
3P	*ha-*	*hegam*

From Zepeda 1983: 35

(111) *Inepo* **enchi** *bo'o-bit-nee*   Yaqui
       I   you   await-FUT
       'I will wait for you.' (Dedrick & Casad 1999: 245; spelling adapted)

According to Guerrero (2006) and Haugen (2004, 2008), only third person singular and plural object pronouns behave like clitics and even then they are optional, as with *aa* in (112).[3]

(112) *Inepo* *Hose-ta* **(aa)**-*vicha-k*   Yaqui
       1S   Hose-ACC   (3S.OBJ)-see-PF
       'I saw Hose.' (Maria Amarillas, from Haugen 2008: 222)

Haugen (2008: 223) shows that object pronouns are obligatory only if the DP object is right dislocated, that is, an adjunct. Table 3.14 shows the paradigm of object pronouns. Dedrick and Casad (1999: 245) provide a slightly different set of object pronouns and a complete paradigm for the dependent ones (mostly similar to the independent ones). Haugen (p.c.) is inclined to see the absence of first and second person dependent pronouns in table 3.14 as evidence of the loss of polysynthesis. This means the language is moving toward stage (c), with first and second person leading the way.

     As mentioned in the previous section, noun incorporation (NI) is often seen as typical for polysynthetic languages. Noun incorporation is a process where objects that are heads can be incorporated into the verb, as in (113a) from Yaqui. In Yaqui, noun incorporation is in complementary distribution with transitive marking on the verb, as shown in (113b).

(113) a. *aapo* **maaso**-*peu-te-n*   Yaqui
         3S   deer-butcher-INT-PST
         'He was deer butchering.'
      b. *aapo* *maaso-ta* *peu-ta-k*
         3S   deer-ACC   butcher-TR-PF
         'He butchered a deer.' (Jelinek 1998: 213)

---

3. In the related Warihío, only the first person singular is clitic-like (see Armendáriz 2007: 29).

TABLE 3.14

Yaqui Object Pronouns

	S		P	
	Independent	Dependent	Independent	Dependent
1	*nee*		*itom*	
2	*enchi*		*enchim*	
3	*apo'ik*	*a*	*apo'im*	*am*

From Guerrero 2006: 5

Incorporation	>	optional	>	either nominal or	> only
of DO nouns and		object agreement		pronominal	pronominal
pronouns					agreement

FIGURE 3.3. Object polysynthesis (adapted from Haugen 2004)

If the object is a full phrase, object NI is ungrammatical, as shown in (114).

(114) **aapo bwe'uu-k maaso-peu-te-n* Yaqui
       3sg   big-ACC   deer-butcher-INT-PST
       [*'He was [big deer]-butchering'] or [*'He was deer-butchering a big one']

Technically speaking, noun incorporation is independent of object polysynthesis though much research has linked them. For instance, in Nahuatl, NI is in complementary distribution with object marking on the verb. Haugen (2004: 336) suggests a grammaticalization path as in figure 3.3. Uto-Aztecan developed (subject and) object polysynthesis and lost it again in certain languages. Thus, it went through the entire cycle. The relationship between Tohono O'odham and Yaqui may tell us that the loss of polysynthesis starts with first and second person.

7. Indirect and Prepositional Object Cycles

As I have shown so far in this chapter, direct objects are frequently indicated by agreement on the verb. Other objects can also be represented on the verb, however. Applicatives "allow the coding of a thematically peripheral argument or adjunct as a core-object argument" (Peterson 2007: 1). Applicatives are also referred to as indirect or benefactive objects. In some languages, they are marked on the dependent nominal, in others on the verbal head. Since this chapter examines head marking, I will only consider head-marked applicatives and their development.

In Cora, a Uto-Aztecan language, there is applicative agreement, as in (115), since the first person indirect object is marked through *nya* on the verbal head.

(115)   *me-tí'i-**nya**-hašu'u-te-'e*   Cora
          3P-DISTR-1S-wall-CAUS-APPL
          'They are building me a wall.' (Casad 1998: 139)

Pima and Tohono O'odham, other Uto-Aztecan languages, also have object incorporation but on the adposition, as in (116). I count these objects as verbal objects since the adpositions must appear immediately before the verb and can be seen as incorporated.

(116)   *ka:lit*   *'a-n-t*   ***ha-da:m***   *melc*   *heg*   *'u'us*   Pima
          Car   AUX-1S-PF   P-over   drive   the   sticks
          'I drove the car over the sticks.' (Munro 1989: 115)

Munro (1989: 120–122) argues that this preposition incorporation adds an argument to the verb. It is very productive, except with temporal adpositions since it is harder to see arguments in their objects.

    In Athabascan, there are similar adpositional objects, that is, objects marked on an adposition. Here too, these are often analyzed as part of the verbal complex: *bí* in Navajo (117) and *beghá* in Chipewyan/Dëne Sųłiné (118).

(117)   ***b-í**-na-bi-ni-sh-tin*   Navajo
          3-against-ASP-3-Q-1S-handle =I handle him against it
          'I teach it to him.' (Young & Morgan 1980: 223; see also Rice 2000: 94)

(118)   ***be-ghá**-yé-n-i-l-tį*   Chipewyan/Dëne Sųłiné
          3S-to-3S-ASP-1S-CL-handle
          'I have given her to him.' (Li 1967: 419)

Young, Morgan, and Midgette (1992) divide Navajo adpositions into three categories, depending on their degree of dependence on the verb: "comparison with Eyak points to the probability that many . . . were originally independent adverbial elements" (922). Rice (1989: 19) notes this closeness of the adposition to the verb in other Athabascan languages, such as Slave: "when the object of a postposition is a pronoun, the phrase is often attracted to the verb." Holton (2000: 284) describes a similar closeness of the adposition and the verb in Tanacross.

    It is easy to see how the adposition in (117) could be reanalyzed as an applicative marker: *bí* could be analyzed as an indirect object marker. This is in fact the trajectory Craig and Hale (1988) and Peterson (2007) suggest. Peterson gives the following example from Kinyarwanda. In (119a), the place is marked by a preposition and *mu maazi* is adverbial; in (119b), the preposition has been incorporated into the verbal complex and *amaazi* is in a different position.

(119)   a.   *umwaana*   *y-a-taa-ye*   *igitabo*   ***mu***   *maazi*   Kinyarwanda
              child   he-PST-throw-ASP   book   in   water
              'The child has thrown the book into the water.'
         b.   *umwaana*   *y-a-taa-ye-**mo***   *amaazi*   *igitabo*
              child   he-PST-throw-ASP-APPL   water   book
              'The child has thrown the book into the water.' (Kimenyi 1980: 89)

Peterson (2007) provides examples of such incorporations from the Sahaptian-Klamath languages Nez Perce and Sahaptin, from the Papuan Yimas, from the Tibeto-Berman Hakha Lai, and from the Muskogean Chickasaw. Many more are discussed in Craig and Hale (1988), Mithun (1999: 244–248), and Siewierska (2004: 145–148).

The introduction of head marking of indirect and prepositional objects on verbs is common, but it can also happen that adpositions acquire head marking.[4] In Dutch (120), German (121), French (122), Middle English (123), and Italian (see Giusti 2001b: 57), a preposition can combine with the article. This is also known as D-to-P incorporation.

(120) *Ik zag haar **in't** museum*   Dutch
       I saw her in-the museum
       'I saw her in the museum.'

(121) ***ins** Kino*   German
       in-the movies
       'in the movie theater'

(122) ***aux** enfants*   French
       to-the children
       'to the children'

(123) *His wyf ful redy mette hym **atte** gate*   Middle English
       'His wife well ready met him at-the gate.'
       (Chaucer, "The Shipman's Tale," 7: 373, in Benson 1987: 207)

Head marking appears in (120) to (123) because the P is a probe with [u-phi] looking for something to agree with. The features are valued on P by a D that has been reanalyzed as an agreement marker on P. As a result, it cannot be left behind in preposition stranding (see chapter 1, section 4).

8. Changes in Argument Structure: Reflexives, Passives, and Intransitives

So far, I have discussed the object cycle, where object pronouns are reanalyzed as agreement markers and then renewed. There are also cases where objects disappear and reappear due to valency changes, that is, changes in how all arguments are expressed. These changes also proceed in cyclical fashion.

8.1 REFLEXIVE TO PASSIVE: SCANDINAVIAN AND SLAVIC

Reflexive (object) pronouns have developed into "passive" markers in the Scandinavian and Slavic languages, a well-studied trend.

---

4. Bakker (2008) reports 63 languages with no adpositions, 209 with no person marking on the adposition, and 106 with person marking.

In (124), the reflexive pronoun is independent and can, as in English, be reinforced by a form of 'self', as (125) shows. In (126), it is either a clitic or an affix (see Ottosson 2004) and the structure is ambiguous between passive or transitive verb.

(124) *hann   nefndi   **sik**   Ola*   Old Norse
       he   called   self   Oli

       'He called himself Oli.' (Faarlund 2004: 149)

(125) *sumir   hǫfðu   sik   sjalfa   deydda*   Old Norse
       some-NOM   had   REFL-ACC   self-ACC   killed

       'Some had killed themselves.' (Faarlund 2004: 90)

(126) a. *kollu-**mk***   Old Norse
         call-1S

         'I call myself; I am called.'

      b. *kalla-**sk***
         call-3S

         'He calls himself; he is called.' (Ottosson 2004)

The pronoun *sik* becomes the passive in the form of *-s*, as in Swedish (127), though it is also frequent as middle or reciprocal.

(127) *Det   dansade**s**   hela   natten*   Swedish
       it   dance-PASS   whole   night

       'There was dancing the entire night.'

The change from pronoun to valency marker can be interpreted as the verb moving through the position that the object is in, that is, stage (b), as in (128).

(128)

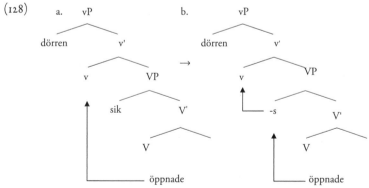

The change from (128a) to (128b) is from phrase *sik* to head *-s*. There is an additional change, but its shape depends on one's analysis of passives. Minimalism hasn't added much to our understanding of passives and I will therefore adopt a relatively old-fashioned approach where the passive morphology absorbs the theta role. This means that the passive *-s* in (128b) will be reanalyzed as a v head (in accordance with Late Merge). I am not sure how this would be expressed in terms of features since an argument disappears.

In Slavic, a similar change occurs from *sebja* to *–sja*, as is shown in (129) to (131).

(129) *Ivan   uvidel   **sebja***   Russian
       Ivan   saw   himself
       'Ivan saw himself.'

(130) *Ivan   moet-**sja***   Russian
       Ivan   wash-REFL
       'Ivan washes himself.'

(131) *Èta   sobaka   kusaet**sja***   Russian
       this   dog   bites
       'This dog bites.' (Faltz 2008)

Full nominal arguments, as in (129), with clear theta roles are reanalyzed to indicate a verb is without a theme, that is, unergative.

8.2 PRONOUN TO PASSIVE: AUSTRONESIAN

In this section, I first briefly discuss the well-known Indonesian verbal prefix *di-*, which is unlikely to have been a pronoun. Then I turn to the history of Austronesian, where it is possible to argue that an ergative pronoun becomes optional and results in a passive.

Guilfoyle, Hung, and Travis (1992) have argued that the Indonesian passive *di-* prefix has its origin in the third person singular pronoun *dia* 'she/he' since the construction is limited to third person agents, as in (132), and resembles the actual pronominal form.

(132) *saya   **dijemput**   oleh   dia*   Indonesian
       I   PASS-met   by   3S
       'I was met by him/her.' (Sneddon 1996: 248)

If we think of this in terms of a tree structure, *dia* would be reanalyzed from Specifier of vP to head and then absorb the theta role. Again, abstracting away from a good way to represent theta-absorption in terms of features, this is an expected change.

However, Wolff (1996) provides evidence against this view: some varieties of Indonesian do allow first and second person agents in *di*-passives. Musgrave (2001: 55) agrees that there are major problems with analyzing *di* as deriving from a pronoun and concludes that it is a verbal prefix. If they are correct, the above account won't work, but it is theoretically possible.

Kikusawa (2007) argues that an ancestor of Austronesian had an obligatory ergative pronoun that became optional and developed into a passive marker on the verb. Her evidence comes from the different stages of Austronesian languages. Some have an obligatory pronoun, others an optional pronoun optionally alternating with a passive, and still others "the remnants of the earlier pronominal forms . . . as agreement markers" (2007: 5). The start of this set of changes occurs when "the agent of a transitive sentence which was typically expressed with a post-genitive clitic pronoun became optional when it had an indefinite reference" (2007: 6).

Obligatory ergatives (in the form of genitives) occur in languages of the Philippines and Taiwan, as in (133) from Hiligaynon, provided in Kikusawa (2007).

(133) *Ipangluto'-**ko**   sang   lumpya   ang   kalaha'*   Hiligaynon
       cook.IV-1GEN   OBL   lumpia   NOM   frying-pan
       'I will use the frying to cook lumpia.' (Wolfenden 1971: 131, from Kikusawa 2007)

In (133), the first person is marked by a genitive on the verb and the verb is in the instrument voice (IV) since the instrument has nominative.

What happened next, according to Kikusawa, is that this marking became optional and could alternate with a verbal prefix, as in (134): "The process was that a passive structure emerged from a system in which the ergative noun phrase had become optional and alternated with a verbal prefix which was originally formally identical to one of the post-genitive third person clitic pronouns, but which lost its pronominal reference and became a passive prefix."

(134) a. ***Ku**-peppe'-ko*   Konjo
           1GEN-hit-2NOM
           'I hit you.'
       b. ***ni**-peppe'-ko*   *(ri   nakke)*
           PASS-hit-2NOM   by   me
           'You were hit by me.' (Friberg 1996: 165)

The ergative subject is present in (134a), but not in (134b), which has a passive marker (reconstructable as perfective aspect).

In some languages, the subject pronoun is reanalyzed as an agreement marker, as in Tetun (135), and follows the subject cycle.

(135) ***(nia)**   **n**-alai   ti'an*   Tetun
       3S   3S-run   already
       'She has run away.' (van Klinken 1999: 179)

In short, there is evidence that an ergative marker on the verb came to be seen as a passive. An analysis as in (128) could be developed for this.

8.3 INTRANSITIVE TO TRANSITIVE AND THE REFLEXIVE CYCLE IN ENGLISH

Nichols, Peterson, and Barnes (2004) argue that languages have a basic valency orientation. In this section, a few examples are given of how valency is marked in Old English (see Plank & Lahiri 2009 for German; van Gelderen 2010 for Old English). Visser (1963–1973: 1: 97–135) argues in some detail that there was an increase in transitive verbs. If true, there are (at least) two consequences: (1) objects become more frequent, also resulting in more reflexive objects, and (2) transitivizing affixes are lost. This is a huge topic that I cannot do justice to here. My main interest for now is the reflexive cycle.

As shown is section 1.1, it is sometimes difficult to distinguish between transitive and intransitive verbs. In some languages, object drop is possible but it may be that Old English, as in (136) and (137), used an intransitive construction (an inherent reflexive) for the verbs *to chide* and *to fear* where Modern English uses a transitive one.

(136)   *Begunnon hi to cidenne*
began they to chide

'They began to chide **themselves**.' (Aelfric, *Homilies*, in Thorpe 1844–1846: 2: 158.13,)

(137)   *Ondreardon*
fear-PST.P

'They feared **them**.' (*Lindisfarne Gospels*, Matthew 9.8, in Skeat [1881–1887] 1970)

If there is an increase in transitivity in Modern English, or a shift in basic type, how did this happen? I will show that there was a loss of prefixes to derive transitive verbs and an increase in strategies to mark intransitive verbs since transitive was now the basic type. In terms of syntactic structure, one could argue there was a solidification of the VP shell with both a light and regular verb.

In section 7, I showed that indirect objects can be added by means of an adverbial/adposition. Old English derived many of its transitive verbs from intransitives by means of prefixes: *ge-* in (138) and (139) and *for-* in (140).

(138)   *Swa **sceal** geong guma gode **gewyrcean***
So shall young man good-DAT accomplish

'So should a young man accomplish through good works.' (*Beowulf*, in Klaeber [1922] 1941: 20)

(139)   *ærnan* 'to run'   *geærnan* 'to reach'
feran 'to go'   *geferan* 'to reach'
gan 'to go'   *gegan* 'to overrun, subdue'
hwitian 'to become white'   *gehwitian* 'to make white'
restan 'to rest'   *gerestan* 'to give rest'
winnan 'to labor, toil'   *gewinnan* 'to gain, conquer'
wadan 'to go'   *gewadan* 'to traverse'
(Visser 1963–1973: 1: 127)

(140)   *þone biscopdom **for**letan sceolde*
that diocese leave should

'should leave that diocese.' (*Life of St. Chad*, in Vleeskruyer 1953: 162)

During the Middle English period, the verbal prefixes are lost and replaced by particles, such as *up* in (141) to (143), and these replace the perfective function though not always the transitivizing one. Thus, phrasal verbs extend their domain in Early Middle English.

(141)   *til he aiauen **up** here castles*

'till they gave up their castles' (*Peterborough Chronicle* [1140], 52).

(142)   *7 ælc unriht for gode and for worulde **up** aras*
        'and every wrong in the sight of God and of the world rose up' (*Peterborough Chronicle* [1100]).

(143)   *asprang **up** to þan swiðe sæ flod*
        'sprang up to such height (the) sea flood' (*Peterborough Chronicle* [1099]).

Old and Early Middle English have no special reflexives, but full pronouns are used, as in (144) and (145). Note the *ge-* and *be-* transitivizing prefixes on the verbs.

(144) | *þæt* | *we* | ***us*** | *gehydan* | *mægon* |
        |------|------|------|---------|-------|
        | that | we | us | hide | may |
        'that we can hide ourselves.' (Christ and Satan, Junius, in Krapp 1931: 100)

(145) | ***him*** | *bebeorgan* | *ne* | *con* |
        |-------|-----------|------|------|
        | (he) him | hide | not | can |
        'He could not hide himself.' (*Beowulf*, in Klaeber [1922] 1941: 1746)

In Old and early Middle English, reflexives start to appear, as in (146) to (148).

(146) | *þæt he hyne* | ***sylfne*** | *gewræc* |
        |-------------|----------|--------|
        | that he him-ACC | self-ACC | avenged |
        'He avenged himself.' (*Beowulf*, in Klaeber [1922] 1941: 2875)

(147) | *ic þa* | *sona eft* | *me* | ***selfum*** | *andwyrde* |
        |-------|---------|------|----------|----------|
        | I then | soon after | me-DAT | self-DAT | answered |
        'I soon answered myself.' (Alfred, *Pastoral Care*, 4.22, in Sweet [1871] 1934)

(148) | *he heo lette nemnen; efter **him-seoluan*** |
        |---------------------------------------|
        | he-NOM it-ACC let name after himself |
        'and had it named after himself.' (Layamon, *Brut*, Caligula, 1454, in Brook & Leslie 1963)

In this development, there are a number of issues. First, the type of verb is relevant (see, e.g., Ogura 1989 and König & Vezzosi 2004), as figure 3.4 shows. So certain verbs start the reflexive cycle. Second, one could think of the introduction of the reflexive as a change from verbal reflexive marking to nominal, as proposed in Faltz (1985, 2008) and represented as (149).

(149) | Pronoun | > clitic | > zero | > pronoun | etc. |
        |---------|----------|--------|-----------|------|
        | nominal | | verbal | nominal | |
        | Gothic | Old Norse | Old English | Middle English | |

In terms of structure, this could be as in (128). The stages of the cycle are interesting: the pronoun loses first and second person features (e.g., Mohave, Yiddish *zich*) and the renewal proceeds along a clear path (third before first and second).

typical towards another (help, kill, attack)	-	ambiguous (see)	-	typical towards oneself (wash, shave, shame, defend)

MORE marking   LESS marking

Judas hine **sylfne** *aheng* Judas him-ACC self-ACC hanged 'Judas hanged himself.'	-	*þæt we* **us** *gehydan mægon* that we us hide may 'that we can hide ourselves.'

FIGURE 3.4. Types of reflexive verb

8.4 HIDDEN REFLEXIVES: LAMAHOLOT

In Lamaholot, a Central Malayo-Polynesian language spoken on several islands of Eastern Indonesia, there are no transitivity markers on verbs and many verbs can be either transitive or intransitive. The ones used intransitively may have a pronominal suffix, as in (150a), which makes them almost reflexive. The verbs that are used transitively have a pronoun but cannot have a suffix, as (150b) and (150c) show.

(150) a. *go   hvbo(-**kvn**)*   Lamaholot
        I   bathe(-1S)
        'I bathe.'

       b. *go   hvbo   **na***
        I   bathe   her/him
        'I bathe her/him/.'

       c. **go   hvbo-**kvn**   **na***
        I   bathe-1S   her/him
        'I bathe her/him.' (Nishiyama & Kelen 2007: 77)

This is also true for noninherently reflexive verbs: *gasik* 'count', *buka* 'open', and *pupu* 'gather'.

Nishiyama and Kelen (2007) discuss two accounts for the restriction in (150). One is that historically there was object marking on verbs and the suffix in (150a) is a remnant of the object marker. Another is that there are a limited set of optional object markers, as in (151), and there is only one suffix position on the verb, reserved for objects in the case of transitives.

(151) a. *go   pehen   (ro)na*   Lamaholot
        I   touch   her/him

       b. *go   pehen-ro*
        I   touch-3S
        'I touch her/him.' (Nishiyama & Kelen 2007: 14)

These data fit with the object cycle if we think of this language as being in stage (b) with either a phrase, as in (151a), or a head, as in (151b), with the reflexive being optional.

There are many (object) arguments that end up incorporated into the verb. I have mentioned a few in this section but most I haven't talked about. For instance, Lehmann and Shin

(2005) provide various strategies of concomitant marking that can be seen of as different stages on a cline, such as from independent verb to adposition to Case and to verbal affix.

9. Conclusion

This chapter is parallel to the previous one, which discussed the subject cycle. Like the subject cycle, the object cycle knows several stages. Urdu/Hindi, Japanese, Malayalam, and Mokilese have object pronouns that are fully phrasal. We can show that other languages are developing from phrasal to head status, that is, are analyzed by the learner as heads in the absence of other evidence. Persian, Cape Verdean Creole, English, Arabic, Hebrew, and Coptic are possible candidates. Object pronouns are reanalyzed as verbal agreement markers in varieties of Spanish, Southern Slavic, Bantu, and Austronesian.

Object polysynthesis arises in Athabascan, and I have argued that it is possible to see this as the head keeping its interpretable features but occupying a position in a functional head.

The start of the object cycle is much less clear than that of the subject cycle where first and second person are the ones first reanalyzed. For the object cycle, it is human objects in Swahili; it is third person objects in early Modern English (animate and inanimate); it may be starting with definite animate objects in Persian, as is also the case in Spanish and Macedonian; and it may be definite human objects in Athabascan. Since first and second person are the most definite arguments, they lead the way in Swahili, and possibly in Sambaa, Albanian, Marshallese, and Uto-Aztecan. I have suggested this is due to their position relative to the verb. Indefinite objects are always arguments, not adjuncts, so once they are doubled, the pronoun has been reanalyzed as agreement. In chapter 5, we will see that definite and animate objects themselves can be marked specially when in object position. Each language that does this has a slightly different set of specially marked objects. This is to be expected since pronouns do not include the same features in every language.

4

THE PRONOMINAL COPULA CYCLE

IN THIS CHAPTER, I show that the reanalysis of a demonstrative or pronoun as an agree-ment marker, discussed in chapters 2 and 3, is also obvious when a subject pronoun is reana-lyzed as an auxiliary or copula verb, initially with its person and number features intact. This change involves a third person pronoun or demonstrative. This is very different from the sub-ject cycle, where first and second person are consistently the first to change. I argue the reason is due to the deictic features of the demonstrative, which translate into locational features on the copula, thus lending support to the feature analysis of third person pronouns in chapter 2.

Li and Thompson (1977) are among the first to examine this change and Katz (1996) is one of the first to note its systematic nature and to discuss it as a cycle. Copula cycles occur in many typologically and genetically different languages: Turkish, Uto-Aztecan, Chinese, Hebrew, Palestinian Arabic, Maltese, Kenya Luo, Lango, Logbara, Nuer, Wappo, West Greenlandic, and Creoles. I will argue that the cyclical changes follow from the Head Prefer-ence Principle and Feature Economy.

There are other sources for copulas, mainly prepositions and verbs (see Hengeveld 1992; Nicholas 1996; Stassen 1997; and Pustet 2003), and they can be accounted for within the framework developed in this book (see Lohndal 2009b). In this chapter, I will mainly be looking at demonstratives and pronouns.

In section 1, I provide some background on copulas. Sections 2 through 6 provide exam-ples of stages of the pronominal copular cycle. Section 7 considers how pronouns have been seen to derive from copulas.

1. Background

First, I provide some examples of copulas from English as well as a structure for representing copulas. Then, I review the literature on grammaticalization of copulas.

1.1 WHAT IS A COPULA?

I use the term *copula* for a verb with no independent meaning; it is also referred to as a linking or equating verb. English has a wealth of copulas, as the incomplete list in (1) shows.

(1)   be, become, seem, appear, look, remain, keep, stay, fall, turn, go

Some consider only *be* a copula since other linking verbs add an aspectual (*remain, keep,* and *stay*) or evidential (*seem* and *appear*) touch. Most copulas in English can also be used as intransitives, as (2) shows.

(2)   a. He **looked** nice (in that outfit)   = copula
       b. He **looked** (for it) everywhere.   = main verb

Many linguists distinguish (at least) two types of copulas cross-linguistically. Hengeveld (1992: 188) calls these predicativizing and discriminating. The predicativizing ones are typically verbs, as in (2a), or verbalizing affixes. The discriminating copulas are markers of non-verbal predication, such as pronouns, as we'll see in Greenlandic, Hebrew, and other languages, and invariant particles, as in (3), which I will not examine further.

(3)   **Te'i**   *ma'inə*   *a*   *gərə*   Gude
       PRT   water   LOC   river

       'There is water at the river.' (Hoskison 1983: 81, from Hengeveld 1992: 191)

This distinction is relevant in grammaticalization since the predicativizing ones derive from verbal sources and the discriminating ones from pronominal and other deictic elements.

Many possible structures for copulas have been suggested (Stowell 1978; Higgins 1979; Rothstein 1995; Adger & Ramchand 2003; and Mikkelsen 2005). In Stowell's analysis, the copula is a raising verb with a small clause complement, as in (4).

(4)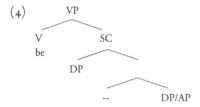

This analysis has a number of advantages: it is simple and could be changed into a vP shell relatively easily. In what follows, I will present an account for the cycle that does not depend on the precise structural representation of the copula but rather on its features, in accordance with Feature Economy.

1.2 THE COPULA CYCLES

As mentioned in the introduction, there are at least three sources of copulas, hence the plural in "copula cycles": pronouns, verbs, and adpositions/adverbs. Classic examples of these cycles are described by Li and Thompson (1977), Hengeveld (1992), Gildea (1993), Devitt (1994), Katz (1996), Stassen (1997: 78–95), Whitman (2000), Pustet (2003: 54), and Lohndal

(2009b). I will give examples of each of the sources for copulas but then focus on the pronominal source for the remainder of the chapter.

In many languages, pronouns end up as copulas: in (5) from West Greenlandic, *tassa* is a linker but can also (still) be used as a demonstrative pronoun.

(5) *Hansi* **tassa** *pisurtaq*   West Greenlandic
     Hansi   that   leader

'Hansi is the leader.' (Fortescue 1984: 72, from Hengeveld 1992: 192)

Positional verbs are also a source of copulas. Thus, Dutch *zitten* 'to sit' can be used as a copula, as in (6).

(6) *Jan* **zit** *in* *Frankrijk*   Dutch
     Jan   be-3S   in   France

'Jan is in France.' (Hengeveld 1992: 238)

The third source is the most diverse. Stassen (1997: 87–90) mentions the focus marking particle –*k* in the Uto-Aztecan Chemehuevi in (7); adpositional sources are also frequent.

(7) *Nɨɨ-k*   *nainc*   Chemehuevi
     1S-FOC   girl

'I am a girl.' (Press 1975: 132)

As mentioned, I will consider only the pronominal source in this chapter. A cycle is easy to notice: a demonstrative is reanalyzed as a copula and a new demonstrative is introduced. The copula, in turn, might disappear. The way this cycle has been explained is through the reanalysis of a topic or focus construction, as in (8).

(8) The elephant   that   happy
     TOP   SU   VP
                    ↓
     SU   copula   VP

The question would be why first (or second) person pronouns are never reanalyzed as copulas since they are frequent topics. I will therefore suggest an addition to (8) that depends on the features of the demonstrative.

It is possible to think about the changes in terms of the Head Preference Principle and Late Merge. The Head Preference Principle predicts that the demonstrative/pronoun could optionally be a head; once that happens, it could be analyzed by the language learner as a (higher) copula. I will be more precise and use features since they account for the renewal. Like Lohndal (2009b: 218), I rely on a version of Feature Economy. However, rather than using [F], as in Lohndal, I will be more specific and use [loc] and [phi] features ([u-T] in (9) represents Case).

(9) demonstrative/pronoun   >   copula   >   grammatical marker
     specifier   >   head   >   affix
     [i-loc]   >   [i-loc] >   --
     [i-phi]   >   [u-phi]
     [u-T]

I haven't seen an analysis of copulas in terms of features.[1] Since the sources of renewal are deictic and aspectual, I'd like to suggest the features in (10) for English copulas. The simplest copula is *be*; most of the others will have additional aspect or mood features.

(10)   *be*   *remain*   *seem*
       [i-loc]   [i-loc]   [i-loc]
                  [i-ASP]   [i-M]

Demonstratives and third person pronouns start the copula cycle, as we will see, and that makes sense given that those have deictic features (as I argued in chapter 2).

I have represented the stages in figure 4.1. In stage (a), the phi features of the T probe are valued by the pronoun or demonstrative in VP, the demonstrative or third person pronoun moves as full phrase to the Spec of TP, and the copula moves to T. Modern English represents that stage. In stage (b), the demonstrative is a head and its phi features are very similar to those of the copula and of the T. A reanalysis may therefore take place of the demonstrative

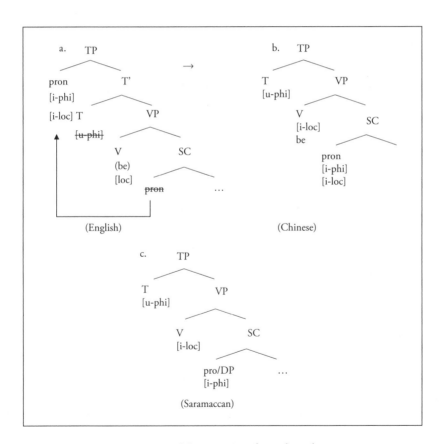

FIGURE 4.1. The pronominal copula cycle

---

1. Katz's (1996: 62) suggestion that copulas and demonstratives share "existence in time and space" focuses on both time and place whereas I think copulas and demonstratives share the location only.

as copula. Chinese is representative of this stage. Stage (c) shows a new demonstrative to provide interpretable phi features for the T probe; this occurs in Saramaccan. Stage (b) and especially stage (c) might start to delete the copula. I will not look at the triggers for that change. There is an enormous literature (see the review in Walker 2000) on copula contraction and deletion in African American English.

In what follows, I provide examples of the various stages languages go through, starting with an overt copula and regular subject.

2. Pronoun and Copula Stage: English

Stage (a) is what we are used to from English, so I will keep this section short. In (11), T is a probe and agrees with the pronoun; the copula *be* and the subject move to T and the Specifier of TP respectively.

(11)

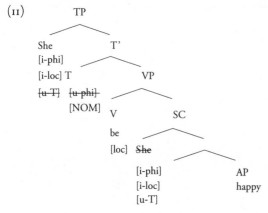

As I argued in chapter 2, third person pronouns and demonstratives usually have deictic features, and hence there is a similarity with the (finite) copula. I suggest this makes a reanalysis possible in some languages. In English, this would probably not happen since (third) person pronouns also have case ([u-T] in [11]). If it didn't have this, the features after valuation would be as in (12) and be very reanalyzable.

(12)   She   T
                be
       [i-loc] [i-loc]
       [i-3S]   [u-phi] > [3S]

In English, the copula *be* is used for permanent as well as nonpermanent qualities, unlike Spanish for example, and [i-loc] for *be* in (10) and (11) is meant to represent individual as well as stage level. Languages where that distinction is relevant would have an ASP(ect) Phrase, as do verbs such as *remain* in English.

3. Demonstrative Pronouns as Ambiguous Copulas: Chinese, Polish, and Russian

The stage from (a) to (b) is here represented by Chinese and by Polish and Russian.

3.1 CHINESE *SHI*

Many have examined the origin of the copula in Mandarin Chinese. For instance, Wang (1958) argues that Ancient Chinese has no copulas, Li and Thompson (1977) put the origin of the Chinese copula (from the demonstrative *shi*) in a broader typological perspective, Peyraube and Wiebusch (1994) provide data for various copulas, and Whitman (2000) formulates the change from pronoun to copula as a change from specifier to head.

In an early period (before 200 BCE), there are no copulas, according to Wang (1958), and *shi* 'this' typically functions as a demonstrative in *shi ri* 'this day.' *Shi* still has this function in very formal contexts, as in (13). In Old Chinese, *shi* also functions as a resumptive pronoun with an empty copula, as in (14).

(13) *jiang* **shi** *xiang* *jing-fei jibo*   *ben* *suo*   Mandarin Chinese
      will   D   CL   funding-transfer D   organization
      'He will transfer these funds to our organization.'
      (Academia Sinica Balanced Corpus of Modern Chinese; Hui-Ling Yang, p.c.)

(14) *fu*   *yu*   *gui*   **shi** *ren* *zhi* *suo*   *yu*   *ye*   Old Chinese
      Riches and honor this men GEN NOM desire PRT
      'Riches and honor, this is men's desire.' (Peyraube & Wiebusch 1994: 393)

Peyraube and Wiebusch (1994) argue, against Wang, that classical Chinese always had copulas but that they were optional. Based on data from Takashima (1990), they show that *hui, wei, yi,* and *ye* function as copulas, and that the last word in (14) is indeed such a copula. I have not looked into *ye*; it could be that *ye* grammaticalized into an affirmative particle and as a result a new copula *shi* appeared.

In (14), it is difficult to determine whether *shi* is a copula or a demonstrative subject. However, examples such as (15) are unambiguous since doubling occurs; in Modern Chinese, this would be rendered as (16) with a demonstrative *zhe*.

(15) **Shi** **shi** *lie*   *gui*   Old Chinese
      this is violent ghost
      'This is a violent ghost.' (Peyraube & Wiebusch 1994: 398)

(16) **Zhe** **shi** *lie gui*   Mandarin Chinese
      'This is a violent ghost.' (Mei Ching Ho, p.c.)

According to Peyraube and Wiebusch (1994: 398), the earliest clear examples like (15) date from 180 BCE.

The demonstrative function of *shi* is (mainly) lost in modern Mandarin Chinese, but the copula function, as in (16), remains. It indicates identity (location, possession, and existence are expressed in different ways). It is also often used as a cleft or in a presentational construction, as in (17) and (18).

(17) **Shi** *wo* *de*   *zuo*   Mandarin Chinese
      be 1S POSS fault

      'It's is me (who is) at fault.' (Hui-Ling Yang, p.c.)

(18)   **Shi**   *wo*   Mandarin Chinese
       be   1S

    'It's me.' (Hui-Ling Yang, p.c.)

Summarizing the situation in Chinese, one can say that this language has seen a reanalysis of the demonstrative *shi* as copula: since the features of the demonstrative are similar to those of the copula and appear in similar functional heads, this reanalysis was possible. The demonstrative *shi* itself is still used, as in (13), but the sources of demonstrative renewal come from demonstratives such as *zhe* in (16). The developments in Chinese follow the copula cycle presented in figure 4.1 very well, namely from phrase to functional head. This basic account would still be correct if Chinese turns out not to include a TP but an ASPP as well as a TopP. Then the copula would occupy the head position and the 'subject' the specifier position. I'll also mention this possibility in connection to Russian.

3.2 POLISH AND RUSSIAN

Most Indo-European languages have a copula derived from a verbal source (e.g., English and Dutch). Slavic languages seem to be an exception, although the change taking place there is not complete.

In Polish, the copula *być* 'be' is optionally preceded by *to*, as (19a) and (19b) show. In the present tense, this particle is also optional, as in (20a) and (20b), but the present tense copula *jest* can be deleted as well, as (20c) shows.

(19)   a.   *Adam **był** lingwistą*   Polish
            Adam was linguist
       b.   *Adam **to był** lingwista*
            Adam PRT was linguist

       'Adam was a linguist.' (Rutkowski 2006)

(20)   a.   *Jan **jest** mój najlepszy przyjaciel*   Polish
            Jan is my best friend
       b.   *Jan **to jest** mój najlepszy przyjaciel*
            Jan PRT is my best friend
       c.   *Jan **to** mój najlepszy przyjaciel*
            Jan PRT my best friend

       'Jan is my best friend.' (Rutkowski 2006)

To is historically a demonstrative and Rutkowski (2006) argues that its presence in addition to the copula provides evidence of an unfinished change. Sentences such as (20c) are of course ambiguous where the status of *to* is concerned and provide the impetus for reanalysis of *to* as a copula with fewer features, according to (9).

Rutkowski argues that *to* hasn't completely reached the head stage. He suggests that *Adam* in (19b) is in Top position, *to* in the Spec of TP, *był* in T, and *lingwista* in the Spec of VP. In a sentence without *to*, such as (19a), *Adam* is in the Spec of TP. One piece of evidence for the different status of *Adam* in (19a) and (19b) is that control by *Adam* is possible in (21) but not in (22). This shows that, in sentences with *to*, the DP subject is in an adjunct position.

(21)   *Adam był lingwistą, mieszkając w New Haven*   Polish
       Adam was linguist living in New Haven
       'Adam was a linguist when he lived in New Haven.'

(22)   **Adam to był lingwista, mieszkając w New Haven*   Polish
       Adam PRT was linguist living in New Haven
       (Rutkowski 2006)

Russian has a very similar construction to the Polish one, as is shown in (23) for the present tense. In all cases, *eto* is optional.

(23)   *Misha **eto** nash doctor*   Russian
       Misha this our doctor
       'Misha is our doctor.' (Markman 2008: 366)

Markman, following others, proposes that *eto* in (23) is in the head of the TopP and suggests a reduced pseudocleft structure. Unfortunately, she (2008: 374) leaves the nature of the pronominal element for further research. If *eto* is in the Top head, it is not technically a copula, however. Olena Tsurska (p.c.) mentions that *eto* in (23) can still be a demonstrative with a comma intonation between *Misha* and *eto*. I think that means the change is very much in progress.

Chinese, Polish, and Russian provide evidence of an ambiguous stage in the development of the demonstrative, one where it can be seen as a specifier or a head. This is of course necessary before a reanalysis can take place. In Chinese, *shi* has reached the head stage but Polish and Russian represent cases where we have a demonstrative that could be reanalyzed as a copula, for example, in the present tense, but hasn't completely been finalized.

4. Pronouns Reanalyzed as Copulas: Creoles, Afro-Asiatic, and Native American Languages

In this section, I discuss languages where demonstratives have been reanalyzed as copulas. There are a number of complexities, as I show.

4.1 CREOLES

Creoles provide evidence that a demonstrative was reanalyzed as a copula and an earlier topic pronoun now functions as subject. This represents stage (b) of figure 4.1. I'll discuss Saramaccan and Cape Verdean Creole in this section; the former provides a good example but the latter only a partial one.

McWhorter (1997) presents examples of demonstrative pronouns being reanalyzed as copula verbs in Saramaccan, as in (24), where *da* derives from the English demonstrative *that*.

(24) a. *Mi*   ***da***   *i*   *tatá*   Saramaccan
         I   COP   your father
      'I am your father.' (McWhorter 1997: 87)
   b. *Hɛn*   ***dà***   *dí*   *Gaamá*
      he   is   the   chief
      'He's the chief.' (McWhorter 1997: 98)

McWhorter (1997: 97) argues that early Saramaccan had a zero copula and the demonstrative subject pronoun *da* 'that' was reanalyzed as an (identificational) equative copula. He also argues that earlier *mi* and *hɛn* in (24a) and (24b) were in topic position but that they are now in subject position. I am assuming this scenario is correct and therefore a clear case of a demonstrative pronoun reanalyzed as copula.

   Apart from the copula *da* in (24), there is another copula in Saramaccan that is derived from the English locative adverb *there*, namely *dɛ* in (25). It is used for class equatives and locatives.

(25) a. *a*   ***dɛ***   *mi*   *tatá*   Saramaccan
         he   is   my   father
      'He is my father.' (McWhorter 1997: 99)
   b. *Dí*   *wómi*   ***dɛ***   *a*   *wósu*
      the   woman   there   LOC   house
      'The woman is at home.' (McWhorter 1997: 88)

McWhorter (1997: 106) calls this *dɛ* 'expressive' since, he argues, its origin is that of a deictic adverb. Putting *dɛ* in tree form (abstracting away from Case), I see this change as one from an empty copula with uninterpretable location features checking with a locative adverb to one where the lexical ***dɛ*** is reanalyzed as copula with [i-loc] features, as in (26).

(26)

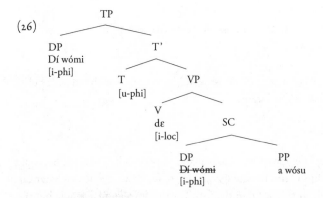

   Baptista (2002) provides sentences from Cape Verdean Creole showing a similar origin of the copula. In (27), the copula form *e* (used with individual-level predicates) derives from the third person pronoun *el* 'he' and has kept the [3S] interpretable features since this copula can be used only for third person singulars.

(27) a. **(El)** e nha pai   CVC
      'He is my father.'
      b. **(El)** e spertu   CVC
      'She/he is smart.' (Baptista 2002: 255)

The copula *e* in (27) has none of the deictic features since it is purely equational. Because (27) is limited to third person singular, we could also argue that *e* still is the subject and that the optional *el* is a topic. This is what Baptista (2002: 102) suggests: "*e* occupies the syntactic position of a copula but behaves like a pronoun." Later on, she argues that it is also used as a focalizer, as in (28).

(28) **E**   mi   ki   ta   fika   ku   kes   minizu   CVC
      FOC   1S   REL   ASP   stay   with   the kids
      'It is me who stays with the kids.' (Baptista 2002: 103)

This means that, as copula, it can also move to the left periphery, and that being a topic or cleft marker is a natural extension of the copula.

CVC also has a stage-level copula, *sta*, that can be used with any subject, as (29) shows; when used without a pronoun, it can be first, second, or third person.

(29) *Bu*   **sta**   *livri*   CVC
      'You are free.' (Baptista 2002: 255)

However, the origin of *sta* is verbal (I assume from *estar* 'be' in Portuguese, which derives from the Latin *stare* 'to stand'). So CVC shows that a third person pronoun can be used as an individual level copula. It doesn't show evidence of a demonstrative being reanalyzed in a more locational way.

Many creoles have a copula verb and, in most, this copula derives from an earlier demonstrative or pronoun, as it does in Saramaccan. Haitian (DeGraff 1992; Déprez 2003), Jamaican (Bailey 1966: 65; Durrleman-Tame 2008: 70), Sranan (Arends 1986), and Tok Pisin (Verhaar 1995: 83) provide further examples.

4.2 AFRO-ASIATIC

The history of Hebrew and Arabic shows that copulas in these languages are derived from demonstratives or third person independent pronouns. The relevant examples come from Reckendorf (1921), Berman and Grosu (1976), Doron (1986), Katz (1996), Zewi (1996), Stassen (1997), and Naudé (2002). I'll start with an example from Egyptian and then continue with the Semitic branch of Afro-Asiatic. Cushitic and Chadic languages also display some evidence of this change, but I will not go into these.

Loprieno (1995: 68) explains that in Old Egyptian there are many series of demonstratives. There is a pronominally based one, with a person marker (*p*- for masculine singular, *t*- for feminine singular, and *jp*- and *jpt*- for the plural) followed by a deictic element (e.g., −*n* and −*w* for different degrees of closeness). This results in demonstratives such as *pn* 'this' in (30a) and *jpw* 'those' in (30b).

(30)   a. *rmt*   **p-n**   Old Egyptian
       man   MS-PROX
       'this man'

       b. *ntr-w*   **jp-w**
       god-P   MP-DIST

       'those gods' (Loprieno 1995: 68)

According to Loprieno, the masculine distal *pw*-pronouns become copulas in Middle Egyptian, as in (31), not agreeing in gender or number with the nominal predicate.

(31)   a. *rmt*   **pw**   Middle Egyptian
       man   be
       'This is a man.' (Loprieno 1995: 68)

       b. *ṯmjt*   **pw**   *jmnt*
       city-F   be   west-F

       'The West is a city.' (Loprieno 2001: 1752)

This change from demonstrative to copula could have happened because of a reanalysis of the demonstrative from an element with phi features to one without but keeping its deictic features, as shown in (32).

(32)   Old Egyptian   Middle Egyptian
       p-w   >   *pw*
       [i-phi]   [i-loc]
       [i-loc]

Note that *pw* in (31a) would still be ambiguous, but not in (31b).

In Modern Hebrew, the third person pronoun can optionally function as a present tense copula, as in (33), or a regular subject, as in (34). This means that the pronoun *hu* is either a pronoun or a copula and could in principle be reanalyzed as a copula head in (33).

(33)   *dani*   **(hu)**   *ha-more*   Hebrew
       Dani   he   the-teacher

       'Dani is the teacher.'

(34)   **hu**   *malax*   *'al*   *jisra'el*   Hebrew

       'He   ruled   over   Israel.' (Katz 1996: 86)

However, this situation is reminiscent of Polish and Russian in that the past tense still requires an overt verb with tense and deictic features. This means reanalysis may not take place for a while.

Eid (1983), among many others, argues that pronouns also serve as present tense copulas in Arabic sentences such as (35). These forms can appear with non-third-person subjects as well, as in (36a),[2] but agree in gender and number with the subject, as (36b) shows.

---

2. Edwards (2006) provides these sentences from Egyptian Arabic but, according to Mohammed Al-Rashed (p.c), they are fine in Standard Arabic as well.

(35) *allahu* **huwa** *'lhayyu*   Arabic
     God   he   the-living
     'God is the living.' (Benveniste [1966] 1971: 165)

(36) a. *'ana* **huwwa** *l-mas'u:l*   Egyptian Arabic
       I   he   the-responsible
       'I am the responsible.' (Edwards 2006: 51)
     b. *il-mushkila* **hiyya** *T-Talaba*
       the-problem(FS)   she   the-students
       'The problem is the students.' (Edwards 2006: 52)

Sentences such as (36a) seem to suggest that a reanalysis has taken place. In addition, the erstwhile pronoun can be negated in the present tense in the same way as a verb. Note (37) where *hiyya* behaves as a regular verb.

(37) *faTma ma-**hiyya:**-sh*   *il-mas'u:la*   Egyptian Arabic
     Fatima NEG-be.3FS-NEG   the-responsible
     'Fatima is not the one responsible.' (Edwards 2006: 53)

The status of the pronominal copula is still controversial, however. Building on Simpson and Wu (2002a), Edwards argues for a pronominal analysis of the copula, noting that the negative surrounds many other nonverbal elements and that (37) is a focusing construction. The most likely development is one where the pronoun (with interpretable phi- and deictic features) in a specifier position of the VP was reanalyzed as a head with uninterpretable features, such as V in (26) (though v in a vP shell would also work). The uninterpretable features would probe a new goal. There is a copula *ka:n* for nonpresent tenses and there a reanalysis would not be taking place.

The status of subjects such as *faTma* in (37) can be either argumental or not. If they are nonarguments, there would be a pro providing new phi features for T, not impossible given that Arabic is a pro-drop language.

A possible piece of counterevidence to the pronoun being a head is that in neither Arabic (38a) nor in Hebrew (38b) can we "double" the pronoun.

(38) a. **huwwa* **huwwa** *l-mas'u:l*   Arabic
       he   he   the-responsible
       'He's the responsible.' (Mohammed Al-Rashed, p.c.)
     b. **hu* **hu** *more*   Hebrew
       he   he   teacher
       'He's the teacher.' (Doron 1986: 326)

This could be a phonetic constraint as well since, even if the second *huwwa* and *hu* in (38) are not copulas, they should be able to function as subjects and the preceding material as topics. Various linguists have formulated antihomophony constraints that could be relevant here: two adjacent elements cannot have the same phonological form.

Naudé (2002) examines an earlier stage of Hebrew, namely Qumran Hebrew, used about eighteen hundred years ago. In Qumran Hebrew, the postcopular element can be only a definite nominal, as in (39), not an indefinite one or an adjective, as in Modern Hebrew.

(39) *'th   hw'   yhwh*   Qumran Hebrew
      You   he   lord

      'You are the Lord.' (Naudé 2002: 162)

This suggests a demonstrative origin, as in Egyptian, which may not yet have been completely grammaticalized in the case of (36a).

Another Semitic language that develops a copula from a demonstrative is Amharic. Stassen (1997: 78) suggests that the "copula *na/ne* in this language may have had a demonstrative origin." It now appears in final position, as in (40), which is typical of verbs.

(40) *Antä   təlləq   nä-h*   Amharic
      2S   big   be-2S

      'You are big.' (Stassen 1997: 78)

Afro-Asiatic languages thus frequently reanalyze demonstratives as copulas. Different languages show different stages: Middle Egyptian clearly has such a copula but the evidence in Hebrew and Arabic is still contested.

4.3 NATIVE AMERICAN LANGUAGES

Native American languages provide many examples of copulas derived from a demonstrative/pronoun. Pustet (2003: 58) shows that the Lakota copula *hécha* goes back to the demonstrative *hé*. I will just mention Zoque.

Faarlund (2005) provides an example from Zoque, a Mixe-Zoque language of southern Mexico. In (41), the demonstrative *te'* is shown as well as its more grammaticalized use as a predicate marker *te* having assimilated to *-de*.

(41) *Te'*   *une*   *che'-bü-de*   Zoque
      The   child   small-REL-PRED

      'The child is small.'

The examples in this section show demonstratives and third pronouns in the process of being reanalyzed as copulas. In Saramaccan, there is evidence for a full cycle but in the other languages discussed here that is not yet the case.

5. Turkish and Hebrew: Possible Counterexamples

Katz (1996) provides many examples of pronouns being reanalyzed as copulas, including the ones mentioned earlier in Chinese and Hebrew. However, she also provides some reconstructed evidence from earlier stages of Turkish and Hebrew of the opposite development, namely that copulas change into pronouns.

Basing her discussion on a dictionary of Turkish from before the thirteenth century, Katz (1996: 118–136) argues that the present-day Turkish pronoun *o(n)* 'she/he' derives from the verb *ol-mak* 'be-INF'. In the early texts, *ol* already appears as demonstrative and pronoun, but Katz argues that the copula use was earlier. Her main reason is that early texts "make sparing use of independent pronouns" (1996: 122). To me, this is not a convincing argument for claiming that the copula was earlier than the pronoun. Arabic, for instance, also avoids subject pronouns such as *huwwa* 'he', as in (42).

(42) **(huwa)** jaa'-a   Arabic
     he   came-3MS
     'he came'.

The case of a possible reverse development in Hebrew is more complex. Katz (1996) argues that the origin of *hu* in Hebrew (33) is the verb *xaja/xawa* 'to live'. Her grammaticalization path for Hebrew is as in (43).

(43) *xaja/xawa* *haja/hawa* *howo*   *hu*   *hu*
     a   b   c
     'to live'   'to be'   'his being' 'he' 'be'
     (Katz 1996: 189)

She provides (44) from biblical Hebrew with most of the stages of (43) represented. According to Katz, the etymology of 'Eve' is connected to 'life' from being 'the mother of all life'.

(44) *wajriqa* *ha'adam* *sem*   *ísto*   **xawa**   Biblical Hebrew
     called   the-man   name   wife   Eve
     ki   **hi**   **hajta**   *'em*   *kol-***xaj**
     because   she   was   mother   all-alive

     'And Adam called the name of his wife Eve because she was the mother of all living things.' (Genesis 3.20, from Katz 1996: 166)

The change from (43a) to (43c), that is, a change to the use of *hu* from copula verb to pronoun, would constitute a counterexample to what I have presented in this chapter since a pronoun has more features than a copula. The argument that this happened seems to rest on the assumption that the pronoun is a cognate of a lexical verb. However, there is no stage with just the lexical verb and not the pronoun. This means that the pronoun was always around and therefore, the counterexamples to a unidirectional cycle are not convincing.

Another possible counterexample is provided in Kwon (2009), who argues that the auxiliary *be* in Old North Russian developed into a pronoun. Old Russian was pro-drop and there was a *be* 'available' after the resultative *l*-participle. This verb became used on its own as a general past tense. Kwon argues that pronouns and auxiliaries were similar enough in their feature specifications for this to happen. I think one of the problems is that, if the new pronoun is indeed a full pronoun, the change would mean that an earlier head is now projecting as a phrase. I don't see evidence of that in Kwon's data.

6. Specialized Demonstratives

In section 4, we saw that both *da* and *dɛ* are used as copulas in Saramaccan. They have specialized functions, such as identificational and locative copulas. Some copulas develop special aspectual uses, as is most obvious in the copulas that have a verbal source. In this section, I provide a brief overview of the data from Panare presented in Gildea (1993).

Panare is a Cariban language where the past and present tense marking auxiliaries, Gildea argues, derive from distal and proximal demonstratives via a copula stage. The proximal *këj* can be used to draw attention to something being in the present, whereas the distal *nëj* is more typically a default or the past tense, as in (45).

(45) *maestro* **nëj** *chu*   Panare
      teacher   DIST   1S

      'I was a teacher.' (Gildea 1993: 61)

A demonstrative indicates the spatial deixis of a nominal; as copula, "the deixis is now of the predications" (1993: 59).

In addition to the development of (45), nominalized verbs are used with copulas, as in (46). The copulas are syntactically the same as other auxiliaries, though their use is extremely complex (and beyond the scope of this chapter).

(46) *ëˀpúmanëpëj*   **këj**   *Toman*   Panare
      detrans-hit-IMPF PROX   Thomas

      'Thomas is falling.' (Gildea 1993: 65)

Thus, Panara shows that, if both distal and proximal demonstratives are reanalyzed, they may be specialized for tense.

7. Conclusion

The pronominal and demonstrative source of copulas examined in this chapter is relevant to the development of head marking. The changes can easily be accounted for either in a Feature Economy framework or with the Head Preference Principle. If demonstratives and third person pronouns have deictic features, they can be "confused" with copulas, that is, they are ambiguous and can be reanalyzed. The "confusion" is in accordance with the Feature Economy cline of (9). If ambiguous, a lexical item will be reanalyzed with fewer features.

Other sources for copulas, such as adpositions and locational verbs, also fit the Feature Economy framework, but see Lohndal (2009b) for more on that.

Part II

5

THE DEPENDENT MARKING CYCLES

Case

THIS CHAPTER ON dependent marking and Case has been the hardest to write and will probably be the most controversial in the book. As Butt (2006: 5) puts it, "no theory can honestly claim to have 'the answer' as to why case works the way it does cross-linguistically." The chapter is an attempt to deal with Case in the same way as I have with agreement, through Feature Economy. I will argue that Case derives from deixis, actual deixis for the semantic cases and grammaticalized deixis (e.g., [uT] in previous chapters) for the grammatical cases.

Of the three main ways in which languages express grammatical and other relations, word order, head marking (or agreement), and dependent marking (or Case), the latter two are very prone to grammaticalization. In chapters 2 to 4, we have seen head marking develop when pronouns are reanalyzed as subject and object markers on the verb. If the subject and object (pro)nominals have special markings for grammatical function, this is often lost in the reanalysis to verbal agreement (since 'light' elements start this cycle). Thus, the increase in head marking of subjects and objects may result in a loss of or change in dependent marking, as has happened in the modern Romance (see Cennamo 2009) and Germanic languages. The agreement and Case cycles are therefore not completely independent of each other, although Case and agreement themselves may be (see also Baker 2009). Dependent marking arises through grammaticalization as well, mainly of deictic markers, as we'll see in this chapter and the next. It is a lot less "well behaved" than head marking.

Dependent marking on a nominal is often referred to as Case (and I will use both *Case* and *dependent marking* in this chapter). Dependent marking can be (a) semantic (marking the thematic relations), (b) grammatical (marking the subject and object), and (c) discourse

This chapter was originally presented at the Oslo Symposium on Universal Grammar, acquisition and change, organized by Jan Terje Faarlund at the Center for the Study of Mind in Nature in August 2008. I would like to thank the participants.

related (marking indefiniteness and definiteness, topic/focus), and of course they overlap. In much generative work, the grammatical relations are seen as structurally determined, and hence (b) is not specially mentioned. Thus, Chomsky (2002: 113) mentions (a) and (c) in arguing that "[t]he semantics of expressions seems to break up into two parts. . .. There's the kind that have to do with what are often called thematic relations, such as Patient, Experiencer, etc.; and there's the kind that look discourse related, such as new/old information, specificity, Topic, things like that."

Marking the thematic roles (i.e., [a]) is done through pure merge in Chinese and English, for example, or through inherent Case and adpositions as in Sanskrit, Latin, Malayalam, Japanese, and Tagalog. Definiteness and specificity (i.e., [c]) can be marked through Case in, for example, Finnish, Turkish, Persian, Japanese, and Limbu (van Driem 1986: 34), through aspect as in Russian (Leiss 1994, 2000; Abraham 1997; Philippi 1997), through position as in Chinese, through a determiner, and through a combination of position and articles in Arabic, Dutch, and German, for example (Diesing 1992). Grammatical function (i.e., [b]) is most consistently marked by agreement on the verb with some structurally special position. The nominal in this special position may be assigned a structural Case. Agreement is represented in the grammar through phi features, and they are responsible for the agreement cycle.

In this chapter and the next, I will argue that deictic features are responsible for the Case cycles. I follow Leiss (2000) in considering definiteness on nouns and aspect on verbs as two sides of the same coin and, as before, I adapt Pesetsky and Torrego (e.g., 2001) and Richards (2004, 2008a) in representing dependent marking as [u-T] (nominative, marked on the D) and [u-ASP] (accusative, also marked on D). The choice of [u-T(ense)] and [u-ASP(ect)] points to the connection between nominal and verbal marking. Grammars of specific languages can have an emphasis on nominal marking of aspect and boundedness or on verbal marking. This can be seen in terms of dependent marking (noun is marked, as in Finnish) or head marking (verb is marked, as in Russian).

The first section provides some background on dependent marking. The second section is predominantly a case study from Old English on the change from a grammar where verbal aspect dominates to one where nominal markers do. Section 3 examines the origins of dependent marking on subjects and objects. Another type of marking, differential (subject and object) marking, is discussed in section 4. This kind of marking can be seen as definiteness. Marking on noncore nominals (e.g., location and instrumental) is discussed in section 5. Section 6 returns to a discussion of the cycle and presents a conclusion.

1. Case, Its Uses, and Its Structure

Case is unlike agreement in that it typically identifies the marked situation. As Comrie (1981: 122) puts it, Case is widespread as an "indication of unnatural combinations of A and P," that is, to indicate that the agent is less animate than the patient or the patient more animate than the agent. Case is also used for definiteness and in that function interacts with animacy, of course. Nichols (1992: 46–96) asserts that head marking and dependent marking "are about equally frequent overall" (1992: 95), but this is not clear. Siewierska and Bakker (2009: 299) say that "case marking of arguments is overall considerably less common cross-linguistically than agreement marking."

This section first focuses on the types of Case and how these may be responsible for a variety of functions, such as marking the semantic, grammatical, and pragmatic roles. It then provides some structural descriptions.

1.1 KINDS OF CASE

As mentioned, three types of information are relevant in a sentence and they are marked by a variety of morphological and syntactic markers that sometimes overlap. In table 5.1, repeated from table 1.7, I have given a very simplified picture of the primary functions of these markers. (See Abraham 2007[1] and Bisang 2006 among others for more detailed views.) Prosodic factors are also important but are left out here. In the remainder of this section, I discuss the markers of table 5.1. Semantic roles can be divided into core roles (agent and theme) and noncore roles (goals and locations, etc). The noncore functions are often expressed by means of a preposition or postposition, as in (1), or by means of a specialized Case, as in (2) and (3). The specialized Case is also known as inherent Case, and when it is lost it is often renewed by adpositions (as probably occurred in Hindi/Urdu).

(1) *Wo*   *šehr*   ***se***   *jʌngl*   ***ko***   *jata*   *hẽ*   Hindi/Urdu
     he   city   from   forest   to   go-M   be-3S
     'He goes from the city to the forest.'.

(2) *nagar**at***   *van**am***   *gacchati*   Sanskrit
     city-ABL   forest-ACC   goes-3S
     'He goes from the city to the forest.'

(3) *Ayodhya-**yam***   *vasa-ti*   Sanskrit
     Ayodhya-LOC   lives-3S
     'He lives in Ayodhya.'

I consider this Case to be an instance of inherent Case though this is not uncontroversial.

Core grammatical roles are typically not marked by semantic Case but by structural (nominative and accusative) Case and by agreement. I argue later that *Case* is the wrong term for structural Case, and this is recognized early on by Schuchardt, for one (quoted in van der Horst 2008: 145): "Der Nominativ ist kein Kasus; ... er ist das nackte Nomen" (The nominative is not a case; ... it is the bare noun").[2] The term *accusative* is not helpful either. According to the *OED*, it is a rendering of the Greek *aitiatike* 'of accusing', but also of *to aitiakon* 'thing directly affected', and that is the semantic Case of theme, not the structural position it moves

---

1. Abraham (2007: 32) uses (and discusses) the terms *paradigmatic* and *syntagmatic Case*. The former concerns the thematic differences, e.g., between *ihn anrufen* 'to telephone him' and *ihm rufen* 'to call him' and the latter the accusative and genitive shift connected to aspectual marking.

2. Faarlund (1990: 145) provides an explanation of why the nominative is different in that it was not needed in early Indo-European since the subject was marked through inflection on the verb. If the subject was there, it was marked as topic.

TABLE 5.1

Morphological and Syntactic Markers

	Semantic	Grammatical	Discourse
Adpositions	Yes	(Some)	(Some)
Case-inherent	Yes	No	No
Case-structural	No	Yes	No
Agreement	No	Yes	No
Aspect	No	(Some)	Yes
D	No	(Some)	Yes
"Word order"	No	Yes	Yes

to. Most of the time, the object has a marker of definiteness, not thematic role. So rather than through Case, core nominals receive their thematic interpretation in the VP shell (as in Hale & Keyser 2002), that is, they are determined by word order (see the Uniformity of Theta Assignment Hypothesis in M. Baker 1988).

Since the agent tends to be in the highest structural position, it is also often the subject and the most topical element, especially in languages where all subjects are agents. Van Valin and Foley (1980: 339; see also Andrews 1985: 119) divide languages into topic-subject and agent-subject. English, Dutch, Finnish, and Chinese would be examples of topic-subject languages and Dakota and Choctaw as agent-subject. Keenan (1976), Schachter (1976), and Mithun (2008b) suggest that not all languages may have the grammatical role of subject. A very helpful observation in this respect is from Donohue (1999), who says that in some languages the pivot (or the grammatical role) is directly tied to the semantic role—he mentions Archi and Aceh—but that in others it is tied to pragmatic or syntactic roles. In Tukang Besi, an Austronesian language, the system is mixed, for example, the addressee of an imperative always has to be a semantic agent, the pronominal indexing on the verb is tied to the grammatical role (S or A), and cases are tied to the pragmatic roles.

Inherent Case, as in (2) and (3), is connected to a particular theta role (see, e.g., Chomsky 1986a) and contrasts with structural Case, which is connected to a particular position such as the Specifier of a TP for the nominative and possibly to the Specifier of ASPP for the accusative. The structural nominative is responsible for subject agreement on the verb; if such a nominative is lacking, a verb can have default agreement or find a nonnominative to agree with (see Woolford 2006 for more discussion on this).

In table 5.1, I mark in brackets that adpositions sometimes mark grammatical information. I have differential object marking in mind, which is grammatical or pragmatic. It marks that the object is unusual (or the subject in an ergative language) and in many languages indirect objects are marked this way. Moravcsik (1978: 283) suggests that the accusative is marking the more definite, animate, or affected nominal. According to Malchukov (2008), animacy is redundant for the semantic role but not for the grammatical one. I come back to DOM in section 4. Subjects can also be differentially marked, as Cennamo (2009) has shown.

Structural Cases such as the nominative and accusative are, in recent minimalism, seen as assigned by finiteness (the T) and transitive verb (v) respectively. The markings signal specificity, volitionalty, and modality (see de Hoop 1992; Diesing 1992; Abraham 1997; Kiparsky 1998; Leiss 2000, to name but a few). Subjects are typically specific or definite, and as DuBois (1987) points out, in a careful analysis of the ergative Mayan language Sacapultec, new information is often presented as the object of a transitive or the subject of an intransitive.[3] Sacapultec has grammaticalized information structure through its Case system. This situation is not rare, as English, Dutch, Finnish, Turkish, Spanish, Persian, and Urdu/Hindi show. Baker (1985: 134) reviews work on the reconstructed accusative marker in Uralic "that [insists] its case function was purely secondary to its main role of marking definiteness."

Thus, the grammatical subject and object positions are connected with discourse information through movement, as well as to their semantic roles through copies in their vP-internal positions. Subjects and objects move from the position relevant for their thematic role to another position. Since Sportiche (1988), floating quantifiers have been used to chronicle the positions an element was copied/moved into, as in (4), which shows the wanderings of the subject through the quantifier that can be left behind:

(4) Those children may (all) ~~those children~~ have (all) ~~those children~~ been (all) ~~those children~~ shouting.

The floating *all* can appear in any of the positions shown in (4) since the QP subject *all those children* moved through those. Why subjects and objects need to be expressed is perhaps one of the most puzzling questions. The marking is not one-to-one between nominative case and subject properties such as relativization or control of a reflexive. In many languages, such as Icelandic, Gujarati, Bengali, Telegu, and Lezgian, nonnominatives control reflexives (see Newmeyer 2008).

VP adverbials mark the boundaries of the thematic/semantic layer from that of the other layers. Objects that move to the left of these adverbials receive a particular interpretation, such as definite or partitive. This marking is different from Differential Object Marking, discussed in section 4, since all objects receive this kind of Case regardless of animacy and definiteness. Meinunger (1995: 92) lists some German sentences relevant in this respect which I list in Dutch. In (5a), when the object *dat boek* 'that book' is inside the VP, either the book was read completely or parts of it were. This would also be the position of indefinite objects. In (5b), however, where the object moves out of the VP (considering the adverb to indicate the left boundary of the VP), the book has been read completely a number of times. In this position, an indefinite object would be ungrammatical.

(5) a. *omdat ik vaak **dat boek** gelezen heb*   Dutch
        because I often that book read have
        'because I've read that book often'
     b. *omdat ik **dat boek** vaak gelezen heb*
        because I that book often read have
        ' because I have often completely read that book'

---

3. That may be why subject pronouns become affixes before object ones do. In English, a nondefinite marked full DP (i.e., new information) is also less common in subject position in spoken discourse.

The reason for the difference is that a DP that moves to a higher position, as in (5b), moves to one where a certain aspect is checked (as well as specificity and boundedness) and the action must be complete. The DP inside the VP, as in (5a), on the other hand, can be partitive.

Other languages raise objects in a similar way. In Yiddish, a nominal object that moves out of the VP, as in (6a), has to be definite; indefinite nominals in that position result in ungrammaticality, as in (6b):

(6) a. *Maks hot **dos bukh** mistome/ nekhtn/ keyn mol nit geleyent*   Yiddish
        Max has the book probably/ yesterday/ no time not read

        'Max has probably/ never read the book (/yesterday).'

     b. **Maks hot **a bukh** mistome/ nekhtn/ keyn mol nit geleyent*
        Max has a book probably/ yesterday/ no time not read

        'Max has probably/never read a book (/yesterday).' (Diesing 1997: 389–390)

In (13), I make use of this insight that the position of grammatical Case is relevant to specificity and aspect. Chomsky (1995) discusses this point in relation to object shift in a number of the Scandinavian (and other Germanic) languages.

Structural Case and specificity are related in other language families, such as in Turkish, as Grönbech (1936: 155) argues early on. Grönbech calls the marking by –*yi* in (7a) an accusative but notes that it is used to prevent the object from becoming indefinite. This "verschmelzen" 'to melt with' occurs in (7b). So technically, –*yi* in (7a) is a definiteness marker not a Case.

(7) a. *Ahmet dün   akşam   **pasta-y**ı   ye-di*   Turkish
        Ahmet yesterday evening cake-DEF eat-PST

        'Yesterday evening, Ahmet ate the cake.'

     b. *Ahmet dün   akşam   **pasta** ye-di*
        Ahmet yesterday evening cake   eat-PST

        'Yesterday evening, Ahmet ate cake.' (Kornfilt 2003: 127)

See also Enç (1991), de Hoop (1992), and Öztürk (2005).

In short, semantic Case can be marked by adpositions, Case markers, and position; grammatical Case is closely related to specificity/definiteness and aspect in many languages; and *Case* is perhaps not the most useful term for an element that has moved away from the position where it is marked semantically.

1.2 DP, KP, AND PP: STRUCTURES FOR CASE

Modifying work by Bittner and Hale (1996a, 1996b), Svenonius (2006), and Asbury (2008), I suggest that semantic/inherent Case is represented by an (expanded) PP and structural Case by just a DP, not a K(ase)P as Bittner and Hale and others argue. In terms of features, I will suggest that inherent Case is represented by interpretable features such as time and place. Structural uninterpretable Case on subjects is checked by T (as in Pesetsky & Torrego 2001) and on objects by ASP/v. It is grammaticalized deictic marking.

Bittner and Hale (1996a: 6) argue (1) that the nominative is unmarked and therefore just a DP (or NP), (2) that the structural accusative has a KP with an empty K, and (3) that inherent Case has a filled K. Their structure (Bittner & Hale 1996a, 1996b: 537) is as in (8) (I show them without specifier positions).

(8)

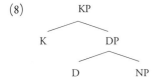

The category K is very similar to P and (9) is therefore the structure that Asbury (2008) argues for. In Finnish, for instance, the addessive *-lla* of *talolla* 'at (a) house' would be in P, and the genitive *-n* in D (though they cannot occur together).

(9)

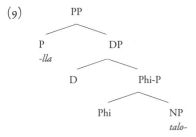

Svenonius, in various publications (e.g., 2007), argues for a split PP with one P head introducing the ground and the other p head introducing the figure. In other work (e.g., 2006), he presents a more articulated PP for the ground, as in (10), without the figure. His (10) can include a DegreeP above PlaceP to accommodate the intensifier *right*. (Again, I show them without specifier positions.) The structure in (10) will be used for complex prepositions and language change when AxPrt, the position for the nominal element in the PP, is reanalyzed as place.

(10)

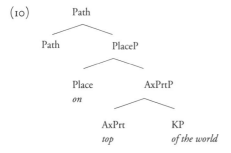

I will use a simple PP, as in (9), when talking about inherent, nonstructural Case, but a DP when structural Case is involved. The respective probes for these are V and P for inherent Case and T and v for structural case. I'll now discuss some of the features involved.

Most people ignore feature checking where inherent Case is involved since it is interpretable (Chomsky 1995). Let's first look at the Case in a regular PP. Van Gelderen (2008e, 2009a) uses (11) as a structure for the temporal preposition *after*.

(11)

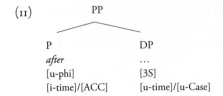

Having interpretable features on the P is somewhat similar to Pesetsky and Torrego's (2004) assumption that prepositions have [i-T(ense)]. I use [time] in (11) to distinguish prepositional objects from nominatives. The [time] feature is interpretable and is licensing the [u-time]. The [u-phi] feature makes an adposition into a probe and thereby different from an adverb, just as a demonstrative is different from an article.

The structure in (11) could be reanalyzed as inherent Case, as has happened with benefactives, comitatives, and locatives. In those cases, the main verb has to be reanalyzed as licensing a goal or other theta role, as in (12). It means adjuncts are made into arguments.

(12)

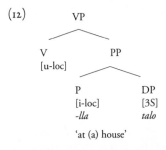

Structural Case, according to Pesetsky and Torrego (2004, 2007), involves an uninterpretable/unvalued T on the nominal that is valued by a finite tense or transitive v. Pesetsky and Torrego connect Case, finiteness, and agreement by having a tense feature in T (and v) look down the tree for a feature on the DP.[4] My adaptation of this is as in (14), leaving out a separate V(P) and an ASPP. Note that, what Pesetsky and Torrego assume for nominative, I assume for accusative. There are other possibilities, as I discuss in more detail, for example, the ASP features may be number or measure.

(13)

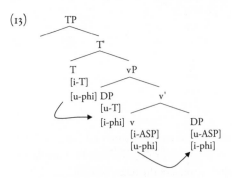

---

4. I think a good alternative is suggested in Asbury (2008: 22), namely that the feature is categorial and uninterpretable on the verb and interpretable on the noun. For the purpose of this chapter, I will stick to a more mainstream version.

In (13), the [u-phi] features in v act as the probe and value the [u-ASP] of the DP as well as the [u-phi] of their own. The same happens with the T. In some languages, the [u-T] can be valued +/- definite, as in Finnish. When "assigned" definite values, the subject moves to Spec TP (the EPP). My proposal in (13) thus represents structural Case as valued by tense and aspect/measure. In (13), I assume it is the D that carries the [u-T] and that having [u-T] implies specificity.

If the structure in (13) is correct, tense and deixis are two sides of the same coin and would be expected on both verbs and nouns. Tense is, however, typical for verbs and deixis is for nouns, but as we'll see in section 3.2, nominals can also be marked for temporal tense and verbs for spatial deixis. Schematically, the possibilities are presented in table 5.2.

Another part of Pesetsky and Torrego's (2001, 2007) work that is relevant to the features of the demonstrative-turned-complementizer *that* is T to C movement, not indicated in (13). Pesetsky and Torrego not only assume that nominative Case is T checking, they also suppose that the complementizer *that* is a T element spelling out the [u-T] features of C. According to them, these assumptions unify four phenomena: (a) the need for an auxiliary to appear with *wh*-movement from object but not from subject position, (b) the *[that trace] filter, (c) the fact that a CP doesn't need Case, and (d) the optionality of the *that* complementizer when the CP is an object adjacent to the higher verb.

To account for (a), Pesetsky and Torrego (2001) adapt an idea by Rizzi (1996), namely the *wh*-criterion. The latter states that an interrogative C needs to be licensed by a *wh*-specifier and a *wh*-head in a Spec-Head relationship. In the case of objects, T moves to C to license the head and the *wh*-element moves to the specifier of the CP. In the case of subjects, only the *wh*-element needs to move since this subject was already in a Spec-Head relationship with T. Pesetsky and Torrego assume that C has a [u-T] feature (with EPP) that needs to be checked. A nominative *wh*-element in (14a) can do this as well as check the [*wh*-]feature, and hence an auxiliary is not wanted. T to C movement of *did* is needed when an object *wh*-element appears, as in (14b), since the object *wh*-element doesn't check [u-T].

(14)   a. Who C[u-T] ~~who~~ bought the book?
       b. What **did** he read ~~what~~?

Thus, both Rizzi and Pesetsky and Torrego argue that an interrogative C connected to a subject is licensed by it.

The *[that* trace] filter is the name of the condition that some languages do not allow extraction of the subject from a clause introduced by *that*, as in (15a). Note that (15b), with extraction of the object, is grammatical.

TABLE 5.2

Tense and Deixis Marking

	DP	V/AUX
Deixis	English, French	Halkomelem
Tense/Aspect	Lardil, Chamicuro, Koasati	English, French

(15)   a.   *Who did John say ~~who~~ **that** ~~who~~ will buy the book?
       b.   Who did John say ~~who~~ ~~who~~ will buy the book?

The "*that* trace" phenomenon has been written about extensively, most recently by Boeckx (2008) and Lohndal (2009a). The latter two accounts rely on Case marking by *that* in the Fin head stopping the English subject in (15a) from moving further, in other words, freezing it in position. Pesetsky and Torrego's account is that the intermediate *wh*-subject copy checks the [u-T] of C and therefore *that* is not wanted, unlike in the case of an object *wh*-element, as in (16). In (16), the object is unable to check the [u-T] and hence *that* lexicalizes C.

(16)   What did John say ~~what~~ **that** Bill will buy ~~what~~?

That in C is thus a spell-out of the interpretable T features that move from T to C to check on the [u-T] in C. This fact also explains optional *that*. Pesetsky and Torrego say that the C in (17) can be checked by the nominative subject, *Jill*, in (17a) or by *that* in (17b).

(17)   a.   I noticed [Jill ~~u T~~ [Jill left]].
       b.   I noticed [that u T [Jill left]]

This means *that* has [i-T]. The subject as licenser of the [u-T] cannot, however, explain the data in (18): when the C is not immediately adjacent to the verb, as in (18a), it is ungrammatical.

(18)   a.   *I noticed yesterday Jill had left.
       b.   I noticed yesterday that Jill had left

The last phenomenon that Pesetsky and Torrego explain is the resistance by a CP to appear in a Case-marked position. However, having [u-T] in C should in fact make it possible for a CP to be checking Case.

So in short, many of the phenomena explained by Pesetsky and Torrego have alternative explanations or cannot be correct explanations. The main problem I perceive has to do with the [i-T] features of *that*. As we'll see in chapter 7, in Old English, there is no C deletion and no "*that*-trace" effects. I will argue that the lack of C deletion is due to the presence of interpretable features in C. As they are reanalyzed as uninterpretable by late Middle English, C becomes deletable. Thus, I keep Pesetsky and Torrego's account of nominative case as [u-T] checked by [i-T] in T but I do not agree with their account of C.

Summarizing, inherent/semantic Case is represented by interpretable features such as time and place on P and structural Case by definiteness or specificity on the dependent DP and through [i-T] on T and [i-ASP] on v. This is reflected in their grammaticalization paths, as we'll see now.

1.3 CASE CYCLES

There is a lot of (early) research on the history of Case but the picture is much less clear than with agreement. Even early on, inherent and structural Cases are distinguished, although those terms are of course not used. Wüllner (1827: 5) emphasizes semantic Case and hence ignores the nominative, which he thinks indicates independence from the verb.

Bopp ([1833–1852] 1868: 248) and Ravila (1945) emphasize grammatical Case and the demonstrative origin of this Case.

Hjelmslev (1935) reviews the different approaches in the literature and identifies localist and antilocalist approaches. The localist approach looks at the genitive, dative, and accusative in spatial terms, namely as distant, at rest, and getting closer respectively. The nonlocalists worry about the function of the nominative. I'll mainly assume a localist origin for semantic case but a verbal/demonstrative one for grammatical Case.

Blake (2001: 161) says "[t]here are two common sources for lexical markers, one verbal and the other nominal, of which the verbal is probably the more fruitful. Adverbial particles also provide a source." Tauli (1956) provides an in-depth overview of the debate on the (pro) nominal sources of Case particles that has gone on at least for the last century and a half. Greenberg's cycle would of course fit since definiteness develops into Case in his scheme. I will argue for the developments in (19) and (20).

(19) **Semantic/Inherent Case**

    Adv

    N   P   >   Semantic/Inherent Case

    V

(20) **Grammatical/Structural Case**

    D   >   Specificity/Tense (=[u-T] and [u-ASP])

    V   >   Measure/ASP (=[u-ASP])

    P   >   Differential (Subject and) Object Marker

In section 5, I examine the adverbial source of semantic Case, followed by the development from N to P and then to semantic Case. The change from V to P (or to coverb) to semantic Case marker, represented in (19), is well known from Asian and African languages, as is the reanalysis of the (converb) V to P in many European and Asian languages. This change is also discussed in section 5.

Linguists know that when inherent Case endings disappear, adpositions may take over (e.g., *with* and *through* replace the instrumental). The choice of the replacement depends on the contents of the P. In a structure such as (12), the inherent Case is represented by [i-loc]. When the affix in P is lost, another P with the appropriate features is used.

The category V can result in either semantic/inherent or grammatical Case, as (19) and (20) show. In section 3, I discuss the development of a V to grammatical Case, emphasizing that the verb is first reanalyzed as v or ASP(ect). The change of D to grammatical Case was widely accepted by the early Indo-Europeanists such as Bopp ([1833–1852] 1868), Uhlenbeck (1901), Pedersen (1907), and Specht (1947) but seems currently not discussed much (exceptions are, e.g., Greenberg 1978 and Kortlandt 1983). This too is discussed in section 3. In (20), I have also listed the sources of differential subject and object marking. In section 4, I discuss this phenomenon. Even though I group it as a grammatical case, it is more a blend between semantic and grammatical Case.

The clines in (19) and (20) show the sources of grammaticalization but don't indicate the features. They can also be represented as in (21) and (22). As I said before, it isn't clear (from the literature on this) what the features of inherent Case are, and in (12) and (21), I suggest [i-time]/[i-loc], or whatever the relevant feature is (e.g., accompaniment, direction). Example (22) shows the deictic features of the demonstrative reanalyzed as [u-T] and this reanalysis in fact keeps the DP cycle going,[5] as we'll see in the next chapter, since new deictic elements will be needed.

(21) Semantic/inherent case

A/N/V		>	P		>	semantic/inherent Case
[semantic]			[i-time/loc]			[u-time] (on V)
([i-phi])			[u-phi]			[i-loc] (on P)

(22) Grammatical
   a. Nominal:

Demonstrative	>	article	>	zero
[i-loc]		[u-loc] = [u-T]		
[i-phi]		[u-phi]		

   b. Verbal:

Adverb/D	>	Aspect/Tense	>	affix on v/ C-T
semantic		[i-ASP]/[i-T]		[u-ASP]/[u-T]

The different stages of feature reduction need further work, such as, when are the phi features affected and when are the others? I briefly mention this in chapter 11.

Having looked at the grammaticalization of head marking in chapters 2 to 4, I will show in this chapter that the development of Case, that is, dependent marking, is less of an automatic development: head marking is more uniform across languages than dependent marking. The reason for the difference is that dependent marking is used for so many different functions. A theoretical account is therefore harder, as I mentioned at the beginning of the chapter.

2. Articles, Aspect, and Case

As mentioned in the introduction, a number of people, in particular Leiss in her 2000 book *Artikel und Aspect*, argue for a close connection between definiteness, aspect, and Case. Languages such as Russian and Finnish can "do without" articles because they have a well-developed head marking and dependent marking system respectively. In section 2.1, I discuss Leiss's proposal on the connection between articles and aspect. I then apply some of those insights to (late) Old English in sections 2.2 to 2.4. Three major changes occur in the early twelfth century: aspectual markers are lost, objective Case is lost, and articles are introduced. There is thus a relation between loss of aspect and case on the one hand and increase in definiteness marking on the other.

---

5. The phi features can be further divided. In some languages, the demonstrative has [u-#], for instance. Later, e.g., in (69) and (75), I indicate some other possibilities.

2.1 LEISS (2000)

In Russian, as Leiss shows, the difference between (23) and (24) is one of verbal aspect, imperfective and perfective respectively, and the definiteness of the object is a consequence of the perfective aspect. Aspect in Russian is expressed through a verbal prefix, *ras-* in (24), which also makes the object definite.

(23) *On* *kolo-l* *drova* Russian
     he   split-PST wood
     'He was splitting **wood**.'

(24) *On* ***ras-kolo-l*** *drova* Russian
     he   PF-split-PST wood
     'He split **the wood**.' (Leiss 2000: 12)

Aspect and definiteness have in common how the action/event and the nominal are measured and seen as complete or incomplete.

In Old Norse (also referred to as Old Icelandic by various researchers), the preverbal aspect markers are lost and definite articles, such as in (25) and (26), arise, with the article either prenominal or postnominal. In the next chapter, I come back to the actual development of the demonstrative and article in both Old Norse and Old English. For now, only the big picture is important.

(25) ***inn*** *vari* *gestr* Old Norse
     'the wise/knowing guest' (*Edda, Hávamál* 7)

(26) *gestr-**inn*** Old Norse
     guest-DEF, 'the guest' (made up to parallel [25])

The difference between (25) and (26) lies in the presence and absence of a (weak) adjective. There are also demonstrative pronouns, as in (27).

(27) *sökkðisk* *síðan* ***sá*** *fiskr* *í* *mar* Old Norse
     sank   then   that fish in sea
     'and the fish sank into the sea' (*Edda, Hymniskviða* 24)

Leiss (2000: 62) suggests that the function of demonstratives such as *sá* in (27) is "textverweisend": "[s]*á* nimmt vorerwähnte Information wieder auf" (it takes up information that was mentioned earlier), as well as information that comes later.

Basing her discussion on work by Delbrück (1907), Koller (1951), and others, Leiss then argues that, even though the perfectivizing prefixes are lost in Old Norse, some aspect remains in the historical present and this present can be seen as a perfective aspect and not an imperfective. The historical present "hat Vergangenheitsbezug und vordergrundiert Erzähltes" (2000: 75) (has reference to the past and foregrounded narrative) whereas the preterite backgrounds information. The definite article "helps" the perfective aspect and so does verb-first word order and adverbs (2000: 95).

How does Case play into this? From Finnish and other languages, we know that a special Case on the object marks aspect. Historically, Leiss (2000: 185) says "[d]ie Artikelexplosion findet . . . im Genitiv statt" (the articles start in the genitive) because the genitive is the Case that is no longer marked aspectually. This is confirmed for Old High German by Glaser (2000: 194–196), who examines the use of articles in Old High German glosses and finds that articles are used with genitives and inside PPs, not with nominatives. According to Leiss (2000: 38, 62), a nominal is not marked with an article in subject or topic position since that position is already definite but that it is so marked when it is in focus. So the new cycle of definiteness marking in Old Norse and Old High German starts in nontopic position.

Summing up Leiss's observations on Old Norse, we can say that Old Norse marks perfective aspect and definite nominals through word order, verbal aspect, and articles. The demonstratives are not part of this; they mark textual reference. Once aspect is lost, demonstratives are used for definites/subjects. The history of English will show a connection between loss of aspect, increase in D-markers, and a loss of (aspectually marked) Case.

2.2 LOSS OF ASPECT: THE PETERBOROUGH CHRONICLE

Many Germanic languages indicate aspect by means of a verbal prefix (and Slavic, of course; see [23] and [24]). Old English is no exception and "[t]he perfective aspect [is] often indicated by means of verbal prefixes" (Mustanoja 1960: 446; see also Quirk & Wrenn 1955: 114). For instance, *þurh-* 'through', *of-*, and *to-*, as in *þurhbrecan* 'break through', *ofsceotan* 'shoot off', *tobrecan* 'break up', render an imperfective verb perfective by specifying the goal (see Brinton's 1988 appendix B for a summary of the different aspectual meanings of the prefixes). *Ge-* expresses perfectivity as well and I will focus on *ge-*.[6]

I examine the *Peterborough Chronicle* (hence *PC*) since its late Old English/early Middle English parts mark the beginning of frequent article use in English. The Peterborough version of the Chronicle (also known as Chronicle E) contains entries for years in the history of Britain from the time of Caesar to 1154. One scribe is responsible for the part up to 1121, which is copied from an earlier manuscript, and for some original additions to the years before 1121 (called the Interpolations), for example, the one for the year 656 in (29), and writes the entries for the years 1122–1131 (called the First Continuation). A second scribe takes over in 1132 and this stage (called the Final Continuation) shows very fast change. The scribe may have been from another dialect area where the change had already taken place. In this subsection, I focus on the aspectual prefix but I come back to other characteristics later.

In the *Peterborough Chronicle*, as in Old English in general, a *ge-* participle is used to mark simple perfective past, as in (28), and a passive, as in (29). These two are the most frequent uses of *ge-*.

(28) *Her . . . **gefuhton** wið Æðelbriht*
'in this year . . . fought against A' (*PC* [861])

(29) *ðes writ wæs **gewriton** æfter ure drihtnes acennedness*
'This writ was written . . . after the birth of our lord.' (*PC* [656])

---

6. There is a frequent separation between *ge-* and the participle in writing, as evidenced by looking at the facsimile of the *Peterborough Chronicle*, but I have no explanation for that.

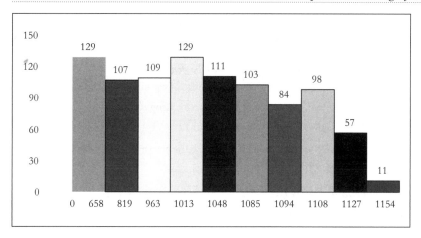

FIGURE 5.1. The *Peterborough Chronicle* divided in ten equal parts covering spans of years with numbers of *ge-*. The X axis represents years and the Y axis represents numbers.

The *Peterborough Chronicle* also has nineteen instances of a form of 'have' connected to a *ge-*marked participle, as in (30), and twenty-seven of one connected to a modal, or what is now a modal, as in (31).

(30)   *Headda abbot **heafde** ær **gewriton** hu Wulfhere . . .*
       'Headda the abbot had before written how Wulfhere . . .' (*PC* [963], interpolation)

(31)   *hwonne man **scolde** þæt mynstre **gehalegon***
       when they should that monastery hallow
       'when that monastery should be hallowed' (*PC* [657])

This system changes in Middle English when the prefixes weaken and disappear; that change starts in the Final Continuation after the entries for the year 1121.

The total number of verbal *ge-*forms in the *Peterborough Chronicle* is 938, and they virtually disappear after 1130 (there are three instances of passive *gehaten* which could be adjectives). Hiltunen (1983: 92) says that they were "swept away overnight." Figure 5.1 shows the distribution of *ge-*marked verbs throughout the *Peterborough Chronicle*. As is clear from this table, the use of *ge-* decreases dramatically during the First Continuation, but especially during the Final Continuation. See also Hiltunen (1983: 93) for a table with other prefixes in the periods between 1122 and 1131 and 1132 and 1154.

Since the *Peterborough Chronicle* is more northern than other versions, such as the Parker version and version D, the disappearance of *ge-* should be further advanced according to Mustanoja (1960: 446), for example, and it is. The *Peterborough Chronicle* also continues longer. Indeed, we see a clear loss of *ge-* in the *Peterborough Chronicle*,[7] for example, *of slean* in (32) where Parker and the other versions have (33), with *a*, the reduced form of *ge-*.

---

7. The loss cannot be reliably determined from the total number of forms (938 in the *Peterborough Chronicle* and 406 in Parker) since the Peterborough is much longer than the Parker.

(32) *Her Offa Myrcena cining het Æþelbrihte þ heafod of* **slean**
(*PC* [792])

(33) *Her Offa Miercna cyning het Æþelbryhte rex þ heafod of***aslean**
In-this-year Offa Mercian king commanded Æthelbryht king the head struck-off
'In this year, the Mercian king Offa ordered to have King Aethelbryht's decapitated.'
(Parker Chronicle [792])

Numen in (34), rather than *genumen*, is such a late occurrence that there is no Parker counterpart.

(34) *hefde* **numen** *Fulkes eorles gingre dohter*
'had taken the younger daughter of count Fulk' (*PC* [1124])

The *ge-* prefix appears in the *Peterborough Chronicle* only three times after 1130 (all three with passive *gehaten*). As mentioned, one sign of weakening of *ge-* is the change to *a-*, and its strengthening by other adverbs, such as *up* in (35) to (38), as well as its replacement, as in (39) to (42).

(35) *til he aiauen* **up** *here castles*
'till they gave up their castles' (*PC* [1140])

(36) *7 ælc unriht for gode and for worulde* **up** **aras**
'and every wrong in the sight of God and of the world rose up' (*PC* [1100])

(37) **asprang** **up** *to þan swiðe sæ flod*
sprang up to such height (the) sea flood
'The flood appeared to such height.' (*PC* [1099])

(38) *swa hine sylf* **upp** **ahebben**
'so raise himself up' (*PC* [1087])

(39) *þær nan þing* **of** *ne nime*
there no thing of not take
'not take a thing thereof' (*PC* [675])

(40) *Sum he iaf* **up**
'Some (castles) he gave up.' (*PC* [1140])

(41) *he uuolde iiuen heom* **up** *Wincestre*
'He would give Winchester up to them.' (*PC* [1140])

(42) *til hi iafen* **up** *here castles*
'till they gave up their castles' (*PC* [1137])

This replacement of *ge-* by an adverb occurs throughout Old English and a major increase of, for instance, *up* is found throughout the *Peterborough Chronicle*. Thus, *up(p)* occurs a total of fifty-six times but starts to reinforce an *a-*prefixed verb only from 1086 (*upp ahebban*) on. Such instances with *up* occur in the entries for the years 1099, 1100, and 1140.

Thus, the Final Continuation of the *Peterborough Chronicle* starting in 1132 indicates a dramatic loss of the prefix *ge-*. I turn now to the changes that may have occurred as a result of the demise of the aspectual markers.

2.3 LOSS OF GENITIVE/OBJECTIVE CASE

In this section, I first use Pysz's (2007) data on the Case loss on demonstratives in the *Peterborough Chronicle* after 1122 but then focus on the loss of genitive Case in the *Peterborough Chronicle* and Layamon's early Middle English *Brut*.

Pysz (2007) provides tables comparing expected Old English endings with attested ones. In the pre-1121 data, there are few unexpected forms. For instance, the masculine nominative *se* is used for masculine nominatives 275 times and only 2 times for a dative and the innovative *þe* is used only 10 times. In the 1122–1131 section, *se* is used as masculine nominative 103 times but 14 times as dative or accusative and *þe/ðe* is used 7 times. In the last section, that is, 1132–1154, *se* is used as masculine nominative only once. The form *te* is used 19 times, *the* once, and *þe* 55 times. Pysz (2007: 73) provides percentages for when all Cases are indicated "correctly," in other words, archaically: 85 percent in the pre-1121 period, 46 percent between 1122 and 1131, and 13 percent in the last period. This shows that the use of all the Case forms by the second scribe is definitely non–Old English. I'll now focus on genitive objects.

Similar to some of the languages discussed in section 1, Old English shows a connection between Case and measure. Thus, the genitive Case is used when the object is partially affected, that is, when the "limit of involvement" of the object is relevant (Allen 2005: 240), as in (43), with verbs of deprivation, or of mental action, as in (44).

(43) *Ðar com eft ongean Swegen eorl to Eadwerde cinge and gyrnde to him* **landes**
There came back again Swegen earl to Edward king and craved of him land-GEN *þæt he mihte hine on afedan.*
that he might it on sustain

'Then Swegen came back again to King Edward and wanted land from him so that he'd be able to sustain himself.' (Chronicle D [1049], 9, in Thorpe 1861)

(44) *þe cyng . . . . gyrnde* **heora fultumes**
the king . . . desired their support-GEN
'The king wanted their support.' (*PC* [1087], 37–39)

However, Allen (2007: 86) writes that even in the pre-1121 Chronicle "we find a trend towards replacement of the genitive objects" and that in the additions "no certain examples of genitive objects" occur. Allen (1995: 177) provides a few examples from the First Continuation, after 1121, of genitive loss. I repeat two as (45) and (46), where the accusative object would have been genitive in Old English.

(45) *benam   ælc   **ðone**   riht   hand*
took   every   the-ACC   right   hand
'deprived each of their right hands' (*PC* [1125], 9)

(46) *him   me   **hit**   beræfode*
    him   man   it-ACC   bereaved

    'He was deprived of it.' (*PC* [1124], 51)

The genitive Case of the object disappears in English in the twelfth century, at the same time as aspectual prefixes, and when specificity/definiteness markings increase. Bungenstab (1933) and Mitchell (1985) list over two hundred verbs that have genitive objects in Old English; very few are left in Middle English. However, there are early thirteenth-century examples of genitive objects, as in (47a) and (48a), although the later versions (47b) and (48b) do not mark these objects as genitive.

(47) a. *For þe king ne mai . . . bruken **nanes drenches***
      Because the king may not . . . use no-GEN drink-GEN

      'Because the king can't use any drink (except . . .)'
      (Layamon, *Brut*, Caligula, 9857, in Brook & Leslie 1963)

    b. *For þe king ne may . . . dringke **none senche***
      because the king can not . . . drink no refreshment
      (Layamon, *Brut*, Otho, 9857, in Brook & Leslie 1963)

(48) a. *he . . . wilnede **þeos mæidenes***
      he . . . desired that maiden-GEN (Layamon, *Brut*, Caligula, 1599, in Brook & Leslie 1963)

    b. *wilnede . . . [t mayd]e*
      'wanted that maiden' (Layamon, *Brut*, Otho, 1599, in Brook & Leslie 1963)

Allen (2005: 239–240) says that the loss of the genitive object is "difficult to attribute . . . to the phonological changes" or to a loss of genitives in general. She partly blames it on the "loss of a coherent and distinctive meaning of the genitive case for objects."

Other objective Case loss is experienced around this time as well. Witness (49) to (51), with the (a) examples found in the earlier *Caligula* version and the (b) examples from the later *Otho* version. In (49b), the inherent dative is not marked clearly and a *to* is used. In (50b) and (51b), the pronominal distinction between accusative *hine* and dative *him* is lost.

(49) a. *þa andswarede Merlin. **þane kinge** þe spac wið him*
      Then answered Merlin the-ACC/DAT king-DAT who spoke with him

      'Then Merlin replied to the king who addressed him.'
      (Layamon, *Brut*, Caligula, 7995, in Brook & Leslie 1963)

    b. *þo answerede Merlyn **to þan king** þat spak wiþ him*

      'Then Merlin answered the king who spoke to him.' (Layamon, *Brut*, Otho, 7995, in Brook & Leslie 1963)

(50) a. *7 to Corinee **hine** sende*
      'and sent him to Corineus' (Layamon, *Brut*, Caligula, 1209, in Brook & Leslie 1963)

    b. *and to Corineus **him** sende.* (Layamon, *Brut*, Otho, 1209, in Brook & Leslie 1963)

(51) a. *7 **hine** fæire on-feng*

'and received him heartily' (Layamon, *Brut*, Caligula, 2442, in Brook & Leslie 1963)

b. *and onderfeng **him** deore.* (Layamon, *Brut*, Otho, 2442, in Brook & Leslie 1963)

I'll now look at what happens as a result of both Case and aspect being reduced.

2.4 INCREASE OF D IN THE PETERBOROUGH CHRONICLE

The first instances of what look like the article *þe* are early but sporadic, as in (52). In (52), *se* is expected and *ðe* may therefore be a variant of *se* (since they are both voiceless fricatives of roughly the same place). The first frequent use of *þe* is in the *Peterborough Chronicle*, as in (53), and this appears in an interpolation so is written in the twelfth century. In (53), a genitive *þæs* would be expected under the archaic system, instead of the *þe* that actually appears.

(52) | *Cueð* | *to* | *him* | *ðe* | | *hælend* |
      | said | to | him | the-NOM | | savior |

'the savior said to him' *(Lindisfarne Gospel*, Matthew 9.15)

(53) *Ic Wulfere gife to dæi Sancte Petre 7 þone abbode Saxulf 7 þa munecas of **þe** mynstre þas landes 7 þas wateres*

I Wulfhere give today Saint Peter and the abbot Seaxwulf and the monks of the abbey the lands and the waters. . . (*PC* [656], 40)

The next chapter will be devoted entirely to the changes in definiteness and the DP structure. For now, I will just show the data about definiteness markers in relation to the loss of aspect and Case. The demonstrative pronoun is originally used to refer to previously mentioned material and articles do not occur in Old English. This picture changes around 1130. See also Irvine (2004) and Allen (1995: 190).

In this section, I first examine some differences in demonstratives between the beginning of the *Peterborough Chronicle*, before the real loss of aspect, and the end, the part we have seen in section 2.2 to be losing aspect. I then examine in what functions the first instances of *the* occur in the final part, and finally look at two versions of a text we already looked at from about a century later, namely Layamon.

The language of the *Peterborough Chronicle* is traditionally seen as representing the change from Old to Middle English. As I noted, the main change comes around the entry for the year 1122, when the scribe starts adding new information; a second change starts with the year 1132 when the second scribe takes over, and there are the additions the first scribe made throughout the text. I will examine an excerpt from the beginning of the Chronicle (the preface), that is, without articles, an excerpt from the changing part (the year 1130), that is, with articles, and will provide some numbers for a year in the Final Continuation (the year 1137).

2.4.1 The Beginning of the *Peterborough Chronicle*

In (54) and following, from the beginning of the *Peterborough Chronicle*, the nominals are in bold and the translation is from the online medieval and classical library (http://omacl.org/Anglo/part1.html) so as not to be biased by my own translation on the use of definites. The first few clauses in (54) have no demonstratives, and the proximal demonstrative *þis* is used to refer to the island mentioned in the first part of that sentence.

(54) ***Brittene igland*** is *ehta hund mila lang. & twa hund brad. & her sind on **þis iglande fif geþeode. Englisc. & Brittisc. & Wilsc. & Scyttisc. & Pyhtisc. & Boc Leden.***

'The island Britain is 800 miles long and 200 miles broad. And there are in the island five nations; English, Welsh, Scottish, Pictish, and Latin.'

In (55), the proximal *þises* is again used for reference to the already-mentioned island, but no other D elements are used. The aspect in the first clause is imperfective—a literal translation would be 'first were living on this island Britons'—and this could be the reason for the lack of a demonstrative. It could also be that the tribes/nations mentioned in (54) were adjectival and not seen as a proper mention of the actual people.

(55) *Erest weron bugend **þises landes Brittes**. þa coman of Armenia. & gesætan suþewearde **Bryttene** ærost. þa gelamp hit þæt **Pyhtas** coman suþan of Scithian. mid **langum scipum** na manegum.*

'The first inhabitants were the Britons, who came from Armenia, and first peopled Britain southward. Then happened it, that the Picts came south from Scythia, with long ships, not many.'

In (56), the first mention of *Scottas* has no D but the second does, and in (57), the *Pihtas* also get a demonstrative since they have been mentioned before, as does the *land* in (57). The *Brittas* in (57) are possibly indefinite.

(56) *& þa coman ærost on norþ **Ybernian** up. & þær bædon **Scottas** þæt hi þer moston wunian. Ac hi noldan heom lyfan. forþan hi cwædon þæt hi ne mihton ealle ætgædere gewunian þær. & þa cwædon **þa Scottas**. we eow magon þeah hwaðere ræd gelæron.'and, landing first in the northern part of Ireland, they told the Scots that they must dwell there. But they would not give them leave; for the Scots told them that they could not all dwell there together; But, said the Scots, we can nevertheless give you advice.'*

(57) *We witan **oþer egland** her be easton. þer ge magon eardian gif ge willað. & gif hwa eow wiðstent. we eow fultumiað. þæt ge hit magon gegangan. Đa ferdon **þa Pihtas**. & geferdon **þis land** norþanweard. & suþanweard hit hefdon **Brittas**. swa we ær cwedon.'We know another island here to the east. There you may dwell, if you will; and whosoever withstandeth you, we will assist you, that you may gain it. Then went the Picts and entered this land northward. Southward the Britons possessed it, as we before said.'*

I have not been able to find a pattern for the function of the nominal marked by a demonstrative. There are subjects with and without a demonstrative. The use of the demonstrative seems to be pragmatic; it refers to already known referents.

2.4.2 The Change Starting

For the transitionary period (the First Continuation), I randomly picked the beginning of the entry of the year 1130. There is a real increase in demonstratives and these demonstratives are often phonologically lighter. Notice that all the nominals in (58) are preceded by a D element; the names are not since they are themselves definite.

(58) ***Ðis geares wæs se mynstre of Cantwarabyri** halgod fram þone ærcebiscop Willelm
     þes dæies iiii Nonæ MAI. Ðær wæron **þas biscopes**. Iohan of Roueceastre. Gilbert
     Uniuersal of Lundene. Heanri of Winceastre. Alexander of Lincolne. Roger of Særesbyri.
     Simon of Wigorceastre. Roger of Couentre. Godefreith of Bathe. Eourard of Noruuic.
     Sigefrid of Cicaestre. Bernard of Sancti Dauid. Audoenus of Euereus of Normandige
     Iohan of Sæis.*

     'This year was the monastery of Canterbury consecrated by the Archbishop William,
     on the fourth day before the nones of May. There were the Bishops John of Roches-
     ter, Gilbert Universal of London, Henry of Winchester, Alexander of Lincoln, Roger
     of Salisbury, Simon of Worcester, Roger of Coventry, Geoffry of Bath, Evrard of
     Norwich, Sigefrith of Chichester, Bernard of St. David's, Owen of Evreux in
     Normandy, John of Sieyes.'

In (59), all arguments are preceded by a demonstrative except *Sancti Andreas mynstre* 'St. Andrews monastery' but this is because *Sancti Andreas* functions as D. Inside PPs, there is typically no D, an indication that the demonstrative is used for structural Case.

(59) ***Ðes feorðe dæges þæræfter wæs se king Heanri** on Roueceastre. & **se burch**
     forbernde almæst. & **se ærcebiscop Willelm** halgede **Sancti Andreas mynstre**
     & **ða forsprecon biscop** mid him. & **se kyng Heanri** ferde ouer sæ into Normandi
     on heruest.*

     'On the fourth day after this was the King Henry in Rochester, when the town was
     almost consumed by fire; and the Archbishop William consecrated the monastery of
     St. Andrew, and the aforesaid bishops with him. And the King Henry went over sea
     into Normandy in harvest.'

In (60) and (61), all the arguments are preceded by demonstratives. The only exception seems to be the quoted proverb. Again, many prepositional objects, such as *ouer sæ* and *on heruest* in (59), lack a demonstrative or article.

(60) ***Ðes ilces geares** com **se abbot Heanri of Angeli** after æsterne to Burch. & seide þæt he
     hæfde forlæten **þone mynstre** mid ealle. Æfter him com **se abbot of Clunni** Petrus
     gehaten to Englelande bi **þes kynges** leue & wæs underfangen ouer eall swa hwar swa he
     com mid mycel wurðscipe.*

     'This same year came the Abbot Henry of Angeli after Easter to Peterborough, and
     said that he had relinquished that monastery withal. After him came the Abbot of
     Clugny, Peter by name, to England by the king's leave; and was received by all,
     whithersoever he came, with much respect.'

(61)   *To Burch he com & þær behet **se abbot Heanri** him þæt he scolde beieton him **þone**
       mynstre of Burch þæt hit scolde beon underðed into Clunni. Oc man seið to biworde.*
       *hæge sitteð þa **aceres dæleth**. **God ælmihtig** adylege iuele **ræde**. & sone þæræfter ferde **se***
       ***abbot of Clunni** ham to **his ærde**.*

       'To Peterborough he came; and there the Abbot Henry promised him that he would
       procure him the ministry of Peterborough, that it might be subject to Clugny. But it
       is said in the proverb, The hedge abideth, that acres divideth. May God Almighty
       frustrate evil designs. Soon after this went the Abbot of Clugny home to his country.'

The *Peterborough Chronicle* shows a real change in demonstratives: used pragmatically in the
early parts but grammatically, marking subjects and objects, in the later parts. The real change
comes in the twelfth century, as we'll see next.

2.4.3 The Final Continuation and Layamon's Caligula Version

The *Peterborough Chronicle* marks the first large number of instances of *the*, as in (53), starting after 1122 and in particular after the year 1132. In this subsection, I look at the entry from
1137 and at the Caligula version of Layamon's *Brut* from a century later.

Leiss suggests for Old High German that the explosion of articles first occurs in genitives, as a
compensation for the loss of Case. This is true somewhat in the First Continuation of the *Peterborough Chronicle* as Allen (1995: 172) also notes. However, the introduction of articles also
occurs in other positions, as the distribution given in table 5.3 for the entry for the year 1137 (from
the Final Continuation) shows. Since *all* is a frequent predeterminer, as in (62), I list it separately.

(62)   *I ne can ne i ne mai tellen **alle þe** wunder ne **alle þe** pines ðæt hi diden.*

       'I don't know nor can I tell all the enormities nor all the pain that they did.' (*PC*
       [1137])

I think *all* is a mark of measure, that is, aspect, especially since it is frequent with objects. It
therefore replaces the inherent aspect accompanying the object Case.

Some examples from this entry are given in (63) and (64), which are from the start of the
entry for this year. Note that names such as *þe king Stephne* and *Henri king* show that the
article is in complementary distribution with the preposed name; both article and name are in
D. The articles occur in subject and object position, but there are no distal demonstratives left.

TABLE 5.3

The Definite Article *the* in the *Peterborough Chronicle* for the Year 1137

	þe	al(le) þe	te	the	al(le) the
Subject	6	1	1	2	—
Object	8	4	2	—	1
PObject	11	2	—	5	—
	25	7	3	7	1

As Irvine 2004: clx notes there are a few other forms.

(63) *ðis gære for **þe** king Stephne ofer sæ to Normandi & ther wes underfangen forþi ðæt hi*
    *uuenden ðæt he sculde ben alsuic alse **the** eom wes. & for he hadde get his tresor. ac he*
    todeld it & scatered sotlice. Micel hadde Henri king gadered gold & syluer. & na god ne
    dide me for his saule thar of.

'This year, (the) King Stephen crossed the sea to go to Normandy and was received
there because they thought he was like the uncle (i.e., his uncle). And because he still
had his treasury, but he divided and scattered it stupidly. King Henry has gathered
much gold and silver and no good did men with it for his soul.'

(64) *Đa **þe** king Stephne to Englalande com þa macod he his gadering æt Oxeneford. & þar*
    *he nam **þe** biscop Roger of Sereberi & Alexander biscop of Lincol & te Canceler Roger*
    hise neues. & dide ælle in prisun. til hi iafen up here castles.

'When King Stephen came to England, he held a gathering at Oxford and there he
took bishop Roger of Salisbury and Alexander bishop of Lincoln and the chancellor
Roger, his nephews. And put all in prison until they gave up their castles.'

Since we looked at Case loss in Layamon in the previous subsection, I'll briefly discuss the
use of definite articles in this text. The distribution is very much the same as in the last part
of the Chronicle, namely spread among subjects, as in (65), objects, as in (66), and prepositional objects, as in (67). Again, *all* is very frequent.

(65) *al swa **þe** boc spekeð þe he to bisne inom*
    All so the book says that he to example took

    'as the book says that he took as example.' (Layamon, *Brut*, Caligula, 37, in Brook &
    Leslie 1963)

(66) *heo nomen al Taurins and Iuorie; & alle **þe** burзewes of Lu[m]bardie*

    'They took all Turin and Ivrea and all the cities of Lombardy.'
    (Layamon, *Brut*, Caligula, 2623, in Brook & Leslie 1963)

(67) *he wes king   of **þe** Amalæh.   þe Wurse him wes ful nieh.*
    'He was king   of the Amalakites   (and) the evil (one) was very close to him.'

    (Layamon, *Brut*, Caligula, 8302, in Brook & Leslie 1963)

Thus, taking Leiss's (2000) insights into aspect and definiteness into account, we can see
that, in English, the twelfth century shows signs of a loss of aspectual prefixes, the loss of
genitive object Case, and an increase in definiteness markers. The latter increase is with subjects and objects and initially less so with prepositional objects. This shows, I think, that the
articles are marking structural Case.

3. D and ASP to Subject and Object Markers

In this section, I examine the origins of grammatical Case. In many languages, nominative
and accusative structural Cases indicate information status. This is part of what a subject and
object do. I will provide further examples in section 3.1. If the account provided in section
1 is correct, one expects verbal markers on nominal DPs to serve as Case and I show that
this is so in 3.2. If grammatical dependent marking is really the marking of specificity and

definiteness by the verb, it makes sense that the origin is a D. In 3.3, I focus on the origin of subject markers and in 3.4 on object markers.

3.1 DEFINITENESS ON SUBJECTS AND OBJECTS

In Finnish, subjects can have nominative, genitive, and partitive and objects can have accusative, nominative, and partitive Case (see Tauli 1966: 17; Comrie 1981: 125; Sands & Campbell 2001). Definiteness determines these (Belletti 1988). Estonian also shows a connection between Case and definiteness, where a nominative is definite/specific, as in (68a), and a partitive, as in (68b), is not.

(68) a. **_Lilled_**   _kasvavad_   _siin_   Estonian
        flowers-NOM   grow-3P   here
        'The flowers are growing here.' (Hiietam nd: 2)
   b. **_Inimesi_**   _soitis_   _maale_
        people-PART   drive-PST.3S   countryside-to
        'Some people drove to the countryside.' (Hiietam nd: 2)

When we use the earlier tree in (13), the T probes the VP in (69) and finds a (plural) DP to agree with. The definiteness of this nominal DP (u-T) is valued at the same time and the subject moves to the specifier of TP.

(69)

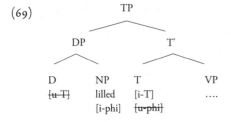

Subjects in Finnish and Estonian can also be marked genitive in nonfinite clauses (as well as in modal contexts). This is expected since the T would not have [i-T]. The Case of the object depends on the aspect of the verb and the definiteness or measure of the object. As pointed out by various people (e.g., Kiparsky 1998), perfective aspect results in accusative, as in (70), imperfective in partitive, as in (71).

(70) _Poiss_   _luges_   **_raamatu_**   _läbi_   Estonian
      boy-NOM   read-PST.3S   book-ACC   through
      'The boy read the book.' (Hiietam nd: 18)

(71) _Poiss_   _luges_   **_raamatut_**   Estonian
      boy-NOM   read-PST.3S   book-PART
      'The boy was reading a book.' (Hiietam nd: 18)

Kiparsky (1998: 267) gives the following Finnish examples, and argues that crucial to the Case of the objects is the aspectual boundedness of the event.

(72) *ammu-i-n*   *karhu-n*   Finnish
      shoot-PST-1S   bear-ACC

      'I shot the/a bear.'

(73) *ammu-i-n*   *karhu-a*   Finnish
      shoot-PST-1S   bear-PART

      'I shot at the/a bear.' (Kiparsky 1998: 267)

To show definiteness in Kamassian, another Uralic language, accusative case is used, as (74) shows. Nominative is used for the subject and for the indefinite object.

(74) *də*   *šüšküm*   *aspa'də'*   *pa'dlobi*   Kamassian
      he   bone-ACC   kettle-LAT   put-3S

      'He put the shoulder bone into the kettle.' (Künnap 1999: 16)

A tree for object marking could be (75), using the Finnish data. The [u-ASP] on D might in fact be the number features on D. (D might have [i-phi] as well, or a [u-phi] probe that is valued by N.)

(75)

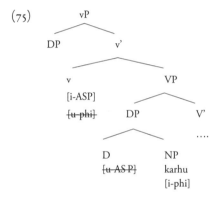

The same connection between Case and definiteness appears in Amharic, a Semitic language, where a special marker on the object DP marks definiteness, as Amberber (2005) shows. In (76), the object marker on the verb is optional because the object is definite but the object marker would be ungrammatical in (77) since the object is indefinite. I do not count these as Differential Object markings.

(76) *ləmma*   **t'ərmus-u-n**   *səbbər-ə-(w)*   Amharic
      Lemma   bottle-DEF-OM   break-3M.SM-3OM

      'Lemma broke the bottle.' (Amberber 2005: 299).

(77) *ləmma*   **t'ərmus**   *səbbər-ə*   Amharic
      Lemma   bottle   break-3M

      'Lemma broke one bottle.' (Amberber 2005: 298).

In Tati, a group of Iranian dialects here represented by Chali, the same is true. The indefinite object, as in (78), is marked by the same Case as the subject, but the definite object, as in (79), bears oblique Case.

(78) **alaf**   *undi*   *cuare*   Chali
      grass   sheep   give

      'Give grass to the sheep.' (Yar-Shater 1969: 98)

(79) **alafe**   *undi*   *cuare*   Chali
      grass-OBL   sheep   give

      'Give the grass to the sheep.' (Yar-Shater 1969: 98)

If Case in Finnish, Estonian, and other languages does not mark semantic roles, what does? In many languages, it is of course the position that arguments occupy through external Merge that is reflected in their spell-out position also. So an agent is relatively high in the vP and usually occupies Spec TP as well. In addition, Sands and Campbell (2001) argue that there is a rich set of affixes on the verbs, as shown in (80). Thus, transitivity and semantic roles are marked on the head, not on the dependent.

(80) *Minu-a*   *pelo-**tta**-a*   Finnish
      1S-PART   fear-CAUS-3S

      'I am afraid'/'Something frightens me.' (Sands & Campbell 2001: 253)

Thus, specificity/definiteness and tense mark the grammatical subject, and measure and aspect mark the grammatical object. If tense is relevant to both a verb and a noun, we expect some evidence of this. In the next section, I therefore provide some indication that nominals are sometimes marked for tense.

3.2 DEIXIS ON THE AUX/V AND TENSE ON THE DP

Section 1.2 mentioned that even though typically verbs are marked for tense and nouns for spatial deixis, the opposite also occurs in rare cases. This is expected if tense and definiteness are reflexes of the same phenomenon. I'll first look at verbs and then nouns.

Suttles (2004: 35) observes that in Halkomelem "[t]he auxiliary *i* 'be here' locates the phenomenon or event (whether real or hypothetical, present, past or future) near the speaker at the time of utterance. The auxiliary *ni* 'be there' locates it somewhere else." This of course often corresponds to present and past, as in (81a) and 81(b).

(81) a. **ʔi**   *cən*   *c'éc'əw-ət*   Downriver Halkolmelem
          AUX   1S   be.helping-TR

          'I am helping him.'

      b. **niʔ**   *cən*   *c'éw-ət*
          AUX   1S   help-TR

          'I helped him.' (Suttles 2004: 35)

Ritter and Wiltschko (2008) provide a theoretical analysis arguing that location is equivalent to tense in Halkomelem (but see Matthewson 2009 for a different view). One of the pieces of evidence that the auxiliaries are indeed spatial markers and not temporal ones is that they can be prepositional as well.

Observations in other Salish languages point to the same connection between space and time. Davis and Saunders (1997: 89) say that Bella Coola has no equivalent of time in the proposition: "the time of the event is to a certain degree inferred from the deictic arrangement of the participants." Thus, in (82), the boy has a proximal demonstrative *ti* and the rope a middle-distance one *ta* and hence the activity cannot be done at the same time as the utterance, that is, not in the present tense.

(82) *mus-is*   *ti-ʔimmllkĭ-tx*   *ta-qlsxʷ-taX*   Bella Coola
      feel-he/it   DEM-boy-DEM   DEM-rope-DEM

      'The boy felt that rope.' (Davis & Saunders 1997: 89)

Dixon (2003: 72–74) argues that verbs in Boumaa Fijian have deictic reference, but they seem to me to have reference to the manner in which the action was done, not the time or place:

(83) *o*   *'ea*   *'eneii*   *tuu*   *gaa*   *'eneii*   Boumaa Fijian
      ART   3S   do-like-this ASP   just   do-like-this

      'He did just like this.' (narrator mimes a spearing action)

Nordlinger and Sadler (2002, 2004) provide a typology of TMA marking on nouns that I follow, though I don't do justice to their detailed account. South American languages such as Guarani, Siriono (both Tupian), Apurinã, Chamicuro (both Arawak), and Tariana and Australian languages such as (Old) Lardil and Kayardild have argument nominals that encode the TMA properties of the verb. Other languages include Yag Dii, Supyire (both Niger Congo), Somali (Cushitic), and Halkomelem (Salish). Koasati, as described in Kimball (1985, 1991), also marks tense/aspect on the noun, as in (84). "The article suffixes locate a noun in time," Kimball notes (1991: 404).

(84) *á:ti*   *loká:casi-k-ok*   *átł-ok*   *ísko-toho:limpáhco-k*   Koasati
      person orphan-ART-SS.FOC   fill-SS.FOC   drink-M/ASP-PST

      'The orphaned man filled it up and drank, so it is said.' (Kimball 1985: 346)

Nordlinger and Sadler distinguish between propositional and independent marking, where propositional marking indicates that the entire clause is of a particular tense (or mood or aspect) and independent marking just indicates something about the nominal. The former are found in Lardil, Kayardild, Chamicuro, Yag Dii, and Supyire and the latter in Tariana, Guarini, Somali, and Halkomelem. For the purposes of this chapter, the former is the most relevant.I give here examples of propositional TMA marking from Chamicuro and Lardil (based on Nordlinger & Sadler) and of independent TMA marking from Tariana.

In Chamicuro, an Arawak language spoken in Peru, tense information is encoded on the definite article accompanying the subject and object arguments: *na*, as in (85a), is used in the present and future; *ka*, as in (85b), is used in the past (the data in Nordlinger & Sadler are from Parker, as indicated).

(85) a. *I-nis-kʹana*   *na*   *ʹcamʹalo*   Chamicuro
         3-see-P   D-NONPST   bat

         'They see the bat.' (Parker 1999: 552)

b. *Y-al'ıyo* **ka** *k'e:ni*
3-fall   D-PST   rain

'The rain fell.' (Parker 1999: 552)

Chamicuro has optional tense marking on the verb as well. Parker provides no instances with more than one nominal in one clause, and such an example would be interesting.

In Lardil, the case markers of the nonsubject nominals depend on the tense of the verb, as discussed by Nordlinger and Sadler (2002:7). For instance, in (86a), the indefinite objects have unmarked Case, but in (86b), they are marked for future.

(86) a. *Ngada*   **niwee**   **maarn-in**   *wu-tha*   Lardil
           1S.NOM 3S.OBJ spear-OBJ give-NF

'I gave him a spear.' (Klokeid 1976: 476)

      b. *Ngada bilaa*   *wu-thur* **ngimbenthar** **diin-kur**   **wangalk-ur**
           1S.NOM tomorrow give-F   2S.F.OBJ   this-F.OBJ   boomerang-F.OBJ

'I'll give you this boomerang tomorrow.' (Klokeid 1976: 493)

Nordlinger and Sadler discuss many more instances, such as independent or inherent marking in Tariana (data from Aikhenvald 2003, but with some glosses left out) where the TAM on the noun is independent of that on the verb. In (87), 'the eagle' is no longer alive.

(87) *Thepi*   *di-mare-pidana*   *eta-miki-ri-nuku*   Tariana
      to.water   3S.NF-throw.CAUS eagle-PST-NF

'He threw the remains of the eagle into water.' (Nordlinger & Sadler 2002: 22)

Nordlinger and Sadler argue that this marking on the noun is inflectional rather than derivational, and that is very plausible since these markings are fully productive.

The instances of languages discussed in the literature as having temporal markings on nouns and spatial markings on verbs provide evidence of the close relationship of tense and time on the one hand and deixis and place on the other.

3.3 D TO SUBJECT AND OBJECT MARKER

Greenberg (1978: 73–74) maintains that the origin of nominative case is often a definite marker (since subjects are most often definite) and König argues the same (2008: 117) for the origin of ergative Case in West Nilotic. Sasse (1984) has argued for a demonstrative origin of the cases in Berber, and Kulikov (2006: 29–30) provides a review of languages for which scholars have similarly argued this point, such as Kartvelian, Georgian, and Caucasian. For instance, the ergative *-man* in Georgian (Lomashvili, p.c.) is a postposed pronoun and the same is probably true of the absolute *–I*, going back to *-igi* 'that' (see Kulikov 2009: 447). McGregor (2008) shows that some ergative suffixes in Australian languages derive from pronouns. Mithun (2008a: 215), based on work by Anderson (1992), argues that the Wakashan language Kwakw'ala's subject marker derives from a proximal demonstrative and the object marker from a distal one. In this subsection, we see further examples of the pronominal origin of nominative and accusative marking.

For early Indo-European, some have argued that the nominative *-s* ending is a demonstrative; see Bopp ([1833–1852] 1868), Uhlenbeck (1901), Pedersen (1907), Delbrück (1919), Specht (1947), and Kortlandt (1983). Bopp ([1833–1852] 1868: 248) is the most definite about Case endings in general. He finds the origin of both the nominative and accusative in the pronoun. For the latter, he lists the forms *ima* 'this one' and *amu* 'that one' ([1833–1852] 1868: 323) and notes:

> Ihrem Ursprunge nach sind sie, wenigstens gröfstentheils, Pronomina. [In origin, they are for the most part pronouns.] (Bopp [1833–1852] 1868: 248)

Others put a "probably" in, and are more specific that it holds for the nominative:

> Es ist wahrscheinlich, daß das *s* aus dem Demonstrativum stammt, mit dem auf das hervorragende Substantivum hingewiesen wurde. [It is likely that the *s* derives from the demonstrative, which referred to the preceding nominal.] (Delbrück 1919: 215)

> ein suffigiertes *-s*, das kaum von dem demonstrativen Pronominalstamme *so* getrennt werden darf und wahrscheinlich als postpositiver Artikel aufzufassen ist [a suffixed *-s*, that can hardly be distinguished from the demonstrative pronoun *so* and is probably to be interpreted as postpositional article]. (Uhlenbeck 1901: 170).

The most common Sanskrit nominal declension is that of noun stems in *-a*, given in table 5.4 for the singular and plural of *deva* 'god', and for the masculine singular demonstrative. These paradigms show the similarities between the endings of the nouns and the demonstratives. The argument would be that the nominative *-s* (or *ta*) was the original deictic and that it combined with the noun and that this original demonstrative is in turn strengthened. Jespersen (1922: 381–383) is a fierce critic of this position. He wonders why neuter nouns would not get a definite ending. This is explained by the work of Gamkrelidze and Ivanov

TABLE 5.4

Cases for Sanskrit *-a* Stems for *deva* 'god' and the Demonstrative Pronoun

	S	P	MS Demonstrative
NOM	*devas*	*devaas*	*sa(s)*
ACC	*devam*	*devaan*	*tam*
INST	*devena*	*devaais*	*tena*
DAT	*devaaya*	*devebhyas*	*tasmai*
ABL	*devat*	*devebhyas*	*tasmaat*
GEN	*devasya*	*devaanaam*	*tasya*
LOC	*deve*	*deveshu*	*tasmin*
VOC	*deva*	*devaas*	—

(1994–1995: 1: 233–276), however, and also by earlier work (see a review in Royen 1929: 877–885). If the Proto-Indo-European system is originally one making a distinction between animate and inanimate nominals, this distinction is reanalyzed as plural (in the genitive) and Case (in the nominative and accusative).[8]

The demonstrative origin of the nominative is widely accepted,[9] certainly in the nineteenth century. As mentioned, Bopp thinks the accusative has a similar origin. This is less widely agreed upon. Finck (cited in Royen 1929: 891–892) sees the -*m* as originating in a locative noun *medhio* 'middle'. This is not impossible, certainly if this accusative started as a DOM.

Tauli (1956: 176, 198, 210) and many others argue that the origin of the accusative ending -*m* in Uralic is a demonstrative pronoun. Baker (1985: 134–135) provides an overview of the different hypotheses. The accusative counts as a DOM rather than as a Case, according to Baker. The evidence from late Latin points to the same. Cennamo (2009) shows that low agentive subjects are marked with accusative, as in (88).

(88) *lucem...*   *caruit*   Late Latin
     light-ACC   failed

     'The light failed.' (Corpus Inscriptionum Latinarum 8.5372, from Herman 1997: 23)

In Japanese, the particle *ga* is described as a nominative marker and *no* as a genitive in Modern Japanese. In older Japanese, as shown in Hashimoto (1969), they were markers of the subject of a nominalized clause which had the verb in the attributive form (before the conclusive and attributive merged), as in (89) and (90).

(89) *morobito*   **no**   *asobu*   *o*   *mireba*   Old Japanese
     all-people   PRT   play-ATTR   ACC   see

     'when I see the playing by all the people'

(90) *imo*   **ga**   *misi*   *ooti*   *no*   *hana*
     beloved   PRT   see-ATTR   sandalwood   PRT   flower

     'the sandalwood flower that my beloved saw' (Shibatani 1980: 348)

Hashimoto's argument is that both *ga* and *no* link two nominals and that only later were they seen as marking the subject. Linking two nominals in a clause may be interpreted as indicating finiteness. Hence, in a framework such as I have suggested, *ga* has [i-T], and *no* is its nonfinite alternative.

---

8. Gamkrelidze and Ivanov (1994–1995) argue that the Proto Indo-European genitive had two forms, *-os* and *-om*, which on the basis of Hittite evidence can be reconstructed as neuter/inanimate versus animate. The distinction between inanimate and animate is reanalyzed as one between plural and singular (see table 5.5, where the genitive singular has an additional pronominal enclitic -*ya*). The *-os* and *-om* Proto-Indo-European forms parallel the later nominative and accusative, which are also reanalyzed from an animate/inanimate distinction (hence, Latin *lupus* 'wolf' as nominative but *iugum* 'yoke' as both nominative and accusative).

9. The genitive is another possible source that I haven't considered. Givón (p.c.) suggests that genitive subjects can be reanalyzed as nominatives when subordinate clauses turn into main clauses, e.g., due to verbs grammaticalizing as TMA.

3.4 V TO ASP TO OBJECT MARKER

Chinese *ba* is perhaps the best known example of a verb being reanalyzed as an object marker, with an enormous literature explaining its properties.[10] *Ba* is originally a lexical verb 'to hold', as in (91a) from the fifth century BCE, but was a frequent serial verb, as Li and Thompson (1974: 202) show with sentences such as (91b).

(91) a. *Yu   qing   **ba**   tian   zhi   rui-ling*...   Old Chinese
        Yu   himself   take   heaven   PRT   mandate

        'Yu himself took the mandate of heaven ...'

        (*Me-zi*, from Li & Thompson 1974: 202)

    b. ... *yin   **ba**   jian   kan*
        should   hold   sword   see

        'I should take the sword and see it.'

        (Tang dynasty poem, from Li & Thompson 1974: 202–203)

In Modern Chinese, *ba* has been analyzed as verb, coverb, preposition (Li 1990), or Case marker (Li & Thompson 1974: 203; Koopman 1984; Yang 2008; Blake 2001: 164). Li and Thompson (1981: 465) mention the definiteness and disposal (the affectedness) of the object in this construction.

(92) *wo   **ba**   **shu**   mai   le*   Chinese
     I   PRT   book   buy   PF

     'I bought the book.' (Li & Thompson 1981: 21)

The *ba* is obligatory when the object is animate and highly affected. This has led many to see it as a differential object marker. This, of course, fits the view that objective/accusative Case is really a definiteness/disposal marker.

    Scholars have argued for various structures, for example, with *ba* as a causative phrase, or *ba* in the v. I will assume it is an ASPP since affectedness is important, as in (93), with *ba* moving to v (see Sun 2008).

(93)

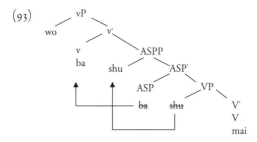

This structure accounts for *ba* and the nominal object not forming a constituent.

---

10. In section 6, I mention the possibility that the Urdu/Hindi object marker *ko* originates from a participial. The possibility is remote but, if it is accurate, the account is roughly the same: a verb and its object are reanalyzed as object marker and object.

How did this structure arise? If a serial verb is analyzed as in, for example, Stewart (2001), *ba* can be reanalyzed from a full verb to an aspect marker in (93). This is of course compatible with both Late Merge and Feature Economy. Compare this type of reanalysis to the discussion of Edo in section 5.

Section 3 has provided more evidence for seeing the grammatical notion of subject as marked by tense and definiteness, and similarly the notion of object as marked by aspect and expressing some kind of measure. The nominative and accusative cases on nouns are therefore grammaticalized definite markers. I'll now turn to a kind of subject and object marking that is a mix between grammatical and semantic Case.

4. Differential Marking of Objects and Subjects

Differential marking (DM) occurs when subjects or objects are specially marked because they "violate" the definiteness/animacy hierarchy, as in, for example, Silverstein (1976), mentioned in chapter 2. If a subject is unexpectedly indefinite or inanimate, or an object is unexpectedly definite or animate, this marking occurs. This may also happen with indirect objects. Aristar (1997) and Viti (2008) note an interesting phenomenon related to differential marking. Aristar argues that if the object of the preposition is animate, as in (94a), it has a goal theta role (dative); if it is inanimate, as in (94b), it has a direction/location (allative) connected to it.

(94)   a.   I sent a letter **to John**
       b.   I sent a letter **to Phoenix.**

Viti (2008) examines this in Ancient Greek and finds that animate objects occur more often with the preverb *en* and inanimate objects with a preposition.

This marking of special status is restricted to dependent marking and does not occur with agreement and word order. The beginning of the subject agreement cycle, discussed in chapter 2, shows that subject agreement typically starts with expected subjects, namely first and second person pronouns, but chapter 3 shows that the types of objects first to be marked by agreement on the verb are definite and animate. So while subject agreement is very different from differential subject marking (DSM) and regular Case marking on the grammatical subject, DOM and object agreement have more in common, though not regular Case marking on the grammatical object. Mahajan (1990: 82, 88) shows for Hindi that, in terms of position, objects with or without the DOM act the same: they can either occur inside the VP or outside. This too makes them different from the object marking that has aspectual consequences. I will therefore regard DM as a special facet of dependent marking.

The literature on DOM is vast: Bossong (1985), Torrego (1998), and Aissen (2003), to name but a few. See also Baker (1985: 117–118) on the function of accusative Case in Komi. Some doubts on the universality of this phenomenon can be found in Bickel and Witzlack-Makarevich (2008). There is also a growing literature on DSM, for example, the essays in the volume edited by de Hoop and de Swart (2008), and on unifying DOM and DSM theoretically, as in Kwon and Zribi-Hertz (2008) and Malchukov (2008).

4.1 DIFFERENTIAL (OBJECT) MARKING

The languages marking DOM can be found in the Indo-European, Pama-Nyungan, and Sino-Tibetan families. Heine and Kuteva (2002: 37) add Lezgian and Tamil to this list. I provide examples from Indo-Iranian and Romance. The source is invariably an adposition and the adposition marks animacy and definiteness, rather than grammatical object. This prompts Richards (2008a) to argue that DOM is the result of [Person] checking by v; if the v has no [Person] probe, only indefinite objects will appear and they would be marked differently. So even though DOM and object agreement superficially look alike, I think they are different: DOM is tied to animacy, and object agreement to definiteness/animacy.

Persian uses a suffix *-ra* to mark definite objects. In chapter 6, I raise the possibility that Persian uses few demonstratives, possibly since it has *-ra*. Windfuhr (1987: 534, 541) argues that *-ra* derives from the noun *radi* 'reason' that is then reanalyzed as a preposition 'for the sake/reason of', and then used to mark topicalized specific indirect and direct objects, as in (95a) from the eleventh century, and (95b) from the twelfth century, and finally only as a direct object marker in Modern Persian, as in (95c).

(95) a. *shah* **ra** *goft* Middle Persian
          king OM   told
          'the king, he told' (*Noruzname*, from Karimi 1989: 104)

   b. *yeki* *az* *moluke* *xorasan* *mahmud*
      one   of   kings   Chorassan Mahmud
      *sobaktegin-**ra*** *be-xab* *did*
      Sobaktegin-OM   in-sleep saw
      'One of the kings of Chorassan saw Mohmud S. in his dream.'
      (Sa'di, *Golestan*, from Bossong 1985: 60)

   c. *kitab* **ra** *xandam* Persian
      book   OM   read-I
      'I read the book.'

Karimi (1989: 100) suggests that *-ra* is a nonnominative topic marker. She (1989: 106) cites Kent (1950) and Brunner (1977) on *-ra* taking on a broader role and marking specific direct objects starting in Middle Persian. Bossong (1985: 57–62) has a similar chronology. He argues that between Middle and New Persian, that is, in the tenth century, DOM becomes "voll ausgebildet" (1985: 58) though some of the original functions such as the dative continue to be marked.

Bossong (1985) studies DOM in twenty-six current Iranian languages, and many reanalyze *radiy* as *-ra*. Apart from Persian, some other languages that use *-ra* are Gilaki, Mazanderani, Natanzi, Gazi, Sivandi, Balochi, as in (96), and Tati:

(96) *a* *shuma-**ra*** *ida* *nelit* Balochi
         he you-OM   here not-leave
         'He won't leave you here.' (Barker & Khan Mengal 1969: 1: 141)

Bossong (1985: 104) finds that there is polygenesis of this construction; in other words, there is no clear genetic relationship between the languages that have introduced DOM.

Urdu/Hindi *–ko* is also typically analyzed as a DOM. If the object is animate or definite, as in (97a), a *–ko* is added, but not if it is indefinite, as in (97b).

(97) a. *aadmii* **nee** *kitaab* **ko** *peRhaa*   Urdu/Hindi
      man   ERG   book   OM   read

      'The man read the book.'

    b. *aadmii* **nee** *kitaab* *peRhaa*
      man   ERG   book   read

      'The man read a book.'

In chapter 3, we saw how the Romance languages use *a* 'to' as an object marker, as in (98), repeated from (63) in that chapter.

(98) *Pedro* **lo** *vió* **a** **Juan**   River Plate Spanish
     Pedro   him   3S-saw   OM   Juan
     'Pedro saw Juan.'

Torrego (1998: 25) argues that the dative preposition is used because it has a D feature. I suggest an alternative in (100).

Indirect object marking shows a similarity with differential object marking (see Malchukov 2009). In languages that have what is known as the dative alternation, such as English, the marker *to* is typically used when the indirect object is in a position nonadjacent to the verb (unless the direct object is a pronoun).

(99) a. I gave **him** a book.
    b. I gave a book **to him**.

The differential object markers in Romance and Indo-Iranian are indirect object markers as well. The direct object marker *a* in (100) derives from a locative preposition; see the pre-Spanish Latin *ad* 'to'. The goal markers *a, ko,* and *ra* start out with interpretable place features, as argued in 1.2. In some languages, these are reanalyzed as [u-loc]/[u-T] starting in a certain position, transitive or specific. This reanalysis of the dependent marker is shown in (100).

(100) DOM Cline
      P   >   Inherent Case   >   DOM
      [i-loc]   [i-loc]   [u-loc] = [u-T]
      [u-phi]

This would make DOM an alternative to definiteness marking. Evidence for this can be found in Neuburger and Stark (2009)'s data that show that the differential object marker is in complementary distribution with a D in Corsican, as shown in (101).

(101) a. *Vigu* **à** *Pedru*   Corsican
      see-1S   OM   Pedru
      'I see Pedru.'

b. *Vigu   l'omu*
   see-1S   the-man
   'I see the man.'

In brief, DOM marks animate/definite objects through originally locative prepositions.

4.2 DIFFERENTIAL (SUBJECT) MARKING

According to Woolford (2008), "DSM (Differential Subject Marking) effects involving Case do not constitute a unified phenomenon. They come in diverse types, requiring different kinds of theoretical accounts." I focus on this aspect of DSM.

The examples of DSM often provided, such as by Woolford (2008: 20), are Urdu (102) and Basque (103).

(102) **Mujhee** *yee*   *pasand*   *hē*   Urdu
       I-DAT   this   pleasant   is
       'I like this.'

(103) **Ni-ri**   *zure*   *oinetako-a-k*   *gustatzen*   *zaizkit*   Basque
       I-DAT   your   shoes-DET-NOM   like   AUX
       'I like your shoes.' (Austin and Lopez 1995: 12, from Woolford 2008)

The grammatical subjects in these are the nominatives *yee* 'this' in (102) and *zure oinetako-a-k* 'shoes' in (103). These are less animate and definite than expected of subjects, and hence the experiencer "subjects" can be marked by DSM. Another example is Dutch (104).

(104) **Mij**   *lijkt*   *dit*   *leuk*   Dutch
       1S-DAT   seems   this   nice
       'This seems nice to me.'

The experiencers in (102) to (104) are datives and can be seen as having inherent Case, connected to their (experiencer) theta role and to their position in the vP, whereas the grammatical subjects are marked with nominative and still act like subjects.

Ergative Case in some languages is different and could be a candidate for being a DSM. A well-studied phenomenon (see Dixon 1994) is that third person pronouns are more likely to be ergative than first person ones, so the ergative on a less animate/definite is a DSM. In languages where certain aspects trigger ergative structures, this explanation cannot be right since animate/definite nominals, as in (99b), repeated as (105), show ergative marking.

(105) *aadmii*   **nee**   *kitaab*   *peRhaa*   Urdu/Hindi
       man   ERG   book   read
       'The man read a book.'

Inanimate/indefinite subjects are less common, with or without DSM.

In section 4's review of both DOM and DSM, we see that DOM markers derive from prepositions, as do DSM markers. There is less agreement that there are DSMs, however, since many seem experiencers and seem clearly marked that way. The reason grammaticalized prepositions are marking DOM is related to the interpretable location features of the preposition. As features are lost, the preposition is reanalyzed as definiteness marker.

5. Semantic Case

In this section, I discuss three sources for semantic Case, each in a different subsection. I show that there is very little evidence for an adverbial source (section 5.1) of Case, contrary to expectations. The nominal and verbal origins (sections 5.2 and 5.3) are most obvious.

5.1 CASE FROM ADVERBS AND ADPOSITIONS

Before I started working on the origin of Case markers, I took it for granted that they were originally adpositions and adverbs. It is, however, very hard to find clear cases of adverbial origins. Blake (2001: 170–171) expresses similar feelings. Tauli (1966: 12) argues for a pronominal origin of many Cases, but many of those are the grammatical Cases. Kuryłowicz (1964: 201) asserts that "all oblique cases and even the acc[usative] go back to expressions of spatial relations" and that may be correct. The "secondary semantic functions" betray this origin and "[t]he polysemy of case-forms, due to the increasing range of their use, calls for a constant renewal of their etymological spatial value" (202). Kahr (1976) argues that adpositions are the only source for Case markers; a noun or verb or adverb always has to go through the stage of adposition before it is reanalyzed as Case.

Kuryłowicz (1964: 171, 179) suggests a change of adverbs to (prepositional) Case markers, as in (106a), noting that some adverbs also can become preverbs, as in (106b).

(106) a. [Verb + Adverb] + oblique noun > Verb + [P + noun]
       b. [Verb + Adverb] > [affix-Verb] (+ Adverb)

Only (106a) is relevant to Case/dependent marking; (106b) will feature in chapter 7. Unfortunately, Kuryłowicz gives ample examples of (106b) but not of (106a). Vincent (1999) provides a few instances where a later preposition is functioning as adverb, such as *úd* in (107a), and Gary Miller (p.c.) provides (107b), with the Latin adverb *forās* 'out' as the precursor of the French preposition *hors* 'outside'. Note the doubling through *ex-*.

(107) a. **úd**   *usríyā*   *jánitā*   *yó*   *jajāna*   Vedic Sanskrit
           out   cows   creator   who   created
           'who as creator created forth the cows'
           (Hock 1996: 221, from Vincent 1999: 1119)

       b. *omnīs*   **ex-ēgit**   **forās**   Latin
           all.ACC.P.M   out-drove.3S   out
           'All (of us) he drove out.' (*Aulularia* 414)

Vincent also provides a scenario as to how this adverb could have been reanalyzed. Because preposing of the adverb was frequent, for instance *úd* in (107b), the reanalysis of an independently marked nominal (in this case *usríyā*) could occur.

Using work by Bréal (1924) and Lehmann (1958) as a base, Fairbanks (1977) reconstructs the Proto-Indo-European Case system as having five cases for the singular with the three additional endings in Sanskrit having been added through adverbial particles. According to Fairbanks,

> Sanskrit had a suffix *-tas* which derived from PIE *-tos* and occurred in Greek and Latin also with the meaning 'from', but was used only as an adverbial form in these languages. In Pali it became used as a case inflection for the abl[ative] s[ingular]. . . . [It] must have derived from some noun form obscured by the passage of time. (Fairbanks 1977: 117, 122)

So the evidence for adverb origins of Case markers exists but such a source is not extremely frequent.

Languages with adpositions do develop or renew semantic Case markers. The Indo-European dative Case provides an instance of a semantic Case marked by an adposition since the goal markers *to* and *for* derive from prepositions of location in the various languages. Other families show similar trends. Finnish has an *-ine* comitative that is lost in Estonian, but renewed by various forms of a postposition. The latter, however, in its turn is derived from a noun *kansa* 'people, company' (Oinas 1961: 12–13) and also used as an adverb, as in (108) from the now extinct Salis Livonian.

(108) *Utak*   *mind*   **kazu**   Salis Livonian
      take   me   with
      'Take me along.' (Oinas 1961: 13)

This comitative surfaces as *kaas* as early as the sixteenth century in North Estonian, as *kaan* in Southern Estonian, and later as *-ga* in Southern Estonian. Different dialects still preserve various forms, as in (109).

(109) *lapsien-**ka***   Sippola Finnish
      children-with
      'with children' (Oinas 1961: 44)

Oinas discusses a range of relatively recent Case markers, such as the *ke*-comitative, originally from a noun *kerta* 'time' (1961: 60), the *mö*-prolative/comitative, from *myö* 'back', and a *sa*-terminative, from a verb meaning 'to receive, get, come, arrive' (1961: 139). So adpositions develop into Case markers but are themselves derived from nouns and verbs.

Turkish has a postposition *ile* 'with' that is starting to be suffixed to the noun, as in (110).

(110) *Mehmet-**le***   Turkish
      Mehmet-with
      'with Mehmet' (Lewis 1967: 88, from Kahr 1976: 121)

This postposition too may have a more lexical origin.

To sum up, adverbs are possibly the least likely source of Case. Some adpositions may derive from adverbs, but most, such as *kazu*, derive ultimately from nouns or verbs. I will therefore not provide an account in terms of Economy for adverbs but will turn to nouns.

5.2 N TO P AND TO SEMANTIC CASE

Nouns form the basis of many prepositions and this development seems to be similar in countless languages. I will argue that a reanalysis of N to P takes place and that the spatial features are reduced in a manner suggested in (21).

First, I provide some instances of nouns that reanalyze to adpositions. The (unusual) English preposition *via* derives from the Latin noun *via* 'road', the Italian *senza* 'without' from Latin *absentia*, *baka* in Sranan from 'back' (see Plag 1998), *tp* 'on' from 'head' in Egyptian (Gardiner 1957: 130), Ewe *ta* from 'head', as in (111), and Swahili *juu* from 'top', as in (112), and similar derivations occur in various Zapotecan languages (Lillehaugen 2006).

(111) a. *e-fe*   **ta**   Ewe
          he-of head
          'his head'

       b. *e-ta*
          he-on
          'on him' (Heine & Reh 1984: 257)

(112) a. ***juu***   *ya*   *mlima*   Swahili
          top   of   hill

       b. ***juu** ya*   *mlima*
          on   hill (Heine & Reh 1984: 101)

Kahr (1975: 45–46) and Heine and Kuteva (2002) provide numerous other examples, such as the Tzotzil 'ear' becoming a locative preposition, the Finnish noun 'earth' reanalyzing to the adverb/preposition 'down', 'shoulder' becoming 'up', and 'heart' becoming 'in'.

The structure in (113) is a representation of the changes from (112a) to (112b).

(113)

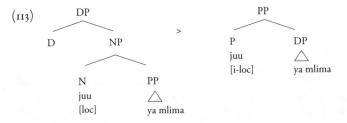

The French preposition *chez* 'with' is related to the Latin noun *casa* (see Vincent 1999; Lightfoot 1999).[11] Longobardi (2001) examines locatives as in Italian (114) and suggests the reanalysis in (115). The noun first moves to D and then to P.

(114) *vago*   *casa*   *(mia)*   Veneto Italian
       go-1S   home   my
       'I am going home.' (Longobardi 2001: 289)

---

11. And, of course, the Scandinavian preposition *hos* 'with' is similarly derived from the noun with the meaning of 'house'.

(115)   a.   PP   b.   P

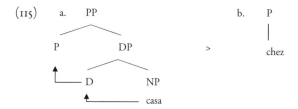

Longobardi argues that *casa* undergoes movement from N to D in Latin and early French (*chies* at this point) and that, once it is in D, it can be incorporated as a P. This clearly is a case of Late Merge.

A cline for this type of change could be as in (116) with the stage through D optional.

(116)   The Nominal Case Cline

>   Noun   >   (D)   >   P   >   Semantic Case
>   [i-phi]   [u-phi]   [i-loc]
>   [loc]   [i-loc]

In the remainder of this section, I give a detailed description of the changes from the noun *side* to the preposition *beside*.

Hopper and Traugott (2003: 110) mention changes involving the preposition *beside*. Using the noun 'side' as an adposition is quite widespread across languages (see also Heine & Kuteva 2002: 271–272). The *OED* claims it is "[f]ound in OE only as two words, but by 1200 used as an adverb and preposition." In fact, *besides* occurs as an adverb and preposition in Old English and can be written as one or two words. Its use is infrequent and, when written as two words, it is a noun accompanied by a determiner or possessor modifying the noun. The typical preposition meaning 'next to' is *be/bi*, as in (117), with a dative object.

(117)   *gesæt him þa se halga holmwearde neah, æðele **be** æðelum*
        sat him then the hallowed pilot near, noble by noble-DAT.P
        'Sat then the pilot near, nobleman besides nobleman.' (*Vercelli Book, Andreas*, 360, in Krapp 1932)

There are four occurrences of *be* and *side* in the DOE corpus, and they are given in (118). They all have a genitive demonstrative or possessive preceding the dative singular noun *sidan*.

(118)   a.   *duru ðu setst **be ðære sidan***
             door you put by its side-DAT.S
             'You will put the door in the side.' (Genesis 6.16, in Crawford 1922: 101)
        b.   *be heora sidan næbben*
             'didn't have by their side'
             (*Rule of Benedict*, 22.10, in Schröer [1885–1888] 1964: 47)
        c.   *be his sidan*
             'by his side' (*Chrodegang of Metz*, 12.20, in Napier 1916: 23.8)
        d.   *be þære sidan*
             'by their side' (*Monasterialia indicia*, 9.57, from Kluge 1885: 118–129)

In the same DOE corpus, there are three instances of prepositional use of *beside(n)*. Sentences (118a) and (119a and 119b) are from the same eleventh-century manuscript. The latter, however, have been added by a later hand (probably the late twelfth century). This puts the one word innovation of (119) around 1100. Notice that *side* is preceding the object; the Case may still be dative.

(119)   a. ***beside þan** wæs adam 7 eue* . . .

      'Next to that were Adam and Eve . . . '

      (Genesis, note 5, in Crawford 1922: 419)

    b. *on ane munte **beside paradise***

      'on a mountain next to paradise'

      (Genesis, note 18, in Crawford 1922: 421)

    c. *þat lond **besiden Thrandestone***

      'the land near Thrandeston'

      (*Will of Thurketel*, in Whitelock 1930: 68.14)

This word order may suggest that *side(n)* is taking the place of the demonstrative, as in (120), or has already been reanalyzed with the P.

(120)

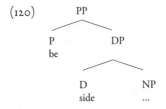

In early Middle English, the one- and two-word instances increase suddenly, compared to Old English, as I'll show by looking at Layamon, as in (121). There remain an amazing number of variants, although only *bi*, not *be* as in (118) and (119), is used.

(121)   *þer fæht Baldulf **bi siden** his broðer*

    'There fought Baldulf besides his brother.' (Layamon, *Brut*, Caligula, 10682, in Brook & Leslie 1963)

Layamon's Caligula version is one of the early texts showing many instances. It has twenty-six instances of a form of *besides* as a preposition or postposition, written as either one or two words.[12] Note that Brook and Leslie's (1963) edition has a hyphen whenever the adposition and *side* occur next to each other. The original manuscript doesn't have hyphens and I have therefore taken the hyphens out. I have grouped the two-word sequences in (122) and the one-word ones in (123). I have not looked at the adverbial types such as (124). Examples (122)–(125) all come from the version of Layamon's *Brut* in Brook and Leslie (1963).

---

12. In addition to *bi*, other prepositions are used, e.g., *on, a, an*, and *to*, but I ignore those here.

(122) a. i. *bi Corineus siden*

'by the side of Corineus' (Caligula, 731)

ii. *bi his side*

'by his side' (Caligula, 10547)

iii. *bi his siden*

'by his side' (Caligula, 12854)

iv. *bi weste siden*

'on the west side' (Caligula, 10880)

v. *bi þæs kinges side*

'at the side of the king' (Caligula, 4640)

vi. *bi his luft side*

'by his left side' (Caligula, 12207)

vii. *bi þere norð side*

'on the north side' (Caligula, 12234)

viii. *bi þire side*

'by your side' (Caligula, 10695)

ix. *bi þere sæ side*

'by the seaside' (Caligula, 12807)

x. *bi mire side*

'by my side' (Caligula, 3929)

b. i. *bi siden Scotlonde*

'toward Scotland' (Caligula, 8429)

ii. *bi side Scot londe*

'by the border of Scotland' (Caligula, 6200)

iii. *bi siden his broðer*

'beside his brother' (Caligula, 10682)

iv. *bi siden his iferen*

'beside his companions' (Caligula, 12982)

c. i. *heom bi sides*

'besides them' (Caligula, 15814)

ii. *heom bi siden*

'beside them' (Caligula, 5349)

(123) a. i. *bisides þere burh*

'outside the borough' (Caligula, 7761)

ii. *bisiden Amberesburi*

'beside Amesbury' (Caligula, 8176)

iii. *Bisiden Allemaine*

'beside Almaigne' (Caligula, 14667)

iv. *biside þere Humbre*

'alongside the Humber' (Caligula, 11077)

v. *bisides Scotlonde*

'alongside Scotland' (Caligula, 5162)

vi. *biside Baðe*

'beside Bath' (Caligula, 10706)

vii. *bisides Bælʒes-ʒate*

'beside Billingsgate' (Caligula, 7519)

b. i. *heom bisides*

'beside them' (Caligula, 13500)

ii. *me biside*

'beside me' (Caligula, 5391)

iii. *Brennes bisides*

'by the side of B' (Caligula, 2584)

(124) *to his iueren bisiden*

'to his comrades by (his) side' (Caligula, 13356)

The difference between (122a) and (122b) is one of Case marking and word order. They correspond to the Old English (118) and (119) respectively: *side* appears to be a noun in (122a) and *be side(n)* a preposition in (122b). The Case on *siden* is much reduced from the Old English. The preposed pronouns (and possibly) names in (122c) and (123b) show that there may be a difference between full phrases and pronominal heads and names, that is, D elements. As a result, (125a) and (125b) are unattested.

(125) a. %besides me/heom/Corineus
       b. %be siden me/heom/Corineus

This could mean that D on its own must incorporate into the P by adjoining to the latter's left. This optional postpositional use of *besides* does not occur in all texts, as (126) shows.

(126) *ða com on angel of heuene to hem, and stod **bisides** hem*

'Then came an angel from heaven to them and stood besides them'

(Trinity College Homilies [c. 1200], 31, from *OED*)

Examples (122c) and (123b) do not occur in Old English, nor does *besides* with an *-s*. The latter form looks like the adverbial genitive also found in *once, twice, hwiles*, and so on. I think it means that *-sides* in *besides* is never a noun, as the unattested (127) indicates, but an adposition. In the constructions in (122a), *side(n)* is still nominal.

(127) %bi his sides

The basic change concerning *beside* is represented in (128), with a reanalysis of the semantic features of the noun *side* as grammatical, possibly via D to P.

(128)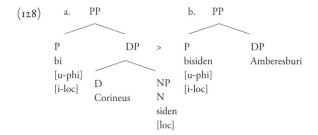

Svenonius (2006: 74) speculates on the origin of these prepositions and assigns a more elaborate structure to (128b), with *bi* in place and *side* in an axial part head. I think that may be the case in more recent innovations, such as *on top of, in front of* where the noun is less nominal. Svenonius's argument for having *side* as axial part is that then *beneath*, *between*, and so on then fit in where the *neath*, *tween* are not nouns but can be axial parts. Even if *side* turns out to be an axial part, I think the change to (128b) is one of conflation of several heads, as Waters (2009) argues.

The change from noun to preposition (and then to semantic Case) is one where the noun (e.g., *casa*) may be reanalyzed as D first. The change involved is a good example of Late Merge. In terms of features, the spatial/locative features are reanalyzed from semantic to interpretable.

5.3 FROM (CO(N))VERB TO ADPOSITION AND SEMANTIC CASE

I now examine the verbal origins of dependent markers for the noncore arguments. There are two main verbal sources, serial verbs and participles. Serial verbs on their way to becoming prepositions are typically called coverbs and participles headed that way are called converbs.

5.3.1 Serial Verbs

I'll first discuss some terminology, examples of serial verbs and coverbs/prepositions, and an analysis using the framework of Baker (1989) and Stewart (2001). Lord (1993) provides some of the background on their origins.

Coverbs occur in the Niger-Congo languages such as Twi, Efik, Ijo, Tagbana, and Zande, in American languages such as Lakhota (Pustet 2000), in many creoles, for example, Sranan, Saramaccan, and Negerhollands, in the Tibeto-Burman family, as in Lahu and Burmese, in Oceanic languages such as Pulawat, Jabêm, Ulithian, and in many others, according to Pawley (1973: 142–147), Lichtenberk (1985), Lord (1993), and Heine &and Kuteva (2002: 149–151).

In a serial verb construction, two or more verbs are juxtaposed in one clause and the verbs share a subject or object as well as TMA and negative markings. The clause lacks complementizers or coordinators. Examples of serial verbs from Yoruba are given in (129) and (130), where in (129) the subject is shared and in (130) the aspect marker, subject, and object are shared. In (131), from Ewe, the negative is shared as well. The serial verbs are in bold.

(129) *Olú* **sáré** **lọ** *sí* *Ìbàdàn*   Yoruba
      Olu   run   go   to   Ibadan
      'Olu went to Ibadan quickly.'

(130) *Adé* *ń*   ***ra*** *ęran* *ję*   Yoruba
    Ade PROGR buy meat eat

    'Ade is buying meat and eating it.'

    (from http://www.africananaphora.rutgers.edu/Grammar-Yoruba.pdf)

(131) *Nye* *me* ***fle*** *agbale* ***na*** *Ama* *o*   Ewe
    1S NEG buy book give Ama NEG

    'I did not buy a book for Ama.'

    (Agbador 1994: 117)

In sentences with a shared locative or object, such as in Yoruba (130) and Ewe (131), one of the verbs could be reanalyzed as a marker of that locative or object rather than an actual verb and this occurs frequently.

    Additional examples of coverbs are the Chinese verb *dao* 'arrive' in (132) that is used as preposition 'to', and the Thai *haj* 'give' in (133), also used as a preposition.

(132) *ta* ***dao*** *Zhongguo* *qu* *le*   Chinese
    he to China go PF

    'He went to China.' (Heine & Kuteva 2002: 45)

(133) *Dɛɛŋ* *sɔɔn* *leeg* ***haj*** *Sudaa* ***haj*** *phyan*   Thai
    Dang teach arithmetic give Suda give friend

    'Dang taught arithmetic to Suda for his friend.' (Bisang 1998: 771)

The change from verb to adposition can be seen as a reduction of features, as in (134) for the Chinese verb *dao*. After I introduce some structures for serial verbs, I come back to this sentence.

(134) *dao* 'arrive'   >   *dao* 'to'
    [move, direction]   [i-direction] (or [i-T])

The coverb/preposition can be the source for semantic Case. Blake (2001: 164) combines semantic Case and the DOM *ba* in table 5.5; they have their origin in verbs.

    Durie (1988) examines serial verbs and coverbs in the Oceanic languages. The dependent markers show quite some variety among the related languages, showing recent change. For instance, the instrumental is often marked by a preposition, such as *nɛ* in Ambrym, *nga* in Jabêm, *eni* in Paama, and *ngan* in Pulawat. Only in the latter can the instrumental "also be used independently as a verb" (Durie 1988: 7), as in (135).

(135) *wo* *pwe* ***ngan***-*iy-ay* *efor*   *suupwa*   Puluwat
    you Hortative give-TR-1S cigarette

    'Give me a cigarette.' (Durie 1988: 7)

Pustet (2000) argues that Lakhota postpositions derive from serial verbs, and Pustet (2008) argues that these postpositions also appear as (semantic) Case affixes. Examples are given in (136) and (137).

(136) *thí-ki*   ***ópta*** *ibláble*   Lakhota
    house-DEF through 1S.go

    'I went through the house.' (Pustet 2008: 270)

TABLE 5.5

V to P in Mandarin

	Verbal Meaning	P/Case Use
ba	'hold'	Object
gei	'give'	Dative
dao	'arrive'	Allative
gen	'follow'	Comitative
yong	'use'	Instrumental
zai	'be at'	Locative
cong	'follow'	Ablative

Adapted from Blake 2001: 164

(137) **thi-ópta**   *ibláble*   Lakhota
       house-through   1S.go

 'I went through the house.' (Pustet 2008: 271)

Pustet discusses the stress, marked in (136) and (137). Postpositions carry independent stress but affixes will carry whatever the word structure demands.

For an analysis of SVCs, I will use Baker (1989), Baker and Stewart (1999), and Stewart (2001). They distinguish two main types of serial verb constructions, the consequential and the resultative. The consequential merges two vPs, as in (138) for (139), and the resultative merges two Vs as in (143) for (144). (I am leaving out the Spec vP, the position where the agent originates.) In the consequential one, the two Vs move to their corresponding light verbs.

(138)

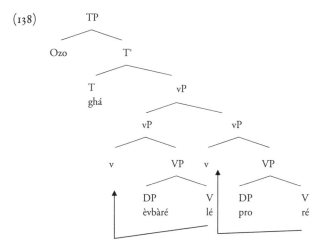

(139) *Òzó*   *ghá*   *(tòbórè)*   *lé*   *èvbàré*   *ré*   Edo
       Ozo   FUT   by.self   cook   food   eat

 'Ozo will by himself cook the food and eat it.' (Baker & Stewart 1999: 13)

In the resultative construction, two verbs are conjoined but only one V moves to the v position, as in (140). The resulting word order is similar to that in (139) but not the interpretation.

(140)

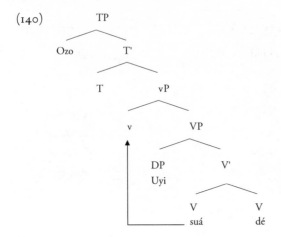

(141) Òzó   suá   Úyì   dé   Edo
      Ozo   push Uyi   fall

'Ozo pushed Uyi, causing him to fall.' (Baker & Stewart 1999: 18)

The resultative construction in (140) is relatively easy to reanalyze so that the first verb in the series is seen as contributing to the cause and to the agent/causer theta role. This change of *suá* from V to v is one of Late Merge (similar to *ba* in Mandarin). It is of course also analyzable in terms of a loss of features from a full verb to a light verb and so on.

A consequential serial verb can be the source of grammaticalization also. The Chinese coverb construction mentioned earlier, and repeated from (132) as (142), could originally have had the structure in (143) (where *ta* originates as the specifier of the highest vP).

(142) ta   **dao**   Zhongguo   qu   le   Chinese
      he   to   China   go   PF

'He went to China.'

(143)

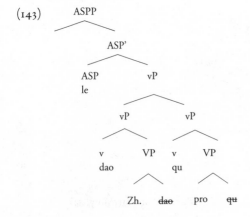

Since the two vPs are independent, there may be a reanalysis, namely of *dao* as the higher v and *qu* as the lower V, as shown in (144).

(144)

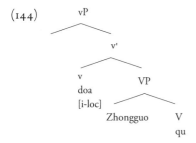

Thus, if we use the examples of serial verbs being reanalyzed as coverbs, we can formulate the coverbal cline as in (145). It is unclear to me at the moment how and if the reanalysis to a preposition takes place.

(145)   The Verbal Case Cline

V	>	v	>	P
[move, finish]		[i-loc]	>	??

5.3.2 Converbs

I'll first discuss some terminology and then give some examples of converbs. Many of these remain verbal or prepositional and do not (yet) mark semantic Case. The exception is the South Asian root *ker*, which some have argued has become a dependent marker in the shape of *ki/ka/ke*. Another example is the development of the topic markers in English.

Converbs involve nonfinite subordinate verbs that function inside adverbials. Haspelmath (1995: 3–7) includes nonfinite in his definition, noting that nonfiniteness may differ across languages. He distinguishes three kinds of converbs depending on whether the subject cannot be expressed, must be expressed, or can optionally be expressed. Converbs are sometimes referred to as conjunct participles or adverbial participles and exemplified in (146) to (148) from Finnish, Tatar, and Balochi. As the gloss to (146) indicates, English has them as well.

(146)   *Kaatu-essa-**an***   *Maija*   *satutt-i*   *jalkansa*   Finnish
fall.over-CONV-3S   Maija   hurt-PST.3S   leg
'When falling over, Maija hurt her leg.' (http://www.ling.helsinki.fi/uhlcs/
LENCA/LENCA-2/information/datei/12-greed.pdf)

(147)   *Janggyr bet-**kach**,*   *bala*   *uram-ga*   *chyq-ty*   Tatar
rain   finish-CONV child   street-DAT   go.out-PST.3S
'After it had stopped raining, the child went out.'
(http://www.ling.helsinki.fi/uhlcs/LENCA/LENCA-2/information/datei/
12-greed.pdf)

(148) | *Guda* | *duz* | ***thartho*** | *akhta* | *wathi* | *logh-a* | Balochi
  | then | thief | return-CONV | came | himself | house-to |

'The thief then returned home.' (Gilbertson 1923: 22)

Converbs are typical for Finno-Ugric (Finnish [146]), Altaic (Tatar [147] and Korean), Indo-European (Balochi [148] and English), Dravidian, and Tibeto-Burman. They have frequently been studied, as in Old Turkish by Gabain (1941: 135–143), in French and English by Haspelmath (1995), in Marathi by Pandharipande (1990), and in Nepali and Maithili by Bickel, Yadava, and Bisang (1999). In many of these languages, the form is (still) quite verbal.

Which original converbs are now clearly marking semantic Case? Künnap (1971: 139) suggests that the instrumental ending in the Samoyedic languages derives from a participial form of the auxiliary 'be', as well as in Hungarian (1971: 149) and Steever (1987: 736) mentions the Dravidian adposition *parttu* 'toward' as deriving from the converb 'looking at' and the Sanskrit *sahita* 'with' from the participle of 'join'. These changes are frequent, yet not as regular and predictable as some other changes. I will consider two instances in more detail, one whose development is not completely clear to me, and another where change is very slow.

The consensus about the development of the Urdu/Hindi converb *kar* (from the verb meaning 'to do') seems to be that it changed from participial *kar* to genitive Case marker. An alternative analysis is that the participial was reanalyzed as the oblique and definite object marker *ko*, and though that has been argued, it is no longer the majority opinion (although see the recent Kulikov 2006: 26). I'll discuss these two options further next.

Urdu/Hindi and many other Indo-European languages in Asia use the verb *karna* 'to do' as a regular verb though it is usually a light verb. Its root *kar* is also used as a converb, as in (149); see, for example, Kellogg (1893: 341). Platts ([1873] 1967: 134) calls the construction in (149) the "past conjunctive participle" and recognizes different forms: *-ke, -e, -ker*, and *ker-ke*. A relatively complex example from Hindi is given in (150), with the two converbs in bold. This example also provides instances of the genitive *ki* and the object marker *ko*, markers that could have developed from the converb.

(149) | *ghar* | *aa-**kar*** | *me* | *nee* | *khaanaa* | *khaayaa* | Urdu/Hindi
  | home | come-CONV | I | ERG | food | ate |

'Having come home, I ate some food.'

(150) | *Sultan* | *nee* | *Rehan* | *ko* | *apne* | *pad* | *see* | *hata-**kar*** | Hindi
  | Sultan | ERG | Rehan | OM | REFL | post | from | remove-CONV |

| *usee* | *Badayu* | *ki* | *jagir* | *de-**kar*** | *udhar* | | *ravana* |
| 3S | Badayu | of | jagir | give-CONV | there | | departed |

kar-di-yaa.
make-for-3S

'The sultan removed Rehan from his (Rehan's) office and, giving him the Badayun jagir, sent him there.' (Hook 1990: 331)

Butt (1997) adds an interesting twist to this story, arguing that the *kar* converb is relatively recent, and that the Sanskrit converb was a verb in *-tva(ya)/ya*, as in (151).

(151) | *stríyam* | *drs-**tvaya*** | *kitavám* | *tatapa* | Sanskrit
       | woman | see-CONV | gambler | distress-PF |

'Having seen the woman, the gambler is distressed.'

(*Rigveda* 10.34.11, Whitney [1889] 1967: 358, from Gary Miller, p.c.)

In Urdu/Hindi, this ending became optional and we therefore have (152) with the endless *gaa*.

(152) | *naadyaa* | *gaa* | *uthii* | Urdu/Hindi
       | Nadya | sing | rise |

'Having sung, Nadya got up' or 'Nadya burst into song.'

Butt remarks (1997: 6) that "this form of the adverbial participial appears to be falling into disuse in Urdu/Hindi, as there is another, preferred, form available in which the conjunction *kar/ke*, . . . is attached to the embedded verb," that is, (149).

In addition to *-tva(ya)/ya*, Kulikov (2006: 25–26) mentions another converb in Rigvedan Sanskrit, as in (153), derived from a verb meaning 'to grasp'.

(153) | *puusáá* | *tvaa* | *itó* | *nayatu* | *hasta-**grhya*** | Sanskrit
       | Pusan | you | from-here | lead-3S-IMPF | hand-grasp-CONV |

'Let Pusan lead you from hear by the hand (=having grasped your hand).' (*Rigveda* 10.85.26, from Gary Miller, p.c.)

This form never "caught on" but could have become analyzed as a Case marker.

To come back to the grammaticalization of the converb *ker*, Payne (1995: 296) asserts that the genitive marker *ka/ki/ke* in Urdu/Hindi, as in (154), derives from this root or participle *ker* of the verb *kerna* 'to do' (or 'be' and 'give').

(154) | *us* | *aadmi* | ***ke*** | *gher* | Urdu
       | that | man | of | house | 'that man's house'

He bases this assertion on Chatterji (1926: 767), who notes possible Dravidian influence for this use. This would mean that a converb is now a marker of possessive Case. To me this scenario, though now generally accepted, seems doubtful and I will provide the (older) alternative.

As mentioned earlier, Urdu has a marker for definite objects, namely *-ko* (also used for datives). Kellogg (1893) looks for the origin of *ko* in the same Sanskrit participle *krta* 'make'. However, in a later edition (Kellogg 1938: 130), Kellogg follows work by Hoernle and Beames in deriving *ko* from a Sanskrit locative noun *kakshe* 'side', so a nominal rather than a converbal root. Platts's ([1884] 1930) dictionary agrees that the oblique object marker *ko* derives from a postposition marking the dative and accusative in Old Hindi through *kahan*, *kahun*, and other forms. McGregor (1968: 184–185), discussing a medieval northern dialect of India, notes *kahum* as an object marker. If this scenario is correct, the development into the object marker would be very similar to Chinese *ba*, discussed earlier.

Some scholars have seen the Hindi/Urdu converb *ker* as the precursor of either the genitive Case marker *ka/ke/ke* or the oblique marker *ko*. One could think of these changes in terms of a verbal cline, as in (145), where a verb with semantic features is reanalyzed as a semantic marker. Since the exact details of the reanalysis are still debatable, I will refrain from a precise formulation and turn to converbs in English.

Kortmann (1992: 438) shows how English verbs, in the shape of participles, become prepositions (and that some of these develop into complementizers). Table 5.6 lists a few of these. Some originate as present participles and some as past participles. This is true in related languages too, such as Dutch, German, and French. Kortmann says they are quite marked as prepositions, due to use in specialized styles, morphological complexity, ambiguous categorial status, and lack of preposition stranding.

Huddleston and Pullum (2002: 610–611) add *barring, counting, including, pertaining to, given, touching, excluding, regarding, respecting, saving*, and *granted* to this list. They distinguish between verbal and prepositional use in the following way. The participle is verbal if one can think of an elided subject, as in (155), and prepositional if one cannot, as in (156). Other distinctions involve adding an auxiliary or adverb, possible in the verbal use, as in (157), but not in the prepositional use, as in (158).

(155)   **Facing** powerful political pressure in Washington for reductions in the defence budget, **the Pentagon** was also keen to overcome the embarrassing memories of the chaotic invasion of Grenada in 1983. (BNC-AAB 239)

(156)   **Concerning** the request you make that I would allow these being copied—; I have no power either to refuse or comply—(BNC-HRB 124)

(157)   **Having** unhappily **faced** powerful pressure, the Pentagon . . .

(158)   *__Having concerned__ the request . . .

The function of the participial is often as an adverbial of space, time, exception, inclusion, topic, concession, and accord. According to Kortmann (1992: 441–442), many of the participles are originally verbs of position (*pend, hang, face, stand*), motion (*follow, (a)go*), duration (*during, continuing*), vision (*seeing, considering*), and agreement (*granted, admitting, according*). Kortmann (1992: 443) provides a functional explanation for this: English particularly lacked prepositions of exception and topic, hence the popularity of verbal prepositions expressing these functions.

Let's examine one such participle more closely, namely that based on the verb *consider*, borrowed from French in the late fourteenth century. Almost as soon as it is borrowed, it is used in its participial shape. Most of these early instances of the participial form of *considering* are ambiguous as to whether they are verb or preposition, as in (159). This example is from Chaucer and is the first use of *considering* as preposition in the *OED*.

(159)   And gentilly I preise wel thy wit, Quod the ffrankeleyn, *__considerynge__ thy yowthe*, So feelyngly thou spekest, sire.

'And gently I praise well your wit, said the Franklin, considering your youth, so feelingly you speak, Sir.' (Chaucer, "Franklin's Tale Prologue," 3)

TABLE 5.6

From V to P (adapted from Kortmann 1992)

Verbal				Prepositional
facing	considering	according to	during	past
preceding	failing	allowing for	except	ago
succeeding	following	owing to	concerning	

The use of *consider* and *considering* is frequent in Chaucer, and especially in his *Astrolabe* (from 1391); examples are given in (160) and (161).

(160)   **Considere** wel that I ne vsurpe nat to haue fownde this werk of . . .

'Consider well that I don't claim to have discovered this work of . . .' (Chaucer, *Astrolabe*, "Prologue")

(161)   And in his herte he caughte of this greet routhe, **Considerynge** the beste on every syde

'And in his heart, he found great pity, considering the best on every side.' (Chaucer, "Franklin's Tale," 1520–1521)

In other early instances from the *OED*, the HC-ME3, and the *Paston Letters, consider* is used as a regular verb, as in (162), as well as a present participle that functions as complementizer, as in (163) and (164). The latter is fairly frequent in the *Paston Letters*.

(162)   that ȝe wole **considere** how that I pursuede diuerse billes by fore oure liege lord kyng henry (1414 petition)

(163)   for this mater touchyth hem, **consideryng** that they have be-gonne. (*Paston Letters* [1452], 45, in Davis 1971: 71)

(164)   to kepe the seid maner with fors, **consideryng** he hath be in possession iij yere and more (*Paston Letters* [1462], 65, in Davis 1971: 115)

Thus, *considering* was a C (and P) almost from the time it first appeared. Since then it has not changed much.

The change from V to P to C can be related to the ending on the participle going from [iF] > [uF], in accordance to Feature Economy. If we assume that the English converbal *-ing* is connected to the (interpretable) aspect features, a reanalysis to preposition would entail a loss of these features. This explains why a converb is never an infinitive.

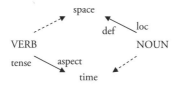

FIGURE 5.2. Anchoring nouns and verbs in space and time

6. Case Cycles and Economy: A Conclusion

In considering the origin of dependent marking, I have focused on grammatical and semantic marking. The change from semantic to grammatical Case is not literally such a change, even though it is often portrayed that way. Semantic Case may be lost (as happened in Old English) and a new marker may arise that we call Case for convenience; its source is always lexical (N or V). Grammatical Case is somewhat different since it is related to specificity marking. Ultimately, that too derives from a deictic source but through a demonstrative.

Arguments need to be located in space and time and that's what structural Case and tense do. I have represented that as [T], [loc], and [ASP], adapting work by Pesetsky and Torrego. Structural Case expresses definiteness, measure, tense, and aspect. As expected under a Feature Economy model, the origin of the markers can be found in location/deixis. The grammatical Case cycle is one where a demonstrative has an interpretable [i-loc] feature that is reanalyzed as an uninterpretable [u-T] feature.

Figure 5.2 is a visual representation of the connection between space and time, indicating that the link between nouns and space and verbs and time is the strongest, but that once in a while a verb is marked for location and a noun is marked for time.

I'll summarize some of the ideas from previous chapters and this chapter in the following points. (1) Subject and object agreement crucially involve phi features. (2) Case on the grammatical subject is grammaticalized definiteness marking. (3) Most Case on the grammatical object is also definiteness marking. (4) Inherent Case is the result of a reanalysis of the location and time features of a V, N, and ADV, via an adpositional stage.

6

THE DP CYCLE

AS WE HAVE seen in the previous chapter, definiteness and specificity can be expressed in a number of ways, through position, structural Case, verbal aspect, and of course through a determiner. In this chapter, I examine changes in determiner systems. Demonstratives are involved in cyclical changes by becoming articles and later class or Case markers (see Greenberg 1978 and Lyons 1999). This involves the grammaticalization of deictic features. For instance, the Old English masculine demonstrative pronoun *se* develops into the definite article *the*. When the demonstrative is renewed, it is often done so through a locative adverb, as in English with the adverb *there/here* (see Brugè 1996).

The changes from demonstrative to article can easily be expressed using a determiner phrase, where the demonstrative is in the specifier position (possibly having moved there) and the article is the head. I will focus on cyclical changes involving the DP rather than definiteness, the more so since there are languages and language families, such as Salish (Matthewson 1998), where definiteness and specificity, scholars have argued, are not part of the determiner system. The structural changes involved in the cycle are from specifier to head to affix of the DP, not surprising given changes described in earlier chapters. Again, I will put these changes in terms of Feature Economy: semantic features are reanalyzed as interpretable and then uninterpretable features. The cycle involves changes both in syntactic position, feature content, and semantic function; I focus on the former two.

In section 1, I first briefly review some views on definiteness and specificity, the structure of the DP, and the (definite) DP cycle. I assume a DP even if a language doesn't have articles. In sections 2 through 8, I look at different language families starting with Indo-European in sections 2 and 3 since so much is known about this family. Each language corresponds to a different stage of the cycle, but by looking at the languages in a family, cyclical change can be seen in some. Some languages are just grouped for convenience, not because of typological or genetic classifications. Uralic is represented in section 4 by Finnish and Hungarian and section 5 examines some families of North America. Section 6 discusses the DP cycle in

Austronesian, section 7 in Afro-Asiatic and Niger Congo, and section 8 looks at creoles. As in previous chapters, I argue that certain grammatical features are lost in this cycle and then replaced by new semantic ones.

1. Definiteness, the DP, and the DP Cycle

I first examine definiteness and specificity in nominals very briefly, and then turn to a structural representation of the nominal in the form of a DP as well as a discussion of the DP cycle.

1.1 DEFINITENESS AND SPECIFICITY

Lots has been written about the difference between definiteness and indefiniteness, and between specificity and nonspecificity. Definite *the* in English is used in familiar contexts where both the speaker and hearer know the referent. Uniqueness is an aspect of definiteness as well, as Russell (1905) argued. Specificity can be defined through identifiability or, as in Frawley (1991: 69), as "the uniqueness of the entity," for example, a particular man in (1), not just any man.

(1)   I'm looking for **a man** who speaks French. (Frawley 1991: 69)

Specificity is relevant for a number of grammatical phenomena, such as whether to use indicative or subjunctive in Spanish in (2). The indicative is used for a specific man in (2a) and the subjunctive for a nonspecific man in (2b).

(2)   a. *Busco*   *a un*   *hombre*   *que*   **habla**   *francés*   Spanish
           look-I   for a   man   who   speak-3S.IND   French

           'I am looking for a man who speaks French.'

       b. *Busco*   *a un*   *hombre*   *que*   **hable**   *francés*
           look-I   for a   man   who   speak-3S.SBJ   French

           'I am looking for any man who may speak French.'
           (Frawley 1991: 70)

Many languages mark specificity through morphological or syntactic means, namely definiteness marks specificity and indefiniteness nonspecificity. However, (1) shows that there is not a one-to-one relationship between the two since (1) is indefinite and yet specific. A very common way to mark definiteness is through a demonstrative or an article. The demonstrative and the article both have an identifying function, but demonstratives have an additional locational or temporal feature.

1.2 THE DP

Since the mid-1980s, a basic structure for nominals is a DP, as in (3).

(3)

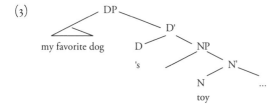

The specifier of the DP contains demonstrative pronouns or possessive nominals (the latter moved from a lower position), and the D head contains articles and possibly the genitive marker *'s* in English. There are restrictions on the co-occurrence of definite markers. Thus, in English, either the specifier or head can be present but not both, as (4a) shows, and *that*, but not *the*, appears independently, as (4b) and (4c) show.

(4)   a.   *That the dog loves their the toys
      b.   I saw that.
      c.   *I saw the

Cross-linguistically, if both a demonstrative and article appear, the order is [DEM ART N] or [ART N DEM], according to Rijkhof's (2002: 179–180) list of languages. This fits (3) well in that [DEM ART N], attested in Abkhaz, Guariní, and Hungarian, among others, is the base order, and [ART N DEM], attested in Berbice Dutch Creole and Galela, for example, has a specifier-last structure. The structure in (3) can be expanded with agreement and Case features, through a number phrase (NumP) or a kase phrase, for example, and I will do so where necessary.

   Adjectives are placed in between the determiner layer and the noun. They have been ana-lyzed in many different ways. Early on, the AP was an adjunct inside the NP, as in (5a); later, the AP was given its own projection, as in (5b).

(5)   a.   b.

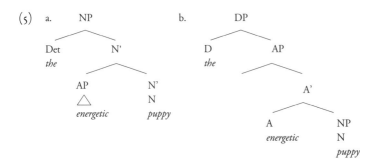

Many researchers, for example, Valois (1991), Laenzlinger (2000), and Cinque (2010), have split up the AP even further. For instance, quality adjectives such as *beautiful* linearly precede size adjectives such as *round*; in other words, they are merged later. Some also distinguish between inherent (Individual Level) and noninherent (Stage Level) adjectives. Chierchia and McConnell-Ginet (2000) use a division of intersective, subsective, and nonpredicating. To map the syntactic position of an adjective to a semantic meaning is a challenge and I will not attempt this here.

For Old Norse and Old English, I will use a DP structure based on Cinque (2010), Spamer (1979), Fischer (2000, 2006), and van Gelderen and Lohndal (2008), where there is a crucial difference between the nominal adjective (mainly prenominal in position and inflected as weak) and the verbal adjective (in both positions, inflected as strong). I argue that strong verbal adjectives originate as reduced relative clauses in postnominal position, and that prenominal weak adjectives are nominal. Cinque describes adjectival positions in Romance and Germanic and notes that they display some mirror effects. His suggestions for Germanic work well for Old English.

> In English (Germanic) the prenominal position is systematically ambiguous between the two values of each property [stage-level and individual-level, etc.], while the post-nominal one (when available) has only one value: stage-level, restrictive, implicit rela-tive clause, and intersective readings. . . . In Italian (Romance), it is instead the postnominal position that is systematically ambiguous between the two values of each property, while the prenominal one only has the individual-level, nonrestrictive, modal, nonintersective, absolute, absolute with superlatives, specific, evaluative, and NP dependent readings (2010: 17).

As to feature checking inside the DP, articles are clear probes located in D, as in (6a), with uninterpretable features checking the phi features of the noun. Since *the* has [u-phi], it cannot occur on its own, as shown in (4c). The demonstrative can occur on its own, as in (4b), and I therefore assume it has [i-ps] or [i-ps] and [i-loc], as shown in (6b) and (6c). Number in (6b) and (6c) has to be checked, as I have indicated,[1] but the exact probe on the demonstrative still has to be determined. That probe might be [u-#] with no probe in the NumP when a demonstrative appears.

(6)

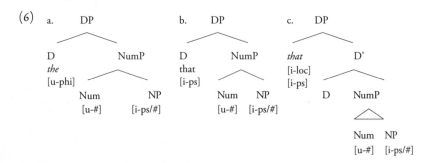

The English D in (6a) and (6b) would also have [u-T] or [u-ASP], valued by the T and v respectively; the DP in (6c) would not and would be expected in a nonstructural Case posi-tion. Not all languages might have all three possibilities.

I have not indicated gender in (6), but in languages with gender such as Dutch, German, Romance, or Hindi/Urdu, the D head would also probe for gender. I assume the same holds for adjectives: they have uninterpretable gender and number and look down the tree to value those features.

---

1. Diessel (1999: 25) shows percentages of inflection on demonstratives in sixty-eight languages that have inflec-tion and shows that number marking is the most frequent, followed by gender and Case.

In the next section, I suggest that the change from demonstrative to article is determined by (a) the shift from specifier to head, and (b) the (complete) loss of interpretable features (i-F). That would mean a reanalysis of (6c) as (6b) as (6a). The exact mechanism of probing/feature checking presented in (6) remains to be made more precise.

1.3 THE CYCLE AND ECONOMY

Greenberg (1978) describes a cycle where demonstratives become articles (stage 1) that in turn become nongeneric markers (stage 2) and finally noun class markers (stage 3). Greenberg's examples come from languages in the Niger-Congo family, and from Semitic and Indo-European. He emphasizes that the cycle "constantly generates concordial phenomena" (Greenberg 1978: 75). Diessel (1999) and Lyons (1999) expand on these stages and see the initial loss of the deictic character as crucial. As we have seen in the previous chapter, articles are also reanalyzed as Case markers, and demonstratives can be reanalyzed as finite complementizers, as we'll see in the next chapter.

The definiteness cycle can be represented as in (7). Using a DP structure, (7a) translates into (7b). The specifier becomes a head which subsequently disappears and is replaced by a new specifier. (7c) lists the changes involving the features.

(7) a. demonstrative >definite article >Case/nongeneric
     b. specifier   >head   >affix
     c. i-F   >u-F   (u-F)

Figure 6.1 shows these changes in tree form (although [6b] is not shown). In stage (a), the demonstrative has interpretable features, which are reanalyzed as uninterpretable in stage (b). Stage (c) shows the renewal of the features by means of an adverb.

Renewal of the demonstrative, as in stage (c), is frequent with locative adverbs, which (8) and (9) show, or with additional demonstratives, as in (10) and (11).

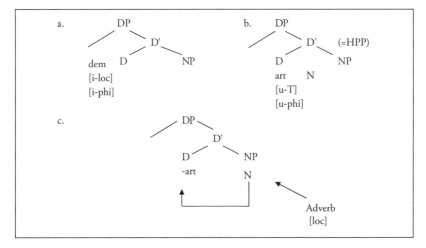

FIGURE 6.1. The DP cycle

(8) *die   man   **hier/daar***   Dutch
     that   man   here/there

(9) *den   **här/där**   mannen*   Swedish
     the   here/there   man-DEF

(10) *el   hombre   **este***   Spanish
     the   man   this

(11) *om-ul   **acesta***   Romanian
     man-the   this

As is known from the grammaticalization literature, when an element grammaticalizes, both
the source and the new element may survive. We see this in (10) and (11) and will see it in a
number of languages later.

The numeral is frequently reanalyzed as indefinite article, as in (12) from Kurdish, a Western Iranian language. In other Iranian languages, there are also indefinite affixes, such as in
Balochi (Royen 1929: 485).

(12) a. ***jek   mal***   Kurdish
         one   house
      b. *mal-**ək***

         'a house' (both from Lyons 1999: 95)

The Old English numeral *ane* corresponds to the Modern English *a(n)* and Sorbian has also
grammaticalized the numeral 'one' into indefinite marker. In Upper Sorbian, *jedyn* 'one' is
usually *jen* when used as article. This change can be represented as in (13a) (see Lehmann
2002: 46–47). The syntactic change, as in (13b), depends on one's theoretical assumptions on
what numerals are and where indefinite articles are in the DP. It could be expressed easily as
a cycle and through a loss of interpretable features as in (13c) (where F is number), though
this chapter will only consider definiteness and specificity marking:

(13) a. numeral   >   indefinite pronoun   >   indefinite article
      b. Q/A   >   D   >   zero
      c. i-F   >   u-F   >   zero

With this background on definiteness, the DP, and the DP cycle, we now turn to examples
of that cycle.

2. Indo-European: Germanic

As mentioned in the previous chapter, in Proto-Indo-European and Proto-Germanic, there
are no definite and indefinite articles, although there is evidence that the Case markers have
reanalyzed from earlier definiteness markers.[2] Germanic seems to have had many cycles,

---

2. Section 2 is based on material from van Gelderen (2007) and on van Gelderen and Lohndal (2008), though
the analysis is a little different.

however. For instance, Ringe (2006: 170) sees in the weak adjectival *-n* ending an original definite article (though Curme 1910: 441 and Lockwood 1968: 40 consider it a nominalizer). Other articles arise later, for example, in Old Norse, in early Middle English, and in High German (see, e.g., Demske 2001 and Philippi 1997 for the latter), mainly originating from demonstrative pronouns or adverbs.

The history of Scandinavian shows that demonstratives go through several cycles of figure 6.1. The complicating factor is the intricate nature of the DP with multiple definite layers. Demonstratives in the history of English are also complex but here I will simplify the structure as a DP. I end the section with some stages in other Germanic languages, for instance, Afrikaans, which analyzed Dutch demonstratives as articles and renewed the demonstratives through an adverb.

2.1 SCANDINAVIAN

The runic inscriptions from the fifth century on show very few demonstratives and no obvious articles. In Antonsen's (1975) set of early runic inscriptions, there are three demonstratives, (14) from the fifth century, (15) from the sixth century, and (16) from the seventh century.

(14) *wate   hali   **hino***   Old Norse
     wet   stone this
     'Wet this stone.' (Strøm stone, from Antonsen 1975: 54–55)

(15) *worte   **þat**   azina*   Old Norse
     'wrought this stone.' (Buskerud stone, from Antonsen 1975: 80–81)

(16) *warait   runaz   **þaiaz***   Old Norse
     wrote   runes   these
     'wrote these runes.' (Istaby stone; Antonsen 1975: 84)

In the nonrunic Old Norse texts, such as the *Poetic Edda* from the twelfth or thirteenth century, there are very still few markers of indefiniteness and definiteness, as the bare noun in (17) shows. The demonstrative pronouns *hinn* and *sa* (and their morphological variants) are typically used independently, as in (18) and (19).

(17) ***Byrði**   betri   berr-at   maðr   brautu at*   Old Norse
     burden   better bear-NEG   man   road there
     'A better burden may no man bear on wanderings (than great wisdom).'
     (*Edda, Hávamál*, 10)

(18) ***Hinn** er sæll er sér of getr lof . . .*   Old Norse
     'He is happy who (for) himself obtains fame.' (*Edda, Hávamál*, 8)

(19)   *Sá er sæll er sjalfr of á lof...*   Old Norse

    'He is happy who self possesses fame.' (*Edda, Hávamál*, 9)

Sentences (18) and (19) are very similar in structure and the pronouns *hinn* and *sá* refer to similar abstract persons, and both start a stanza. There is also an *inn* which is less independent since it only occurs before weak adjectives and nouns, as in (20) and (21). The form of the adjective is always the weak one, and this will feature in my analysis.

(20)   *at **ins** fróða Fjalars*   Old Norse
    with the-GEN wise-W Fjalar
    'with the wise Fjalar' (*Edda, Hávamál*, 14)

(21)   ***inn** vari gestr*   Old Norse
    the-NOM wise-W guest
    'the wise/knowing guest' (*Edda, Hávamál*, 7)

There is also a suffixed form of *inn* but these are rare (e.g., in *Hávamál*, there are 10 instances, as in [20], of independent *ins* but none of a suffixed form).

    The use of the demonstrative *sa* and its variants before a noun is less frequent in the *Poetic Edda* but does occur, as in (22).

(22)   *sökkðisk   síðan   **sá**   fiskr í mar*   Old Norse
    sank   then   that   fish in sea
    'and the fish sank into the sea' (*Edda, Hymniskviða*, 24).

In later texts, there are even more ways to express definiteness, as shown most recently by Faarlund (2004, 2007, 2009), Abraham and Leiss (2007), and Lohndal (2007). An independent definite article *(h)inn* continues to be used before a weak adjective as in (23), and the noun can be marked for definiteness, as in (24), when no adjective precedes the noun.[3] There can also be just a demonstrative pronoun, as in (25).

(23)   *ok   **hinn** síðasta vetr   er   hann var í Nóregi*   Old Norse
    and   the   last   winter   that   he was in Norway
    (*Bjarni's Voyage*, 41.8, from Gordon 1956)

---

3. Though Faarlund provides two instances of doubling that I don't discuss because they are rare:

(i)   ***ins** versta   hlutar**ins***   Old Norse
    the   worst-W   part-DEF
    'of the worst part' (*Bandamanna Saga*, 46.21, from Faarlund, 2004: 58)

(ii)   ***hinir**   beztu   menninn-**ir***
    the.MP.NOM   best-W   men-DEF
    'the best men' (*Konungs Skuggsiá*, 54.38, from Faarlund 2004: 58)

(24) *konung-ar-**nir***   Old Norse
      king-P-DEF
      'the kings'

(25) *ok*   *var*   ***þann***   *vetr*   . . .   Old Norse
      and   was   that   winter
      'and he was during that winter . . .' (*Fóstbræðra Saga*, 78.11, from Faarlund 2004: 82)

The article and demonstratives (both proximal and distal) in Old Norse are inflected for Case, gender, and number. Thus, *hinn* in (23) is a nominative singular masculine, *nir* in (24) is a plural masculine nominative, and *þann* in (25) is an accusative masculine singular.

   Having the demonstrative and article occur together is also possible, as in (26) to (28), and this could indicate that *it* is in the D head and the demonstrative *þat* in the specifier position of a DP, as I argue later. Notice again that the adjectival endings are weak:

(26) ***þat***   *it*   *helga*   *sæti*   Old Norse
      that   the   holy-W   seat
      'the holy seat' (Gordon 1956: 312)

(27) ***þau***   *in*   *storu*   *skip*   Old Norse
      those   the   big-W   ships
      'those big ships' (*Heimskringla* 1: 437.13, from Faarlund 2004: 82)

(28) ***þat***   *it*   *mikla*   *men*   *Brisinga*   Old Norse
      that   the   mighty-W   necklace (of Freyja)
      'the mighty Brisinga necklace' (*Thrym's Lay*, 13)

A possessive pronoun can also precede the article, as in (29), though of course a possessive precedes a noun regularly on its own, as in *þinn hamar* 'your hammer.'

(29) ***þitt***   *hitt*   *milda*   *andlit*   Old Norse
      your   the   mild-W   face
      'your mild face' (*Barlaams ok Josaphats Saga*, 187, from Faarlund 2004: 60)

Faarlund (2004, 2007) suggests a double DP for the sentences in (26) to (31) (one DP and one RP, for reference phrase). His main argument for the double structure is that a noun may appear before the demonstrative, as in (30) and (31). I argue that in these sentences the demonstrative (*þat* in [30] and *sa* in [31]) is a D head and that the preposed nominal is in the specifier of DP. The article *inn* is in a low position. Thus, demonstratives in Old Norse are ambiguous between specifier and head.

(30) *fé*   *þat*   *allt*   Old Norse
      money   that   all
      'all that money' (*Egil's Saga*, 232.9, from Faarlund 2007, 2009)

(31) **kvistr** sa inn fagri   Old Norse
      twig   that the fair

'that beautiful twig' (*Barð*, 3.8, from Faarlund 2007, 2009)

Building on recent work by Julien (2005), Lohndal (2007), and Roehrs (2009), I suggest
that the basic DP in Old Norse is as in (32), with the article *hitt* in a low position and the
weak (nominalized) adjective more like a compound, indicated by the Adj head. The demonstratives *sa, þat,* and *þau* are in the specifier or in the head.[4]

(32)

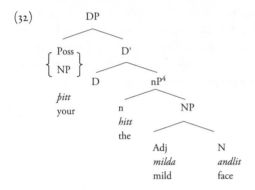

I have not found sentences with a possessive and a demonstrative (e.g., *þitt þat andlit* [your
that face] or *þat þitt andlit* [that your face]). I will take this absence to indicate that the possessive can also check deictic features (see Wood 2003, 2007b) and that its typical position is
(still) in the specifier position.

The DP in (32) has a specifier that can be occupied either by a possessive, as in (29), or a
nominal, as in (30) and (31). I assume that the demonstrative is analyzable as specifier, as in
(26), or as head D, as in (30), since there is evidence for both positions to the language
learner. The head position has the grammaticalized demonstrative. The n head is what
renders the noun root referential and this head can be joined by the head noun, as in (30).
When the (weak) adjective precedes the noun, *inn* plays a role in nominalizing the adjective. Nygaard (1906: 48) formulates the individual-level character of the weak adjective as
"[a]djektivet betegner da en bekjendt egenskab . . . eller en egenskap, der tillhører gjen-
standen efter dens natur og væsen" (the adjective denotes a known characteristic . . . or a
characteristic that belongs to the thing according to its nature). Prokosch (1939: 260) and
others similarly suggest that these weak adjectives "denote permanent quality," much like
the noun.

A (mainly postnominal) strong adjective is predicative and individualizes, and could
be represented as a reduced relative clause (see also Cinque 2010). A tree for strong
adjectives is given in (33), with the words of (35) below filled in. It is similar to the
structure in van Gelderen and Lohndal (2008), with the structure of the relative clause
undetermined.

---

4. The nP in (32) is used in parallel to the vP, i.e., in order to accommodate the argument structure of verbal
   nouns.

(33)

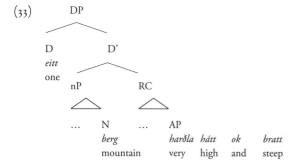

In the case of prenominal strong adjectives, the AP moves into a higher position (with the A in D picking up the strong inflection). The strong ending is often called the pronominal one.

The difference between the weak and strong adjectives explains why prenominal adjectives do not stack and are typically heads, not phrases. Postnominal adjectives can be phrasal, of course, as in (34) and (35).

(34) *ok   sá   þar   **mikinn**   her*
     and   saw   there big-S   army

     'and saw a big army there' (*Heimskringla* 2.229.7, from Faarlund 2004: 68)

(35) *eitt   berg   **harðla   hátt   ok   bratt***
     one   mountain   very   high   and   steep

     'one very high and steep mountain' (*Barlaams ok Josaphats Saga*, 47.36, Faarlund 2004: 95)

I'll now turn to features. When a demonstrative occurs on it own (and is in the specifier position), as in *Hinn er sæll* in (18), it has interpretable features that do not need to probe for a noun. I argued earlier that a D head has uninterpretable phi features and that the phrase in the specifier position has (mainly) interpretable features. The Old Norse uninterpretable phi features on D include number and gender and are valued by the noun's interpretable features. If a demonstrative with interpretable locative/deictic features is used, the D can be empty. As to the features of the n probe, they probe for phi features (in fact before the D does so) to ensure that the root is a noun (in Chomsky 1995, these would be categorial features).

In terms of the cycle, the historical development described here is what we would expect in terms of demonstratives being reanalyzed as articles. How about the nominalizer in n? At some point, let's say Proto–Old Norse, a locative adverb *hinn/hitt* 'here' is incorporated as part of the nP, as in *hali hino* 'stone this'. Then it is reanalyzed as a head and as a clitic nominal marker in Old Norse sentences such as (24). The latter is the origin of the Modern Norwegian and Swedish *-en/-et*, which Faarlund (2007) argues is an affix. Old Norse then renews its locative marker through a demonstrative, such as *sa, þat*, or *þann*, possibly appositive initially. Since these are deictic elements, a DP is triggered and they are incorporated as specifiers of the DP. Aspectual prefixes are also lost and this may have contributed to this reanalysis as well (see chapter 5). These demonstratives correspond to *det* and *den* in Modern Norwegian and Swedish (*det* for neuter nouns and *den* for the others). Examples of this later stage are modern Swedish (36) and (37).

(36) ***den** nya bok-**en***   Swedish
      the new book-the

(37) *bok-**en***   Swedish
      book-the 'the book'

Renewal of deixis in Scandinavian has two sources, one locative adverb that is incorporated into the DP in a low position and an appositive demonstrative pronoun that is incorporated quite high in the DP. Similarly, Dahl (2004: 178) argues that there are two grammaticalizations going on independently in Scandinavian but that external factors make the situation opaque. He says the suffix strategy in addition to a demonstrative, as in (36) from Swedish, is basically the option Scandinavian languages of the northeastern areas use and the prenominal demonstrative without nominal affix, as in (38), is the pattern the southwestern languages use (i.e., most Danish dialects). The pattern in (36) is commonly referred to as double definiteness. When no adjective occurs, as in (37) and (39), both varieties have an affix.

(38) ***det**   store   hus*   Danish
      the   big   house

(39) *hus-**et***   Danish
      house-the
      'the house'

From the point of view of the DP cycle, the northeastern situation represents the older stage where the head has not yet gone to zero and the southwestern situation gives evidence for the stage where the head has been replaced.

The analysis of the double definite constructions, as in (36), has remained controversial. Taraldsen (1990), Delsing (1993), and Julien (2005) provide different analyses. Julien accounts for the phenomenon of double definiteness in terms of an nP structure, where *–en/-et* are in n with the noun in N moving to n. If no modifier is present to block the movement of the nP to the specifier of DP, the nP moves to the specifier of the DP, as shown in (40).

(40)

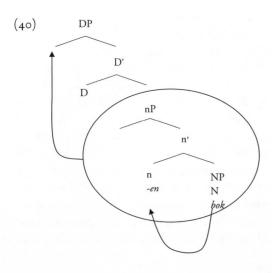

In this way, it is possible to see the *-en* as making a nominal out of the root *bok*. If an adjective is present, the AP that contains the adjective would be closer to the D and, not containing a definiteness feature, the AP would not be able to move to Spec DP. Hence, an expletive *den* would appear with adjectives.[5]

How does this work in the older stages, such as in (23)? I suggest that the weak adjective is inside the NP and that the *hinn/hitt* element precedes that weak adjective, as in (41).[6] In the spirit of Spamer and Fischer, this adjective is really a nominal, and I have therefore added another n to (32), resulting in (41).

(41)

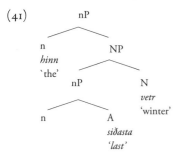

We have seen renewal of the definite marker (*h*)*it* by more deictic elements, such as *þat* in (26). With a possible erosion of the deictic element in (37) and (38), a renewal of demonstratives is indeed going on in the modern Scandinavian languages. Josefsson (2000: 738) mentions (42) and Bondi Johannessen (2006) argues that Norwegian encodes psychological deixis, for example, uncertainty about the hearer's knowing the person, in (43).

(42) *Känner   du   **han**   den   gamle   vaktmästeren*   Swedish
      know   you   he   the   old   janitor-DEF
      'Do you know the old janitor?'

(43) *Men   **hun**   søster-en   min   er   sånn* ...   Oslo Norwegian
      but   she   sister-DEF   my   is   like
      'But my sister is the kind ...'

There is of course also the adverb reinforcement with *där*, as in (44), and the use of a more specific *denna* in (45).

(44) *den   **där**   bok-en*   Swedish
      the   there   bok-DEF
      'that book'

(45) ***denna***   *bok(en)*   Swedish variety
      that   book-DEF
      'that book'

---

5. There are other alternatives. Roehrs (2009) has an article phrase (ArtP) above the nP, and his demonstrative moves from the specifier of the ArtP to that of the DP. Roehrs uses this to account for Old Norse, where both noun-demonstrative and demonstrative-noun orders occur. The modern languages would have lost the N-fronting option.

6. The glosses of 'that' and 'the' in (32) and of 'the' in (41) are for convenience; they may not be accurate.

We will see this type of renewal in other languages as well. In fast speech, the two demonstratives in (44) become one, according to Gisle Andersen[7] for her Bergen variety of Norwegian presented in (46).

(46) *den   der   bilen*   >   *denner   bilen*   Norwegian variety
      the   there   car-DEF   >   that/this   car-DEF

      'that/this car'

To summarize, Scandinavian has seen a number of changes in its DP. They can be accounted for through the Head Preference Principle and Late Merge of the adjectives or, alternatively, through Feature Economy. The latter also provides insight into the renewal: if a particular feature is uninterpretable, it will automatically find a renewal.

2.2 ENGLISH

There are many thoughts on how the demonstrative pronoun in English was reanalyzed as an article (some reviewed in McColl Millar 2000). In what follows, I'll extend the analysis for the demonstrative, article, and adjective given for Old Norse to Old English.

In Old English, there are no articles but there are demonstratives, such as *ða* before *æþelingas* in (47). This demonstrative refers back to an earlier *þeod cyninga* 'kings'. We have seen in section 2 of the previous chapter that demonstratives are a lot less frequent in Old English than articles are in Modern English.

(47) *hu   ða   æþelingas   ellen   fremedon*
      how   those-NOM.P   nobles-NOM.P   courage   did

      'how those nobles performed heroic acts.' (*Beowulf*, 3, in Klaeber [1922] 1941)

As in Old Norse, adjectives can be weak (definite) or strong (indefinite) with the weak ones in pre- or postnominal position or on their own, as in (48), and the strong ones in either pre- or postnominal position, as in (49), with (originally) indefinite or definite meaning. The situation is quite complex in Old English, as for example, Mitchell (1985: 1: 51–80) shows.

(48) *Ic þæm **godan** sceal for his modþræce madmas beodan.*
      I (to) the **good-W** (one) shall for his daring precious-things give

      'I'll give treasures to the good one for his daring acts.' (*Beowulf*, 384–385, in Klaeber [1922] 1941:)

(49) *þæt wæs **god** cyning*

      'That was a good-S king.' (*Beowulf*, 11, in Klaeber [1922] 1941)

In (48), *þæm* is in the specifier of the DP with interpretable features, and in (49), the adjective (or noun) moves to D, and checks the features.

Demonstratives occur together with possessives, as in (50). This shows the demonstrative is not yet article-like.

---

7. As reported in 1995 on Linguist List 6-799.

(50)   ***Se heora*** *cyning ongan ða singan 7 giddian*   Old English
         the their king began then to sing

         'Their king began to sing.' *(Orosius,* in Bately 1980: 35.14–15)

Tables 6.1 and 6.2 show the different forms. The masculine nominative *se* is the form that is reanalyzed as *the* and the neuter *þæt* is reanalyzed as the singular distal demonstrative *that.* Both of these changes occur first in the north (according to the *OED*). In addition, the plural *þa* ends up as *those.* Rupp (2008) and others have argued that *þæt* is the precursor of the reduced article *t'.* This could be the case and, toward the end of the section, I argue that the present-day demonstrative *that* is grammaticalizing again.

It is hard to determine when the article first appears in English. In the northern *Lindis-farne Gospels,* there is a nominative masculine *ðe/þe,* as in (51) and (52), but this may be a variant of *se,* since they are nominative forms.

(51)   *Herodes* ***ðe***   *cynig*
         Herod   the-NOM   king

         'King Herod' *(Lindisfarne Gospels,* Matthew 2.3, in Skeat [1881–1887] 1970)

(52)   *Cueð* *to* *him* ***ðe***   *hælend*
         said   to   him   the-NOM   savior

         'the savior said to him' *(Lindisfarne Gospels,* Matthew 9.15, in Skeat [1881–1887] 1970)

TABLE 6.1

Demonstratives in Old English

	Masculine	Feminine	Neuter	Plural
NOM	*se*	*seo*	*þæt*	*þa*
GEN	*þæs*	*þære*	*þæs*	*þara*
DAT	*þæm*	*þære*	*þæm*	*þæm*
ACC	*þone*	*þa*	*þæt*	*þa*

TABLE 6.2

Proximal Demonstratives in Old English

	Masculine	Feminine	Neuter	Plural
NOM	*þes*	*þeos*	*þis*	*þas*
GEN	*þisses*	*þas*	*þisses*	*þissa*
DAT	*þissum*	*þisse*	*þisum*	*þisum*
ACC	*þisne*	*þas*	*þis*	*þas*

Mitchell (1985: 1: 102) mentions the accusative *þe* in (53), which could be the first article.

(53) *Ða   geseah   ic **þe**   gedriht*
      then   saw   I   the   host/company

      'Then I saw that nation.' (*Daniel* 22, Junius, in Krapp 1931)

Wood (2003: 69–71) suggests two additional Old English ones (one from Bede's *Ecclesiasti-cal History* and one from *Appolonius of Tyre*). Generally, however, it is thought that the demonstratives are weakening phonologically by late Old English. The *OED* gives examples from the *Peterborough Chronicle* and the *Ormulum* as the first. In the late Old English (54), there is a *þe* instead of *þæs* and in the early Middle English (55), *þe* is very frequent.

(54) *Ic Wulfere gife to dæi Sancte Petre 7 þone abbode Saxulf 7 þa munecas of **þe** mynstre þas landes 7 þas wateres*
      I Wulfhere give to ... St Peter and the abbot Saxulf and the monks of the abbey the lands and the waters ... (*Peterborough Chronicle* [656], 40, in Thorpe 1861).

(55) *& gaddresst   swa **þe** clene corn All fra **þe** chaff togeddre*
      and gather-2S   so the clean wheat all from the chaff together

      'and so you gather the clear wheat from the chaff' (*Ormulum* [1485], in Holt 1878)

In (54), the demonstrative forms do not show the forms expected either, such as the accusative *þone* should be the dative *þæm* according to table 6.1.

More evidence for the changing status of the demonstrative can be found in data provided by Traugott (1992), Wood (2003, 2007a, 2007b), and others, namely that the possessive often precedes the demonstrative, as in (56a), even if in the original Latin there is no demonstrative. Wood (2007a, 2007b) argues that the demonstrative is in the head position by late Old English. One of her arguments is that toward the end of the Old English period, the possessive is in complementary distribution with the demonstrative, as is shown by the (100 to 150 years) later scribe's rendering of these sentences as (56b).

(56) a. ***his þone** onfangenan   lichaman*
          his that   received   body
      b. ***his** underfanzenan lichaman*

          'his received body' (*Gregory's Dialogues*, 155.9, from Wood 2007a: 181)

(57) a. ***min   þæt**   ungesælige   mod*
          my   that   unhappy   spirit
      b. ***min** ungesælige   mod*

          'my unhappy spirits' (*Gregory's Dialogues*, 4.9, from Wood 2007b: 355)

As Wood shows, of the sixteen Possessive-Demonstrative constructions that occur in both the earlier C-text and the later H-text, fifteen are replaced by just the demonstrative in the later text. The reason is, according to Wood, a reanalysis of the possessive between Old and Middle English from indefinite to definite features. In Old English, the possessive can be adjectival or originate from below the D to move to the specifier of DP if the demonstrative is (already) a head. The disappearance of the combination of possessive and demonstrative pronouns shows the possessive being reanalyzed as a D head. The complementarity means that both possessive and demonstrative are in the head D.

As noted in chapter 2, Traugott (1992: 173) and Kiparsky (2002) argue that *se* in (58) is a demonstrative that is used as third person 'he' with more topic shifting possibilities than the (regular) pronoun *he*.

(58)   **Hi** habbað mid **him** awyriedne engel, mancynnes feond, and **se** hæfð andweald...

   'They have with them corrupt angel, mankind's enemy, and he [the angel] has power over...' (Ælfric, *Homilies*, 2.488.14, from Traugott 1992: 171)

I agree with this scenario and, in chapter 2, phrased it in terms of deictic features. The pronoun, lacking clearly deictic features, can be used as a reflexive and is syntactically a clitic (according to Pintzuk 1996).

When, as I argue in this section, *se* reanalyzes as an article, schematized in (59a), it loses interpretable features. However, there are other shifts in the pronominal system. These other changes are presented in (59b). The Old English third person pronouns show an initial *h-*, but are very variable (*hi* can be singular and plural, etc.) and change in the late Old English period. Thus, a new third person feminine singular pronoun *she* and third person plural *they* appear first in the same texts as the articles first appear in. The *OED* has the first instance of *she* in the text that has the first clear articles, namely in (54), and *they* first appears in the same text as (55) does.[8]

(59)   Old English   Middle English
   a.   *se*   >   *the*
        [i-loc]/[i-phi]   [u-T]/[u-phi]
   b.   *he/hi*   is replaced by   *he*
        heo/ha   is replaced by   *she*
        hi/hie   is replaced by   *they*
        [i-phi]   [i-phi]/[i-loc]

The change represented in (59b) would go against Feature Economy. It is, however, often argued that the shift toward both a special feminine pronoun and a plural one were caused externally, through Scandinavian influence. Some texts, such as the northern *Ormulum*, have the definite article as well as the feminine and plural pronouns. The shift in (59b) is therefore not one where one lexical item gains features but one where a lexical item is replaced by another and causes a reorganization. These changes then enable the third person pronouns to shift topic and be more deictic.

The independent use of *se* in (58) stops, as Wood (2003: 69) also shows, and the third person pronoun loses its reflexive character. So when one of the demonstratives (the masculine singular) is reanalyzed as article, another (the neuter singular) is reanalyzed as the regular demonstrative. Replacing the independent demonstrative is the personal pronoun. Once

---

8. There are many other forms of demonstratives, but I give just the most frequent ones in (59).

the appears, it cannot be used independently and this is important in showing that it is in the head position: D on its own doesn't license an empty noun, or to put it in terms of features, uninterpretable features (in the head D) need interpretable features on the N.

Three other stages of the cycle can be found in the history of English, namely further reduction of *the* to *t(h)'* (and of *that* to *t'* in certain dialects), the renewal of the demonstrative by a locative, and the frequent use of *that* instead of *the* in spoken English. I'll start with the first.

In early Modern English, there is a stage with a definite clitic, as in (60a) and (60b).

(60) a. Morret's brother came out of Scoteland for **th'**acceptacion of the peax
          (*The Diary of Edward VI*, in Nichols 1963: 265)
      b. There's a Letter for you Sir:
          It comes from **th'** Ambassadours that was bound for England.
          (*The Diary of Edward VI*, Nichols 1963: 265)

These do not just occur before nouns that start in vowels, as (61) and (62), from Shakespeare's First Folio, show. The examples in (61) are before the consonant /b/ and the ones in (62) before /f/, but there are many more.

(61) a. When he was brought agen to **th'** Bar, to heare . . .
          (*Henry 8*, 2.1.31)
      b. Turne all to **th'** best: these Proclamations (*Winter's Tale*, 3.1.15)
      c. on certaine Speeches vtter'd By **th'** Bishop of . . . (*Henry 8*, 2.4.171)

(62) a. To **th'** fairenesse of my power. (*Coriolanus*, 1.9.72)
      b. Expos'd this Paragon to **th'** fearefull vsage (*Winter's Tale*, 5.1.153)
      c. She workes by Charmes, by Spels, by **th'** Figure (*Merry Wives*, 4.2.185)
      d. To **th'** fire ith' blood: be more abstenious,. . . (*Tempest*, 4.1.53)
      e. They'll sit by **th'** fire, and presume to know. (*Coriolanus*, 1.1.186)

One would expect the early Modern English stage to experience renewal, and we see quite a number of pronouns such as *them* being used as demonstratives, as in (63) and (64). According to the *OED*, this occurs from the sixteenth century on. From the eighteenth century on, we find (65) and (66).

(63) To Samaria and **them** partes (H. Clapham, *Bible History* [1596] 92, from *OED*, s.v. *them*)

(64) The warres and weapons are now altered from **them** dayes. (Barret, *Theor. Warres* [1598], 1.1.4, from *OED*, s.v. *them*)

(65) On leaving yours and Mr. B.'s hospitable House, because of **that there** Affair. (Richardson, *Pamela* [1742], 3.404, from *OED*, s.v. *there*)

(66) As for staying with **them there** French rascals, it was never the near. (*Ora and Juliet*, [1811], 4.93)

Standard English never develops into a stage where the article is weakened and needs a new reinforcement, but many contemporary dialects continue the pattern of (63) and (64) with just *t'* or *th'*, as in the fictional (67) and (68).

(67)   "**T'** maister nobbut just buried, and Sabbath no o'ered, und **t'** sound o' **t'** gospel still
        i' yer lugs, and ye darr be laiking! Shame on ye! Sit ye down, ill childer; there's good
        books eneugh if ye'll read 'em. Sit ye down, and think o' yer sowls!" (Emily Bronte,
        Wuthering Heights)

(68)   "Ah'm gettin' **th'** coops ready for **th'** young bods," he said, in broad vernacular.
        (D. H. Lawrence, *Lady Chatterley's Lover*, chapter 8)

Barry (1972) and Jones (2002) have made studies of this definite article reduction phenomenon. Rupp and Page-Verhoeff (2005: 326) argue that older speakers at the North Yorkshire–Lancashire border used *t'* when referring to something identifiable, as in (69), but use demonstratives for other uses.

(69)   They had a baby and when **t'**baby arrived he got jealous.

As mentioned, Rupp (2008) and others show that this use arises from the demonstrative *that*. That is quite possible and would mean an additional application of a phrase being reanalyzed as a head.

Many varieties (both in Britain and the United States) also continue the trend of (65) and renew demonstratives, as in (70) to (73), where the first may be a slip of the tongue. This use is nowadays typical for nonstandard urban dialects (see, e.g., Cheshire, Edwards, & Whittle 1993).

(70)   It was just I I was just looking at **there them** down there (BNC-FME, 662).

(71)   The things showing round **there them** (BNC-KBD, 7334).

(72)   Oh they used to be ever so funny houses you know and in **them** days and The er you
        never used to see in the oh a lot of houses and you never used to see big windows like
        these. They used to have big windows, but they used to a all be **them there** little tiny
        ones like that. . .. Used to have to be very rather experienced in **them** days to do **this
        here** net mending. (BNC-FYD, 72, 112)

(73)   then the Headmistress, cos we had a Headmistress there cos it was a mixed school,
        and she recommended me for **this here** errand boy's job, his name was. (BNC-
        H5G, 117)

We can put the list of changes in English in terms of changes to the structure, as in (74), namely a reanalysis of the demonstrative *þat* as a head *the* and an incorporation of the postmodifying locative as a higher element.

(74)

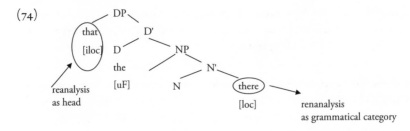

The similarities between Old Norse and Old English are that (a) both incorporated locatives, *(h)inn/(h)itt* in Old Norse and *there* in English and (b) the demonstrative was reanalyzed as a D head that is in its turn being renewed.

Apart from the reduction of the article *the* and the reinforcement of the demonstrative *that* by a locative, there is a third change in progress that can be seen by comparing written and spoken texts. In spoken texts, the demonstrative *that* is more frequent compared to the definite article; in written, more formal texts, the article *the* is more frequent. This is of course directly relevant to the DP cycle: *the* is being replaced by *that*.

Early Modern English shows this tendency because, as mainly a written set of texts, it favors definite articles over demonstrative pronouns. Just looking at the Helsinki Corpus EMOD1–3 texts, minimal use of *that/those* is made compared to *the*. Table 6.3 gives some numbers for nouns immediately following these but there is no difference when an adjective intervenes.

The percentage of definite articles in the Helsinki Corpus EMOD1–3 texts—*the* consti-tutes 4.98 percent of the total number of words—is very close to that of modern written texts. Academic texts are even higher; for example, this book has *the* at 5.25 percent. The percentage of the definite article *the* (as measured against all words in a text) varies enor-mously in English texts (and in French as we'll see) but mainly between spoken and written genres. For instance, in a spoken formal corpus of Modern American English (CSE), *the* is used only once in a hundred words (1.1 percent to be precise).

Comparing *the* and *that* in the same texts results in very interesting differences. In the BNC 10-million-word spoken part, the definite article appears more than 400,000 times, as table 6.4 shows, and the demonstrative less than 150,000 times. In the BNC 15.3-million-word academic part, the definite article is much more frequent than the demonstrative. The article appears more than a million times and the demonstrative only about 30,000 times.

Table 6.4 shows that in spoken English, *that* is more frequent than in other registers and could be a sign of renewal of the [u-phi] in D, a change in progress. It might be that the numbers of *that* are higher for spoken English because of the frequent independent use (i.e., without a noun). This is not the case, however: sequences of *that* and a noun or an

TABLE 6.3

That and *the* Followed by Frequent Nouns in the Helsinki Corpus EMODE

	Woman	Man	Child	King	Building	Number
the	45	61	119	192	10	17
that	0	3	1	3	0	1

TABLE 6.4

The Article *the* and Demonstrative *that* in the BNC as a percentage of the total number of words

	Spoken	Fiction	Newspapers	Academic Writing
the	409,960 (4.1%)	836,836 (5.3%)	644,043 (6%)	1,129,235 (7.4%)
that	147,335 (1.5%)	78,129 (.5%)	19,501 (.2%)	32,284 (.2%)
Total	10,000,000	15,900,000	10,500,000	15,300,000

TABLE 6.5

That and *there* in the BNC

	Spoken	Fiction	Newspapers	Academic Writing
that (A) N	26,470 (.27%)	23,718 (.14%)	7,148 (.07%)	16,330 (.1%)
that (A) N *there*	281	34	2	0
% with *there*	1%	.14%	.03%	0%

adjective and noun are still much higher in the spoken part of the corpus. I provide these numbers in table 6.5, and add the numbers of reinforcements with *there*. The latter, as expected, are much more frequent in spoken English.

As this subsection shows about changes in the history of English concerning demonstrative pronouns, in the Old English period, there are no articles; they are the result of the grammaticalization of demonstratives in late Old English. In Old English, demonstratives were used more like personal pronouns.

2.3 AFRIKAANS, DUTCH, AND VARIETIES OF GERMAN: RENEWAL

In Afrikaans, arguably a creole based on Dutch with some lexical and syntactic borrowings from English, Malay, Bantu languages, Khoisan languages, Portuguese, and other European languages, *die* is the definite article where, in Dutch, *die* 'that' is a demonstrative. *Dié, hierdie,* and *daardie* (or *daai*) are the demonstratives, as in (75) and (76).

(75) **Hierdie** plaatjie laat jou 'n gedetaileer boom van **hierdie** taal familie sien. Afrikaans
This picture lets you a detailed tree of this language family see

'This picture lets you see a detailed family tree of this language family.'
(http://home.unilang.org/main/families.php?l=af)

(76) **Daardie** teenstrydighede was egter nie soseer in die man Bram Fisher nie Afrikaans

'Those contradictions were however not so much in the man Bram Fisher not
(but in . . .)' (Mandela speech, 1997, http://www.anc.org.za/ancdocs/history/
mandela/1997/sp971128.html)

There has been prescriptive pressure against *hierdie* en *daardie* in the past (see Donaldson 1993: 142–143), but this is no longer evident in the media. To a Dutch speaker reading newspapers, however, it seems that *hierdie* en *daardie* are still not as frequent as demonstratives in Dutch.

In short, one of the Dutch demonstratives, namely *die*, was analyzed in Afrikaans as the article. The reason for this may be that the Dutch article shows a gender distinction and the demonstrative does not. The Dutch demonstratives show a proximal (*dit/deze* 'this/these') and distal (*dat/die* 'that/those') distinction and this distinction appears in Afrikaans in *hierdie* and *daardie*.[9] In terms of the cycle, the specifier *die* is analyzed as head and new specifiers appear reanalyzed from the Dutch locative adverbs *hier* 'here' and *daar* 'there'.

In Dutch, there are two definite articles depending on the gender of the noun, *de* and *het*. These originate from demonstratives as also happened in the other Germanic languages. I won't go into that history but would just like to point out a renewal in the independent use in certain Dutch dialects: the original article *den* is reinforced with the (inflected) demonstrative *die* or *dieje*.

(77) *Ik wil **den dieie/deze***   Brabant Dutch
        I want the that/this
        'I want that/this one.'

(78) *Dat is maar seriewerk bij **den die**!*   Brabant Dutch
        That is only mass production with the that
        'With him, it is just mass production.'
        (From *Woordenboek van de Brabantse Dialecten* 1996: 2597 Assen)

Van der Horst (2008: 597) shows that this use goes back to at least Erasmus, in the sixteenth century, next to the use of a locative *g(h)ene*.

Pennsylvania Dutch has a construction with an agreeing demonstrative (*sell* 'that') and a locative (*datt* 'there') as well, as in (79), from Old Order Amish speakers. Putnam (2006) shows that the younger generation of Pennsylvania Dutch speakers is introducing a new form with the specifier and the head merged, as in (80).

(79) ***seller   datt***   *gross   mann*   Pennsylvania Dutch
        that   there   tall   man
        'that tall man' (Putnam 2006: 170)

(80) *mit   **selldatt**   grosse   mann*   Pennsylvania Dutch
        with   that-there   tall   man
        'with that tall man' (Putnam 2006: 170)

The emerging "street languages" in European countries show similar uses of the Head Preference Principle. These languages are multiethnic youth languages and they have emerged, for example, in the Netherlands, Germany, Sweden, and Denmark. For instance, *so* 'such' has

---

9. Dutch *dit* 'this' corresponds to the same form in Afrikaans but with the meaning 'it', Dutch *dat* is restricted in Afrikaans to the complementizer, and Dutch *deze* 'this' is not present in Afrikaans.

become an article in (81), though it is an adverb in the standard languages. Himmelmann (1997: 20) reports the same for Swiss German, as in (82), where *säb* derives from *selbst* 'same'.

(81) Ich   such'   nicht   **so**   Ausbildungsplatz   Kanak German
      I   search not   that   education-place

      'I am not looking for that kind of position.' (Wiese 2006)

(82) *i säbem huus*   Swiss German

      'in that house' (Himmelmann 1997: 20)

We can thus describe the DP cycle as going from deictic to definite since deictic features are lost, as in (83), slightly adapting (6) and (7) above. This follows from Feature Economy but also from the Head Preference and Late Merge Principles.

(83) a. demonstrative   >   definite article   >   zero
          [i/u-phi]   [u-phi]
          [i-loc]   [u-T]
      b. specifier   >   head   > affix >   zero

From the renewal of the demonstrative by means of locative adverbs, it is clear that the article loses those features. I have not said much on the loss of the phi features of the demonstrative. This remains a subject for further work.

3. Indo-European: Romance, Slavic, and Indo-Iranian

In Romance, the most well-known case of the DP cycle is Latin demonstrative *ille* 'that' appearing, for instance, in French as the article *le* (and the weak accusative pronoun), and in Romanian as an enclitic. As this grammaticalization took place, another set of demonstratives came into being, for example, *ce(tte)* in French. This development fits the cycle very well: the Latin demonstrative was in the Spec of DP (as also argued by Boucher 2003) and its French and Romanian descendants in the head. In what follows, I give some of the well-known facts about Romance, add a few comments on Slavic, and provide some information on Persian, Balochi, and Urdu. In the latter, definiteness is not marked by demonstratives but through an Object Marker (*-ra* and *ko*), as we saw in the previous chapter.

3.1 THE DP CYCLE IN ROMANCE, FRENCH IN PARTICULAR

In this section, I show some stages of the DP cycle in the different Romance languages, discuss the variation among them, and review the (extensive) literature on where these forms come from. The results show that the DP cycle from Latin to Old French is as predicted; French, from the seventeenth century on, shows two kinds of renewal.

Three different stages of the cycle are given in (84) to (86). In (84), Latin *ille* is a demonstrative indicating location away from the speaker and addressee, which has become the definite marker *le*, *la*, or *l'* in French (85), and a definite marking suffix in Romanian (86):

(84) **ille**   *liber*   Latin
      that   book,
      'that book'

(85) *l'hiver*   French
      the-winter

(86) *om-**ul***   *bun*   Romanian
      man-DEF   good,
      'the good man'

This represents a change from specifier to head to affix.

In many of the Romance languages, the article is a clitic. Interestingly, the French article (*le/la*) was reanalyzed by African and North American learners as part of the noun, as in French (87) but (88) in Haitian Creole.

(87) *la*   *rivière*   French
      'the   river'

(88) *larivyè*   *a*   Haitian Creole
      river   DEF
      'the river'

The article in Modern French is phonologically quite weak. It cannot occur on its own, as (89) shows, and is repeated between different instances of nominals, as in (90).

(89) **Je pratique le*   French
      'I play the'

(90) *Je pratique **le** tennis, **le** badminton, **le** squash, **la** natation.*   French
      'I play tennis, badminton, and squash, and I swim.'
      (Corpus d'entretiens spontanés)

There is a lot of variation in Romance. Table 6.6 provides more details on the descendants of Latin *ille* 'that'. Some languages have D elements showing different Cases; some have two and some three genders.

Vincent (1997) has shown that the Latin demonstratives *ille* 'that' and *ipse* 'self' were both candidates for articlehood. The former is traditionally a marker of distal deixis and the latter one of emphasis. Leiss (2000), on the basis of data in Selig (1992), suggests that *ille* is first used with (definite) focus and *ipse* for anaphoric use, that is, topic. *Ille* was reanalyzed as the French article *le* (among other things). Descendants of *ipse* functioned or function as articles in Catalonia, Gascony, parts of Provence, Sicily, Sardinia, and parts of southern Italy (Vincent 1997: 154). Since the demonstratives lose some locative/deictic function in the daughter

TABLE 6.6

Different Ds in Romance

	Masculine S/P	Feminine S/P	Neuter S/P	Case
Latin	*ille/illi*	*illa/illae*	*illud/illa*	(NOM)
	illum/illos	*illam/illas*	*illud/illa*	(ACC)
Roma	*o/le*	*e/le*		(NOM)
	le/le	*la/le*		(OBL)
French	*l(e)/les*	*la/les*		
Spanish	*el/los*	*la/las*		
Catalan	*(e)l/els*	*l(a)/les*		

	prefixed #/gender	definite article	proximity marker
Classical Latin	-	-	hic, iste, ille
Vulgar Latin	-	ille	ecce iste, ecce ille
Old French	-	le	cest, cel
Modern French	le	ce	ce ... ci, ce ... là

FIGURE 6.2. The development of Romance determiners. From Harris 1977, 1978

languages, they are reinforced in Vulgar Latin as *ecce iste* 'see this' and *ecce ille* 'see that' (see Greenberg 1978: 76; Giusti 2001a: 169), which in turn grammaticalize to *cest/cist* and *cel/cil* in Old French and become *ce(tte)* in Modern French.

Harris (1977: 256) asserts that the latter forms are articles since they do not mark distance, and that "only forms with . . . -*ci* and -*là* can be regarded as demonstratives" (260). Harris (1977: 256, 1978: 76) uses figure 6.2 to illustrate his arguments for the developments between Latin and French. According to Giusti (2001a), *ecce* was introduced in a specifier position after *iste* and *illum* had become heads. As Epstein (1993: 113) argues, and as figure 6.2 shows, *le* and *li* in Old French DPs, such as *li empereres* 'the emperor', are articles since the emperor is Charlemagne, easily identifiable. Boucher (2003: 57) confirms that the articles were already in the D head position by Old French since contractions such as *au, a(u)s, del, du, dou*, and so on occur from the very beginning. Thus, one set of cyclical changes takes place between Latin *ille* and Old French *le/li*.

Between Old French and present-day French, there are two kinds of renewal. There are "new" demonstratives, namely *ce(t), cette*, and *ces* and *celui, celle(s)*, and *ceux*, and adverb-like elements that reinforce the demonstrative, namely -*là*, as in (91), or -*ci*:

(91)   *mais ma femme elle vivait à **ce moment-là** encore*   French
       but my wife she lived at that moment-DEM still

       'but my wife was still alive at that moment' (Corpus d'entretiens spontanés)

Comparing the use of the old and new variants in the last four hundred years, one can con-clude that *le* and its forms mark definiteness, *ce* and its forms refer back to something in the context, as in (92), and *-là* or *-ci* mark real deixis, as in (91).

(92)   *On essaie justement **dans ces moments** de . . . méditation, de . . . d'éch. . .*

'One tries exactly in those moments of meditation to . . . to esc[ape].'

(Corpus d'entretiens spontanés)

The use of the *ce* forms has not increased considerably in the last four hundred years, but that of *-là* and *-ci* has. The use seems stylistically determined.

Table 6.7 shows a very rough approximation of the situation in Jules Verne's late nine-teenth-century fiction *De la Terre à la Lune* and (Kate Beeching's) twentieth-century spoken French Corpus d'entretiens spontanés. This may provide some insight as to how frequently *ce(t)*, *cette*, and *ces* are used (12 percent and 6 percent respectively) in comparison with the regular articles. The numbers of *ce* include only a D in combination with a noun, as in (92), and not independent *ce* 'it'. These numbers give just a rough sense for the relations between the article and *ce*-forms because the percentages of demonstratives relative to the total number of demonstratives and articles may be lower. The reason is that the contracted arti-cles *au*, *aux*, *du*, and *des* are not included. Some of the instances of *le* and *l'* are object clitics, however. What is important to notice is that the instances of *ce(t)*, *cette*, and *ces* are not very high and, as we'll see next, have not been increasing.

Using the same method for Descartes's *Discours de la Methode*, a philosophical text from the year 1637, renders a percentage of 8 percent demonstratives out of a total of demonstra-tives and articles combined, and for Molière's *L'Avare*, a comedy from 1668, the percentage is 11 percent (table 6.8). (Again contracted forms are not among these and the object clitics have not been eliminated.) This would mean that the demonstrative forms have stayed stable, as between Molière and Verne, but that the text type (academic, spoken, fiction, etc.) plays a major role, something we saw in English too. However, unlike in English, the special demon-stratives are low in spoken French, and the article is still frequent.

If the difference between the *le*- forms and *ce*- forms is stylistically motivated and probably hasn't changed much, has anything? For instance, has the number of *ce* forms enhanced by *–là* increased? Table 6.9 shows, of all the instances of *ce(t)*, *cette*, and *ces*, how many nominals have *-là* following in Descartes, Molière, Verne, and the spoken French corpus. This may

TABLE 6.7

Articles and Demonstratives in Modern French							
	Jules Verne				Cd'ES		
MS	*le*	1225	*ce*	196	*le*	2556	*ce*	231
FS	*la*	1534	*cette*	228	*la*	2804	*cette*	195
MFS	*l'*	1120	*cet*	54	*l'*	1234	*cet*	31
P	*les*	1090	*ces*	193	*les*	2790	*ces*	139
Total		4969 (88%)		671 (12%)		9384 (94%)		596 (6%)

TABLE 6.8

Articles and Demonstratives in Descartes's *Discours de la Méthode* and Molière's *L'Avare*

	Descartes				Molière			
MS	*le*	272	ce	31	*le*	330	ce	46
FS	*la*	407	cette	31	*la*	316	cette	48
MFS	*l'*	234	cet	8	*l'*	274	cet	12
P	*les*	597	ces	57	*les*	215	ces	28
Total		1510 (92%)		127 (8%)		1135 (89%)		134 (11%)

TABLE 6.9

Numbers of *-là* and Percentages Relative to All *ce-* Forms

	Descartes	Molière	Verne	Modern Spoken
-là	2 (1.6%)	10 (7%)	20 (3%)	96 (16%)

indicate that *ce(t)*, *cette*, and *ces* were not reanalyzed as demonstratives but that *-là* and *-ci* are reanalyzed as such, especially in modern spoken French. This requires more research into different text types, however. Note that Molière's comedy with spoken dialogues has a much higher percentage of *-là* than the prose of both Descartes and Verne. Danton (2010) notes that the use of *–là* is mainly anaphoric to something already mentioned in the text and that French doesn't seem to make much use of spatially deictic demonstratives.

Turning to Romanian, in which language Latin *ille* develops into a suffix *-ul*, in other words, makes a full cycle, we see an additional demonstrative *cel* that can be added, as in (93). The renewal is similar to the form in French and of course expected. This *cel* is more deictic and there is a proximal one as well, as in (94).

(93) *om-ul*   **cel**   *bun*   Romanian
      man-DEF that   good
      'that good man' (Greenberg 1978: 76)

(94) *băiat-ul*   **acesta**   *frumos*   Romanian
      boy-the   this   nice
      'this nice boy' (Giusti 2001a: 161)

Could these new specifiers *cel* and *acesta* have become heads in (95)?

(95) **acest**   *băiat*   *frumos*   Romanian
      this   boy   nice
      'this nice boy'

If yes, the development of Romanian demonstratives shows another stage in the cycle from specifiers to heads.

In Romance, there is thus quite a bit of evidence for a DP cycle where a demonstrative such as *ille* (in the specifier of the DP) is reanalyzed as an article *le* (in the D head). The demonstrative then gets renewed two ways, via *ecce* (which ends up in the demonstrative *ce(t[te])*) and via *-là* and *–ci*. The changes in features would be very similar to those in English.

3.2 SLAVIC

There is a lot of variation in Slavic, with Russian showing no evidence of an article, and Bulgarian and Macedonian having suffixed ones. I'll just mention some stages here that are in between, but an entire chapter could be devoted to the variation in Slavic. As mentioned in the previous chapter, Slavic languages also use aspect and Case to mark definiteness (accusative is definite whereas genitive is indefinite).

Serbian, Polish, Sorbian, Czech, and Slovenian have grammaticalized demonstrative adjectives as definiteness markers, though these languages do not yet have full-fledged articles (Heine & Kuteva 2006: 97–139). This development has not taken place in their standard varieties but it certainly has in their colloquial varieties. An example from Czech of an optional demonstrative is given in (96).

(96) *Chci   vodu   ale   **ta**   voda   musi   by't   čistá*   Czech
      want   water   but   DEM   water   must   be   clean

      'I want water but the water must be clean.' (Heine & Kuteva 2006: 115)

In Sorbian, the changes are perhaps most obvious. In Upper Sorbian, there is evidence that the use of a demonstrative goes back to the sixteenth century. Heine and Kuteva (2006: 113), based on Lötzsch (1996), suggest that with the grammaticalization of the demonstratives *tón*, *ta, te*, and *te*, the demonstrative use was strengthened by means of *tu-* 'here'. There is a lot of extralinguistic pressure against this grammaticalization. For some speakers, the use of articles is seen as a German influence.

Bosnian/Serbian/Croatian has a reinforced demonstrative, as in (97), that functions as a phrase, according to Brugè (1996).

(97) ***ona tamo** nova kniga*   Bosnian/Serbian/Croatian
      that there new book

      'that new book there' (Brugè 1996: 23)

The renewal of the deictic features of *ona* 'that' and *ova* 'this' is of course by overt locative elements. According to Brown and Alt's (2004: 80–81) description of Bosnian/Serbian/Croatian, *ona* and *ova* have complex roles as textual markers and that may be responsible for their reanalysis and subsequent renewal.

Slavic languages show a lot of variation in their DPs, with only demonstratives in Russian, reinforced demonstratives in Bosnian/Serbian/Croatian (97), grammaticalization of demonstratives in for example Czech (96), and clitic articles in Macedonian. Language contact is a major influence: the development of articles is typical of the European Sprach-bund (Standard Average European) and the clitic article is typical of the Balkan Sprachbund. As Heine and Kuteva (2006) argue grammaticalization and hence also cyclical change is accelerated in these contexts.

3.3 INDO-IRANIAN: PERSIAN, BALOCHI, AND URDU/HINDI

In Persian, all the (demonstrative) ingredients are present for a definiteness/DP cycle but, as I show, there is very little change going on. This is even more so in Balochi and in Urdu/Hindi. This means there are other ways to mark definiteness. One possibility is through the DOM object markers *–ra* and *–ko*, another is through the well-developed aspect system, and a third possibility is that the compound verb system is used to indicate indefinite objects.[10]

Persian has a suffix article *-i* that would in principle be a candidatefor renewal. The suffix marks both the indefinite and definite and is therefore marked as a D in (98) and (99). However, it is rare in a definite context.

(98)   *ketaab-i*   *ke*   *didam*   Persian
         book-D   that   saw-1S
         'the book that I saw'

(99)   *(yek) ketaab-i*   Persian
         a book-D

The suffix derives from an older *aiva* 'one' or 'this' respectively. Infrequently, the definite *-i* occurs with a relative clause, as in (98); the indefinite may be doubled by *yek* 'one', either as reinforcement, as in (99), or as sole marker. Lazard (1957: 66) notes that *ketaabi* on its own is more formal than *yek kitaab(i)*, showing the *yek* is probably a renewal of the indefinite article.

There is no renewal, however, for the definite suffix *–i* in the form of a new demonstrative. There are demonstrative pronouns in Persian, *an* and *in*, but these are also used as personal pronouns and emphatically, as in (100), not for specificity.

(100)   *chun*   *hævaye*   ***an***   *ruz*   *kæmi*   *særd*   *bud,...*   Persian
          because   weather   that   day   little   cold   was
          'because the weather was a little cold that day...' (Dresden et al. 1958: 66)

These demonstratives are specifiers since they can occur on their own. Specific nouns such as the bolded ones in (101) lack special markings by definite markers but they have locative prepositions.

(101)   *be*   ***molla***   *xæbær*   *dadænd*   *ke*   *be*   ***meydan***   *berævæd*   Persian
          to   mullah   news   gave-3P   that   to square   go-SBJ
          'They told the mullah that he should go to the square.' (Dresden et al. 1958: 68)

---

10. Leiss (2000: 216), in a note, mentions the unpublished work of Shahram Ahadi in this context.

As mentioned in the previous chapter, the regular definite is marked only when it is an object, as in (102), as a DOM.

(102)   *ketaab-**ra***   *didam*   Persian
        book-OM   saw-1S
        'I saw the book.'

Another Indo-Iranian language that has no definite or indefinite articles is Balochi; it is "the context of the sentence" (Gilbertson 1923: 12) that determines definiteness. For indefinites, there is a numeral *yak* 'one' that can be used, and for definites, the demonstrative pronouns *e* 'this' and *án* 'that' can be used and can be made emphatic with *ham*, as in (103).

(103)   **haw-án**   *zál*   Balochi
        EMPH-that   woman
        'that woman' (Gilbertson 1923: 12

Looking through some Balochi texts in Gilbertson, I find that the use of demonstratives is rare. As in Persian, there is an object marker -*(r)a* (Gilbertson 1923: 20; Barker & Mengal 1969: 1: 141) used for definite objects, as in (104a), whereas indefinite objects have no ending, as in (104b).

(104)   a. *mən*   *koh-**a***   *gyndin*   Balochi
           I   mountain-DOM   see
           'I see the mountain.'
        b. *mən*   *kohe*   *gyndin*
           I   mountain   see
           'I see a mountain.' (Barker & Mengal 1969: 1: 141)

Urdu is quite close to Persian regarding demonstratives, as well as in other respects, such as the DOM and the compound verb system. Hindi is grammatically almost identical to Urdu but the examples below are Urdu in vocabulary choice and therefore marked as such. In Urdu, there is no -*i* suffix as in Persian but the distal demonstrative *woo* 'that', as in (105), is very infrequent and hard to find in texts, except in more set phrases, as in (106). Another function is as third person pronoun, as in (107), which I have argued in chapter 2 is phrasal.

(105)   *Elly*   *kii*   **woo**   *doo*   *laal*   *kitaaabēē*   Urdu
        Elly   of   DEM   two   red   book-P
        'Elly's two red books'

(106)   **woo** *vakt*   *merii*   *xaan*   *bahot*   *duur*   *nehii*   *hē*   Urdu
        that time   my   love   very   far   not   is
        'That time isn't very far, my love.' (Iqbal, *axrii xat*)

(107) **woo** *kitaab* *parhtaa*   *hē*   Urdu
       he   book   reading -MS   is

     'He is reading a book.'

As in Persian, a specific/definite noun is often not marked, especially when inanimate. For instance, in (108), the football was the cause of trouble and quite specific; yet it is not marked. Again, as in Persian, to make an object definite, a differential object marker is used, namely *-ko* in (109).

(108) **fuutbo** *kal*   *suuba*   *tak*   *mere* *pas*   *rah-egaa*   Urdu
       football tomorrow morning till   me   with   stay-FUT

     'The football will stay with me till tomorrow morning.' (Barker 1975: 1: 248)

(109) *mē* *nee* *kitaab* **ko**   *parhaa*   Urdu
       I   ERG   book   DEF   read

     'I read the book.'

I suggest that the structure of a simple Urdu DP with a demonstrative *woo* is as in (110). *Woo* is in a specifier position with interpretable features, because *woo* can appear on its own and be emphasized through *hii*. (As mentioned in connection with (6), the number features on Num may be uninterpretable as well.)

(110)

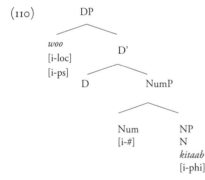

Though infrequent, the structure with a *woo* marked nominal is quite complex, with a possessive phrase that precedes the demonstrative, as in (105), or follows it, as in (111).

(111) **woo** *phalvaalee* *kii* *duukaan*   Urdu
       that   fruitseller of   shop

     'that fruitseller's shop' (Barker 1975: 1: 107)

Barker (1975: 1: 107) says the unmarked construction is (111) but that three other possibilities occur, as in (112) to (114).

(112) *phalvaalee* *kii* **woo** *duukaan*   Urdu
       fruitseller of   that   shop

     'that shop of the fruitseller' (there may be more than one owned by the same person)

(113) **us** *phalvaalee*   *kii* *duukaan*   Urdu
       that-OBL fruitseller   of   shop

       'that fruitseller's shop'

(114) **us** *phalvaalee*   *kii* **woo** *duukaan*   Urdu
       that-OBL fruitseller   of   that   shop

       'that shop of that fruitseller' (Barker 1975: 107).

In these sentences, *woo* and its oblique variant *us* are used for deictic reference. The possessor *phalvaalee kii* can move higher to a position preceding *woo* and then its function is deictic, and replaces *woo*, as in (112). In (113), the demonstrative is modifying *phalvaalee* and, in (114), there are two demonstratives. The analysis of (112) to (114) will involve a higher topic position to which the possessor moves. The analysis of the genitive *kii* is debated; it shows suffixaufnahme (Payne 1995; Plank 1995) in that it indicates the genitive as well as the Case and agreement of the entire DP. It also goes with entire phrases, like English *'s*.

Thus, in Persian, Balochi, and Urdu/Hindi, there is very little evidence of a DP cycle going on. I think this is because there are other means of indicating definiteness on objects (and subjects).

4. Uralic

Uralic includes Finnish, Sami, Samoyed languages, Hungarian, and a few others. In this section, I examine Finnish and Hungarian. Though Finnish conveys definiteness through Case, it is developing an article; Hungarian has a well-developed D system.

Finnish, as is well known from the work of Belletti (1988) and de Hoop (1992), expresses definiteness on objects through accusative Case (see the previous chapter). Finnish also has demonstratives *tämä* 'this', *tuo* 'that', and *se* 'it, that, the', with three separate plurals, *nämä*, *nuo*, and *ne* and they are of course marked for Case. The exact relationship between the three demonstratives is debated, especially for spoken Finnish. Laury (1997: 58–59) tends toward a dynamic approach in which these demonstratives are "used by speakers . . . to express their orientation and stance toward referents." The morphologically appropriate form of *tämä* 'this', namely *tällä* in (115), places a referent within the speaker's current sphere and is used when objects are focused on and manipulated. *Tuo* 'that' places the object outside that sphere, and its accusative form in (116) does this. *Se* 'the', with a partitive given in (117), defines the addressee's sphere.

(115) *Mä* *leikin* **tällä**   Finnish
       I   play   tämä-ADE

       'I'll play with this one.' (Laury 1997: 63)

(116) *Nääthän* *sä* **on**   *lipun*   Finnish
       see-2S   2S   tuo.ACC   flag

       'You can see that flag, right?' (Laury 1997: 75)

(117) | te | rakensitte | **sitä** | taloo | sitte | vai | Spoken Finnish
| 2P | build-PST | se.PRTV | house-PRTV | then | PRT |

'You were building the house then, right?' (Laury 1997: 118)

Laury's book is a study of the emergence of the definite article in spoken Finnish. The texts she cites from the 1890s indicate that *se*-marked referents are more often discourse-prominent, that is, topics, and that *se* is (becoming) an article. In (118), the food has been mentioned and is very important since 'the girl' (Cinderella-like) is supposed to cook it.

(118) | kun | tyttö | näytti | **sen** | muanan | Older Finnish
| when | girl | showed | se.ACC | food-ACC |

'when the girl showed him the food'. (Laury 1997: 184)

Laury also shows that these nominals more often have an object (O) role than a subject (S) or agent (A) role (1997: 177). Laury's explanation is that "*se*-marking can be seen as an accessory device. ... [A]n addressee is likely to read a lexical noun phrase in the O or Oblique role as a new mention" (1997: 179), and this needs to be marked.

The data from the 1930s and 40s show more *se*- marking, particularly when these indicate new information. Laury's data from the 1970s, '80s, and '90s show that *se*- marking has increased for noun phrases in all roles, especially those identifiable to the addressee, and that *tämä* is now used for prominent referents. This use to identify would suggest that *se* is an article and Laury agrees, while mentioning dissenting voices that say it is not yet obligatory.

In Hungarian, the situation is very different. A noun is (mostly) preceded by an article, the definite one being *a(z)* 'the', as in (119). This form shows allomorphy depending on the first sound (consonant or vowel) of the word following, and is therefore more clitic or affix-like. The article is not inflected for Case or number.

(119) | a | ház | Hungarian
| 'the | house' |

A phrase can have two definiteness markers, as in (120) and (121), with the demonstrative preceding the article and (heavily) inflected for Case and number.

(120) | **az-t** | **a** | filmet | akarom | megnézni | Hungarian
| that-ACC.S | DEF | movie | want-1S | watch-INF |

'I want to watch that movie.' (Rounds 2001: 132)

(121) | **ez-ek-röl** | **a** | part-ok-ról | Hungarian
| this-P-ABL | DEF | shore-P-ABL |

'from these shores' (Szabolcsi 1994: 185

The uninflected definiteness marker looks like a reduced form of the demonstrative, and would be in the head of the DP while the demonstrative is in the specifier position. There are also reinforced forms such as *amaz* 'that there'.

The two Uralic languages reviewed in this section have different definiteness strategies. Finnish is developing a definite article from a demonstrative and, according to many, this is happening on the basis of contact with Swedish. In Hungarian, there is evidence of previous cyclical change from the synchronic forms.

5. North American Languages

North American languages provide examples of how demonstrative pronouns are reanalyzed as heads and how new demonstratives develop, all evidence of cyclical change. I am grouping these languages by geographic area for the sake of convenience more than for typological reasons. Yuman languages, such as Mohave, Tiipay (or Diegueño), Havasupai, and Yavapai, all have some incipient form of the article, as do several Uto-Aztecan, Salish, and Algonquian languages. Of these, I'll discuss Pima Bajo, Tohono O'odham, Cupeño, and Cora (all Uto-Aztecan), Maricopa and Tiipay (Yuman), St'át'imcets, Lushoodseed, Bella Coola (all Salish), and Cree (Algonquian). However, there are many others, such as Siouan (Riggs 1893: 18; Pustet 1995), Wakashan (Anderson 2005: 101), and Athabascan (see, e.g., Lovick 2009).

5.1 UTO-AZTECAN AND YUMAN

Shaul (1986, 1995) provides a description of an earlier stage of the Tepiman branch of Uto-Aztecan, namely Nevome, on the basis of texts and grammars starting from the seventeenth century. He shows that there are no articles in this stage but that there are Case-marked demonstratives, *hugai* 'that', *huca* 'that-OBL', *hugama* 'those-NOM', and *hucama* 'those-OBL', whose system is breaking down (1986: 51). Direct descendants of Nevome are Pima Bajo and Tohono O'odham.

In Pima Bajo, the more conservative of the two in this respect, Estrada Fernández (1996: 8) calls *ig* and *ik* in (122) articles but notes that they are homophonous with the demonstrative.

(122) *ig   kɨl   ik   gogosi   gɨvim*   Pima Bajo
      the   man   the   dog   strike-IMPF

      'The man is striking the dog.' (Estrada Fernández 1996: 8)

This indicates that the article stage has not quite been reached. According to Estrada Fernández (1996: 19), Case is also marked on the article in (122), *ig* for the nominative and *ik* for the oblique. This is of course not surprising given what Shaul has illustrated regarding the earlier stage.

Pima Bajo's close relative Tohono O'odham (Zepeda 1983) has *heg(ai)* 'that' and *heg(am)* 'those' as demonstratives. They also serve as third person pronouns. There is an article *g* (see also Langacker 1977: 100–101), as in (123), that looks like a contraction or shortening of the demonstrative.

(123) *'Ab   'o   hihim   g   cewagi*   O'odham
      there   AUX   walk-P   the   clouds

      'Here come the clouds.' (*D'ac 'O'odham*, from Zepeda 1982)

In O'odham, *g* does not occur sentence-initially, probably due to its reduced phonology (at least compared to Pima Bajo), but otherwise seems to be frequent. Payne (1987: 787) says that its distribution "is strictly syntactic, identifying the beginning of" the NP. Nevome, Pima Bajo, and O'odham are thus in different stages of the DP cycle.

Langacker (1977: 100–101) provides many other examples of Uto-Aztecan languages with emerging and established articles, such as Nahuatl, Southern Paiute, Cupeño (124), and Cora (125).

(124) **ət**   **pə'**   *pulini-š*   Cupeño
    DEM   ART   child-ABS

    'that child' (Hill & Nolasquez 1973: 127)

(125) **áihna** **i**   *tyaata'a*   Cora
    that   ART   man

    'that man right here' (Casad 1984: 246)

In their syntax, these constructions fit the DP cycle since there is in (124) and (125) what looks like a specifier followed by a head. Semantically, they are quite complex. Cora has three articles, agreeing with the demonstratives with respect to the position of the object to the speaker. The demonstratives can be inflected for Case and, in the case of objective demonstratives, agreement with the subject. The demonstrative can be dislocated too.

The Yuman languages have complex systems of demonstratives, some of which are developing into articles. For instance, Gordon (1986: 53) discusses the system in Maricopa, where demonstrative suffixes (*-ny, -s, -v*), prefixes (*ny-, s-, v-*), and roots (*aany, aas, va, da*) all work together. The suffix *–ny*, as used in (126), comes closest to being a definite marker but it is not obligatory.

(126) *'iipaa-**ny**-sh*   *hmii-k*   Maricopa
    man-DEM-SM   tall-REAL

    'The man is tall.' (Gordon 1986: 53)

This suffix is the one most closely connected (in phonological shape) to the root *aany*, which is also used as the regular third person pronoun.

Epstein (1993) argues that Jamul Tiipay (Diegueño) possesses an article *pu*, as in (127), that derives from a distal demonstrative *puu* 'that' (128). Note that the article in (127) is clitic-like since *wa* 'house' precedes it. Relevant examples can be found in Miller (2001), who refers to *pu* in (127) as a "demonstrative clitic," not an article.

(127) *wa-**pu***   *nyaa-ch*   *shin*   *chaw*   Jamul Tiipay
    house-DEF   1S-NOM   along   made

    'I built that house myself.' (Miller 2001: 153)

(128) ***puu**-ch*   *xiipuk-ch*   *w-aa*   Jamul Tiipay
    that-NOM   be.first-SS   3-go

    'That one went first.' (Miller 2001: 151).

The article is used in discourse-prominent positions, according to Epstein; compare (129) and (130) where, in the latter, a preposed specific object is marked.

(129) *nyaach* **vuur**   *wiiw*   Jamul Tiipay
       I   burrow   see

       'I saw a/the burrow.' (Epstein 1993: 121)

(130) *vuur-**pu***   *nyaach*   *wiiw*   Jamul Tiipay
       burrow-DEF   I   saw

       'I did see that burrow.' (Epstein 1993: 121)

Miller (2001) analyzes a few stories and notes that the first time a nominal is introduced, it does not have -*pu* but that subsequently it typically does. Other references that are specific are also marked by -*pu*.

(131) *'ii-**pu***   *achkatt*   Jamul Tiipay
       wood-DEF   cut into pieces

       'She cut the wood into little pieces.' (Miller 2001: 346)

This seems quite clear evidence for the start of an article phase. The structural position is in accordance with the DP cycle: an independent demonstrative in (129) and a head in (128).

The Uto-Aztecan languages are in various stages of losing dependent marking on DPs through the demonstratives and are developing articles. Structurally, this process follows the stages in the DP cycle. The Yuman languages show various stages in their synchronic shapes.

5.2 SALISH

I will show that Salish languages are in different stages of the DP cycle. Even though the semantics of demonstratives are controversial, the actual structural positions are not. It is harder in this family to show a diachronic development.

Lots is written on the determiner system in the Salish family, partly because there is a debate as to whether or not there are articles (see Himmelmann 1997: 204). Kroeber (1999), in his comparison of the Salish languages, uses the term *article* and notes that they code gender in most languages but that their degree of definiteness may just be "known to the speaker" (1999: 66) and that *referential* may be a better term. Matthewson (1998) argues (convincingly, I think) that D elements do not convey definiteness or specificity but assertion of existence. The various Salish languages express different features on the D from among visibility, proximity, gender, number, and Case and they differ widely in complexity. Bella Coola has eighteen different distinctions but Sechelt only five (Matthewson 1998: 28–31). I will first discuss the semantic properties of the D but my main interest is where the different elements are situated in the DP and what that tells us about the DP cycle.

Matthewson (1998) defines definiteness as the novel-familiar distinction. She shows in detail for seven Salish languages that this distinction known from English is not relevant. Some examples from Sechelt are given in (132). The determiner *lhe* presents the first mention of the snake woman and (133) a later one, but the determiner is the same.

(132)   t'i   súxwt-as   **lhe**   ʔúlhkaʔ   slhánay   Sechelt
       FACT   saw-he   DET   snake   woman
       'He saw a snake woman.'

(133)   t'i   tl'um   s-kwal-s   **lhe**   slhánay   Sechelt
       FACT   then   NOM-speak-her   the woman
       'then the woman said' (Beaumont 1985: 188).

Matthewson (1998: 58) then shows that specificity is not relevant either but that assertion of existence is. In (132), *lhe* indicates that the snake woman exists, whereas in (134) *she* indicates that the cloud isn't there yet.

(134)   t'i   tl'um   s-ʔút-s   **she**   ts'ámkwelh   Sechelt
       FACT   then   calling her   DET   cloud
       'Then she called a cloud.' (Beaumont 1985: 191)

Though the semantic features of the determiner system are different, the syntactic representation of the DP can still be used and I turn to the representation of determiners and provide different stages of the DP cycle in Salish. St'át'imcets (or Lillooet) has a specifier and a head as well as a suffix in (135), but the demonstrative is clearly proximal, as (136) shows.

(135)   **cʔa**   **ti-sxwápmǝx-a**   St'át'imcets
       this   ART-Shuswap-DEF
       'this Shushap' (van Eijk 1997: 169)

(136)   táyt   **ti-sqácw-a**   St'át'imcets
       hungry   ART-man-DEF
       'The man is hungry.' (Demirdache 1996)

The structure for (135) might look like (137). The proximal demonstrative *cʔa* is in the specifier position, the article *ti* in the head position, and the suffix in the light n.

(137)   St'át'imcets

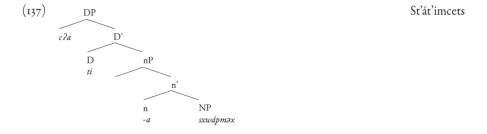

Matthewson (2005: 19–20) provides full paradigms for the determiner, for example, *ti ... a* and the demonstrative. Her table makes clear that the *-a* suffix indicates that there is an assertion and the choice of the *ti/ta, ni/na, ku* prefixes indicate present, absent, or remote in the singular. The demonstrative shows a three-way distinction: number, proximity, and visibility. The deictic markers 'here' and 'there' in St'át'imcets show interesting similarities to the specifier in (135). For instance, *l-č̓a* means visible, proximal 'here'. This similarity to the specifier *c̓a* is not surprising considering the typical renewal sources.

Demonstratives co-occur with possessives, as in (138). This fits with the structure in (137) since the possessive would be closer to the noun, possibly in the sepcifier of the nP.

(138) **niʔ**   **na**   *n-stá̓ʔ-a*   St'át'imcets
        DEM   DET   1S.POSS-aunt-DEF
        'my aunt' (Matthewson 2005: 51)

In Lushoodseed, another Salish language, there are differing analyses and sets of demonstratives, depending on the researcher. Hess and Hilbert (1977: 5) list the group in (139).

(139) *ti*   'the'
        tiʔəʔ   'this'
        tiʔił   'that'
        kwi   "remote, hypothetical, or conjectured"

Hess (1995: 77) adds a fifth to this list, namely the noncontrastive *tə* and provides a list of these five sets of adnominal demonstratives with their neutral and marked (feminine) forms too. Himmelmann (1997: 206) notes that the *ti* is not very frequent in Lushoodseed texts and that the longer forms *tiʔəʔ* 'this' and *tiʔił* 'that' are much more frequent. This suggests an absence of the article, and that Lushoodseed is in an earlier stage of the DP cycle than St'át'imcets.

In the related Bella Coola (Davis & Saunders 1997: 86, 89), two sets of deictic prefixes are listed, with masculine, feminine, and plural forms, as well as six sets of deictic suffixes. For instance, in (140), *ti-* indicates proximal masculine and *-tx* the same but also that it is not gestured; *ta-* is distal and *-t̓aχ* distal and pointed.

(140) *mus-is*   **ti-ʔimmllkī-tx**   **ta-q̓lsxw-t̓aχ**   Bella Coola
        feel-3S   DEF-boy-DEF   DEF-rope-DEF
        'The boy felt that rope.' (Davis & Saunders 1997: 89)

The system Davis and Saunders describe is extremely complex and I will not go into this more except to note that the preverbal Bella Coola *ti* is similar to the Lushoodseed and St'át'imcets *ti* and that the Bella Coola suffixes seem to be deictic renewals. Why they appear as suffixes is not clear; the St'át'imcets pattern of demonstrative is more expected cross-linguistically.

In Skwxwú7mesh (or Squamish), there are again a number of determiners and demonstratives. Gillon's (2009) table of determiners is given here as table 6.10. She distinguishes between determiners and demonstratives on syntactic grounds: the determiner cannot occur by itself (is comparable to *the* in English) whereas the demonstrative can (is comparable to *this* and *that* in English). They cannot occur together.

TABLE 6.10

The Determiner System of Skwxwú7Mesh

	Deictic/Locatable			Nondeictic/ Nonlocatable
	Neutral	Proximal	Distal	
Gender neutral	*ta*	*ti*	*kwa*	*kwi*
Feminine	*lha*	*lhi*	*kwelha*	*kwes*

From Gillon 2009: 188

Gillon argues that determiners are used for domain restriction within a context, following Westerståhl (1984) and others. There are numerous other semantic analyses, such as Mat-thewson's (1998) mentioned earlier. Sentence (141) shows that the same form *ta* is used for novel and familiar nominals.

(141) | *Chen* | *nam* | *ch'áatl'am* | *kwi* | *chel'áklh.* | | Skwxwú7mesh |
I	go	hunt/track	DET	yesterday		
S-en		*men*	*kw'ách-nexw*	***ta***	***míxalh.***	
NOM-1S.sbj		just	look-TR	DET	bear	
S-en		*men*	*kw'élash-t*	***ta***	***míxalh.***	
NOM-1S.SBJ		just	shoot-TR	DET	bear	

'I went hunting. I saw a bear. I shot the bear.' (Gillon 2009: 193 [43])

The nondeictic determiner *kwi* refers back to a previously mentioned referent, here *ta schí7i*, but can also restrict this referent, as it does in (142).

(142) | *Chen* | *wa* | *lhém-n* | *ta* | *schí7i.* | Skwxwú7mesh |
I	IMPF	pick-TR	DET	strawberry	
Chen	*húy-s*		***kwi***	*schí7i.*	
I	finish-CAUS		DET	strawberry	

'I picked strawberries. I ate one strawberry.' (Gillon 2009: 197)

The difference between deictic and nondeictic in Skwxwú7mesh, according to Gillon, is that the deictic determiners have wide scope whereas the nondeictic determiners, such as the one introducing *stá7uxwlh* in (143), have narrow scope.

(143) | *Na* | *múkst-s-t-as* | *í7xw* | *slhen-lhánay'* | ***kwi*** *stá7uxwlh* | Skwxwú7mesh |
| REAL | kiss-CAUS-TR-3ERG | all | woman | DET child | |

'Every woman kissed a (different) child.' (Gillon 2009)

The nondeictic determiners are analyzed by Gillon as part of the predicate, somewhat like bare nouns. Though Gillon doesn't draw this conclusion, I suggest this means they are in a different position: the deictic DP being able to escape into a position of wide scope and the nondeictic NP not.

Demonstratives in Skwxwú7mesh are more morphologically complex than determiners and, as mentioned, they can appear on their own. I think this means that they are in specifier positions with interpretable features, whereas determiners are in the head position with uninterpretable features, hence they need a noun. Salish languages present a variety of options: either the specifier is filled or the head or both.

5.3 ALGONQUIAN

Cree languages, a group of closely related Algonquian languages, have a very complex set of demonstratives, as Cyr (1993: 199) shows. I will just provide a short description showing that the current system is quite old and that it provides some evidence for earlier cyclic development.

Cyr argues, on the basis of textual evidence from Montagnais Cree, that "the so-called demonstratives should be classified as definite articles" (Cyr 1993: 198). They are most often used after the nominal they go with has already been introduced in the text by nothing or by a demonstrative. The sentence in (144) follows a discussion on how to build a house and the house is known to all participants, in other words, very topical.

(144) *eukun*   ***ne***   *mitshuap*   Montagnais Cree
       that-was   DEF   house

       'and that was the house' (Cyr 1993: 208)

The marker *ne* can occur together with proper nouns and locative and possessive constructions, and is used by monolingual older speakers. This prompts Cyr not to see it as French influence, which I think is correct since even the reconstructed Proto-Algonquian (see Proulx 1988) was already shifting toward article use.

Three families in North America, therefore, show evidence of a DP cycle. In Uto-Aztecan, the historical data show an absence of an article in older varieties but various articles that derive from demonstratives in the modern versions. In Salish, it is harder to see a diachronic development. The languages in this family vary tremendously: either the specifier is filled or the head or both; the locative adverb is related to the demonstrative and could have served as its source. In Cree, there is perhaps the beginning of an article stage.

6. Austronesian

In Austronesian, there are demonstrative pronouns, article-like elements, as well as frequent linkers/ligatures and adverbial renewals. These four elements represent the stages in the DP cycle since linkers derive from demonstratives, according to Himmelmann (1997), and would be the last stage in the cycle (with demonstratives being specifiers and articles heads and adverbials the renewals). I'll start with Maori.

Maori has definite (the singular *te* and plural *ngaa*) and indefinite (*he*) articles, as well as proximal (*tenei*) and distal (*tenaa* and *teraa*) demonstratives (Bauer 1993: 355–361, 381–387). The definite article is shown in (145) and the demonstratives can be 'divided', as (146ab) shows, where (146b) is the most common strategy.

(145)   **te**   *tangata*   Maori
        DEF   man,

        'the man'

(146)   a. **tenei**   *tangata*   Maori
           'this   man'
        b. **te**   *tangata*   **nei**
           DEF   man   this

           'this man' (Prytz Johansen 1948: 5–6)

Waite (1994) analyses these phrases using a DP with *te* as head D and Dooley-Collberg (1997) argues that the demonstrative involves a (postnominal) proximal particle incorporated in the D head. More information is needed on the difference between (145), (146a), and (146b) in terms of emphasis or formality. For now, I'll describe the cyclical mechanisms most likely occurring. The interesting point for the cycle is that the D head is reinforced by an adverb-like element.

Example (145) has a very basic structure with *te* in the D head. To derive (146a), *nei* moves to a position between the D and the N in Dooley-Collberg's analysis; more specifically, it incorporates into D. The sentence in (146b) requires no movement.

(147)

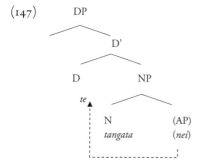

The position that *nei* moves to is right-adjoined to D, which is a bit unusual (using Kayne's 1994 antisymmetry). In addition, *nei* may be phrasal, which Dooley-Collberg's analysis of possessives requires for possessives anyway. I therefore extend Dooley-Collberg's analysis of possessives to *nei* in (146) as well. This provides an analysis of renewal very similar to, for example, that in English earlier.

Possessive nominals, as in (148a), can be preposed as well in (148b). In the singular, the genitive marker[11] attaches to the article *te* to form *too*.

(148)   a. *te*   *whare*   **o**   **Hone**   Maori
           DEF.S   house   GEN   John

           'John's house'
        b. **too**   **Hone**   *whare*
           DEF.S-GEN   John   house

           'John's house' (Dooley-Collberg 1997: 30)

---

11. There are two kinds of genitive markers in Maori, *o* and *a*, which I will not go into.

The analysis Dooley-Collberg suggests for (148b) is one where the *o Hone* moves to the specifier of the DP. The head of this DP, *te*, will in its turn move to the head of the phrase *o Hone*, resulting in *too Hone*, as in (149).

(149)

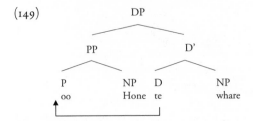

The advantage of (149) is that *te* left-adjoins to *oo* and that we could extend this analysis to the demonstrative in (146a); the disadvantage is that the movement is to a position that doesn't obviously c-command the D. What speaks for movement of *nei* in (146a) is that movement is limited to occurring only once: either *te* moves to join a demonstrative in (150) or a possessive in (151) but not both.

(150) **teenaa**   *huu*   *ooku*   Maori
       DEF.S-DIST   shoe   GEN-1S

       'that shoe of mine' (Dooley-Collberg 1997: 36)

(151) **tooku**   *whare*
       DEF.S-GEN-1S   house

       'my house' (Dooley-Collberg 1997: 33)

That means that the specifier of the DP in (149) can be filled only by one phrase at the time.

In Austronesian languages with a topic-focus system such as Tagalog, the topic marker *ang* is a definiteness marker as well. Technically, only *a* is the definiteness marker since *-ng* is a ligature linking the article to the noun. In (152), the verbal prefix *b-* identifies the theta role of the topic DP that is marked by *ang* as agent. The other dependent markers are used when the DP is a nontopic: *ng* is used when the actor, patient, and instrument are nontopics; *sa* is used to mark the goal, source, location, and benefactive of the nontopics.

(152) *b-um-ili*   *ng*   *kotse*   **ang**   *lalake*   Tagalog
       AF-PF-buy   P   car   TOP   man

       'The man bought a car.' (Frawley 1976: 106)

If the ligature *–ng* derives from a demonstrative that reanalyzed as a D, *a-* must be the renewal. In Ilokano, that reanalysis of the ligature as D head is clearer.

In Ilokano (Frawley 1976: 29), another Austronesian language spoken in the Philippines, the article *ta* in (153) can be "lengthened" to a demonstrative *dayta* in (154). This may have happened, as in Maori, through the incorporation of a more deictic element either in the specifier or the head of the DP.

(153)   **ta**   *aso*   Ilokano
    the   dog

(154)   **dayta**   *aso*   Ilokano
    that   dog

What is interesting is *ta*'s and *dayta*'s interaction with the ligature. In the case of the simple article, there can be no ligature, as (155) shows, but in the case of the demonstrative, shown in (156), the ligature is optional.

(155)   *****ta**   *nga*   *aso*   Ilokano
    the   LIG   dog,
    'the dog'

(156)   **dayta**   *(nga)*   *aso*   Ilokano
    that   LIG   dog,
    'that dog' (Frawley 1976: 31)

Example (155) suggests an analysis where *ta* and *nga* are in complementary distribution in the head D and where *dayta* is analyzable as either head (in [154]) or specifier when *nga* is present (in [156]). Thus, *nga* is an original demonstrative (e.g., Himmelmann 1997: 172),[12] but after having become a D head, it may now be replaced by another D, namely *ta*.

The instances from the literature on Austronesian languages show that here too there is a head that marks nouns, though not a definiteness marker, that derives from a more specific, more independent element. As the head becomes less specific, it may be reinforced by adverbial material, as in Maori. In Tagalog, *a-* might have reinforced the head *ng* in D. In Ilokano, a reinforcement of the article *ta-* by the demonstrative element *day* is reminiscent of the Maori. The demonstrative in Ilokano shows an ambiguity as to whether it is a head (as in Maori) or a specifier. This will no doubt lead to a reanalysis. The data in this section fit stages of the DP cycle very well. I have not phrased this in terms of features since less is known what the features involve.

7. The Afro-Asiatic and Niger-Congo Families

As mentioned, each language represents a different stage in the cycle. Evidence from Egyptian, Arabic, and Amharic, all Afro-Asiatic, shows that their cliticized articles derive from more elaborate pronominal forms. The Niger-Congo languages Gourmanchéma and Fongbe also show evidence of various stages. I'll start with Egyptian, where evidence exists for a complete cycle.

The DP cycle has been noticed in the history of Egyptian where, for instance, the feminine ending *-t* in Middle Egyptian *śn-t* 'sister' is reinforced by a demonstrative *t3*, as in (157). The demonstrative in turn becomes a *t-* prefix in Coptic, as do the masculine *p3* and plural *n3* demonstratives.

---

12. The linker is often *na* and *nga* and this is the same form as demonstratives, e.g., *nana* 'that' in Kambera.

(157)   *t-ȝ*   *śn-(t)*   Middle Egyptian
         F-DIST   sister-F

'that sister' (Schenkel 1990: 18)

In chapter 4, I showed that the masculine distal demonstrative pronoun *pw* in Old Egyptian is reanalyzed as a copula through a loss of phi features. There are four levels of closeness represented in Old Egyptian demonstratives, the *w-* series being only one (Loprieno 1995: 68). The *-ȝ* series, used in (157), is reanalyzed as an article. Whereas the copula *pw*, originally one of the demonstrative *–w* series, loses its phi features, this doesn't happen with the articles *pȝ*, *tȝ*, and *nȝ*; masculine, feminine, and plural continue to be marked. The reanalysis can therefore be formulated as in (158), with a loss of deictic features rather than a loss of phi features as in the case of the copula. Example (158a) represents the feminine demonstrative reanalyzed as article, (158b) represents the masculine, and (158c) the plural.

(158)   Middle Egyptian   Coptic
         a. *t-ȝ*   >   *t-*
         b. *p-ȝ*   >   *p-*
         c. *n-ȝ*   >   *n-*
            [i-phi]   [u-phi]
            [i-loc]

Amharic, a Semitic language of Ethiopia, has an enclitic inflected for gender and number, as in (159). As in Romanian, the adjective (or numeral) when it precedes is thus marked, as (160) shows.

(159)   *bet-u*   Amharic
         house-DEF.MS

'the house'

(160)   *tələq-u*   *bet*   Amharic
         big-DEF   house

'the big house'

This means *u-* is a head in D that the closest head (either N or A) moves to.

Both Hebrew and Arabic DPs have received a lot of attention. Scholars know that, especially for Arabic, the article is quite clitic-like in that it assimilates to the consonant of the noun or adjective it attaches to; the Hebrew article *ha-* seems less phonologically attached. Benmamoun (2000) and Shlonsky (2004) provide some data where new deictic material is added to the DP and this is relevant for the cycle in that different varieties are in different stages.

The demonstrative in standard Arabic agrees in person, number, and gender with the noun and is free to appear both prenominally and postnominally, as in (161).

(161)   a. **haaðihi**   **l**   jaami͑at-u   Standard Arabic
            this-3FS   the   university

b. *l   jaamiᶜ at-u   haaðihi*
   the   university   this-3FS
   'this university' (Shlonsky 2004: 1494)

Levantine Arabic similarly has agreeing demonstratives precede and follow the noun, as in (161), but in addition has an invariable *hal* in prenominal position, as in (162).

(162) **hal** *bint*   Levantine Arabic
   'this girl' (Shlonsky 2004: 1500)

Shlonsky (2004) argues that *hal* is bimorphemic and includes the article *l*. Evidence for this is the assimilation that is typical for the article. Example (163) shows the article *l* and demonstrative *hal* assimilating to the consonant of the next word.

(163)   a. **z**   zalame   Levantine Arabic
      'the man'
   b. **haz**   *zalame*
      'this man' (Shlonsky 2004: 1500)

The cyclical stages represented are standard Arabic with the (proximal) demonstrative in the specifier of the DP and the article showing some evidence of phonological reduction. Levantine Arabic shows how the demonstrative is no longer in the specifier but together with the article occupies the head position.

Frajzyngier (1997) shows that Chadic languages, also Afro-Asiatic, have plural markers that may derive from demonstratives. Put in terms of features, this would mean a reanalysis from interpretable phi features and deictic features to possibly just number features. Plurals, however, are often restricted to definite nouns in Chadic and it is therefore possible that some deixis remains. In the most widely spoken Chadic language, Hausa (Lyons 1999: 52–53; Jaggar 2001), there are several definite/specific markers. Schuh (2002) provides data from three related Chadic languages, Western Bade, Gashua Bade, and Ngizim: "The *-n* of WB [Western Bade] nunation is clearly cognate with the GB [Gashua Bade] masculine distal demonstrative."

The Niger-Congo language Gourmanchéma, or Gurma, spoken mainly in Burkina Fasso, has two definite forms for 'the men', namely those in (164). The semantic difference between the two is not clear but, in terms of the DP cycle, it is interesting to see the renewal of *ba* in (164b).

(164)   a. *nita-**ba***   Gourmanchéma
      men-DEF
      'the men'
   b. **ba**   *nita-**ba***   Gourmanchéma
      DEF   men-DEF
      'the men' (Greenberg 1978: 55)

Languages closely related to Gourmanchéma show a variety of differences. Some have a suffix or a prefix or the renewed "prefix" has lost the definite meaning, as in Gangam. According to Greenberg (1978: 55), this group shows all the stages in the cycle.

In Fongbe, a Niger-Congo language spoken mainly in Benin, there is a doubling as well, as (165) shows. I assume that ɔ́ is a reduced form of élɔ 'reinforcing the deixis.

(165) *àsɔ́n*   *nyɛ̀*   *tɔ̀n*   **élɔ́**   *ɔ́*   *lɛ́*   Fongbe
        crab   me   GEN   DEM   DEF   P

       'these/those crabs of mine.' (Lefebvre 2004: 89)

According to Lefebvre (2004), Haitian Creole has used French lexical items *ça, cela*, and *celui-là* but uses the syntax of Fongbe, as (166) shows.

(166) *krab*   *mwen*   **sa/sila**   **a**   *yo*   Haitian Creole
        crab   me   DEM   DEF   P

       'these/those crabs of mine' (Lefebvre 2004: 89)

There are apparently some speakers that use *sa* as proximate and *sila* as distal, but this is not common. Other speakers use *sila* as distal but *sa* as general definite. A third set of speakers makes no distinction at all, and a fourth group has only *sa*. The latter group may be gaining in influence, according to Lefebvre (2004: 257). Lefebvre argues that the differences can be traced back to substratum differences, in that Fongbe, Ewe, and other languages show the same variation.

The data from Egyptian, Arabic, and Amharic, all Afro-Asiatic, and from Gourmanchéma and Fongbe, Niger-Congo languages, reviewed in this section all show evidence of various stages of the DP cycle.

8. Creoles

Recent work on the structure of the creole nominal includes Bruyn (1995), Déprez (2003, 2007), and especially Baptista and Guéron (2006). Bickerton (1981) suggests that a typical creole language distinguishes between specific and nonspecific but there is enormous variation and no two creoles have the same nominal system. Number marking seems crucial in many to mark referentiality. In this section, I provide a few examples and show how they may fit in the stages of the cycle.

Bruyn (1995: 98) examines the history of Sranan Tongo, a creole of Surinam. In Modern Sranan, the definite articles are singular *(n)a* and plural *den*, but in earlier forms these are *da* and *den* respectively. Bruyn provides examples of definite markers from the eighteenth century, as in (167), where *da boote* 'the boat' has been mentioned previously.

(167) *Cezar joe*   *bin*   *tey*   **da**   *boote*   *bon* ...   Early Sranan
        Caesar you   PST   tie   the   boat   well

       'Caesar, did you tie the boat well?' (van Dyk 110, from Bruyn 1995: 99)

She notes (see also 2006: 359) that the articles are sometimes still seen as having deictic value because they do not occur together with the more deictic *dati*. The latter is used as third person independent pronoun as well. This situation changes by the end of the eighteenth century, as (168) shows, where *dati* is used as an additional marker of deixis, that is, a renewal.

(168) **den**   *dey*   **dati**   Sranan
     the-P   day   that

     'those days' (Leys 735, from Bruyn 1995: 107)

Bruyn also examines the relative frequency of the articles *da/(n)a*, as in (167), and *den*, as in (168), over three centuries and notes that their frequency goes up, expected if they are grammaticalizing. The relative frequency of reinforcing demonstratives also goes up.

Deprez (2007) develops a very comprehensive account of grammaticalization of the elements in DP, also in terms of changes in the features, in a way very similar to what I have suggested. She argues, as I have, that specifiers have interpretable features and heads uninterpretable ones. Some heads trigger movement to their specifier and thus appear postnominally, as in Mauritian Creole (169) with a structure as in (170); other heads do not.

(169) **sa**   *bann*   *zom*   **la**   Mauritian Creole
     DEM   P   men   DEF

     'these men' (from Deprez 2007)

(170)

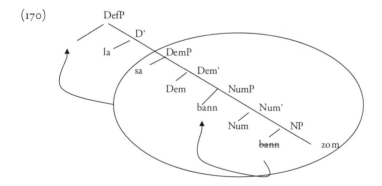

If a determiner is in the specifier position, it will always be initial to its phrase; if it is a head, it will trigger movement of a lower phrase to its specifier. The changes are from specifier to head, and from interpretable to uninterpretable, though this might involve triggering movement into the specifier position, itself not economical.

Jamaican Creole has a definite and indefinite article, *di* and *wan* respectively. The demonstratives are interesting in that they can be split, as in (171) and (172).

(171) a. *dat-de*   *bwai*   Jamaican Creole
       'that boy'
     b. *da*   *bwai-de*
       'that boy'
       (Bailey 1966 : 29)

(172)   a. *dem-de bwai*   Jamaican Creole

'those boys'

b. *dem   bwai-de*

those boys' (Bailey 1966 : 29)

This is very reminiscent of the data in English, where the locative *there* is used to reinforce a demonstrative.

Creoles can thus be characterized as using a DP system where cyclical renewal takes place.

9. Conclusion

Demonstratives are very frequent across the world's languages and express definiteness and location relative to the speech event. Articles convey just definiteness and appear, for instance, in Indo-European, Hungarian and Finnish, Uto-Aztecan, Yuman, Salish, Algonquian, Austronesian, Afro-Asiatic, Niger-Congo, and Creoles. Apart from those discussed in this chapter, articles appear in the Indo-European Armenian, Bengali, and Kashmiri; in Dravidian (e.g., Sinhalese); in Basque (Trask 1997: 199); in Oto-Manguean, Mixe-Zoque, Mayan, and Wakashan. Huang (1999) argues they can even be found in Chinese. Royen (1929), Himmelmann (1997: 195–198), Diessel (1999), Lyons (1999), and Anderson (2005) provide further references and examples.

I have suggested that some of the stages and changes that demonstratives undergo can be seen in terms of a DP cycle where demonstratives in specifier positions are reanalyzed as heads. The deictic meaning that was earlier connected with the demonstrative is lost when it bleaches to an article but this deictic function can then be renewed through other means, such as a deictic adverb or a demonstrative. This change can be formulated in terms of features being reanalyzed from semantic to formal, as in (83).

Part III

7

THE TENSE, MOOD, AND ASPECT (TMA) CYCLES

IN THE PRECEDING chapters, we have looked at how subject and object arguments are marked on the verb (chapters 2 to 4) as well as at how nominals display a variety of functions (chapters 5 and 6). Space/deixis marked on nouns is comparable to time/tense marked on verbs. In this chapter, I consider only the tip of the iceberg of how tense, mood, and aspect are indicated on verbs and how time, space, evidence, and manner grammaticalize. Links to the other cycles could also be made but what I want to emphasize here are the cyclical TMA patterns.

The mechanisms of the TMA cycles much resemble those in earlier chapters in that the Head Preference Principle and Late Merge are very obvious. These can again be translated as Feature Economy. Each cycle is a little different. For instance, future auxiliaries derive from verbs and aspectual markers from verbs, adverbs, and adpositions. Markers of TMA are found throughout the clause. The CP layer has mood and tense, in the shape of adverbs and complementizers; the TP layer has mood, tense, and aspect, in the shape of auxiliaries and adverbs; and the VP layer has aspect, in the shape of adverbs. As is common, I use the term *adverbial* when the function is relevant and *adverb* when the form is. Sometimes, they are hard to distinguish.

After some general remarks in section 1, I look at expressions of mood and tense in the CP layer in section 2. In sections 3 to 5, I focus on the TP—on tense in section 3, on future in section 4, and on mood in section 5. Analysis of the future cycle is the easiest since it builds on work by Harris (1969), Roberts (1993), Hopper and Traugott (2003), Roberts and Roussou (2003), and others. The other cycles have been less documented. I then turn to aspect in section 6, which is represented in both the TP and the VP. The organization is therefore from the top layer to the bottom one.

1. Tense, Mood, and Aspect

I won't provide much introduction on tense, mood, and aspect; for good background, see Comrie (1976, 1985), Bybee (1985), Bybee, Perkins, and Pagliuca (1994), and Abraham and Leiss (2008). Dahl and Velupillai (2008) give evidence that only half of the languages in their sample express present and nonpresent tense and that only half indicate perfective and imperfective aspect. This of course doesn't mean that the other languages don't express when and in what manner an action took place; some do this lexically. Putting aspect and tense together, Dryer (2008a) shows that 87 percent of the languages in his sample have tense or aspect inflection or both. Similarly, most languages have some kind of future marker but only half express that through inflection. Mood is much harder to estimate and the *World Atlas of Linguistic Structures* (*WALS*) (Haspelmath et al. 2006) has many maps dealing with modal categories.

Cross-linguistically, tense, mood, and aspect are marked through adverbs, as in (1), or by auxiliaries, as in (2), or by affixes, as in (3), or by preverbs/particles, as in (4), from Old English.

(1) I [possibly] saw him [quickly] [some time ago]
     mood   aspect   tense

(2) I [may] [have] seen him before
     mood   tense + aspect

(3) I walk[ed] around
     tense

(4) ... *þæt* *[ge]sawon*
          that   PF-saw-P
                 aspect

'[they] saw that' (*Beowulf*, in Klaeber [1922] 1941: 1591)

Apart from what we have seen in section 4.2 of chapter 5, these categories are not normally marked on the noun. I am listing the sequence of these elements as TMA, but nothing hinges on that. There are other ordering possibilities, as (1) and (2) show. Not all types of TMA markers are grammaticalized; the ones in (1) are fairly lexical. Cinque (1999) and Haumann (2007) incorporate them all in the clausal structure and so will I for expository convenience.

I will be dividing the clause into three layers, the highest CP layer where pragmatic information is provided, the middle TP layer where grammatical agreement is marked, and the VP layer that provides mainly lexical and thematic information. Cinque (1999: 106) provides the ordering of adverbs in (5) for the higher adverbs and in (6) for the TP ones. Haumann's (2007: 403) list in (7) provides a nice skeleton for aspect in the VP, where DegPerf, Freq, Rep, AspPcompl, and Rest stand for degree of perfection, frequency, repetition, and completion adverb respectively.

(5) CP Layer
     Mood $_{speech\ act}$ Mood $_{evaluative}$ Mood $_{evidential}$ Mod $_{epistemic}$
     frankly   *fortunately*   *allegedly*   *probably*
     honestly   *evidently*

(6) TP Layer

Tpast	Tfut	Moodir	Modnec	Modpos	ASPhab	ASPrep	ASPfreq
once	*then*	*perhaps*	*necessarily*	*possibly*	*usually*	*again*	*often*

(7) VP Layer

SpaceP	> AgentP	> DomainP	> MannerP	> DegPerfP >
here	*deliberately*	*universally*	*loudly*	*slightly*
MeansP	> FreqP	> RepP	> AspPcompl	> RestP
manually	*rarely*	*again*	*completely*	*again*

TABLE 7.1

Order and Kind of Tense Marking

	Number	%		Number	%	Total examined
V+T	202	72	T V	63	23	
T+V	60	21	V T	33	12	
Total						280

From Julien 2002: 48

+ indicates affixation

I will provide trees for each of these layers in the relevant sections.

Julien (2002) provides data from a typological study of 530 languages from 280 genera/ families,[1] and one can draw theoretical conclusions regarding the base order. She focuses on how tense is represented (and tense combined with aspect). There are four basic possibilities and they are given in table 7.1 together with the percentages of language genera in Julien's corpus.

Since some language genera can have a combination of these strategies, the total of the percentages are above 100 percent.

Patterns [V+T] and [T V] should be the most common under a Kaynian approach of movement to the left and adjunction to the left, and they are. To get [V+T], the V moves to the c-commanding T in (8) and [T V] is the base order:[2]

(8)

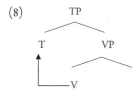

Patterns [T+V] and [V T] are unexpected assuming (8). However, Julien notices that in many prefix languages speakers consider the prefix less connected to the verb than suffixes.

---

1. *WALS* does not include a section on analytic versus synthetic marking of TMA. It includes chapters on affix order and prefixing or suffixing tendencies.

2. Julien's (2002: 48) numbers include "tense or aspect" morphemes, and that makes the data more complicated.

Therefore, it could be that many of the [T+V] instances are really [T V]. It could also be that the tense prefix is an (adverb-like) head, base generated lower than V, and moving to join V. For tense, this is less likely but it has happened in the case of aspectual prefixes, as we'll see in section 6.3. If Julien is right that prefixes are in fact independent morphemes, the percentages in table 7.1 would be less skewed: the suffixes would be found in 72 percent of the genera examined and auxiliaries in 44 percent (again noting that the total is above 100 percent since some language genera have a combination of the two).

Tree (8) together with the assumption that [T+V] is really [T V] explains three of the four patterns, namely [V+T], [T+V], and [T V]. The remaining pattern, [V T], could be derived through (remnant) movement of the VP to Spec TP, or through Long Head Movement. Julien's numbers therefore make (8) into the most likely structure and the one I'll use.

So far, I have reviewed the possible morphological shapes of TMA markers in (1) to (4), their orders in each of the three clausal layers in (5) to (7), and the order of T vis à vis V. The variety of the markings displayed in (1) to (4) represents cyclical change: (1) and (2) are analytic and (3) and (4) are synthetic stages. The adverbs and auxiliaries in (1) and (2) could be precursors to the affixes in (3) and (4). Figure 7.1 shows a generic cycle from analytic auxiliaries to synthetic TMA markers, where F stands for T, M, or ASP, and [f] for the features connected to that position. Stage (a) is the analytic stage where the TMA auxiliary verb is base generated in the TMA head. In most languages, there will be a probe with [u-phi] that the TMA combines with and that may be responsible for the movement of the V to F. Stage (b) is synthetic and the lexical verb may move to the TMA head. Stage (c) is similar to (a), analytic again, but with the erstwhile lexical verb as auxiliary.

The auxiliary in F has interpretable features in stage (a) but in stage (b) it has been reanalyzed as a probe with uninterpretable features. V-a in stages (a) and (b) and V-b in stage (c) are main verbs, with V-a reanalyzed as auxiliary in stage (c). Late Merge is relevant to most changes affecting TMA: it occurs between stages (b) and (c) in figure 7.1.

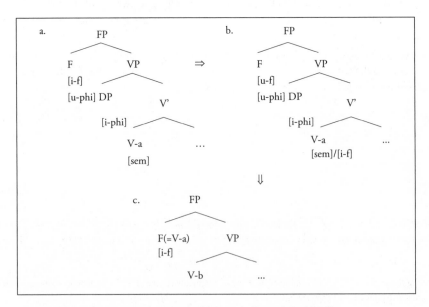

FIGURE 7.1. A generic TMA cycle (F stands for TMA)

In a number of cycles, once something is a functional head it has uninterpretable features. Since some heads have multiple features, the relevant point is that at least one feature is uninterpretable. That is most likely the (person) phi-feature. It could also be that the tense or aspect features in (a) of figure 7.1 are uninterpretable and that interpretable features, in the form of –*ed* and –*ing*, are part of the lexical verb. This would account for affix-hop in English.

Late Merge is also relevant when VP adverbs are reanalyzed as CP or TP adverbs, as shown in figure 7.2, and as preverbs, as shown in section 6.3. The changes in figure 7.2 are harder to formulate as changes in features and I will not (see also Roberts 2010a for difficulties in this regard). The next section starts with cyclical change in the CP layer.

2. Mood and Tense in the CP

Section 2.1 provides a structural description of the CP; it is based on Rizzi (1997, 2001) and Cinque (1999). Section 2.2 focuses on the changes in (mood) adverbs that have occurred in this layer throughout Old English. Later changes are very similar so I provide a few examples in the appendix. As just mentioned, I don't know of a characterization of adverbials in terms of features, so the explanation of the changes in 2.2 is in terms of Late Merge only. In 2.3, I examine how tense is represented in the CP. If C has [u-T], as I argued in chapter 5, the grammaticalization path is not unexpected, having as a source demonstrative pronouns and locative and temporal prepositions.

2.1 THE CP

I assume that the high adverbials in (5) can be part of the high CP layer (see also van Gelderen 2001, 2004).[3] This happens either through base generation or through movement to prominence) phrase (PromP), with the PromP added for the preposed adverbials. The rough structure of the CP layer is as in (9). Note the high position of *that*. The latter can also be lower cross-linguistically.

(9)

---

3. This is unlike the system developed in Cinque (1999), who considers them situated below the FinP.

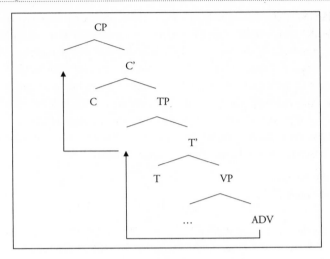

FIGURE 7.2. Late Merge of adverbials

Haumann (2007: 408) has a slightly different cartography, but also fits all the adverbials of
(5) into the CP. There is of course a debate as to whether a top-down approach, as in (9), or
a bottom-up approach, as in much Minimalism, is correct. This is a fundamental question
that I don't address in this book. I will therefore just use (9) descriptively.

2.2 MODAL ADVERBIALS: FROM LOW TO HIGH

Many English higher adverbials derive from lower adverbials (and many of these from adjectives); the high ones disappear and are replaced by new ones. Hence, one can speak of a cycle.
The rate of change is quite fast; for instance, during the Old English period there is at least
one full cycle that adverbials undergo. Swan (1991: 409) writes that there has been a "tremen-
dous growth of a certain class of adverbials in English."

There are alternative analyses to the one I advocate here. For instance, Berry (2009) argues
that the CP-adverbial speech act adverb *frankly*, and he would argue the same is true for other
high adverbials, is the result of a lexicalization of an independent clause containing *frankly*.
Lexicalization is a process where lexical categories are created from phrases (see Brinton &
Traugott 2005). Berry, using data from the Corpus of Contemporary American, argues that
frankly as a CP adverb is a relatively recent development and he suggests the scenario in (10).

(10)   a.   "May I speak frankly?" Farrell nodded. "Always, . . ."
        b.   I must speak frankly now and tell you that I see no reason . . .
        c.   If I might speak frankly, there's others . . .
        d.   To speak frankly, Barbara, do you think . . .
        e.   Frankly speaking, if you're looking . . .
        f.   Frankly, in the spirit of free speech, that's good (Berry 2009: 6 [9])

I think this analysis of *frankly* is correct, but I don't think it holds for Old English adverbials,
mainly because the preposing from VP to CP happens slowly, as we'll see in table 7.3. Such
gradual change is typical of grammaticalization.

There are (infrequent) sentences such as (11) that might provide evidence for a lexicalization account if we could find intermediate stages where the adjectives of the higher clause reanalyze as adverbials in the lower clause.

(11) a. *Wæs eac **wundorlic** þæt seo ðruh wæs geworht . . .*
          'It was also wonderful that the coffin was made . . .
          (Aelfric, *Lives of Saints*, 20.102, in Skeat 1881–1900: 1: 438)

      b. *Nes þet naht **wunderlic** þet he þone deaþes deg swa unforht abad . . .*
          not-is that not wonderful that he the death's day so unfearfully awaited . . .

          'Isn't that wonderful that he . . .' (*Saint Chad*, 148, in Vleeskruyer 1953: 174, DOE segment 18)

Fischer (2007: 286) also thinks these constructions are the source of the later CP adverbials. Even though I argue for a grammaticalization account in Old English, that doesn't mean the origin of all CP adverbials would have to be that way.

Old English adverbs can either be positioned in the left periphery (and are then sentence adverbials) or closer to the verb "in the middle" of the sentence (and then function more like VP adverbials). The marking of adverbs by *-lice* increases in the course of Old English, as does their preposed position, and their incorporation into the higher layer. This means Old English VP adverbials are reanalyzed as CP ones, after frequent preposing. I will first look at the origin of CP adverbials, their position and position of the verb, and their marking by *-lice*, and then at the different rates of preposing of the different adverbs. Finally, I look at the demise of the high adverbials.

Some Old English CP adverbials are *witodlice* 'surely, certainly, undoubtedly', as in (12), *wundorlice* 'wonderfully, remarkably', as in (13), and *soðlice* 'truly', as in (14). In the classification of (5), these would be evidential and epistemic adverbs, that is, in the low CP domain.

(12) ***Witodlice** [æfter þam þe ic of deaþe arise] ic cume to eow on galilee*
      Surely after that that I of death arise I come to you in Galilee

      'Surely, after I arise from the dead, I come to you in Galilee.' (Gospels, West Saxon version, Matthew 26.32, Hatton, in Skeat [1881–1887] 1970).

(13) *& **wundorlice** nædran wæron geseogene on Suðseaxna lande*

      'and remarkably serpents were seen in the South Saxon's land'
      (*Peterborough Chronicle*, 774.5, in Thorpe 1861)

(14) **Soðlice** monn   ðes   sunu   godes   wæs.
      Surely   man   of-the   son   God's   was

      'Surely this man was the son of God.' (Gospels, Lindisfarne, Mark 15.39, in Skeat [1881–1887] 1970, from *OED*)

Note that (12) could still be a VP adverbial modifying *cume to eow* and how none of these adverbials have the verb immediately following, that is, they show a lack of verb-second. Swan (1988) considers that a sign of adjunction, and not of proper incorporation.

The Old English CP adverbials are derived from adjectives or are noun compounds, as in *wundor* 'miracle' and *soð* 'truth', and the noun *lice* 'body'. *Witod* is an adjective in Old English with the meaning of 'appointed, certain' (though it ultimately derives from a noun meaning 'law'). In early Old English, for instance in the Junius manuscript, *witod* is typically used as an adjective, as in (15) and (16), and so is *sweotol* in (17). These adjectives can be attributive as well as predicative.

(15) *Ne bið þec mælmete . . . ne rest **witod***
      not is you-DAT food . . . nor resting-place fixed

      'You shall have no food, nor a fixed resting-place.'
      (Daniel, Junius, 574–575, in Krapp 1931)

(16) *here stille bad **witodes** willan,*
      host silent awaited fixed will

      'The host awaited in silence his fixed will.' (Exodus, Junius, 551–552, in Krapp 1931)

(17) *þæt wæs tacen **sweotol***
      That was sign clear

      'That was a clear sign.' (*Beowulf*, in Klaeber [1922] 1941: 833)

The adverb is formed with an -*e* initially; for example, *sweotole* 'clearly, openly' is used as a VP adverb especially in the early Old English period, as Swan (1988: 107) also observes. Some examples appear in (18a) and (18b).

(18) a. *Hit wæs eac **sweotole** gesiene þæt hit wæs Godes stihtung*

          'It was also clearly seen that it was God's dispensation.'
          (*Orosius*, 133.21, in Bately 1980)
      b. *Hu ne is þe nu **genoh sweotole** gesæd þæt . . .*
          how not is you now enough clearly proven that . . .

          'Is it not now clearly enough proved to you that . . .'
          (Alfred, *Boethius*, 11: 25.28, in Sedgefield 1899)

Later in the Old English period, VP adverbs are increasingly marked by -*lice*, as in (19) and (20).

(19) *ic gelyfe **witodlice** þæt eallswa God unc geuþe þæt wit unc gemetton, þæt . . .*
      I believe truly that so God us gave that we us met that . . .

      'I believe verily that just as God granted us that we met that . . .'
      (Aelfric, *Lives of Saints*, 2: 30.369, in Skeat 1881–1900: 212)

(20) a. *se þe **soðlice** gelyfð*

          'he who truly believes'
          (Aelfric, *Lives of Saints*, 1: 246, in Skeat 1881–1900, from Swan 1988: 99)
      b. *Ic þe **soðlice** andette þæt . . .*
          I you truly confess that . . .

          'I confess truly to you that. . . .'
          (Bede, 134, Miller 1890–1898, from Swan 1988: 99)

Preposing of the adverbial increases in the Old English period. Since preposed adverbials are often ambiguous between VP and CP adverbial, as in (20), I assume they initially prepose and are then reanalyzed in that position.

(21)   **soðlice**   unc   gecypeþ   *ure Drihten Hælend Crist his mægen*
       surely   us   manifests   our Lord Savior Christ his power

       'Surely our Lord will manifest his power to us.' (*Blickling Homilies*, 159, Morris 1874–1880, from Swan 1988: 90)

To see a few of the changes from early Old to late Old English, I'll provide some examples of adverbs in the Junius manuscript (in Krapp 1931) and compare them with some homilies by Aelfric. The Junius manuscript comprises Genesis, Exodus, Daniel, and Christ and Satan and is from around the year 1000, but parts are assumed to be from the eighth century (see Krapp 1931: xxvi). In this manuscript, I found no preposed adverbs ending in *-lice*, and as seen earlier, *witod* and *sweotol* are used as adjectives. Typical adverbials appear in (22).

(22)   *We þe **arlice** gefeormedon and þe **freondlice** on þisse werþeode wic getæhton*
       we you with-honor entertained and you friendly in this realm dwelling gave

       'We harbored you with honor and gave you a dwelling in this realm in a friendly way.' (Genesis, Junius, 2686–2688, in Krapp 1931)

In this manuscript of a little less than thirty thousand words, there are only thirty-four adverbs that end in *-lice*, as in (22), or one in a thousand words. Adverbs that end in *-e*, such as *georne* in (23), are few as well and, although some of them are clause-initial, it is often hard to see where that clause starts.

(23)   **Georne** *þurh godes gife gemunan gastes bled*
       Eagerly through God's grace to mind spirit's joy

       'Gladly by God's grace, to be mindful of the spirit's joy.' (Christ and Satan, 644)

In these texts, there are phrases where speech act and other CP adverbials might be used in present-day English. Some of these are listed in (24ad). I add only a word-by-word gloss and not a translation because I don't think a literal one would do it justice.

(24)   a.   *Swa he sylfa cwæð*
           so he self said (Christ and Satan, 305)
      b.   *Segdest us to soðe*
           say-2S us to truth (Christ and Satan, 63)
      c.   *þa geseah selfa*
           then saw self (Genesis, 1270)
      d.   *Ah ic þe hate þurh þa hehstan miht*
           but I you command through the highest power (Christ and Satan, 693)

Constructions such as (11) do not occur in the Junius manuscript with adjectives ending in *-lic*, suggesting that there were no conditions favorable to a lexicalization account.

TABLE 7.2

Some Frequent Adverbs in Part of Aelfric

	Gloss	Total	Clause-Initial	V-2
soðlice	truly	52	24 (46%)	0
witodlice	surely	28	24 (86%)	2
rihtlice	rightly	23	6 (26%)	4
gastlice	spiritually	14	0 (0%)	0
lichamlice	physically	14	0 (0%)	0
geornlice	eagerly	13	0 (0%)	0
georne	eagerly	5	0 (0%)	0

Late Old English manuscripts, for example, the works of Aelfric, are quite different and abound with preposed adverbs, as in (25).

(25)   **Witodlice** *on swa micelre sibbe wæs crist acenned*

'Verily in such great peace was Christ born.'
(*Homilies* 1: 32.15, in Thorpe [1844–1846] 1971)

One part of the Aelfric's *Homilies* (segment 5 in the DOE corpus), comprising around sixty thousand words, has 376 adverbs that end in *–lice*, that is, six in a thousand words. This is quite an increase compared to the earlier text. It has twenty-eight instances of *witodlice* and all but four are in clause-initial position; *soðlice* is a little less frequent in initial position, twenty-four of fifty-two instances. Table 7.2 lists some frequent adverbs. The last column lists the number of clause-initial adverbs that trigger verb-second.[4] Thus, the main difference between the early and late Old English is in the number of adverbs (certainly those ending in *–lice*) and their position.

Swan (1991: 415) shows that many of the sentence-initial adverbs are evaluative or subject intensifying. She argues that they are on their way to being disjuncts, that is, no longer topicalized. In the framework I use, this means they are base generated in the high positions. I reproduce Swan's data (Swan 1988: 89, 103, 130, 160, 164) as table 7.3 and use the terms for the adverbs she does. These data are from a corpus of Old English texts that Swan selected. As is obvious, there is a lot of difference, but *witodlice* is most often preposed and most often results in verb-second. Swan says that *soðlice* on its own does not cause inversion but often has another element before the inverted verb, as in (22). For my purposes the column of preposed adverbials is the relevant one, and one sees a real difference between the different types.Many of the preposed adverbs have a degree adverb accompanying them, as in (26), making them clear phrases.

---

4. Interestingly, the two verbs that follow *witodlice* are negatives.

TABLE 7.3

Preposing of Adverbials in Old English

Swan's Label		Meaning	Total	Clause-Initial	V-2
Truth intensifier	*witodlice*	surely	67	43 (64%)	8/43 (19%)
	soðlice	truly	135	30 (22%)	0
Evaluative	*wundorlice*	wonderfully	24	3 (13%)	2/24 (.08%)
	sweotolice	clearly	14	3 (21%)	0
	sweotole	clearly	20	3 (15%)	0
Subject oriented	*rihtlice*	rightly	62	4 (.06%)	1 (.16%)
	rihte	rightly	32	8 (.25%)	1 (.03%)

From Swan 1988

(26) **Suiðe ryhte** *se bið geteald to ðæm liceterum se ðe . . .*
very rightly he is counted to that hypocrisy who that . . .

'He is very rightly considered a hypocrite, who . . .'
(Alfred, *Pastoral Care*, Hatton, 121.23, in Sweet [1871] 1934)

Though quite a few Old English sentence adverbials are clause-initial, not all are, as (27) to (29) show.

(27) *Ne deþ **witodlice** nan man niwes claðes scyp on eald reaf.*
Not does surely no man new cloth piece on old garment

'Surely, no man will put an old cloth onto a new one.'
(Gospels, West Saxon version, Matthew 9.16, in Skeat [1881–1887] 1970)

(28) *Gað nu **witodlice** to weʒa.*
Go now surely to ways

'Go therefore on the highways . . .' (Gospels, West Saxon version, Matthew 22.9, in Skeat [1881–1887] 1970)

(29) *Næron hi **witodlice** naðor ne godes scep, ne godes bearn þa gyt.*
not-were they surely neither not God's sheep nor God's children then yet.
(Aelfric, *Homily*, Corpus 162, in Assmann [1889] 1964: 70, from *OED*)

Some of the CP adverbials are very frequent. In the entire Old English corpus (DOE), *witodlice* occurs 1,629 times and *soðlice* 4,902 times. Other such adverbs are *sicerlice* 'surely', *wærlice* 'truly', *wiselice* 'wisely', and *rihtlice* 'justly, correctly' (with varying spellings, of course).

The position of these is variable. In (25), *witodlice* is very high but in (29), it occurs probably after Fin. The assumption is that the lower position is an intermediate stage between a VP adverbial and a CP one.

(30)

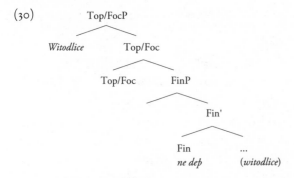

In the *OED*, the last instances of *witodlice* and *wundorlice* are from late Old English (using the *OED*'s advanced search); and of *soothly* they are from the nineteenth century, but these are archaisms. The Helsinki Corpus confirms that for *witodlice*, *soðlice*, and *wundorlice* the last examples are in the early Middle English part (ME1). Looking at the Helsinki Corpus gives a sense of frequency. Because the sizes of these parts are not equal—e.g. OEI-2 is less than half the size of OE-3[5]—I have also given the percentages these adverbs appear among total words in the text (table 7.4).

This section has so far shown a number of Old English adverbs that speakers of Modern English might classify as high adverbials, that is, as expressing the speaker's sentiments. In Old English, many of these adverbials are VP adverbials, not placed sentence-initially. Those that are initial are often marked by -*lice*. Since manner adverbials are often preposed, they can be reanalyzed as mood adverbials in higher positions. This is because manner adverbials are inherently ambiguous. As a result of these changes, new VP and CP adverbials appear in Middle English, as shown in the appendix to the chapter.

Section 2.2 shows that the high adverbials in English have undergone fairly fast grammaticalization: they originate inside the VP and, after a stage of frequent preposing, they are reanalyzed as base generated in the CP. An explanation in terms of Late Merge is easy to

TABLE 7.4

Adverbial Uses in the Helsinki Corpus

	Meaning	OE 1–2	OE 3	OE 4	ME1	ME2
witodlice	surely	2	84	20	9	—
wærlice	truly	5	10	5	5	—
soþlice	truly	72	205	19	37	2
wiselice	wisely	—	6	3	9	—
wundorlice	wonderfully	3	21	1	7	—
rihtlice	rightly	3	27	10	4	1
Numbers		85	353	58	71	3
Percentage of total		.09	.14	.09	.06	.003

---

5. See http://www.helsinki.fi/varieng/CoRD/corpora/HelsinkiCorpus/period.html.

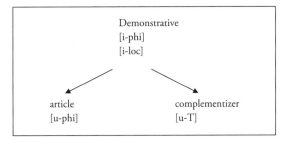

FIGURE 7.3. Feature Economy and the demonstrative pronoun

formulate. My conclusion is similar to Traugott and Dasher's (2002: 188), namely that "different languages may favor different kinds of ADVs at different times in their histories" but that the changes are unidirectional. From mood markers in the CP, we now turn to tense markers.

2.3 THE TENSE MARKERS IN THE CP

Complementizers such as *that, for, while, since, once, after*, and *before* appear in Fin or in Force in (9). They are mostly deictic demonstratives or are related to words of time and place. Germanic is not the only group of languages to have developed a complementizer from a demonstrative. Diessel (1999: 125–126) lists many more languages (Hixkaryana, Epena Pedee, and Khasi among them). Noonan (1985) and Frajzyngier (1991) provide further examples. In 2.3.1, I'll restrict myself to English *that* and give a brief history as well as a possible account for the change. The change from preposition to complementizer is a frequent one, too; see, for example, Heine and Kuteva (2002). In 2.3.2, I'll also consider some English examples.

2.3.1 *That*

The history of *that* is very complex. As we have seen in the previous chapter, the masculine demonstrative *se* evolves from a demonstrative into an article around the end of the Old English period. It loses deictic features in the process and becomes a D head with uninterpretable features. If the complementizer also derives from the demonstrative (the neuter singular demonstrative in this case), demonstratives are reanalyzed in two ways, in accordance with Feature Economy, as heads D with loss of deictic and phi features (discussed in chapter 6) and as complementizers with loss of interpretable deictic features. Figure 7.3 shows both developments.The demonstrative has locative and person features. If it loses the locative ones, we end up with an article (with a possible in-between stage of a demonstrative that still has interpretable person features). If the demonstrative loses phi features, it can end up as a complementizer with u-T (with a possible in-between stage as well). I'll focus on the latter change in this section.

In chapter 5, we have seen that the complementizer C has uninterpretable [u-T] features and that is represented in the figure. According to Pesetsky and Torrego (2001), *that* is the spell-out of a T with interpretable tense features. Some problems occurred with Pesetsky and Torrego's analysis, in particular regarding the lack of C-deletion in Old English (and no "*that*-trace" effects). I mentioned some alternatives; for example, *that* could have [u-T]. I will argue that the lack of C deletion is due to the interpretable features of C in the older period. As they are reanalyzed as uninterpretable, C becomes deletable.

Some linguists have argued that the complementizer *that* in Germanic is a reanalyzed form of the demonstrative pronoun *that*; see Lockwood (1968: 222) and Hopper and Traugott (2003: 191–192). Many linguists have arged that the clause that it introduces in present-day Germanic is an adjunct (see Kiparsky 1995). Wessén (1970: 299), discussing the history of Swedish, says "[d]ieses *þat* hatte anfangs determinative Funktion und gehörte daher zum Hauptsatz . . . und der nachfolgende Satz war appositive Bestimmung dazu" (This *that* originally had a determinative function and therefore belonged to the main clause . . . and the sentence that followed was appositive). However, this change must have happened before Old English split off from Germanic since complementizer *that* is frequent from the oldest texts on, as in (31).

(31) *þæt hit þus gelomp **þæt** hi sceawodon scyppend engla.*
      (thanked) that it thus happened that they saw prince angles

      'that it thus happened that they saw the Prince of angles'
      (Christ and Satan, Junius, 532–533, in Krapp 1931)

The complementizer *þæt* cannot be misunderstood for an actual argument with an independent clause because *hit* is there in (31). Many times, due to the more paratactic nature of Old English, the *þæt* clause seems a little more independent. I'll argue that, even though *that* is part of the CP in Old English, it is in the specifier position, not yet in the head C.

One piece of evidence that the conjunction originally belongs to the main clause is that the morphological Case of the demonstrative in Old English often reflects its function in the main clause, unlike in Modern English. Hock (1991: 342) mentions that "similar patterns are found in Old Norse and traces also in Gothic." Thus, the "heralding object" (Visser 1963–1973: 459), as in (32a) and (32b), is Case marked by the main verb: accusative and genitive respectively.

(32) a. *Ic **þæt** gehyre [þæt þis is hold weorod frean Scyldinga]*
          I that-ACC heard that this is strong company (of the) lord (of the) Scyldings

          'I hear that this is a company loyal to the lord of the Scyldings.' (*Beowulf*, 290–291, in Klaeber [1922] 1941)

      b. *þæs ne wendon ær witan Scyldinga*
          that-GEN not believed before (the) wise (of) Scylding-P
          [þæt hit . . . manna ænig . . . tobrecan meahte]
          that it men any destroy could

          'The Scylding elders didn't believe before that anyone could destroy [the hall].'
          (*Beowulf*, 778–780, in Klaeber [1922] 1941)

I am not certain that this is good evidence to prove that *þæt* and *þæs* reanalyzed as complementizers since they are still demonstratives in (32) and the second *þæt* is clearly part of the embedded clause. I follow the traditional account, however, and the development in figure 7.3 that *that* reanalyzes from demonstrative to complementizer in a change from deictic location features to tense. I argue that change didn't proceed in one step but in two: *that* was first merged as a specifier and then as a head.

If Pesetsky and Torrego are right that the finite C has tense features that must be checked by either a nominative, by *that*, or by an auxiliary, then two phenomena that are explained by this checking are the optionality of *that* in English complement clauses (since either the subject DP or *that* can check [u-T]) and the *that*-trace effect in Modern English. This is where a problem turns up for their analysis. If *that* is reanalyzed as [i-T] before the Old English period, it should be deletable in Old English as well and there should also be a "*that* trace" effect. However, van Gelderen (1993: 59–84) shows that the optionality of the complementizer appears around 1380 and *that*-trace is not ungrammatical in Old English, as (33) shows, taken from Allen (1977).

(33) *Ac hwaet saegst ðu ðonne **ðaet hwæt** sie forcuðre ðonne sio ungesceadwisnes?*
       But what say you then that is wickeder than be foolishness

       'But what do you say is wickeder than foolishness?' (Alfred, *Boethius*, 36.8, from
       Allen 1977: 122)

A solution to this could be that the second *that* in (32ab) is still a demonstrative in the specifier of the CP and that those are not deletable. Evidence for such a view can in fact be found in van Gelderen (2004), even though there it is not phrased in terms of features. There is in Old and Middle English a complementizer *þe/te* (a bleached descendant of the demonstrative *þa* according to the *OED*) that follows *that*, as in (34). That makes it look like *that* is a specifier preceding a head (see van Gelderen 2004: 82–87) with interpretable tense features.

(34) *monig oft gecwæð **þæt te** suð ne norð . . . oþer . . . selra nære*
       many often said that that south nor north, other better not-was

       'It was often said that no better one could be found north or south.'
       (*Beowulf*, 858, in Klaeber [1922] 1941)

An account for the introduction of *that*-deletion would be to have a reanalysis of the interpretable features as uninterpretable and optional.

   In short, the change from older English to Modern English involves deictic features on *that* being reanalyzed as tense features, as in figure 7.4. Demonstratives are first reanalyzed as specifiers of CPs and later as their heads. I turn now to temporal complementizers where semantic temporal and locational features are likewise reanalyzed.

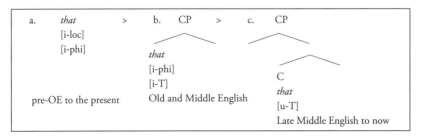

FIGURE 7.4. Demonstrative to complementizer

2.3.2 Temporal Complementizers

I consider a complementizer a word that introduces a clause, such as *that* but also *while, for, before*, and *after*, whereas a preposition introduces a nominal. In van Gelderen (2008e, 2009a), the tree for the P and C is presented as (35a) and (35b) respectively.

(35)   a.   PP   b.   CP

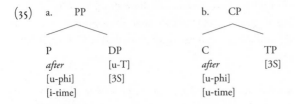

P	DP	C	TP
after	[u-T]	*after*	[3S]
[u-phi]	[3S]	[u-phi]	
[i-time]		[u-time]	

Both P and C are probes for a goal with phi features, hence the [u-phi]. The [u-time] on C expresses that it needs to probe for tense. This need for an (empty) [i-time] is compatible with the observations made by Geis (1970), cited in Larson (1990), that sentences such as (36) have two readings. In (36a), if the [i-time] appears in the clause with *claim*, it means I saw her in New York before she claimed something; if [i-time] is in the lower clause, she arrived unexpectedly. The same ambiguity occurs in (36b).

(36)   a.   I saw Mary in New York before
            [she claimed **i-time** [that she would arrive **i-time**]].
       b.   I encountered Alice after [she swore [that she had left]].
            (Geis 1970, from Larson 1990: 170)

C is also relevant for the tense interpretation of the T. I have ignored that in (35). Chomsky (2007: 20) argues that "[t]ense is a property of T, but receives only some residual interpretation unless selected by C. . . . One advantage of the latter option is that T will then have at least some feature in the lexicon." Chomsky considers the case only of *that*. I argue that the [u-time] in (35b) probes the [i-T] of the T but that the latter is connected with the empty adverbial in (36). The exact details remain for further work.

The history of "prepositional" complementizers is relatively well known (see van Gelderen 2008e, 2009a). In the case of *for* and *after*, as mentioned in chapter 1, the preposition was part of a PP that was often preposed and did double duty in introducing the clause temporally and in modifying the verb. The other complementizers, *while, once, ær*, and *before*, are less often discussed.

The origin of *while* is a noun, used as an adverbial in Old English, as in (37), but the use continues up to early Middle English (38) and the present.

(37)   **Lytle hwile** *sceolde he his lifes niotan*
       little while should he his life enjoy

       'For a little while he might enjoy this life.' (Genesis, 486, Junius, in Krapp 1931)

(38)   *þa lifede he **litle hwile** þær æfter buton þry gear.*
       then lived he little while there after only three years

       'Then he lived a little while, only three years, after that.'
       (*Peterborough Chronicle* [1066], 42)

By the time of Alfred and Aelfric, but not in the earlier poetic works such as *Beowulf* or those represented in the Junius manuscript, the noun forms part of a complex complementizer as well, as in (39). It changes to a simple one in early Middle English, as in (40), with a short period of *while that*.

(39) *Eall hie us þyncað þy leohtran **ða hwile þe** þa oncras fæste bioð*
      All they us seem the lighter the while that the anchors fast are

      'They all seem the lighter to us, as long as the anchors are fast.'
      (Alfred, *Boethius*, 10.23, in Sedgefield 1899: 14–15)

(40) *þet lastede þa .xix. wintre **wile** Stephne was king*

      'That lasted the 19 winters while Stephen was king.'
      (*Peterborough Chronicle* [1137])

In the early poetic texts of Old English, the preposed form in (38) is rare, but I haven't looked into the preposing of *while* in great detail. A head preference, however, is definitely at work from (39) to (40), very much like the history of the complementizers *after* and *for*, discussed in chapter 1.

Once is also an adverb in Old English, namely *ænes*, as in (41), but it isn't that frequent and so I can't compare early and late use.

(41) *Soðlice þa se broður þas word gehyrde **ænes**, ...*
      Truly then that brother that word heard once . . .

      'Truly when that brother heard that word once . . .'
      (Gregory, *Dialogues*, 4: 49.338.3, in Hecht [1900–1907] 1965)

The use of *once* in (41) is classified by Cinque (1999) as a tense use and I will therefore come back to it in the next section.

Ær (*ere*) is very frequent as adverb, meaning 'before, at an early hour', a preposition in (42), and a conjunction in (43). The grammaticalization is complete in Old English, however, as (43) shows.

(42) *Swa hi wærun on þam daȝum **ær** þam flode.*

      'as they were on those days before the flood'
      (*Anglo-Saxon Gospel*, Matthew 24.38, from *OED*)

(43) *Oft hio . . . secge sealde **ær** hie to setle geong*
      Often she . . . man-DAT gave before she to seat went

      'She often gave . . . to a warrior before she sat down herself.' (*Beowulf*, 2019, in
      Klaeber [1922] 1941)

The use of *ær* peters out; it probably became too phonologically reduced, as in the Middle English (44).

(44) *Thei asken hure hyure **er** þey hit haue deserued*

      'They ask their wages before they it have deserved.'
      (Langland, *Piers Plowman* C, 4: 303, from *OED*)

TABLE 7.5

Possible Feature Choices

ADV	P	C
[loc]/[time]	[i-loc]/[i-time]	[u-T]/[u-time]
Up/now	on/at	that/after

The use of *before* is much later than *ær* and is probably a renewal: the first use as C is the early Middle English (45); (46) is from the middle of the fourteenth century.

(45)　**Biforenn þatt** *te Laferrd Crist Wass borenn her to manne*

'before (that) the lord Christ was born here to mankind'
(*Ormulum*, 964, in Holt 1878)

(46)　*On oure **byfore** þe sonne go doun He se3 . . .*

'An hour before the sun goes down, he saw . . .' (*Pearl*, 9: 530, Andrew and Waldron 1978: 78)

The two sources of [T] features on C discussed in this section, a demonstrative source (for the finite *that* C) and a prepositional one (for *after, before*, etc.), are reminiscent of the clines in chapter 5. The interpretable temporal or spatial features of the preposition are reanalyzed as [T]. Table 7.5 lists possible settings for the locative/temporal features. Change involves the loss of semantic and interpretable features.

3. Tense in the TP Layer

In this section, I look at adverbs (in 3.1) and auxiliaries (in 3.2) used for tense marking. I'll start with a structure for the TP layer, based on (6) but with fewer positions. The adverbials in (47) are in the specifier positions and the auxiliaries in the head positions for a sentence as in (48).

(47)

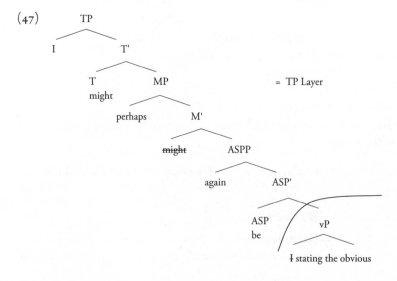

(48)   I guess I **might perhaps again be** "stating the obvious" and I apologise to FTers who feel annoyed by this. (http://flyertalk.com/forum/archive/index.php/t-63529.html)

3.1 ADVERBS IN THE TP LAYER

Cinque (1999) classifies only *once* and *then* as tense adverbials (see [6]). Compared to the number of aspectual and modal adverbs, that is meager indeed. Haumann (2007: 263) explains that there are many other temporal adverbs, such as *afterwards, before, now, since, today, tomorrow*, and *yesterday*, but that many are not grammatical in the area between the subject and the VP for a variety of reasons. For instance, the calendar adverbials (*Sunday, last week*, and *next year*) can occur in the left periphery and inside the VP, so are much more like circumstantial adverbs; they are almost PP-like. Hence, they are assumed to have moved to the PromP of structure (9), as in (49).

(49)   **Last week**, they were very happy ~~last week~~.

The history of *once* and *then* is extremely complex and I can't begin to do justice to it. *Once* in Old English means 'at one time in the past', as in (50), repeated from (41).

(50)   *Soðlice þa se broður þas word gehyrde ænes*, ...
        Truly then that brother that word heard once

        'truly when that brother heard that word once'
        (Gregory, *Dialogues*, 4: 49.338, Hecht [1900–1907] 1965)

The *OED* distinguishes "at one time only (not twice or more)," in other words, aspect, as in (50), from "at one time (as opposed to another)," that is, tense, as in the earliest example in (51).

(51)   *Ðises geares com þet leoht to Sepulchrum Domini innan Ierusalem twiges, ænes to Eastron, and oðre siðe to Assumptio sanctae Marie.*

        'This year came the light to Sepulchre (of the) Lord in Jerusalem twice, once at Easter and other time at (the) Assumption (of) St Mary.' (*Peterborough Chronicle* [1120])

The aspectual use is therefore older, as expected; *once* is still ambiguous between tense and aspect, as in (52) and (53).

(52)   I've only met him **once**. (BNC-EA5, 1807)

(53)   In all the years that Halifax held office I never met him **once**. (BNC-G12, 707)

Once is often used after a preposition (*at once* or *for once*) and is then probably a VP adverbial. It also has mood overtones and, starting around 1500, can also be used as a complementizer. Tracing its function as tense marker, one can probably say that it derives from a VP adverb as in (51) and then moves up.

Then has referred to past and future from the earliest Old English on, and unlike Cinque who refers to it as future, I will assume it is a nonpresent tense.

(54)   *Ond þæt ʒeweorþeþ on domes dæʒe . . . **þonne** forhtiaþ ealle ʒesceafta.*

    'And that happened on doom's day . . . then feared all creatures.'
    (*Blickling Homilies*, 11, in Morris 1874–1880)

The *OED* lists it from the beginning as "[r]eferring to a specified time, past or future." Even in Old English it is used as a complementizer, as in (55), a correlative structure.

(55)   ***þonne** se mona wanað, **þonne** tacnað he ure deaþlicnesse*

    'When the moon wanes, then marks he our mortality.' (*Blickling Homilies*, 17, in Morris 1874–1880)

This *þonne* was a temporal complementizer, replaced by *when* in the middle of the thirteenth century.

As to the adverbs expressing tense, there is certainly not the richness as for the other adverbs in the TP. This may be because there are other possibilities in head positions—auxiliaries and tense morphemes. The origin of the tense adverb *once* may derive from a VP adverbial, as in (51), but not much seems to be changing, and *once* is still both a tense and aspect adverb. *Then* has not changed much either and is still used as an adverb. It may have resisted grammaticalization because it is a pro form for a temporal PP, typically situated in the VP.

3.2 VERBAL TENSE

Cross-linguistically, there are very few auxiliaries expressing pure tense. For instance, most tense marking in creole languages by auxiliaries/particles is in fact aspect or future/irrealis, not present or past tense. Siewierska (2000: 380–381) mentions three origins for "tense markers," namely serial verbs, adverbs, and auxiliaries/verbs. Of the examples she gives, two are future and aspect, and one is past tense. As pointed out by Andrej Malchukov (p.c.), Nenets (Salminen 1997: 94) shows an interesting pattern of a tense suffix following the subject agreement, perhaps indicating that it was recently grammaticalized. I will focus on *do* possibly being reanalyzed as a past tense marker in Germanic.

As Kiparsky (2003: 1) remarks, "[t]he dental preterite of weak verbs remains one of the most troublesome chapters of Germanic historical-comparative grammar." Scholars have argued that in the history of Germanic, the weak verbal past tense endings -*ed* derive from a proto-Germanic auxiliary *do* (see, e.g., Bopp 1816; Tops 1974; Lass 1994; Lahiri 2000). Lahiri (2000: 99) recognizes three stages, shown slightly adapted in (56).

(56)   Compounding $[\text{Verb} + j + \text{affix}]$ + $[do + \text{T}/[\text{phi}]]$
      Cliticization $[[\text{Verb} + j + \text{affix}]$ + $[do + \text{T}/[\text{phi}]]]$
      Suffixation $[[\text{Verb} + j + \text{t/d}]$ + $[\text{phi}]]$

The past tense ending arose from a nonfinite verb (either an infinitive or participle, indicated by the affix in [56]) followed by an inflected form of the past tense of *do*. The *j-* in (56) is a derivational affix typical for weak verbs. Because of this –*j-* suffix, changes occur to the stem vowel and this makes the strong past (through ablaut) impossible and hence the need for a light verb. In Lass's (1994: 165) words, *do* "was obscured . . . with no semantic content except 'past.'" I'll schematize the changes in (56) and Lass's insight in terms of features.

In (57a), using Modern English words, the change from light verb (or auxiliary) *did* to affix is given. I label this as tense but technically the Old English preterite is perfective aspect. The (remaining) main verb *do* could participate in other cycles of TMA marking in later Germanic, as suggested in (57b). Depending on which features are grammaticalized, *do* can be reanalyzed as tense, (realis) mood, or aspect.

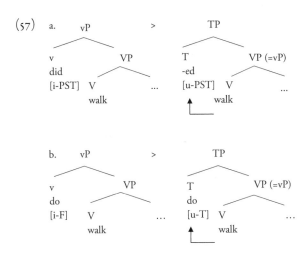

(57) a. ...

Initially, *do* is a verb, then a light verb (or auxiliary), and it is subsequently joined by the verb. In some varieties of Germanic, a periphrastic *do* is used again, as in (58), be it for a different tense. This conforms to the cycle of figure 7.1.

(58) *This man what **do** own this, ...*   West Somerset

   'This man who owns this, ...' (Kortmann 2004: 246)

The history of auxiliary *do* in English has been explored a lot. One story is that the causative verb *do* (in v) is reanalyzed as a progressive aspect marker. This is possible since the semantic features of *do* presumably include [action] and [duration]. Grammars from around 1700 provide evidence for the latter change. Miège ([1688] 1969) gives as the present tense *I love* or *I do love*. Lane ([1700] 1969: 44) says: "The Auxiliaries of the Present Tense, are, *do, dost, ...*; *am, art, ...*; as *I do call ...*; *I am calling*." Duncan ([1731] 1967: 22) provides the following for the present tense: *I carry*, or *I do carry*, or *I am carrying*. Lowth ([1762] 1967: 40) remarks: "*Do* and *did* mark the action itself, or the time of it, with greater distinction." Subsequently, *do* is reanalyzed as in (57b), at least in a number of dialects. As Kortmann (2004: 246) points out, there is "an interesting range of grammaticalized uses of *do* across varieties of English": completive, progressive, habitual aspect, and tense. That makes this cycle unlike the others. It may depend on the variety as to what positions *do* occupies. In standard English, *do* is in quite a high position, namely the T.

   In Dutch and German, *do* is also used as auxiliary, especially in colloquial language, as in (59) and (60), but also in relatively formal texts, as in (61). These, however, seem to me more progressive aspect, so lower in the tree than the T in (57).

(59) *Ik **doe** die   pop   aankleden*   Dutch
      I   do   that   doll   put-clothes-on

      'I am putting clothes on that doll.'

(60) *Ik **deed** denken aan de gekke maar memorabele uitgaansnacht*   Dutch
      I did think of the crazy but memorable going-out-night

      'I was thinking of the crazy but memorable night out.'

(61) *Ich **tue** denken, dass wir hier eine erbärmliche Übersetzung haben*   German
      I do think that we here a miserable translation have

      'I am thinking that we have a very bad translation here.'
      (http://www.zeit.de/2007/12/O_ja_tue_ich)

For more on this use of *do*, see van der Auwera (1999), Auer (2004), and Abraham (2002). There are interesting areal developments: European English (and German and Dutch) are losing the inflected past tense in favor of the periphrastic one (see Abraham & Conradie 2001) but American English is not.

Thus, if the *-ed* ending in Germanic is the result of a reanalysis of an originally independent form of the past tense auxiliary *did*, this represents one stage of the cycle. A renewal, as in (58), is expected, and represents the next stage in the cycle, although it is important to take into account the lexical items that are available.

4. The Future Cycle

There are many indications that future auxiliaries merge morphologically with the verb. For instance, in Navajo, there is a *-d-* future on the verb that could be related to *doo(leeł)*, the future auxiliary; in Melanesian Pidgin, the future auxiliary *bai* 'will' can cliticize as *b-* (Crowley & Bowern 2010: 222); and in Greek *tha* 'will' is an affix originating from *thelo* 'to want' (see, e.g., Joseph 2003: 480; Roberts & Roussou 2003: 58). I quoted Dahl and Velupillai (2008) earlier as showing that half of the languages in their sample have future marked inflectionally. In French and Urdu/Hindi, the future form of the verb is very synthetic but can be related (as I discuss later) to a more analytic origin. I will mainly discuss French, Spanish, and Urdu/Hindi. Future is really ambiguous between being a tense (future) or a mood (irrealis). I prefer the latter, but sometimes leave it open by using an FP, meaning that it can be any functional category.

Future auxiliaries develop from verbs (e.g., *will* from *willan* 'to want' and *gonna* from *going to*). Figure 7.5, very similar to figure 7.1 but starting in a different stage, shows the typical development that main verbs undergo. Stage (a) has a main verb's semantic features satisfy the [u-FUT] of T (or M) and stage (b) shows the main verb reanalyzed as auxiliary. Stage (c) is one where the features are uninterpretable and need a reinforcement, which means we are back at stage (a) but with a new element providing the semantic features.

I will now turn to the well-known history of Romance futures. If one wants to derive futures derivationally in modern French (and other Romance varieties), they need to have head movement. Thus, if we follow an early analysis of Harris (1969: 94–95), the verb *arrivera*

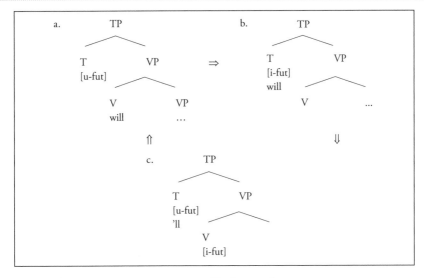

FIGURE 7.5. The future cycle

in *Brigitte arrivera* 'Brigitte will arrive' first checks the future and then the third person ending when the verb moves to higher functional categories in (62).

(62)

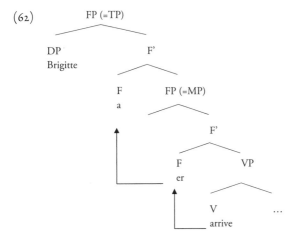

In (52), the highest functional category F can be seen as AGRsP and the lower functional category is for the future, possibly T or M (Harris has V rather than F or T).

The history of this construction is well known (and apparently was first written about in the fifteenth century; see Royen 1929: 489; Benveniste 1968; and Hopper & Traugott 2003: 9). Latin has two futures, a synthetic one *canta-bi-mus* (sing-FUT-1P) 'we will sing' (itself grammaticalized from a Proto-Latin *canta bhu-mos* [sing be-1P]) and an analytic one *cantare habe-mus* (sing have-1P) 'we will sing'. This latter form comprises the infinitive and the present tense form of *haber* 'to have'. These words are initially quite separate, as Lloyd (1987: 311) notes, and as the early Spanish (63) and Middle French (64) show.

(63) **ama-r**   *lo*   *è*   Early Spanish
      love-INF   him   have

      'I'll love him.' (Lloyd 1987: 311)

(64) *Jo* **ai**   *paiens*   **veüz**   Middle French
      I   have   heathens   seen

      'I have seen heathens.' (*Song of Roland*, from Schwegler 1990: 135)

Provençal, Old Italian, and Modern Portuguese are all similar to early Spanish and Middle French in that the object can still come between the verb and the subject agreement (see Royen 1929: 490).

If the modern structure in (62) is correct, the original could be something like (65a) or (65b). The Latin infinitival ending is probably in an M position (for irrealis mood) and since irrealis and future are often ambiguous, a reanalysis is easy of –*er* from M to T. In order to get the finite verb last, we could either have MP movement to a higher position in (65a), or a head-final structure, as in (65b). I don't go into that.

(65)

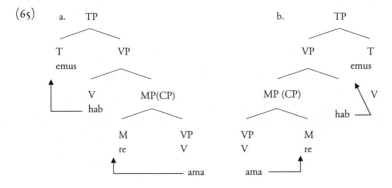

The verb *habere* may be a main verb in Latin, as represented in (65), that is reanalyzed as a functional category (from (a) to (b) in figure 7.5). For clarity, I summarize that change in (66).

(66)

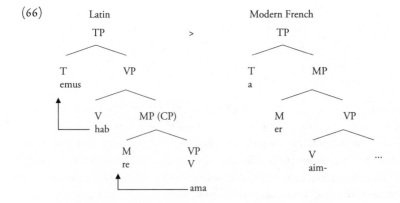

That change is not surprising according to Late Merge since the verb *hab*- would have to move to T. So the development from Latin to French and Spanish shows a full cycle, from main verb *hab-* to tense marker. There is, of course, an analytic renewal in the form of *aller* 'go', as in (67).

(67)   *Je*   **vais**   *le*   *faire*   Colloquial French
       I   go   it   make

'I am going to do it.'

In the normally quite analytic Urdu/Hindi, the future is formed synthetically from a conditional form of the verb followed by the originally present participle of the verb 'go'. Thus, *kerūgi* [do-1S-FUT-FS] 'I-FEM will do (it)' consists of the stem *ker* 'do-INF', the first person singular ending, a future marker *-g-* derived from the older *ga* 'go', and an inflection for singular number and feminine gender. Lahiri (2000) and Butt and Lahiri (2002), based on Kellog (1893), suggest the development in (68), which I have slightly adapted.

(68)   a.   [*mar* + *ũ*]   [*ga* + *tah*]
            hit   1S   go   MS

           ' I will hit.'
       b.   [*mar* + ps/#] + [*ga* + gender/#]
       c.   [*mar* + ps/# + fut + gender/#]

Butt and Lahiri don't suggest a contemporary analysis. One of the puzzling aspects of the Urdu/Hindi future is that agreement is marked on both sides of the future marker. If one drew a structure, the changes might look as in (69), with simplified functional structure, and head-last. Example (69a) presents a fairly straightforward biclausal structure, but a structure for the modern stage in (69b) is problematic. What set the change in motion was a reanalysis of the semantic features of *ga-* 'to go' as grammatical ones.

(69)

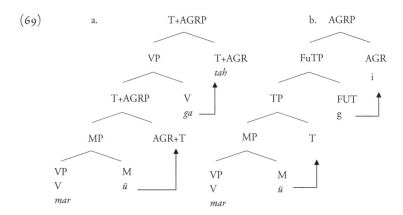

This construction is different from the Romance ones, since the agreement marking is unusual: gender very high up, person low, and number marked twice. This means that the construction hasn't totally changed from biclausal to monoclausal.

The well-known future cycle's stages can thus be represented as in figure 7.5. An explanation of the changes can be found in Feature Economy (from semantic to interpretable to uninterpretable) or in terms of Late Merge.

5. Mood in the "Middle"

Mood is the least grammatical of the TMA complex, at least in Modern English. As we saw in section 2, it is expressed by lexical means in the CP layer. In this section, I first look at subjunctive mood marked on the verb in Old English and then at its replacement through analytical markers in M and T in Middle English. I will be relatively brief about this topic since there is a huge literature on it.

In the Old English period, there are subjunctive endings on verbs. For instance, typical singular present endings are *–e*, as in *ic fremme* 'I do', and the plural *–en*, as in *we fremmen* 'we do'. The meaning of the subjunctive resembles that in Modern English of an irrealis wish or command, as in (70), but also a speaker reporting an opinion, as in (71), not doubting it!

(70)   *Ic wille . . . þæt þu **forgyte** þæt ic þe nu secge*
       I want that you forget-SBJ that I you now say

       'I want you to forget what I am telling you now.' (*Byrhtferth's Manual*, 154.14, in Visser 1963–1973: 2: 841).

(71)   *þæt folc . . . cwæð þæt Crist **wære** soð witega.*
       that people . . . said that Christ was-SBJ wise prophet
       'The people . . . said that Christ was a wise prophet.' (Aelfric, *Homilies*, in Thorpe [1844–1846] 1971, segment 5 in DOE)

The subjunctive endings weaken during that period. Two sources of renewal are available: modals and the nonfinite markers *for* and *to*.

Scholars know that modal auxiliaries are reanalyzed from verbs; deontic uses, as in (72) and (73), are first, and epistemic uses develop by late Old and early Middle English. Traugott (1989: 41–42) lists (74) as an early epistemic. This makes it likely that the verb first reanalyzed as a v (for the deontic) and then as M (for the epistemic).

(72)   *Swa **sceal** geong guma gode **gewyrcean***
       So shall young man good-DAT accomplish

       'So should a young man through good works accomplish.' (*Beowulf*, 20, in Klaeber [1922] 1941)

(73)   *þæt ic sænæssas **geseon mihte***
       that I sea-bluffs see might
       'so that I could see the cliffs' (*Beowulf*. 571, in Klaeber [1922] 1941)

(74)   *& to þam Pentecosten . . . wæs gesewen blod weallan of earþan. swa swa mænige sæden þe hit **geseon sceoldan***
       and at that Pentecost was seen blood well-up from earth as many said that it seen should

       'At Pentecost, blood was seen to well up from the earth, as many said who supposedly saw it.' (*Peterborough Chronicle* [1100], in Thorpe 1861)

If (72) to (74) are renewals for subjunctive markers, we can think of this change in terms of figure 7.5: a [u-F] in M values its features with a lexical verb. If that verb is semantically appropriate, for example, *sceal* in (72), that verb can be reanalyzed as generated higher (merged later) with [i-F], especially if there are other features checked by this verb. This renders a biclausal structure into a monoclausal one.

The second way to renew the subjunctive is, of course, the infinitive. This is more complex since the subjunctive is licensed by the main verb but expressed on C and T of the subordinate clause. Again, much has been written about the introduction of the *to*- infinitive, as in (75). See Fischer (1990), van Gelderen (1993, 2004), Roberts and Roussou (2003). Most syntacticians would put *to* in M, in complementary distribution with the epistemic modal. I would argue that it is indeed in M with [i-F], where F is irrealis mood.

(75) *echn(e) cniht. þat lofde **for to** segg(e) riht*
      every knight who loved for to say truth

      'every knight who loved to say the truth' (Layamon, *Brut*, Otho, 5523, in Brook & Leslie 1963)

Thus, concerning modal marking in the TP, modal auxiliaries follow the cycle of renewal from main verb to light verb to auxiliary. Modals, like the CP adverbials, are hard to characterize in terms of precise semantic features, so I haven't.

6. The Aspect Cycles

In this section, I examine some aspectual auxiliaries in section 6.1, adverbs in section 6.2, and preverbs in section 6.3. Aspect is marked in the lower layers—in the lower part of the TP and in the VP. In the TP, auxiliaries (*have* and *be*) and adverbs (*often, again*, etc.) are used; in the vP shell, adverbials (mostly PPs) are. The clearest cycles involve the aspectual prefixes discussed in section 6.3.

The Modern English adverbials in (76) and (77) show broad patterns of agreement with the hierarchy in (7), repeated for convenience as (78). In (76), *again* is the repetitive aspectual and *completely* the completive; in (77), *rarely* is the frequentive and *again* the repetitive.

(76) until the Sun is once **again completely** uncovered.
      (http://csep10.phys.utk.edu/astr161/lect/time/eclipses.html)

(77) I will **rarely again** be so privileged
      (http://www.earthfoot.org/lit_zone/seals.htm)

(78) VP layer

SpaceP	> AgentP	> DomainP	> MannerP	> DegPerf >
here	*deliberately*	*universally*	*loudly*	*slightly*
MeansP	> FreqP	> RepP	> AspPcompl	> RestP
manually	*rarely*	*again*	*completely*	*again*

One problem with the hierarchy in (78) is that some combinations are frequently units even though they appear quite far apart in (78). For instance, *once again* occurs as a combination 3,580 times in the BNC and this occurs about 10 percent of the time that *once* appears. Another problem is that v and the aspect internal to the VP are not listed.

6.1 ASPECTUAL AUXILIARIES

Unlike the case with tense auxiliaries, there are numerous aspectual auxiliaries. In English, they include perfect *have*, progressive *be*, and inceptive *start* and *begin*. Dutch positional verbs function as progressives; for example, *staan*, *liggen*, and *zitten* 'stand', 'lay', and 'sit' are all instances that could be explored. The Chinese perfective marker *le* derives from the verb *liao*, meaning 'to complete', and the Nupe perfective *á* derives from the light verb *lá*, meaning 'take'; see Kandybowicz (2008) for Nupe. In this section, I will look at an example from English based on data from Sims (2008) where cyclical change occurs and one example from Polish that shows a loss of aspect in favor of tense, and an interaction with the subject agreement cycle.

In Old English, there are a number of verbs to indicate the beginning of an action, namely *-ginnan* (and its prefixed variants *onginnan*, *aginnan*, *ingannan*, and *beginnan*), *fon* (and its prefixed variants *gefon*, *onfon*, and *underfon*), *weorþan*, *tacan*, and *niman* (see Brinton 1988: 116; Sims 2008). According to the *OED*, the most common is *onginnan*. *Beginnan* and (*on*) *fon* are rare, and *niman*, *tacan*, and *weorþan* even rarer. Typical examples for *onginnan* and *beginnan* are provided in (79) and (80).

(79)   *þa **ongan** ic . . . þa boc **wendan** on Englisc . . .*
       the began I . . . the book translate in English . . .

       'then I began, . . . , to translate the book into English . . .'
       (Alfred, *Pastoral Care*, preface, 6.17, from Sims 2008: 98)

(80)   Israhela *folc **begunnon to geeacnienne** heora ealdan synna . . .*
       Israel folk begun to increase their old sins . . .

       'The people of Israel began to multiply their old sins . . .'
       (Ælfric, *Judg.*, 10.6, from Sims 2008: 112)

According to Sims (2008), there are three main differences between the inceptive variants of *-gin*: (a) the phonological reduction and the use of the preterit form by *onginnan/aginnan* (cf. also Ogura 1997), (b) the type of prefix on the preauxiliary, and (c) the morphology and syntax of the following verb. *Onginnan* (and *aginnan*) show more characteristics of auxiliaries than *beginnan*. *Onginnan* experiences phonological reduction to *aginnan* and *ginnen*, becomes a frozen preterit construction, and disappears during the Middle English period. *Beginnan* does not experience this reduction and continues into Modern English, where it "competes" with a new verb, *start*. *Start* appears in the early Modern English period.

The more grammaticalized *anginnan* appears with a bare infinitive or participle, as in (81), whereas *beginnan* has a frequent *to*- infinitive, as in (82).

(81) . . . **anginne gehealde** *na mid ege helle ac mid cristes lufan*
      . . . begin hold not with fear hell but with Christ's love

      '[You] . . . begin to hold not with fear of hell but with love of Christ'
      (*Rule of St. Benet*, G1 36.15, from Sims 2008: 109)

(82) *þurh þa lufe he **beginþ to healdenne** swylce gecyndelice and gewunlice*
      through the love he begins to hold such natural and common

      'Through the love [of Christ] he begins to hold as if natural and innate.'
      (*Rule of St. Benet*, 7.31.18, from Sims 2008: 109)

Table 7.6 shows that the *on*-prefixed variant occurs very frequently, and with the bare infinitive (96 percent), while the *be*-prefixed variant is less frequent in Old English and selects the *to*-infinitive (67 percent) (see Sims 2008: 113; Los 1999).Sims (2008: 119–120) argues that "it is the individual aspect marker (*onginnan* vs. *beginnan*) that influences the form of the infinitival complement": the *on*- prefix is strong during the time of Alfred but weakens by the time of Ælfric and *to*- helps renew the aspect. However, by the Middle English period, the successor of *onginnan*, namely *gon/gunnen*, is no longer an inceptive marker and *beginnan* has taken over.

In early Middle English, we also see a renewal of the bare infinitive, so to speak, in the *–ing* complement. Further changes are that, by the early Modern English period, *start* has become an inceptive marker. The *OED* lists its origin in the verb "to leap into something," cognate to Dutch *storten* 'fall in a violent manner', for example. This use is shown in (83).

(83) *Among the serpentis in the pit sche **styrte***

      'jumped among the snakes into the pit.' (Chaucer, *Legend of Good Women*, 697, from *OED*)

TABLE 7.6

| Old English *aginnan* and *beginnan* | | | | |
	Bare Infinitive	%	*to-* Infinitive	%
onginnan				
Alfred	246	99	2	1
Ælfric	82	77	25	23
Other texts	649	98	10	2
Total *onginnan*	977	96	37	4
beginnan				
Alfred	0	—	0	—
Ælfric	19	26	54	74
Other texts	9	75	3	25
Total *beginnan*	28	33	57	67

From Sims 2008: 113, based on Callaway 1913: 279–287

I cannot provide the entire history of the inceptive markers but what is important in terms of the cycle is loss and renewal of the sense of the start of the action. As (83) shows, *start* has a meaning of 'going into something' and this grammaticalized as inceptive auxiliary. Figure 7.6 shows that *beginnan* replaces *onginnan*, but *start* has not done that with *beginnan*. I have also added the complements without much discussion. In figure 7.6, I have just represented a few of the changes but have not taken into account the meaning differences between *beginnan*, *(on)ginnan*, and *start*.

I'll now turn to Polish. In the Common Slavic period, as explained at length in Andersen (1987), analytic forms arise for retrospective aspect, using a resultative participle inflected for gender and number and a finite form of '*be*', as in Old Polish (84).

(84) *mlŭvilŭ*   *jestŭ*   Old Polish
      spoken.MS   is.3S
      'He has spoken.' (Andersen 1987: 24)

These forms continue to be used until the sixteenth century or so. However, already in prehistoric Polish, variants develop where the forms of 'be' are reduced phonologically into subject clitics placed in second position (the Wackernagel position), as *–ś* is in (85), from Old Polish, with the lexical verb still in participial form.

(85) *Ani-ś*   *mię*   *zepchnął....*   Old Polish
      NEG-2S   me   repulsed, ...
      'You didn't repulse me.' (Andersen 1987: 28)

The third person singular independent auxiliary form is *jest* but it is usually zero. The independent *jest* is increasingly only used for "emphatic predication," as in (86).

(86) *To-m*   *jest*   *ogląda-ła*   Old Polish
      that-1S   EMPH   see-PST
      'That I did see.' (Andersen 1987: 28)

Subsequently, but still in prehistoric Polish, the tense/aspect system is reduced (and imperfect and aorist aspectual forms are lost) and the analytic uses such as in (86) take over more

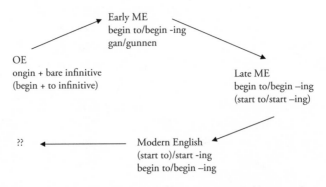

FIGURE 7.6. The inceptive cycle (from Sims & van Gelderen 2010)

functions. As a result of the reduction in the aspect system, a reanalysis takes place (Andersen 1987: 26) of the forms of 'be' as person and number markers and the participle as a finite past tense. When subject pronouns are present, as in (86), the person and number markers can be omitted.

(87) Jest   **ja**   ciebie   zepchnął   albo...   Old Polish
      EMPH   1S   you   repulsed   or

      'Did I repulse you, or . . . ' (Andersen 1987: 28)

The last change involves the change of the person and number markers to inflectional morphemes. Statistics from Rittel (1975) show that, from 1500 to the present, the person and number markers change their position and become increasingly attached to the finite verbs (which used to be participles), the singular before the plural and the first person before the second person. As Andersen points outs, this development toward inflectional endings is not complete but the end point is clear. The variation is now conditioned pragmatically and stylistically.

In the history of Polish, the retrospective aspect combination of an inflected auxiliary and past participle was reanalyzed as a past finite verb, an agreement clitic, and an optional particle *jest*. This means the auxiliary lost its function as aspect marker. Agreement with the subject is initially marked on the auxiliary but then on C (Wackernagel position) and increasingly on the main verb. A next stage might be for another auxiliary to arise.

6.2 ADVERBIAL ASPECT MARKERS

In this section, I discuss a few adverbs. Cinque doesn't mention *soon* but I am taking that as an aspectual adverb, certainly in Old English, and discuss it as well as *often*, *usually*, and *again*.

Soon as an adverb appears in Old English with the meaning "without delay," as in (88), as well as with a less definite time indicated.

(88)   *Ac he him **sona** ondwyrde, & him swiðe stiernlice stierde.*

       'But he answered him without delay, and guided him sternly.'
       (Alfred, *Pastoral Care*, 196, in Sweet [1871] 1934)

"Without delay" indicates something about how the action is viewed, so I consider it aspect, modifying the verb and inside the VP. In Modern English, *soon* can still be used in this meaning but it also shifted to a temporal adverb, as in (89). It is also a degree adverb in *soon enough* but most often a complex complementizer part of *as soon as*[6] in (90).

(89)   I'll **soon** do that.

(90)   **As soon as** it's official, the President will clearly have a statement. (CSE-WH94)

So *soon* has grammaticalized from VP-adverb to complementizer; its Old English near synonym also did, as we'll now see.

The Old English *hraðe* 'quick, soon' in (91) and (92) has a similar meaning as *sona* 'without delay'.

---

6. In the CSE, *soon* occurs 228 times and 108 instances of those are part of the complementizer *as soon as*.

(91) *Ða wæs him swiðe **braðe** geandwyrd: Ic eom se Nazarenisca Hælend, se...*
      Then was he very quickly answered: I am the of-Nazareth Savior who

      'He was very soon/quickly answered with 'I am the Savior of Nazareth, who
      ...'(Alfred, *Pastoral Care*, 443.23, Hatton, Sweet [1871] 1934)

(92) *...þætte geherde aras **braeðe** & cuom to him.*
      ... that heard arose quickly and came to him
      'On hearing that, she arose quickly and came to him.' (Gospels, Lindisfarne,
      John 11.29, in Skeat [1881–1887] 1970)

Note that the ambiguity between "without delay" and "in the future" occurs already in the Old English, especially with the frequent preposings of *hrædlice*, as in (93) to (95).

(93) *Ac ða ða he ongeat ða scylde on Annanian & on Saffiram,*
      But then that he saw the sin of Ananias and Sapphira,
      *suiðe **hrædlice** he oðiewde hu micelne onwald he hæfde ofer oðre menn*
      ...very soon/quickly he showed how great power he had over other men

      'But when he saw the sin of Ananias and Sapphira, he soon showed how great his
      authority was over others.' (Alfred, *Pastoral Care*, 115.12, Hatton, in Sweet [1871] 1934)

(94) *& syððon **hrædlice** wendon westweard on Oxnafordscire.*

      'and then soon turned westwards to Oxfordshire'
      (*Peterborough Chronicle* [1010], 15)

(95) *Ac ðonne he gemette ða scylde ðe he stieran scolde,*
      But then he saw the sin which he punish should
      ***hrædlice** he gecyðde ðæt he wæs magister & ealdormonn.*
      soon he showed that he was master and lord

      'But when he discovered the sin he had to punish, he soon showed that he was
      master.' (Alfred, *Pastoral Care*, 117.5, Hatton, Sweet [1871] 1934)

At the end of the Old English period, forms such as *hrædlice* and (less frequently) *raðor* lose the temporal meaning. Some are ambiguous, as in (96).

(96) *But do nou als Y wile **rathe:***
      'But do now as I want rather.' (*Havelok* [1335], in Skeat 1868: 41)

Gergel (2009) examines this change in *rather* from lower temporal VP adverb, as in (91) to higher modal one, as in (96) and (97).

(97) I would **rather** go than stay.

Early uses of *rath(er)* induce a temporal scale, but since there is a "side-message," it is reanalyzed as a scale over situations, according to Gergel. This too is a case of Late Merge.

Usually, *again*, and *often* are clear aspect markers and are labeled habitual, repetitive, and frequentive respectively in Cinque (1999). *Oft(en)* may etymologically be derived from *up*.

It is used as an adverb in (98). Looking at the use of *often* in the CSE, there are very frequent instances of preposed adverbs, as in (99), making it much more of a TP adverb.

(98) *forðon **oft** fallas in fyr and symle in wætre.*
      Therefore often falls into fire and often into water

      'Therefore he often falls into the fire and often into the water.'
      (Gospels, Lindisfarne, Matthew 17.15, in Skeat [1881–1887] 1970)

(99) I mean, I think too **often** that is used as an excuse to exclude students.
      (CSE-COM 97)

Usually appears in the fifteenth century, after the adjective *usual* had been introduced, and means 'in the usual manner' modifying the verb called in (100). Again, in the modern spoken corpus, it seems frequently preposed, as in (101) and (102), and definitely outside of the VP.

(100) All the Membres **usuelly** called to the forseid Parlementes.
       (*Rolls of Parliament* [1477], 6: 191 –192, from *OED*)

(101) But **usually**, when you're reading informational text, it's framed in a bigger picture.
       (CSE-COMM 97)

(102) **Usually** the original paper form gets stored at the office that generated it.
       (CSE-FACMT 95)

Again has the meaning of "in the opposite direction, back," as in (103), and changes in Middle English to "once more," as in (104), and repetitive aspect.

(103) *Her com Cnut **aʒan** to Englalonde*

       'Then came Cnut back to England.' (*Anglo-Saxon Chronicle*, Parker [1031], in Thorpe 1861)

(104) As of the lef **agayn** the flour to make.
       (Chaucer, *Legend of Good Women*, 72)

We have seen a number of adverbs reanalyzed from VP adverbs modifying the verb to adverbs modifying the time or aspect of the event. This remains to be formulated in terms of Feature Economy. For instance, the quickness of the action in *hrædlice* is reanalyzed as temporal quickness.

6.3 PREVERBS

In many languages, perfective aspect goes through a cycle in which an aspectual prefix weakens and is replaced by an adverb or adposition. For instance, Lehmann (1993: 97) and Diessel (1999: 142) argue that aspectual preverbs derive from relational adverbs and adverbial demonstratives, such as *hin/her* in German *hinweisen/hinfahren/herbringen*.

Miller (1993: 118–124) provides instances of preposition incorporation in Ancient Greek and Latin, as well as an analysis. Booij and van Marle (2003) bring together a number of studies on many languages that show a development from adverb to preverb. These cycles occur in Indo-European, but also in the Amazonian language Nadëb, as described by Weir (1986), in spoken Hungarian, as reported by Kiss (2006), in Athabascan languages such as Dëne Sųłiné/Chipewyan, as described by Li (1967), and in the Uto-Aztecan Tohono O'odham.

I'll focus on Indo-European in 6.3.1, mainly on English and Dutch, and add a little on Athabascan and Pomoan in 6.3.2. See also Butt (2003) who uses Deo (2002) to argue that preverbs in Sanskrit are taken over by light verbs in the modern languages. Bowern (2008) discusses preverbs in Nyulnyulan. These preverbs are uninflected verbs that precede fully inflected verbs, such as *balygarr-nganka* 'swearing-speak' in Bardi, to reinforce the inflected verb.

6.3.1 Indo-European

I show here that Greek, Latin, Bulgarian, and Paduan Italian have incorporated a preposition, whereas English has incorporated an adverb.

Familiar from Greek and Latin (see Horrocks 1981 and Smyth [1920] 1974) is the change shown in (105) from preposition to preverb.

(105)   *eo **trans** flumen* >   ***trans**-eo flumen* >   *transeo **trans** flumen*   Latin
          go through river   through-go river   go-through through river
          'Go through the river.'

As Smyth ([1920] 1974: 366) puts it, "[t]he addition of a preposition ... to a verbal form may mark the completion of the action of the verbal idea (perfective action)." Thus, in Greek (106), δια 'through' renders the predicate perfective. As seen in chapter 5 for Latin, the preverb can be doubled by a preposition, as in (107), for the preverb *eis*.

(106)   **διαφεύγειν**   Greek
          [through-flee]
          'succeed in escaping' (Smyth [1920] 1974: 366)

(107)   ***eis**-elthen*   **eis**   *ton*   *oikon*   New Testament Greek
          in-came   in   the   house
          'He entered the house.' (Luke 1.40, from Goetting 2007: 317)

Miller (1993: 119) argues for the incorporation, that is, movement, of the P into the V. In chapter 5 (section 1.2), I suggested that verbs may be probing for a theta role (a locative one) in (107) and because, after valuation of the [u-loc] on V, the features on V are the same as the features on the P.

Slavic languages have gone through the same changes. In Bulgarian, both (108) and (109) occur, where the latter is the innovation. The two sentences have different interpretations, with the PP in (108) an adjunct but the DP in (109) an object.

(108)   *Ivan skoči **prez** ogradata*   Bulgarian
        Ivan jumped over fence-the 'Ivan jumped over the fence.'

(109)   *Ivan **preskoči** ogradata*   Bulgarian
        Ivan over-jumped fence-the
        'Ivan jumped the fence.' (Mariana Bahtchevanova, p.c.)

In Standard Italian, as noted by Vedovato (2008), verbs such as *accendere* 'to turn on (the light)' and *spegnere* 'to turn off' are not reinforced by adverbs, but in the Paduan dialect they are used. Where standard Italian uses *chiudere* 'close', Paduan uses *sarar su*, as in (110).

(110)   *Sara   su   a   porta*   Paduan
        close   up   the   door
        'Close the door.' (Vedovato 2008: 13)

Other such verbs are *inpisar su* 'turn on', *far su* 'collect', and *magnar for a* 'eat up'.

English renews aspect through adverbs. In Old English, as mentioned in chapter 5, there is an aspectual prefix, such as *upp* in (111), similar to the prefixes in Latin, Greek, and Bulgarian.

(111)   *Hu lange sceal min feond beon **upp**ahafen ofer me*
        'How long shall my enemy be elevated over me?' (*Paris Psalter*, 19, from HC OE3)

This prefix disappears in early Middle English and perfective aspect is not expressed grammatically but lexically. As we have also seen in chapter 5, there is a perfective *ge-* prefix in Old English that disappears at the beginning of the early Middle English period. Some of these changes are represented in figure 7.7, where I assume the adverb *up* provides the semantic features for the probe in ASP.

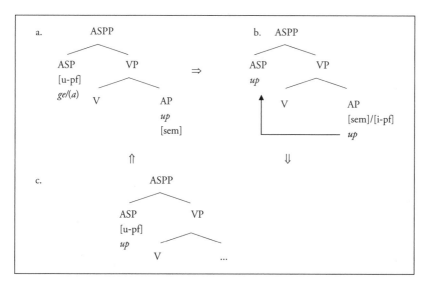

FIGURE 7.7. The aspect cycle and feature change

There is some evidence for a movement analysis as in (b) from varieties that don't always delete the lower copy, for example, Sea Island Creole (112), and many of these in colloquial English (113) to (115).

(112)   *If I was somebody could turn **up** that hospital **up**, I'd do it*   Sea Island Creole
        'If I were somebody who could tear up that hospital, I'd do it.'
        (Cunningham 1992: 95)

(113)   To evaluate whether there is air mixed with water in the radiator, turn **on** it **on** for a little while. (http://www.wisegeek.com/what-is-radiator-bleeding.htm)

(114)   Then turn **on** it **on**, and it should be okay.
        (http://answers.yahoo.com/question/index?qid=20080106133423AAs8d5b)

(115)   and help the congregation tear **down** it **down**.
        (http://bayridgebrooklyn.blogspot.com/2008/02/rally-to-save-bay-ridge-method-ist.html)

Starting in early Modern English, as in (116), perfective aspect is again expressed through grammatical adverbial particles with verbs such as *offer up*. The order of adverb and object as in (116) is more frequent in the examples provided by the *OED* than that in (117).

(116)   to offer **up** his only son.
        (Udall [1548], from the *OED*)

(117)   those that offer it **up**.
        ([1657], from the *OED*)

With other verbs this is not the case; for example, *receive in* followed by an object is less frequent than the pattern *receive* followed by an object and then *in*. The earliest instances of each pattern from the *OED* are shown in (118) and (119). These examples suggest that both orders are introduced around the same time.

(118)   they . . . did **receive in** such booties of catell or other things.
        (Cowell [1607], from the *OED*)

(119)   Each grape to weep, and crimsin streams to spin
        Into the Vate, set to **receive** them **in**. (Sylvester [1605], from the *OED*)

Other recent innovations are provided in table 7.7. All except the two indicated were recently uttered or written by native speakers of American English.

As mentioned, two different word orders are possible, one with a definite object typically preceding the adverb and one with the indefinite object typically following the adverb. The second word order with the verb and the particle together has become more frequent recently, according to Gardner & Davies (2007), even with definite nominals. The use of pronominal objects, typical for the first order, with these verbs has gone down too. The difference in

TABLE 7.7

Aspectual Renewal

They'll issue them **out**.

I ordered one **up.**

They offered **up** that suggestion.

Include it **in.**

Copy them **out/down**.

NPs may . . . become compacted **down**. (Vincent 1999: 1113)

To boost **up** tourism (ICE-Tanzania)

to calculate **out** the cognates.

---

frequency patterns is evident for the verb *receive* followed by a particle. In the 100-million British National Corpus, *receive* occurs nine times in constructions such as (120) and four times in constructions such as (121) (twice with a pronoun and twice with a DP).

(120)   Elizabeth's accession allowed him to **receive back** his wife (BNC-GTB938)

(121)   a husband who changed his mind to **receive** his wife **back** without ceremony (BNC-HTX2122).

In the Kuczaj corpus (see Kuczaj 1976), there are a few interesting instances of the verb, particle, and object pattern, as in (122) and (123). Abe, around age three, is analyzing the pronoun as a regular object of the verb and particle.

(122)   You can't **open up it** because it is glued on. (Abe, 2;11.21, Kuczaj corpus)

(123)   to **pick up it** (Abe, 3;4.08, Kuczaj corpus)

I'll provide an account for Abe's use of (122) and (123) and the corpus preference for (120) next.

The trees in (124) represent perfective aspect by means of an ASP head where the adverb could either be part of the VP or in ASP. The order in (120) is derived by merging the adverb *back* with the VP and the verb *receive* moving to (merging internally with) the ASP and then the v. This is shown in (124a).

To check perfective aspect, it is also possible for the nominal object to move to the specifier of the ASPP (i.e., internally merge in that position). This is typical for definite objects, as in (121). Before the definite object moves, the verb will have moved to ASP. The verb then merges in the v position and the word order will be as in (121). This is shown in (124b).

If the object is pronominal, it can (internally) merge in the head of the ASPP to check definiteness and perfective aspect and the verb will left-adjoin to it on its way to v. This is shown in (124c).

(124)

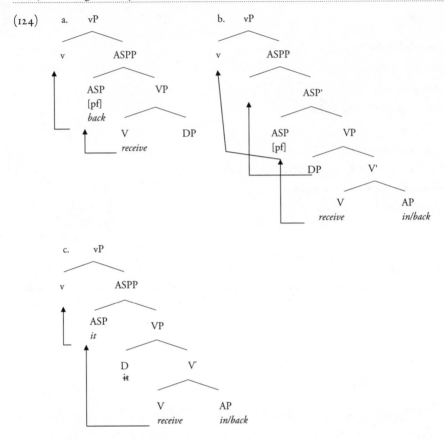

In terms of number of operations, (124a) is the most economical because there is late merge of *back* and regular V movement. This construction turns out to be the one that is more frequent as well and the one for which there are some unusual instances in child language. The additional movement of the DP and pronoun to express aspect is eliminated.

In (124), I have left the [pf] features unspecified for interpretable or uninterpretable. These features depend on the status of the erstwhile adverb *back*. In (124a), it could be merged in the specifier position and result in the same word order. The features in the specifier would be [i-pf], whereas they might be [u-pf] in the head. Some evidence for the (124a) with *back* in the head of the ASPP comes from modification. When the adverb is in the VP, it is a full phrase and can therefore be modified, as by *right* as in (125a); when it is the head of ASP, it cannot, as in (125b).

(125)   a. He received that package **right back**.
        b. *He received **right back** that package.

I'll add a little more on the specifier possibility, which I advocated erroneously in van Gelderen (2004). Elenbaas (2007) explains the patterns in (122) and (123) by arguing that adverbs optionally project as head or as phrase, for adverbs in the history of English. Then, in accordance with the Head Preference Principle, a language learner will reanalyze the phrase as an aspectual head. Middle Dutch would provide nice evidence for this change in (126) and (127).

(126)   *mer tis een flaute die hem **over ghe**comen is*   Middle Dutch
        But it-is a swoon that him over PART-come is
        'He fainted.' (Blom 2004: 66).

(127)   *Hem is een flauwte **overkomen***   Dutch
        Him is a fainting-spell happened
        'He fainted.'

If it is a general tendency for adverbs to become aspectual markers (perfective), these adverbs would initially be positioned in the specifiers of the aspect phrases, as in (126), and later in heads, as in (126). The change is represented in (128).

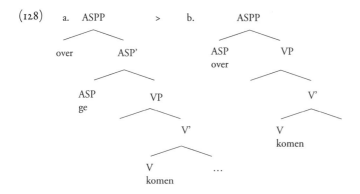

(128) a. ASPP   >   b.   ASPP

However, Fertig (2005) has convincingly argued that (127) was already an early Germanic form (Old English *ofercuman* and Old High German *ubarqueman*) and that there is no direction to this change. Different forms stayed around, so the change in (128) cannot be proven and it is therefore likely that the reanalysis was from adverb to ASP head.

    A scenario for further change after (124a) is that the adverb becomes reanalyzed as an affix. After the adverb stage in (129a), the adverb initially becomes reanalyzed as ASP in (129b), and since the V moves to ASP on its way to v, the element in ASP automatically loses its independence, as in (129c).

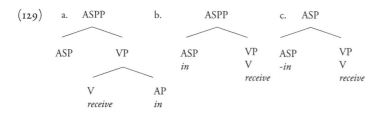

(129) a. ASPP   b.   ASPP   c. ASP

I'll now turn from Indo-European examples of the aspect cycle to two other languages.

6.3.2 Athabascan and Pomo

In this section, I just briefly look at layers of aspect marking, and speculate on their development. I first discuss aspect in Athabascan and then sketch the account given in Mithun (2000b) on Central Pomo, a Hokan language of California.

In Athabascan, there are several areas in the verbal complex that express aspect. A simplified list of prefixes in Athabascan is given in (130).

(130)   Object P **outer-Aspect** Number // DO **inner-Aspect** Su Voice Stem-**ASP**

The slashes mark the boundary between disjunct and conjunct prefixes with the latter being closer to the verb and probably older. According to Young and Morgan (1987: 164), "[t]here are at least 11 Primary Aspectual categories in Navajo," marked by adverbial elements in the disjunct and conjunct domains and by what is called the mode on the verb stem. The mode on the verb determines the type of subject prefix. There is a discussion on how best to represent aspect, and in particular the inner aspect, marked around the subject. Faltz (1998: 17) explains that issue by using the imperfective, perfective, and future modes of *to play* in Navajo. In (131), the mode of the verb (*né*, *ne'*, or *neeł*) determines the shape of the subject conjugation (*sh*, *sé*, and *deesh*), which in turn determine the phonological shape of the outer prefix *na*.

(131)   a. *naashné*   Navajo
            around-1S-play.IMPF

            'I am playing'

        b. *niséne'*
            around-1S-play.PF

            'I played.'

        c. *nideeshneeł*
            around-1S-play.FUT

            'I will play.'

Other examples from Navajo and Chipewyan are given in (118) and (119), with the iterative outer prefix *na* and the stem and subject conjugation marked for aspect as well.

(132)   *b-í-na-bi-nish-tin*   Navajo
        3-against-ASP-3–1S-handle-IMPF =I handle him against it

        'I teach it to him.' (Young & Morgan 1980: 223; see also Rice 2000: 94)

(133)   *bɛyɛ́   xá-dá-na-'ɛ-s-d-zis*   Chipewyan/Dëne Sułiné
        it-in   out-P-ITERATIVE –INDEF.O–1S.SU-VOICE-sip.CUSTOMARY

        'I sip out of several vessels.' (Li 1967: 417)

Young and Morgan (1987) speak of 'ancient' strata in the language (e.g.,1987: 190) and Givón (2000) uses internal reconstruction to solve the typological puzzles of the Athabascan language Tolowa. The many layers of aspect are due to different times of grammaticalization.

The adverbial outer prefixes are still fairly recognizable as adverbs (e.g., *xá* in Chipewyan) as are the plural (*dá* in [133] Dine Sułine and *da* in Navajo) and the iterative (*na* in [131] to [133]). There is variation in the ordering of some of these elements; for example, *dá* precedes *na* in Chipewyan/Dëne Sųłiné (133) and Slave but not in Hupa, Apache, and Navajo (134) (see Rice 2000: 80–81 for the ordering). Rice argues this is due to the fact that these are items not related by scope. I think the plural has reanalyzed closer to the subject prefix.

(134) *ni-de-ii'-né*   Navajo
       Around-P-1-play.IMPF
       'We (three or more) are playing.'

There are many more prefixes in the disjunct domain but I will not go into that further.

As for the conjunct domain, these prefixes are less often immediately recognizable. In (133), the object is *'ɛ* and the subject prefix is *s* and, in (132), the object is zero and the subject *sh*. There are often inner aspectual, thematic (TH), and adverbial prefixes (position VI in Young & Morgan 1987) which have lost their original meaning, such as *di* in (135), which can be used to relate to arms and legs.

(135) *biih*   *di-nó-sh-níih*   *lágo*   Navajo
       it-in   TH-OPT-1S-stuck   PRT
       'If I were to get stuck in it' (Mary Willie, p.c.)

The Athabascan languages provide some evidence of different (historical) layers of aspectual marking. The aspect marked on the verb may be the oldest and the subject mode may have originated from an incorporated adverb. Currently, these are renewed by outer aspectual markers.

Mithun (2000b), in an article with "Recycled Aspect" as part of the title, shows that Central Pomo, spoken in Northern California, contains a very rich system of aspectual marking. Looking at the list of markers, reproduced in table 7.8, Mithun remarks that they are drawn from a restricted set and that they repeat themselves, so to speak. For instance, a continuative was "created by the addition of an extra aspectual marker to verbs already

TABLE 7.8

Central Pomo Aspect Markers	
Imperfective	*-an*
Perfective	*-w*
Progressive	*-wan*
Continuative	*-(h)duw*
Habitual imperfective	*-adan*
Habitual perfective	*-(h)duwan*
Frequentative	*-(h)duwandan*

From Mithun 2000b: 261

inflected for aspect" (Mithun 2000b: 269) and "[a] frequentive was formed by qualifying the habitual perfective . . . with yet another imperfective marker" (Mithun 2000b: 272), as in (136).

(136)   *Wá.ymin-wa   ma   ʔé.y-yo-h-du-w-a-d-anʔ*   Central Pomo
         Often-Q   you   away-go-PF-IMPF-PF-IMPF-IMPF

         'Do you go away a lot?' (Mithun 2000b: 273)

When a native speaker was asked about the difference between the habitual perfective and the frequentative, she said "not much difference" (Mithun 2000b: 276).

So both Athabascan and Pomo show layers of aspectual affixes. Hence this cycle is a little different from the one in Indo-European where previous "evidence" disappears.

7. Conclusion

In this chapter, I have examined some tense, mood, and aspect cycles; some are full cycles and others show stages. How an event is situated in time and how speaker attitudes and manner are expressed differ tremendously from language to language. The cyclical patterns also differ dependent on whether their source is a phrase or head. I have used Feature Economy to discuss the future and aspect cycles and Late Merge with changes in the adverbials.

As we have seen, the specific changes range from VP to CP adverbial with subsequent renewal of both VP and CP adverbials (section 2.1), the demonstrative *that* losing some of the interpretable deictic features to be reanalyzed as finite C (section 2.3.1), the temporal prepositions undergoing a reduction in the features to become complementizers (section 2.3.2), adverbs and auxiliaries reanalyzed as tense (section 3), future cycles having verbs reanalyzed as auxiliaries and affixes (section 4), modal auxiliaries appearing (section 5), and finally two aspect cycles occurring (section 6).

TABLE 7.9

	Gloss	EME	LME	Total	Preposed
Adverbials in Middle English					
certes	certainly	3	185	188	178 (94.6%)
trewly	truly	17	134	151	83 (54.9%)
forsoothe	in truth	25	60	85	64 (75.2%)
verily	in truth	11	53	64	1 (1.5%)
sikerly	certainly	21	24	46	15 (32.6
sothly	truly	43	26	69	43 (62.3%)

From Swan 1988: 292, 289
EME = early Middle English; LME = late Middle English

Appendix : More Adverbial Renewals

What happens in early Middle English after so many VP adverbials become CP ones and are then lost (see table 7.4)? The adverbials are renewed. Adding this information to section 2.1 would give too much focus to one particular change in the chapter. I therefore provide some of this material in an appendix.

There is lots of renewal in Middle English. This is what one would expect after what we saw in section 2.1. Swan (1991: 415) says that the situation in Middle and early Modern English is similar to that in Old English and that the real increase comes in the seventeenth and eighteenth centuries. She does say that there is an increase in evaluative adverbs such as *possibly, actually, peradventure, certes*, and a continuation of *soothly*. I think the adverbs keep renewing themselves throughout the period, as in Middle English.

There is quite a shift in the inventory of adverbials during Middle English, as shown in table 7.9; for example, *certes* is introduced and the numbers of *trewly* increase. The table also shows a lot of preposing.

Some of these are CP adverbials from the start, as in (137) and (138), the earliest from the *OED*, and also obvious from their preposed position.

(137) **Certes** *cwaþ þe ule þat is soþ.*
 Certainly said the owl that is true (*Owl and Nightingale* [1250], 1769)

(138) '**Sertes**', said þai, 'leue lauerdinges, Haue we noght þan o þe kinges.'
 (*Cursor Mundi* [1300], 4907, in Morris 1874–1880)

Sertes/certes is a loan from French and borrowed as CP adverbial.
 Others are introduced as VP adverbials, as in (139), and become preposed, as in (140).

(139) *Alle heo sworen þene að* **trouliche** *þat heo wolden mid Arðure halden*
 All they swore then oath faithfully that they wanted with Arthur keep

 'They all had to swear an oath that they would remain faithfully with Arthur.'(Layamon, *Brut*, Caligula, 9979–9980, in Brook & Leslie 1963)

(140) **Truely** I will not goe first: **truely**-la: I will not doe you that wrong.
 (Shakespeare, *Merry Wives of Windsor*, 1.1.322).

The adverbials *siker*, as in (141) and (142), and *sekirly*, as in (143) to (145), derive from Old English adjectives, like *truly*.

(141) *Dead is Vortimer þe king, &* **siker** *þu miht hider comen.*
 'Dead is Vortimer the king and safely you can come here.'
 (Layamon, *Brut*, Caligula, 15092, in Brook & Leslie 1963)

(142) **Siker** *þu ert myd him a galilewis mon.*
 'Certainly you are with him a Galilean man.'
 (*Passion of Our Lord* [1275], 286, in *Old English Miscellany*, 45, in Morris 1872)

(143)   ***Sikerlichen*** *we sculden uaren & fehten wið þon kæisere*

      'Confidently, we will go and fight against the emperor.'

      (Layamon, *Brut*, Caligula, 7883, from *OED*)

(144)   **sekirly** he schal erre and faile of his purpos

      'Certainly he'll err and fail regarding his purpose.' (HC ME3)

(145)   **Sekirly** wiþ-outyn comparison moche more mercy wil he haue

      'Certainly, without comparison much more mercy will he have.' (HC ME 3)

They become frequent in early Middle English, as table 7.10 shows. This table includes spelling variations such as *sekirly*, *sikirly*, *sikerlike*, and so on.

    In Old English, there is just a very infrequently occurring adjective *sicor(e)* 'sure', inside VP, as in (146).

(146)   *ȝif we ðæt ȝedone mid nanum ðingum ne betað ne ne hreowsiað,ne bio we no ðæs* **sicore**.

      if we that do with no things not atone nor not repent not are we not of-that sure

      'Even if we never do so again, unless we somehow atone for and repent, we are not

      sure [of forgiveness].' (Alfred, *Pastoral Care*, 425. 6, Hatton, in Sweet [1871] 1934)

Seker/siker is one of the adverbs that has an Old English origin and is reanalyzed from VP to CP adverbial in early Middle English (see [142]). This is the same pattern that occurred with *witod* and *sweotol* in Old English, from adjective to low adverb to high adverb.

    Traugott and Dasher (2002: 159, 165) provide other examples of new adverbials, one of them is *indeed*. In the thirteenth century, it is a PP with the meaning of "in the act" but is reanalyzed as an epistemic adverbial in the fifteenth century with the meaning of "in truth." It ends up as a discourse marker beginning in the seventeenth century.

    There are a lot of other changes in the high adverbial inventory in the Old English and early Middle English period. The pattern is the same: from low to high adverbial. By the time of Chaucer, many of the adverbials ending in *-ly* and *-lie* occur sentence-peripherally, mostly on the left but some on the right. Examples (147) through (154) are taken from the General Prologue to the *Canterbury Tales*.

(147)   *Ful **semely** after hir mete she raughte.*

      Very seemly for her food she reached (136)

(148)   *And **sikerly** she was of greet desport,*

      and truly she was of excellent deportment (137)

TABLE 7.10

Forms of Adverbial *sicer(lice)* 'surely' in the Helsinki Corpus

	OE 1–4	ME1	ME2	ME3	ME4
sicerlice	—	5	12	—	—
sicerly/ig	—	1	—	26	5
sicer	—	3	1	3	—

(149)   *Ful **semyly** hir wympul pynched was,*
        Very properly her head dress pleated was (151)

(150)   *But **sikerly** she hadde a fair forheed;*
        but certainly she had a fair forehead (154)

(151)   *For, **hardily**, she was nat undergrowe*
        Because certainly she wasn't small (156)

(152)   *Now **certeinly** he was a fair prelaat;*
        Now certainly he was a fair prelate (204)

(153)   *Ful **swetely** herde he confessioun,*
        Very sweetly heard he confession (221)

(154)   *And **certeinly** he hadde a murye note:*
        and certainly he had a pleasing voice (235)

Some of these are of course loans from French, such as *certainly*, which was first borrowed as an adjective around 1300.

Thus, in the aftermath of the loss of Old English CP adverbials, as expected, they continue to be renewed.

8

THE NEGATIVE CYCLES

IN THIS CHAPTER, I provide examples of (partial) negative cycles from a variety of languages and show that there are two grammaticalization paths, one involving an indefinite phrase and one a verbal head. Old Norse provides a good instance of the first cycle and Chinese of the second. Other languages mix the two, for example, those in the Uralic, Afro-Asiatic, and Athabascan families. Compared to the agreement cycle, the negative cycle (and technically it is not one cycle but two) is a minor one since no language will be characterized as synthetic or analytic just on the basis of the negative. Perhaps because it has a minor typological impact, the negative cycle may be one of the most pervasive of cyclical changes.

Van der Auwera and de Vogelaer (2008) credit Gardiner (1904) as being the first to identify cyclical changes in the negative in different stages of Egyptian, though Jespersen ([1917] 1966) is most often given credit for it. Jespersen's focus is on Indo-European, especially French and English, and he shows how negation arises out of indefinite objects or adverbs. Givón (1976: 89) adds a second source: "negative markers . . . most often arise, diachronically, from erstwhile negative main verbs, commonly 'refuse', 'deny', 'reject', 'avoid', 'fail', or 'lack'." Croft (1991) discusses a related cyclical development, namely how the negative and existential verb are merged together and used as a negative. Some recent work on negative cycles includes Poppe (1995), van Kemenade (2000), Simpson and Wu (2002a), Abraham (2003), Roberts (2005), Ingham (2006), Willis (2006), Jäger (2008), Biberauer (2009), Hoeksema (2009), Tsurska (2009), and van der Auwera (2009). It is mainly focused on Indo-European, however.

Structurally, sentential negation involves full negative phrases or negative verbs or both. The full phrase can be accommodated in a negative phrase as the specifier and the verb as head. All elements in the NegP work together to form one single negative meaning. This is known as negative concord; the term *double negative* will be used only if the two negatives are independent and hence cancel each other out, as Horn (2001: 296) explains. I show that a reanalysis of the specifier of the NegP as a head is responsible for one stage of one cycle, a reanalysis of one head as a negative head for a stage in another cycle. It will also become clear that negation is not placed in a single structural position in all languages. In some languages, it is in initial position, that is, structurally quite high; in others it is placed more in the middle, or structurally low; and in some languages more than one position is involved.

There is sometimes confusion over what counts as multiple negation. Of the over one thousand languages surveyed in the *World Atlas of Language Structures* (Dryer 2008b), only sixty-six are shown to have (what is there called) double negation. This is unexpected if languages are continually undergoing negative cycles. Looking at the map, however, we notice that several negative agreement languages are missing under that label. The accompanying essay justifies not including standard French and Mupun since the second negative is optional, but Navajo, Haida, Apache, Tanacross, and various Berber languages have clear multiple negatives, as I show, but are marked on the map as having a single negative. The map and essay are not really focusing on negative agreement and one should not therefore count my discussion as criticism. In what follows, I will examine any case where more than one negative expresses a single negation. These are typically of two kinds.

This chapter is a much reorganized and updated version of van Gelderen (2008c, 2008d). In section 1, I provide a discussion of the two negative cycles and a possible explanation in terms of the Economy Principles used in previous chapters. Section 2 describes the indefinite source of negatives in Indo-European, Uralic, Afro-Asiatic, Athabascan, and Creoles. Section 3 provides instances of verbs and copulas that are the source of negatives. In many cases, all we have evidence for are parts of cycles. When there is a lack of historical depth, I examine variation among different members of a language family. In section 4, I provide some instances where negatives grammaticalize so high that they are reanalyzed as C, that is, as interrogative markers. Section 5 investigates where these cycles start.

1. Two Cycles

In sections 1.1 and 1.2, I introduce the two sources of negatives, the phrasal and nonphrasal ones, to which I come back in great detail in sections 2 and 3. In 1.3, I also outline in some detail how the Economy Principles used earlier in the book apply to negatives and their cycles.

1.1 INDEFINITE PHRASES

Pollock (1989), Ouhalla (1990), and others working in a generative framework have suggested the phrase structure for a typical negative as given in (1), for example, for formal, standard French.

(1)

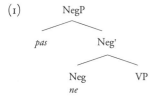

The *ne* is in the head position and attaches to the verb as the latter moves through on its way to a higher position above the NegP and the phrasal *pas* remains in the specifier position, as in (2).

(2) *Je* **n'ai** **pas** *vu* *ça*   Standard French
     I   NEG-have NEG seen that

   'I haven't seen that.'

As argued in Ouhalla (1990) and in more depth in Cinque (1999), the position of the NegP can be relatively high (just below the CP) or relatively low (just above the VP). A possible structure for standard French (2) is given in (3) with the NegP relatively low.

(3)

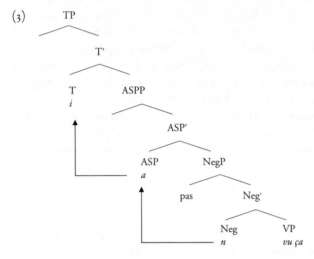

One can also argue for special polarity and focus positions in connection with negation. For instance, Simpson and Wu (2002a: 292) posit a FocP just below the NegP. Historically, the *pas* 'step' is an adverbial minimizer that was late merged into the Spec of the NegP. Simpson and Wu argue that it was first in the specifier of the FocP. This has happened in a number of Romance languages, though typically not in the standard varieties (see Schwegler 1988; Parry 1998).

   Scholars have also argued that, in addition to a FocP, the CP layer includes a polarity phrase (PolP) with an overt or nonovert head. Laka (1994) calls it a Sigma-Phrase. In many languages, such as Arabic and Basque, emphatic nonnegatives can be marked, as in (4). The structure for that would be in (5).

(4) *Irune* **ba-da** *etorri*   Basque
     Irune so-has arrived

   'Irune has arrived.' (Laka 1994: 77)

(5)

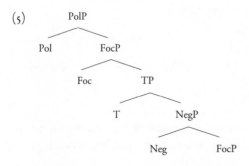

Polarity phrases are also relevant to *yes-no* questions and, as I discuss in section 4, negatives reanalyze as interrogatives, that is, to a position in the CP layer. Negatives are specified for the negative value of the PolP and if the negative quality somehow weakens, it is reanalyzed as a Pol head whose polarity is not specified.

Studying language variation and change, we can see that the element in the head position of (1), *ne*, typically disappears, mostly via an affix stage (see [2]). The negative in the specifier position is then reanalyzed as a head, which in its turn disappears. Before that happens, a fully lexical element gets utilized to express negation. Jespersen's ([1917] 1966) cycle can thus be accounted for by means of a reanalysis of the specifier as head, the subsequent renewal of the specifier position, and the disappearance of the head, as represented in figure 8.1.

An example of a negative cycle comes from the history of English, of course: an early Old English *no*, as in (6), corresponds to a later Old English *n(e)*, as in (7) and (8), where *nan heafodman* and *noht* strengthen the *ne*.

(6) **No** hie *fæder* *cunnon*
   NEG they father know
   'They don't know their father.' (*Beowulf*, 1355, in Klaeber [1922] 1941)

(7) *Æt nyxtan* **næs** **nan** *heafodman þæt fyrde gaderian wolde*
   At last NEG-was no headman who force gather wanted
   'In the end there was no chief man who would gather a force.' (*Peterborough Chronicle* [1010], in Thorpe 1861)

(8) *Næron ȝe* **noht** *æmettiȝe, ðeah ge wel* **ne** *dyden*
   NEG-were you not unoccupied. though you well not did
   'You were not unoccupied, though you did not do well.' (Alfred, *Pastoral Care*, Cotton, in Sweet [1871] 1934: 206, from *OED*).

Once *ne* disappears and *noht/not* weakens to *-n't*, as in Modern English, one expects other elements with semantic negative features to appear, and this happens. However, a reinforcement of the negative by adverbs such as *never* is said to have been stopped for prescriptive reasons. Early reinforcements occur, as in (9), and many dialects use *never* or a negative nominal, as in (10) and (11) respectively.

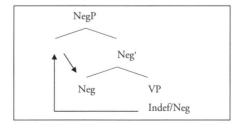

FIGURE 8.1. The negative cycle

(9)   *that the sonne dwellith therfore **nevere** the more ne lasse in oon signe than in another*

    'that the sun therefore doesn't dwell more nor less in one sign than in another'
    (Chaucer, *Astrolabe*, 665 C1)

(10)   No, I **never** see him these days (BNC-A9H, 350)

(11)   You could have **no clue** of their passion for snooker (BNC-ECU, 10)

Never could have weakened too, but there is a lot of discussion of the "vulgar" use of *ne'er* in the nineteenth century (see Trudgill & Cheshire 1998: 129). Horn (2001: 453–462) reviews some of the theories looking into why certain renewals took place, for example, because of internal reasons such as word order changes. I won't go into those here. I think that the negative cycle is so pervasive because there are always ready-to-be-recycled negative objects and adverbials and minimizers, such as *pas* 'step' in French and *a bit* in English, as well as verbs. Part of the choice depends on the semantic features of the renewer but part is also chance (i.e., external).

1.2 VERBAL HEADS

The phrasal strategy sketched in section 1.1 is only one strategy. Givón (1978), Dahl (1979), Payne (1985), and Croft (1991) provide instances of languages where negative heads develop from verbal heads. There may be structural reasons for the choice of the one over the other. For instance, polysynthetic languages lack quantifier arguments (see Baker 1995) and therefore may renew their negatives through verbs. Typical for the verbal strategy is that the negatives may be marked for aspect and mood, as in the Athabascan and Semitic families and in Chinese. That is a result of the grammaticalization path, first as a full verb, then as aspectual or mood marker retaining the negative feature. Hindi/Urdu negative forms *nahii* and *na* also differentiate between indicative and nonindicative (e.g., conditional and subjunctive) contexts, probably due to the origin of *–hii* as auxiliary.

    Croft formulates a negative-existential cycle, where in one stage a negative particle marks both existential and nonexistential predicates (Type A). English is an example of that stage. Subsequently, a special negative existential may arise (Type B), as in for instance Amharic. This form is then used as the general negative, to be reinforced by another existential in existential sentences (Type C). This cycle is shown in figure 8.2, reproduced from Croft (1991: 6). Of course, there are in-between stages too.

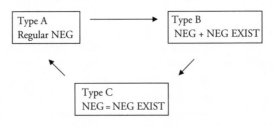

FIGURE 8.2. Croft's existential cycle

Another verbal strategy is to use negative verbs such as *to refuse*, as in Beja, an Afro-Asiatic language, discussed in section 3.3. A last strategy is employed in the grammaticalization of prohibitives. As Heine and Kuteva (2002: 283) show, the verb *stop* becomes *don't* in a number of languages, as in (12).

(12) **Aret**   *vol*   *sitrô!*   Seychelles Creole
Stop   steal   lime

'Stop stealing the limes!'
(Corne 1977: 184, from Heine & Kuteva 2002: 284)

In the remainder of this section, I provide one example of a verb being reanalyzed as a negative from Chinese, but I give many more instances in section 3.

In Chinese, one of the negatives is *mei*, as in (13). *Mei* is derived from a verb meaning "to not exist; to die," as shown in (14) and (15).

(13) *wo*   **mei**   *you*   *shu*   Chinese
I   not   exist   book

'I don't have a book.'

(14) *Yao*   *Shun*   *ji*   **mo**   ...   Old Chinese
Yao   Shun   since   died

'Since Yao and Shun died, . . .' (Mengzi, Tengwengong B, from Lin 2002: 5)

(15) *yu*   *de*   *wang*   *ren*   **mei**   *kunan,*   ...   Early Mandarin
wish   PRT   died   person   not-be   suffering

'If you wish that the deceased one has no suffering, . . .'
(*Dunhuang Bianwen*, from Lin 2002: 5–6)

In many languages (Payne 1985: 222), the negative develops from a verb meaning "not exist" and "to die" and Chinese had that step too, as (15) shows. Later, *mei* is also found, but always with the aspect marker *you*, as in (16).

(16) *dayi*   *ye*   **mei**   *you*   *chuan,*   *jiu*   *zou*   *le chulai*   EarlyMandarin
coat   even   not   PF   wear,   then   walk   PF out

'He didn't even put on his coat and walked out.' (Rulin Waishi, from Lin 2002: 8)

According to Lin (2002), the transition from verb to negative proceeds via a perfective aspect stage, as in (16). Since *mei* appears only in perfective contexts, it is assumed that it helps to express aspect. *Mei*, in this use, gradually replaces the Old and Middle Chinese negative existential *wu* in the early Mandarin period. This change is shown in figure 8.3 and is due to a reanalysis of *mei* in a higher position.

Thus, there are two strategies for changes in negatives: one is when an (indefinite) phrase is reanalyzed as a phrasal negative and then as a head; the other when a negative head is replaced by a lower head. In section 1.3, I outline the by now well-known mechanisms for these two negative cycles.

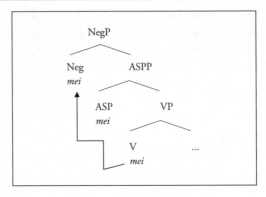

FIGURE 8.3. The negative head cycle

1.3 ECONOMY PRINCIPLES

As mentioned in earlier chapters, Chomsky (2007: 3) identifies three factors that are crucial in the development of language in the individual; the genetic endowment or UG, the data a learner is exposed to, and principles not specific to the faculty of language.The latter are called third factor principles and my attempts in this book to explain cycles have used such principles, such as those as in van Gelderen (2004) and in (17).

(17)   **Head Preference Principle (HPP):**
       Be a head, rather than a phrase.

For negatives, this means that an (English) learner and speaker will build structures such as (18a) rather than (18b) if given evidence that is compatible with either.

(18)   a.   NegP   b.   NegP

The evidence for something being a specifier/phrase is that it can be expanded; for example, *completely not* is a possible negative in languages such as Dutch or German and hence a full phrase like (18b). A head is not expandable in such a way and can be adjoined to by a head, as *ne* in Standard French is joined by the auxiliary, shown in (1), as opposed to the specifier *pas*.

The second principle that I discussed in earlier chapters is relevant to both kinds of cycles, namely (19).

(19)   **Late Merge Principle (LMP):**
       Merge as late as possible

Where negatives are concerned, the LMP would help reanalyze a verb that is functioning both as a verb in VP (responsible for argument structure) and as a means to express negation above VP as one just expressing negation. This reanalysis would involve merging the element directly outside VP, in NegP.

It is also possible to reformulate Head Preference and Late Merge in terms of feature change and loss. This will also account for the stage where a head disappears, a stage neither the LMP nor the HPP include. Changes in negatives can be accounted for by arguing that their (initially) semantic features are reanalyzed as interpretable ones connected to the specifier of the NegP and then as uninterpretable ones, as in (20a), connected to the head. Changes connected to the negative cycle occur because the interpretable negative features of an indefinite negative are reanalyzed as uninterpretable. The uninterpretable features function as probes that need to connect with something that is negative through semantic or interpretable features. The changes represented in (20b) involve heads being reanalyzed as higher heads. Typically, as higher heads, they are connected with a number of other features (tense, aspect) and may weaken that way, and become probes.

(20) **Feature Economy**

		Specifier (of NegP)		Head (of NegP)		affix
a	Adjunct/Argument semantic	> [i-NEG]	>	[u-NEG]	>	--
b.	Lexical Head [neg]	> (higher) Head [i-NEG]/[u-F]	>	(higher) Head [u-F]/[u-F]	>	o

The changes in (20) mirror changes in acquisition and language change and also account for the need for renewal, which the LMP and the HPP do not do on their own. After a semantic feature is reanalyzed as interpretable and then as uninterpretable, the latter uninterpretable feature is not enough on its own and will trigger a renewal.

The view of negation expressed in (20a) is somewhat compatible with recent probe-based accounts of negative concord, as in Ouali (2006), Roberts (2007: 69), Tsurska (2009), and Haegeman and Lohndal (2010), and to some extent Zeijlstra (2004). Haegeman and Lohndal and Zeijlstra, however, posit empty operators with interpretable features. In addition, the probe can be lower than the goal. I stick to a more traditional agree relationship. The changes in (20b) have not received much attention within the Minimalist framework. The situation here is more comparable to for example, the renewal of future auxiliaries discussed in chapter 7.

Having briefly discussed two cycles of negation and some possible explanations, I examine other cycles or partial cycles in the remainder of this chapter, showing that the grammaticalization cycle is either as in figure 8.1 or figure 8.3.

2. The Reanalysis of Indefinites

This section provides examples of phrasal indefinites being reanalyzed as negatives. For purely practical purposes, I group the examples by language family.

2.1 INDO-EUROPEAN

Good examples of the first kind of negative cycle can be found in Germanic (as we've seen for English in [6] to [8]), Celtic, Greek, and Romance, less so in Slavic (but see Tsurska 2009). The pattern is for a preverbal negative to be strengthened by an adverbial. The changes in negatives occurring in English have been well documented (see Iyeiri 1999; van Kemenade

2000; Ingham 2006, 2007a, 2007b) and I won't go into those, except in section 5 where I discuss triggers of the change.

For the Celtic languages, the data in Poppe (1995), Willis (1998, 2006), and Roberts (2005: 159) show that there may be a cycle from single preverbal marker *ny* in Middle Welsh (21), reinforced by *(d)dim* 'at all/anything' in contemporary Welsh, and then losing the original negative in spoken Welsh (22). Breton represents an older stage and still has a discontinuous negative *ne . . . ket*.

(21) . . . **ny** wnn i pwy wytti.   Middle Welsh
      NEG know 1S who are-2S

      '. . . I don't know who you are.' (*Pedeir Keinc y Mabinogi*, 2.22–23, from Willis 2006: 63)

(22) Wn I **ddim** pwy wyt ti   Spoken Welsh
      Know 1S NEG who are you

      'I don't know who you are.' (Willis 2006: 63)

Cowgill (1960) shows that the (Classical and Modern) Greek negative *ou* derives from *ne oiu kwid [not life anything] 'not ever/not on your life'. It first loses *ne* and becomes *oiukid*, and then further weakens to *oukí* and *ou(k)* (see also Kiparsky & Condoravdi 2006). Romance languages have all the makings of cyclical renewal but this seems to be happening typically in nonstandard varieties (see Parry 1998).

In early Germanic, the negative element *ne/ni* precedes the verb (as in other Indo-European languages). This independent negative *ne* survives in some Germanic languages, such as in the Old Norse *Poetic Edda*, composed between the tenth and thirteenth centuries and preserved in a thirteenth-century manuscript (from which the following examples in Old Norse are drawn).[1] It appears either alone immediately preceding the finite verb, as in (23), or with a verbal suffix *-a(t)*, as in (24). In the main clause, the negated verb often appears in sentence initial position.

(23) er hjör **né** rýðr   Old Norse
      that sword not redden

      'that do not redden a sword' (*Fáfnismál*, 24)

(24) bíta preftönnum ef Gunnarr **né** kemr-**at**   Old Norse
      bite teeth if Gunnar not return-not

      'will bite with their teeth if Gunnar doesn't return' (*Atlakviða*, 11)

In most of the Germanic daughter languages, *ne* weakens and is reinforced. In Old Norse, *ne* weakens phonologically and is strengthened by *a(t)* in (24). The reinforcement *-a(t)* probably derives from the indefinite *ain 'one' and its neuter indefinite *ainata and this negative can also occur without *ne*, as (25) shows, though I haven't been able to find this form on its own.

---

1. All my references to the *Poetic Edda* are taken from http://www.heimskringla.no/original/edda/gudrun-arkvidaintridja.php unless otherwise noted.

(25) | *Kemr-a* | *nu* | *Gunnarr* | *kalli-g-a* | *ek* | *Högna* | Old Norse
come-not | now | Gunnarr | call-I-not | I | Hogna

     se-kk-a | *ek* | *siðan* | *svasa* | *brœðr*
see-I-not | I | again | dear | brothers

'Now Gunnar will not come and I will never call Hogna and I will never see my dear brothers again.' (*Guðrunarkviða*, 3: 8)

The position and status of *ne* and *-at* are unclear at this point. They both look like heads, prompting Eythórrson (2002) to say that *ne* is a verbal prefix and is in the head position.

Since both *ne* and *-at* markings are weak, a new strengthening comes in the form of indefinites with an enclitic *-gi* attached, as in (26).

(26) | *er-at* | *maðr* | *svá* | *góðr* | *at* | *galli* | *né* | *fylgi* | Old Norse
is-NEG | man | so | good | that | blemishes | not | belong

     né | *svá* | *illr* | *at* | ***einugi*** | *dugi*
nor | so | bad | that | nothing | is-fit-for

'Nobody is so good that he doesn't have faults nor so bad that he is not good for something.' (*Hávamál*, 133).

Ei(nu)gi does not, however, occur together in the same clause with any other negatives, as far as I have been able to determine, at least in the *Poetic Edda*. A few negatives with *eigi* 'not' are given in (27) and (28), but there are also instances of *aldrigi* 'never' and *eitgi/ekki* 'nothing'.

(27) | *þat* | *mæli* | *ek* | ***eigi*** | Old Norse
that | say-1S | I | not

'I am not saying that.' (*Njalssaga*, 219, from Faarlund 2004: 225).

(28) | ***eigi*** | *em* | *ek* | *haftr* | Old Norse
not | am | I | bound

'I am not bound.' (*Fáfnismál*, 8)

Faarlund (2004: 225) asserts that the *-gi* suffix is no longer productive in Old Norse but rather that it is part of the negative word. That means that *eigi* and other negatives in Old Norse are phrasal adverbs, as is obvious because they trigger V-second, as in (28).

Eigi is first clearly in the specifier position, as in (28) but it may have also been in either specifier or head, because of sentences such as (29), also from Old Norse, where the negative immediately precedes the verb.

(29) | *Heyrðu nú, Loki, hvat ek nú mæli* | Old Norse
Hear-you now Loki what I now say

     *er **eigi veit** jarðar hvergi*
what not knows earth nobody

né upphimins: áss er stolinn hamri
and-not heaven Ass is stolen hammer

'Hear now Loki what I am telling you, what nobody on earth or in heaven knows: the hammer of the God Ass is stolen.' (*Lay of Thrym*, 2).

Old Norse *eigi* corresponds to Modern Norwegian *ikke* 'not' and between Old Norse and Modern Norwegian, the negative is reanalyzed from specifier to head. For instance, Bondi Johannessen (2000) argues that Modern Norwegian *ikke* is a head. If this is true, an expected further change would be for the head to weaken phonologically and this is indeed the case as is fairly obvious from sentences such as (30) and (31), very common according to native speakers.

(30)   *Men detta æ'kke et forslag som vi har interesse av*   Norwegian
       but that is-not a proposal that we have interest in

       'But that's not a proposal we are interested in.' (Solstad *Svik*, 1977: 70).

(31)   *Trøtt. . . jeg? Ha'kke tid*   Norwegian
       tired . . . me? have-not time

       'Me, tired? I don't have the time.'
       (http://www.vg.no/pub/vgart.hbs?artid=9131849; 14 June 2006)

Christensen (1985) in fact argues that *ikke* is a clitic. This is similar to the development in English with negative auxiliaries such as *don't*, argued by Zwicky and Pullum (1983) to be affixes.[2] As mentioned, the reason that English doesn't reinforce the weakened *-n't* through another negative specifier may be a prescriptive one. Norwegian varieties may be freer from prescriptive pressures.

    Many linguists have connected having a negative head to the possibility of a system of negative concord, for example, Wood (1997) and Rowlett (1998). The intuition behind this claim is that once the negation is in the head position, it is weakened to the point where it no longer 'interferes' with a second or third negative. If *ikke* is a head in varieties of Modern Norwegian, one would expect negative concord. This is indeed what may be occurring in certain varieties of Norwegian. Thus, Sollid (2002) argues that in the northern Norwegian dialect of Sappen, negative concord is starting to occur, as in (32), where *aldri* 'never' is optional.

(32)   *Eg har ikke aldri smakt sånne br Od*   Sappen Norwegian
       I have not never tasted such bread

       'I haven't ever tasted that kind of bread.' (Sollid 2002).

---

2. The negative in Norwegian is probably not an affix since it reportedly can be attached to a pronoun too, as in (i):

(i)   *Har   du   ikke   gjort   det* [harükə yurt dE]?   Norwegian
     have you not done that

     'Haven't you done that?'

She argues this is under the influence of Finnish, which may well be the case. This would, however, not be possible if the grammar wasn't ready for this, in other words, if *ikke* weren't already a head, and negative concord a possibility. Jespersen ([1917] 1966: 66) mentions that "cumulative negation" of *aldrig* and a negation is rare in Danish, but later he writes that reinforcement is "very frequent in Danish dialects" ([1917] 1966: 73). Searching Norwegian websites brings up quite a number, as in (33) and (34).

(33) *Men det var nok ikke mye oppvartning de fikk, for jeg merket*   Norwegian
     ikke aldri *at noen hadde kjærestebesøk den tiden jeg jobbet der.*

     'But that wasn't much attention that they got, because I never noticed
     (=not never) that anyone had visits from loved ones the time I worked there.'
     (http://www.nkbf.no/Nyheter/2004/Brunborg_1_04.htm)

(34) *USA bør* ***ikke ALDRIG*** *være et forbilde når det kommer til integrering*   Norwegian

     'The US should never (=not never) be an example when it comes to integration.'
     (www.superserver.no/invboard/index.php; 21 June 2005)

Giannakidou (2005) writes that languages that employ Negative Concord and languages that don't are obviously clearly different. There are, however, languages that sometimes allow negative concord, according to her. She notes that these cases may be marginal or be emphatic. This may include the Norwegian in (33) and (34), or those constructions might be the first step in a renewal. Colloquial (Southern) Dutch[3] has similar constructions, as in (35), even though the regular negative *niet* is not yet a head, as (36) shows.

(35) *Ik zie hier* ***nooit niemand/geen*** *mens*   Colloquial Southern Dutch
     I see here never nobody/no person

     'I never see anyone here.'

(36) **Ik zie hier* ***niemand/geen mens niet.***   Colloquial Southern Dutch
     I see here nobody/no person not

     'I don't see anyone here.'

The changes for *ne*, *eigi*, and *ikke* (though not *-a[t]*) can be summarized in figure 8.4, where (a) and (b) represent Old Norse, (c) is Modern Norwegian, and (d) represents a variety such as Sappen Norwegian with the verb moving through the negative head and negative concord being possible. In figure 8.4, I have indicated the changes in the features as well, from semantic to interpretable to uninterpretable. I am not sure if stage (c) exists or if (b) is reanalyzed as (d) in one step. I have therefore left the features of *ikke* unspecified.

Thus, Old Norse *ne* disappears and is replaced by a reanalyzed indefinite *eigi*, which becomes *ikke* 'not' in Modern Norwegian. *Ikke* is being reanalyzed from phrase to head in present-day Norwegian and is renewed by yet another indefinite *aldri* 'never'.

---

3. Van der Auwera, de Cuypere, and Neuckermans (2006: 307) provide a map for this use by Belgian Dutch speakers.

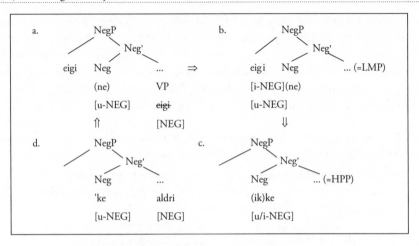

FIGURE 8.4. The negative cycle in Scandinavian

2.2 URALIC

Most Uralic languages have a negative auxiliary that indicates negation and may mark person, number, tense (past and present), and very infrequently mood.[4] That aspect of those languages is discussed in section 3. In this section, I discuss the phrasal renewal prevalent in languages such as Sami, Finnish, and Kamassian. I also briefly mention the origins of *nem* in Hungarian, which saw a "Neuerung" (Honti 1997: 81) through a particle *nem*, possibly an indefinite.

In Southern Sami, as in other Uralic languages, the negative is expressed by an inflected auxiliary *idtjim*, as in (37).

(37) **Idtjim**   *(manne)*   *daejrieh*   Southern Sami
      NEG-PST-1S   (I)   know
      'I didn't know.' (Bergsland 1994: 44)

In Northern Sami, the auxiliary also appears, though less fully inflected (Lagercrantz 1929: 195, 203–204). It can be accompanied by a reinforcing element, glossed as 'never', which works together with the negative auxiliary (negative concord) since the end result is a negative meaning.

(38) *In*   *leat*   **goassege**   *dahkan*   *dan*   Northern Sami
      NEG-1S   be   never   do-PART   it
      'I have never done that.' (Trosterud, p.c.)

In Finnish, Sami's linguistic relative, the negative is also inflected but only for subject agreement not for tense, as (39) shows.

---

4. A project has started at the University of Vienna to develop a typology of negation in these languages. See www.univie.ac.at/negation.

(39) *Liisa*   ***ei***   *osta-nut*   *kirjaa*   Finnish
      Liisa-NOM   NEG-3S   buy-PST   book
      'Liisa did not buy a/the book.'

As in Northern Sami, the negative auxiliary or particle is reinforced with a negative polarity adverb, as (40) shows, again resulting in one negative sense—in negative concord.

(40) *En*   *ole*   ***koskaan*** *maistanut* *sellaisia* *leipiä*   Finnish
      NEG   have   ever   tasted   such   bread
      'I have never tasted such bread.' (Sollid 2002)

In Finnish varieties, the auxiliary can be deleted if this adverbial is present (see Honti 1997: 164, who quotes Savijärvi 1977). This is of course expected if one considers a typical negative cycle.

Kamassian, a Northern Samoyedic language in Siberia whose last native speaker died in 1989, had an auxiliary for general negation, as in (41), and one to negate existence and possession, as in (42).

(41) *(man)* *e-m*   *nere-ʔ*   Kamassian
      I   NEG-1S   fear-CONNEG
      'I will not be frightened.' (Künnap 1999: 25)

(42) *bilä*   *kuza*   *man*   ***naɣa-m***   Kamassian
      bad   man   I   NEG-1S
      'I am not a bad man.' (Simoncsics 1998: 594)

Croft (1991) argues that it is typical for the existential negative to be generalized as a negative. Thus, if *em* was weakening, one could have expected *naΦa* to become the general negative. This did not occur. Instead, probably because of influence from Russian, a newer (43) developed. The negative auxiliary is in a higher position in (43), no longer moving via the position that has the agreement features.

(43) *oʔb-l*   ***ej***   *moo-lja-m*   Kamassian
      collect-PART   NEG   AUX-PRES-1S
      'I can't collect.' (Simoncsics 1998: 594)

The data from Northern Sami, Finnish, and Kamassian show how the two negative cycles are relevant in the Uralic family. In Sami and Finnish, the negative auxiliary shows signs of being reanalyzed in a higher position, as we'll see in sections 3 and 4. As this happens, emphatic negation is expressed through an additional adverb and in some varieties the auxiliary is left out. In Kamassian, a negative existential could have been used to renew the older verbal form. Because of Russian influence, the adverbial was used instead.

I end with a speculation on Hungarian. As mentioned, Hungarian is unlike its Uralic relatives in not having an inflected negative auxiliary. Honti (1997: 164) suggests that the negative particle *nem* possibly derives from a *n and *ma 'what, thing'. This would be in accordance with Jespersen's cycle and the other languages we have seen so far. In current Hungarian, *nem* often immediately precedes the predicate and seems a head and occurs with other negatives, such as *senki* 'nobody' in (44).

(44)   **senki**   **nem**   *olvas*   Hungarian
     nobody   NEG   read-3S
     'Nobody is reading.'

So Uralic has a negative head, with interpretable features. As the head moves to other head positions, its negative features become uninterpretable and a probe for another negative adverb.

2.3 AFRO-ASIATIC

In this section (focusing on phrasal renewal) and in section 3.3 (focusing on the negative head), I consider negation in several Afro-Asiatic languages. Afro-Asiatic is usually divided into Berber, Semitic, Egyptian, Cushitic, Omotic, and Chadic, and many languages and varieties of these groups show multiple negatives agreeing to make one negative. The cyclical pattern is present in these languages too, namely a verbal head that is common in all but a specifier, derived from an indefinite, that is new. Many of these languages display more than one of the stages; coexistence of older and newer patterns is to be expected when language changes. (Old) Egyptian has a single negation that is renewed by a different negative in Coptic (see Gardiner 1904), but I will leave that outside this discussion. All languages in this section have in common an original negative head, which in some languages is reinforced. The head is older than the indefinite.

Ethnologue lists at least twenty varieties of Berber, including the Northern Tamazight, Tarifit, Taqbaylit (Kabyle), the Eastern Augila, and the Southern Tamashek (Tuareg). Mettouchi (1996) and Chaker (1996) review negation in Berber and the etymologies of the negative morphemes. They identify a preverbal *wer* (informally *ur*)[5] with a possible source as negative verb, but other sources are possible, as from *ara* 'thing'. The second negative morpheme, one I will suggest is the renewal, is an often optional indefinite *ara, k(ra), š(ra)*, and so on.

Ouali's (2003: 245) examples in (45) to (47) show that all (Northern) Berber dialects have a preverbal negative element *ur/wer* and that most have an optional postverbal element that is different in different dialects.

(45)   **ur**   *ssex*   **(sha)**   Tamazight
     NEG   drink-PF.1S   NEG
     'I don't drink.'

(46)   **ur**   *kshimegh*   **(ara)**   Taqbaylit
     NEG   entered.PST.1S   NEG
     'I didn't enter.'

---

5. Chaker (1996: 11) suggests that *wer* is the older form; Sudlow (2001: 65) uses *wər* but says it can be contracted to *u(r)*.

(47) **u-sn**   *twshi*   **(sha)** *arbii*   Tarifit
      NEG-them   give.PST.3S   NEG   grass
      'She didn't give them grass.'

Ouali (2003) argues that the preverbal negative element *ur* is base generated as a polarity
head and the second negative as the specifier of NegP. It is also possible that *ur* is in the head
of a high NegP, as in (48), and that the optional element is still lexical, with semantic negative
features. This is in fact what Ouali (2006: 134) argues.

(48)

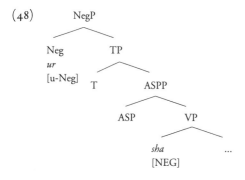

The T and ASP are probably in the position indicated in (48) since tense and aspect can
come in between (see Ouali 2008: 51).

   In Tamazight, the optional *sha* may precede *ur* as well. This means that *sha* is attracted to
the specifier of the NegP and may become reanalyzed as originating in that position.

(49) **sha**   **ur**   *ssex*   Tamazight
      NEG   NEG   drink-PF.1S
      'I don't drink.' (Ouali 2006: 131)

Chris Lucas (p.c.) reports that at least one variety, Augila Berber, has an obligatory postverbal *sha*, expected if the indefinite is reanalyzed as the specifier of the NegP. This means that
ur now has [u-NEG].

   As also expected if *ur* is a head that probes for another negative, a second negative *walu*
'nothing' or *agidge* 'no-one' is grammatical, as in (50) and (51).

(50) **ur**   *as-wshi.x*   **walu**   Tamazight
      NEG   him-give.3S   nothing
      'I didn't give him anything.' (Ouali 2003: 246)

(51) **agidge**   **ur**   *iddin*   Tamazight
      no-one   NEG   go-PF-3S
      'No one left.' (Ouali 2008: 147)

If both *sha* and *walu* are specifiers, the reinforcing negative *sha* of (45) cannot co-occur with
the quantifier in (50), and this is the case.

Ouali's analysis and data fit with what we know about the negative cycle: the head *ur* is older than the specifier *sha* and hence the specifier, but not the head, varies across the different varieties and not all varieties have introduced one yet; for example, Touareg (Heath 2005) and Tashlhit lack it. The specifier is also in complementary distribution with another indefinite. In Touareg, there is evidence that the negative is a head (clitics attach to it) and also that it soon will be reinforced. Notice (52).

(52)   *wər*   *i-ja*   **wæla**   **əndərræn**   Tamashek
        NEG   3MS-be.done   even   little
        'Nothing happened at all.' (Heath 2005: 589)

I turn now to Arabic. Much has recently been written about Arabic negation; see, for example, Comrie (1991), Fassi Fehri (1993), Ouhalla (1997), Shlonsky (1997), and Benmamoun (2000). There is a lot of variation, particularly where co-occurrence with certain aspects is concerned. The oldest forms are probably the *l*-initial ones. Walker (1896: 233) speaks of the Semitic "common negative stem" *l*- and Lipiński (1997:455) argues that it is related to the Berber form *wər/ur* just discussed. Levin (2004: 438) speculates that that form is possibly cognate with Egyptian *–n*.

As in Berber, more recent negative elements originate as indefinite interrogative pronouns—*maa* 'what' is used often in positive rhetorical questions—and as indefinites, such as -*sh* from *shay'un* 'thing'. *Maa* is no longer used as an interrogative pronoun in modern varieties and has become the most general negative. In Classical Arabic, the negative preverbal elements are the heads *laysa, laa, lam, lan* (where *lam* and *lan* are marked for past and future respectively, *laysa*- bears agreement, and *la* is not marked), as in (53), or the preverbal *maa*. The latter has become the general form in modern varieties of Arabic (Fischer 1982: 85), with a postverbal -*sh*, as in (54) in some dialects.

(53)   **lam**   *yuhibba*   *Zayd*   *ʔal*   *qiraaʔ*   Standard Arabic
      NEG-PST   3MS-like   Zayd   the   reading
      'Zayd did not like reading.' (Shlonsky 1997: 95)

(54)   *Omar*   **ma-kteb-sh**   *l-bra*   Moroccan Arabic
      Omar   NEG-write.PST.3M-NEG   the-letter
      'Omar didn't write the letter.' (Benmamoun 2000: 81)

There is enormous variation and different stages of the cycle are represented in the various languages. For instance, Benmamoun (2000: 69–70) says the pattern of (54) also occurs in Egyptian, Palestinian, and Yemeni Arabic, and Ouhalla (1997) adds Lebanese and shows that the postverbal –*sh(i)* is optional in the Middle Eastern group but not the Western groups. The postverbal negation can be on its own in certain dialects. Vanhove (1996) and Simeone-Senelle (1996) show for Yemeni dialects that either *maa* or -*sh* or both occur; *laa* is possible as well with an optional -*sh*. According to most accounts, the -*sh* is grammaticalized from Classical Arabic *'ayyu šay'in* 'what thing', *maa* is older, and *l*- the oldest.

Based on the data presented in Fassi Fehri (1993: 165–166, 207), one could argue that *ma* appears in a relatively high position. It isn't inflected, can be together with a question particle, as in (55), and doesn't interact with other auxiliaries.

(55) *ʔa-**maa***   *raʔay-ta*   *r-rajul-a*   Standard Arabic
       Q-NEG   saw-you   the-man-ACC

       'Haven't you seen the man?' (Fassi Fehri 1993: 166)

This high position of *maa*, possibly as head of a polarity phrase, fits with its origin as an interrogative pronoun *ma* 'what' (Rubin 2005: 50). This would have been an instance of *maa* in the specifier position being reanalyzed as a polarity head. Arabic has a positive emphatic, namely *qad*, which is in complementary distribution with *maa* (see Bahloul 1996: 41) and could be in the PolP as well. Shlonsky (1997: 16), following Benmamoun (1992: 68), argues that *maa* is the head and *-sh* the specifier, though in later work Benmamoun (1996: 50) acknowledges that the "status [of *sh*] is not clear." It seems most plausible that *maa* has become a head in most varieties. The postverbal suffix *-sh* still has specifier-like characteristics because it is in complementary distribution with polarity phrases, as shown in (56) for Moroccan Arabic.

(56) ***maa***   *shaft*   **(*shi)**   *Nadia*   *hette*   *haja*   Moroccan Arabic
       NEG   saw   (NEG)   Nadia   anything

       'Nadia didn't see anything.' (Benmamoun 1996 : 47)

In Amharic, another Semitic language, the negative is formed with *al-* preceding the perfective verb as well as a suffix, as in (57) from Zway.

(57) *hoytäñä*   ***al-agrägäb-o***   Zway Amharic
       again   NEG-answer-3MS-NEG [o = ä 3MS + u NEG]

       'Again he didn't answer.' (Leslau 1999: 177)

In other aspects, the suffix is optional and another preverbal particle or affix is used, as in (58), and in the subordinate the suffix disappears.

(58) *äyä*   ***ənku***   *dämam-**(u)***   Zway Amharic
       I   not   rich-1S-NEG

       'I'm not rich.' (Leslau 1999: 58)

The doubling occurs in other varieties of Amharic as well, for example, that described in Leslau's (1995) *Reference Grammar*. Here the suffix disappears in a subordinate clause (Leslau 1995: 292). As in colloquial Arabic, it is hard to decide which is the head and which is the specifier.

(59) ***al-säbbärä-mm***   Amharic
       NEG-break.3S-NEG

       'He did not break.' (Leslau 1995: 292)

So what does this mean for the cycle? In standard Classical Arabic, there is a negative (verbal) head *l(a)-* that starts out as a negative head and moves to a higher position. When this happens, its features become opaque and reinforcements, present in many varieties, are expected. These are *ma* 'what' and *shay'un* 'thing'. The Afro-Asiatic languages thus show discontinuous negation. In most cases, there is clear evidence for a head and a specifier that functions as a reinforcer. In section 3, we'll see some other Afro-Asiatic languages renewing their heads with other heads.

2.4 ATHABASCAN, EYAK, TLINGIT, AND HAIDA

The Athabascan languages, as well as Tlingit and Eyak, are considered members of the Na-Dene family, but it is controversial whether Haida is related to them or is an isolate. I combine all these languages in one section since, typologically, they have similar negative systems. In this family, there is evidence for the two cycles discussed earlier, one based on an auxiliary, the other on a phrasal element. In this section, I discuss the latter.

Krauss says that it is "difficult to establish what the negative forms in Proto-Athapaskan were like" (1969: 73). As we will see, this is indeed the case, since the forms are very different from each other, making it an ideal family in which to study the negative cycle. Most varieties have an independent word that occurs before the verb complex and one or more affixes inside the verb complex. Rice (2000: 318) also shows that the negative affix is very variable across the languages: "The variable position of the negative is allowed by the scope hypothesis: negation is always expressed by a syntactic suffix that has scope over the entire verb word."

The most variable part is the negative word or particle that precedes the verb, so this is the most recent addition to the renewal. The position of the affix inside the verb word is also variable and it disappears in some variants. The general cycle seems to be one where the negative auxiliary verb is incorporated in the verbal complex and then renewed by an element outside the verbal complex. Unlike Old Norse, Finnish, and Sami, Athabascan is generally polysynthetic. This is relevant to the cycle since indefinite arguments are rare in polysynthetic languages. There are, however, adverbs in these languages, for instance, *łahágóó* 'a few places' and *t'áá ałch'įįdígo* 'a little bit' (Young & Morgan 1987: 13) that could be used as emphatic minimizers and then reanalyzed. As I argue, indefinite elements are indeed a source of renewal.

I start with a general description of negatives in Navajo, one of the Southern Athabascan languages, focusing on their structural characteristics, and then I describe the variation in some other Athabascan languages (Ahtna, Koyukon, Upper and Lower Tanana, Chipewyan/Dëne Sųłiné) as well as in Haida, Eyak, and Tlingit. This section also provides some speculations on the historical spread of the Athabascan phrasal renewal. In section 3.4, I add more on the head strategy.

Negation in Navajo consists of two parts, a specifier *doo*, with interpretable negative features, and a head *da*, with uninterpretable negative featrues. I provide frequent trees to show where negatives, and NegP, are situated in the Navajo sentence. In (60), the preverbal *doo* and postverbal *da* are shown.

(60) **Doo** dichin nishłįį **da**   Navajo
      NEG hungry 1S-be NEG

    'I'm not hungry.' (Young & Morgan 1987: 350)

Doo is a specifier since it forms a constituent with *t'áá* 'just' or by *t'ah* 'ever', as in (61), and *da* is a head and is always immediately to the right of the verb (and is in complementary distribution with the complementizer –*go*).

(61) **T'ah   doo**   *tónteel   yiistséeh   da*   Navajo
      ever   NEG   ocean   1S-see-PF   NEG

      'I've never seen the ocean.' (Young & Morgan 1987: 710)

Assuming a head-initial structure, a possible structure for a regular negative in (62) is given in (63a), but a head-final one would be possible too, as in (63b).

(62) *doo   (bił)   hózhǫ́ǫ -da*   Navajo
      NEG   3S-with   happy-NEG

      'He is not happy.'

(63) a.

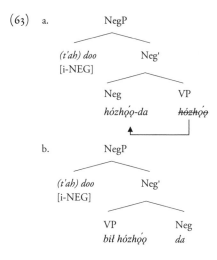

      b.

There is, however, evidence that a position higher than NegP may be involved in Navajo negation (as in other languages) since *doo* can be sentence-initial and interacts with the question marker as in (64). The interrogative marker is part of the CP layer and is in fact a head in (64), since a *t'ah* cannot be added to the *doo* to make it 'Are you never happy?' (Mary Willie, p.c., but see Young & Morgan 1987: 472).[6]

---

6. The question would be asked as in (i) or (ii), with (ii) better than (i).

   (i)   *Da'   ts'ídá   doo   nił   hózhǫ́ǫ -da*   Navajo
         Q   really   NEG   you-with   happy   NEG
         'Are you really not happy?' (Mary Willie, p.c.)

   (ii) *Da'   łahda-ísh   nił   hózhǫ́ǫ   nt'ee'*   Navajo
         Q   sometimes-Q   you-with   happy-NEG   PST
         'Were you ever happy once?' (Mary Willie, p.c.)

(64) ***Doó-sh***   *nił*   *hózhǫ́ǫ -da*   Navajo
       NEG-Q   you-with   happy-NEG

       'Aren't you happy?' (Wilson 1995: 84)

In (65), I use a structure with a polarity and focus phrase. These indicate whether the sentence is negative or not. Constituents that precede *doo* would be in the left periphery.

(65)

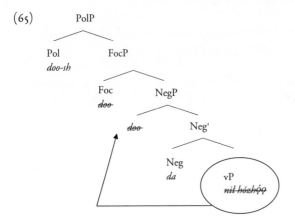

I discuss this further in section 4.

     As to the position of other functional categories, (66) shows that the TP is higher than the NegP. This could be represented as in (67).

(66)   *T'ah*   ***doo***   *kwii*   *nisháah*   ***da***   *ńt'éé'*   Navajo
       Yet   not   here   I-went   not   PST

       'I had never before been here.' (Mary Willie, p.c.)

(67)

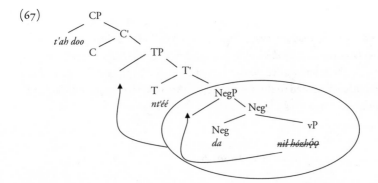

Looking at changes in other languages, one might expect for *da* to weaken at some point and for *doo* to become the head. Reichard (1951: 308) mentions that *da* is sometimes optional in Navajo but this seems not very accepted by native speakers. In Apache, negatives are generally very similar, as the Western (San Carlos) Apache in (68) shows, though here *doo* may be left out in fast speech (Willem de Reuse, p.c., 2006: 59).

(68) **(doo)**   nchad   **da**   (Western) Apache
     NEG   2S-cry   NEG

     'Don't you cry?' (Bray & the White Mountain Apache Tribe 1998: 109)

Thus, Apache shows that the specifier can also be left out. If it is a fast-speech phenomenon, it makes sense to not use the specifier since that is less economical. In San Carlos Apache, *(ha) k'eh* 'at all' optionally follows *doo* (de Reuse 2006: 59), whereas in White Mountain Apache, another form of Western Apache, *-haa* 'yet' is attached to *doo*. This is interesting since it is the same form as the interrogative/indefinite base in Apache (see Greenfield 1995). All this points to *doo* still being a fully phrasal specifier, optional in Apache though not in Navajo.

As mentioned earlier, if *doo* is a negative specifier, negative indefinites are not expected and this turns out to be correct in Navajo. There are words such as *(t'áá) háiida* 'anyone, no one', *(t'áá) haa'ida* 'anywhere, nowhere', and *háadida* 'anytime, never' (Young & Morgan 1987: 817).[7] Perkins and Fernald (2010) say that, as negatives, they "can only appear within a negative frame or a limited number of other environments," as in (69).

(69) *Hastiin*   *doo*   **háágóóda**   *ootbąsda*   Navajo
     man   NEG   somewhere   drive-NEG

     'The man isn't driving anywhere.' (Perkins & Fernald)

They appear infrequently, and are often rendered with what looks like a nominalized verb (70).

(70) *Doo*   *nisíní*   *da*   Navajo
     NEG   want-NM   NEG

     'I want nothing.' (Young & Morgan 1987: 953)

Young and Morgan in their 1987 work avoid translating these as negatives; they use them when free choice *any-* is used in English, rather than with *no-*. If *doo* is a specifier, the absence of negative definites fits, since negative concord would not be allowed, but then indefinites are incompatible with a polysynthetic language too.

Analyzing Navajo negation as a combination of a phrase *doo* and a head *da* seems a likely possibility. If the stages of the cycle as represented in, for example, figure 8.1 or figure 8.4 are correct, *doo* is the newer specifier (although the interaction with the question marker is puzzling). In section 3, I quote some work that argues that the original negative is probably an aspectual verb. In Navajo and Apache and in some other Athabascan languages, this negative is replaced by phrases such as *doo*.

---

7. Languages typically do not use double negation (when two negatives make a positive). In Navajo, as in (i), they are judged "confusing" by native speakers, even though Reichard gives some examples:

(i) **doo**   **doo**   *bił*   *hózhǫǫ*   **da**   Navajo
     NEG   NEG   3S-with   happiness   NEG

     'He is not angry' (Reichard 1951: 309)

If these are genuine examples, it is interesting to notice that only the specifiers are doubled, not the heads.

Turning to other Athabascan languages, one finds incredible variety in the negatives. Examples (71) to (81) provide some instances that show some commonalities, such as forms that are based on an –*l*-, as well as an initial *do*, despite quite a diversity.

(71) ***lh*-*e*-'*z*-*us*-'*al***   Carrier
   NEG-OM-NEG-1S-eat

   I am not eating (an unspecified object).' (Poser 2009: 26)

(72) ***dō*** *he* *tce* *niñ* *yai*   Hupa
   not EMPH out 3-PST come

   'He didn't come out.' (Goddard 1905: 31; Goddard's spacing)

(73) ***du*** *rágwe* ***yíle***   Hare (K'áshgot'ine)
   NEG 3.stay NEG

   'She/he is not staying.' (Rice 1989: 24)

(74) ***k'á*** *šudíhkéd*   Tanacross
      š-u-di-í'-h-ké't-ɛ
   NEG 1S-TH-TH-M-CL-ask-NEG

   'He didn't ask me.' (Holton 2000: 232)

(75) ***gam*** *sangaay* '*la* *q'wiid-ang-**ang**-gan*   Haida
   not morning he be.hungry-ASP-NEG-PRES

   'He is never hungry in the morning.' (Enrico 2003: 41).

(76) ***'ele'*** *k'e-s-t'aaz-**e***   Ahtna
   NEG it-NEG-cut-NEG

   'He isn't cutting it.' (Kari 1992: 123)

(77) *nɛzú-**hílɛ***   Chipewyan/Dëne Sųłiné
   be.good-NEG

   'It is not good.' (Li 1967: 420)

(78) *Edna* ***ʔədu*** *Mary* *əʔį'h*   Kwadacha (Ft. Ware Sekani)
   Edna NEG Mary 3.see

   'Edna doesn't see Mary.' (Hargus 2002: 110)

(79) ***X̌éł*** *wusgíd*   Tlingit
   NEG fall.IRR

   'He didn't fall.' (Krauss 1969: 72)

(80) *etl-chon-ą*   Lower Tanana
     NEG-rain-NEG

     'It's not raining.' (Frank, Kari, & Tuttle 2006: 6)

(81) **dik**   *dəsłεqahGł-G*   Eyak
     NEG   fall-NEG

     'He didn't fall.' (Krauss 1969: 72).

In this section, I focus on the phrase-like elements such as *doo* in Navajo (60); *doo* in Apache (68), Hupa (72),[8] Bear River Athabascan, and Mattole; the *dú/du* in Sarcee and Hare (73); *k'aa* in Upper Tanana and Tanacross (74); and *gam* in Haida (75). In section 3.4, I examine the *l*-shaped auxiliaries such as the Ahtna (76), Chipewyan/Dëne Sųłiné (77), and Hare (73), to which the Kwadacha (78) and Tlingit (79) negative auxiliaries are possibly related as well. Lower Tanana (80) and Carrier (71) show an affix that might be an incorporated auxiliary. As mentioned, I won't go into the origin of the postverbal affix, as in Ahtna (76) and Eyak (81).

In figure 8.5, I have indicated the occurrence of *doo/du/dú* in Athabascan in terms of geography. It becomes clear that the Pacific Coast, Southern, and some of the Eastern languages are reinforced by *doo*. The distribution is geographically very much the opposite of that for the verbal *–l* form shown in figure 8.7. I suggest this complementary distribution is due to a loss of the *l-* form and a renewal by *doo*.

In addition to the languages just discussed, the Pacific Coast languages Mattole (Li 1930), as in (82), and Bear River Athabascan (Goddard 1929) have been added to figures 8.5 and 8.7. They show negative *do* and have lost the affix. The extinct Pacific Coast language Kato (Goddard 1912) also has *doo*.

(82) **do-bin**   **do-diɣiłyél**   Mattole
     Not-probably   NEG-2S.win

     'Not probably. You will not win.' (Li 1930: 141)

The Alaskan languages have not developed a reinforcing *do(o)*, but some of the Canadian Athabascan ones have, for example, an optional *du* in Hare (Rice 1989: 1103), and *dú* in Sarcee (Cook 1984: 51), though the latter's single example looks more like a prohibitive. Looking at the geographic spread, that is, assuming Athabascan spread from the Northwest to the Pacific Coast (Mattole and Hupa), to its east in Canada (Slave and Sarcee), and to the Southwest (Navajo and Apache), we see a predominance of *do* in the languages that are not in the Northwest, indicating *doo/du* is an innovation.

To the best of my knowledge, not much is known about the etymology of *doo* and *da* or about Upper Tanana *k'aa* and other renewals. If we look for possible cognates, there are a few around. In Koyukon, *doo'* is a sentence initial emphatic and a sentence final interrogative, as in (83), and *do* an emphatic and interrogative head, as in (84).

---

8. Hupa, as do most of the other languages, has an optional emphatic *heh* to add to *do:* 'not at all' (Golla 1996), showing *do:* is a specifier.

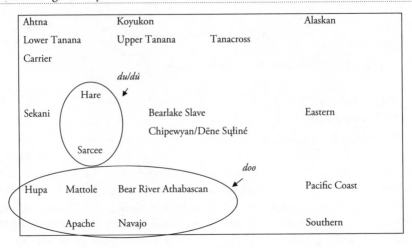

FIGURE 8.5. Geographical grouping of *doo-* forms in Athabascan

(83) *see* **doo'** Koyukon
1S Q

'What about me?' (Jetté, Jones, & Kari 2000: 149)

(84) **do**-*hoo-deyoh* Koyukon
what-place-happened

'What happened?' (Jetté et al. 2000: 139)

This means that in Koyukon, *doo* might have originally been an indefinite that was reanlyzed as part of the FocP. *Doo* may be related to an interrogative in Ahtna too, as with *nduu* 'where' (see Kari 1990: 158), *du'* 'who' in Eyak (Krauss 1976), and possibly *aadoo* 'ho' and *daa* 'what' in Tlingit (Story & Naish 1973: 390).

The origin of Upper Tanana *k'aa* is unknown but may be related to the negative *k'ali'i/k'alii/k'ali'* in varieties of Ahtna. There is a negative prefix *cha-* in some Southern Carrier dialects (though Bill Poser, p.c., thinks those are not connected). The first part *k'a* could be an emphatic and the second part similar to the Ahtna negative auxiliary *'ele'*.

The structure for Navajo suggested in (63), with a specifier and a head, can be adapted for some of the other languages, for instance, Hupa, Hare, Haida, and Upper Tanana. The grammaticalization of *doo* may have been from an indefinite to a negative specifier, as also happened in Afro-Asiatic and Indo-European.

I'll now add a little bit on the structural differences between some of the languages. Haida (75), repeated here as (85), presents evidence for the NegP being lower than the TP, as in (86), similar to Navajo (66), with the verb moving leftward. The separate negative *gam* would, as in Navajo, be situated in the CP.

(85) **gam** *sangaay* '*la* *q'wiid-ang-***ang**-*gan* Haida
not morning he be.hungry-ASP-NEG-PRES

'He is never hungry in the morning.' (Enrico 2003: 41).

(86)

In languages such as Slave, a Canadian Athabascan language, the future can follow the negative (Rice 1989: 1101, ex. [8]), indicating possibly a tree similar to (86), with TP above NegP. In Chipewyan/Dëne Sųłiné (Cook 2004: 106, 109), past tense and aspect enclitics also follow the negative, as in (87).

(87) *Dëne   tsąba   dábets'į   **híle**   łí   nį*   Chipewyan/Dëne Sųłiné
      man money 3P-have NEG ASP PST
      'People usually didn't have money.' (Cook 2004: 109)

The variation in Athabascan negation can be accounted for if we recognize two slightly different cycles in this family, one where indefinites renew the weakening negative features as I suggest here. In 3.4, I outline another cycle where negatives derive from verbal sources. The Northern, more conservative languages such as Ahtna, Koyukon, Lower Tanana, Sekani, Bearlake Slave, and Chipewyan/Dëne Sųłiné show evidence of an original negative auxiliary whereas the Pacific Coast and Southwestern languages such as Hupa, Mattole, Bear River Athabascan, Apache, and Navajo show replacement by an interrogative or indefinite. Of the Eastern languages, Hare has both and Sarcee shows the replacement. More research is needed especially regarding these languages.

More work is also needed on the possibility of negative concord in certain languages. The Navajo situation is as expected; with a specifier present, negative concord should not occur, and that's in fact the case. The same is true for Hare (Rice 1989: 1105, ex. [40]).

The examples in this section come from various families in which a renewal by a phrasal element is quite common. The phrase provides a new set of negative features.

3. The Reanalysis of Negative Verbs

In this section, I provide examples of verbs and auxiliaries being reanalyzed as negatives. Again for purely practical purposes, the examples are grouped by language family.

3.1 CHINESE

In this section, I discuss an analysis of the two main negative markers *bu* and *mei* in Chinese. The second of these, *mei*, has already been discussed in section 1. The main point is that, due to negative heads moving to other head positions, reanalyses take place and lexical verbs are used to renew the features.

There are many negatives in present-day Chinese, and their use is limited by the mood and aspect of the clause. The most general negative is *bu*, as in (88) and (89).[9]

(88)   wo   **bu**   jide   ta   Chinese
        I   not   remember   he

        'I don't remember him.' (Li & Thompson 1981: 415)

(89)   wo   **bu**   hui   tan   gangqin   Chinese
        I   not   can   play   piano

        'I can't play the piano.'

When the verb is *you* 'exist', the negative is *mei*, as in (90), repeated from (13). *Mei(you)* also occurs with verbs marked with certain aspect markers, as in (91).

(90)   wo   **mei**   you   shu   Chinese
        I   not   exist   book

        I' don't have a book.'

(91)   ta   **meiyou**   kan   wan   nei   ben   shu   Chinese
        He   NEG   read   finish   that   CL   book

        'He didn't finish reading the book.'

Li and Thompson (1981: 421) argue that *bu* is the neutral negation, but that *mei(you)* negates the completion of an event. A number of interesting differences follow from this: *bu* negates states and auxiliaries, such as *hui* 'know', as in (89), but not bounded events; *mei(you)* on the other hand marks boundedness, and is used for the perfective (as an alternative to *le*). Other analyses exist as well. The occurrence of *mei(you)* is relevant to Croft's cycle discussed in section 1, in which with the negative *mei*, there is an optional *you* 'to exist', a verbal renewal so to speak.

The syntactic analysis of the negatives is a matter of debate. Both *bu* and *mei* seem to be heads (as in Xu 1997: 111). This is not surprising since *mei* and *bu* originate as verbs, as we have seen for *mei* and will see for *bu*, and both usually occur just before the verb or auxiliary. Li and Thompson (1981: 340), however, consider them negative adverbs, since they occur in the typical posttopic position. Ernst (1995) argues that *bu* is in a specifier position but that it (pro)cliticizes. I will assume that *bu* and *mei(you)* are generated in or move through an ASP phrase, as in (92) and (93) respectively, where (93) is similar to figure 8.3. This means that they have features for negation as well as aspect. Example (92) shows the tree for (89) and (93) for (90). In (92), the *bu* is attracted all the way up to Neg but making small steps.

---

9. I have left a representation of tones out of the discussion. Wiedenhof (1993: 95) discusses differences between the variants *bú*, *bù*, and *bu*. The latter is very common at normal conversation speeds.

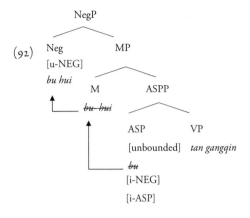

(92)

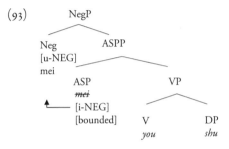

(93)

These structures explain the complementary distribution between the two types of aspectual negatives, and also that *mei* is in complementary distribution with perfective *le* (but see Scurfield 1991: 43 about the meaning with 'change of state' *le*).

As has been widely discussed, there is no negative concord in Chinese and the quantifiers *shei dou* and *shei ye* are translated into English as 'everyone' or 'anyone' depending on whether a negative *bu* appears.

(94) *wo   shei   dou   xihuan*   Chinese
       I   who   all   like

       'I like everyone.'

(95) *wo   shei   dou   **bu**   xihuan*   Chinese
       I   who   all   not   like

       'I don't like anyone.' (Li & Thompson 1981: 529).

If the tree in (92) is correct, it is not surprising that negatives and modals reanalyze as one unit, and this indeed has happened a lot in the history of Chinese. For instance, the negative *bie* in (96) is a merged form of *bu* and *yao* 'need' and *beng* 'not have to' from *bu* and *yong* (see Xu 1997: 111).

(96) **bie**   *guan   men*   Chinese
      don't   close   door

       'Don't close the door.' (Li & Thompson 1981: 415)

Zhang (2005) provides an example from Shaoxing Chinese, one of the Wu languages, of the negative of *have* which is [niΦ], where [n] is the negative prefix, as in (97).

(97) *No* **n-iΦ** *kē* *ʈɕiē*   Shaoxing Chinese
      I   NEG-have   look   see

      'I haven't seen it.' (from Zhang 2005: 71)

Another negative [veʔ] 'not' is used with other verbs, as in [veʔʔiaɒ] 'don't want to' and [veʔɦioN] 'don't use' (Zhang 2005: 76), and these may be reinforcements. Let's look at some older forms now.

As we saw in section 1, *mei* derives from a verb meaning "to die; to not exist" and the history of some of the others is similar. Old Chinese negatives are similarly numerous (see, e.g., Djamouri 1991: 8) and are usually divided into a stop (**p-*) and a nasal (**m-*) group depending on their initial consonants, though these may change. Pulleyblank (1995: 103–111) provides lists of the different negatives in each of the two groups: the modern and older form *bù* and the older forms *fǒu* and *fú* in the stop group express simple negation, and *wú*, *wù*, *wáng*, *mò*, *miè*, and others in the nasal group express nonexistence. Djamouri (1991) examines seven negative markers in the earliest Chinese and shows that *bù* is used with intransitive predicates or with adjectives whereas *fú* is used with transitives and functions as an adverbial. It is possible that *fú* is a specifier since it might be modified. Others have modal meanings, such as *wú* and *wù*.

Apart from *fú* possibly, these negatives are head-like and may derive from verbs. For instance, Sagart (1999: 84) suggests that negative *fú* is cognate with the verb "to eliminate" and that the *m* may have been a prefix to mark deontics or imperatives. According to Pulleyblank, *wú* is the same as the verb "not have," *wù* is an aspectual variant of *wú* (but see Djamouri 1996: 291), and *wáng* is a verb meaning "to die, disappear" in the classical period. *Mò* modifies a subject and means "no one," whereas *miè* is a negative particle or a verb meaning "to destroy."

In the history of Chinese, lexical verbs are reanalyzed as higher functional ones on the basis of certain semantic features. A NegP with a head containing [u-NEG] may check its features with a verb. This verb might be reanalyzed as having [i-NEG] features and later as [u-NEG] and disappear.

3.2 URALIC

The origin of the negative auxiliary so prevalent in Uralic "may well be related to the verb 'is' (*i-*)" (Simoncsics 1998: 594) and more precisely to a negative copula (Honti 1997: 173). The nonfinite main verb is also marked as negative (connegative), an original nominal form (see Honti 1997: 249). In section 2.2, I showed that, in three Uralic languages, the negative is now reinforced through an adverb. In this section, I argue that the negative auxiliary is a head moving from a relatively low NegP to a higher position, even to C. As that happens, it is likely to be reanalyzed in a higher position.

Sami, a collection of languages spoken in northern Scandinavia, has a negative construction where the negative word is inflected for person, number, and tense, as shown in (98) and (99), with (99) repeated from (37).

(98) **Im**   *(manne)*   *daejrieh*   Southern Sami
     NEG-PRES-1S   (I)   know

     I don't know.'

(99) **Idtjim**   *(manne)*   *daejrieh*   Southern Sami
     NEG-PST-1S   (I)   know

     'I didn't know.'   (Bergsland 1994: 44)

Using a structure with separate positions for agreement and tense, one can argue that negation is a head *-i*, moving to T and AGR, as in (100), (and to C since imperative and declara-
tive have different forms).

(100)

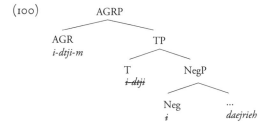

The reason for the movement of the negative (auxiliary) will need to be worked out in terms
of features. Once the notions of weak and strong heads were abandoned in Minimalism,
accounting for overt movement is much less intuitive. The EPP forcing movement is in many
ways ad hoc, especially for heads.

Very synthetic forms are prone to reanalysis; that is, the negative in (100) is related to
many positions and one might therefore expect a reanalysis of the NegP in a higher position
and a reinforcement of another negative element, and this is definitely true in some varieties.

In Finnish (101), repeated from (39), the negative is a head also moving to a higher position. The Finnish tree in (102) differs from the one in Southern Sami in the order of Neg and
T, and hence Neg moves to AGR and the main verb moves to T.

(101) *Liisa*   **ei**   *osta-nut*   *kirjaa*   Finnish
      Liisa   NEG-3S   buy-PST   book

      'Liisa did not buy a/the book.'

(102)

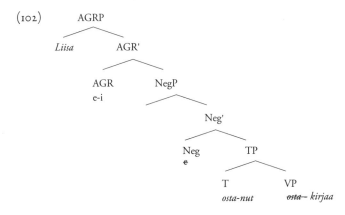

The AGR in this tree probably needs to be split into number and person features. For instance, Savijärvi (1977: 286) says that in some dialects, there is only person agreement, not number, on the negative. This suggests that the person features are higher than NegP in those varieties but not the number ones.

Honti (1997: 88) remarks that almost all negative verbs in Uralic show subject agreement, that many have tense, and that a few have mood, aspect, or definite object agreement. If the NegP is relatively high, only subject agreement will be marked; if it is lower, other inflection is too. In figure 8.6, the different positions are marked and NegP can in principle be in between any of them.

As evidence that the negative moves from a position below CP to a position above it, Holmberg, Nikanne, Oraviita, Reime, and Trosterud (1993) provide (103), which only has the meaning indicated in its gloss. This indicates that the negative originates below *varmaan* since otherwise the negative could have scope over the CP adverb *varmaan* 'surely'.

(103) *Jussi e-i   varmaan ole ostanut sitä kirjaa*   Finnish
      Jussi NEG-3S   surely   has bought that book

    'It is certain that Jussi didn't buy that book.' (Holmberg et al. 1993: 201–202).

This is different with TP or aspectual adverbs such as *aina* 'always', as in (104), showing that the negative is merged above the TP.

(104) *Jussi e-i   aina   ole pitänyt sinusta*   Finnish
      Jussi NEG-3S   always has liked   you

    'Jussi hasn't always liked you.' (Holmberg et al 1993: 202)

The negation in Finnish and Sami is originally a verbal head (existential or copular) but since it is related to so many positions, it is prone to reanalysis. We can see it "go up the tree" in figure 8.6. The negative replacement doesn't come from another verb but from an indefinite adverb, as we saw in section 2.2.

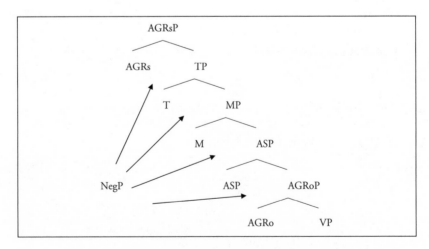

FIGURE 8.6. NegP positions in Uralic

3.3 AFRO-ASIATIC

Section 2.3 examined how Berber and Semitic reanalyze indefinites as negative in the specifier of the NegP, and how subsequently these specifiers can become heads. Negatives in Omotic, Cushitic, and Chadic show a different grammaticalization path. In many, such as the Omotic language Kooreto, there is evidence of a main verb being reanalyzed as a negative auxiliary. I just list a few patterns of discontinuous negation without giving precise positions for the negatives. Such an analysis would need a detailed grammatical analysis, not yet available. Clear, however, is that negative verbs with negative features are reanalyzed as negative heads, that is, with interpretable features.

Negation in Kooreto, an Omotic language of Ethiopia, is expressed by means of a negative auxiliary *ba* 'not exist', as in (105) and (106).

(105) *nen-i*   *doro*   *woon-do*   **ba-nna-ko**   Kooreto
      you-NOM   sheep   buy-PF   NEG-2S-DEC

      'You didn't buy sheep.' (Binyam 2008: 123)

(106) *is-i*   *dana*   *ush-iya*   **ba-nni-ko**   Kooreto
      she-NOM   beer   drink-PROG   not.exist-3FS-DEC

      'She is *not* drinking beer.' (Binyam 2008: 151)

As Binyam (2008) shows, there is still a lexical verb *ba* in Kooreto with the meaning "disappear," as in (107a), which can itself be negated, as in (107b).

(107) a. *is-i*   *ba-d-o*   Kooreto
         she-NOM   disappear-PF-PST

         'She disappeared.'

     b. *is-i*   *ba-d-o*   *ba-nni-ko*
         she-NOM   disappear-PF-PST   not.exist-3FS-DEC

         'She did *not* disappear.' (Binyam 2008: 150)

There is also an emphatic negative, as in (108), using an extra adverbial *petto* 'never' indicating a renewal as we saw in Uralic.

(108) *es-i*   *keele*   *petto*   *han-g-u-waa-s-so*   Kooreto
      he-NOM   Keele   never   go-IMF-PRES-not_exist-3MS-AFOC:DEC

      'He will never go to Keele.' (Binyam 2008: 160)

There are some puzzling aspects, such as why the negative auxiliaries are inflected but not the main verbs, as seen in nonnegative sentences, as (105) and (106) show. The grammaticalization is clear, however, and the form *ba* may be related to that in Chadic, discussed later.

Cushitic languages have interesting sets of negatives as well with similar patterns to the other languages of the Afro-Asiatic family. In Somali, the negative is expressed through *má* and a special form of the verb, as in (109). *Má* is also used as an interrogative, as in (110).

(109) *Ku* **má** *uu garánéyn*   Somali
      you   not   he   understand-NEG

'He didn't understand you.' (Saeed 1999: 186)

(110) **Muu**   *kúu*   *dhiibay*   Somali
      Q-he [=ma+uu]   you-to   hand-PST

'Did he hand it to you?' (Saeed 1999: 197)

From the data discussed here, we know that it is quite common for an indefinite or inter-rogative to be reanalyzed as a (high) negative. That makes *má* an innovation with a possibly earlier negative on the verb.

Beja, a relatively isolated Cushitic language, has a regular negative, marked for aspect and mood, which Hamid Ahmed and Vanhove (2002) discuss. I will leave that outside the discussion here. Noteworthy is that Beja has developed a contrastive negative auxiliary from the verb *rib* 'to refuse', as in (111).

(111) *yiinaat a-sni   naat   rh-at   a-***reb***   Beja
      days   I-waited   thing   see-PART   I-refused

'I waited for days and could not see anything.' (from Hamid Ahmed & Vanhove (2002: 157)

This is used in pragmatically highly salient situations.

Negation in Hausa, a Chadic language of the Afro-Asiatic family, is as in (112a) and (112b).

(112) a. **Bà**   *kà*   *kāwō àbinci*   **ba**   Hausa
         NEG   you   bring   food   NEG

'You didn't bring food.' (Kraft & Kirk-Greene 1973: 38)

      b. **Bà**   *zăn*   *tàfi*   **ba**   *sai   gō'be*
         NEG   1S-FUT   go   NEG   till   tomorrow

'I won't go till tomorrow.' (Kraft & Kirk-Greene 1973: 187)

The main restriction on word order is that *bà* immediately precede the subject pronoun with which it assimilates phonologically when relevant. This first *bà* is a head that moves from the NegP to left-adjoin to *kà* and *zăn*. The second *ba* is movable and can be followed by an adverbial, as in (112b).

Negative polarity items occur, as expected, such as *tabà* in (113).

(113) *matsalōli* **bà`**   *zā*   *sù*   **tabà**   *kāre-'wā*   **ba**   Hausa
      problems   NEG   FUT   3P   ever-do   end-PART   NEG

'The problems will never end.' (Jaggar 2009: 61)

As Jaggar (2009) shows, there are many such negative polarity items and they derive from verbs, e.g *tabà* 'ever do something', or PPs, such as *dàɗai* '(not) once' [=*dà* 'with' and *ɗaya* 'one'], or DPs, for example, *kō kàɗan* '(not) even a bit'. According to Jaggar, there is quite a bit of variation where speaker judgments vary. For instance, some negative polarity items appear initially, sometimes with final *ba* and sometimes without.

(114) **dàɗai/fàufau**   **bàn**   *gan* *shì* **ba**   Hausa
      once/ever   NEG.1S.PF see 3M   NEG

      I"ve never once/ever seen him.' (Jaggar 2009: 61)

(115) **dàɗai/fàufau**   **bā**   *nà*   *yàrdā*   Hausa
      once/ever   NEG   1S.IMPF agree.VN

      'I will never ever agree!' (Jaggar 2009: 61)

To summarize negation in Hausa, the presubject negative is a head (with uninterpretable features) reinforced by a second negative, either a phrasal *ba* or a negative indefinite.

3.4 ATHABASCAN, EYAK, TLINGIT, AND HAIDA

Section 2.4 examined the variability of phrasal negatives, such as *doo* and *k'aa*, that precede the verbal complex. These are of more recent, possibly indefinite, origin. In this section, I first argue that the older negatives derive from verbs and that some (still) look like auxiliaries, cognate with verbs meaning "to be" and "to be missing." I then suggest that the origin of the inner affix, still present in Ahtna, Koyukon, and Lower Tanana, is verbal as well.

Section 2.4 looked at a number of negatives in the different languages. Kari (1990) suggests that *'ele'* in Ahtna (116) is perhaps related to the verb *lae* 'to be', and I think one could argue that the suffix *–leh* is also related to the verb. Kwadacha (117), Chipewyan/Dëne Sųłiné (118), and Tlingit (119) have the same forms but no affix, and in Carrier (120), it may be a prefix. (These are repeated from 78, 77, 79, and 71 respectively.)

(116) *'ele'*   *ugheli* *ghi-leh*   Ahtna
      NEG   good   3-PF.be.NEG

      'He is not good.' (Kari 1990: 272)

(117) *Edna* *ʔədu* *Mary* *əʔi,'h*   Kwadacha (Ft. Ware Sekani)
      Edna   NEG   Mary   3.see

      'Edna doesn't see Mary.' (Hargus 2002: 110)

(118) *nɛzú-hílɛ*   Chipewyan/Dëne Sųłiné
      be.good-NEG

      'It is not good.' (Li 1967: 420)

(119) *ɬél*   *wusgíd*   Tlingit
      NEG   fall.IRR

      'He didn't fall.' (Krauss 1969: 72)

(120) *lh-e'-z-us-'al*   Carrier
      NEG-OM-NEG-1S-eat

      'I am not eating (an unspecified object).' (Poser 2009: 26)

Leer reconstructs a Proto-Athabascan *-he suffix, "originally an enclitic" (2000: 102), and a Proto-Atabaskan-Eyak-Tlingit particle *(ʔi)le? 'it is not' (Leer 2000: 123). He argues that it "seems probable that the Tlingit negative particle l is by origin a contraction of the prohibitive interjectional particle (ʔi)li 'don't' which is a phonologically perfect cognate with Pre-PA [Pre-Proto-Athabascan] *(ʔi)le?" (Leer 2000: 123–124). Willem de Reuse (p.c.) also suggests a link of the sentence-final prohibitive particles to this root. In Western Apache, for instance, there is hela' and in Navajo lágo, both meaning 'don't'.

The Pre-PA form *(ʔi)le? may originally be a third person negative of the verb to be that was reanalyzed as a negative particle during Proto-Athabascan-Eyak-Tlingit; see Tlingit X̱él and Ahtna 'ele', as in (117). Rice (1989: 1108, n. 1) suggests that the negative yíle in Slave, for example, Hare (73) and Bearlake (121), "may historically be an auxiliary verb in the perfective aspect."

(121) *bebí* *nedá* **yíle**   Bearlake
      baby heavy NEG

      'The baby is light.' (Rice 1989: 1101)

Hare, apart from having both du and yíle, can have either of these alone. Chipewyan/Dëne Sųłiné (119) would fit this pattern with -híle as head. The Slave forms are therefore very similar to the preverbal negatives 'ele' in Ahtna and X̱él in Tlingit. A speculation might be that this preverbal auxiliary became phonologically too light (evidenced in frequent change from yíle to -le in Slave) and the verb moved to its left.

Before the –l- form was a form of "not to be," it could have been another verb. There is some evidence—Navajo hólǫ́ means 'there is'; one of the 'be' verbs has an –l- shape, for example, nishłį́ means 'I am'; and Minto kula means 'is missing'. Rice (1989) has many examples from Bearlake and Hare with the same verb.

(122) *nįhtsʼi* **whíle**   Bearlake
      wind   absent

      'There is no wind.' (Rice (1989: 1107)

So both the affix inside the verb complex and the independent form may derive from the same verbal root.

Let's go back to the affixes. Kari (1993) shows that Koyukon (123) has a clear l-affix. Example (123) is rendered as (124) in the more conservative Lower Tanana (transcription as in Kari). That means that the –l-form was incorporated later in Lower Tanana. In Tanacross (125), there is a special negative perfective mode marker and in the innovative Upper Tanana (126), the affix is totally lost.

(123) *ghiitenleeghtletenee*   Koyukon

gh	+t	+n	+l	+gh	+es	+ł	ten	+ee
QUA	FUT	QUA	NEG	3S	1S	CAUS	ice	NEG

      'I won't freeze it solid.' (Kari 1993: 55)

(124) *tendhghaaghetltenęę*   Lower Tanana

t	+n	+dh	+gh	+gh	+es	+ł	+ten	+ęę
FUT	QUA	NEG	QUA	QUA	1S	CAUS	ice	NEG

'I won't freeze it solid.' (Kari 1993: 55)

(125) **k'á** **šudíhké'd**   Tanacross

k'á š-u-di-í'-h-két-ɛ

NEG 1S-TH-TH-M-CL-ask-NEG

'He didn't ask me.' (Holton 2000: 232)

(126) **k'aa** **tinak-tän**   Upper Tanana

NEG 1S.FUT-freeze

'I won't freeze it solid.' (Kari 1993: 55)

The negative in (124) varies between *T/ð* in Minto Tanana and *ð/h* in Salcha Tanana in nonperfective forms (see Tuttle 1998: 111). In many varieties of Lower Tanana, the prefix disappears and just the final -ą appears (Siri Tuttle, p.c.).[10]

The preverb root negative affixes, for example, the *tl* in (127), the *s* in (128), and the *l* in (129), repeated from 80, 76, and 123 respectively, are related to the verb's aspect and are sometimes in complementary distribution with the aspect marker (whose origin is verbal). This suggests a grammaticalization path very similar to that of Chinese, with an *l*-based verb first becoming an aspect marker and then a negative.

(127) *etl-chon-ą*   Lower Tanana

NEG-rain-NEG

'It's not raining.' (Frank et al. 2006: 6)

(128) **'ele'** **k'e-s-t'aaz-e**   Ahtna

NEG it-NEG-cut-NEG

'He isn't cutting it.' (Kari 1992: 123)

---

10. The variant forms of the suffix in Koyukon Athabascan depend on where they appear in the sentence: *-éé* [iː] is an emphatic, *-aa* [æː] is used sentence-finally, and *e* [ə] or zero appears in nonfinal position:

(i) a. *etlkon-éé*   Koyukon Athabascan
     b. *etlkon-aa*
     c. *etlkon-(e)*
         raining-NEG
         It wasn't raining.' (Jetté et al. 2000: 5)

Keren Rice (p.c.) notes that there is still a (zero) suffix in (ic) even if the ending is not visible. A comparison with the (different) nasal in (ii) shows this. The weakening is typical of heads. As the nonnegative version in (ii) shows, there is also a negative prefix *-l* or *ł* (slashed l) in (i) in addition to the variable suffix (before another slashed *l*, the two become *tl*):

(ii) *etkonh*   Koyukon Athabascan
      raining
      'It is raining.' (Jetté et al. 2000: 299).

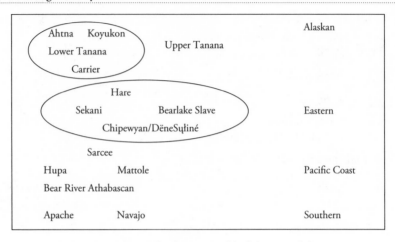

FIGURE 8.7. Geographical grouping of the *l-* form in Athabascan

(129) *ghiitenleeghtletenee*   Koyukon Athabascan

gh	+t	+n	+l	+gh	+es	+ł	ten	+ee
QUA	FUT	QUA	NEG	3S	1S	CAUS	ice	NEG

'I won't freeze it solid.' (Kari 1993: 55)

I have quoted Kari, Leer, and Rice that the *l*-like affix and the separate forms such as *'ele'*, *yile*, *-hilɛ*, and *ʔéł* are likely negative forms of the verb 'be', in accordance with what we know about one of the two negative cycles. Athabascan languages have spread from an Alaskan "homeland" to the east and south. If one looks at the geographical spread, as in figure 8.7, one could argue that the *l-* form is an older one since the languages closer to Alaska have it. Auxiliaries typically derive from full verbs and there is some evidence for this in Athabascan. In fact, there are languages such as Ahtna where negatives can be marked three times. Some of the affixes are negative as well as aspectual, so I would suggest they go through a cycle as in figure 8.3. They are then renewed by the same verb if that verb kept the original meaning.

3.5 CREOLES

Using data from creoles is controversial since it isn't always clear where the forms come from—the substratum or the superstratum —or are instead new "inventions." However, creoles are ideal languages in which to test the cognitive principles that learners/speakers used to build up their grammars, and different variants of the linguistic cycle are evident. Creoles typically have a pre-TMA negative marker, as in English-lexified creoles that use a preverbal *na*, *don*, and *didn*, as in (130),[11] or a sentence-final emphatic, or both, as in Portuguese-based creoles.

---

11. Note, however, that the epistemic modal precedes, as in (i)

(i) *Yu* *shud-n* *en* *tel* *im*   Jamaican Creole
    You should-NEG have tell him

    'You shouldn't have told him.' (Bailey 1966: 91)

(130)   *Shi **didn** laik tu taak tu eni and eni man*   Jamaican Creole
        she NEG like to talk to any and any man

        'She didn't like to talk to just any man.'
        (Bailey 1971: 342)

In most creoles, the negative is a head on a par with the other TMA heads and this means they have interpretable negative features. They can double with another negative, which means they are optional probes. See Holm (1988: 171–174) for an excellent overview of negatives in creoles.

Bailey (1971: 342) provides two varieties of Jamaican Creole; (130) is closer to the lexifier English and (131) more creolized. The latter variety uses *neba* 'never' as *na* 'not' (Bailey 1966: 54–55).

(131)   *Im **neba** laik fi taak tu eni an eni man*   Jamaican Creole
        3 never like for talk to any and any man

        'She didn't like to talk to just any man.'
        (Bailey 1971: 345)

Palenquero, a Spanish-based creole described by Bickerton and Escalante (1970), Friede-mann and Patiño (1983), and Schwegler (1991), has negatives, as in (132), where the preverbal negative is optional, used for emphasis. Holm (1988: 173) mentions that *nu* in (133) has scope over the entire sentence. This means the NegP is quite high, as in (134).

(132)   *tata*   *si*   ***(nu)***   *ten*   *losa*   ***nu***   Palenquero Creole
        father   your   NEG   have   field   NEG

        'Your father doesn't have a field.' (Schwegler & Morton 2003: 142)

(133)   *i sabé*   *si ané*   *ba*   *rreklamá*   *mí*   *ele*   ***nu***   Palenquero Creole
        I know   if they   will   complain   me   about   NEG

        'I don't know if they'll complain to me about it.'
        (Friedemann & Patiño 1983: 171)

(134)

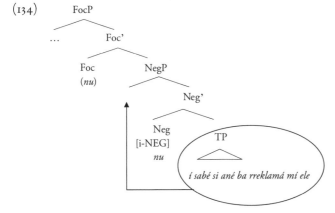

French-lexified creoles often use a *pa*, as in Haitian Creole (135). DeGraff (1993) argues that, unlike in its sub- or superstratum languages (the Kwa languages of the Niger-Congo family and French respectively), the NEG *pa* in Haitian Creole is in a head position in (135) with interpretable negative features. It precedes the TMA heads.

(135) *Jan* **pa** *t-* *av-* *ale* *nan* *mache*   Haitian Creole
     Jan   not   ANT IRR go   in   market

Jan wouldn't have gone to the market.' (DeGraff 1993: 65)

There are some other varieties that are renewing *pa*, as in (136) from Bahamian Creole, and that means *pa* is becoming a probe.

(136) *li* **pa** *repon* **naye**   Bahamian Creole
     He NEG answer nothing

'He isn't answering.' (Shilling 1976)

In standard French, it is commonly assumed that *ne* is in the head of the NegP and *pas* in the specifier. DeGraff's main arguments for *pa* as head in Haitian Creole are based on word order and differences in negative concord. Standard French (137) and Haitian Creole (138) differ in their interpretation of negative quantifiers, and Haitian Creole *pa* in (138) patterns with standard French *ne* in (139).

(137) *Personne n'est pas venu*   Standard French
     'Nobody hasn't come = everyone came.'

(138) *Pèsonn pa vini*   Haitian Creole
     'Nobody has come.' (DeGraff 1993: 67)

(139) *Personne n'est venu*   Standard French
     'Nobody has come.'

If negatives in the specifier position make negative concord impossible, the difference is accounted for. Thus, Haitian Creole *pa* patterns with the French head *ne*. Haitian Creole *pa* cannot modify an adjective either, as it can it French, again expected if it is a head. DeGraff doesn't mention features, but I have suggested that some varieties have optional probes with uninterpretable features.

    DeGraff (1993: 87), based on unpublished work, says that Fongbe *ma* is also a head. Fongbe and Ewe, two of the substratum Kwa languages, show no real evidence that they have a negative specifier (see Lefebvre & Brousseau 2002: 140; Aboh 2003; Lefebvre 2004). Instead, there seems to be evidence for a regular NEG head in (140), or a negation in the focus position in (141), which sentence is used to express the speaker's attitude. But both are heads, and under special conditions can occur together.

(140) *Kòkú* **mà** *wá*   Fongbe
     Koku NEG arrive

     'Koku hasn't arrived.' (Lefebvre & Brousseau 2002: 120)

(141) *Kòkú* *xò* *àsón* *lé* *ǎ*   Fongbe
     Koku buy crab P NEG

     'It is not the case that Koku bought the crabs.' (Lefebvre & Brousseau 2002: 128)

Aboh (2003) mentions that other Kwa languages have related systems: Gungbe has just pre-verbal *má* and Ewegbe has both a Neg and C head.

The instances of negative heads in this section are being renewed, originate as verbs, and are somehow interpreted in higher positions. We will see more of such reanalyses to higher position in the CP layer next.

4. Negatives as Yes-No Questions

As we have seen so far, negatives develop from main verbs, often via aspect markers. We have already encountered a few instances where they are reanalyzed in even higher positions, namely in the CP layer. In this section, I show that negatives are reanalyzed as interrogatives in Finnish, Latin, Arabic, Navajo, Quechua, and Chinese. I start with Finnish, where the negative moves to the CP layer but hasn't been reanalyzed as an interrogative; in the other languages it has. I discuss each case and then argue that this grammaticalization happens because the negative is attracted to a FocP, much in the spirit of Simpson and Wu (2002a), that is licensed by a PolP, as Biberauer (2009) argues for Afrikaans. Once there, it can be reanalyzed as having unvalued polarity features.

Sections 2 and 3 show that Uralic languages use a negative auxiliary that derives from a form of 'to be / not to be'. In some languages, this auxiliary moves from NEG to T to AGR and in some from NEG to AGR (or whatever position agreement is situated in). It can further move to C in questions, as (142) shows, and as Holmberg, Nikanne, Oraviita, Reime, and Trosterud (1993) show.

(142) **e-i-kö**   *Pekka*   *ole*   *kaupungi-ssa*   Finnish
      NEG-3S-Q   Pekka   be-PRES   town-INE
      'Isn't Pekka in town?' (Brattico & Huhmarniemi 2006: 12)

In Finnish, the T is situated below the NEG and hence the NEG moves to AGR. In (49), it then moves to C, indicated as a polarity phrase in (143). The negative features are still present, even though as we saw in section 2.2, they may be weakening to [u-F], that is, being reanalyzed as [u-NEG]. The reason that the negative auxiliary moves may be because the question marker *kö* is a clitic; it may also be the case that a focus phrase is triggered when there is a PolP, as we'll see.

(143)

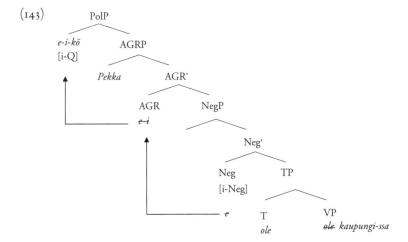

In Latin, yes-no questions can be introduced by a clitic *–ne* added to an emphatic word, as in (144). This *–ne* is an original negative, but the negative in Latin has of course been reinforced (to *non*), so the situation in Latin is one where an original negative is now an interrogative in the CP layer without a negative meaning attached.

(144)   *tu-**ne***   *id*   *veritus*   *es*   Latin
        you-Q   that   fear   be
        'Did you fear that?' (Greenough et al. 1931: 205)

Before the reanalysis, since the *–ne* is added to an emphatic word (not phrase), it makes sense that the focused element moves to the head of a FocP, originally connected to a NegP, as in (145). The negatively marked focus element would move to FocP.

(145)

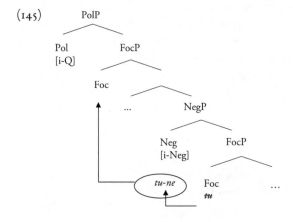

Both Pol and Neg are connected to Foc; this much is uncontroversial. Since a polarity question is really +/- positive, negative features can be reanalyzed in a broader sense.

In Arabic, we have seen a negative *–sh(i)* in section 2.3. This is also used in yes-no questions, as in (146), with V movement, or as in (147), with TP movement. As is obvious from the translation, *shi* has lost its negative features.

(146)   *ʔatal*   ***shi***   *Kariim*   *l-maasle*   Lebanese Arabic
        Kill   Q   Kariim   the-actress
        'Did Kariim kill the actress?'

(147)   *ʔatal*   *Kariim*   *l-maasle*   ***shi***   Lebanese Arabic
        Kill   Kariim   the-actress   Q
        'Did Kariim kill the actress?' (Choueiri 1995, from Ouhalla 1990: 27)

Shi is originally an indefinite, so could have been involved in two grammaticalization schemes, reanalyzed in the specifier of the NegP, as in (56), or reanalyzed in the manner of (145). More dialect evidence is needed for determining the steps of the second path.

In Athabascan, there are negative affixes (in those languages that still have them) that differ depending on the aspect of the construction (see Kari 1993). There is some evidence that these affixes were verbal at one time and that the negative is a remnant of a perfective auxiliary. Negatives also derive from indefinites, and this indefinite ends up as interrogative marker also. For instance, the Navajo *da* is indefinite in *háágóóda* 'some place', and part of the negative *doo . . . da*, as we've seen in section 2.4, and *da'* introduces a yes-no question, as in (148). In Ahtna (Kari 1990: 138), *da* is also an interrogative, as in (149) and (150).

(148)   **da'**   *kintahgóó*   *díníyá*   Navajo
        Q   town-to   2S-go
        'Are you going to town?' (Young & Morgan 1987: 301)

(149)   *natidaas*   **da**   Ahtna
        back-2-go   Q
        'Are you going back?' (Kari 1990: 138)

(150)   *nen*   **da**   *natidaas*   Ahtna
        you   Q   back-2-go
        'Are *you* going back?' (Kari 1990: 138)

Historically, *da* was probably an indefinite that was reanalyzed as a negative and subsequently as an interrogative. Both forms stayed around.

The negative in (64), repeated as (151), has *da* in the head of the NegP, but *doo* is moving quite high up, as in (152).

(151)   *doo-sh*   *(nił)*   *hózhǫ́ǫ́*   **-da**   Navajo
        NEG   2S-with   happy   -NEG
        'Are you not happy?'

(152)

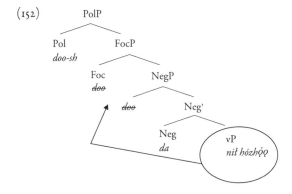

I have put *doo* in the specifier of the NegP, but it may already have reanalyzed in a higher position. Example (152) is very close to (145). *Doo* is still carrying negative features, but could at some point be reanalyzed, and the same could have happened to *da'*. Some evidence for the connection between a PolP and a FocP comes from another set of interrogative markers in

Navajo, namely *-ísh* and *-shá* (Schauber 1979; Young & Morgan 1987: 472). The form *sh* is used in (151) to question the entire sentence, but these markers are perhaps more typically used to question a phrase, as in (153), connected to focus.

(153) a. *Dinéé-sh*   *bilagáana*   *nilį̨?*   Navajo
        man-Q   white.man   is

        'Is the man a white man?' (Goossen 1995: 4)

    b. *ashkii-shą́*   *łį́į́'*   *nabíílgo'*
        boy-Q   horse   3.3-throw

        'Was the boy thrown by the horse?' (Schauber 1979: 111)

Quechua is in an intermediate stage: the negative is made by a sentence-initial *mana* and a verbal suffix *-chu*, as in the second part of (154), but *-chu* is also used, as in the first part of (154), as a question marker.

(154) *kawalla-y-ta*   *ensilla-rqa-nki-chu*   Bolivian Quechua
     horse-1S-ACC   saddle-PST-2S-Q
     arí   **mana**   *ri-saj-chu*
     yes   not   go-FUT1S-NEG

     'Did you saddle my horse? Yes, I will not go.' (van de Kerke 1996: 23)

This could mean that *mana* is a renewal, with *-chu* now mainly functioning as interrogative. I have given data in (154) for Bolivian Quechua but the same forms appear in other varieties of Quechua. I'll now turn to Chinese, Cantonese, and Southern Min, where more work has been done on the connection between negation and question marking.

As is well known, Chinese questions can be formed by using a sentence-final *ma*. Chao (1968: 800–801, 807–808) may be the first to mention this in recent times. Ji (2007: 189) discusses the development of *ma* from the verb *wu* 'lack, not have' in Old Chinese (155) to a question marker in early Chinese (156), and to *ma* in Modern Mandarin (157).

(155) *ren*   *er*   **wu**   *xin*   Old Chinese
     person   but   lack   trust

     'A person lacks trustworthiness.' (*Analects of Confucius*, from Ji 2007: 189)

(156) *shan*   *yan*   *xianren*   *yi*   *wo*   **wu**   Early Chinese
     good   eye   immortal   recall   I   Q

     'The immortal with sharp eyes, can you recognize me?' (Ji 2007: 189)

(157) *ta*   *lai*   *le*   **ma**   Mandarin
     He   come   PF   Q

     'Did he come?'

Similarly, contemporary Chinese negatives such as *bu* and *mei(you)* can be used as question markers, as in (158) and (159).

(158) *ta   chang   qu   **bu***   Chinese
       he   often   go   not

       'Does he go often?' (Cheng, Huang, and Tang 1996: 43)

(159) *hufei   kan-wan-le   nei-ben   shu   **meiyou***   Chinese
       Hufei   read-finish-PF   that-CL   book   not

       'Has Hufei finished the book?' (Cheng et al. 1996: 41)

The distribution of the negative particles *bu* and *mei(you)* is aspectually determined: *bu* negates states and auxiliaries, such as *hui* 'know', but not bounded events; *mei(you)* on the other hand marks boundedness, and is used for the perfective. In Chinese, this aspectual relation also holds when the negatives are sentence-final particles. According to Cheng et al., this indicates that these forms are still moving from Neg to C. Cheng et al. don't add ASP to the tree, but as I have argued in section 3.1, having the negative be base generated in the ASPP and then move to NegP nicely explains the distribution. In the case of *meiyou*, the aspect would be [bounded]; in the case of *bu*, it could be [unbounded].[12] Structure (160) represents how *bu* moves in (158).

(160)

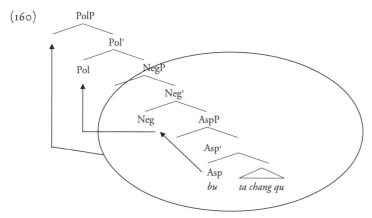

Cheng et al. (1996) argue in favor of a movement analysis on the basis of embeddings. If the negative in C is compatible with the aspect of both the embedded and main clause, as in (161), the question is ambiguous since the negative can be seen as having moved from either the subordinate or the main clause.

(161) *ta   yiwei   ni   qu   **bu***   Chinese
       he   think   you   go   not
       (a) 'Does he think or not think that you are going?'
       (b) 'Does he think that you are going or not going?' (Cheng et al. 1996: 58)

If, however, the embedded clause is perfective and the main clause nonperfective, as in (162), the question particle will be *meiyou*, and if the main clause is nonperfective it will be *bu*, as in (163). These sentences are then not ambiguous.

---

12. The jury (e.g., Li & Thompson) is still out on how best to represent the class of verbs that occurs with *bu*.

(162) *ta*   *hui* *yiwei* *ni*   *qu-guo*   ***meiyou?***   Chinese
       he   will   think   you   go   not

      'Will he think that you have or haven't been there?'

(163) *ta*   *yiwei* *ni*   *qu-guo*   ***bu?***   Chinese
       he   think   you   go   not

      'Does he think or not think that you have been there?' (Cheng et al. 1996: 59)

Cantonese has three negatives, also aspectually determined, but only one of these appears as a yes-no marker, namely *mei* as in (164) and (165).

(164) *wufei*   *lei-zo*   ***mei?***   Cantonese
       wufei   come-PF   not

      'Has Wufei come yet?' (Cheng et al. 1996: 41)

(165) *ngo*   *hoyi*   *ceot-heoi*   ***mei***   Cantonese
       I   can   go-out   NEG

      'Can I go out?' (Cheng et al 1996: 54)

This *mei* in C is no longer aspectually determined and therefore base generated as a question marker in C.

Yang (2009) examines four interrogatives, *m*, *bo*, *buei*, and *be*, in (Taiwanese) Southern Min and concludes that some are aspectually determined and therefore moving while others are base generated in C. She thereby argues against Cheng et al., who assert that the situation in Southern Min is the same as in Cantonese. These four markers originally are the negative forms of *beh* 'want', *u* 'have', *a* 'yet', and *e* 'will'. For instance, in (166a), *bo* is used as negative, but in (166b), it is used as a question marker with the verb *u*.

(166) a. *i*   ***bo***   *lai*   Southern Min
           she/he   not   come

        'He didn't come.'

     b. *i*   *u*   *chiN*   ***bo***
           she/he   have   money   Q

        'Does he have money?' (Yang 2009: 7)

For Yang (2009: 17), in a construction such as (167), only *bo* and *be* are possible, indicating that the others are still modally or aspectually conditioned. *Be* is expected in this sentence since it is the negative connected to the future; used with the verb *u*, it is not grammatical, as (168) shows.

(167) *i*   *e*   *lai*   ****m/bo/*buei/be**   Southern Min
       she/he   will   come   Q

      'Will she/he come?' (Yang 2009: 17)

(168)   **I   u   chin   be*   Southern Min
         she/he   have   money   QM

'Does she/he have money?' (Hui-Ling Yang, p.c.)

Yang argues that *m* is not used as question marker in (167), possibly because of being phonologically weak, but that it has lost its link to the modal *beh*. *Bo* likewise has lost its link to the verb *u*, and can be used as question marker in any construction.

Thus, in Chinese, the negative moves to the CP layer in negative questions, but in Cantonese, it is no longer moving, and in Southern Min, some are and some aren't. What triggered the initial movement to the CP layer is still to be determined. In Latin, Arabic, and Athabascan, the reanalysis seems to have gone through a stage where focus was relevant—a word moved to the FocP below the NegP, and the negative then moved to the FocP in the CP layer. That may be true in Chinese as well. Negatives have a negative value and, if they end up in the PolP, the negative quality somehow weakens and is reanalyzed as a Pol head whose polarity is not specified.

Apart from negatives, other elements end up marking yes-no questions. These are mainly elements marking a choice—*whether* in English was a yes-no question marker for some time and Heine and Kuteva (2002: 226–227) report that the disjunctive *either* and *or* are often used that way.

5. Triggers

In (20), repeated as (169), I provide a possible scenario of the changes involving negatives, but haven't said anything yet about what triggers the changes.

(169) a. Adjunct/Argument   Specifier (of NegP)   Head (of NegP)   affix
           semantic   >   [i-NEG]   >   [u-NEG]   >   —
       b. Lexical Head   >   (higher) Head   >   (higher) Head >   o
           [neg]   [i-NEG]/[u-F]   [u-F]/[u-F]

In this section, I contemplate two possible starts, a pragmatically marked situation and a specific syntactic context.

One good place to look is in what constructions "doubling" starts. That would give an indication of which features in the head are really relevant and reanalyze as grammatical (interpretable initially). I only briefly discussed Old English in section 1.1 since so much is known about negatives in the history of English. After a period with a solitary *ne* negative, the negative meaning of the sentence is reinforced by phrases such as *na wiht* and *noht*. Here, I'll examine possible starts since less is known about that.

At first glance, there seem to be a large number of doubly negated forms involving the noun *God*, as (170) and (171) show. This could show that the reason behind the introduction is pragmatic and the additional semantically negative features of *na God* enable the reanalysis of the regular negative features.

(170) *forðan swa hwæt swa læsse bið. 7 unmihtigre þæt **ne** bið **na god***
        therefore so what so smaller is and weaker that not is no God
        'Therefore what is so small and weak that is no God.'
        (Aelfric, *Homilies*, 228.26, in Thorpe [1884–1886] 1971)

(171)   *hwæðere heo **ne** bið **na of godes** agenum gecynde*
        whether she (the soul) not is never of God's own kind

        'Is she ever of God's own kind?'
        (Aelfric, *Homilies*, 292.25, in Thorpe [1884–1886] 1971)

Such pragmatic causes have been argued for the start of *self* as an emphatic and for the initial use of the relative *who*. However, most of the 154 instances of *na* in (a part of) Aelfric's *Homilies* precede *man*. And this text already has so many instances of negative concord that it is hard to see this period and text as the start. In Alfred's writings, the same is true. Out of 97 instances of *nan* in the *Pastoral Care* (Sweet [1871] 1934), 8 precede *god* or *godes*, but most precede a form of *man/mon* rather than the pragmatically more salient *god*. I argue looking at another text that this more grammaticalized form *na man*, used in a very specific syntactic context, was in fact the trigger of the change.

The translation into West Saxon Old English of Bede's (originally Latin) *Ecclesiastical History of the English People* shows both negative concord, as in (172) to (174), and sentences without it, such as (175). Of the 65 forms of *nænig*, 15 occur together with *ne*, and some in questions or conditionals (following examples from Bede in Miller 1890–1898).

(172)   *Mid þy hine þa **nænig mon ne** gehabban ne gebindan meahte*
        Therefore that him then no man not hold not bind could

        'because no one could hold or bind him' (Bede, 184.27)

(173)   ***ne nænig** his agen wiif forlæte.*
        nor no one his own wife leave

        'that nobody leave his own wife' (Bede, 278.30)

(174)   *Ac **nænig mon** in þære mægðe **ne** heora lif onhyrgan wolde ne heora
        lare gehyran*
        but no man in that province not their life imitate would nor their
        teaching heed

        'But no man in that province imitates their life nor heeds their teaching.'
        (Bede, 302.21)

(175)   *Gehet he him, þæt he wolde in þam fyrrestum dælum Ongolcynnes, þær **nænig** lar ær
        cwom, þa sæd sawan þæs halgan geleafan.*
        'He promised him that he would sow the seed and the holy faith in the
        most remote parts of England where no teaching had come before.'
        (Bede, 166.25)

In this "intermediate" text, the generalization is that, in the negative concord cases, the indefinite is a subject, hence can move via the specifier of the NegP, as in (176). The quantifier "picks up" negative concord from the negative head.

(176)

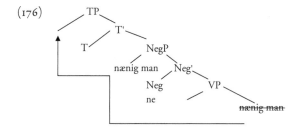

These data show that negative concord is first introduced when an indefinite moves through the specifier of the NegP on its way to a higher position. This remains true in the early Middle English of Layamon's Caligula version of *Brut*. To phrase the change in tearms of features, the negative in (176), by moving through the Spec of NegP checks the negative uninterpretable features of the head.[13]

6. Conclusion

The descriptions in this chapter of (partial) negative cycles in Old Norse, Modern Scandinavian, Finnic, Sami, Kamassian, Berber and Arabic dialects, Amharic, Koorete, Hausa, Athabascan, Eyak, Tlingit, Haida, Creoles, and Chinese show that there are two main grammaticalization strategies, one from lower head or phrase to a higher one (e.g., Chinese verbs to negatives), accounted for through Late Merge, and another from specifier to higher specifier to head (e.g., Scandinavian negative indefinites or adverbs to negative heads). The first strategy is responsible for the fact that in many languages the form of negatives depends on the mood or aspect, as seen for Athabascan and Chinese. The second strategy takes minimizers and indefinites as source.

Parts of these two cycles can be accounted for in terms of the Head Preference Principle and Late Merge. The stage where the head disappears could be explained in a number of ways. I have suggested that the changes involved in both complete cycles can be understood in terms of Feature Economy, as in (20).

I have also shown that speakers analyze their negatives in different positions in the sentence. The Uralic languages are good examples, in that in some the negative is inflected for tense as well as agreement and is lower (more to the right) than the negative inflected just for agreement. Arabic dialects and Hungarian show that indefinite *wh*-elements are reanalyzed as negatives too. This may in fact be the origin of the innovative *doo* in Athabascan.

---

13. Ingham (2006, 2007b) argues in a similar way that negative objects that precede the verb move to the Spec of NegP, and in these cases *ne* is optional.

Part IV

9

TYPOLOGY, WORD ORDER, AND PARAMETRIC VARIATION

IN THIS CHAPTER, I consider the relevance of the macrocycles discussed so far for linguistic typology. The difference between head marking and non-head-marking languages—between synthetic and analytic languages—depends on what stage of the agreement cycle they are in. I explore whether the head-marking cycle can be seen as an analytic-synthetic-analytic cycle. Dependent-marking cycles are in principle also relevant to the synthetic-analytic cycle but are harder to relate to a cycle of change since they are more idiosyncratic, as chapter 5 shows. The microcycles involving TMA marking, negatives, and interrogatives are less crucial to the general character of a language than those of head or dependent marking.

I also return to parameters and the language faculty. There are currently two major approaches to parameters, a micro and a macro approach, and I will try to combine insights from both. I have been arguing that Feature Economy is an alternative for Late Merge and Head Preference and that it accounts for the cyclical change seen in much of this book. This principle presupposes that cross-linguistic variation is the result of different lexical choices by the child acquiring the language. The question is how the child knows what features to pay attention to. To answer this, I articulate feature macroparameters in figure 9.6.

In addition to head and dependent marking, word order distinguishes grammatical and pragmatic roles. Word order may determine a subject and object as well as mark specificity. In this chapter, I ask the question whether there are cycles of word order change, for example, from SOV to SVO to SOV. I chronicle some of the stages and connect them to parametric choices. Remarkably little turns out to be known about those changes apart from the ones from SOV to SVO and not much evidence for a full word order cycle can be found.

In section 1, I provide some background to the use of analytic and synthetic and how they are regarded by some scholars as stages in a cycle. In section 2, I review how the cycles discussed in chapters 2 to 8 fit into the discussion on stages in an analytic-synthetic cycle. Looking at cycles in terms of Minimalist features brings up many questions on the nature of features. This section therefore includes a plea to revisit the characteristics of features in a more systematic way. In section 3, I discuss parameters and provide two different views on parameters, feature based (as in Chomsky 1995 and others) and non-feature-based (as in Baker 2001, 2008a). I argue that a feature-based approach best represents the cyclical changes, but present the choices language learners have to make about features in terms of a macroparameter (as in Roberts & Holmberg 2010 and Richards 2008b). Section 4 mostly discusses cyclical changes in word order and briefly how these are related to parameters.

1. Analytic and Synthetic

In this section, I briefly discuss some of the problems in characterizing a language as analytic or synthetic. It is, of course, impossible to do justice to the vast literature on this topic. I just list a few views. See Schwegler (1990) for more literature review.

Analytic languages have words with few morphemes, with the most analytic showing a one-to-one relationship between word and morpheme. Chinese is often cited as a good example of this, and I come back to this language later. Words in synthetic languages contain more than one morpheme. Languages with verbal agreement are candidates for being synthetic. As is obvious from this description, it is easy to decide on a purely analytic language but hard to decide on what counts as a synthetic language: is it having words that contain three morphemes or words with five morphemes? Humboldt (1836) proposes a third type of language, namely polysynthetic, that is widely accepted. As Sapir (1921: 128) puts it, polysynthetic languages are "more than ordinarily synthetic."

August Wilhem von Schlegel seems to be the first in 1818 to use analytic and synthetic where languages are concerned. As Schwegler (1990) points out, from the beginning, the terms were not used in precise ways since they include gradations, such as "elles penchent fortement vers" (they lean strongly toward) and "une certaine puissance de" (a certain power of). Schlegel's reasons for postulating the terms may have been to distinguish the more "perfect" synthetic languages from the less perfect ones. He sees the reason for change toward an analytic language "les conquérans barbares" (the barbarian conquerors) (1818: 24) who acquired Latin imperfectly.

Apart from morphemes per word, a second distinction is made as to whether the morphemes in the synthetic languages are agglutinative, as in Inuktitut and Korean, or (in)flectional, as in English and Navajo. Sometimes this is put as a cycle as well, as in Crowley (1992: 170), reproduced in figure 9.1.

The distinction between agglutinative and inflectional doesn't really say anything and moreover is not always straightforward either. Another question in such a framework would be what to do with clitics. Do they count as independent words or not?

Sapir (1921: 135–136) tries to distinguish syntax, morphology, and meaning where analytic and synthetic are concerned. The result is very complex and the system is not used today.

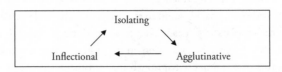

FIGURE 9.1. Attachment type

Proto-Afroasiatic	*Sm
Old Egyptian	sM
Late Egyptian	Sm
Coptic	sM

FIGURE 9.2. Developments in Egyptian (from Hodge 1970: 5)

Greenberg ([1954] 1960) provides a system where words are assigned values depending on their complexity. A completely analytic language (one word, one morpheme) would have the value 1.00, a mildly synthetic language would be 2.00 (two morphemes in a word), and a polysynthetic language would average above 3.00. There are many drawbacks to Greenberg and, as Schwegler (1990: 22) points out, that may be the reason Greenberg stopped pursuing it. Nichols (1992) formulates a point system to determine how head marking or dependent marking a language is. She is less concerned with how extreme a language is in its marking but more with whether it is head marking or dependent marking consistently. Hodge (1970) uses lower and upper case to give a visual representation of full cycles from synthetic (sM) to analytic (Sm) and back, but this approach mainly concerns head marking. Figure 9.2 illustrates his representation.

The approach taken in this book is to look at analytic and synthetic as stages in a cycle. I agree with Sapir (1921: 128), who says, "the terms are more useful in defining certain drifts than as absolute counters." Languages can be in one stage for agreement and in another for TMA and negation. The often-cited Chinese language is analytic in that mood, negation, and aspect are expressed as separate words but might be becoming more synthetic because, for instance, the perfective marker *-le* in (1) cannot be on its own and has grammaticalized from the verb *liao* meaning 'to complete' among other meanings (Sun 1996: 85, 178).[1]

(1) *ta   ba wenjian-jia   qingqingde   fang **zai le** zhuo shang*   Mandarin
   she   BA document folder   gently   put on PF table up
   'She put the documents gently on the table.' (yahoo.com.tw)

There are many other such words that can no longer be independent, such as the question marker *ma* and object marker *ba*.

Synthetic languages such as Old English change into more analytic languages. For instance, verbs inflected for mood and aspect/tense come to be replaced by auxiliaries generated in positions just expressing mood and aspect/tense, originating in verbs. Modern English cannot, however, be characterized as a completely analytic language since, as we saw, futures and negatives are becoming affixes, as in (2).

(2) *I **shouldna**   done   that*   Colloquial English
   'I should not have done that.'

It is really hard to give a precise definition of synthetic and analytic (and of agglutination/inflection, etc.). A language with more than one morpheme per word is synthetic and a

---

1. Example (1) was provided to by Hui-Ling Yang.

language where most arguments are marked on the verb but where nominals are optional is polysynthetic.

2. Cycles, Features, and Typology

The cycles discussed in this book can be divided into three kinds: the agreement cycles in chapters 2 to 4, the dependent-marking cycles in chapters 5 and 6, and the functional category cycles in chapters 7 and 8. Descriptively, one could say that analytic languages have heads with interpretable features and synthetic languages heads/probes with uninterpretable ones. That is more or less correct, but caution is in order since much more work on the nature of interpretable and uninterpretable features is needed, and I start with that.

Chomsky (1995 and later) talks about interpretable features as those features that are interpretable at the conceptual-intentional interface. These presumably include tense on T (or C), negation on a negative element, aspect, and person and number on nouns. These features are in principle independent (not in need) of checking. There is cross-linguistic variation, however, as to whether there is a second element with uninterpretable features. In many languages, the negative features are uninterpretable in the NegP head and probe for interpretable negative features. The agreement features—phi features—in nonpolysynthetic languages are always uninterpretable on T and on v and on D heads. They keep the derivation going. What has been missing from the discussion, it seems to me, is what the possible feature settings are: can tense on T be uninterpretable, is tense independent of phi features, why do we have u-phi on both T and V, and so on.

With this problem noted, let's see if we can link type of feature to stage in the cycle. The agreement cycles show a very strong correlation with the change from analytic to synthetic to analytic (and so on). In chapter 2, I have suggested that the change from subject pronoun to agreement is as in (3). The head pronoun stage is considered synthetic in this approach.

(3) | Adjunct | | Specifier | | Head | | affix |
|---|---|---|---|---|---|---|
| emphatic | > | full pronoun | > | head pronoun | > | agreement |
| [i-phi] | | [i-phi] | | [u-1/2] [i-3] | | [u-phi] |

The analytic stage is where the phi features on the pronoun are interpretable and the synthetic one where the phi features on T are uninterpretable. The latter are always uninterpretable in nonpolysynthetic languages, so the change involves mainly the nominal element. The stages in this cycle can be represented as in figure 9.3, repeated from figure 2.2. In stage (a), the phi features in T act as a probe and value their person and number with the DP (or pronoun); the [u-T] of the DP is valued at the same time (as 'nominative'). In (b), the pronominal head is reanalyzed as having fewer features. Notice that the [u-T] features on the goal are absent, but as discussed in chapter 2, other features can be too. In (c), the pronoun in T has [u-phi] and needs to probe for another DP (empty or not). Note that we are ignoring the tense features and that they are irrelevant for this particular cycle.

As mentioned in chapters 2 and 3, I use Roberts's and Holmberg's (2010: 13–14) insights into the clitic/head distinction in (b). They argue that if the valuation of the features results

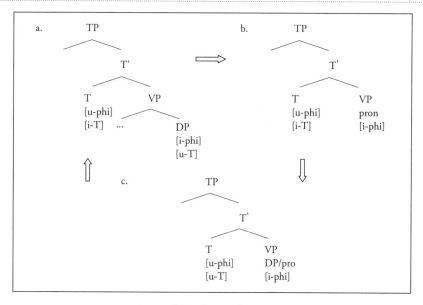

FIGURE 9.3. Stages of the subject cycle using Feature Economy

in a situation (after valuation) as if movement had taken place, the features of the goal can be reanalyzed as those on the probe. So instead of moving as in figure 9.3 (b), the head stays where it is, but the result is as if it had moved.

In chapter 2, I also provided an analysis for a polysynthetic stage. If one argues for a Baker-like approach with empty *pro*, as in (4), the correlation between uninterpretable features on T/V and a (poly)synthethic stage would work too.

(4)

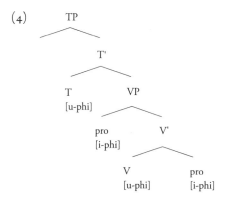

However, in chapter 2, I argued against an analysis such as in (4) and do so again because, even if (4) gives a nice typology, we would still need to see the stages in terms of how language is acquired and why it is the way it is.

The other way of thinking about stage (b) and polysynthesis besides that in (4) is as in (5), which would be an updated Jelinek (1984). In chapter 2, I argued that stage (b) can result in a reanalysis of the pronoun as T [u-phi], as in colloquial French and some varieties of Italian, or as a loss of features on T in polysynthetic languages, as in (5).

(5)

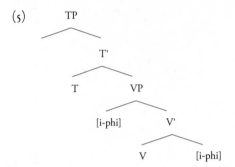

One can think of the "affixes" as incorporated pronominal arguments, having [i-phi] features, and bearing a theta role. If (5) is correct, the correlation between interpretable and analytic doesn't hold since polysynthetic languages also have [i-phi]. The argument in favor for (5) came from being able to use third factor explanations for changes involving polysynthetic languages. See section 4 in chapter 2 for more on this.

I'll now turn to dependent marking. Case-marked nouns are synthetic (using, e.g., Greenberg's [1954] 1960 criteria), whereas nouns just preceded by articles are not. This means that the reanalysis of a demonstrative to an article to an affix increases the synthetic nature of a language. In the case of agreement, there is a relationship between the features of the probe on the T/V and those of the DP goal. The same is true with dependent marking and its stages. On the DP, they show a loss of (interpretable) deictic and temporal features in favor of (uninterpretable) specificity and measure, as shown in (6), repeated from (22a) in chapter 5.

(6)   Demonstrative   >   article   >   zero
      [i-loc]   [u-loc] = [u-T]
      [i-phi]   [u-phi]

The features on D can also be reanalyzed as Tense, as shown in (7), but an uninterpretable [u-T] on C or T need not result in a synthetic structure. That depends on the phi features of T (i.e., whether or not it triggers a reanalysis of the V as T).

(7)   D   >   Tense   >   affix on C-T
      [i-loc]   [i-T]   [u-T]

Let's look at a sentence to make this more concrete, (8). If we follow Pesetsky and Torrego (2001, 2007), as in chapter 5 and 7, the complementizer *that* is an element used to spell out the [u-T] feature on C but a nominative can also do this; hence the optionality of *that* in my cases.

(8)   a. … that they saw Mary
      b. … [[that u̶-̶T̶] [they t̶h̶a̶t̶ saw Mary]]

Thus having [u-T] in C, this [u-T] doesn't make the language more synthetic. If anything does that, it is the agreement features, in other words, the [u-phi], as explained earlier. So the dependent features do not contribute to an increase in synthesis.

The TMA and Negative cycles in chapters 7 and 8 also, as I have shown, lose semantic and interpretable features; this loss means an increase in synthetic nature. However, the correlation is not straightforward. For instance, the future cycle can be represented as in figure 9.4, repeated from figure 7.5, and as is obvious, stage (a) is analytic but has uninterpretable features checking with *will*. Again, if there is a correlation at all it is only with agreement features.

Thinking about analytic and synthetic languages, we could say descriptively that the features on the verb, its agreement features, determine the synthetic or analytic character of a language. Adding polysynthetic languages, under the analysis I have argued for, makes this correlation invalid, however. So we are back at the problem faced in section 1: intuitively we know what analytic and synthetic languages are but the difference is hard to define. Looking at cycles provides some insight because one sees what features change. We also notice that more theoretical discussion of features is necessary.

3. Parameters and Cycles

In this section, I review some ideas on how to account for typological differences, especially the stages of the various cycles, using a parametric approach. I will suggest a model as in figure 9.6, which needs to be developed more in future work.

3.1 THE PRINCIPLES AND PARAMETERS FRAMEWORK

Parameters have been used in generative grammar since the so-called Principles and Parameters approach. Principles are valid for all languages but parameters need to be set. Principles

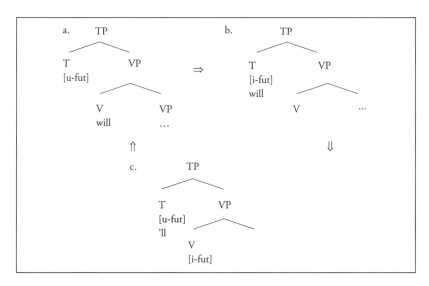

FIGURE 9.4. The future cycle

include the Structure Preserving Hypothesis (Emonds 1976), the Head Movement Constraint (Travis 1984), Relativized Minimality (Rizzi 1990), the Phase Impenetrability Condition (Chomsky 2001), the Inclusiveness Condition (Chomsky 1995: 225–228), No Tampering (Chomsky 2004: 117), and many others, including possibly the Head Preference Principle, Late Merge, and Feature Economy. Principles continue to be valid.

Early examples of parameters include determining if a language is pro-drop (Rizzi 1982), its headedness, and whether it moves its *wh*-elements. Pro-drop is the cover term for a set of related phenomena, and, as seen in chapter 2, there are many ways to account for having empty subjects. Nobody, however, believes that it is a +/- setting of an actual parameter called "pro-drop." Headedness is a great way to characterize a language, with Arabic being head-initial and Japanese head-final. Following work by Kayne (1994), headedness has been abandoned as a formal parameter. In this framework, the basic word order is SVO and other word orders come about through movement, possibly due to feature strength. I come back to this in section 4. Likewise the *wh*-movement parameter is now often seen as dependent on feature strength or EPP. Setting the Binding Domain (Chomsky 1981) and finding the relevant barriers for Subjacency (Chomsky 1973) are two other early parameters. They are now part of a theory of phases.

Though most introductory generative syntax books continue to cite a set of three parameters, pro-drop/null subject, headedness, and *wh*-movement, these are often used in very descriptive ways, not to explain what goes on in language acquisition. There are practical problems on how to formulate the parameters, as we have seen, but currently the main question is how these parameters would have arisen in the brain. If the shift in humans from no language to language was immediate, it makes sense that there is one crucial change in the way the brain functions and that change could have been Merge. Complex parameters of the pro-drop variety don't really fit in this picture.

3.2 THE MINIMALIST PROGRAM: MICRO- AND MACROPARAMETERS

Within the Minimalist Program, there are currently two lines of thought where parameters are concerned. Chomsky (e.g., 2004, 2007, 2008), Lohndal (2009c), Richards (2008b), on the one hand, attribute as little as possible to the role of parameters and to Universal Grammar in general. Minimalist parameters consist of choices of feature specifications as the child acquires a lexicon, as in Borer (1984), dubbed the Borer-Chomsky Conjecture by Baker (2008a). All parameters are lexical and determine linearization; therefore, they account for the variety of languages. Chomsky assumes that language is perfectly designed to interface with the conceptual-intentional system (the old LF) but not with the sensori-motor one (the old PF). In Richards's (2008b: 146) words, parameters find a place "as PF-repair strategies."

Most principles have been attributed to Universal Grammar. At the moment, however, the emphasis in the Minimalist Program is on principles not specific to the language faculty (UG), but to "general properties of organic systems" (Chomsky 2004: 105), "third factor principles" in Chomsky (2005, 2007). My emphasis in the book has been on these as well.

Baker (2001, 2008b), on the other hand, has suggested macroparameters. In Baker (2001), following Sapir, he argues that a language has a basic character. Thus, the choice of

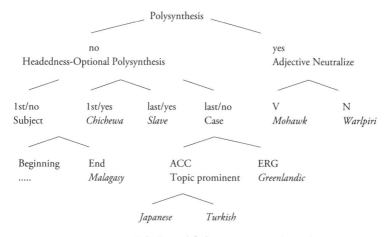

FIGURE 9.5. Baker's simplified macroparameter hierarchy

polysynthesis, for example, implies that the language will have many other characteristics. Figure 9.5 is repeated from figure 1.2 and provides a simplified version of Baker's hierarchy.[2]

The major choice in figure 9.5 is between polysynthesis and no polysynthesis. Polysynthetic languages treat adjectives as nouns or verbs, and that is the second parameter to set. Nonpolysynthetic languages have many parameters to set. One familiar parameter is headedness. The main objection is that the approach has a flavor of arbitrariness and is difficult to envision as part of Universal Grammar (see also Baltin 2004: 551). The settings may change fast in some languages without too many other characteristics changing. For instance, as shown in chapter 3, the Northern Athabaskan languages lack object polysynthesis whereas the Southern ones have it; otherwise, the two are quite similar. This is a problem for the hierarchy of macroparameters. In addition, the question arises how this would have come about as an evolutionary shift.

Baker (2008a: 155) has two macroparameters, as in (9) and (10).[3] The choices are "shallower" than those in figure 9.5 and one choice can be easily made, without having to go down a set of choices, as in figure 9.5.

(9) The Direction of Agreement Parameter (DAP)
F agrees with DP only if DP asymmetrically c-commands F.
(Yes: most Bantu languages; No: most Indo-European languages)

(10) The Case Dependence of Agreement Parameter (CDAP)
F agrees with DP/NP only if F values the Case feature of DP/NP (or vice versa).
(No: most Bantu languages; Yes: most Indo-European languages)

The 108 languages that Baker (2008a) examines fall into four groups, a distribution predicted by the DAP and CDAP: those with yes/yes, yes/no, no/no, and no/yes. Therefore,

---

2. Baker (2008a) is not concerned with the macroparameters of figure 9.5. In that work he devises two parameters concerned with agreement.

3. To these, Baker (2008a: 100) adds a parameter on how many times a functional head can search.

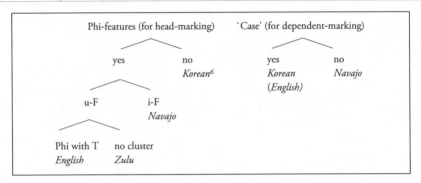

FIGURE 9.6. Feature macroparameters

according to Baker, the DAP and CDAP "cannot be recast as the assignment of special feature values to individual lexical items; that view would allow different kinds of agreement to
be found within a single language" (Baker 2009).

The DAP reminds one of the discussion in the 1990s of the differences between Spec-Head
agreement[4] (in SVO languages) and agreement under government (in VSO languages). If
specifier positions are important in a language, that language has EPP features triggering
movement to these positions. If the DAP is about agreement (and possibly about the EPP),
the CDAP requires us to rethink the usual Case assignment rules in languages where Case and
agreement are not dependent on one another. In English, as explained in chapter 5, [u-phi]
and [i-T] are part of the T probe, so agreement and Case are connected. In some languages,
Case is not evident at all. The parameters can be stated in a simplified form as (11) and (12).

(11) a. Spec-Head or Agree;
      b. Agree up or Agree down

(12) a. Cluster [u-T] and [u-phi] or not
      b. Case and agreement depend on each other or not

It would be good if the DAP and CDAP could be generalized, for example, to *wh*-movement.

3.3 COMBINING MICRO- AND MACROPARAMETERS

In this book, I have argued that Case and agreement are not necessarily connected, so that
position fits with Baker's CDAP. Agreement is the more basic phenomenon in language,
more widespread than Case.[5] It is therefore possible to formulate a Baker-like macroparametric hierarchy in terms of head marking and dependent marking and see some differences
between languages as different feature choices. I attempt in figure 9.6, adapted from figure
1.3, to incorporate the CDAP.[6]

---

4. Baker (2008a) does make a point of saying that (9) is in accordance with bare phrase structure, and (11) is not.
5. What isn't captured in figure 9.6 is that [i-F] is often linked to [no-Case].
6. As mentioned in chapter 1, Baker (2008a: 39, 153) argues that T is not a probe in, for instance, Japanese, which
   is similar to not having probing phi-features. In these languages, I assume that independent subjects may be
   absent too, with radical pro-drop as the result.

TABLE 9.1

Languages with and without Case and Agreement

	Agreement	No Agreement
Case	Yaqui, Amis, Urdu, Basque	Japanese, Korean, Khoekhoe
No Case	Navajo, Zulu, Lakhota, Ainu	Sango, Haida, (French), Thai, Haitian Creole

This means that languages could be head marking, dependent marking, both, or neither, and that is what we find, as shown in table 9.1.

The model in figure 9.6 goes against the current thinking that both phi and Case features are relevant for all languages. Other attempts involving features are found in Biberauer and Richards (2006), Richards (2008b), and Roberts and Holmberg (2010). Initially, a child would use lexical categories (as well as demonstrative pronouns) with interpretable features (see Radford 2000). The child would then hear evidence in English for phi features but would have a preference principle and, if not enough external data were available, would analyze the features differently from a previous generation.

In approaches such as those represented in figure 9.6, the choices are not as deep and are feature based. This means that the child may get hints to pay attention to certain features. For instance, if modals are around, a child might postulate an MP and then needs to decide on the types of features connected to it. The parametric differences expressed in figure 9.6 are also in accordance with the view that parameters are only relevant to lexical and grammatical items, the approach used in this book. If all parameters are feature based, word order should be looked at in those terms as well, and I turn to that next.

4. Word Order Cycles

In this section, I look at the possible effect of the Economy Principles on word order changes. For instance, according to the Head Preference Principle, head movement of V might be more economical than phrasal movement of VP. Since Chomsky (1995), there has been a lot of discussion of the status of head movement: is it in the syntax or the PF and does it exist at all or is it really remnant XP movement? I will keep this section conservative and assume there is head movement. The conclusions regarding word order change are quite disappointing in that no clear patterns for word order change emerge. This is not a new observation, but one that has been made in early work on the markedness of certain word orders.

The classification using S (and A) and O is relevant for dependent-marking languages though not really for head-marking ones such as the polysynthetic languages (where S and O are optional adjuncts). Other well-known problems for the classification of languages in terms of S, V, and O involve languages such as German and Dutch with word orders depending on the clause type. I will nevertheless stick to it, focusing on nonpolysynthetic languages.

In this section, I first outline the approach taken by many generative syntacticians, namely that SVO is basic (section 4.1). I then examine the different orders and widely attested changes between them (sections 4.2 and 4.3). In section 4.4, I discuss how these word order changes play into the typological changes and conclude that too little is known to think of this in terms of economy.

4.1 SVO AS BASIC?

I briefly survey the possible word orders and the argument that all languages have one basic word order (as in Kayne 1994; Chomsky 1995: 334–340; Fukui & Takano 1998).[7] Since word order is not relevant to the narrow syntax (Chomsky 2004: 109), c-command and hierarchy are the crucial notions and the hierarchical structure has to be translated into linear order. See the approaches by Nunes (2004) and Richards (2004, 2008b).

Typological work of the 1960s, especially Greenberg (1963), and later (e.g., Dryer 1992) distinguishes six word orders: SOV, SVO, VSO, VOS, OSV, and OVS. SVO and SOV are by far the most frequent, followed by VSO, and this prompts Greenberg's Universal 1, repeated in (13), with a note to some exceptions.

(13) Universal 1
      In declarative sentences with nominal subject and object, the dominant order is always one in which the subject precedes the object (Greenberg 1963: 77).

Another universal relevant to basic word order is Universal 6, repeated in (14).

(14) Universal 6
      All languages with dominant VSO order have SVO as an alternative or as the only alternative basic order. (Greenberg 1963: 79)

Since SOV and SVO are so frequent cross-linguistically, an estimated 80 percent to 90 percent of languages, Universal 6 might lead us to think that VSO is derived from SVO or SOV through V movement. That is indeed what many (generative) linguists assume for VSO languages such as Celtic and Arabic, as in (15), with the original position of the verb indicated by means of a copy.

(15) **kataba**   *r-rajul-u*   ~~kataba~~   *r-risaalat-a*   Standard Arabic
      wrote   DEF-man-NOM   wrote   DEF-letter-ACC
      'The man wrote the letter.'

If we assume that all languages derive from a basic SVO structure (but see Fukui & Takano 1998, who argue for a universal head-last order), a VSO structure would then be derived through V movement to sentence-initial position; SOV and OSV through object shift; VOS

---

7. Fukui and Takano (1998) derive a VO order from an OV basic word order through V to v movement, e.g., in English but not Japanese. This is an interesting alternative but it would be hard to entertain this possibility for the shift in English from OV to VO since verbs in English stopped moving to T and C around the same time.

through VP fronting; and OVS would be the least obvious one. Later in this section, I examine whether any of these movements are more economical than others.

Let's look at the argument of having SVO as basic and not having a headedness parameter. Kayne (1994) argues that linear order is read off the hierarchical structure. If an element *a* c-commands *b* but not vice versa, this is an asymmetric c-command relation and *a* has to precede *b* at spell-out. This principle is also known as the Linear Correspondence Axiom (LCA) and has been used in a number of ways. For instance, Nunes (2004) argues that it is the reason behind the non-spell-out of lower copies, and Richards (2004) that language can ignore one of the c-command relations at PF. Notice that all of this assumes that word order is just relevant to the spell-out (at the sensorimotor interface), but that c-command is the basic notion (at the conceptual-intentional interface).

As to word order, the LCA predicts that languages either branch to the right or to the left, as in (16), with the linearization underneath. Note that one of the lower elements must be moved, since *cd* in (16a) and *ab* in (16b) cannot be linearized when they c-command each other.

(16)

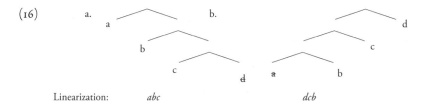

Linearization: *abc*   *dcb*

Because subjects are more frequent in initial position, Kayne (1994) chooses (16a), with the subject as *a*, the verb as *b*, and the object as *c*. Fukui and Takano (1998) provide a more principled reason for why the subject is so often first. They argue that Merge starts a derivation from bottom to top in the narrow syntax, but that spell-out is a process of "demerge," a decomposition of the structure from top to bottom. Since the specifier is always at the top, not matter what order it is in, they predict subjects to be initial.

Head-initial structures such as (16a) also predict that languages can be verb-second but never verb-almost-last (see Zwart 2006). Note that the SVO as underlying means that the order in the vP shell is agent before theme, not really S before O.

With regard to parameters and Universal Grammar in general, Chomsky (2004, 2007, etc.) tries to limit their role and to ascribe as much as possible to nonlinguistic principles. This skepticism as to parameters holds for the headedness parameter as well. Chomsky (2008: 7) says, "I think that there is by now substantial evidence that ordering is restricted to externalization of internal computation to the sensorimotor system, and plays no role in core syntax and semantics." See also Chomsky (1995: 334–340) and Richards (2004). In 4.3, I entertain a way to rephrase the headedness effects in terms of features, where most of these choices would involve EPP features or strong features, a mysterious phenomenon in itself.

The alternative to one basic word order is the headedness parameter. In Japanese, Hindi/Urdu, and Korean, it would be set as head-final since the verb and adposition follow their complements; in English, Arabic, and Thai, it would be set as head-initial because the verb and adposition precede their complements. There are languages, however, where the headedness varies among categories (Dutch, Persian, and Chinese), and languages that have both prepositions and postpositions (German, Old English) or prenominal and postnominal adjectives (French). This variation seems to point toward a featural approach: some heads trigger object movement whereas others don't.

I now turn to frequent word order changes and will try to formulate them as feature changes.

4.2 SUBJECT-INITIAL: CHANGE INVOLVING SOV AND SVO

In this section, I examine the evidence for a cycle of SVO to SOV to SVO and so on. The conclusion reached in most of the literature on this subject is that the change from SOV to SVO is well attested but that the one from SVO to SOV is less likely to be a language-internal development. It occurs in cases of language attrition and contact.

The change from SOV to SVO is a frequent one in Indo-European, as in Latin to Italian, Old Spanish to Modern Spanish, and Old English to Modern English. Canale (1978) sketches the development in the history of English (as do Lightfoot 1999; Trips 2001; and many others), Delsing (2000) does so in Swedish, and Hróarsdóttir (2000) in Icelandic. The change is often ascribed to the loss of dependent marking (or as a case of positional licensing taking over from morphological, as in Kiparsky 1997), but this is complicated. For instance, Pinkster (1990) argues that grammatical and thematic function in Latin is signaled by Case only 5–10 percent of the time even though the word order is fairly free, and Hróarsdóttir (2000) shows the change to VO in Icelandic occurs without loss of dependent marking.

Universal 1 in (11) suggests that the subject is always first and SVO can therefore come about through no movement or through movement of the subject to the specifier of a higher functional category. SOV can be derived by having the object move to before the verb, not strange from what we know about scrambling languages that move definite objects outside the VP. The change from SOV to SVO might be one where the object stops moving, probably due to a shift in the features, not at all an unexpected change. I next give examples of how the shift to VO took place in Icelandic and Norwegian. The former is a language with rich overt Case and the latter one without it. In Old English, the shift to VO was first in finite clauses and then in nonfinite; the last OV structures occurred with indefinite negative objects (as we'll also see in Scandinavian). Object shift was lost in Spanish, shifting the word order to VO as well, according to Parodi (1995), but she doesn't go into the steps the loss takes.[8] The shifts give some indication of what was going on with features.

In Icelandic, the shift from predominantly SOV to SVO took place somewhere in the nineteenth century, according to Hróarsdóttir (2000: 60), when the OV order drops to 25 percent. Note that OV had never been predominant, with 45 percent OV in the thirteenth century. Modern Icelandic still allows OV when the object is definite.

---

8. An example of object shift in Old Spanish is given in (i); it disappears in the modern period.

(i)   ...*cuemo*   *avie*   *su*   *obra*   *acabad-a*   Old Spanish
       how   had-3S   his   work   finished-F

       '... that he had finished his work' (Parodi 1995: 371)

Assuming that the underlying order is SVO at all stages, Hróardsdóttir (2000: 272) provides one possible analysis (among some others) that Old Icelandic has three kinds of movement: the nominal objects obligatorily move to the left of the main verb (to a position either inside or outside of the VP), prepositional and other complements also move to the left, and nonfinite verbs move optionally to the left, as in (17), resulting in VO when they do.

(17)

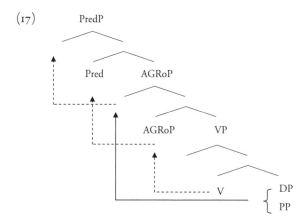

The change to Modern Icelandic is not the loss of object movement but the introduction of obligatory verb movement. This account is preferable, according to Hróardsdóttir, since the morphology on the objects undergoes no change.

In Norwegian, a change from OV to VO also takes place. Sundquist (2006: 105) paints a complex picture. Consistent with what we saw in Icelandic, he asserts that "fluctuation between [O]V and V[O] is more attributable to information structure and interpretive restrictions on leftward movement than presence of rich morphological case" (2006: 107). Pronominal objects are very frequent in OV structures, and nominal objects are more often definite/specific when preceding the verb. Sundquist's table on a phase of this change is reproduced here as table 9.2. Sundquist's conclusion is that Modern Norwegian "resembles Yiddish and Icelandic in that it is a VO language with leftward movement of certain objects for interpretive reasons, yet it also resembles such languages as Old and Middle English in which the VP-structure can be either head-initial or head-final." He introduces a sociolinguistic component as well. Because Middle Danish was more VO and used in Norway in the late fifteenth century, "there was simply less evidence available in the speech community that XV word order was possible" (2006: 132).

Thus, Sundquist's analysis supports work cited earlier: the loss of OV was not due to the loss of morphological Case. The OV patterns that remain are similar to the ones discussed in chapter 5 for German, Dutch, and Yiddish. Kiparsky (1996) reviews accounts of Lightfoot (1991), for instance, and concludes that the reanalysis to VO is made possible by languages that front the verb to T in all clause types. This in turn is made possible by the rise of T(P), as in van Gelderen (1993).

A lot has been written about Germanic, especially about Old English, and Indo-European in general so I will now focus on the loss of SOV in some non-Indo-European languages, although the evidence is more controversial.

TABLE 9.2

Types of Preverbal Objects in the Norwegian of 1250–1450

	Pre-V/All Objects	%
Bare NPs with antecedent in previous discourse	24/33	70
Bare NPs with light verbs	17/26	65
Quantified NPs	39/71	55
Demonstrative NPs	26/57	46
Definite NPs	12/44	27
Possessive NPs	22/86	26
Indefinite NP plurals	30/169	17
Bare NPs (not in previous discourse)	10/60	17
Indefinite NPs with article	1/9	11
Proper names	4/66	6
Cardinal numbers	0/56	0
Total	185/677	26

from Sundquist (2006)

The Niger-Congo family has long seen a debate as to whether SOV or SVO was the order in Proto-Niger-Congo. Givón (1975) and Hyman (1975) suggest it is SOV; Heine (1976), Heine and Reh (1984), Marchese (1986), and Claudi (1994) argue it is SVO. The entire family shows traces of an OV order. For instance, in the Kru languages, the nonfinite verb follows the object while the finite verb moves to T (Koopman 1984); in Mande, Dogon, and Ijo objects precede all types of verb; the very SVO-like Bantu languages have preverbal object clitics; and a few languages have straight SOV (Tunen and Bandem). If the family went from SOV to SVO, what are some of the stages? Givón (e.g., 1971) looks at current Bantu morphology to get an indication. The modality markers are prefixes and of recent verbal origin. Verb-deriving suffixes are also originally verbal and grammaticalized very early from main verbs. Givón hypothesizes an OV structure with widespread serialization and a reinterpretation of the main verb as a suffix: "At some later date, the core Bantu-proper group changed its verb phrase syntax" to VO (Givón 1971: 159). This latter change is the one left unmotivated. Other work doesn't help clarify how the VO switch took place.

Some linguists, such as the very influential Li &and Thompson (1974), have argued that the change from SOV to SVO took place in Chinese as well. The argument goes as follows: Sinitic shares OV with its Tibetan sister family and develops SVO. However, Djamouri (2001: 146) finds only 6 percent OV, as in (18), and 94 percent VO, as in (19), in the Archaic Chinese oracle-bone inscriptions. Most objects in the archaic OV constructions are

(18) *Wáng wù wéi **lóng fāng** fá*   Archaic Chinese
     king NEG be Long tribe fight

'It must not be the Long tribe that the king will fight.' (*Heji*, 6476, from Djamouri 2001: 157)

(19) *Wáng   fá   **gōng   fāng***   Archaic Chinese
       king fight Gong tribe

       'The king will fight the Gong tribe.' (*Heji*, 6223, from Djamouri 2001: 157)

interrogative pronouns and demonstratives that are focalized, as in (18). If Li and Thompson are right, the change to SVO could involve the loss of object movement, as in Norwegian, with certain pronouns the last to be still moving. If Djamouri and others are right, and not taking Proto-Sino-Tibetan into account, one could also argue that OV was the innovation, with certain pronouns as the first to move. The controversy remains therefore, with scholars such as Djamouri (2001) solidly on the SVO side.

The changes to VO discussed so far have been internally motivated. Ma'a, an originally Cushitic language, shifted from SOV to SVO under the influence of contact with Bantu (Thomason 1983). I turn now to the change from SVO to SOV where external motivation for the change is much more common.

The change from SVO to SOV occurs less frequently, and scholars have mostly argued it occurs on the basis of language contact, as in Thomason and Kaufman (1988) and Heine (2007). I will provide a brief review here without much discussion from a variety of language families: Austronesian, Tai-Kadai, Afro-Asiatic, and Austroasiatic.

Crowley (1992: 173–174) cites Austronesian languages as typically having SVO, as in Tolai in (20), but some of the Papuan Austronesian languages, such as Motu in (21), as having reanalyzed to SOV under the influence of their neighboring languages on the island of Papua.

(20) *a   pap-i   gire   **tikana   tutana***   Tolai
       NM   dog-3S see   one   man

       'The dog saw a man.' (Crowley 1992: 173)

(21) *sisia   ese   **tau   ta**   eitaia*   Motu
       dog   the   man   one   it-saw-him

       'The dog saw a man.' (Crowley 1992: 173)

Crowley provides no further references but suggests language contact with the non-Austronesian languages of Papua for Motu. The Western Oceanic language Takia may similarly have changed from SVO to SOV order under the influence of the Papuan language Waskia (Ross 2001).

Khanittanan (1986) argues that Kamti Tai, a Tai-Kadai language spoken in India and Burma, went from SVO to SOV probably due to language contact. Cushitic languages in northeastern Africa are blamed for a change from SVO (or VSO) of Proto-Semitic, to SOV in Amharic languages (Leslau 1945).

Donegan and Stampe (1983) mention that the Munda languages of India, of the Austroasiatic family, have developed OV (and other head-final structures) with morphological marking of subject and object (sometimes by head marking, sometimes by dependent marking) and relatively free word order. Proto-Austroasiatic, as represented by the Mon-Khmer languages, has VO order without any inflectional markings.

In short, the change from SVO to SOV is much less frequent than the one from SOV to SVO (and to other orders as we'll see). Assuming an underlying SVO, an SOV can be derived straight-forwardly through object preposing. The shift to SVO would be a loss of object movement.[9] Word order changes in other languages have been linked to other factors (loss of verb movement and grammaticalization of a verb), however, and I think there is no one reason, so it is "chance" which word order a language ends up with. The diachronic change from SVO to SOV is less frequent. The most frequent mechanism to introduce OV seems to involve the introduction of object shift, moving definite objects to a position higher than the VP. It is not clear to me why this wouldn't happen more frequently, for example, if definiteness marking changed.

4.3 CHANGES INVOLVING VERB-FIRST (AND OBJECT-FIRST)

In this section, I list changes from verb-initial languages, that is, VSO and VOS, to other word orders (e.g., SVO) and changes to verb-initial languages (e.g., from SOV to VSO). Analyses of verb-initial languages are debated. I list some of the changes that are known to have happened and end with a paragraph on the shift to object-initial languages.

Verb-initial languages are widespread and occur for instance among the Austronesian, Indo-European (Celtic), Salish, Mayan, Semitic, and Zapotecan families. Assuming an SVO base, verb-initial constructions derive from verb movement (or remnant movement) or VP movement. The shift from VSO to SVO could mean the loss of verb movement and the shift from VOS to SVO the loss of VP movement. Both of these would be economical but might interact with the drift toward head marking that we have seen with accompanying Merge in a higher position.

Carnie, Harley, and Dooley (2005) summarize the current lack of consensus about a uniform analysis. Even for the same language, such as Irish, Bury (2005) argues for verb movement, whereas Oda (2005) argues for remnant VP movement. VOS languages intuitively seem to need VP preposing, and Rackowski and Travis (2000) and Chung (2005) provide evidence that the VO sequence in VOS languages such as Malagasy, Seediq, and Tzotzil is indeed a fronted constituent. However, Chung (2005: 27–28) concludes her survey on VOS with this comment:

> [L]anguages with VOS clauses differ significantly from one another in the transparency with which they conform to the prediction of the VP raising hypothesis. The evidence from Seediq and Malagasy for the islandhood of VP is automatically explained if VPs in these languages must raise to the specifier of TP. But the evidence from word order patterns and specificity effects in Chamorro seem far less amenable to a VP raising account.

Even when an analysis of verb-initial languages is hard to agree on, how much do we know about the word order changes affecting these languages? A change from VSO to SVO affects Teso, a member of the Nilo-Saharan family, described in Heine, Claudi, and Hünnemeyer (1991: 217–218). The regular word order in Teso is VSO but, when a negative appears, the order is SVO. This order is the result of *mam*, a negative and form of 'to be', reanalyzing as a

---

9. See Hróardsdóttir (2000) for a more complex picture of the change in Old Icelandic, as also outlined above.

negative, as in (22), and the clause grammaticalizing from a biclausal ('It is not Peter...') to a monoclausal structure ('Peter doesn't...').

(22) **mam** *petero* *e-koto* *ekiŋok*   Teso
      NEG Peter 3S-want dog
      'Peter doesn't want a dog.' (Heine et al. 1991: 218)

From older Egyptian to Coptic, a similar change from VSO to SVO has taken place.

According to Cumming (1991), a change from VSO to SVO is also taking place in Indonesian. Cumming compares nineteenth-century Malay with present-day spoken Indonesian and finds (1) that the trigger system on the verb is used less often, and (2) that verb-initial structures do too. A patient-trigger verb, marked for example, by *di-*, must have a patient in the clause clearly present or implied, and an agent-trigger verb an agent (but no patient). The patient can occur either before or after the verb but the agent when present must be preverbal.

Greenberg (1995: 156) mentions Proto-Ethiopian Semitic as an SOV language changing to VSO but is light on the details of the change. Celtic undergoes the same change to VSO, which Hock (1991) sketches in detail. Though "the reasons for this development are complex" (1991: 340), he concludes that the switch from SOV to VSO in Celtic "was an indirect consequence of a fairly minor process (univerbation)" (1991: 362). That makes it similar to Teso.

Arawakan, a group of languages spoken across large parts of South America, shows evidence for an original SOV order. Wise (1986: 568) argues that the Pre-Andine Arawakan languages of Peru are changing from SOV, as in Piro in (23), to VSO, as in Amuesha and Campa varieties such as Asheninca in (24). In the latter, SVO is option for topic marking of the subject.

(23) *hita* **kašri** *mexita*   Piro
      1S arrow attach-feathers-to
      'I attach feathers to the arrow.'
      (Matteson 1965, from Wise 1986: 604)
(24) *i-kamaa-waiȼ-i-siNpi*   **hiñaa-ki**   Asheninca
      3M-dive for-CONT-NONFUT-fish water-LOC
      'He dove for fish in the river.' (Payne 1981, from Wise 1986: 605)

Derbyshire (1986: 558), looking at Brazilian Arawakan, agrees that there is a "move away from an earlier SOV" but he finds that this may be a move to either VSO or SVO.

Some other languages can be added to the list. The Tupi-Guarini language Guajajara of Brazil is currently a VSO language but as Harrison (1986: 429) argues it "is a latecomer to the VSO ranks." Linguists have argued that Fijian, an Oceanic language, has undergone a change from SOV to VOS, and England (1991) that Proto-Mayan is VOS, with currently many languages allowing both VOS and VSO.

In table 9.3, I summarize some of the changes. There is not enough evidence to think about possible cycles or even to formulate a pattern of change.

The languages with OVS and OSV are rare cross-linguistically and are found only in Amazonian languages (Derbyshire & Pullum 1986: 17). Derbyshire (1981) provides some evidence for a shift from SOV to OVS in some Carib languages. Carib of Surinam still has SOV but Hixkaryana and Makúsi are moving to OVS. It is of course hard to speak of OVS if subject and object are obligatorily expressed on the verb and the free subject and object "are often deleted" (Derbyshire 1985: 32). Derbyshire comments that it isn't the loss of Case (so often 'blamed' for the loss of SOV) that is causing this pulling apart of the SO sequence since Carib is SOV and has no Case and Makúsi has Case even though it is OVS. He notices that subjects are often (optionally) expressed as afterthoughts, and are also marked on the verb. This could result in a reanalysis of the adjoined subject as an argument.

4.4 WORD ORDER AND PARAMETRIC CHANGE

In sections 4.1 to 4.3, I have outlined a general approach to word order, with SVO as basic, and have indicated how word order change might come about. There are, however, relatively few data of changes involving languages other than SOV, as table 9.4 shows. The ones I described are indicated by *v*.

Word order shifts are not necessarily related to a loss of marking of the thematic or grammatical roles. For example, Icelandic has shifted to VO seemingly for no particular reason. Its dependent marking is strong and it always had some preverbal objects to indicate definiteness. If Proto-Niger-Congo is SOV, the development toward a largely SVO Bantu involved an increase in head marking. Like the retention of Case in Icelandic, this too is unexpected if the explanation for the preference of SVO is a functional one, to keep the subject and object separate.

In this discussion, I have indicated some feature changes that may be relevant; from SOV to SVO, the features triggering object movement could be lost or weakened, as in Norwegian. The various mechanisms reviewed that may lead to word order are loss of object shift (Norwegian, Icelandic), loss of verb movement to C (Old English), auxiliation of one of the verbs (Bantus), definite objects starting to shift (Chinese), loss of V and VP movement (V-initial languages), and grammaticalization of a biclausal (Teso). The trigger for object loss would be indefinite objects and for the loss of verb movement possibly a loss of inflection. My unsatisfactory conclusion is that there is no straight answer for how word order interacts with marking the various roles of the arguments and hence a feature account is difficult as well.

TABLE 9.3

Changes Involving Verb-Initial and Object-Initial Languages

SOV > VSO	VSO > SVO	SOV > OVS	SOV > VOS	VOS > VSO
Celtic, Semitic, Arawakan, Guajajara	Teso, Indonesian, Egyptian to Coptic	Carib	Fijian	Mayan

TABLE 9.4

Possible Shifts in Word Order

SOV > SVO *v*	SVO > SOV *v*	VSO > VOS	VOS > VSO *v*
SOV > VSO *v*	SVO > VSO	VSO > SVO *v*	VOS > SVO
SOV > VOS *v*	SVO > VOS	VSO > SOV	VOS > SOV
SOV > OSV	SVO > OSV	VSO > OSV	VOS > OSV
SOV > OVS *v*	SVO > OVS	VSO >OVS	VOS > OVS
OSV >OVS	OVS > OSV		
OSV >SVO	OVS > SVO		
OSV >SOV	OVS > SOV		
OSV >VSO	OVS > VSO		
OSV >VOS	OVS > VOS		

v = possible shifts in word order described in the text

5. Conclusion

In sections 1 and 2, I have considered if we can speak of a macrocycle, so to speak, a cycle that explains the basic character of a language as analytic or synthetic. The best candidate for a macrocycle is the agreement cycle. I have suggested how this cycle can be seen in terms of changes in the phi features of the functional categories. Thus the phi features keep the cycle going.

In section 3, in reviewing differing views on parameters, I considered how parametric hierarchies could perhaps be formulated to incorporate cycles of change. In section 4, in turning to word order cycles, I was surprised to find how little is really known about the patterns that change and what the triggers are. I probably missed a lot of relevant literature in specialized venues, however.

10

LANGUAGE EVOLUTION

IN THIS CHAPTER, I suggest that cyclical unidirectional changes give us insight into the question of language evolution. I argue that semantic features are part of what is known as pregrammar, responsible for the VP domain with arguments and theta roles relating to an event. Uninterpretable and interpretable features account for setting that event in place and time in the higher layers of the clause and arise later. As lexical items acquire nonsemantic features, this grammatical stage evolves, resulting in a full-fledged grammatical system. Grammar and lexicon therefore evolve together. There are several major steps in the evolution of language; one introduces Merge, recursion, and thematic function, using already existing concepts expressed by nouns and verbs; another involves changes in grammatical and pragmatic marking, in accordance with Economy Principles.

Many agree that "cognitive representation preceded communication in evolution" (Givón 2009: 1; see also Chomsky 2005). Pragmatics in the form of pointing was probably an early characteristic as well (see Tomasello, Carpenter, and Liszkowski 2007). A major debate is taking place about how language evolved, through adaptive selection or through exaptation (a shift in function that was not selected for). Connected with this is whether these changes are gradual or gapped. Givón argues they are gradual and that "grammar is an adapted code for the mental representation of other minds" (Givón 2009: 13). I agree that grammar (morphosyntax) is indeed that code but that it is hard to find evidence about whether it evolved through selection or exaptation. If it happened through selection, language could have evolved in many parts of the world and in other species.

In section 1, I briefly introduce the topic of language evolution and justify using cyclical processes to shed light on early language. Merge is the focus of section 2 and grammaticalization of section 3. I argue how grammaticalization follows from economy and how it and linguistic cycles are relevant to language evolution.

Africa Asia America Europe Oceania

FIGURE 10.1. Genetic relationships between people (from Cavalli-Sforza 2000: 39)

1. Language Evolution and the Shape of Early Language

Language evolution is a huge topic examined in many recent works, such as Christiansen and Kirby (2003), Botha and Knight (2009), and Givón (2009). As mentioned, there are at least two views as to why and how language evolved: gradual adaptation (Pinker & Bloom 1990; Givón 2009) and a sudden mutation or exaptation (Chomsky 2005; Piattelli-Palmarini & Uriagereka 2005). I will not discuss this debate in detail but will provide a little bit of background on the genetic and archeological evidence and on two types of view of early grammar.

Estimates about the origin of modern human language range from dates of 50,000 to 150,000 to 500,000 years ago. These estimates are based on archeological findings, the presence of tools and beads in such sites as the Blombos cave in Southern Africa at 70,000 years ago, and mutations in a gene connected to speech (FOXP2) at about 120,000 years ago. The latter is controversial since some songbirds have similar mutations. From the work on mutations in the mitochondrial DNA and Y chromosome (see, e.g., Cavalli-Sforza 2000), scholars argue that the continent of origin for modern humans is Africa. The genetic similarities and differences between the various populations, as shown in figure 10.1, suggest that humans migrated from Africa to Australia and Oceania, then to Asia, then to Europe and America. This figure implies the greatest affinity between the people of Asia and those of the Americas, indicating that the Americas were settled by Asian (Siberian) peoples.

There are also people, mainly anthropologists, who argue that prehumans evolved into *Homo sapiens* in a variety of places. This is called the regional continuity model and is advocated by Milford Wolpoff (e.g., 2005).[1] In this model the ultimate ancestor of modern humans was *Homo erectus*, who lived in Africa 1.8 million years ago and moved to other parts of the world. From their ancestors, modern humans developed independently in various regions.

The human fossil record points to an anatomically modern human at possibly 195,000 years ago. These are the remains found at Omo Kibish, in Ethiopia (see, e.g., Sisk & Shea 2008). In Europe, the Middle East, and Asia, younger early modern humans have been found, for example, 100,000 BP at the Skhul and Qazfah caves. What the genetics and the

---

1. There are other accounts that humans developed in similar ways outside of Africa too (see, e.g., Morwood & van Oosterzee 2007). In Asia, for instance in Indonesia, very old prehuman and early human remains have been found.

archeology confirm is where language may have originated and how it spread (although there are huge gaps in the fossil record), not what it looked like.

What can linguistics contribute to the picture of early language? Genetic and areal linguistics might be the places to start. Genetic linguistics provides insights into linguistic relationships, and areal linguistics shows which features are typical for a particular area. Genetic linguistic groupings such as the four families in Africa and the three in the Americas are much contested (see the criticism Greenberg received throughout his life). The only superfamily that has been constructed is Nostratic (with Eurasiatic as alternative), and this reconstruction is not without problems (see the debates between Ruhlen and Manaster-Ramer, for instance). Many linguists think it is unlikely that we can reconstruct beyond these so we won't get insight into the early shape of language from genetic reconstruction.

Areal linguistics might tell us where language could have started if features remained constant in an area. However, Nichols (1992) and the *World Atlas of Language Structures* by Haspelmath et al. (2006) show us more about recent trends that languages in proximity undergo than about original features. So neither genetic nor areal linguistics help us. Recently, a group of linguists has started to explore what is called "complexity" (Miestamo, Sinnemäki, & Karlsson 2008; Sampson, Gil, & Trudgill 2009), though these linguists draw no clear conclusions for language evolution. Another group is examining the language of hunter-gatherers (see Güldemann, McConvell, & Rhodes. forthcoming). What has come out of these discussions are tendencies, not pictures of linguistic systems; for example, Comrie (2009) finds variable word order, initial interrogatives, and subject clitics to be common among hunter-gatherer languages. The search for differences between preliterate and literate languages has not given us insight either since many preliterate languages are extremely complex and vice versa.

In this chapter, I briefly review what (historical) syntax has to say. I argue that recurrent processes in language change provide us some insight into the original state of human language. Grammaticalization and cyclical change are such easily observable processes in the history of languages that they can be seen as involved in the evolution of language from its earliest stage to the present. I agree with Heine and Kuteva (2007: 30) that the "processes of language change were the same in the past as they are in the present." There are many views on the shape of early language. The one most compatible with the cyclical changes explained in this book is that it was analytical.[2] Early authors who agree with this include Humboldt (1836); the current proponent is Bickerton (1990). There is another view, as in Schlegel (1806), which holds that suffixes were there from the beginning. A modern variant of this view is that protolanguage was holophrastic, and evolved out of animal calls (e.g., Wray 1998) that were reanalyzed as synthetic sequences. Many variants exist, such as that proposed by Gil (2005), who argues that an early stage in language evolution was isolating, monocategorial, and associational.

In the next section, I turn to the importance of Merge, the recursive mechanism so typical of human language.[3]

---

2. Confusingly, some authors use *synthetic* for this stage to indicate opposition to the view that language was holophrastic.

3. Some of the next section appears as van Gelderen (2009d).

2. Merge

Starting in the 1950s, Chomsky and the generative model he develops present an alternative to then current behaviorist and structuralist frameworks. Chomsky focuses not on the structures present in the language and outside world but on the mind of a language learner/user. The input to language learning is seen as poor (the "poverty of the stimulus" argument) since speakers know so much more than what they have evidence for in their input. How do we know so much on the basis of such impoverished data? The answer to this problem, Plato's problem in Chomsky (1986a), is Universal Grammar, the initial state of the faculty of language, a biologically innate organ. Universal Grammar helps the learner make sense of the data and build up an internal grammar.

Initially, many principles were attributed to Universal Grammar but currently (e.g., Chomsky 2004, 2005, 2007), there is an emphasis on principles not specific to the faculty of language, to Universal Grammar, but to "general properties of organic systems" (Chomsky 2004: 105), also called "third factor principles" in Chomsky (2005). A consensus is therefore emerging that the faculty of language relies on much that is not specific to language and this is due to how it evolved. Chomsky (2007: 7) says that syntactic Merge is an operation that can be seen as one possibly "appropriated from other systems." A non-Minimalist, but similar, view is that of Givón (2002: 3), who argues that "a large chunk of the neurology that supports human language processing is an evolutionary outgrowth of the primate visual-information system."

Although Merge could possibly have been appropriated from other systems, Hauser, Chomsky, and Fitch (2002) argue that recursion sets human language apart from animal communication and Chomsky (2005: 11) specifies this further by saying that Merge, linking two elements, was the "'Great Leap Forward' in the evolution of humans." Likewise, Piattelli-Palmarini and Uriagereka (2005) emphasize the role of recursion and Merge. Some principles follow for free from Merge and some from general cognitive principles. The emergence of Merge brings with it certain relations such as complements (merged once with a head), specifiers (merged twice), heads (initiator of Merge), and c-command. What drives Merge is the edge features on the heads. An understanding of these, to me, still needs refining and I therefore pay little attention to them. Heads, complements, and specifiers in turn define argument structure or thematic structure. The thematic layer is one aspect of language evolution. I argue that grammaticalization was the other step responsible for markings in the grammatical layer. Typical grammaticalizations are adverbs starting to function as deictic markers, verbs as markers of aspect, and pronouns as agreement morphemes. These changes can be seen in terms of cognitive economy, namely semantically 'lighter' elements over 'heavier' ones.

Within the Minimalist Program (Chomsky 1995, 2004, 2007), there is a narrow syntax (with Merge) and mappings to two interfaces, the sensorimotor interface, PHON, and the conceptual-intentional one, SEM. As mentioned, Chomsky has suggested that some rewiring of the brain, a small mutation or the result of one, brought about Merge. "The individual so endowed [with Merge] would have the ability to think, plan, interpret, and so on." Then, "[a]t some stage modes of externalization were contrived" (Chomsky 2007: 14). Phonology and morphology are involved in the externalization and highly varied since there would be no universal principles involved unlike with Merge.

Work on animal communication has shown that animals use symbols. Bickerton (1990) and Calvin and Bickerton (2000) have argued that animal communication probably uses thematic structure, but no recursion of structures, that is, Merge. We know that some animals have an impressive set of sounds, but not a large vocabulary. The vocabulary develops after sounds are abundant enough (see Carstairs-McCarthy 1999). Tomasello et al. (2007) have shown that nonhuman primates don't use pointing to draw attention to locations but that it's innate in humans (and possibly dogs).

Chomsky entertains both the possibility that syntax was "inserted into already existing external systems," namely PHON and SEM (Chomsky 2002: 108), and that externalization develops after Merge (Chomsky 2007: 13–14). Figure 10.2 shows the three components of human language. Merge appears after SEM and PHON are already developed, and subsequently grammaticalization creates more syntax and grammatical categories. In addition to this, there is a lexical component as well, of course, that provides a link between SEM and PHON without the computational system.

Merge comes in two kinds, internal and external Merge. Chomsky (2005: 14) suggests that external Merge is relevant to the argument structure, whereas internal Merge is relevant for scope and discourse phenomena, as in figure figure 10.3. The longest utterance that Nim, a chimpanzee trained by Terrace in the 1970s, uttered is apparently (1).

(1)   Give orange me give eat orange me eat orange give me eat orange give me you.

This sentence obviously has thematic structure, but this is not expressed in the hierarchical way that human language is. It also has a very basic set of categories. The introduction of (external) Merge helped organize the thematic structure in human language. In many languages, marking the thematic positions is done through pure Merge (e.g., Chinese and English), but in some languages, inherent Case and adpositions mark thematic roles (e.g., Sanskrit, Latin, Malayalam, Japanese, Tagalog). This special marking has come about through grammaticalization of location to Case markers (see, e.g., chapter 5). Definiteness and specificity are the second aspect that needs to be marked. Many languages use internal Merge for this purpose (movement to a subject position indicates specificity). The differences between the two kinds of Merge are listed in figure figure 10.3.

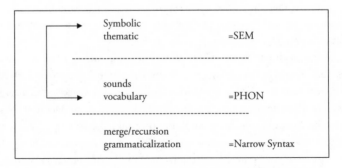

FIGURE 10.2. The separate systems of the faculty of language

Merge:	External Merge	-	Internal Merge
	=		=
	Theta		Discourse/Grammar
Grammaticalized through:			
	adpositions/inherent Case		definiteness
	word order in the VP		displacement

FIGURE 10.3. The two kinds of Merge

Austronesian languages that mark Topic show a difference in morphology for the two systems of Merge. As is well known, Tagalog marks its topic through *ang*. This topic marker is a definiteness marker as well (technically, only *a-* is, and *-ng* is a ligature linking the article to the noun, according to Frawley 1976). The other markers *ng* (actor, patient, or instrument) and *sa* (goal, source, location, or benefactive) mark the theta roles of the nontopics, and derive from location markers (Finney 1999).

(2) *b-um-ili* **ng** *kotse* **ang** *lalake*   Tagalog
    AF-PF-buy P   car   TP   man
    'The man bought a car.' (Frawley 1976: 106)

This picture suggests that syntax and morphology evolved independently. Some, such as Jackendoff (2002: 260), have argued that they are therefore separate systems. Bobaljik (2006) too has agreement adding features after narrow syntax. I will argue that external Merge emerged first, followed by internal Merge. Grammaticalization affected both, however.

Apart from Merge, there are "atomic elements, lexical items LI, each a structured array of properties (*features*)" (Chomsky 2007: 6). Each language learner selects the features compatible with the input. Thus, the features are parameterized, not the syntax. The main kinds of features involve Case (T features), agreement (phi features), and displacement to subject position (EPP or OCC). The features come in different types: semantic, interpretable, and uninterpretable. I suggest that the uninterpretable features were not present during the stage at which Merge appeared originally. Currently, within Minimalism, there are edge features as well, as mentioned earlier. Where earlier Chomsky argues that phase heads "may have" displacement features, in later work edge features on all heads drive the derivation. Languages closer to the protolanguage will have external Merge but there is no reason they would have move and agree, though Newmeyer (2000: 385, note 4) suggests that protolanguages may have been inflectional. My focus on grammaticalization as a process responsible for morphology assumes that inflection arises later.

So the first step in the evolution of syntax is the appearance of Merge. It brings with it notions of headedness (once you merge two elements, one determines the resulting label) and binarity. These notions also determine possible argument structures. The next step is for grammatical heads, such as auxiliaries and prepositions, to appear.

3. Grammaticalization and Language Evolution

As I argued, Merge could have been the first step in creating syntax from a stage that consisted of either words or gestures (e.g., Corballis 2002), and as Traugott (2004: 134) puts it as "an exaptation of thematic role structure." This section provides a scenario for subsequent steps. Bickerton (1990) assumes there was a stage between protolanguage and full-fledged language that has negation, question words, the lexical modals *can* and *may*, expressions of place, and quantifiers. He stresses wisely that most of our speculations are "conjectural." Heine and Kuteva (2007) suggest layers of lexical and grammatical categories and take nouns and verbs to be "evolutionary primitives" (2007: 59). I assume that as well.

Once external Merge applies, certain structural and thematic relationships start to crystallize between nouns and verbs, unlike those obvious in (1), uttered by Nim. Chomsky (2007) talks about edge features as determining what merges externally, and at the vP level, this is probably determined by thematic features. Thus a V selects a DP to merge and a (little) v a VP (in which a DP with a specific theta role occurs). The vP represents the thematic level, and one that adult native speakers employ when they speak or write in "fragments," as in (3a). Children reach this stage too, as (3b) shows and as I discussed in chapter 1, though they understand grammatical categories before they produce them.

(3) a. Work in progress
     b. like a cookie (Abe, 3.7)

So thematic roles are initially marked through basic word order, but this makes complex sentences really hard. There appear other ways to mark thematic structure, for instance, adpositions or inherent case (Chomsky 1986a: 193), as in (4), with a dative as a goal theta role.

(4) *þæt* *he* **sæmann-um** *onsacan* *mihte*
     that he sailors-DAT strive-against might
     'that he might strive against the sailors' (*Beowulf*, 2954, in Klaeber [1922] 1941)

This inherent Case can be argued to be derived through grammaticalization of adpositions (see chapter 5) and used for another reason.

How do grammatical elements relevant to tense, aspect, specificity, and definiteness arise? Feature Economy provides an answer. Lexical items are rich in semantic features but these categories can also be reanalyzed to mark a more abstract time and place, as we have seen happen. There is no absolute need for these markers to arise. A language where definiteness is expressed by preposing is Chinese, as is well known from the work by Li and Thompson (1978). See (5), repeated from (12) in chapter 1.

(5) a. *chi* *le* **fan**   Chinese
        eat PF rice
        'I ate some rice.'

b. ***fan***   *chi*   *le*
    rice   eat   PF

    'I ate the rice.' (Yi Ting Chen, p.c.)

Definite time adverbials also precede the verb whereas durative ones follow in Chinese. There are other languages, however, in which such grammatical functions are not purely achieved through movement but through grammatical elements. They develop when one feature of a lexical element is emphasized over others (hence the slight semantic loss). Similar data exist for other complementizers as well as CP adverbs and auxiliaries.

I have portrayed this as if the language had a mind of its own, which is obviously not the case. We know that children's language suddenly becomes more complex around two years of age. Bickerton (1990) would say that their latent protolanguage is replaced by a language, as long as they have input during the critical period. The stage where nouns and verbs (with semantic features) are "recruited" into functional elements (with interpretable and uninterpretable features) is one that we have seen in cyclical change and also in language acquisition (in chapter 1). I review now how the three principles discussed in this book (HPP, LMP, and FE) are responsible for language evolution beyond Merge.

If the thematic stage has nouns and verbs, these can be reanalyzed as, for instance, adpositions and auxiliaries, respectively, by the LMP but also through using the item with fewer features, as in (6). The two sets of features can both continue to be used.

(6)   a.   'house'   >   'house'   (N to P)
          [3S]   [u-phi]
          [place, live]   [i/u-place]
      b.   'go'   >   'go'   (V to AUX)
          [motion, forward]   [i/u-future]

The adposition and auxiliary in turn can be reanalyzed.

Once an element has reached the stage of uninterpretable features, it looks for another element that provides the interpretable features. Sometimes, these "renewals" are innovations from inside the language, as in the case of the Old English negative DP *na wiht* 'no creature' to mark negation, but other times, these renewals are borrowed through contact with other languages. One such possible borrowing is the introduction into English of the *wh*-relative. In Old English, there are a number of relative strategies, but by early Middle English, the complementizers *þat* and *þe* are typical. This is predicted under the HPP since those forms are heads (see van Gelderen 2004: 83–87). By later Middle English, this form is competing with the *wh*-pronoun still existing in present-day English (be it mainly in written English). Mustanoja (1960) cites Latin influence for the introduction of the *wh*-pronoun. Romaine (1982) shows that the introduction of the *wh*-pronouns was stylistically influenced, and Rydén (1983) shows both Latin and French influence. The first instances of *who* occur in epistolary idioms that are very similar to those in French letters of the same period. For instance, in many of the collections of letters from the fifteenth century, the same English and French formulaic constructions occur, such as in (7a) from Bekynton and (7b) from the *Paston Letters*:

(7) a. *a laide de Dieu notre Seigneur,* **Qui** *vous douit bonne vie et longue.*
     with the-help of God our lord, who us gives good life and long
     'with the help of God, our Lord, who gives us a good and long life' (Bekynton,
     from Rydén 1983: 131)
   b. *be the grace of God,* **who** *haue yow in kepyng*
     'by the grace of God, who keeps you' (*Paston Letters*, 410, in Davis 1971)

The *wh*-pronoun is in the specifier position (since it can pied pipe a preposition and is inflected).

In this section, I have suggested that the emergence of syntax could have followed the path that current grammaticalization also follows. The merging of nouns and verbs brings with it a set of relations. Economy Principles reanalyze the structures and lexical items. These Economy Principles are responsible for what is traditionally called grammaticalization but can also be seen as building new grammatical items.

4. Conclusion

I have discussed two steps that are required in the evolution from presyntactic language to language as we currently know it. The one is Merge and the structural and thematic relations it entails to build a basic lexical layer (the VP). The second consists of the Economy Principles that enable learners to choose more economical lexical items and to expand the lexical categories. These principles result in what is known as grammaticalization and build the nonlexical layers (the TP and CP). Grammaticalization leads to renewal (and cyclical change) and the FE results in lexical items with uninterpretable features. These become probes and find other elements that supply semantic material. This principle allows the speaker to creatively include new material, for example, as negative reinforcement in special stylistic circumstances.

It is thus possible to formulate economy in terms of features and incorporate the HPP and LMP into FE: the computational load is less when semantic or interpretable features are not included in the derivation. Full phrases have more features (to check) and they are more likely to be interpretable. Apart from the preference for heads, there is also a preference for positions higher in the tree, in other words, merged later in the derivation. For instance, a PP base generated in the VP can come to be used as a sentence connector. These changes too can be accounted for through computational economy: the lower (externally merged) element in the tree has more semantic features whereas the grammatical/functional element has uninterpretable features (uF). Thus, this approach eliminates the "imperfection" of uF.

What does this tell us about the shape of the original language? The emergence of syntax followed the path that current change also follows, one that children take acquiring the language. Chomsky (2002: 113) sees the semantic component as expressing thematic as well as discourse information. If thematic structure was already present in protolanguage (Bickerton 1990), the evolutionary change of Merge made them linguistic. What was added through grammaticalization is the morphology, the second (grammatical) and third (pragmatic) layers of information.

11

CONCLUSIONS

IN THIS BOOK, I have examined a number of linguistic cycles. The linguistic cycle can be seen as grammaticalization followed by renewal of a similar feature followed by grammaticalization and so on. Thus, agreement in many languages is lost and renewed by pronouns that are in turn reanalyzed as agreement. I use the word *cycle* to emphasize that these changes are unidirectional and they are caused by internal factors, that is, principles the language learner/user employs. The renewed item doesn't have to be identical to the eroded one and typically isn't. The cycles that are most robust are the agreement, definiteness, and negative cycles.

Patterns of where these cycles start and how they are renewed show which features are relevant to the particular grammatical phenomenon. In this book, I have identified and examined a few such patterns (though some of these were known before). I hope to contribute to descriptions of several cycles in a variety of languages and language families and types. The families looked at in some detail are Afro-Asiatic (especially for the negative, copula, object agreement, and DP cycles), Altaic (regarding dependent marking), Athabascan (mainly for the object agreement cycle and the negative cycle), Austronesian (for the object agreement and DP cycles), creoles (for the subject and object agreement, the DP, negative, and copula cycles), Indo-European (for subject and object agreement, dependent marking, the DP cycle, TMA, and negatives), Niger-Congo (agreement and DP cycles), Pama-Nyungan (subject agreement), Salish (the DP cycle), Sino-Tibetan as represented by varieties of Chinese (for the copula, object marking, and negative cycles), Uralic (negatives and DPs), and Uto-Aztecan (the subject and object agreement cycles and the DP one).

In section 1, I review the different cycles discussed in chapters 2 to 8. In section 2, I highlight the major findings with respect to the triggers and features. In section 3, I discuss parameters and language evolution, and in section 4, I provide a list of specific findings. Section 5 covers the picture of language change that the book presents. The limitations and areas for future research are sketched in section 6.

1. The Cycles

Cross-linguistically, the grammatical subject and object are often marked by agreement, and cyclical change involving agreement is extremely common. The subject agreement cycle has the clearest patterns of triggers and renewal. For instance, as shown in chapter 2, the change from an Old French pronoun to the colloquial French agreement marker is an instance of a full cycle, and one where the trigger is first (and second) person. The explanation I provide is that the features of first and second person (singular and plural) subject pronouns are very similar to those on the verb, that is, the phi features in the T position, and are therefore reanalyzed as agreement. Third person pronouns have features in addition to phi features and are therefore less easily reanalyzed.

There are languages that do not show agreement on the verb (Mandarin, Korean, and Japanese) and where the subject is optional. These are topic-oriented languages and possibly have no subject argument. I have found no evidence that these languages undergo the agreement cycle. The presence of the topic position without a structural subject position would make them similar to, for instance, the Athabascan languages.

Object cycles are also frequent cross-linguistically, but which nominals start the cycle is less uniform. Chapter 3 shows that the definite or animate object is the most frequent initiator of this change. In some languages it is the third person while in others it is first and second person. The sources for renewal are therefore new pronouns.

The copula cycle shares some characteristics with the subject cycle since demonstrative pronouns are reanalyzed as the copula verb. Copulas have locational features that can be renewed by verbs of position, prepositions, and demonstratives. I have focused on renewals by the demonstrative.

The Case cycle is extremely complex, as discussed in chapter 5, since marking on dependents can be used to mark semantic/thematic and grammatical (and to a lesser extent pragmatic) information. These different functions are reflected in different grammaticalization paths: lexical items such as verbs, nouns, and adverbs provide the source for semantic marking, whereas demonstratives and aspect markers can provide the source of renewal for the grammatical dependent markers. I have not looked in much detail at the origin of pragmatic markers but they seem to be similar to those of grammatical markers.

In chapter 6, I examine the definiteness cycle that contributes to both grammatical and pragmatic marking. The cycle is clear and some instances of full cycles are recorded, for instance, in Germanic. The demonstrative pronoun is reanalyzed as definiteness marker and then renewed through a new deictic/locative marker.

Minor cycles involve markers of tense, mood, aspect, and negation. In chapter 7, I look at a broad range of lexical and grammatical phenomena involving TMA marking and note that certain cycles are extremely common. Aspect can be expressed on the verb or through an adverb, and full cycles are evident in Germanic, Athabascan, and Pomoan. Future cycles prevail as well, as in Romance and Hindi/Urdu. I suggest a feature-based account for the reanalysis of demonstratives as complementizers marking (finite) tense and of prepositions as temporal complementizers. The renewal of these complementizers is related to a number of changes driven by the grammaticalization of deictic elements. It has been discussed in chapters 1, 5, as well as 7 and more detail can be found in van Gelderen (2009a).

Of all the cycles, the negative one is no doubt the best known. In chapter 8, I discuss a number of full cycles from negative argument to negative adverb to zero and from negative verb to aspect marker to loss and renewal. Indo-European and Semitic show many instances of the first kind of cycle, renewal by a negative indefinite. Chinese shows renewal through verbs and Uralic and Athabascan show evidence of an early verbal pattern but are now experiencing renewal through indefinites.

2. Triggers and Features

There are two major types of grammaticalization, those reanalyzing full phrases to words to affixes and those reanalyzing lexical items to grammatical ones. Both involve a change from semantic to formal features. The main features I have looked at are phi features, deictic features (abbreviated [loc]/[time]), negative, and question features. Since heads such as T are probes, they typically have uninterpretable phi features, and will be looking for another element with interpretable phi features to agree with. The latter elements are therefore typically full phrases such as full pronouns or nouns. The agreement cycle is driven by the phi features of both T and the nominal.

Phi features can be divided in person, number, and gender and the complexity of the features, or rather lack thereof, may be the trigger for the start of the agreement cycle. Deictic features drive the dependent-marking cycle, or rather cycles. I distinguish three kinds of dependent marking: semantic, grammatical, and pragmatic. Grammatical Case is related to specificity marking and derives from a deictic source through a demonstrative. The change from semantic to grammatical Case is not literally such a change, even though it is often portrayed that way. Semantic Case may be lost (as happened in Old English) and a new marker may arise that we call Case for convenience; its source is always lexical (N or V).

The negative cycle involves negative features. Languages vary if the negative marker in the NegP has interpretable or uninterpretable features. In the latter case, interpretable or semantic features have to appear as well. Tense, mood, and aspect features still require some elaboration in the Minimalist framework (e.g., for an account of affix-hop in English). I show that, like negative features, TMA features vary cross-linguistically in whether or not the marker in the TP, MP, and ASPP has interpretable or uninterpretable features. Table 11.1 lists the features discussed in this book.

One of the problems, mentioned in chapters 1, 7, and 9, is that there are so many possible combinations of features. A more restrictive theory needs to take into account languages that seem to rely on heads (polysynthetic languages) with only interpretable features and those where cycles do not rely on phi features at all (Chinese). The features determine the (grammatical) categories. For instance, a category with interpretable deictic as well as phi features is a demonstrative.

Chomsky (1995 and later) argues for the notion of numeration and transfer of a phase on the basis of lessening the computational load. The numeration is needed so that elements can be selected from the lexicon and the lexicon need not stay accessible during the derivation. In addition, once a chunk (a phase) is ready it is also no longer accessible. When we list a numeration, we put words down, but technically the items in the numeration are feature

TABLE 11.1

Grammatical Features and Their Sources

[u-F] and [i-F]	[T] on C + T	[T] on D	[phi] on T, V, and N	[Q]	[NEG]
Semantic features as source	[loc] [time]	[loc]	[person, number, gender]	[wh] [negative]	[negative]

bundles only. Throughout the book, I have assumed that learners build up the lexical items in their mental lexicon first by including semantic and interpretable features. As their language develops they include items with uninterpretable features, sometimes through grammaticalizing items they already know. Data from language acquisition can provide insight as to what is interpretable or not. For instance, children acquire the *–ing* on verbs very fast as well as the plural on nouns. That suggests these are interpretable for them. Agreement on the verb can be quite late, as expected if those features are not salient.

3. Parameters, Cycles, and Language Evolution

We need an account for typological differences, especially the stages of the various cycles, using a (feature) parametric approach. In this book, I assume that there are two macroparameters (very similar to Baker's 2008a approach). They can be put as follows: does a language have agreement and does it have structural case? These are feature macroparameters; see figure 9.6. Even though Nichols (1992) suggests that head and dependent marking occur almost equally cross-linguistically, I think they are very different types of marking, which is reflected in the figure. The head-marking phi features are therefore different from the dependent-marking deictic features. As Comrie (1981) has put it, dependent marking is used to mark something extraordinary (e.g., inanimate subjects) whereas agreement marks the expected subject or object.

The minor cycles will have feature choices based on whether or not the negative or definiteness marker connected to the NegP and DP have interpretable or uninterpretable features (i.e., whether they are in the Spec of head position of their respective functional category). The choice of these is triggered by direct evidence in the language.

I argue that cyclical unidirectional changes give us insight into the question of language evolution. Grammar relies on a semantic core that is its argument structure, and humans most likely had that in a prelanguage stage. Grammaticalization helped situate the arguments in space and time by reanalyzing lexical items as functional or grammatical ones.

4. Specific Findings

In this section, I list some of my findings. The ones specifically relevant to cycles appear in (1) through (9).

1. In the languages I explore, the subject cycle starts with first and second person. Number seems not to influence this. The cycle is driven by phi features.

2. The object cycle does not start as uniformly as the subject cycle. It is driven by animacy or deictic features.

3. Polysynthetic languages do not employ uninterpretable phi features, a condition that distinguishes them from others. It has sometimes been claimed that Romance languages are changing to polysynthetic ones but, if we look carefully at the changes they are undergoing discussed in chapter 2, they are not.

4. Copulas consist of locative features. They therefore grammaticalize from three sources: demonstratives, locative verbs, and adpositions.

5. Dependent marking of grammatical roles is definiteness marking.

6. Differential object marking is (still) a mysterious phenomenon. There is some evidence that it is really definiteness marking. Differential subject marking does not exist.

7. Inherent Case is represented by interpretable features such as time and place. Structural uninterpretable Case on subjects is checked by T (as in Pesetsky & Torrego 2001) and on objects by ASP/v.

8. The position of the NegP is variable. Cyclical change indicates that there is perhaps always a polarity phrase in the expanded CP since negatives are often reanalyzed as very high question markers.

9. Cross-linguistically, TMA cycles are very varied. They rely on adverbs, PPs, and demonstratives.

10. Pronouns such as *he* and *hi* in Old English were not the same referentially independent entities as they are today. They are renewed in late Old English, possibly through contact with another language. Currently, they again show signs of grammaticalization.

11. Arguments have semantic roles but that is not enough. They also need to be located in time and place; that's what Case and tense do.

5. Language Change

As mentioned in chapter 1, language change comes from "inside" the language faculty, not from the outside. The internal Economy Principles, such as Feature Economy, drive grammaticalization and ultimately the cycles. Cycles are the result of reanalysis by the language learner and of renewal. I argue that the real sources of change are internal principles that bias the learner toward certain structures.

As should be obvious from the preceding chapters, I take grammaticalization and renewal—the linguistic cycle—as excellent tools to describe and understand language change and the language faculty. Within a generative approach, grammaticalization is often said to be an epiphenomenon. Linguists also often deny that language change is unidirectional. I agree with neither view.

The speed of the changes is highly variable in different languages. If they are driven by internal Economy Principles, one might expect fast cyclical change. This is where external factors play a role, the need for cross-generational communication being one of these.

6. Limitations

There are a few limitations to this framework, although they are not all unique to it.

First, in a cartographic approach (Cinque 1999), the features to be relied on are not spelled out very well. My analysis suffers from the same problem, especially when I am examining mood and aspect. However, the book does identify [loc], [time], and [ps] as important semantic features. All languages have semantic features but not all grammaticalize these.

For good reasons, I have made no commitments as to which grammatical or formal features are needed in grammar. The macroparameters I suggest in, for instance, figure 9.6 can be set for no phi features and no Case. Languages such as Chinese might fall in this category.

Second, within the person features, I have not clearly differentiated first and second person features since I am not sure what distinguishes them empirically.

Third, the need for dependent marking and Case is mysterious. It can indicate semantic, grammatical, and pragmatic roles. It is not clear to me why we need grammatical markings at all: semantic and pragmatic roles should suffice. If, as in Chomsky (2005), we are asking why language is the way it is, this is not clear.

References

Aalberse, Suzanne. 2009. Inflectional Economy and Politeness. Dissertation, University of Amsterdam.

Aboh, Enoch. 2003. On the Right Peripheral Typing Morphemes: The Case of Negation in Gbe (Kwa). Ms.

Abraham, Werner. 1997. The Interdependence of Case, Aspect, and Referentiality in the History of German: The Case of the Genitive. In Ans van Kemenade & Nigel Vincent (eds.), *Parameters of Morphosyntactic Change*, 29–61. Cambridge: Cambridge University Press.

Abraham, Werner. 2002. Substandard German *tun* as an Auxiliary and Its Structural Implications. In W. Bublitz et al. (eds.), *Philologie, Typologie und Sprachstruktur: Festschrift für Winfried Boeder zum 65. Geburtstag*, 225–240. Frankfurt: Peter Lang.

Abraham, Werner. 2003. Autonomous and Non-Autonomous Components of 'Grammatic(Al)ization': Economy Criteria in the Emergence of German Negation. *Sprachtypologie und Universalienforschung (STUF)* 56.4: 325–365.

Abraham, Werner. 2007. Introduction. In Daniel Hole et al. (eds.), *Datives and Other Cases*, 3–46. Amsterdam: John Benjamins.

Abraham, Werner & Jac Conradie. 2001. *Präteritumschwund und Diskursgrammatik*. Amsterdam: John Benjamins.

Abraham, Werner & Elisabeth Leiss. 2007. On the Interfaces between (Double) Definiteness, Aspect, and Word Order in Old and Modern Scandinavian. *Working Papers in Scandinavian Syntax* 80: 17–44.

Abraham, Werner & Elisabeth Leiss. 2008. Introduction. In Werner Abraham & Elisabeth Leiss (eds.), *Modality Aspect Interfaces*, xi–xxiv. Amsterdam: John Benjamins.

Adger, David & Gillian Ramchand. 2003. Predication and Equation. *Linguistic Inquiry* 34.3: 325–359.

Agbador, Paul. 1994. Verb Serialization in Ewe. *Nordic Journal of African Studies* 3.1: 115–135. Available at http://www.njas.helsinki.fi/pdf-files/vol3num1/agbedor.pdf.

Aikhenvald, Alexandra. 2003. *The Tariana Language of Northwest Amazonia*. Cambridge: Cambridge University Press.

Aissen, Judith. 2003. Differential Object Marking: Iconicity or Economy. *Natural Language and Linguistic Theory* 21: 435–483.

Akhtar, Raja Nasim. 1999. Aspectual Complex Predicates in Punjabi. Dissertation, University of Essex.

Allen, Cynthia. 1977. Topics in Diachronic English Syntax. Dissertation, University of Massachusetts.

Allen, Cynthia. 1995. *Case Marking and Reanalysis*. Oxford: Clarendon Press.

Allen, Cynthia. 2005. Changes in Case Marking in NP. In Mengistu Amberber & Helen de Hoop (eds.), *Competition and Variation in Natural Languages*, 223–250. Amsterdam: Elsevier.

Allen, Cynthia. 2007. The Case of the Genitive in the *Peterborough Continuations*. In Alexander Bergs & Janne Skaffari (eds.), *The Language of the Peterborough Chronicle*, 77–92. Frankfurt: Peter Lang.

Amberber, Mengistu. 2005. Differential Subject Marking in Amharic. In Mengistu Amberber & Helen de Hoop (eds.), *Competition and Variation in Natural Languages*, 295–320. Amsterdam: Elsevier.

Andersen, Henning. 1987. From Auxiliary to Desinence. In Martin Harris & Paolo Ramat (eds.), *Historical Development of Auxiliaries*, 21–52. Berlin: Mouton de Gruyter.

Andersen, Henning. 2008. Grammaticalization in a Speaker-Oriented Theory of Change. In Thórhallur Eythórsson (ed.), *Grammatical Change and Linguistic theory: The Rosendal Papers*, 11–44. Amsterdam: John Benjamins.

Anderson, Stephen. 1992. *A-morphous Morphology*. Cambridge: Cambridge University Press.

Anderson, Stephen. 2005. *Aspects of the Theory of Clitics*. Oxford: Oxford University Press.

Andrew, Malcolm & Ronald Waldron (eds.). 1978. *The Poems of the Pearl Manuscript*. Berkeley: University of California Press.

Andrews, Avery. 1985. The Major Functions of the Noun Phrase. In Timothy Shopen (ed.), *Language Typology and Syntactic Description* 1: 62–154. Cambridge: Cambridge University Press.

Anttila, Raimo. 1989. *Historical and Comparative Linguistics*. Amsterdam: John Benjamins.

Antonsen, Elmer. 1975. *A Concise Grammar of the Older Runic Inscriptions*. Tübingen: Niemeyer.

Arends, Jacques. 1986. Genesis and Development of the Equative Copula in Sranan. In Pieter Muysken et al. (eds.), *Substrata versus Universals in Creole Genesis*, 103–127. Amsterdam: John Benjamins.

Armendáriz, Rolando Félix. 2007. *A Grammar of River Warihío*. Munich: Lincom Europa.

Ariel, Mira. 1990. *Accessing NP Antecedents*. London: Croom Helm.

Ariel, Mira. 2000. The Development of Person Agreement Markers. In Michael Barlow & Suzanne Kemmer, *Usage-based Models of Language*, 197–260. Stanford: CSLI Publications.

Aristar, Anthony. 1997. Marking and Hierarchy Types and the Grammaticalization of Case-Markers. *Studies in Language* 21.2: 313–368.

Asbury, Anna. 2008. The Morphosyntax of Case and Adpositions. Dissertation, Utrecht University.

Assmann, Bruno. [1889] 1964. *Angelsächsische Homilien u. Heiligenleben*. Darmstadt: Wissenschaftliche Buchgesellschaft.

Auer, Peter. 2004. Non-standard Evidence in Syntactic Typology. In Bernd Kortmann (ed.), *Dialectology Meets Typology*, 69–92. Berlin: Mouton de Gruyter.

Auger, Julie. 1994. Pronominal Clitics in Québec Colloquial French. Dissertation, University of Pennsylvania.

Austin, Jennifer & Luis Lopez. 1995. Nominative, Absolutive and Dative Languages. *Proceedings of the North East Linguistic Society* 25: 1–15.

Axel, Katrin. 2007. *Studies on Old High German Syntax*. Amsterdam: John Benjamins.

Axelsson, Margareta. 1998. *Contraction in British Newspapers in the Late 20th Century*. Dissertation, Uppsala University.

Babaev, Kirill. 2008. Personal Pronoun Origins. *LinguistList* 19.2189.

Baerman, Matthew & Dunstan Brown. 2008. Syncretism in Verbal Person/Number Marking. In Martin Haspelmath et al. (eds.), *The World Atlas of Language Structures Online*, chapter 29. Munich: Max Planck Digital Library. Available at http://wals.info/feature/29.

Bahloul, Maher. 1996. Extending the NegP Hypothesis: Evidence from Standard Arabic. In Mushira Eid (ed.), *Perspectives on Arabic Linguistics VIII: Papers from the Third Annual Symposium on Arabic Linguistics*, 31–46. Amsterdam: John Benjamins.

Bailey, Beryl Loftman. 1966. *Jamaican Creole Syntax*. Cambridge: Cambridge University Press.

Bailey, Beryl Loftman. 1971. Can Dialect Boundaries Be Defined? In Dell Hymes (ed.), *Pidginization and Creolization of Languages*, 341–348. Cambridge: Cambridge University Press.

Baker, Mark. 1988. *Incorporation: A Theory of Grammatical Function Changing*. Chicago: University of Chicago Press.

Baker, Mark 1989. Object Sharing and Projection in Serial Verb Constructions. *Linguistic Inquiry* 20: 513–543.

Baker, Mark. 1995. *The Polysynthesis Parameter*. Oxford: Oxford University Press.

Baker, Mark. 2001. *The Atoms of Language*. New York: Basic Books.

Baker, Mark. 2003. Agreement, Dislocation, and Partial Configurationality. In Andrew Carnie et al. (eds.), *Formal Approaches to Function in Grammar*, 107–132. Amsterdam: John Benjamins.

Baker, Mark. 2008a. *The Syntax of Agreement and Concord*. Cambridge: Cambridge University Press.

Baker, Mark. 2008b. The Macroparameter in a Microparametric World. In Theresa Biberauer (ed.), *The Limits of Syntactic Variation*, 351–374. Amsterdam: John Benjamins.

Baker, Mark. 2009. Agreement Parameters and Modes of Case Assignment. Paper presented at Workshop on Features and Parameters, February, Arizona State University.

Baker, Mark & Osamuyimen Stewart. 1999. On Double-Headedness and the Anatomy of the Clause. Ms. Available at http://rci.rutgers.edu/~mabaker/SVCarch-ss.pdf.

Baker, Robin. 1985. *The Development of the Komi Case System*. Helsinki: Suomalais-Ugrilainen Seura.

Bakker, Dik. 2008. Person Marking on Adpositions. In Martin Haspelmath, Matthew Dryer, David Gil, & Bernard Comrie (eds.), *The World Atlas of Language Structures Online*, chapter 48. Munich: Max Planck Digital Library. Available at http://wals.info/feature/48.

Baltin, Mark. 2004. Remarks on the Relation between Language Typology and Universal Grammar. *Studies in Language* 28.3: 549–553.

Baptista, Marlyse. 2002. *The Syntax of Cape Verdian Creole*. Amsterdam: John Benjamins.

Baptista, Marlyse & Jacqueline Guéron. 2006. *Noun Phrases in Creole Languages*. Amsterdam: John Benjamins.

Barker, Mohammed. 1975. *Spoken Urdu*. 3 vols. Ithaca: Spoken Language Services.

Barker, Mohammed & Aquil Khan Mengal. 1969. *A Course in Baluchi*, 2 vols. Montreal: McGill University Press.

Barry, M. V. 1972. The Morphemic Distribution of the Definite Article in Contemporary Regional English. In M. F. Wakelin (ed.), *Patterns in the Folk Speech of the British Isles*, 164–181. London: Athlone Press.

Bately, Janet. 1980. *The Old English Orosius*. Early English Text Society S.S. 6. Oxford: Oxford University Press.

Bauer, Winifred. 1993. *Maori*. London: Routlege.

Beaumont, Ronald. 1985. *She Shashishalhem, the Sechelt Language: Language, Stories, and Sayings of the Sechelt Indian People of British Columbia*. Penticton: Theytus Books.

Belletti, Adriana. 1988. The Case of Unaccusatives. *Linguistic Inquiry* 19.1: 1–34.

Belletti, Adriana. 2008. Pronouns and the Edge of the Clause. Ms. Available at http://www.ciscl. unisi.it/doc/doc_pub/Book.Pronouns%20and%20the%20edge%20of%20the%20clause.1.pdf.

Benincà, Paola. 2001. The Position of Topic and Focus in the Left Periphery. In Guglielmo Cinque et al. (eds.), *Current Studies in Italian Syntax*, 39–64. Amsterdam: Elsevier.

Benmamoun, Elabbas. 1992. Inflectional and Functional Categories. Dissertation, University of Southern California.

Benmamoun, Elabbas. 1996. Negative Polarity and Presupposition in Arabic. In Mushira Eid (ed.), *Perspectives on Arabic Linguistics VIII: Papers from the Third Annual Symposium on Arabic Linguistics*, 47–66. Amsterdam: John Benjamins.

Benmamoun, Elabbas. 2000. *The Feature Structure of Functional Categories*. New York: Oxford University Press.

Benson, Larry. 1987. *The Riverside Chaucer*. Boston: Houghton Mifflin.

Bentahila, Abdelali & Eirlys Davies. 1983. The Syntax of Arabic-French Code-Switching. *Lingua* 59: 301–330.

Benveniste, Emile. [1966] 1971. *Problèmes de linguistique générale*. Paris: Gallimard.

Benveniste, Emile. 1968. Mutations of Linguistic Categories. In Y. Malkiel & W. P. Lehmann (eds.), *Directions for Historical Linguistics*, 83–94. Austin: University of Texas Press.

Berg, René van den. 1996. The Demise of Focus and the Spread of Conjugated Verbs in Sulawesi. In Hein Steinhauer (ed.), *Papers in Austronesian Linguistics* 3, 89–114. Canberra: Pacific Linguistics.

Bergsland, Knut. 1994. *Sydsamisk grammatik*. Karasjok: Davvi Girji o.s.

Berman, Ruth & Alexander Grosu. 1976. Aspects of the Copula in Modern Hebrew. In Peter Cole (ed.), *Studies in Modern Hebrew Syntax and Semantics*, 265–284. Amsterdam: North Holland.

Berndt, Rolf. 1956. *Form und Funktion des Verbums im nördlichen Spätaltenglischen*. Halle: Max Niemeyer.

Berry, James. 2009. Sentence Adverbs: The Result of Grammaticalization or Lexicalization? Ms. Arizona State University.

Biberauer, Theresa. 2009. Jespersen off Course? In Elly van Gelderen (ed.), *Cyclical Change*, 91–130. Amsterdam: John Benjamins.

Biberauer, Theresa & Marc Richards. 2006. True Optionality: When the Grammar Doesn't Mind. In Cedric Boeckx (ed.), *Minimalist Essays*, 35–67. Amsterdam: John Benjamins.

Bickel, Balthasar & Alena Witzlack-Makarevich. 2008.Referential Scales and Case Alignment: Reviewing the Typological Evidence. In Marc Richards & Andrej Malchukov (eds.), *Scales*, 1–37. Linguistische Arbeits Berichte 86. Available at http://www.uni-leipzig.de/~witzlack/ LAB86_Bickel_Witzlack.pdf.

Bickel, Balthazar, Y. Yadava, & Walter Bisang. 1999. Face vs. Empathy: The Social Foundation of Maithili Verb Agreement. *Linguistics* 37: 481–518.

Bickerton, Derek. 1981. *Roots of Language*. Ann Arbor: Karoma.

Bickerton, Derek. 1990. *Language and Species*. Chicago: University of Chicago Press.

Bickerton, Derek & Aquiles Escalante. 1970. Palenquero: A Spanish-based Creole of Northern Colombia. *Lingua* 32: 254–267.

Binyam. 2008. Aspects of Koorete Verb Morphology. Dissertation, Oslo University.

Bisang, Walter. 1998. The View from the Far East: Comments on Seven Thematic Areas. In Johan Van der Auwera & Dónall P. Ó Baoill (eds.), *Adverbial Constructions in the Languages of Europe*, 641–812. Berlin: Mouton de Gruyter.

Bisang, Walter. 2006. Argumenthood and Syntax in Chinese, Japanese, and Tagalog. In Daniel Hole et al. (eds.), *Datives and Other Cases*, 331–381. Amsterdam: John Benjamins.

Bittner, Maria & Ken Hale. 1996a. The Structural Determination of Case and Agreement. *Linguistic Inquiry* 27.1: 1–68.

Bittner, Maria & Ken Hale. 1996b. Ergativity. *Linguistic Inquiry* 27.4: 531–604.

Blake, Barry. 2001. *Case*. Cambridge: Cambridge University Press.

Blom, Corrien. 2004. On the Diachrony of Complex Predicates in Dutch. *Journal of Germanic Linguistics* 16.1: 1–75.

Bloom, Lois. 1970. *Language Development*. Cambridge: Massachusetts Institute of Technology Press.

Bloom, Lois. 1973. *One Word at a Time*. The Hague: Mouton.

Bobaljik, Jonathan. 2006. Where's Phi? Agreement as a Post-Syntactic Operation. Available at http://web.uconn.edu/bobaljik/papers/Phi.pdf.

Boeckx, Cedric. 2008. *Bare Syntax*. Oxford: Oxford University Press.

Boeckx, Cedric & Kleanthes Grohmann. 2005. Left Dislocation in Germanic. In Werner Abraham (ed.), *Focus on Germanic Typology*, 131–144. Berlin: Akademie.

Boer, R. C. 1920. *Oergermaansch Handboek*. Haarlem: Tjeenk Willink & Zoon.

Bondi Johannessen, Janne. 2000. Negasjonen *ikke*: Kategori of syntaktisk posisjon. Ms. Oslo University.

Bondi Johannessen, Janne. 2006. Just Any Pronoun Anywhere? Pronouns and New Demonstratives in Norwegian. In Torgrim Solstad, Atle Grønn, & Dag Haug (eds.), *A Festschrift for Kjell Johan Sæbø: In Partial Fulfilment for the Requirements for the Celebration of His 50th Birthday*. Oslo: Unipub.

Bonneau, José & Pierre Pica. 1995. On the Development of the Complementation System and Its Relation to Switch Reference. *Proceedings of the North East Linguistic Society* 25: 135–150.

Booij, Geert & Jaap van Marle (eds.). 2003. *Yearbook of Morphology*. Dordrecht: Kluwer.

Bopp, Franz. 1816. *Über das Conjugationssystem der Sanskritsprache in Vergleichung mit jenem der griechischen, lateinischen, persischen und germanischen Sprachen*. Frankfurt.

Bopp, Franz. [1833–1852] 1868. *Vergleichende Grammatik des Sanskrit, Zend, Griechischen, Lateinischen, Litauischen, Gotischen und Deutschen*. 3rd ed. Paris.

Borer, Hagit. 1984. *Parametric Syntax*. Dordrecht: Foris.

Borsley, Robert & Ian Roberts. 1996. Introduction. In Robert Borsley & Ian Roberts (eds.), *The Syntax of the Celtic Languages*, 1–52. Cambridge: Cambridge University Press.

Bossong, Georg. 1985. *Empirische Universalienforschung: Differentielle Objektmarkierung in den neuiranischen Sprachen*. Tübingen: Gunter Narr.

Botha, Rudie & Chris Knight (eds.). 2009. *The Prehistory of Language*. Vol. 1. Oxford: Oxford University Press.

Boucher, Paul. 2003. Determiner Phrases in Old and Modern French. In Martine Coene & Yves D'Hulst (eds.), *From NP to DP*, 1: 47–69. Amsterdam: John Benjamins.

Bowern, Claire. 2008. The Reconstruction of the Nyulnyulan Complex Predication. *Diachronica* 25.2: 186–212.

Brandi, Luciana and Patrizia Cordin. 1989. Two Italian Dialects and the Null Subject Parameter. In Osvaldo Jaeggli & Ken Safir (eds.), *The Null Subject Parameter*, 111–142. Dordrecht: Kluwer.

Brattico, Pauli & Saara Huhmarniemi. 2006. Finnish Negation, the EPP Feature and the Valuation Theory of Morphosyntax. *Nordic Journal of Linguistics* 29.1: 5–44.

Bray, Dorothy & the White Mountain Apache Tribe. 1998. *Western Apache-English Dictionary*. Tempe: Bilingual Press.

Bréal, Michel. 1924. *Essai de sémantique*. Paris: Hachette.

Bresnan, Joan & Sam Mchombo. 1987. Topic, Pronoun, and Agreement in Chichewa. *Language* 63: 741–782.

Brinton, Laurel. 1988. *The Development of English Aspectual Systems*. Cambridge: Cambridge University Press.

Brinton, Laurel & Elizabeth Traugott. 2005. *Lexicalization and Language Change*. Cambridge: Cambridge University Press.

British National Corpus (BNC). Available online at http://www.thetis.bl.uk.

Brook, G. & R. Leslie. 1963. *Layamon: Brut*. Early English Text Society 250. Oxford: Oxford University Press.

Brown, Wayles & Theresa Alt. 2004. A Handbook of Bosnian, Serbian, and Croatian. Available at http://seelrc.org:8080/grammar/mainframe.jsp?nLanguageID=1.

Brugè, Laura. 1996. Demonstrative Movement in Spanish. *University of Venice Working Papers in Linguistics* 6.1: 1–53. Available at http://dspace-unive.cilea.it/bitstream/10278/436/1/6.1.1.pdf.

Brunner, Christopher. 1977. *A Syntax of Western Middle Iranian*. Delmar: Caravan Books.

Bruyn, Adrienne. 1995. *Grammaticalization in Creoles*. Dissertation, University of Amsterdam.

Buell, Leston. 2002. Non-Agreeing Subjects in Zulu. Ms. University of California, Los Angeles.

Bullokar, William. [1586] 1977. *Bref Grammar*. Delmar: Scholars.

Bungenstab, E. 1933. *Der Genitiv beim Verbum und sein Ersatz im Laufe der englischen Sprachgeschichte*. Breslau: Eschenhagen.

Bury, Dirk. 2005. Preverbal Particles in Verb-Initial Languages. In Andrew Carnie, Heidi Harley, & Sheila Dooley (eds.), *Verb First: On the Syntax of Verb-Initial Languages*, 135–154. Amsterdam: John Benjamins.

Butt, Miriam. 1997. Interfaces as Locus of Grammatical Change. *Proceedings of the LFG 1997 Conference*. Stanford: CSLI Publications. Available at http://csli-publications.stanford.edu/LFG/2/lfg97-toc.html.

Butt, Miriam. 2003. The Light Verb Jungle. 2003. *Harvard Working Papers in Linguistics* 9: 1–49.

Butt, Miriam. 2004. Case, Agreement, Pronoun Incorporation and Pro-Drop in South Asian Languages. Ms.

Butt, Miriam. 2006. *Theories of Case*. Cambridge: Cambridge University Press.

Butt, Miriam & Tracey Holloway King. 1997. Null Elements in Discourse Structure. Ms.

Butt, Miriam & Aditi Lahiri. 2002. Historical Stability versus Historical Change. Ms.

Bybee, Joan. 1985. *Morphology*. Amsterdam: John Benjamins.

Bybee, Joan, Revere Perkins, & William Pagliuca. 1994. *The Evolution of Grammar*. Chicago: University of Chicago Press.

Callaway, Morgan. 1913. *The Infinitive in Anglo-Saxon*. Washington: Carnegie Institution.

Calvin, W. & Derek Bickerton. 2000. *Lingua ex Machina: Reconciling Darwin and Chomsky with the Human Brain*. Cambridge: Massachusetts Institute of Technology Press.

Canale, W. M. 1978. Word Order Change in Old English: Base Reanalysis in Generative Grammar. Dissertation, University of Toronto.

Cardinaletti, Anna & Michael Starke. 1996. Deficient Pronouns: A View from Germanic. In Höskuldur Thráinsson et al. (eds.), *Studies in Comparative Syntax*, 2: 21–65. Dordrecht: Kluwer.

Carlson, Anita. 1978. A Diachronic Treatment of English Quantifiers. *Lingua* 46: 295–328.

Carnie, Andrew, Heidi Harley, & Sheila Dooley (eds.). 2005. *Verb First: On the Syntax of Verb-Initial Languages*. Amsterdam: John Benjamins.

Carstairs-McCarthy, Andrew. 1999. *Origins of Complex Language*. Oxford: Oxford University Press.

Casad, Eugene. 1984. Cora. In Ronald Langacker (ed.). *Studies in Uto-Aztecan Grammar*, 4: 151–459. Arlington: Summer Institute of Linguistics.

Casad, Eugene. 1998. Lots of Ways to GIVE in Cora. In John Newman (ed.), *The Linguistics of Giving*, 135–174. Amsterdam: John Benjamins.

Cavalli-Sforza, Luigi Luca. 2000. *Genes, Peoples, and Languages*. New York: North Point Press.

Cennamo, Michaela. 2009. Argument Structure and Alignment Varieties and Changes in Late Latin. In Johanna Barðdal & Shobhana Chelliah (eds.), *The Role of Semantic, Pragmatic, and Discourse Factors in the Development of Case*, 307–346. Amsterdam: John Benjamins.

Chaker, Salem. 1996. Quelques remarques préliminaires sur la négation en Berbère. In Salem Chaker & Dominique Caubet (eds.), *La Négation en Berbère et en Arabe Maghrébin*, 9–22. Paris: L'Harmattan.

Chao, Yuen Ren. 1968. *A Grammar of Spoken Chinese*. Berkeley: University of California Press.

Chatterji, Suniti Kumar. 1926. *The Origin and Development of the Bengali Language*. 2 vols. Calcutta: Calcutta University Press.

Cheng, Lisa, James Huang, & Jane Tang. 1996. Negative Particle Questions. In James Black et al. (eds.), *Microparametric Syntax and Dialect variation*, 41–78. Amsterdam: John Benjamins.

Cheshire, Jenny, Viv Edwards, & Pamela Whittle. 1993. Non-standard English and Dialect Levelling. In James Milroy & Lesley Milroy (eds.), *Real English*, 53–96. London: Longman.

Chierchia, Gennaro & Sally McConnell-Ginet. 2000. *Meaning and Grammar: An Introduction to Semantics*. 2nd ed. Cambridge: Massachusetts Institute of Technology Press.

Chomsky, Noam. 1973. Conditions on Transformations. In Stephen Anderson & Paul Kiparsky (eds.), *A Festschrift for Morris Halle*, 232–285. New York: Holt, Rinehart and Winston.

Chomsky, Noam. 1981. *Lectures on Government and Binding*. Dordrecht: Foris.

Chomsky, Noam. 1986a. *Knowledge of Language*. New York: Praeger.

Chomsky, Noam. 1986b. *Barriers*. Cambridge: Massachusetts Institute of Technology Press.

Chomsky, Noam. 1995. *The Minimalist Program*. Cambridge: Massachusetts Institute of Technology Press.

Chomsky, Noam. 2001. Derivation by Phase. In Michael Kenstowicz (ed.), *Ken Hale: A Life in Language*, 1–52. Cambridge: Massachusetts Institute of Technology Press.

Chomsky, Noam. 2002. *On Nature and Language*. Cambridge: Cambridge University Press.

Chomsky, Noam. 2004. Beyond Explanatory Adequacy. In Adriana Belletti (ed.), *Structures and Beyond*, 104–131.New York: Oxford University Press.

Chomsky, Noam. 2005. Three Factors in Language Design. *Linguistic Inquiry* 36.1: 1–22.

Chomsky, Noam. 2007. Approaching UG from Below. In Uli Sauerland et al. (eds.), *Interfaces + Recursion = Language*, 1–29. Berlin: Mouton de Gruyter.

Chomsky, Noam. 2008. The Biolinguistic Program: Where Does It Stand Today? Ms.

Choueiri, Lina. 1995. Yes-No Questions and the Question Particle *shi* in Lebanese Arabic. Ms. University of Southern California.

Christensen, Kirsti Koch. 1985. Subject Clitics and A-bar-Bound Traces. *Nordic Journal of Linguistics* 8: 1–23.

Christiansen, Morten & Simon Kirby. 2003. *Language Evolution*. Oxford: Oxford University Press.

Chung, Sandra. 2005. What Fronts? In Andrew Carnie, Heidi Harley, & Sheila Dooley (eds.), *Verb First: On the Syntax of Verb-Initial Languages*, 9–29. Amsterdam: John Benjamins.

Cinque, Guglielmo. 1990. *Types of A'-Dependencies*. Cambridge: Massachusetts Institute of Technology Press.

Cinque, Guglielmo. 1999. *Adverbs and Functional Heads*. New York: Oxford University Press.

Cinque, Guglielmo. 2010. *The Syntax of Adjectives*. Cambridge: Massachusetts Institute of Technology Press.

Clark, Eve. 1971. On the Acquisition of the Meaning of *before* and *after*. *Journal of Verbal Learning and Verbal Behavior* 10.3: 266–275.

Claudi, Ulrike. 1994. Word Order Change as Category Change: The Mande Case. In William Pagliuca (ed.), *Perspectives on Grammaticalization*, 191–231. Amsterdam: John Benjamins.

Coar, Thomas. 1796. *A Grammar of the English Tongue*. London.

Collins, Chris. 1997. *Local Economy*. Cambridge: Massachusetts Institute of Technology Press.

Comrie, Bernard. 1976. *Aspect*. Cambridge: Cambridge University Press.

Comrie, Bernard. 1980. Morphology and Word Order Reconstruction. In Jacek Fisiak (ed.), *Historical Morphology*, 83–96. The Hague: Mouton.

Comrie, Bernard. 1981. *Language Universals and Linguistic Typology*. Chicago.

Comrie, Bernard. 1985. *Tense*. Cambridge: Cambridge University Press.

Comrie, Bernard. 1991. On the Importance of Arabic for General Linguistic Theory. In Bernard Comrie & Mushira Eid (eds.), *Perspectives on Arabic Linguistics III: Papers from the Third Annual Symposium on Arabic Linguistics*, 3–30. Amsterdam: John Benjamins.

Comrie, Bernard. 2009. Linguistic Complexity in Hunter-Gatherers. Paper presented at Max Planck Institute, Leipzig, April.

Condillac, Etienne Bonnot de. 1746. *Essai sur lórigine des connaissances humaines*. Paris.

Cook, Eung-Do. 1984. *A Sarcee Grammar*. Vancouver: University of British Columbia Press.

Cook, Eung-Do. 1996. Third-Person Plural Subject Prefix in Northern Athapaskan. *International Journal of American Linguistics* 62.1: 86–110.

Cook, Eung-Do. 2004. *Dëne Sųłiné (Chipewyan)*. Algonquian and Iroquoian Linguistics, Memoir 17, Special Athabaskan Number, Winnipeg.

Corballis, Michael. 2002. Did Language Evolve from Manual Gestures? In Alison Wray (ed.), *The Transition to Language*, 163–180. Oxford: Oxford University Press.

Corne, Chris. 1977. *Seychelles Creole Grammar: Elements for Indian Ocean Proto-Creole Reconstruction*. Tübingen: Narr.

Corpus d'entretiens spontanés (Cd'ES) : Enregistres et transcrits par Kate Beeching. Available at http://www.uwe.ac.uk/hlss/llas/iclru/corpus.pdf.

Corpus of Spoken Professional American English (CSE). See http://www.athel.com.

Cowgill, Warren. 1960. Greek *ou* and Armenian *oč'*. *Language* 36.3: 347–350.

Craig, Colette. 1977. *The Structure of Jacaltec*. Austin: University of Texas Press.

Craig, Colette & Ken Hale. 1988. Relational Preverbs in Some Languages of the Americas. *Language* 64: 312–344.

Crawford, S. J. (ed.). 1922. *The Heptateuch*. London: Humphrey Milford.

Croft, William. 1991. The Evolution of Negation. *Journal of Linguistics* 27: 1–27.

Crowley, Terry. 1992. *An Introduction to Historical Linguistics*. Auckland: Oxford University Press.

Crowley, Terry & Claire Bowern. 2010. *An Introduction to Historical Linguistics*. 4th ed. Oxford: Oxford University Press.

Cumming, Susanna. 1991. *Functional Change: The Case of Malay Constituent Order*. Berlin: Mouton.

Cunningham, Irma. 1992. *A Syntactic Analysis of Sea Island Creole*. Tuscaloosa: University of Alabama Press.

Curme, George. 1910. The Origin and Growth of the Adjective Declension in Germanic. *Journal of English and Germanic Philology* 9: 439–482.

Cyr, Danielle. 1993. Cross-linguistic Quantification: Definite Article vs. Demonstratives. *Language Sciences* 15.3: 195–229.

Cysouw, Michael. 2003. *The Paradigmatic Structure of Person Marking*. Oxford: Oxford University Press.

Dahl, Osten. 1979. Typology of Sentence Negation. *Linguistics* 17: 79–106.

Dahl, Osten. 2004. Definite Articles in Scandinavian. In Bernd Kortmann (ed.), *Dialectology Meets Typology*, 147–180. Berlin: Mouton de Gruyter.

Dahl, Östen & Velupillai, Viveka. 2008. Perfective/Imperfective Aspect. In Martin Haspelmath, Matthew S. Dryer, David Gil, & Bernard Comrie(eds.), *The World Atlas of Language Structures Online*, chapter 65. Munich: Max Planck Digital Library. Available at http://wals.info/feature/65.

Danton, Naomi. 2010. The French Definiteness Cycle: A Diachronic Study of French Determiners. Master's thesis, Arizona State University.

Davis, Norman (ed.), 1971. *Paston Letters and Papers of the Fifteenth Century*. Part I. Oxford: Clarendon Press.

Davis, Philip & Ross Saunders. 1997. *A Grammar of Bella Coola*. Missoula: University of Montana.

de Cat, Cécile. 2005. French Subject Clitics Are Not Agreement Markers. *Lingua* 115: 1195–1219.

de Cat, Cécile. 2007. *French Dislocation*. Oxford: Oxford University Press.

Déchaine, Rose-Marie & Martina Wiltschko. 2002. Decomposing Pronouns. *Linguistic Inquiry* 33.3: 409–442.

Dedrick, John & Eugene Casad. 1999. *Sonora Yaqui Language Structures*. Tucson: University of Arizona Press.

DeGraff, Michel. 1992. The Syntax of Predication in Haitian. *Proceedings of the North East Linguistic Society* 22: 103–117. Graduate Linguistic Student Association, University of Massachusetts, Amherst.

DeGraff, Michel. 1993. A Riddle on Negation in Haitian. *Probus* 5: 63–93.

Delbrück, Berthold. 1907. *Synkretismus*. Strassburg.

Delbrück, Berthold. 1919. *Einleitung in das Studium der Indogermanischen Sprachen*. 6th ed. Leipzig: Breitkopf & Härtel.

Delsing, Lars-Olof. 1993. The Internal Structure of Noun Phrases in the Scandinavian Languages. Dissertation, Lund University.

Delsing, Lars-Olof. 2000. From OV to VO in Swedish. In Susan Pintzuk, George Tsoulas, & Anthony Warner (eds.), *Diachronic Syntax: Models and Mechanisms*, 255–274. Oxford: Oxford University Press.

Demirdache, Hamida. 1996. The Temporal Reference of Noun Phrases in St'at'imcets. Paper presented at Linguistic Society of America.

Demske, Ulrike. 2001. *Merkmale und Relationen*. Berlin: Walter de Gruyter.

Denison, David. 1993. *English Historical Syntax*. London: Longman.

Deo, Ashwini. 2002. A Diachronic Perspective on Complex Predicates in Indo-Aryan. Workshop "Complex Predicates, Particles and Subevents," Constance.

Déprez, Viviane. 2003. Determiner Architecture and Phrasal Movement in French Lexifier Creoles. In Joseph Quer et al. (eds.), *Romance Languages and Linguistic Theory: 2001*, 49–74. Amsterdam: John Benjamins.

Déprez, Viviane. 2007. Grammaticalizing Number and Definiteness in French Based Creoles. Paper presented at International Conference on Historical Linguistics.

Derbyshire, Desmond. 1981. A Diachronic Explanation for the Origin of OVS in Some Carib Languages. *Journal of Linguistics* 17: 209–220.

Derbyshire, Desmond. 1985. *Hixkaryana and Linguistic Typology*. Dallas: Summer Institute of Linguistics.

Derbyshire, Desmond. 1986. Comparative Survey of Morphology and Syntax in Brazilian Arawakan. In Desmond Derbyshire & Geoffrey Pullum (eds.), *Handbook of Amazonian Languages*, 1: 469–566. Berlin: Mouton de Gruyter.

Derbyshire, Desmond & Geoffrey Pullum. 1986. Introduction. In Desmond Derbyshire & Geoffrey Pullum (eds.), *Handbook of Amazonian languages*, 1: 1–28. Berlin: Mouton de Gruyter.

Devitt, Daniel. 1994. Copula Constructions in Crosslinguistic and Diachronic Perspective. Dissertation, State University of New York, Buffalo.

Dictionary of Old English Corpus (DOE). Available at http://www.doe.utoronto.ca.

Diesing, Molly. 1992. *Indefinites*. Cambridge: Massachusetts Institute of Technology Press.

Diesing, Molly. 1997. Yiddish VP Structure and the Typology of Object Movement. *Natural Language and Linguistic Theory* 15.2: 369–427.

Diessel, Holger. 1999. *Demonstratives*. Amsterdam: John Benjamins.

Diessel, Holger. 2004. *The Acquisition of Complex Sentences*. Cambridge: Cambridge University Press.

Dixon, R. M. W. 1980. *The Languages of Australia*. Cambridge: Cambridge University Press.

Dixon, R. M. W. 1994. *Ergativity*. Cambridge: Cambridge University Press.

Dixon, R. M. W. 2003. Demonstratives: A Crosslinguistic Typology. *Studies in Language* 27(1): 61–112.

Djamouri, Redouane. 1991. Particules de negation dans les inscriptions sur bronze de la dynastie des Zhou. *Cahiers de Linguistique—Asie Orientale* 20.1: 5–76.

Djamouri, Redouane. 1996. Comptes rendus-Pulleyblank. *Cahiers de Linguistique—Asie Orientale* 25.2: 289–298.

Djamouri, Redouane. 2001. Markers of Predication in Shang Bone Inscriptions. In Hilary Chappell (ed.), *Synchronic and Diachronic Perspectives of the Grammar of Sinitic Languages*, 143–171. Oxford: Oxford University Press.

Donaldson, Bruce C. 1993. *A Grammar of Afrikaans*. Berlin: Mouton de Gruyter.

Donegan, Patricia & David Stampe. 1983. Rhythm and Holistic Organization of Language Structure. In John Richardson, Mitchell Marks, & Amy Chukerman (eds.), *Papers from the Parasession on the Interfaces of Phonology, Morphology, and Syntax*, 337–351. Chicago: Chicago Linguistic Society.

Donohue, Mark. 1999. *A Grammar of Tukang Besi*. Berlin: Mouton de Gruyter.

Donohue, Mark. 2005. Comment. *Linguist List* 16.645.

Dooley-Collberg, Sheila. 1997. Determiners and Incorporation in Maori. *Lund Working Papers* 46: 25–44.

Doron, Edit. 1986. The Pronominal 'Copula' as Agreement Clitic. In Hagit Borer (ed.), *The Syntax of Pronominal Clitics*, 313–332. New York: Academic Press.

Dresden, Mark et al. 1958. *A Reader in Modern Persian*. New York: American Council of Learned Societies.

Driem, George van. 1986. *A Grammar of Limbu*. Berlin: Mouton de Gruyter.

Dryden, John. [1691] 1965. *Letter to William Walsh*. Charles Ward (ed.). New York: AMS Press.

Dryer, Matthew. 1992. The Greenbergian Word Order Correlations. *Language* 68: 81–138.

Dryer, Matthew. 2008a. Position of Tense-Aspect Affixes. In Martin Haspelmath, Matthew S. Dryer, David Gil, & Bernard Comrie (eds.), *The World Atlas of Language Structures Online*, chapter 69. Munich: Max Planck Digital Library. Available at http://wals.info/feature/69.

Dryer, Matthew. 2008b. Negative Morphemes. In Martin Haspelmath, Matthew S. Dryer, David Gil, & Bernard Comrie (eds.), *The World Atlas of Language Structures Online*, chapter 112. Munich: Max Planck Digital Library. Available at http://wals.info/feature/112.

DuBois, John. 1987. The Discourse Base of Ergativity. *Language* 63.4: 805–855.

Duncan, Daniel. [1731] 1967. *A New English Grammar*. Menston: Scolar Press.

Durie, Mark. 1988. Verb Serialization and 'Verbal-Prepositions' in Oceanic Languages. *Oceanic Linguistics* 27.1–2: 1–23.

Durrleman-Tame, Stephanie. 2008. *The Syntax of Jamaican Creole*. Amsterdam: John Benjamins.

de Vogelaer, Gunther & Annemie Neuckermans. 2002. Subject Doubling in Dutch. *Sprachtypologie und Universalienforschung (STUF)* 55.3: 234–258.

Eckardt, Regine. 2006. *Meaning Change in Grammaticalization*. Oxford: Oxford University Press.

Edwards, Malcolm. 2006. Pronouns, Agreement, and Focus in Egyptian Arabic. *School of Oriental and African Studies Working Papers in Linguistics* 14: 51–62. Available at http://www.soas.ac.uk/linguistics/research/workingpapers/volume-14/file37817.pdf.

Eid, Mushira. 1983. The Copula Function of Pronouns. *Lingua* 59: 197–207.

Eijk, Jan van. 1997. *The Lillooet Language: Phonology, Morphology, Syntax*. Vancouver: University of British Columbia Press.

Elenbaas, Marion. 2007. *The Synchronic and Diachronic Syntax of the English Verb-Particle Combination*. Dissertation, Radboud University, Nijmegen.

Embick, David & Alec Marantz. 2006. Architecture and Blocking. Available at http://web.mit.edu/marantz/Public/Recent/block-dist.pdf

Emonds, Joseph. 1976. *A Transformational Approach to English Syntax*. New York: Academic Press.

Enç Mürvet. 1991. The Semantics of Specificity. *Linguistic Inquiry* 22.1: 1–25.

England, Nora. 1991. Changes in Basic Word Order in Mayan Languages. *International Journal of American Linguistics* 57: 446–486.

Enrico, John. 2003. *Haida Syntax*. Lincoln: University of Nebraska Press.

Epstein, Richard. 1993. The Definite Article: Early Stages of Development. In Jaap van Marle (ed.), *Historical Linguistics, 1991*, 111–134. John Benjamins.

Ernst, Thomas. 1995. Negation in Mandarin Chinese. *Natural Language and Linguistic Theory* 13: 665–705.

Estrada Fernández, Zarina. 1996 *Pima Bajo*. Munich: Lincom.

Everett, Daniel. 1996. *Why There Are No Clitics*. Arlington: Summer Institute of Linguistics.

Eythórrson, Thórhallur. 2002. Negation in C: The Syntax of Negated Verbs in Old Norse. *Journal of Nordic Linguistics* 25: 190–224.

Eythórrson, Thórhallur. 2004. The Syntax of the Older Runic Inscriptions, Paper presented at.

Faarlund, Jan Terje. 1990. *Syntactic Change: Towards a Theory of Historical Syntax*. Berlin: Mouton de Gruyter.

Faarlund, Jan Terje. 2004. *The Syntax of Old Norse*. Oxford: Oxford University Press.

Faarlund, Jan Terje. 2005. Zoque Relative and Focus Constructions. Paper presented at the Center for Advanced Studies, Oslo.

Faarlund, Jan Terje. 2007. From Clitic to Affix: The Norwegian Definite Article. Ms.

Faarlund, Jan Terje. 2008. A Mentalist Interpretation of Grammaticalization Theory. In Thórhallur Eythórsson (ed.), *Grammatical Change and Linguistic Theory: The Rosendal Papers*, 221–244. Amsterdam: John Benjamins.

Faarlund, Jan Terje. 2009. On the History of Definiteness Marking in Scandinavian. *Journal of Linguistics* 45.3: 617–639.

Fairbanks, Gordon. 1977. Case Inflections in Indo-European. *Journal of Indo-European Studies* 5: 101–132.

Faltz, Leonard. 1985. *Reflexivization: A Study in Universal Syntax*. New York: Garland.

Faltz, Leonard. 1995. Towards a Typology of Natural Logic. In Emmon Bach et al. (eds.), *Quantification in Natural Languages*, 271–319. Dordrecht: Kluwer.

Faltz, Leonard. 1998. *The Navajo Verb*. Albuquerque: University of New Mexico Press.

Faltz, Leonard. 2008. A Reflexive Cycle? Paper presented at Linguistic Cycles Workshop, Tempe, April.

Fassi Fehri, Abdelkader. 1993. *Issues in the Structure of Arabic Clauses and Words*. Dordrecht: Kluwer.

Fertig, David. 2005. The History of the Separable and Inseparable Complex Verbs in West Germanic. Paper presented at 11th *Germanic Linguistics Annual Conference*, University of California, Davis.

Finney. Joseph. 1999. General Diachronic Course of Proto-Austronesian Casemarkers. Southeast Asian Linguistic Society 9, ASU Monograph Series. Tempe: Arizona State University.

Fischer, Olga. 1990. Syntactic Change and Causation: Developments in Infinitival Constructions in English. Dissertation, University of Amsterdam.

Fischer, Olga. 2000. The Position of the Adjective in Old English. In Ricardo Bermúdez-Otero, David Denison, Richard M. Hogg, & C. B. McCully (eds.), *Generative Theory and Corpus Linguistics: A Dialogue from 10 ICEHL*, 153–181. Berlin: Mouton de Gruyter.

Fischer, Olga. 2006. On the Position of Adjectives in Middle English. *English Language and Linguistics* 10: 253–288.

Fischer, Olga. 2007. *Morphosyntactic Change*. Oxford: Oxford University Press.

Fischer, Wolfdietrich. 1982. Das Neuarabische und seine Dialekte. In Wolfdietrich Fischer (ed.), *Grundriß der Arabischen Philologie*, 1: 83–95. Wiesbaden: Ludwig Reichert.

Fleischer, Jürg. 2002. *Die Syntax von Pronominaladverbien in den Dialekten des Deutschen*. Wiesbaden: Franz Steiner.

Fonseca-Greber, Bonnibeth. 2000. The Change from Pronoun to Clitic and the Rise of Null Subjects in Spoken Swiss French. Dissertation, University of Arizona.

Forchheimer, P. 1953. *The Category of Person in Language*. Berlin: de Gruyter.

Foreman, John. 2006. The Morphosyntax of Subjects in Macuiltianguis Zapotec. Dissertation, University of California, Los Angeles.

Fortescue, Michael. 1984. *West Greenlandic*. London: Croom Helm.

Fortescue, Michael. 2002. The Rise and Fall of Polysynthesis in the Eskimo-Aleut Family. In Nicholas Evans & Hans-Jürgen Sasse (eds.), *Problems of Polysynthesis*, 257–275. Berlin: Akademie Verlag.

Foulet, Lucien. [1919] 1961. *Petite Syntaxe de L'ancien Français*. 3rd ed. Paris: Honoré Champion.

Fox, Danny. 2000. *Economy and Semantic Interpretation*. Cambridge: MIT Press.

Frajzyngier, Zygmunt. 1991. The De Dicto Domain in Language. In Elizabeth Traugott & Bernd Heine (eds.), *Approaches to Grammaticalization*, 219–251. Amsterdam: John Benjamins.

Frajzyngier, Zygmunt. 1997. Grammaticalization of Number: From Demonstratives to Nominal and Verbal Plural. *Linguistic Typology* 1: 193–242.

Franco, Jon Andoni. 1993. On Object Agreement in Spanish. Dissertation, University of Southern California.

Frank, Ellen, James Kari, & Siri Tuttle. 2006. *Lower Tanana Athabaskan Language Lessons*. Fairbanks: Alaska Native Language Center.

Franzén, Torsten. 1939. *Etude sur la syntaxe des pronoms personnels sujets en ancien français*. Uppsala: Almqvist & Wiksells Boktryckeri.

Frawley, William. 1976. Comparative Syntax in Austronesian. Dissertation, University of California, Santa Barbara.

Frawley, William. 1991. *Linguistic Semantics*. Hillsdale: Lawrence Erlbaum Associates.

Friberg, Barbara. 1996. Konjo's Peripatetic Person Markers. In Hein Steinhauer (ed.),. *Papers in Austronesian Linguistics No.3*, 137–171. Pacific Linguistics A-84. Canberra: Pacific Linguistics.

Friedemann, Nina & Carlos Patiño Rosselli. 1983. *Lengua y sociedad en el Palenque de San Basilio*. Bogotá: Instituto Caro y Cuervo.

Friederici, Angela. 1983. Children's Sensitivity to Function Words during Sentence Comprehension. *Linguistics* 21.5: 717–740.

Fukui, Naoki & Yuji Takano. 1998. Symmetry in Syntax: Merge and Demerge. *Journal of East Asian Linguistics* 7: 27–86.

Fuß, Eric. 2005. *The Rise of Agreement*. Amsterdam: John Benjamins.

Gabain, Annemarie von. 1941. *Alttürkische Grammatik*. 3rd ed. Leipzig: Otto Harrossowitz.

Gabelentz, Georg von der. [1901] 1972. *Die Sprachwissenshaft: Ihre Aufgaben, Methoden und bisherigen Ergebnisse*. Tübingen: Narr.

Gamkrelidze, T. & V. Ivanov. 1994–1995. *Indo-European and the Indo-Europeans*. 2 vols. Berlin: Mouton de Gruyter.

Gardiner, Alan H. 1904. The Word . *Zeitschrift für Ägyptische Sprache und Altertumskunde* 41: 130–135.

Gardiner, Alan H. 1957. *Egyptian Grammar*. Oxford: Oxford University Press.

Gardner, Dee and Mark Davies. 2007. Pointing Out Frequent Phrasal Verbs: A Corpus-Based Analysis. *TESOL Quarterly* 41: 339–59.

Garrett, Andrew. 1990. The Syntax of Anatolian Pronominal Clitics. Dissertation, Harvard University.

Gavel, Henri & Georges Henri-Lacombe. 1929–1937. *Grammaire Basque*. 2 vols. Bayonne: Le Courrier.

Geis, M. 1970. Adverbial Subordinate Clauses in English. Dissertation, Massachusetts Institute of Technology.

Gelderen, Elly van. 1993. *The Rise of Functional Categories*. Amsterdam: John Benjamins.

Gelderen, Elly van. 2000. *A History of English Reflexive Pronouns*. Amsterdam: John Benjamins.

Gelderen, Elly van. 2001. The Force of ForceP in English. *South West Journal of Linguistics* 20.2: 107–120.

Gelderen, Elly van. 2004. *Grammaticalization as Economy*. Amsterdam: John Benjamins.

Gelderen, Elly van. 2007. The Definiteness Cycle in Germanic. *Journal of Germanic Linguistics* 19.4: 275–305.

Gelderen, Elly van. 2008a. Linguistic Cycles and Economy Principles: The Role of Universal Grammar in Language Change. In Thórhallur Eythórsson (ed.), *Grammatical Change and Linguistic Theory: The Rosendal Papers*, 245–264. Amsterdam: John Benjamins.

Gelderen, Elly van. 2008b. Economy of Merge and Grammaticalization: Two Steps in the Evolution of Language. In Regine Eckardt, Gerhard Jäger, & Tonjes Veenstra (eds.), *Variation, Selection, Development: Probing the Evolutionary Model of Language Change*, 179–197. Berlin: Mouton de Gruyter.

Gelderen, Elly van. 2008c. Cycles of Negation in Athabaskan. *Working Papers in Athabaskan Languages* 7: 49–64.

Gelderen, Elly van. 2008d. Cycles of Negation. *Linguistic Typology* 12.2: 195–243.

Gelderen, Elly van. 2008e. Where Did Late Merge Go? Grammaticalization as Feature Economy. *Studia Linguistica* 62.3: 287–300.

Gelderen, Elly van. 2009a. Renewal in the Left Periphery: Economy and the Complementizer Layer. *Transactions of the Philological Society* 107.2: 131–195.

Gelderen, Elly van. 2009b. Feature Economy in the Linguistic Cycle. In Paola Crisma & Pino Longobardi (eds.), *Historical Syntax and Linguistic Theory*, 93–109. Oxford: Oxford University Press.

Gelderen, Elly van. 2009c. Introduction. In Elly van Gelderen (ed.), *Cyclical Change*, 1–12. Amsterdam: John Benjamins.

Gelderen, Elly van. 2009d. Grammaticalization from a Biolinguistic Perspective. In Rudie Botha & Chris Knight (eds.), *The Prehistory of Language*, 1: 225–243. Oxford: Oxford University Press.

Gelderen, Elly van. 2010. Changes in Valency Marking in the History of English. Ms.

Gelderen, Elly van & Terje Lohndal. 2008. *Working Papers in Scandinavian Syntax* 82: 1–22.

Gergel, Remus. 2009. *Rather*—on a Modal Cycle. In Elly van Gelderen (ed.), *Cyclical Change*, 243–264. Amsterdam: John Benjamins.

Ghomeshi, Jila. 1996. Projection and Inflection: A Study of Persian Phrase Structure. Dissertation, University of Toronto.

Giacalone Ramat, Anna. 1998. Testing the Boundaries of Grammaticalization. In Anna Giacalone Ramat & Paul Hopper (eds.), *The Limits of Grammaticalization*, 107–127. Amsterdam: John Benjamins.

Giannakidou, Anastasia. 2005. N-words and Negative Concord. In Martin Everaert and Henk van Riemsdjik (eds.), *The Blackwell Companion to Syntax*, 327–391. Oxford: Blackwell.

Gil, David. 2005. Word Order without Syntactic Categories: How Riau Indonesian Does It. In Andrew Carnie, Heidi Harley, & Sheila Dooley (eds.), *Verb First: On the Syntax of Verb-Initial Languages*, 243–263. John Benjamins, Amsterdam.

Gilbertson, George W. 1923. *The Balochi Language: A Grammar and Manual*. Hertford: Stephen Austin & Sons.

Gildea, Spike. 1993. The Development of Tense Markers from Demonstrative Pronouns in Panare (Cariban). *Studies in Language* 17: 53–73.

Gillon, Carrie. 2009. The Semantic Core of Determiners: Evidence from Skwxwú7mesh. In Jila Ghomeshi, Ileana Paul, & Martina Wiltschko (eds.), *Determiners: Variation and Universals*, 177–213. Amsterdam: John Benjamins.

Giusti, Giuliana. 2001a. The Birth of a Functional Category: From Latin ILLE to the Romance Article and Personal Pronoun. In Guglielmo Cinque & Giampaolo Salvi (eds.), *Current Studies in Italian Syntax: Essays Offered to Lorenzo Renzi*, 157–171. Amsterdam: North Holland.

Giusti, Giuliana. 2001b. The Functional Structure of Noun Phrases. In Guglielmo Cinque (ed.), *Functional Structure in DP and IP*, 1: 54–90. New York: Oxford University Press.

Givón, Talmy. 1971. On the Verbal Origin of the Bantu Verb Suffixes. *Studies in African Linguistics* 2.2: 145–197.

Givón, Talmy. 1975. Focus and the Scope of Assertion: Some Bantu Evidence. *Studies in African Linguistics* 6: 185–205.

Givón, Talmy. 1976. Topic, Pronoun, and Grammatical Agreement. In Charles Li (ed.), *Subject and Topic*, 151–188. New York: Academic Press.

Givón, Talmy. 1978. Negation in Language. In Peter Cole (ed.), *Syntax and Semantics*, 9: 69–112. New York: Academic Press.

Givón, Talmy. 1979. *On Understanding Grammar*. New York: Academic Press.

Givón, Talmy. 2000. Internal Reconstruction: As Method, as Theory. In Spike Gildea (ed.), *Reconstructing Grammar*, 107–159. Amsterdam: John Benjamins.

Givón, Talmy. 2002. *Bio-Linguistics: The Santa Barbara Lectures*. Amsterdam: John Benjamins.

Givón, Talmy. 2009. *The Genesis of Syntactic Complexity*. Amsterdam: John Benjamins.

Glaser, Elvira. 2000. Der bestimmte Artikel in den althochdeutschen Glossen. In Yvon Desportes (ed.), *Zur Geschichte der Nominalgruppe im älteren Deutsch*, 187–212. Heidelberg: Carl Winter.

Goddard, Pliny Earle. 1905. *The Morphology of the Hupa Language*. Berkeley: University of California Press.

Goddard, Pliny Earle. 1912. *Elements of the Kato Language*. Berkeley: University of California Press.

Goddard, Pliny Earle. 1929. *The Bear River Dialect of Athapascan*. Berkeley: University of California Press.

Goetting, Lauren. 2007. Greek Textual Influence on Gothic Complex Verbs. *Journal of Germanic Linguistics* 19.4: 309–347.

Golla, Victor. 1996. *Hupa Language Dictionary, Na:tinixwe Mixine:whe'*. 2nd ed. Hoopa: Hoopa Valley Tribe.

Goossen, Irvy. 1995. *Diné Bizaad: Speak, Read, Write Navajo*. Flagstaff: Salina Bookshelf.

Gordon, E. V. 1956. *Introduction to Old Norse*. Oxford: Clarendon Press.

Gordon, Lynn. 1986. *Maricopa Morphology and Syntax*. Berkeley: University of California Press.

Green, Lisa. 1998. Inversion Phenomena and Expletive Subjects in African American English. Ms.

Greenberg, Joseph. [1954] 1960. A Quantitative Approach to the Morphological Typology of Language. *International Journal of American Linguistics* 26: 178–194.

Greenberg, Joseph (ed.), 1963. *Universals of Language*. Cambridge: Massachusetts Institute of Technology Press.

Greenberg, Joseph. 1978. How Does a Language Acquire Gender Markers? In Joseph Greenberg (ed.), *Universals of Human Language*, 3: 47–82. Stanford: Stanford University Press.

Greenberg, Joseph. 1995. The Diachronic Typological Approach to Language. In Masayoshi Shibatani & Theodora Bynon (eds.), *Approaches to Language Typology*, 145–166. Oxford: Clarendon Press.

Greenfield, Philip. 1995. Some Special Morphological Characteristics of the White Mountain Dialect of Apachean. Ms. San Diego State University.

Greenough, J. B. et al. (eds.). 1931. *Allen and Greenough's New Latin Grammar*. Boston: Ginn.

Grierson, G. 1895. On Pronominal Suffixes in the Kačmiri Language. *Proceedings of the Asiatic Society*: 336–375.

Grimes, Barbara (ed.). 2000. *Ethnologue*. Dallas: Summer Institute of Linguistics International.

Grönbech, K. 1936. *Der Türkische Sprachbau*. Copenhagen: Levin & Munksgaard.

Guerrero, Lilián. 2006. *The Structure and Function on Yaqui Complementation*. Munich: Lincom.

Guilfoyle, Eithne, Henrietta Hung, & Lisa Travis. 1992. Spec of IP and Spec of VP: Two Subjects in Austronesian Languages. *Natural Language and Linguistic Theory* 10: 375–414.

Güldemann, Tom, Patrick McConvell, & Richard Rhodes. Forthcoming. *Hunter-Gatherers and Linguistic History: A Global Perspective*. Cambridge: Cambridge University Press.

Gunlogson, Christine. 2001. Third Person Object Prefixes in Babine-Witsuwit'en. *International Journal of American Linguistics* 67.4: 365–395.

Haegeman, Liliane & Terje Lohndal. 2010. Negative Concord and (Multiple) Agree: A Case Study of West Flemish. *Linguistic Inquiry* 41: 181–211.

Hagège, Claude. 1993. *The Language Builder*. Amsterdam: John Benjamins.

Hale, Ken. 1973. Person Marking in Warlbiri. In Stephen Anderson & Paul Kiparsky (eds.), *A Festschrift for Morris Halle*, 308–344. New York: Holt, Rinehart and Winston.

Hale, Ken. 1983. Warlpiri and the Grammar of Non-configurational Languages. *Natural Language and Linguistic Theory*, 1.1: 5–47.

Hale, Ken. 1989. On Nonconfigurational Structures. In László Marácz & Pieter Muysken (eds.), *Configurationality: The Typology of Asymmetries*, 293–300. Dordrecht: Foris.

Hale, Ken & S. J. Keyser. 2002. *Prolegomenon to a Theory of Argument Structure*. Cambridge: Massachusetts Institute of Technology Press.

Hamid Ahmed, Mohamed-Tahir & Martine Vanhove. 2002. Contrastive Negation in Beja. *Africa und Übersee* 85: 149–169.

Hanson, Chris. 2001. A Description of Basic Clause Structure in Bugis. In Peter Austin et al. (eds.), *Explorations in Valency in Austronesian Languages*, 143–160. La Trobe Papers in Linguistics 11. Available at http://www.latrobe.edu.au/linguistics/LaTrobePapersinLinguistics/Vol%2011/6Hanson.pdf.

Hargus, Sharon. 2002. Negation in Kwadacha (Ft. Ware Sekani). *Alaska Native Language Center Working Papers* 2: 106–120.

Harris, James. 1969. *Spanish Phonology*. Cambridge: Massachusetts Institute of Technology Press.

Harris, Martin. 1977. 'Demonstratives', 'Articles' and 'Third Person Pronouns' in French: Changes in Progress. *Zeitschrift für romanische Philologie* 93: 249–261.

Harris, Martin. 1978. *The Evolution of French Syntax*. London: Longman.

Harrison, Carl. 1986. Verb Prominence, Verb Initialness, Ergativity, and Typological Disharmony in Guajajara. In Desmond Derbyshire & Geoffrey Pullum (eds.), *Handbook of Amazonian Languages*, 1: 407–439. Berlin: Mouton de Gruyter.

Harrison, Sheldon. 1976. *Mokilese Reference Grammar*. Honolulu: University Press of Hawaii.

Harrison, Sheldon. 1978. Transitive Marking in Micronesian Languages. In S. A. Wurm & Lois Carrington (eds.), *Second International Conference of Austronesian Linguistics Proceedings*, 1067–1127. Canberra: Pacific Linguistics.

Hashimoto, S. 1969. *Zyoshi zyodoshi no kenkyu*. Tokyo: Iwanami.

Haspelmath, Martin. 1995. The Converb as a Cross-linguistically Valid Category. In Martin Haspelmath & Ekkehard König (eds.), *Converbs in Cross-linguistic Perspective*, 1–55. Berlin: Mouton de Gruyter.

Haspelmath, Martin, Matthew S. Dryer, David Gil, & Bernard Comrie (eds.). 2006. *The World Atlas of Language Structures*. Oxford: Oxford University Press.

Haugen, Jason. 2004. Issues in Comparative Uto-Aztecan Morphosyntax. Dissertation, University of Arizona.

Haugen, Jason. 2008. *Morphology at the Interfaces*. Amsterdam: John Benjamins.

Haumann, Dagmar. 2007. *Adverb Licensing and Clause Structure in English*. Amsterdam: John Benjamins.

Hauser, Marc, Noam Chomsky, & Tecumseh Fitch. 2002. The Faculty of Language: What Is It, Who Has It, and How Did It Evolve? *Science* 298: 1569–1579.

Hawkins, John A. 2004. *A Performance Theory of Order and Constituency*. Cambridge: Cambridge University Press.

Heath, Jeffrey. 2005. *A Grammar of Tamashek (Tuareg of Mali)*. Berlin: Mouton de Gruyter.

Hecht, Hans. [1900–1907] 1965. *Dialoge Gregors des Grossen*. Darmstadt: Wissenschaftliche Buchgesellschaft.

Heine, Bernd. 1976. *A Typology of African Languages Based on the Order of Meaningful Elements*. Berlin: Dietrich Reimer.

Heine, Bernd. 2007. Typology and Language Contact. Ms. Available at http://www.fl.ut.ee/orb.aw/class=file/action=preview/id=228326.

Heine, Bernd, Ulrike Claudi, & Friederike Hünnemeyer. 1991. *Grammaticalization: A Conceptual Framework*. Chicago: University of Chicago Press.

Heine, Bernd & Tania Kuteva. 2002. *World Lexicon of Grammaticalization*. Cambridge: Cambridge University Press.

Heine, Bernd & Tania Kuteva. 2005. *Language Contact and Grammatical Change*. Cambridge: Cambridge University Press.

Heine, Bernd & Tania Kuteva. 2006. *The Changing Languages of Europe*. New York: OUP.

Heine, Bernd & Tania Kuteva. 2007. *The Genesis of Grammar*. New York: OUP.

Heine, Bernd & Mechthild Reh. 1984. *Grammaticalization and Reanalysis in African Languages*. Hamburg: Buske Verlag.

Helsinki Corpus (HC). OE1–2 before 950; OE3 950–1050; OE4 1050–1150; ME1 1150–1250; ME2 1250–1350; ME3 1350–1420; ME4 1420–1500; EMOD1 1500–1570; EMOD2 1570–1640; EMOD3 1640–1710. Available at www.ling.upenn.edu/mideng.

Hengeveld, Kees. 1992. *Non-verbal Predication*. Berlin: Mouton de Gruyter.

Herman, J. 1997. À Propos du débat sur le pluriel des noms italiens (et roumains). In G. Holtus et al. (eds.), *Italica et Romanica*, 19–30. Tubingen: Niemeyer.

Hess, Tom. 1995. *Lushootseed Reader with Introductory Grammar*. University of Montana Occasional Papers in Linguistics 11, Missoula.

Hess, Tom & Vi Hilbert. 1977. *Lushootseed*. 2 vols. Seattle: Daybreak Star Press.

Hicks, Glyn. 2009. *The Derivation of Anaphoric Relations*. Amsterdam: John Benjamins.

Higashiizumi, Yuko. 2006. *From a Subordinate Clause to an Independent Clause*. Tokyo: Hituzi Syobo.

Higgins, F. R. 1979. *The Pseudo-cleft Construction in English*. New York: Garland.

Hiietam, Katrin. N.d. Case Marking in Estonian Grammatical Relations. Ms.

Hill, Jane. 1987. Spanish as a Pronominal Argument Language: The Spanish Interlanguage of Mexicano Speakers. *Coyote Papers* 6: 68–90.

Hill, Jane & Kenneth Hill. 1986. *Speaking Mexicano*. Tucson: University of Arizona Press.

Hill, Jane & Rosinda Nolasquez. 1973. *Mulu'wetam: The First People; Cupeño Oral History and Language*. Banning: Malki Museum Press.

Hiller, Ulrich. 1988. Contracted forms im Englishen. In Wolf-Dietrich Bald (ed.), *Kernprobleme der englischen Grammatik*, 91–105. Munich: Langenscheidt.

Hiltunen, Risto. 1983. *The Decline of the Prefixes and the Beginnings of the English Phrasal Verb*. Turku: Turun Yliopisto.

Himmelmann, Nikolaus. 1996. Person Marking and Grammatical Relations in Sulawesi. In Hein Steinhauer (ed.), *Papers in Austronesian Linguistics*, 3: 115–136. Canberra: Pacific Linguistics.

Himmelmann, Nikolaus. 1997. *Deiktikon, Artikel, Nominalphrase*. Tübingen: Niemeyer.

Hjelmslev, Louis. 1935. *La Catégorie des Cas*. Munich: Wilhelm Finke.

Hock, Hans. 1991. *Principles of Historical Linguistics*. Berlin: Mouton de Gruyter.

Hock, Hans. 1996. Who's on First? Toward a Prosodic Account of PS Clitics. In Aaron L. Halpern & Arnold Zwicky (eds.), *Approaching Second: Second Position Clitics and Related Phenomena*, 199–270. Stanford: CSLI Publications.

Hodge, Carleton. 1970. The Linguistic Cycle. *Linguistic Sciences* 13: 1–7.

Hoeksema, Jack. 2009. Jespersen Recycled. In Elly van Gelderen (ed.), *Cyclical Change*, 15–34. Amsterdam: John Benjamins.

Hofling, Andrew. 2006. A Sketch of the History of the Verbal Complex in Yukatekan Mayan Languages. *International Journal of American Linguistics* 72.3: 367–396.

Holm, John. 1988. *Pidgins and Creoles*. Vol. 1. Cambridge: Cambridge University Press.

Holmberg, Anders, Urpo Nikanne, Irmeli Oraviita, Hannu Reime & Trond Trosterud. 1993. The Structure of INFL and the Finite Clause in Finnish. In Anders Holmberg & Urpo Nikanne (eds.), *Case and Other Functional Categories in Finnish Syntax*, 177–206. Berlin: Mouton de Gruyter.

Holt, Robert (ed.), 1878. *The Ormulum*. Oxford: Clarendon Press.

Holton, Gary. 2000. The Phonology and Morphology of the Tanacross Athabaskan Language. Dissertation, University of California, Santa Barbara.

Honti, Lásló. 1997. Die Negation im Uralischen. Parts 1–3. *Linguistica Uralica* 2: 81–96, 161–176, 241–252.

Hook, Peter Edwin. 1990. Experiencers in South Asian Languages: A Gallery. In Manindra Verma & K. P. Mohanan (eds.), *Experiencer Subjects in South Asian Languages*, 319–34. Stanford: CSLI Publications.

Hoop, Helen de. 1992. Case Configuration and Noun Phrase Interpretation. Dissertation, Groningen University.

Hoop, Helen de & Peter de Swart (eds.). 2008. *Differential Subject Marking*. Dordrecht: Springer.

Hopper, Paul & Elizabeth Traugott. 2003. *Grammaticalization*. Cambridge: Cambridge University Press.

Horn, Laurence. 2001. *A Natural History of Negation*. Stanford: CSLI Publications.

Hornstein, Norbert & Amy Weinberg. 1981. Case Theory and Preposition Stranding. *Linguistic Inguiry* 12: 55–91.

Horrocks, Geoffrey. 1981. *Space and Time in Homer*. New York: Arno Press.

Horst, J. M. van der. 2008. *Geschiedenis van de Nederlandse syntaxis*. Leuven: Universitaire Pers.

Hoskison, James. 1983. A Grammar and Dictionary of the Gude Language. Dissertation, Ohio State University.

Hróarsdóttir, Thorbjörg. 2000. *Word Order Change in Icelandic: From OV to VO*. Amsterdam: John Benjamins.

Huang, James. 1984. On the Distribution and Reference of Empty Pronouns. *Linguistic Inquiry* 15: 531–574.

Huang, Shuanfan. 1999. The Emergence of a Grammatical Category Definite Article in Spoken Chinese. *Journal of Pragmatics* 31.1: 77–94.

Huddleston, Rodney & Geoffrey Pullum. 2002. *The Cambridge Grammar of the English Language*. Cambridge: Cambridge University Press.

Humboldt, Wilhelm von. [1822] 1972. *Über die Entstehung der grammatischen Formen und ihren Einfluss auf die Ideenentwicklung: Abhandlungen der Akademie der Wissenschaften zu Berlin*. Darmstadt: Wissenschaftliche Buchgesellschaft.

Humboldt, Wilhelm von. 1836. *Über die Verschiedenheit des menschlichen Sprachbaus und seinen Einfluss auf die geistige Entwicklung des Menschengeschlechts*. Berlin.

Hyman, Larry. 1975. On the Change from SOV to SVO: Evidence from Niger-Congo. In C. N. Li (ed.), *Word Order and Word Order Change*, 113–147. Austin: University of Texas Press.

Ingham, Richard. 2006. On Two Negative Concord Dialects in Early English. *Language Variation and Change* 18: 241–266.

Ingham, Richard. 2007a. NegP and Negated Constituent Movement in the History of English. *Transactions of the Philological Society* 105.3: 365–397.

Ingham, Richard. 2007b. A Structural Constraint on Multiple Negation. *Medieval English Mirror* 3: 55–67.

Ingram, David. 1978. Personal pronoun typology and universals, In Joseph Greenberg (ed.), *Universals of human language*, Vol. 3. Stanford, CA: California Stanford University Press, 213–247.

Irvine, Susan (ed.). 2004. *The Anglo-Saxon Chronicle*. Vol. 7. Cambridge: D. S. Brewer.

Iyeiri, Yoko. 1999. Multiple Negation in Middle English Verse. In Ingrid Tieken-Boon van Ostade et al. (eds.), *Negation in the History of English*, 121–146. Berlin: Mouton de Gruyter.

Jackendoff, Ray. 2002. *Foundations of Language*. Oxford: Oxford University Press.

Jacobs, Roderick. 1975. *Syntactic Change: A Cupan (Uto-Aztecan) Case Study*. Berkeley: University of California Press.

Jaeggli, Osvaldo. 1982. *Topics in Romance Syntax*. Dordrecht: Foris.

Jäger, Agnes. 2008. *History of German Negation*. Amsterdam: John Benjamins.

Jaggar, Philip. 2001. *Hausa*. Amsterdam: John Benjamins.

Jaggar, Philip. 2009. Quantification and Polarity. In Norbert Cyffer et al. (eds.), *Negation Patterns in West African Languages and Beyond*, 57–69. Amsterdam: John Benjamins.

Jayaseelan, K.A. 2000. *Parametric Studies in Malayalam Syntax*. New Delhi: Allied.

Jelinek, Eloise. 1983. Case and Configurationality. *Coyote Papers* 4: 73–108.

Jelinek, Eloise. 1984. Empty Categories, Case, and Configurationality. *Natural Language and Linguistic Theory* 2: 39–76.

Jelinek, Eloise. 1987. Auxiliaries and Ergative Splits. In Martin Harris & Paolo Ramat (eds.), *Historical Development of Auxiliaries*, 85–105. Berlin: Mouton de Gruyter.

Jelinek, Eloise. 1989. The Case Split in Choctaw. In Laszlo Maracz & Pieter Muysken (eds.), *Configurationality*, 117–141. Dordrecht: Foris.

Jelinek, Eloise. 1995. Quantification in Straits Salish. In Emmon Bach et al. (eds.), *Quantification in Natural Languages*, 487–540. Dordrecht: Kluwer.

Jelinek, Eloise. 1998. Voice and Transitivity as Functional Projections in Yaqui. In Miriam Butt & Wilhelm Geuder (eds.), *The Projection of Arguments: Lexical and Compositional Factors*, 195–224. Stanford: CSLI Publications.

Jelinek, Eloise. 2001. Pronouns and Argument Hierarchies. Paper presented at Perspectives on Aspect, Utrecht, December.

Jespersen, Otto. [1917] 1966. *Negation in English and Other Languages*. 2nd ed. Copenhagen: A.F. Høst.

Jespersen, Otto. 1922. *Language*. London: Allen & Unwin.

Jetté, Jules, Eliza Jones, & James Kari. 2000. *Koyukon Athabaskan Dictionary*. Fairbanks: Alaska Native Language Center.

Ji, Ming Ping. 2007. The Left-Periphery in Chinese. Dissertation, Arizona State University.

Jones, Mark. 2002. The Origin of Definite Article Reduction in Northern English Dialects: Evidence from Dialect Allomorphy. *English Language and Linguistics* 6.2: 325–345.

Josefsson, Gunløg. 2000. Scandinavian Pronouns and Object Shift. In Henk van Riemsdijk (ed.), *Clitics in the Languages of Europe*, 731–757. Berlin: Mouton de Gruyter.

Josefsson, Gunløg & Gisela Håkansson. 2000. The PP-CP Parallelism Hypothesis and Language Acquisition. In S. Powers et al. (eds.), *The Acquisition of Scrambling and Cliticization*, 397–422. Dordrecht: Kluwer.

Joseph, Brian. 2003. Morphologization from Syntax. In Brian Joseph & Richard Janda (eds.), *Handbook of Historical Linguistics*, 472–492. Oxford: Blackwell.

Julien, Marit. 2002. *Syntactic Heads and Word Formation*. New York: Oxford University Press.

Julien, Marit. 2005. *Nominal Phrases from a Scandinavian Perspective*. Amsterdam: John Benjamins.

Kahr, Joan. 1975. Adpositions and Locationals: Typology and Diachronic Development. *Working Papers on Language Universals* 19: 21–54.

Kahr, Joan. 1976. The Renewal of Case Morphology: Sources and Constraints. *Working Papers on Language Universals* 20: 107–151.

Kaiser, Georg. 1992. *Die klitischen Personalpronomina im Französischen und Portugiesischen*. Frankfurt: Vervuert.

Kalluli, Dalina & Liliane Tasmowski. 2008. *Clitic Doubling in the Balkan Languages*. Amsterdam: John Benjamins.

Kandybowicz, Jason. 2008. *The Grammar of Repetition*. Amsterdam: John Benjamins.

Kari, James. 1990. *Ahtna Dictionary*. Fairbanks: Alaska Native Language Center.

Kari, James. 1992. Some Concepts in Ahtna Athabaskan word formation. In Mark Aronoff (ed.), *Morphology Now*, 107–131. Albany: State University of New York Press.

Kari, James. 1993. Diversity in Morpheme Order in Several Alaskan Athabaskan Languages. *Berkeley Linguistic Society Proceedings* 19: 50–56.

Karimi, Simin. 1989. Aspects of Persian Syntax, Specificity, and the Theory of Syntax. Dissertation, University of Washington.

Katz, Aya. 1996. Cyclical Grammaticalization and the Cognitive Link between Pronoun and Copula. Dissertation, Rice University.

Kayne, Richard. 1994. *The Antisymmetry of Syntax*. Cambridge: Massachusetts Institute of Technology Press.

Kayne, Richard. 1999. Prepositions as Attractors. *Probus* 11: 39–73.

Kayne, Richard 2005. Some Notes on Comparative Syntax, with Special Reference to English and French. In Guglielmo Cinque & Richard Kayne (eds.), *The Oxford Handbook of Comparative Syntax*, 3–69. New York: Oxford University Press.

Keenan, Edward. 1976. Toward a Universal Definition of 'Subject'. In Charles Li (ed.), *Subject and Topic*, 303–334. New York: Academic Press.

Kellogg, Samuel. 1893. *Grammar of the Hindi Language*. Delhi.

Kellogg, Samuel. 1938. *A Grammar of the Hindi Language*. Delhi.

Kemenade, Ans van. 2000. Jespersen's Cycle Revisited. In Susan Pintzuk et al. (eds.), *Diachronic Syntax*, 51–74. Oxford: Oxford University Press.

Kent, Roland. 1950. *Old Persian*. New Haven: American Oriental Society.

Kerke, Simon van de. 1996. *Affix Order and Interpretation in Bolivian Quechua*. Meppel: Krips Repro.

Khanittanan, W. 1986. Kamti Tai: From an SVO to an SOV Language. In B. H. Krishnamurti (ed.), *South Asian Linguistics: Structure, Convergence and Diglossia*, 17–48. Delhi: Motilal Banarsidass.

Kikusawa, Ritsuko. 2007. Optional Ergative Marking and the Emergence of Passive Structures in Austronesian Languages. Ms.

Kimball, Geoffrey. 1985. A Descriptive Grammar of Koasati. Dissertation, Tulane.

Kimball, Geoffrey. 1991. *Koasati Grammar*. Lincoln: University of Nebraska Press.

Kimenyi, A. 1980. *A Relational Grammar of Kinyarwanda*. Berkeley: University of California Press.

Kiparsky, Paul. 1982. *Explanation in Phonology*. Dordrecht: Foris.

Kiparsky, Paul. 1995. Indo-European Origins of Germanic Syntax. In Ian Roberts & Adrian Battye (eds.), *Clause Structure and Language Change*, 140–167. New York: Oxford University Press.

Kiparsky, Paul. 1996. The Shift to Head-Initial VP in Germanic. In H. Thráinsson et al, *Studies in Comparative Germanic Syntax*, 2: 140–179. Dordrecht: Kluwer.

Kiparsky, Paul. 1997. The Rise of Positional Licensing. In Ans van Kemenade & Nigel Vincent (eds.), *Parameters of Morphosyntactic Change*, 460–494. New York: Oxford University Press.

Kiparsky, Paul. 1998. Partitive Aspect and Case. In Miriam Butt & Wilhelm Geuder (eds.), *The Projection of Arguments: Lexical and Compositional Factors*, 265–307. Stanford: CSLI Publications.

Kiparsky, Paul. 2000. Analogy as Optimization. In Aditi Lahiri (ed.), *Analogy, Levelling, Markedness*, 15–46. Berlin: Mouton.

Kiparsky, Paul. 2002. Disjoint Reference and the Typology of Pronouns. In Ingrid Kaufmann & Barbara Stiebels (eds.), *More than Words*, 179–226. Berlin: Akademie.

Kiparsky, Paul. 2003. The Germanic Weak Preterite. Ms. Available at http://www.stanford.edu/~kiparsky/Papers/lahiri_weakpreterite.pdf.

Kiparsky, Paul & Cleo Condoravdi. 2006. Tracking Jespersen's Cycle. In Mark Janse, Brian Joseph, & Angela Ralli (eds.), *Proceedings of the 2nd International Conference of Modern Greek Dialects and Linguistic Theory*, 179–197. Mytilene: Doukas.

Kiss, Katalin. 2006. The function and the syntax of the verbal particle. In Katalin Kiss (ed.), *Event Structure and the Left Periphery*, 17–56. Dordrecht: Kluwer.

Klaeber, Frederick. [1922] 1941. *Beowulf*. Boston: Heath.

Klamer, Marian. 1997. Spelling Out Clitics in Kambera. *Linguistics* 35: 895–927.

Klamer, Marian. 1998. *A Grammar of Kambera*. Berlin: Mouton de Gruyter.

Klinken, Catharina van. 1999. A Grammar of the Fehan Dialect of Tetun, an Austronesian Language of West Timor. Ms., Australian National University.

Klokeid, Terry. 1976. Topics in Lardil Grammar. Dissertation, Massachusetts Institute of Technology.

Kluge, F. (ed.), 1885. Zur Geschichte der Zeichensprache Angelsächsische Indicia Monasterialia. *Techmers internationale Zeitschrift für Sprachwissenschaft* 2: 116–137.

Koller, Hermann. 1951. Praesens historicum und erzählendes Imperfekt. *Museum Helvetikum* 8: 63–99.

König, Christa. 2008. *Case in Africa*. Oxford: Oxford University Press.

König, Ekkehard & Letizia Vezzosi. 2004. The Role of Predicate Meaning in the Development of Reflexivity. In Walter Bisang et al. (eds.), *What Makes Grammaticalization?* 213–244. Berlin: Mouton de Gruyter.

Koopman, Hilda. 1984. *The Syntax of Verbs: From Verb Movement in the Kru Languages to Universal Grammar*. Dordrecht: Foris.

Korn, Agnes. 2008. A Case for the Accusative. Ms. University of Freiburg. Available at http://orient.ruf.uni-freiburg.de/dotpub/korn.pdf.

Korn, Agnes 2009. The Ergative System in Balochi from a Typological Perspective. *Iranian Journal of Applied Language Studies* 1.1: 43–79. Available at http://titus.uni-frankfurt.de/personal/agnes/ergativ.pdf.

Kornfilt, Jaklin. 2003. Scrambling, Subscrambling, and Case in Turkish. In Simin Karimi (ed.), *Word Order and Scrambling*, 125–155. Oxford: Blackwell.

Kortlandt, Frederik. 1983. Demonstrative Pronouns in Balto-Slavic, Armenian, and Tocharian. *Studies in Slavic and General Linguistics* 3: 311–322.

Kortmann, Bernd. 1992. Reanalysis Completed and in Progress. In Günter Kellermann et al. (eds.), *Diachrony within Synchrony*, 429–453. Frankfurt: Peter Lang.

Kortmann, Bernd. 2004. Do as a Tense and Aspect Marker in Varieties of English. In Bernd Kortmann (ed.), *Dialectology Meets Typology*, 245–276. Berlin: Mouton de Gruyter.

Kraft, C. & A. Kirk-Greene. 1973. *Hausa*. London: Hodder & Stoughton.

Krapp, G. P. 1931. (ed.), *The Junius Manuscript*. Anglo-Saxon Poetic Records 1. New York: Columbia University Press.

Krapp, G. 1932. (ed.), *The Vercelli Book*. Anglo-Saxon Poetic Records 2. New York: Columbia University Press.

Krause, W. 1971. *Die Sprache der urnordischen Runeninschriften*. Heidelberg: Carl Winter.

Krauss, Michael. 1969. On the Classification in the Athabascan, Eyak, and Tlingit Verb. *International Journal of American Linguistics supplement* 35.4: 53–83.

Krauss, Michael. 1976. Eyak Morpheme List. Russell Gould (ed.), 1996. Ms.

Kroeber, A. L. & George Grace. 1960. *The Sparkman Grammar of Luiseño*. Berkeley: University of California Press.

Kroeber, Paul. 1999. *The Salish Language Family*. Lincoln: University of Nebraska Press.

Kuczaj, S. 1976. -Ing, -s, -ed: A Study of the Acquisition of Certain Verb Inflections. Dissertation, University of Minnesota.

Kulikov, Leonid. 2006. Case Systems in a Diachronic Perspective. In Leonid Kulikov et al. (eds.), *Case, Valency and Transitivity*, 23–47. Amsterdam: John Benjamins.

Kulikov, Leonid. 2009. Evolution of Case Systems. In Andrej Malchukov & Andrew Spencer (eds.), *Handbook of Case*, 439–457. Oxford: Oxford University Press.

Künnap, Ago. 1971. *System und Ursprung der kamassischen Flexionssuffixe I: Numeruszeichen und Nominalflexion*. Helsinki: Suomalais-Ugrilainen Seura,

Künnap, Ago. 1999. *Kamass*. Munich: Lincom.

Kuno, Susumu. 1973. *The Structure of the Japanese Language*. Cambridge: Massachusetts Institute of Technology Press.

Kuryłowicz, Jerzy. 1964. *The Inflectional Categories of Indo-European*. Heidelberg: Carl Winter.

Kwon, Joon. 2009. The Subject Cycle of Pronominal Auxiliaries in Old North Russian. In Elly van Gelderen (ed.), *Cyclical Change*, 157–184. Amsterdam: John Benjamins.

Kwon, S. M. & A. Zribi-Hertz. 2008. Differential Function Marking, Case, and Information Structure: Evidence from Korean. *Language* 84.2: 258–299.

Kytö, Merja. 1993. *Manual to the Diachronic Part of the Helsinki Corpus of English Texts*. 2nd edition. Department of English, University of Helsinki.

Laenzlinger, Christopher. 2000. French Adjective Ordering: Perspectives on DP-Internal Movement Types. *Generative Grammar in Geneva* 1: 55–104.

Lagercrantz, Eliel. 1929. *Sprachlehre des Nordlappischen*. Oslo: Oslo Etnografiske Museum.

Lahiri, Aditi. 2000. Hierarchical Restructuring in the Creation of Verbal Morphology in Bengali and Germanic: Evidence from Phonology. In Aditi Lahiri (ed.), *Analogy, Levelling, Markedness*, 71–123. Berlin: Mouton.

Laka, Itziar. 1994. *On the Syntax of Negation*. New York: Garland.

Lakoff, Robin. 1972. Another Look at Drift. In Robert P. Stockwell & Ronald K. S. Macaulay (eds.), *Linguistic Change and Generative Theory*, 172–198. Bloomington: Indiana University Press.

Lambrecht, Knud. 1981. *Topic, Antitopic, and Verb Agreement in Non-Standard French*. Amsterdam: John Benjamins.

Lane, Archibald. [1700] 1969. *A Key to the Art of Letters*. Menston: Scolar Press.

Langacker, Ronald. 1977. *An Overview of Uto-Aztecan Grammar*. Dallas: Summer Institute of Linguistics and University of Texas at Arlington.

Larson, Richard. 1990. Extraction and Multiple Selection in PP. *Linguistic Review* 7.2: 169–182.

Lass, Roger. 1994. *Old English*. Cambridge: Cambridge University Press.

Laury, Ritva. 1997. *Demonstratives in Interaction*. Amsterdam: John Benjamins.

Law, Danny, John Robertson, & Stephen Houston. 2006. Split Ergativity in the History of the Ch'olan Branch of the Mayan Language Family. *International Journal of American Linguistics* 72: 415–450.

Law, Paul. 1998. A Unified Analysis of Preposition Stranding in Romance and Germanic. *Proceedings of the North East Linguistic Society* 28: 219–234.

Lazard, Gilbert. 1957. *Grammaire du Persan Contemporain*. Paris: Klincksieck.

Lee, Kee-dong. 1975. *Kusaiean Reference Grammar*. Honolulu: University Press of Hawaii.

Leer, Jeff. 2000. The Negative/Irrealis Category in Athabaskan-Eyak-Tlingit. In Ted Fernald & Paul Platero (eds.). *The Athabaskan Languages*, 101–138. Oxford: Oxford University Press.

Lefebvre, Claire. 2004. *Issues in the Study of Pidgin and Creole Languages*. Amsterdam: John Benjamins.

Lefebvre, Claire & Anne-Marie Brousseau. 2002. *A Grammar of Fongbe*. Berlin: Mouton de Gruyter.

Lehmann, Christian. [1982] 1995. *Thoughts on Grammaticalization*. Munich: Lincom.

Lehmann, Christian. 2002. *Thoughts on Grammaticalization*. 2nd ed. Erfurt: ASSidUE.

Lehmann, Christian & Yong-Min Shin. 2005. The Functional Domain of Concomitance: A Typological Study of Instrumental and Comitative Relations. In Christian Lehmann (ed.), *Typological Studies in Participation*, 9–104. Berlin: Akademie.

Lehmann, Winfred. 1958. On the Earlier Stages of the Indo-European Nominal Inflection. *Language* 34: 179–202.

Lehmann, Winfred. 1993. *Theoretical Bases of Indo-European Linguistics*. New York : Routledge.

Leiss, Elisabeth. 1994. Die Entstehung des Artikels im Deutschen. *Sprachwissenschaft* 19: 307–319.

Leiss, Elisabeth. 2000. *Artikel und Aspekt*. Berlin: Walter de Gruyter.

Leslau, Wolf. 1945. *Short Grammar of Tigré*. New Haven: American Oriental Society.

Leslau, Wolf. 1995. *Reference Grammar of Amharic*. Wiesbaden: Harrasowitz.

Leslau, Wolf. 1999. *Zway: Ethiopic Documents, Grammar and Dictionary*. Wiesbaden: Harrasowitz.

Lewis, G. L. 1967. *Turkish Language*. Oxford: Oxford University Press.

Levin, Saul. 2004. The Two Negatives {n} and {m} in Egyptian and Their Counterparts in Distantly Related Languages. In Gabor Takacs (ed.), *Egyptian and Semito-Hamitic Studies in Memoriam W. Vycicichl*, 437–440. Leiden: Brill

Li, Charles & Sandra Thompson. 1974. An Explanation of Word Order Change: SVO > SOV. *Foundations of Language* 12: 201–214.

Li, Charles & Sandra Thompson. 1977. A Mechanism for the Development of Copula Morphemes. In Charles Li (ed.), *Mechanisms of Syntactic Change*, 414–444. Austin: University of Texas Press.

Li, Charles & Sandra Thompson. 1978. An Exploration of Mandarin Chinese. In W. A. Lehmann (ed.), *Syntactic Typology*, 223–265. Austin: University of Texas Press.

Li, Charles & Sandra Thompson. 1981. *Mandarin Chinese*. Berkeley: University of California Press.

Li, Fang-Kuei. 1930. *Mattole, an Athabaskan Language*. Chicago: University of Chicago Press.

Li, Fang-Kuei. 1967. *Chipewyan*. New York: Viking Fund Publications in Anthropology.

Li, Yen-Hui Audrey. 1990. *Order and Constituency in Mandarin Chinese*. Dordrecht: Kluwer.

Lichtenberk, Frantisek. 1985. Syntactic Category Change in Oceanic Languages. *Oceanic Linguistics* 24: 1–84.

Lightfoot, David. 1979. *Principles of Diachronic Syntax*. Cambridge: Cambridge University Press.

Lightfoot, David. 1991. *How to Set Parameters*. Cambridge: Massachusetts Institute of Technology Press.

Lightfoot, David. 1999. *The Development of Language*. Oxford: Blackwell.

Lightfoot, David. 2006a. *How New Languages Emerge*. Cambridge: Cambridge University Press.

Lightfoot, David. 2006b. Cuing a New Grammar. In Ans van Kemenade & Bettelou Los (eds.), *The Handbook of the History of English*, 24–44. Oxford: Blackwell.

Lillehaugen, Danielle. 2006. Expressing Location in Tlacolula Valley Zapotec. Dissertation, University of California, Los Angeles.

Lin, Nina Yuhsun. 2002. A Corpus-Based Study on the Development of Mandarin Negative Marker *mei*. Paper presented at 35th *International Conference on Sino-Tibetan Languages and Linguistics*, Arizona State University, Tempe.

Lipiński, Edward. 1997. *Semitic Languages: Outline of a Comparative Grammar*. Leuven: Peeters.

Littlefield, Heather. 2006. *Syntax and Acquisition in the Prepositional Domain*. Dissertation, Boston University.

Lloyd, Paul. 1987. *From Latin to Spanish*. Philadelphia: American Philosophical Society.

Lockwood, W. 1968. *Historical German Syntax*. Oxford: Clarendon Press.

Lohndal, Terje. 2006. Labels and Linearization. Ms.

Lohndal, Terje. 2007. On the Structure and Development of Nominal Phrases in Norwegian. In Elisabeth Stark, Elisabeth Leiss, & Werner Abraham (eds.), *Nominal Determination: Typology, Context Constraints, and Historical Emergence*, 287–310. Amsterdam: John Benjamins.

Lohndal, Terje. 2009a. *COMP*-T Effects: Variation in the Position and Features of C. *Studia Linguistica* 63: 204–232.

Lohndal, Terje. 2009b. The Copula Cycle. In Elly van Gelderen (ed.), *Cyclical Change*, 209–242. Amsterdam: John Benjamins.

Lohndal, Terje. 2009c. Spelling Out Parametric Variation. Paper presented at Workshop on Parameters and Features, Arizona State University, Tempe, February.

Longobardi, Guiseppi. 2001. Formal Syntax, Diachronic Minimalism, and Etymology. *Linguistic Inquiry* 32.2: 275–302.

Lopez, Cristian. 2007. Comparison of Subject Pronoun Expression in the Spanish of a Native Mexican and a Mexican-American Speaker. Master's thesis, Arizona State University.

Loprieno, Antonio. 1995. *Ancient Egyptian*. Cambridge: Cambridge University Press.

Loprieno, Antonio. 2001. From Ancient Egyptian to Coptic. In Martin Haspelmath et al. (eds.), *Language Typology and Language Universals*, 2: 1742–1761. Berlin: Walter de Gruyter.

Lord, Carol. 1993. *Historical Change in Serial Verb Constructions*. Amsterdam: John Benjamins.

Los, Bettelou. 1999. Infinitival Complementation in Old and Middle English. Dissertation, Free University, Amsterdam.

Lötzsch, Ronald. 1996. Interferenzbedingte grammatische Konvergenzen und Divergenzen zwischen Sorbisch und Jiddisch. *Sprachtypologie und Universalienforschung* 49.1: 50–59.

Lovick, Olga. 2009. Demonstratives in Dena'ina Discourse. Paper presented at Athabascan Languages Conference, July.

Lowth, Robert. [1762] 1967. *Short Introduction to English Grammar*. Menston: Scolar Press.

Lühr, Rosemarie. 1984. Reste der athematischen Konjugation in den germanischen Sprachen. In J. Untermann & B. Brogyanyi (eds.), *Das Germanische und die Rekonstruktion der Indogermanischen Grundsprache*, 25–90. Amsterdam: John Benjamins.

Lyons, Christopher. 1999. *Definiteness*. Cambridge: Cambridge University Press.

Mahajan, Anoop. 1990. The A/A-bar Distinction and Movement Theory. Dissertation, Massachusetts Institute of Technology.

Malchukov, Andrej. 2008. Animacy and Asymmetries in Differential Case Marking. *Lingua* 118: 203–221.

Malchukov, Andrej. 2009. Ditransitive Constructions: Some Problematic Patterns. Paper presented at Max Planck Institute, April.

Marantz, Alec. 1997. No Escape from Syntax: Don't Try Morphological Analysis in the Privacy of Your Own Lexicon. In A. Dimitriadis et al.(eds), *University of Pennsylvania Working Papers in Linguistics* 4.2: 201–225.

Marchese, Lynell. 1986. *Tense/aspect and the development of auxiliaries in Kru languages*. Dallas: Summer Institute of Linguistics.

Markman, Vita. 2008. Pronominal Copula Constructions Are What? In Charles Chang & Hannah Haynie (eds.), *Proceedings of the 26th West Coast Conference on Formal Linguistics*, 366–374. Somerville: Cascadilla Proceedings Project.

Marten, Lutz, Nancy Kula, & Nhlanhla Thwala. 2007. Parameters of Morphosyntactic Variation in Bantu. *Transactions of the Philological Society* 105.3: 253–338.

Matteson, Esther. 1965. *The Piro (Arawakan) Language*. Berkeley: University of California Press.

Matthewson, Lisa. 1998. *Determiner Systems and Quantificational Strategies: Evidence from Salish*. The Hague: Holland Academic Graphics.

Matthewson, Lisa. 2005. *When I Was Small—I Wan Kwikwis*. Vancouver: University of British Columbia Press.

Matthewson, Lisa. 2009. Tense and Modality in the Pacific Northwest. Paper presented at the Linguistic Society.

Mayer, Elisabeth. 2003. Clitic Doubling in Limeño. Ms. Australian National University.

McCloskey, Jim & Ken Hale. 1984. On the Syntax of Person-Number Inflection in Modern Irish. *Natural Language and Linguistic Theory* 1: 487–533.

McColl Millar, Robert. 2000. *System Collapse, System Rebirth*. New York: Peter Lang.

McGregor, R. S. 1968. *The Language of Indrajit of Orcha*. Cambridge: Cambridge University Press.

McGregor, W., 2008. Indexicals as Sources of Case Markers in Australian Languages. In F. Josephson & I. Söhrman (eds.), *Interdependence of Diachronic and Synchronic Analyses*,299–321. Amsterdam: John Benjamins.

McWhorter, John. 1997. *Towards a New Model of Creole Genesis*. New York: Peter Lang.

Meillet, Antoine. [1912] 1958. *Linguistique historique et linguistique generale*. Paris: Honoré Champion.

Meinunger, André. 1995. *Topic and Comment*. Amsterdam: John Benjamins.

Mettouchi, Amina. 1996. La Négation dans les langues du Maghreb: Synthèse. In Salem Chaker & Dominique Caubet (eds.), *La Négation en Berbère et en Arabe Maghrébin*, 177–195. Paris: L'Harmattan.

Miège, Guy [1688] 1969. *The English Grammar*. Menston: Scolar Press.

Miestamo, Matti, Kaius Sinnemäki, & Fred Karlsson. 2008. *Language Complexity: Typology, Contact, Change*. Amsterdam: John Benjamins.

Mikkelsen, Line. 2005. *Copular Clauses: Specification, Predication and Equation*. Amsterdam: John Benjamins.

Miller, Amy. 2001. *A Grammar of Jamul Tiipay*. Berlin: Mouton de Gruyter.

Miller, D. Gary. 1993. *Complex Verb Formation*. Amsterdam: John Benjamins.

Miller, Thomas. 1890–1898. *The Old English Version of Bede's Ecclesiastical History of the English People*. London: Trübner.

Mitchell, Bruce. 1985. *Old English Grammar*. 2 vols. Oxford: Oxford University Press.

Mithun, Marianne. 1987. Is Basic Word Order Universal? In R. Tomlin (ed.), *Grounding and Coherence in Discourse*, 281–328. Amsterdam: John Benjamins.

Mithun, Marianne. 1991. The Development of Bound Pronominal Paradigms. In Winfred Lehmann & Helen-Jo Jakusz Hewitt (eds.), *Language Typology, 1988*, 85–104. Amsterdam: John Benjamins.

Mithun, Marianne. 1999. *The Languages of Native North America*. Cambridge: Cambridge University Press.

Mithun, Marianne. 2000a. The Reordering of Morphemes. In Spike Gildea (ed.), *Reconstructing Grammar*, 231–255. Amsterdam: John Benjamins.

Mithun, Marianne. 2000b. The Legacy of Recycled Aspect. In John Charles Smith & Delia Bentley (eds.), *Historical Linguistics 1995*, 1: 261–277. Amsterdam: John Benjamins.

Mithun, Marianne. 2003. Pronouns and Agreement: The Information Status of Pronominal Affixes. *Transactions of the Philological Society* 101.2: 235–278.

Mithun, Marianne. 2008a. Borrowed Rhetorical Constructions as Starting Points for Grammaticalization. In Alexander Bergs & Gabriele Diewald (eds.), *Constructions and Language Change*, 195–230. Berlin: Mouton de Gruyter.

Mithun, Marianne. 2008b. Does Passivization Require a Subject Category? In Greville Corbett & Michael Noonan (eds.), *Case and Grammatical Relations*, 211–240. Oxford: Oxford University Press.

Moravcsik, Edith. 1978. On the Case Marking of Objects. In Joseph Greenberg (ed.), *Universals of Human Language*, 4: 249–289. Stanford: Stanford University Press.

Morris, Richard (ed.) 1865. *The Story of Genesis and Exodus*. London: Trübner.

Morris, Richard 1872. *Old English Miscellany*. London: Trübner.

Morris, Richard (ed.). 1874–1880. *The Blickling Homilies of the Tenth Century*. Early English Text Society OS 58, 63, and 73. London: Oxford University Press.

Morris, Richard (ed.), 1874–1893. *Cursor Mundi*. 7 parts. London: Trübner.

Morwood, Mike and Penny van Oosterzee. 2007. *A New Human*. New York: Smithsonian Books.

Mufwene, Salikoko. 2001. *The Ecology of Language Evolution*. Cambridge: Cambridge University Press.

Munro, Pamela. 1989. Postposition Incorporation in Pima. *South West Journal of Linguistics* 9: 108–127.

Musgrave, Simon. 2001. Non-Subject Arguments in Indonesian. Dissertation, University of Melbourne.

Mustanoja, Tauno. 1960. *A Middle English Syntax*. Helsinki:.

Napier, A.S. 1916. *The Old English Version, with the Latin Original, of the Enlarged Rule of the Chrodegang*. Early English Text Society 150. London: Oxford University Press.

Naudé, Jacobus. 2002. The Third Person Pronoun Tripartite Verbless Clauses of Qumran Hebrew. In Horst Simon & Heike Wiese (eds.), *Pronouns*, 161–181. Amsterdam: John Benjamins.

Neeleman, Ad & Kriszta Szendroi. 2008. Case Morphology and Radical Pro-Drop. In Theresa Biberauer (ed.), *The Limits of Syntactic Variation*, 331–348. Amsterdam: John Benjamins.

Neuburger, Kathrin & Elisabeth Stark. 2009. Why Differential Case Marking in Corsican? Ms. Available at http://exadmin.matita.net/uploads/pagine/1697748327_DOM_Neuburger_Stark.pdf.

Newmeyer, Frederick. 1998. *Language Form and Language Function*. Cambridge: Massachusetts Institute of Technology Press.

Newmeyer, Frederick. 2000. On the Reconstruction of 'Proto-World' Word Order. In Chris Knight et al. (eds.), *The Evolutionary Emergence of Language*, 372–388. Cambridge: Cambridge University Press.

Newmeyer, Frederick. 2001. Deconstructing Grammaticalization. *Language Sciences* 23: 187–229.

Newmeyer, Frederick. 2008. Holmberg and Platzack: The Typological Dimension. Paper presented at Nordic center of Excellence in Microcomparative Syntax, October.

Nichols, J. G. (ed.). 1963. *The Diary of Edward VI*. New York.

Nichols, Johanna. 1992. *Linguistic Diversity in Space and Time*. Chicago: University of Chicago Press.

Nichols, Johanna, David Peterson, & Jonathan Barnes. 2004. Transitivizing and Detransitivising Languages. *Linguistic Typology* 8.2: 149–211.

Nicholas, Nick. 1996. Copulas from Pronouns. *Linguist List* 7.1776.

Nishiyama, Kunio & Herman Kelen. 2007. *A Grammar of Lamaholot, Eastern Indonesia: The Morphology and Syntax of the Lewoingu Dialect*. Munich: Lincom Europa.

Noguchi, Tohru. 1997. Two Types of Pronouns and Variable Binding. *Language* 73.4: 770–797.

Noonan, Michael. 1985. Complementation. In Timothy Shopen (ed.), *Language Typology and Syntactic Description*, 2: 42–140. Cambridge: Cambridge University Press.

Nordlinger, Rachel & Louisa Sadler. 2002. The Typology of Nominal Tense. Ms. Available at http://privatewww.essex.ac.uk/~louisa/newpapers/lt-final.pdf.

Nordlinger, Rachel & Louisa Sadler. 2004. Nominal Tense in Crosslinguistic Perspective. *Language* 80.4: 776–806.

Nunes, Jairo. 2004. *Linearization of Chains and Sideward Movement*. Cambridge: Massachusetts Institute of Technology Press.

Nygaard, Marius. 1906. *Norrøn Syntax*. Kristiania: Aschehoug.

Oda, Kenji. 2005. V1 and wh-Questions. In Andrew Carnie, Heidi Harley, & Sheila Dooley (eds.), *Verb First: On the Syntax of Verb-Initial Languages*, 107–133. Amsterdam: John Benjamins.

Ogura, Michiko. 1989. *Verbs with the Reflexive Pronoun and Constructions with 'self' in Old and Early Middle English*. Cambridge: D. S. Brewer.

Ogura, Michiko. 1997. On the Beginning and Development of the 'begin to' Construction. In J. Fisiak (ed.), *Studies in Middle English Linguistics*, 403–428. Berlin: Mouton de Gruyter.

Oinas, Felix. 1961. *The Development of Some Postpositional Cases in Balto-Finnic Languages*. Helsinki: Suomalais-Ugrilaisen Seura.

Oppenrieder, Wilhelm. 1991. Preposition Stranding im Deutschen? Da wil ich nichts von hören. In Gisbert Fanselow & Sascha Felix (eds.), *Strukturen und Merkmale syntaktischer Kategorien*, 159–172. Tübingen: Narr.

Ordóñez, Francisco. 1995. The Antipassive in Jacaltec. *Catalan Working Papers in Linguistics* 4.2: 329–343. Available at http://ddd.uab.cat/pub/cwpil/1132256Xv4n2p329.pdf.

Ordóñez, Francisco & Esthela Treviño. 1999. Left Dislocated Subjects and the Pro-Drop Parameter: A Case Study of Spanish. *Lingua* 107: 39–68.

Ottosson, Kjartan. 2004. *The Old Nordic Middle Voice*. Paper presented at Center for Advanced Studies, Oslo.

Ouali, Hamid. 2003. Sentential Negation in Berber: A Comparative Study. In John Mugany (ed.), *Linguistic Description: Typology and Representation of African Languages*, 243–256. Vol. 8 of *Trends in African Linguistics*. Trenton: Africa World Press.

Ouali, Hamid. 2006. Unifying Agreement Relations. Dissertation, University of Michigan.

Ouali, Hamid. 2008. Agreement Relations Unified. Ms.

Ouhalla, Jamal. 1990. Sentential Negation, Relativised Minimality and the Aspectual Status of Auxiliaries. *Linguistic Review* 7.2: 183–231.

Ouhalla, Jamal. 1997. Remarks on Focus in Standard Arabic. In Mushira Eid & Robert Ratcliffe (eds.), *Perspectives on Arabic Linguistics*, 10: 9–45. Amsterdam: John Benjamins.

Oxford English Dictionary (OED). 1933. Oxford: Oxford University Press. Available at http://www.oed.com.

Öztürk, Balkiz. 2005. *Case, Referentiality and Phrase Structure*. Amsterdam: John Benjamins.

Pandharipande, R. 1990. Serial Verb Construction in Marathi. In Brian Joseph & Arnold Zwicky (eds.), *When Verbs Collide: Papers from the 1990 Ohio State Mini-Conference on Serial Verbs*, 178–199. Columbus: Ohio State University.

Parker, Steve. 1999. On the Behavior of Definite Articles in Chamicuro. *Language* 75: 552–562.

Parodi, Claudia. 1995. Participle Agreement and Object Shift in Old Spanish. In Henning Andersen (ed.), *Historical Linguistics, 1993*, 371–378. Amsterdam: John Benjamins.

Parry, Mair. 1998. On Negation in the Ligurian Hinterland. In Paola Beninca & Cecilia Poletto (eds.), *Atti della terza giornata italo-americana di dialettologia: La negazione nelle lingue romanze, Quaderni di lavoro*. 2: 85–112. Available at http://asis-cnr.unipd.it/documenti/ql2/PAD_NEG2.rtf.

Partridge, A. C. 1964. *Orthography in Shakespeare and Elizabethan Drama*. Lincoln: University of Nebraska Press.

Pawley, Andrew. 1973. Some Problems in Proto-Oceanic Grammar. *Oceanic Linguistics* 12: 102–188.

Payne, David. 1981. Activity as the Encoding of Foregrounding in Narrative. Ms.

Payne, Doris. 1987. Information Structuring in Papago Narrative Discourse. *Language* 63: 783–804.

Payne, John R. 1995. Inflecting Postpositions in Indic and Kashmiri. In Frans Plank (ed.), *Double Case*, 283–298. Oxford: Oxford University Press.

Payne, Thomas. 1985. Negation. In Timothy Shopen (ed.), *Language Typology and Syntactic Description*, 1: 197–242. Cambridge: Cambridge University Press.

Pearson, Matthew. 2001. The Clause Structure of Malagasy: A Minimalist Approach. Dissertation, University of California, Los Angeles.

Pedersen, Holger. 1907. Neues und nachträgliches. *Zeitschrift für vergleichende Sprachforschung* 40: 129–217.

Perkins, Ellavina & Ted Fernald. 2010. Navajo Grammar. Ms.

Pesetsky, David & Esther Torrego. 2001. T-to-C Movement: Causes and Consequences. In Michael Kenstowicz (ed.), *Ken Hale: A Life in Language*, 355–426. Cambridge: Massachusetts Institute of Technology Press.

Pesetsky, David & Esther Torrego. 2004. Tense, Case and the Nature of Syntactic Categories. In Jacqueline Guéron & Jacqueline Lecarme (eds.), *The Syntax of Time*, 495–538. Cambridge: Massachusetts Institute of Technology Press.

Pesetsky, David & Esther Torrego. 2007. The Syntax of Valuation and the Interpretability of Features. In Simin Karimi et al. (eds.), *Phrasal and Clausal Architecture*, 262–294. Amsterdam: John Benjamins.

Peterson, David. 2007. *Applicative Constructions*. Oxford: Oxford University Press.

Peyraube, Alain & Thekla Wiebusch. 1994. Problems Relating to the History of Different Copulas in Ancient Chinese. In Matthew Y. Chen & Ovid J. L. Tseng (eds.), *In Honor of William S. Y. Wang*, 383–404. Taipei: Pyramid Press.

Philippi, Julia. 1997. The Rise of the Article in Germanic Languages. In Ans van Kemenade & Nigel Vincent (eds.), *Parameters of Morphosyntactic Change*, 62–93. Cambridge: Cambridge University Press.

Phillott, D.C. 1919. *Higher Persian Grammar*. Calcutta: Calcutta University.

Piattelli-Palmarini, Massimo & Juan Uriagereka. 2005. The Evolution of the Narrow Faculty of Language. *Lingue e Linguaggio*: 1–52.

Pinker, Steven & Paul Bloom. 1990. Natural Language and Natural Selection. *Behavioral and Brain Sciences* 13: 707–784.

Pinkster, Harm. 1990. *Latin Syntax and Semantics*. London: Routledge.

Pintzuk, Susan. 1996. Cliticization in Old English. In Aaron Halpern & Arnold Zwicky (eds.), *Approaching Second: Second Position Clitics and Related Phenomena*, 375–409. Stanford: CSLI Publications.

Plag, Ingo. 1998. The Syntax of Some Locative Expressions in Sranan: Preposition, Postposition, or Noun? *Journal of Pidgin and Creole Languages* 13.2: 335–354.

Plank, Frans. 1995. *Double Case*. Oxford: Oxford University Press.

Plank, Frans & Adit Lahiri. 2009. Microscopic and Macroscopic Typology: Basic Valence Orientation. Paper presented at Association of Linguistic Typology, Berkeley, July.

Platts, John. [1873] 1967. *A Grammar of the Hindustani or Urdu Language*. Bombay: Oxford University Press.

Platts, John. [1884] 1930. *A Dictionary of Urdu, Classical Hindi, and English*. London: Oxford University Press.

Poletto, Cecilia. 1993. *La Sintassi del soggetto nei dialetti italiani settentrionali*. Padova: Unipress di Padova.

Poletto, Cecilia. 2000. *The Higher Functional Field*. Oxford: Oxford University Press.

Poletto, Cecilia. 2004. Dialectology from a Language Internal Perspective. Ms.

Poletto, Cecilia. 2007 Doubling as Economy. Ms.

Pollock, Jean-Yves. 1989. Verb Movement, Universal Grammar, and the Structure of IP. *Linguistic Inquiry* 20: 365–424.

Poole, Joshua. 1646. *The English Accidence; or, A short and Easy Way for the More Speedy Attaining to the Latine Tongue*. London.

Poppe, Erich. 1995. Negation in Welsh and Jespersen's Cycle. *Journal of Celtic Linguistics* 4: 99–107.

Poser, William. 2009. *The Carrier Language: A Brief Introduction*. Ms.

Press, Margaret. 1975. A Grammar of Chemehuevi. Dissertation, University of California, Berkeley.

Prokosch, Eduard. 1939. *A Comparative Germanic Grammar*. Philadelphia: Linguistic Society of America and University of Pennsylvania Press.

Proulx, Paul. 1988. The Demonstrative Pronouns of Proto-Algonquian. *International Journal of American Linguistics* 54.3: 309–330.

Prytz Johansen, J. 1948. *Character and Structure of the Action in Maori*. Copenhagen: Munksgaard.

Pulleyblank, Edwin. 1995. *Outline of Classical Chinese Grammar*. Vancouver: University of British Columbia Press.

Pustet, Regina. 1995. The Lakota Article. In Michael Dürr & Heinz-Jürgen Pinnow (eds.), *Language and Culture in Native North America: Studies in Honor of Heinz-Jürgen Pinnow*, 173–198. Munich: Lincom.

Pustet, Regina. 2000. Lakota Postpositions. *International Journal of American Linguistics* 66.2: 157–180.

Pustet, Regina. 2003. *Copulas: Universals in the Categorization of the Lexicon*. Oxford: Oxford University Press.

Pustet, Regina. 2008. Discourse Frequency and the Collapse of the Adposition vs. Affix Distinction in Lakota. In Elena Seoane & María José López-Couso (eds.), *Theoretical and Empirical Issues in Grammaticalization*, 269–292. Amsterdam: John Benjamins.

Putnam, Michael. 2006. Those There Demonstratives. *Leuvense Bijdragen* 95: 159–177.

Pysz, Agnieszka. 2007. The Usage of Demonstratives in the Peterborough Chronicle against the Background of the Old English Paradigm. In Alexander Bergs & Janne Skaffari (eds.), *The Language of the Peterborough Chronicle*, 57–75. Frankfurt: Peter Lang.

Quinn, Heidi. 2005. *The Distribution of Pronoun Case Forms in English*. Amsterdam: John Benjamins.

Quirk, Randolph & C. L. Wrenn. 1955. *An Old English Grammar*. London: Methuen.

Rackowski, A. & Lisa Travis. 2000. V-initial Languages: X or XP Movement and Adverbial Placement. In Andrew Carnie & Eithne Guilfoyle (eds.), *The Syntax of Verb-Initial Languages*, 117–141. New York: Oxford University Press.

Radford, Andrew. 2000. Children in Search of Perfection: Towards a Minimalist Model of Acquisition. *Essex Research Reports in Linguistics* 34: 57–74. Available at http://privatewww.essex.ac.uk/~radford/PapersPublications/perfection.htm.

Ramchand, Gillian. 2008. *Verb Meaning and the Lexicon: A First-Phase Syntax*. Cambridge: Cambridge University Press.

Ravila, Paavo. 1945. Nomen verbale suomalais-ugrilaisissa kieliss (Nomenverbum forms in Finno-Ugric languages). *Virittäjä* 49:148–158.

Reckendorf, H. 1921. *Arabische Syntax*. Heidelberg: Carl Winter.

de Reuse, Willem. 2006. *A Practical Grammar of the San Carlos Apache Language*. Munich: Lincom.

Rehg, Kenneth. 1981. *Ponapean Reference Grammar*. Honolulu: University Press of Hawaii.

Reichard, Gladys. 1951. *A Navajo Grammar*. Publications of the American Ethnological Society, no. 23. New York: Augustin.

Reinhart, Tanya & Eric Reuland. 1993. Reflexivity. *Linguistic Inquiry* 24.4: 657–720.

Reintges, Chris. 1997. *Passive Voice in Older Egyptian*. Leiden: Holland Institute of Linguistics Publications.

Reintges, Chris. 2001. Aspects of the Morphosyntax of Subjects and Objects in Coptic Egyptian. In Ton van der Wouden et al. (eds.), *Linguistics in the Netherlands*, 18: 177–188. Amsterdam: John Benjamins.

Rice, Keren. 1989. *A Grammar of Slave*. Berlin: Mouton de Gruyter.

Rice, Keren. 2000. *Morpheme Order and Semantic Scope*. Cambridge: Cambridge University Press.

Rice, Keren. 2003. Doubling Agreement in Slave. In Andrew Carnie et al. (eds.), *Formal Approaches to Function in Grammar*, 51–78. Amsterdam: John Benjamins.

Rice, Keren. 2008. On Incorporation in Athapaskan Languages: Aspects of Language Change. In Thórhallur Eythórsson (ed.), *Grammatical Change and Linguistic Theory: The Rosendal Papers*, 375–409. Amsterdam: John Benjamins.

Rice, Keren & Leslie Saxon. 2005. Comparative Athapaskan Syntax: Arguments and Projections. In Guglielmo Cinque & Richard S. Kayne (eds.), *The Oxford Handbook of Comparative Syntax*, 698–774. New York: Oxford University Press.

Richards, Marc. 2004. Object Shift, Scrambling, and Symmetrical Syntax. Dissertation, University of Cambridge.

Richards, Marc. 2008a. Defective Agree, Case Alternations, and the Prominence of Person. In Marc Richards & Andrej L. Malchukov (eds.), *Scales*, 137–161. Linguistische Arbeits Berichte 86. Available at http://www.uni-leipzig.de/~asw/lab/lab86/LAB86_Richards.pdf.

Richards, Marc. 2008b. Two Kinds of Variation in a Minimalist System. In Fabian Heck, Gereon Müller, & Jochen Trommer (eds.), *Varieties of Competition*, 133–162. Linguistische Arbeits Berichte 87. Available at http://www.uni-leipzig.de/~asw/lab/lab87/LAB87_richards.pdf.

Richardson, Murray. 1968. *Chipewyan Grammar*. Cold Lake: Northern Canada Evangelical Mission.

Rickford, John & Renee Blake. 1990. Copula Contraction and Absence. *Berkeley Linguistic Society Proceedings* 16: 257–268.

Riedel, Kristina. 2009. The Syntax of Object Marking in Sambaa: A Comparative Bantu Perspective. LOT Dissertation Series. Utrecht: LOT.

Riemsdijk, Henk van. 1978. *A Case Study in Syntactic Markedness. The Binding Nature of Prepositional Phrases*. Dordrecht: Foris.

Riggs, Stephen. 1893. *Dakota Grammar, Texts, and Ethnography*. Washington: Government Printing Office.

Rijkhof, Jan. 2002. *The Noun Phrase*. Oxford: Oxford University Press

Ringe, Don. 2006. *A Linguistics History of English*. Vol 1. Oxford: Oxford University Press.

Rittel, Leokardia. 1975. *Szyk członów czasu przeszłego i trybu przypuszczającego w języku polskim*. Warsaw: Ossolineum.

Ritter, Elizabeth & Martina Wiltschko. 2008. Anchoring Events to Utterances without Tense. *Proceedings of the 24th West Coast Conference on Formal Linguistics*. Available at http://www.lingref.com/cpp/wccfl/24/paper1240.pdf.

Rizzi, Luigi. 1982. *Issues in Italian Linguistics*. Dordrecht: Foris.

Rizzi, Luigi. 1990. *Relativized Minimality*. Cambridge: Massachusetts Institute of Technology Press.

Rizzi, Luigi. 1996. Residual Verb Second and the Wh-Criterion. In Adriana Beletti & Luigi Rizzi (eds.), *Parameters and Functional Heads*, 63–90. New York: Oxford University Press.

Rizzi, Luigi. 1997. The Fine Structure of the Left Periphery. In Liliane Haegeman (ed.), *Elements of Grammar*, 281–337. Dordrecht: Kluwer.

Rizzi, Luigi. 2001. On the Position 'Int(errogative)' in the Left Periphery of the Clause. In Guglielmo Cinque et al. (eds.), *Current Studies in Italian Syntax*, 287–296. Amsterdam: Elsevier.

Rizzi, Luigi. 2004. Locality and Left Periphery. In Adriana Belletti (ed.), *Structures and Beyond*, 223–251. New York: Oxford University Press.

Roberge, Yves & Nicole Rosen. 1999. Preposition Stranding and *Que*-delation in Varieties of North American French. *Linguistica Atlantica* 21: 153–168.

Roberts, Ian. 1993. *Verbs and Diachronic Syntax*. Dordrecht: Kluwer.

Roberts, Ian. 2005. *Principles and Parameters in a VSO language: A Case Study in Welsh*. New York: Oxford University Press.

Roberts, Ian. 2007. *Diachronic Syntax*. Oxford: Oxford University Press.

Roberts, Ian. 2010a. Semantic Bleaching, Grammaticalisation and the Clausal Hierarchy. In Elizabeth Traugott & Graeme Trousdale (eds.), *Gradience, Gradualness and Grammaticalization*, 45–73. Amsterdam: John Benjamins.

Roberts, Ian. 2010b. A Deletion Analysis of Null-Subjects. In Theresa Biberauer, Anders Holmberg, Ian Roberts, and Michelle Sheehan (eds.), *Parametric Variation: Null Subjects in Minimalist Theory*, 58–87. Cambridge: Cambridge University Press.

Roberts, Ian & Anders Holmberg. 2010. Introduction. In Theresa Biberauer, Anders Holmberg, Ian Roberts, and Michelle Sheehan (eds.), *Null Subjects: The Structure of Parametric Variation*, 1–57. Cambridge: Cambridge University Press.

Roberts, Ian & Anna Roussou. 2003. *Syntactic Change*. Cambridge: Cambridge University Press.

Robertson, John. 1980. *The Structure of Pronoun Incorporation in the Mayan Verbal Complex*. New York: Garland.

Roehrs, Dorian. 2009. *Demonstratives and Definite Articles as Nominal Auxiliaries*. Amsterdam: John Benjamins.

Romaine, Suzanne. 1982. *Socio-historical Linguistics*. Cambridge: Cambridge University Press.

Rosengren, Per. 1974. *Presencia y ausencia de los pronombres personales sujetos en español moderno*. Stockholm: Almqvist & Wiksell.

Ross, Malcolm. 2001. Contact-Induced Change in Oceanic Languages in North-West Melanesia. In Alexandra Aikhenvald & R. M. W. Dixon (eds.), *Areal Diffusion and Genetic Inheritance*, 134–166. Oxford: Oxford University Press.

Rothstein, Susan 1995. Small Clauses and Copular Constructions. In Anna Cardinaletti & M. T. Guasti (eds.), *Small Clauses*, 27–48. New York: Academic Press.

Rounds, Carol. 2001. *Hungarian*. London: Routledge.

Rowlett, Paul. 1998. *Sentential Negation in French*. Oxford: Oxford University Press.

Royen, Gerlach. 1929. *Die nominalen Klassifikations-Systeme in den Sprachen der Erde*. Vienna: Anthropos.

Rubin, Aaron. 2005. *Studies in Semitic Grammaticalization*. Winona Lake: Eisenbrauns.

Rupp, Laura. 2008. The (Socio)-Linguistic Cycle of Definte Article Reduction. *Folio Linguistica Historica* 28: 215–249.

Rupp, Laura & Hanne Page-Verhoeff. 2005. Pragmatic and Historical Aspects of Definite Article Reduction in Northern English Dialects. *English World-Wide* 26.3: 325–346.

Russell, Bertrand. 1905. On Denoting. *Mind* 56: 479–493.

Rutkowski, Paweł. 2006. From Demonstratives to Copulas: A Cross-Linguistic Perspective and the Case of Polish. *Journal of Universal Language* 7.2: 147–175.

Rydén, Mats. 1983. The Emergence of *who* as Relativizer. *Studia Linguistica* 37: 126–134.

Saeed, John. 1999. *Somali*. Amsterdam: John Benjamins.

Sagart, Laurent. 1999. *The Roots of Old Chinese*. Amsterdam: John Benjamins.

Salminen, Tapani. 1997. *Tundra Nenets Inflection*. Helsinki: Suomalais-Ugrilaisen seuran Toimituksia.

Sampson, Geoffrey, David Gil, & Peter Trudgill. 2009. *Language Complexity as an Evolving Variable*. New York: Oxford University Press.

Sands, Kristina & Lyle Campbell. 2001. Non-canonical Subjects and Objects in Finnish. In Alexandra Aikhenvald et al. (eds.), *Non-canonical Marking of Subjects and Objects*, 251–304. Amsterdam: John Benjamins.

Sapir, Edward. 1921. *Language*. New York: Harcourt, Brace.

Sasse, Hans-Jürgen. 1984. Case in Cushitic, Semitic and Berber. In James Bynon (ed.), *Current Progress in Afro-Asiatic Linguistics*, 111–126. Amsterdam: John Benjamins.

Savijärvi, Ilkka. 1977. *Itämerensuomalaisten kielten kieltoverbi*. Vol. 1. Helsinki: Suomalaisen Kirjallisuuden Seura.

Schachter, Paul. 1976. The Subject in Philippine Languages. In Charles Li (ed.), *Subject and Topic*, 493–518. New York: Academic Press.

Schauber, Ellen. 1979. *The Syntax and Semantics of Questions in Navajo*. New York: Garland.

Schenkel, Wolfgang. 1990. *Einführung in die altägyptische Sprachwissenschaft*. Darmstadt: Wissenschaftliche Buchgesellschaft.

Schiering, René. 2006. *Cliticization and the Evolution of Morphology*. Dissertation, University of Konstanz.

Schlegel, August Wilhem von. 1818. *Observations sur la langue et la literature provençales*. Paris.

Schlegel, Friedrich von. [1806] 1977. *Über die Sprache und die Weisheit der Indier*. Amsterdam: Benjamins.

Schröer, Arnold (ed.). [1885–1888] 1964. *Die Angelsächsischen Prosabearbetungen der Benediktinerregel*. 2nd ed. Darmstadt: Wissenschaftliche Buchgesellschaft.

Schuh, Russell. 2002. Gender and Determiners. Ms. University of California Los Angeles. Available at http//:www.linguistics.ucla.edu/people/schuh/Bade_Ngizim/Handout_05.pdf.

Schütze, Carson. 1997. INFL in Child and Adult Language. Dissertation, Massachusetts Institute of Technology.

Schütze, Carson. 2009. What It Means (Not) to Know (Number) Agreement. In José Brucart et al. (eds.), *Merging Features*, 80–103. Oxford: Oxford University Press.

Schwan, Eduard. 1925. *Grammatik des Altfranzösischen*. Leipzig: Reisland.

Schwegler, Armin. 1988. Word-Order Changes in Predicate Negation Strategies Revisited. *Diachronica* 5: 21–58.

Schwegler, Armin. 1990. *Analyticity and Syntheticity*. Berlin: Mouton de Gruyter.

Schwegler, Armin. 1991. Negation in Palenquero: Synchrony. *Journal of Pidgin and Creole Languages* 6: 165–214.

Schwegler, Armin. 2002. On the (African) Origins of Palenquero Subject Pronouns. *Diachronica* 19.2: 273–332.

Schwegler, Armin & Thomas Morton. 2003. Vernacular Spanish in a Microcosm: Kateyano in El Palenque de San Basilio (Colombia). *Revista International de Lingüística Iberoamericana* 1: 97–159.

Scurfield, Elizabeth. 1991. *Mandarin Chinese*. Sevenoaks: Hodder & Stoughton.

Sedgefield, Walter John (ed.). 1899. *King Alfred's Old English Version of Boethius*. Oxford: Clarendon Press.

Selig, M. 1992. *Die Entwicklung der Nominaldeterminanten im Spätlatein*. Tübingen: Niemeyer.

Shaul, Dave. 1986. *Topics in Nevome Syntax*. Berkeley: University of California Press.

Shaul, Dave. 1995. Reconstructed Proto-Core Grammars. Paper presented at Friends of Uto-Aztecan, Albuquerque, July.

Shibatani, Masayoshi. 1980. *The Languages of Japan*. Cambridge: Cambridge University Press.

Shilling, Allison. 1976. Some Non-standard Features of Bahamian Dialect Syntax. Dissertation, Hawaii University.

Shlonsky, Ur. 1997. *Clause Structure and Word Order in Hebrew and Arabic: An Essay in Comparative Semitic Syntax*. Oxford: Oxford University Press.

Shlonsky, Ur. 2004. The Form of Semitic Nominals. *Lingua* 114.12: 1465–1526.

Siewierska, Anna. 2000. On the Origins of the Order of Agreement and Tense Markers. In John Charles Smith & Delia Bentley (eds.), *Historical Linguistics, 1995*, 377–392. Amsterdam: John Benjamins.

Siewierska, Anna. 2004. *Person*. Cambridge: Cambridge University Press.

Siewierska, Anna. 2008. Verbal Person Marking. In Martin Haspelmath, Matthew Dryer, David Gil, & Bernard Comrie (eds.), *The World Atlas of Language Structures Online*, chapter 102. Munich: Max Planck Digital Library. Available online at http://wals.info/feature/102.

Siewierska, Anna & Dik Bakker. 1996. The Distribution of Subject and Object Agreement and Word Order Type. *Studies in Language* 20.1: 115–161.

Siewierska, Anna & Dik Bakker. 2009. Case and Alternative Strategies. In Andrej Malchukov & Andrew Spencer (eds.), *The Oxford Handbook of Case*, 290–303. New York: Oxford University Press.

Silverstein, Michael. 1976. Hierarchy of Features and Ergativity. In R. M. W. Dixon (ed.), *Grammatical Categories in Australian Languages*, 112–171. Canberra: Australian Institute of Aboriginal Studies.

Simeone-Senelle, Marie-Claude. 1996. Negation in Some Arabic Dialects of the Tihaamah of the Yemen. In Mushira Eid et al. (eds.), *Perspectives on Arabic Linguistics*, 9: 207–221. Amsterdam: John Benjamins.

Simoncsics, Péter. 1998. Kamassian. In Daniel Abondolo (ed.), *The Uralic Languages*, 580–601. London: Routledge.

Simpson, Andrew & Xiu-Zhi Zoe Wu. 2002a. Agreement Shells and Focus. *Language* 78.2: 287–313.

Simpson, Andrew & Xiu-Zhi Zoe Wu. 2002b. From D to T—Determiner Incorporation and the Creation of Tense. *Journal of East Asian Linguistics* 11: 169–202.

Sims, Lynn. 2008. Ingressive Aspect in the History of English. Dissertation, Arizona State University.

Sims, Lynn & Elly van Gelderen. 2010. Aspectual Cycles. Ms.

Sisk, Matthew & John Shea. 2008. Intrasite Spatial Variation of the Omo Kibish Middle Stone Age Assemblages: Artifact Refitting and Distribution Patterns. *Journal of Human Evolution* 55.3: 486–500.

Skeat, Walter (ed.). 1868. *The Lay of Havelok the Dane*. London: Trübner.

Skeat, Walter (ed.). 1886. *The Vision of William concerning Piers the Plowman*. Oxford: Clarendon Press.

Skeat, Walter (ed.). [1881–1887] 1970. *The Gospel according to St. Matthew, St. Mark, St. Luke and St. John*. Darmstadt: Wissenschaftliche Buchgesellschaft.

Skeat, Walter (ed.). 1881–1900. *Aelfric's Lives of Saints*. 2 vols. London: Trübner.

Smyth, Herbert [1920] 1974. *Greek Grammar*. Cambridge: Harvard University Press.

Sneddon, James. 1996. *Indonesian*. London: Routledge.

Snyder, William. 2007. *Child Language: The Parametric Approach*. Oxford: Oxford University Press.

Sollid, Hilde. 2002. Features of Finnish in a Northern Norwegian Dialect. Ms. Available at www. joensuu.fi/fld/methodsxi/abstracts/sollid.html.

Solstad, Dag. 1977. *Svik, Førkrigsår*. Oslo.

Somers Wicka, Katerina. 2007. *Theih, theiz*, and *theist*: A Case of Form Fossilization in Otfrid's *Evangelienbuch*. Paper presented at Germanic Linguistics Annual Conference.

Song, Jae Jung. 1994. The Verb-Object Bonding Principle and the Pronominal System: With Special Reference to Nuclear Micronesian Languages. *Oceanic Linguistics* 33.2: 517–565.

Spamer, James. 1979. The Development of the Definite Article in English. *Glossa* 13: 241–250.

Specht, Franz. 1947. *Der Ursprung der Indogermanishen Deklination*. Göttingen: Vandenhoeck & Ruprecht.

Sportiche, Dominique. 1988. A Theory of Floating Quantifiers and Its Corollaries for Constituent Structure. *Linguistic Inquiry* 19.2: 425–451.

Spuy, Andrew van der. 1993. Dislocated Noun Phrases in Nguni. *Lingua* 90.4: 335–355.

Stassen, Leon. 1997. *Intransitive Predication*. Oxford: Oxford University Press.

Steele, Susan. 1976. Clisis and Diachrony. In Charles Li (ed.), *Mechanisms of Syntactic Change*, 539–579. Austin: University of Texas Press.

Steever, S. 1987. Tamil and the Dravidian Languages. In Bernard Comrie (ed.), *The World's Major Languages*, 725–746. London: Croom Helm.

Stewart, Osamuyimen. 2001. *The Serial Verb Construction*. New York: Garland.

Story, Gillian & Constance Naish. 1973. *Tlingit Verb Dictionary*. Fairbanks: Alaska Native Language Center.

Stowell, Tim. 1978. What Was There before There Was There? In D. Farkas et al. (eds.), *Proceedings of the 13th Regional Meeting of the Chicago Linguistics Society*, 458–471. Chicago: Chicago Linguistics Society.

Stroik, Tom. 2009. *Locality in Minimalist Syntax*. Cambridge: Massachusetts Institute of Technology Press.

Sudlow, David. 2001. *The Tamasheq of North-East Burkina Faso*. Cologne: Köppe.

Sun, Chaofen. 1996. *Word-Order Change and Grammaticalization in the History of Chinese*. Stanford: Stanford University Press.

Sun, Chen Chen. 2008. Variations in the BA Construction and Its Relevance to DP: A Minimalist Perspective. Dissertation, Arizona State University.

Sundquist, John. 2006. Syntactic Variation in the History of Norwegian and the Decline of XV Word Order. *Diachronica* 23.1: 105–141.

Suñer, M. 1988. The Role of Agreement in Clitic-Doubled Constructions. *Natural Language and Linguistic Theory* 6.3: 391–434.

Suttles, Wayne. 2004. *Musqueam Reference Grammar*. Vancouver: University of British Columbia Press.

Svenonius, Peter. 2006. The Emergence of Axial Parts. *Nordlyd* 33.1: 49–77.

Svenonius, Peter. 2007. Adpositions, Particles and the Arguments They Introduce. In Eric Reuland et al. (eds.), *Argument Structure*, 63–103. Amsterdam: John Benjamins.

Swan, Toril. 1988. *Sentence Adverbials in English*. Dissertation, University of Tromsø.

Swan, Toril. 1991. Adverbial Shifts: Evidence from Norwegian and English. In Dieter Kastovsky (ed.), *Historical English Syntax*, 409–438. Berlin: Mouton de Gruyter.

Sweet, Henry. [1871] 1934. *King Alfred's West-Saxon Version of Gregory's Pastoral Care*. London: Oxford University Press.

Szabolcsi, Anna. 1994. The Noun Phrase. In Ferenc Kiefer & Katalin É. Kiss (eds.), *The Syntactic Structure of Hungarian*, 179–274. San Diego: Academic Press.

Takashima, K. 1990. A Study of the Copulas in Shang Chinese. *Memoirs of the Institute of Oriental Culture* 42: 1–92.

Taraldsen, Tarald. 1990. D-Projections and N-Projections in Norwegian. In Juan Mascaro & Marina Nespor (eds.), *Grammar in Progress*, 217–249. Dordrecht: Foris.

Tauli, Valter. 1956. The Origin of Affixes. *Finnisch-Ugrische Forschungen* 32.1–2: 170–225.

Tauli, Valter. 1958. *The Structural Tendencies of Languages*. Helsinki: Annales Academiae Scientiarum Fennicae.

Tauli, Valter. 1966. *Structural Tendencies in Uralic Languages*. The Hague: Mouton.

Tesnière, Lucien. 1932. Synthétisme et Analytisme. In *Charisteria Gvilelmo Mathesio*, 62–64. Prague: Prague Linguistic Circle.

Thomason, Sarah. 1983. Genetic Relationship and the Case of Ma'a (Mbugu). *Studies in African Linguistics* 14:195–231.

Thomason, Sarah & Terrence Kaufman. 1988. *Language Contact, Creolization, and Genetic Linguistics*. Berkeley: University of California Press.

Thorpe, Benjamin. [1844–46] 1971. *The Homilies of the Anglo-Saxon Church*. 2 vols. New York: Johnson Reprint.

Thorpe, Benjamin. 1861. *Anglo-Saxon Chronicle*. 2 vols. London: Longman.

Tomasello, Michael. 1987. Learning to Use Prepositions: A Case Study. *Journal of Child Language* 14: 79–98.

Tomasello, Michael, Malinda Carpenter, & Ulf Liszkowski. 2007. A New Look at Infant Pointing. *Child Development* 78. 3: 705–722. Available at http://email.eva.mpg.de/~tomas/pdf/Liszkowski_ChildDevlp_07.pdf.

Tomić, Olga Mišeska. 2004. The Balkan Sprachbund Properties: Introduction. In Olga Tomić (ed.), *Balkan Syntax and Semantics*, 1–57. Amsterdam: John Benjamins.

Tomić, Olga. 2006. Variation in Clitic Doubling in South Slavic. Ms. Available at http://www.meertens.knaw.nl/projecten/edisyn/abstracts/Abstract_Tomic.pdf.

Tomić, Olga. 2008. Towards Grammaticalization of Clitic Doubling: Clitic Doubling in Macedonian and Neighbouring Languages. In Dalina Kallulli & Liliane Tasmowski (eds.), *Clitic Doubling in the Balkan Languages*, 65–87. Amsterdam: John Benjamins.

Tomlin, Russell. 1986. *Basic Word Order*. London: Croom Helm.

Tooke, John Horne. 1786–1805. *The Diversion of Purley*. London.

Tops, Guy. 1974. *The Origin of the Germanic Dental Preterit*. Leiden: Brill.

Torrego, Esther. 1998. *The Dependencies of Objects*. Cambridge: Massachusetts Institute of Technology Press.

Trask, R. L 1997. *The History of Basque*. London: Routledge.

Traugott, Elizabeth. 1989. On the Rise of Epistemic Meanings in English: An Example of Subjectification in Semantic Change. *Language* 57: 33–65.

Traugott, Elizabeth. 1992. Syntax. In Richard Hogg (ed.), *The Cambridge History of the English Language*, vol. 1,*Old English*, 168–289. Cambridge: Cambridge University Press.

Traugott, Elizabeth. 2004. Exaptation and Grammaticalization. In Minoji Akimoto (ed.), *Linguistic Studies Based on Corpora*, 133–156. Tokyo: Hituzi Syobo.

Traugott, Elizabeth & Richard Dasher. 2002. *Regularity in Semantic Change*. Cambridge: Cambridge University Press.

Traugott, Elizabeth & Bernd Heine. 1991. *Grammaticalization*. Amsterdam: John Benjamins.

Travis, Lisa. 1984. Parameters and Effects of Word Order Variation. Dissertation, Massachusetts Institute of Technology.

Trips, Carola. 2001. *From OV to VO in Early Middle English*. Amsterdam: John Benjamins.

Trudgill, Peter & Jenny Cheshire. 1998. *The Sociolinguistics Reader*. Vol. 1. London: Arnold.

Tsakali, Vina & Elena Anagnostopoulou. 2008. Rethinking the Clitic Doubling Parameter. In Dalina Kalluli & Liliane Tasmowski (eds.), *Clitic Doubling in the Balkan Languages*, 321–357. Amsterdam: John Benjamins.

Tsurska, Olena. 2009. The Negative Cycle in Early and Modern Russian. In Elly van Gelderen (ed.), *Cyclical Change*, 73–90. Amsterdam: John Benjamins.

Tuttle, Siri. 1998. *Metrical and Tonal Structures in Tanana Athabaskan*. Dissertation, University of Washington.

Uhlenbeck, C. C. 1901 Agens und Patiens im Kasussystem der indogermanischen Sprachen. *Indogermanische Forschungen* 12: 170–171.

van der Auwera, Johan. 1999. Periphrastic *do*: Typological Prolegomena. In Guy Tops et al. (eds.), *Thinking English Grammar*, 457–470. Leuven: Peeters.

van der Auwera, Johan. 2009. The Jespersen Cycles. In Elly van Gelderen (ed.), *Cyclical Change*, 35–71. Amsterdam: John Benjamins.

van der Auwera, Johan, Ludovic de Cuypere & Annemie Neuckermans. 2006. Negative Indefinites: A Typological and Diachronic Perspective on a Brabantic Construction. In Terttu Nevalainen, Juhani Klemola, and Mikko Laitinen (eds.), *Types of Variation*, 305–319. Amsterdam: John Benjamins.

van der Auwera, Johan & Gunther De Vogelaer. 2008. Negation and Quantification. In Sjef Barbiers et al. (eds.), *Syntactic Atlas of the Dutch Dialects*, 2: 58–72. Amsterdam: Amsterdam University Press.

Vaissier, Johannes. 1960. *A Deuout Treatyse Called the Tree and xii Frutes of the Holy Goost*. Groningen: Wolters.

Valois, Daniel. 1991. The Internal Syntax of DP. Dissertation, University of California, Los Angeles.

Vanhove, Martine. 1996. The Negation *maaši* in a Yaafi'i Dialect. In Mushira Eid et al. (eds.). *Perspectives on Arabic Linguistics*, 9: 195–206. Amsterdam: John Benjamins.

Van Valin, Robert & William Foley. 1980. Role and Reference Grammar. In Edith Moravcsik & J. Wirth (eds.), *Current Syntactic Theories*, 329–352. New York: Academic Press.

Vedovato, Diana. 2008. On Some Similarities between English Aspectual Particle Verbs and Paduan Phrasal Verbs: A Look into Inner Aspect. Ms. Padua University

Verhaar, J. 1995. *Toward a Reference Grammar of Tik Pisin*. Honolulu: University of Hawaii Press.

Vincent, Nigel. 1997. The Emergence of the D-System in Romance. In Ans van Kemenade & Nigel Vincent (eds.), *Parameters of Morphosyntactic Change*, 140–169. Cambridge: Cambridge University Press.

Vincent, Nigel. 1999. The Evolution of C-Structure Prepositions and PPs from Indo-European to Romance. *Linguistics* 37.6: 1111–1153.

Visser, F. 1963–1973. *An Historical Syntax of the English Grammar*. Vols. 1–3b. Leiden: Brill.

Viti, Carlotta. 2008. The Case of Ancient Greek *en* 'in'. *Transactions of the Philological Society* 106.3: 375–413.

Vleeskruyer, Rudolf. 1953. *The Life of Saint Chad*. Amsterdam: North-Holland.

Waite, J. 1994. Determiner Phrases in Maori. *Te Reo* 37 : 55–77.

Wald, Benji. 1979. The Development of the Swahili Object Marker. In Talmy Givón (ed.), *Syntax and Semantics*, 12: 505–524. New York: Academic Press.

Wald, Benji. 1993. Longterm Evolution of the Syntax of Discourse and the Swahili Person Markers. In Jaap van Marle (ed.), *Historical Linguistics, 1991*, 325–341. Amsterdam: John Benjamins.

Walker, Dean. 1896. The Semitic Negative with Special Reference to the Negative in Hebrew. *American Journal of Semitic Languages and Literatures* 12: 230–267.

Walker, James. 2000. Rephrasing the Copula: Contraction and Zero in Early African American English. In Shana Poplack (ed.), *The English History of African American English*, 35–72. Malden: Blackwell.

Wang, Li. 1958. *Hanyu Shi Lunwen Ji* [Collected essays on the history of Chinese). Beijing: Kexue Chubanshe.

Waters, Cathleen. 2009. The Preposition Cycle in English. In Elly van Gelderen (ed.), *Cyclical Change*, 285–300. Amsterdam: John Benjamins.

Weir, Helen. 1986. Footprints of Yesterday's Syntax: Diachronic Development of Certain Verb Prefixes in an OSV Language (Nadëb). *Lingua* 68: 291–316.

Wenger, Anelale'a. 2005. Floating Quantifiers. Master's thesis, Arizona State University.

Wessén, Elias. 1970. *Schwedische Sprachgeschichte*. Vol. 3. Berlin: Walter de Gruyter.

Westergaard, Marit. 2009. *The Acquisition of Word Order*. Amsterdam: John Benjamins.

Westerståhl, D. 1984. Determiners and Context Sets. In Johan van Benthem and Alice ter Meulen (eds.), *Generalized Quantifiers in Natural Languages*, 45–71. Dordrecht: Foris.

Whitelock, Dorothy (ed.). 1930. *Anglo-Saxon Wills*. Cambridge: Cambridge University Press.

Whitman, John. 2000. Relabelling. In Susan Pintzuk, George Tsoulas, & Anthony Warner *Diachronic Syntax*, 220–238. Oxford: Oxford University Press.

Whitney, William. [1889] 1967. *Sanskrit Grammar*. Cambridge: Harvard University Press.

Wiedenhof, Jeroen. 1993. Standard Mandarin. In Peter Kahrel & René van den Berg (eds.), *Typological Studies in Negation*, 93–124. Amsterdam: John Benjamins.

Wiese, Heike. 2006. Ist Kanak Sprak grammatisch reduziertes Deutsch? Paper presented at Munich.

Williams, Edwin. 1994. *Thematic Structure in Syntax*. Cambridge: Massachusetts Institute of Technology Press.

Willie, Mary. 1991. *Navajo Pronouns and Obviation*. Dissertation, University of Arizona.

Willis, David. 1998. *Syntactic Change in Welsh*. Oxford: Oxford University Press.

Willis, David. 2006. Negation in Middle Welsh. *Studia Celtica* 40: 63–88. Available at http://people.pwf.cam.ac.uk/dwew2/willis_negation_stc.pdf.

Willson, Heather. 2008. Subject Positions in Marshallese. Dissertation, University of California, Los Angeles.

Wilson, Garth. 1995. *Conversational Navajo*. Blanding: Conversational Navajo Publications.

Windfuhr, G. 1987. Persian. In Bernard Comrie (ed.), *The World's Major Languages*, 523–546. London: Croom Helm.

Winters, Richard. 2008. Matrix Wh-questions without Subject Inversion. Paper presented at Linguistic Association of the Southwest, October.

Wise, M. R. 1986. Grammatical Characteristics of PreAndine Languages of Peru. In Desmond Derbyshire & Geoffrey Pullum (eds.), *Handbook of Amazonian Languages*, 1: 567–642. Berlin: Mouton de Gruyter.

Wolfenden, Elmer. 1971. *Hiligaynon Reference Grammar*. Honolulu: University of Hawaii Press.

Wolff, John U. 1996. The Development of the Passive Verb with Pronominal Prefix in Western Austronesian Languages. Ms. Cornell University.

Wolpoff, Milford. 2005. Multiregional Evolution. In Colin Renfrew et al. (eds.), *Archeology: The Key Concepts*, 176–181. New York: Routledge.

Wood, Johanna. 1997. Negation in the *Paston Letters*. Master's thesis, Arizona State University.

Wood, Johanna. 2003. Definiteness and Number: Determiner Phrase and Number Phrase in the History of English. Dissertation, Arizona State University.

Wood, Johanna L. 2007a. Is There a DP in Old English? In Joseph Salmons & Shannon Dubenion-Smith (eds.), *Historical Linguistics, 2005*, 167–187. Amsterdam: John Benjamins.

Wood, Johanna. 2007b. Demonstratives and Possessives: From Old English to Present-Day English. In Werner Abraham, Elisabeth Leiss, & Elisabeth Stark (eds.), *Evolution and Function of Nominal Determination—DPs in Synchrony and Diachrony*, 339–361. Amsterdam: John Benjamins.

Woolford, Ellen. 2006. Case-Agreement Mismatches. In Cedric Boeckx (ed.), *Agreement Systems*, 299–316. Amsterdam: John Benjamins.

Woolford, Ellen. 2008. Differential Subject Marking at Argument Structure, Syntax, and PF. In Helen de Hoop & Peter de Swart (eds.), *Differential Subject Marking*, 17–40. Dordrecht: Springer.

Wray, A. 1998. Protolanguage as a Holistic System for Social Interaction. *Language and Communication* 18: 47–67.

Wu, Zoe. 2004. *Grammaticalization and Language Change in Chinese*. London: Routledge Curzon.

Wüllner, Franz. 1827. *Casus und Modi*. Münster.

Xu, Ding. 1997. Functional Categories in Mandarin Chinese. Dissertation, Leiden University.

Yáñez-Bouza, Nuria. 2004. An Historical Approach to Preposition Stranding in Early Modern English. Ms.

Yáñez-Bouza, Nuria. 2007. Preposition Stranding and Prescriptivism in English from 1500 to 1900. Dissertation, University of Manchester.

Yang, Hui-Ling. 2009. The Loss of Negative Features in Interrogatives. Ms.

Yang, Ning. 2008. *The Indefinite Object in Mandarin Chinese*. Leiden: Holland Institute of Linguistics Publications.

Yar-Shater, Ehsan. 1969. *A Grammar of Sourthern Tati Dialects*. The Hague: Mouton.

Young, Robert & William Morgan. 1980. *The Navajo Language: A Grammar and Colloquial Dictionary*. Albuquerque: University of New Mexico Press.

Young, Robert & William Morgan. 1987. *The Navajo Language: A Grammar and Colloquial Dictionary*. Albuquerque: University of New Mexico Press.

Young, Robert, William Morgan, & Sally Midgette. 1992. *Analytical Lexicon of Navajo*. Albuquerque: University of New Mexico Press.

Zeijlstra, Hedde. 2004. Sentential Negation and Negative Concord. Dissertation, University of Amsterdam.

Zepeda, Ofelia. 1983. *A Papago Grammar*. Tucson: University of Arizona Press.

Zewi, Tamar. 1996. The Definition of the Copula and the Role of Third Independent Personal Pronouns in Nominal Sentences of Semitic Languages. *Folia Linguistica Historica* 17: 41–55.

Zhang, Jisheng. 2005. A Phonological Approach to Clitics in Shaoxing Chinese. *Leiden Papers in Linguistics* 2.2: 69–79.

Zribi-Hertz, Anne. 1994. La Syntaxe des clitiques nominatifs. *Travaux de Linguistique et Litterature* 32 : 131–147.

Zwart, Jan-Wouter. 1996. 'Shortest Move' versus 'Fewest Steps'. In Werner Abraham et al. (eds.). *Minimal Ideas*, 305–327. Amsterdam: John Benjamins.

Zwart, Jan-Wouter. 2006. Complementizer Agreement and Dependency Marking Typology. *Leiden Working Papers in Linguistics* 3.2: 53–72.

Zwicky, Arnold & Geoffrey Pullum. 1983. Cliticization vs. Inflection: English *n't*. *Language* 59.3: 502–513.

Author Index

Topic Index

Languages and Language Families Index

Indo-European, Romance, Old, Middle and Modern English are not listed; please see the table of contents for references there. The varieties of different languages are listed under, for instance, Italian, Spanish, French, Dutch, Arabic and Berber.